ISBN 978-1-332-98578-4
PIBN 10446495

1 MONTH OF
FREE
READING

at

www.ForgottenBooks.com

By purchasing this book you are eligible for one month membership to ForgottenBooks.com, giving you unlimited access to our entire collection of over 1,000,000 titles via our web site and mobile apps.

To claim your free month visit:
www.forgottenbooks.com/free446495

English
Français
Deutsche
Italiano
Español
Português

www.forgottenbooks.com

Mythology Photography **Fiction**
Fishing Christianity **Art** Cooking
Essays Buddhism Freemasonry
Medicine **Biology** Music **Ancient**
Egypt Evolution Carpentry Physics
Dance Geology **Mathematics** Fitness
Shakespeare **Folklore** Yoga Marketing
Confidence Immortality Biographies
Poetry **Psychology** Witchcraft
Electronics Chemistry History **Law**
Accounting **Philosophy** Anthropology
Alchemy Drama Quantum Mechanics
Atheism Sexual Health **Ancient History**
Entrepreneurship Languages Sport
Paleontology Needlework Islam
Metaphysics Investment Archaeology
Parenting Statistics Criminology
Motivational

HANDBOOK OF GERMAN LITERATURE,

CONTAINING:

SCHILLER'S MAID OF ORLEANS,
GOETHE'S IPHIGENIA IN TAURIS,
TIECK'S PUSS IN BOOTS,
THE XENIA BY GOETHE AND SCHILLER,

WITH

CRITICAL INTRODUCTIONS AND EXPLANATORY NOTES;

TO WHICH IS ADDED

AN APPENDIX

OF SPECIMENS OF GERMAN PROSE

FROM THE MIDDLE OF THE SIXTEENTH TO THE MIDDLE OF
THE NINETEENTH CENTURIES.

BY G. J. ADLER, A.M. 1821-18...

PROFESSOR OF GERMAN LITERATURE IN THE UNIVERSITY
OF THE CITY OF NEW-YORK.

_____

NEW-YORK:

D. APPLETON & CO., 200 BROADWAY.

1854.

Stereotyped by HENRY LUDWIG, 45, Vesey-street, N.-Y.

ADVERTISEMENT.

In adding another volume to the series of text-books for the study of the German, which among the friends of liberal culture have met with the most favorable reception, the Author, judging from personal experience, feels confident of of supplying a desideratum, of which every instructor and every student at a certain stage of his progress must be sensible. The latter, after having once vanquished the rudimental difficulties of his new study, is of course anxious to extend his knowledge of the language by forming an early acquaintance with the classical productions of its prominent authors; indeed with many such acquaintance constitutes the main, perhaps the only motive for the acquisition of the language. To these authors, however, he has not always ready access, and even if he has, a guide to the immense treasures now open before him, is in all cases as acceptable, and in most even as necessary as are the "Guides" to London or to Paris to the knowledge-seeking traveller.

To furnish such an aid constitutes the aim of the following pages. Instead of repeating, however, the plan pursued in my Progressive Reader, and of offering a new series of mere extracts, I have deemed it preferable to select a few literary monuments of undisputed excellence, which I have attempted to furnish with such elucidations, as the student of a new literature would be likely to require. In doing so I have diligently availed myself of all the lights, which the critical and biographical contributions of the countrymen of the commented authors have brought to bear upon the subject, and I may confidently hope, that I have placed at the command of the student all the necessary conditions for a complete and thorough appreciation of the monuments selected.

In regard to the introductions and notes to the leading pieces of the volume I may perhaps even incur the censure of an unnecessary and disproportionate prolixity. In my remarks on the Maid of Orleans I have given a *résumé* both of the historical event and of the ante-Schilleric treatment of the subject, and in the prolegomena to the Iphigenia I have even ventured into a parallelism between the Greek dramatist and the German. As in the one of these dramas, however, a world-historic movement, and in the other a clearly defined national Mythos (the fruitful source of tragic pathos among the Ancients) constitute the basis, the framework of the composition, it will at once become apparent that a proper appreciation of the works in question can only be attained by him who has previously formed a clear conception, in the one case, of the events as presented by history, and in the other, of the legendary records as exhibited in the works of those who were the poetic predecessors of the modern author.

The series of Epigrams, the *Xenia*, I have ventured to introduce as a complemental comment to Tieck's polemic comedy. These are so closely interwoven with the history of the culminating period of German taste and literary culture, that a full exposition of the import of their various allu-sions, direct and remote, could only be expected from a com-prehensive history of the age, by which they were produced. I have endeavored to make them as intelligible as the limits of my task would admit. On this subject the student will find some additional light in his own language by consulting Professor Felton's excellent translation of Menzel's "German Literature."

To these volumes I must (for the present at least) like-wise refer the reader for further information respecting the writers, from whom I have given the specimens of German prose contained in the Appendix. To furnish such informa-tion (biographical and critical) myself, and to introduce those authors, as I have introduced these in the main part of the work, would have been as great a source of pleasure to my-self, as it might have been of interest and profit to the stu-dent. The limits assigned to the volume, however, made the feasibility of such an undertaking questionable, while my absentment from my library towards the close of my work (for reasons which the gentle reader may perchance learn hereafter) made it altogether impossible, for this first edition at least.

In regard to the selections themselves I regretted to be under the necessity of excluding entirely many authors, both living and departed, whose genius gives them an unquestion-able claim to rank among the first. This omission, however, ceases to be culpable, when it is remembered, that a manual of this size cannot possibly aspire to completeness. If in the hands of a competent instructor, and in connexion with some such literary history, as I have mentioned, it can serve as the point of departure for a more extended course of German literature, and if the intelligent learner can find therein a guide to the wider field of self-selection from the classics of the language, or an incentive for further enquiry, then my design is fully accomplished, and it is with such expectation that the volume is now submitted to the enlightened judgment of the Public.

G. J. ADLER.

New-York University,
Washington-Square,
Dec. 1st, 1853.

CONTENTS.

Pages.

Introduction to Schiller's Maid of Orleans............... 1— 44

Die Jungfrau von Orleans, eine romantische Tragödie von
Friedrich Schiller....................... ...... 45—197*

Introduction to Goethe's Iphigenia in Tauris, including a
parallelism between Euripides and Goethe............ 198—240

Iphigenia auf Tauris, ein Schauspiel von Goethe...... 241—319

Introduction to Tieck's Puss in Boots.................. 320—328

Der gestiefelte Kater, ein Kindermährchen in fünf Acten von
Ludwig Tieck (1773—1853) .... 329—398

Introduction to the Xenia of Goethe and Schiller .... 399—404

Xenien von J. W. v. Goethe und Friedrich Schiller 405—424

APPENDIX:

Specimens of German Prose, from the middle of the sixteenth
to the middle of the nineteenth centuries .... 425—550

Jacob Böhme. (1575 — 1624.)

1. Aus der Morgenröthe im Aufgang 427

Abraham a Sancta Clara. (1642 — 1709.)

2. Der Kupferstecher 429

Gottlieb Wilhelm Rabener. (1714 — 1771.)

3. Wem Gott ein Amt giebt, dem giebt er auch Verstand 435

Johann Winckelmann. (1717 — 1768.)

4. Beschreibung des Torso im Belvedere zu Rom 445

Gottlieb Ephraim Lessing. (1729 — 1781.)

5. Laokoon 449

Johann Georg Hamann. (1730 — 1788).

6. Aus den biblischen Betrachtungen 452

Matthias Claudius. (1743 — 1815).

7. Ueber's Genie 455

Johann Jacob Engel. (1741 — 1802).

8. Der Traum des Galiläi 457

---

* Pp. 197 and 198 contain the additional notes to Schiller's tragedy, which the
student will find important to consult in commencing the piece.

Pages.

Johann Gottfried Herder. (1744 — 1803.)

9. Unsere Humanität ist nur Vorübung, die Knospe zu einer zukünftigen
  Blume 462

Johann Wolfgang Goethe. (1749 — 1832.)

10. Bekenntnisse einer schönen Seele 466

Friedrich Schiller. (1759 — 1805.)

11. Ueber das Erhabene und Schöne 469
12. Selbstkritik über die Räuber 473

Jean Paul Friedrich Richter. (1763 — 1825.)

13. Ueber die Unsterblichkeit der Seele 475
14. Das Verhältniß der Griechen und der Neuern 477

August Wilhelm Schlegel. (1767 — 1845.)

15. Der Unterschied des Classischen und Romantischen 480

Friedrich Schlegel. (1772 — 1829.)

16. Charakteristik des neuen Testaments 485
17. Der Minnegesang 488

Wilhelm von Humboldt. (1767 — 1835.)

18. Ueber Schiller und den Gang seiner Geistesentwickelung 491

Johann Gottlieb Fichte. (1762 — 1814.)

19. Ueber die Bestimmung des Gelehrten 496

Georg Wilhelm Friedrich Hegel. (1770 — 1831.)

20. Ueber den Werth und die Nothwendigkeit des Studiums der griechischen
  und römischen Sprache und Literatur auf Gymnasien 500

Friedrich Wilhelm Joseph Schelling. (1775 — —.)

21. Ueber das Studium der Historie 507

Berthold Georg Niebuhr. (1777 — 1831.)

22. Ueber römische Geschichte 512

Friedrich Wilken. (1777 — 1840.)

23. Richard's Löwenherz Gefangenschaft 516

Friedrich von Raumer. (1781 — —.)

24. Des Kaisers Friedrich II. Charakter 522

Leopold Ranke. (1795 — —.)

25. Papst Sirtus V. 524

Ludwig Uhland. (1787 — —.)

26. Ueber nordische Mythologie 528

Wolfgang Menzel. (1798 — —.)

27. Nationalität 533

Georg Gottfried Gervinus. (1805 — —.)

28. Regeneration der Poesie unter den Einflüssen der religiösen und weltlichen Moral und Kritik 540

THE

MAID OF ORLEANS,

A ROMANTIC TRAGEDY.

BY FREDERICK SCHILLER.

*Εστιν οὖν τραγῳδία μίμησις πράξεως σπουδαίας καὶ τελείας, μέγεθος ἐχούσης· ἡδυσμένῳ λόγῳ, χωρὶς ἑκάστῳ τῶν εἰδῶν ἐν τοῖς μορίοις· δρώντων, καὶ οὐ δι᾽ ἀπαγγελίας· δι᾽ ἐλέου καὶ φόβου περαίνουσα τὴν τῶν τοιούτων παθημάτων κάθαρσιν.

ARISTOTELES DE POEΓ. c. 6.

INTRODUCTION

TO SCHILLER'S MAID OF ORLEANS.

I. THE HISTORICAL GROUND OF THE DRAMA.

CHARLES VII. was the fourth reigning prince of the house of Valois, which in the drama is represented as struggling for the maintenance of its claim to succession. The founder of the dynasty was Charles, count of Valois, whose son Philip VI. ascended the throne of France in 1328. The rigid enforcement of the Salic Law, to which the elevation of Philip was due, as well as that elevation itself, were chiefly directed against the pretensions of Edward III., of England, who, being a son of Isabella, the daughter of Philip IV. of France, considered his claim to the crown of France more valid, than that of the new house. This gave rise to the long and obstinate struggle for the succession, which lasting for one hundred and twenty years, ruined the cause of the nobles, converted the country into a desert, and plunged the entire nation into a temporary state of barbarity.

Philip commenced the contest with his rival (in 1338), whose movements, however, both by sea and by land, were from the first attended with signal success, until at last the French were totally defeated in the bloody battle of Cressy (1346). The truce soon after established (1348), was of but short duration and after the death of Philip, his successor John I. was again compelled to resort to arms (1350). The so-called Black Prince, who was now at the head of the English forces, had entered into an alliance with Charles the Bad, King of Navarre, and availing himself of the weakness of John, surprised the latter at Poitiers, where the French army in spite of its great numerical superiority was completely routed (there are said to have been 60,000 French to 8,000 English??), and the king himself taken prisoner (1356). The victory was followed by a truce of two years. In 1358, Edward again invaded France and the result of this expe-

3

dition was again in his favor. By the treaty of Bretigni, which restored John to his liberty, he even acquired the sovereign title to Ancient Aquitaine. During the captivity of John, the Dauphin, afterward Charles V., had assumed the responsibilities of the government and of the war. Meanwhile the country was lacerated by intestine disorders of the gravest kind. The " Estates-General," which the Dauphin had assembled for the purpose of organizing his regency, took the power into their own hands, and their insubordination was seconded by the turbulent Charles of Navarre ; in Paris there was a popular insurrection headed by Marcels, and in the North the so-called *Jacquerrie* (peasantry) joined hands with riotous hordes of disbanded soldiers for the common purpose of pillaging the provinces.

In spite of all these internal difficulties, the struggle against the alien Pretender was again revived immediately upon the succession of Charles V. (1364), and continued even after the deaths of Edward and of his son, the Black Prince ; so successfully on the part of Charles, that in 1377, when peace was made with Richard II., France had recovered nearly the whole extent of her former territory. Charles improved this prosperous turn of events for reorganization and reform. He suppressed the States-General, that had been the cause of so much difficulty to him during the period of his regency, and created in their stead the so-called *Lits de Justice*, or Parliamentary Assemblies. After his decease, the minority of his son and successor, Charles VI., again induced the necessity of a regent. Louis, duke of Anjou, uncle to the dauphin, placed himself at the helm ; whose shameless extortions again revived the civil broils at the capital and in the North, while princes of the blood, were busily engaged in fomenting mutinies and intestine commotions in other parts of the land. It was here, that the international quarrel began now to assume a still graver aspect.

Soon after the king had reached his maturity of age, and with it the exclusive exercise of his royal power, he was suddenly overtaken by a fit of insanity, which continuing with only an occasional intermission during the whole remainder of his life, made a regent administration again necessary. This gave rise to the most ruinous jealousies and contentions among those in power. Philip the Bold, duke of Burgundy, and Louis duke of Orleans, the king's brother, were rivals for the regency, and their bitter enmity divided the whole nation into two parties, viz.

that of Orleans and the Burgundian. After the death of Philip
of Burgundy (who had been the successful candidate), the
struggle between the two parties increased in virulence and
extent. His son and successor, John the Intrepid, instigated the
murder of the duke of Orleans, his antagonist, without, however,
being able to suppress the party of the latter. All the princes
of royal blood, together with the young duke of Orleans, united
with his father-in-law, the duke Armagnac, to revenge the crime,
and in their attempt they were joined by all the nobility of the
South, whilst the duke of Burgundy, was supported by the com-
monalty of Paris and the North. All France was, thereupon,
divided into *Armagnacs* and *Bourgignons*, and of the bloodshed
both on the scaffold and on the battle-field there was no end.
   Meanwhile Henry V. of England again invaded France with a
strong force, annihilated the army of the enemy in the battle of
Agincourt (1415), and subsequently formed an alliance with the
duke of Burgundy, who (1417) took the city of Paris, and instituted a reign of terror there. The dauphin Charles, supported
by the Orleans party soon assumed the cares of the administration
himself, at the same time banishing with the consent of his royal
father the profligate and intriguing queen mother, Isabella of
Bavaria. The latter in her chagrin threw herself into the arms
of the enemy; and deluded by a forced interpretation of an
antiquated law, she herself laid claim to the regency, which in
connection with Burgundy and the English, she hoped to become
possessed of. Soon afterwards, and on the occasion, when a
public reconciliation was to be effected between the dauphin and
the duke of Burgundy, the latter was murdered by the followers
of the former; an event which determined the Burgundy party and
the Queen to unite their cause with that of the English. By the
treaty of Troyes, king Henry V. of England, who had previously
married Catherine, the daughter of the crazy king, was declared
heir to the throne of France, and during the illness of the monarch, provisional regent of the country. An edict of his father,
issued soon after, and confirmed by a decision of the Parliament
of Paris, excluded the dauphin entirely from the succession.
   Henry V. was at the head of affairs as long as he lived. His
death was soon followed by that of Charles VI. (the Maniac),
and according to the stipulations of the treaty above-named,
Henry VI., son of the former—though but nine months old—was
declared king of France. The affairs of the young king were

administered by his regent and uncle, the duke of Bedford. But the proscribed dauphin, who now assumed the title of Charles VII., was far from giving up his pretensions in opposition to his alien rival. The chance of arms was to decide, which one of the two was to be supplanted by the other. At first the English were the favorites of fortune, while Charles, whom only a section of France recognized as king, was erring about on the other side of the Loire, destitute of the means necessary for the successful prosecution of the war. The capital had declared itself in favor of the English, who after their victory at Verneuil, had marched on to the siege of Orleans, with the intention of passing the Loire, after the taking of that city. Charles, now reduced to the verge of despair, was already entertaining the design of repairing to a remoter part of the kingdom, or, if reduced to the last choice, of retreating into the Provence. The bastard of Orleans, count Dunois, was, however, still defending the city bravely. This was still a source of encouragement to the Dauphin, which Mary of Anjou, his wife, and Agnes Sorel, his mistress, did not fail to improve in their attempts to inspire this indolent and diffident prince with nobler sentiments of honor, of self-reliance and of confidence in the possibility of success. Their persuasive appeals induced him to remain.

In this difficult state of affairs, two circumstances occurred, that reanimated his hope again. The marriage of the Duke of Glouster, the brother of Bedford, to *Jacqueline* of Hainault, lead to a rupture with Burgundy; in consequence of which Philip, the Good, who felt himself aggrieved by this match, abandoned the cause of the English altogether. The other and more important source of hope was as unexpected and sudden as it was extraordinary. A simple country-maid, seventeen years of age, from the village of Dom Remy near Vaucouleurs, on the borders of Lorraine and Champagne, publicly declared herself commissioned by heaven to retrieve the lost fortunes of her country, and to lead its native and legitimate Lord from the gloom of despair to sunny hopes, to signal victories and final coronation at Rheims. Her personal confidence, her ingenuous enthusiasm subdued every obstacle, which incredulity and the anxious apprehensions of her friends at first opposed to the accomplishment of her purpose. Her plans once formed, and her course begun, her every act and very presence inspired all who witnessed them and her with faith in the divinity of her mission. An imposing personal appearance of unusual beauty, a lively imagination long fed in rural solitude by legends of saints, by historic traditions and by rumors of wars, an uncommon share of sagacity, a fervent love for her native land and its rightful prince, and lastly a confidence in the reality of her visions, which no gainsaying could shake, appear to have been at once the secret and the powers of her success. This was so signal, that her mission from above (or according to her own account, her commission from the Virgin), which her own father had anxiously questioned (in the play at least), and which the enemy ascribed to supernatural agencies of a different sort, was soon no longer a matter of doubt in the minds of any of her countrymen.

Armed with a sword from the church at Fierboys* and bearing a white banner, she no sooner had placed herself at the head of the army (1429), than victory followed upon victory in rapid succession. Her wonderful appearance suddenly resuscitated a feeling of national honor and patriotism among the troops, who had for years before been disheartened by perpetual defeat, while among the masses at large it made her an object of religious veneration. It was in vain, that men of experience in the military art opposed her plans or contradicted her pretensions, she maintained them by an appeal to her higher commission, and by the resistless evidence of their magic results. It was thus, that the siege of Orleans was raised in consequence of her destructive sallies on the enemy, a few days after she had fought her way into the city. The impression she produced on the enemy on this occasion, was so terrible, that the very report of her approach spread consternation and ruin into their ranks forever thereafter. After the accomplishment of this victory, which was deemed decisive, she hastened to join the Dauphin, for the purpose of directing his future movements. Châlons, Troyes and Rheims were taken without any difficulty, and on the 17th of June of the same year, in which she had commenced her career, Charles could celebrate his coronation-festival in the cathedral at Rheims. On this

---

* Shakspeare's metrical vein seems to have been at a low ebb when he makes Joanna say:

> Here is my keen-edged sword,
> Decked with five flower-de-luces on each side;
> The which at Touraine, in St. Katherine's church-yard,
> *Out of a great deal of old iron* I chose forth.

occasion, the happiest of her brief but brilliant career, she stood
with the victorious banner in her hand, by the side of the honored
monarch, whom with tearful eyes and prostrate knees, she then
saluted as sovereign of his native land; at the same time solemnly
declaring, that her mission ended here, and that her part was now
to return to her former humble station.

In spite of her inward misgivings, however, she was prevailed
upon to remain with the army, and to aid its future efforts to ex-
tirpate the last vestige of the enemy from the soil of her country.
But her inward resources failing her, her outward movements
were henceforward, if not less heroic and determined, still less
happy and auspicious than before. At a descent which she made
upon the Burgundians in defence of Compiegne, her return was cut
off by a premature close of the gates of the town, in consequence
of which she fell into the hands of the enemy. The duke of
Burgundy left the dreaded Amazon to the mercy of the English
who forthwith transported the prisoner to Rouen, the seat of their
power. The latter had long detested her as a sorceress in league
with the powers of darkness, as the terrible "witch of Orleans,"
and it was now for their interest to bring her before an ecclesias-
tical court as such.

By a long and scandalous trial, at which the bishop of Beauvais,
assisted by a number of Doctors of Divinity and Doctors of the
Laws, members of the faculty of the Sorbonne, presided, she was
in spite of her own earnest protestations *made guilty* of heresy
and witchcraft,* and the process ended in her condemnation to
the stake (1431), After a brief imprisonment, attended with
shameful abuses, by which a recantation of her error was extorted
from the helpless victim, the odious sentence was executed, and
she ended with a resignation that moved even the obdurate hearts
of her executioners to pity; whilst by-standing witnesses of every
rank describe the scene as one that in point of thrilling interest
was not inferior to any of those depicted in the legends of the primitive martyrs.

Was it cowardice or inability on the part of her princely

---

* "C'était un spectacle étrange, de voir ces théologiens, ces docteurs tra-
vailler de toute leur force à ruiner ce qui faisait le fondement de leur doctrine et le principe religieux du moyen âge en général, la croyance aux
révélations, à l'intervention des êtres surnaturels.... *Ils doutaient du*
moins de celles des anges; mais leur foi au diable était tout entière."
MICHELET.

friends, that in the mortal anguish of her last extremity she was so basely forsaken? On this point history is silent. The account of the trial, however, as it still exists in documentary evidence, shows clearly, that in that section of France the enemies of Charles considered themselves still strong enough to dispose of the prisoner according to their pleasure without any fear of evil consequences from the newly crowned king.

How little, however, the learned theological and legal decision affected the convictions of the people (whose voice is not unfrequently that of the Divinity) may—apart from the emotions betrayed by the hangmen on the occasion of her painful death—be learned from the beautiful popular legend, said to be still current in those parts, that out of her ashes a snow-white dove ascending, winged its way to heaven! *

* Nor has the Nemesis of history been slow in dealing out just recompense to those engaged in this scandalous affair; ridicule and shame on the absurdity of her judges; honor and deathless fame to the martyr-heroine! As early as 1456 a revision of her process was instituted by Pope Calixtus III., by which she was declared innocent. At a more recent period, and particularly since the appearance of Schiller's drama, the subject has undergone repeated scrutiny. Most of the original documents containing the records of the court, as well as the subsequent depositions of those who witnessed the miseries of her captivity, the agony of her death, have been collected and published. Of late years Guido Gœrres has pilgrimised to every spot where Joanna's presence might have left some traditional legend, and ransacked every library of Europe, in search of new materials, that might possibly shed some additional light on this his darling object of research. Michelet has reared to her an imperishable monument in his erudite History of France. The care with which he has evidently sifted the existing evidence, the tact exhibited in the collection and reconstruction of the prominent traits of her character, especially as they appear in her sayings and replies, give to this biographical episode not only the moral certitude of history, but almost the charm of poetry itself. "Humility, *bon sens, douceur*, patriotism, enthusiasm, artless simplicity, piety, immaculate purity of heart and purpose made her triumphant in her cause."—"La vierge secourable des batailles que les chevaliers appelaient, attendaient d'en haut, elle fut ici-bas .... dans la simple fille des campagnes, du pauvre peuple de France!" Vol. V., p. 177.

The nation itself has at different times testified its grateful remembrance of the heroine by the erection of artistic monuments in her honor. The group on the Loire-bridge at Orleans, commemorating the deliverance of the city on May 8th 1429, represented Joanna and King Charles VII. in a kneeling attitude before the Saviour. This was destroyed by the iconoclasts of 1793, but replaced by another statue of la Pucelle on the Place du Martroy. Another monument of the kind stands on the Place de la Pucelle at Rouen. The third,

1*

This ignominious termination of Joanna's remarkable career did not, however, affect the cause of Charles as detrimentally as might have been expected. The success that had attended the movements of the heroine was of enduring importance in the future destiny of her country. It had elevated the nation again to the consciousness of its own strength, which the insolence of its oppressors could now no longer shake. This was its grand, its last result.

The death of the regent, the duke of Bedford, and the rupture between the English and Philip of Burgundy, who by the peace of Arras had joined the legitimist party, were additional and fatal blows to the cause of the invaders, whose subsequent efforts to maintain the possession of their conquered territory were but a feeble shadow of their former strength.

Paris surrendered, and the king could hold a public entrance into his capital, from which he had so long been exiled, on the 12th of November, 1437. Frequent truces and negotiations began now to interrupt the sluggish course of the war, until the Bastard of Orleans in the battle of Castillon completely destroyed the power of the English, who now had lost all their continental possessions with the exception of Calais and the islands of Jersey and Guernsey. It was thus, that the war ended without any formal treaty of peace.

No sooner had the country become tranquil, than Charles zealously undertook the work of reorganizing the disordered affairs of the state. The reforms, which he made in the financial and judicial departments of the administration, exhibited the

and by far the most attractive (because the most artistic) little monument, is the statue executed by a fair and illustrious hand (by princess Mary of France), which in 1851 adorned one of the galleries of Versailles. The national heroine, as represented by this exquisite figure, is a Maiden of fair, but rather slender and by no means athletic proportions, as if thereby the artist had particularly desired to remove the impression, that her achievements might have been accomplished by any physical strength. She is in a standing attitude, clasping a sword to her bosom. A chaste and timid expression of womanly grace is diffused over the whole form. Intensity and piety of mind, clouded, however, by a melancholy reverie, are depicted on her countenance; but her pensive eyes are fixed on the ground, as if she did not venture to raise them up towards heaven. The figure was undoubtedly suggested by the first scene of the fourth act of Schiller's drama; which is still the most complete vindication of Joanna's character, the most gorgeous monument ever erected in honor of woman.

characteristic wisdom and moderation of this monarch. By the
Pragmatic Sanction of Bourges (1438), he had already established
on a decidedly firmer basis the liberties of the Gallican Church,
which by this act had become identified with the nation, and in
a measure independent of the assumptions of the See of Rome.

The discipline and more perfect organization of the army were,
moreover, the object of the king's particular attention. This last
measure, important as it was, in a political point of view, to the
maintenance of peace and internal order, was a thorn in the side
of the nobles, who in the manifest decline of their feudal independence of the crown, regarded all attempts at centralization
with jealousy, and as innovations ruinous to their cause. Hence
the new mutinies and insurrections in the South, into which the
young dauphin even (Louis XI.) was inveigled—source of bitter
sorrow to the declining age of the king.

The whole of this long struggle had, as we have seen, not
been a struggle against an alien enemy simply, but a civil (or
perhaps rather a *feudal*) contest of Frenchmen against Frenchmen, in which sectional and even ethnological enmities were
kindled. So true was this, that in most of the international
engagements, the great bulk of the English army was composed
of the followers of the nobles from the south western part of
France, and not only the Burgundians but also the Gothic descendants of the Aquitaines fought under English banners against
their Northern brethren, who were of Frankish origin.

II. SCHILLER'S POETICAL PREDECESSORS, ANTONIO ASTEZANO,
CHAPELAIN, VOLTAIRE, SHAKSPEARE; HIS METHOD OF
TREATING THE SUBJECT; COMPLETION; THEATRICAL RE-
PRESENTATION.

The mysterious character and brilliant career of Joanna have
made her the subject of poetic composition among several
nations. The first attempt of the kind was made a few years after
her death by the secretary of the duke of Orleans, Antonio Astezano (Ms. de Grenoble, 1435), but this is said to be remarkable
rather from its being the work of a contemporary of the event,
than from any intrinsic æsthetical merit.

The French themselves have made the Maid the heroine of two
epic-poems of a very opposite character. The first of these is

by Chapelain, composed at the beginning of the 17th century, and now almost forgotten in France itself. This poet, however, has done Joanna the justice of representing her in a manner not unbecoming the part which she acted in the actual history of her country. She is here the humble and yet heroic virgin, whose courage and enthusiasm brave every danger, until she has vanquished the foe and accomplished the redemption of her country by the sacrifice of her own life.

At a later period, Voltaire deigned to treat the subject anew, and with express reference to his predecessor. He did it in his characteristic style. "To him whose trade it was to war with every kind of superstition, this child of fanatic ardor seemed no better than a monstrous zealot, and the people who followed her and believed in her to be something worse than lunatics." Of this "wittiest and most profligate poem, for which literature has to blush," Schiller says to Wieland: "You will easily grant me that Voltaire has done his utmost, to make the task of a dramatic successor as difficult as possible. If he has pulled down his Pucelle too deeply into the mire, I have perhaps placed mine too high. But here there was no other remedy, if the infamy, with which he has branded his fair subject, was to be wiped away."*

Shakspeare has not done much better than Voltaire in his characterization of the Pucelle, which is so singular, that it has led a late critic to infer that the whole of the first part of king Henry VI. was one of the early, premature productions of the author, written at a time, when his principles of dramatic composition were as yet but imperfectly established. This becomes so much the more plausible when we consider that Malone, and some others of the earlier editors of Shakspeare, have attempted to prove, that this part of the historical trilogy *never* proceeded from the pen of Shakspeare, and that at the utmost it could only have been retouched by him, and adapted to the other parts, that are undoubtedly his own. The discussion of this point, however, is not necessary here. But the fact, that Joanna figures in an

* Voltaire would seem to have had no real intention to dishonor the maid, on whom in his more sober writings he bestows the highest encomium :

"Cette héroïne .. fit à ses juges une réponse digne d'une mémoire éternelle. Ils firent mourir par le feu celle, qui pour avoir sauvé son roi, *aurait eu des autels*, dans les temps héroïques, où les hommes en élevaient à leurs libérateurs."—*Essai sur les Meurs et l'Esprit des Nations.* C. 80.

English drama is in itself an interesting one, and if national prejudice is even allowed to act a part in poetic composition, the poet's mode of treatment might easily have been predicted. It is in vain that we look here for any of those naïve and charming qualities, which history with hardly a dissenting voice has attributed to the character of Joanna; but on the contrary she, like many of Shakspeare's personages of an inferior order, is represented as using language of dubious import, utterly at variance with our idea of a pure-minded virgin; she is likewise subjected to the most opprobrious abuses from the warriors, whom she encounters in single combat, and such terms as "giglot wench" and even worse are made to wound her ear with impunity.

Not a vestige of those delicate touches of female tenderness and loveliness of soul that adorn so many of the other characters in Shakespeare's tragedies. It is true, that she forms on the part of the French, what Talbot does on that of the English, the very soul of the cause, in which she has enlisted. She succeeds in resuscitating the enthusiasm of patriotism, and with that a belief in a higher assistance, in her nation, and with her appearance the fortune of the war suddenly inclines towards her countrymen. The poet does not deny that she is possessed of supernatural resources, but as an Englishman, he makes her a sort of Walkyrie or Weird Sister, who by incantations derives her aid from demons of an ungodly sort; and all the enthusiastic exultation of the French is to him the operation of an evil principle, the movement of the nightside of our nature. There is, moreover, a singular incongruity in her personal account of herself and her mission.

At her first interview with the dauphin, she makes in substance the same narration, which Schiller has put into her mouth for that occasion. She is here, too, by birth the humble shepherd's daughter, " on whose contemptible estate, it hath pleased heaven and the gracious Lady to shine, who, having appeared to her in a vision full of majesty had willed her to leave her base vocation, and to free her country from calamity." She is, moreover, possessed of a personal beauty, that heaven's clear ray had directly infused on her, of a sagacity that readily can answer any question without premeditation, of a courage that exceeds her sex. After she has become a captive of the enemy, she still pretends to have been a virgin from her tender infancy, chaste and imma-

culate in very thought, whose maiden blood would cry for vengeance at the gates of heaven. She blames the English, that
from want of grace, that others have, they judge it straight a thing
impossible, to compass wonders, but by help of devils; at the same
time asserting, that she never had to do with wicked spirits, that
she was "virtuous and holy, chosen from above, by inspiration of
celestial grace, to work exceeding miracles on earth." But all
these asseverations of hers appear like empty rhetoric, with which
her conduct is in direct conflict. In a previous part, it appears,
that she repelled the almost ludicrously aggressive love of Charles
but for a moment, and her last confession exhibits her veracity
as well as her chastity in a scandalous light. She absurdly
denies her parentage by affirming, in opposition to what she had
told the dauphin, that she was not begotten of a shepherd swain,
but issued from the progeny of kings.

In Scene third, Act V., the nature of her supernatural assistance, which is now even on the point of failing her, is given in
detail. The familiar spirits which she invokes, the speedy helpers,
are substitutes under the lordly monarch of the North (of Zimi-
mar) and are culled out of powerful regions of the earth, to gain
whose present aid she vainly makes use of incantations, staking
first her body and at last her soul as promise for their wonted
furtherance. The " charming spells and periapts " are no longer
of any avail; the demons, that through her mediation had
aided her countrymen, now shake their heads; hell is too strong
for her to buckle with; and France must vail her lofty plumed
crest. Upon the whole, it must be confessed that Joanna's
character is but imperfectly developed; nor does the poet in
this representation rise above the vulgar national prejudice of
his bigoted ancestors, to whom her prowess and enthusiasm was
of impure origin, simply because it had frustrated their ambitious
projects.

The most charitable conclusion, that we can possibly arrive
at, in examining this singular delineation, would be, that
Joanna, originally a pure and heaven-commissioned heroine,
became gradually corrupted by the deteriorating influences of
her military life. But this even is contrary to all historic evidence. Her mind was so thoroughly imbued with sentiments
of piety, that her appearance in the camp produced a sudden

change in its morality *; God and the Virgin received alone the glory of her victories.

It cannot be denied, therefore, that Shakspeare's entire representation of this most wonderful movement in modern history, and of its leading personage, falls below the requisitions both of historic fidelity, and of dramatic consistency; and Schlegel's opinion in this matter, which gives the English bard the preference over Schiller, might surprise us, were not that learned critic's bias of judgment already known to us beforehand. Equally strange is his repugnance to the supernatural machinery of Schiller's work; the poet would in his opinion have done better, if in compliance with the sceptical tendencies of his age, he had entirely omitted all preter-natural interference in the treatment of the subject; if, like his English predecessor he had simply aimed to furnish an objectively real mirror of the times; and still he admits it to be an historically attested fact, that the higher mission of Joanna was believed both by herself and by the majority of her contemporaries.

Schiller's bold aberration from the truth of history, in regard to the end of Joanna's career proved another stumbling-block to both the Schlegels, who maintained in opposition to the general approval of the poet's course, that the real ignominious martyrdom of the forsaken and betrayed heroine would have stirred up our sympathy more profoundly than the rosy serenity which the poet in the face of historic evidence has poured around the triumphant close of her eventful life. This delicate point, however, was duly considered by the poet himself, nor did he adopt the present arrangement without a previous careful examination of all its bearings. After much hesitation he arrived at the conviction, that this change of the catastrophe was *dramatically necessary*, in order that the late and tardy verdict of justice, by which posterity had redeemed the fair name and honor of the deeply injured heroine, of which an evil destiny had robbed her for a time, might be brought within the compass of the career itself, and close together with it, before our eyes.

As was usually the case with all the former dramatic produc-

---

* "It was a risible and touching spectacle to witness the sudden conversion of the veteran brigands of the Armagnac faction ... La Hire did not venture to swear any more. Joanna perceiving the violence, this self-denial cost him, had compassion on him, and permitted him to swear: "Par son bâton!"—MICHELET.

tions of the author, he commenced by an earnest application to the historical sources; he carefully studied for this purpose De l'Auverdy's *Notices et Extraits des Mss. de la bibliothèque du Roi*, (Paris, 1790), which contained a series of twenty-eight Mss. documents, relating to the sentence of Joanna and its subsequent reversal. It was a whole year, that he pondered over the subject before he proceeded to its execution. The piece was begun in the year 1800. Joanna was to him a "*sujet sui generis*, an enviable material for the poet, somewhat like the Iphigenia of the Greeks." In his letters to Goethe, however, with whom he now was in frequent communication on the subject, he complains of its difficulty, which arose, he says, partly from his own poverty of outward experience, and partly from the fact that in all his efforts he needed a method of his own, and much expenditure of time, to infuse the necessary poetic life into the outward clay of his materials. The subject, moreover, was new to him, and none of the easiest. So many poets and poetasters had already stumbled, blundered and sinned against it, that he must needs atone for the error of his predecessors, and attempt its restoration to the rights of the Romantic age, to which it properly belonged. The process of revision in the several poetical acts appeared to him as necessary, as was that real revision of Joanna's trial, which pope Calixtus in 1456 had instituted against the twelve calumniating articles.

The poet had, moreover, now arrived at that period in the development of his mind, when he began to distrust his former notions in regard to the philosophy of art. A poetical work, in so far as it forms also *in hypothesi* an intrinsically organized whole, must be judged by its own inner standard, and not according to general, and consequently empty formulæ, between which and the actual facts there cannot be any possible connection. The two operations of poetic creation and of theoretical analysis now appeared to him to be as far apart as is the north pole from the south; and metaphysical theory, which at one time he had placed so high, was now to him the grave of his activity. This change of conviction turned out greatly to the advantage of the poet, who, throwing aside every shackle, with which formerly he had encumbered himself, entered now into the spirit of his new subject with all the earlier energies of his own enthusiastic nature. For full nine months he was incessantly at work, without even allowing himself the necessary recreation.

The solitude of his residence in upper Weimar, and of his lonely garden in Jena, witnessed the ardor, with which the recluse combatted the difficulties of his new task, which the fear of not getting it ready in time to meet the publisher's engagement (he had already sold the Ms. in advance to Unger of Berlin, who wanted it for the next fair at Leipsic), only served to augment. Add to this all the annoying interruptions from the excessive heat of August, and subsequently, from the chilling winds and rainy spells of March, and on one occasion from the tumultuous hymeneal rejoicings in the house opposite to his, and you will have a faithful picture of the poet's agonies during the production of this darling child of his imagination. On the 16th of April, 1801, the drama was at length completed; and Goethe could inform his friend: "It is so bravely done, so good, so beautiful, that I know nothing to compare with it."

The practicability of its dramatic representation was at first a matter of doubt; and Schiller himself shrunk from the responsibility of it. He dreaded the loss of time, and still more the loss of patience, that the supervision of the "empirical process" of memorizing the different rôles, and the tedious rehearsals would inevitably entail on him. Still he subsequently yielded to the importunities of Goethe, who desired him to arrange the piece, which at first was printed without any division into scenes, for the boards. Letters had already arrived from managers at Berlin, Leipsic, Munich and Hamburg, requesting the play for representation. It was at Leipsic, that the poet, in company with the Kœrner family, attended the first public exhibition of his Joanna, on which occasion he had an opportunity of witnessing the powerful effect of his genius on the public mind. When the curtain dropped at the end of the first act, the enthusiasm of the spectators burst out into the universal shout: "Long live Frederick Schiller!" and the sound of drums and trumpets accompanied and echoed the reiterated congratulations. At the conclusion of the play, the whole audience rushed in hurried confusion out of the house, in order to get a closer view of the poet, as he passed out, and to testify their admiration and their thanks. When Schiller made his appearance, the assembled spectators uncovering their heads, arranged themselves into two long files, and through this avenue of men, who manifested their profound respect by a reverential silence, the poet passed along. During this interesting spectacle a father and a mother might now and then be seen lifting up a child, and whispering: " *That is he!* "

This sincere expression of approbation and esteem, coming as it did from those, who were still intoxicated by the magic influences of his inspired muse, must have given rise to proud emotions in the poet's breast, especially, when he remembered that in his youth, a poor and homeless fugitive, he had appealed from the hard sentence of his prince to the enlightened humanity of his countrymen, whose highest expectations were now more than realized, as was the faith of all his earlier hopes!

At Berlin the piece was first produced on new year's day, 1802, on the occasion of the opening of the new theatre. Zelter wrote to Goethe: " If Schiller wants to see his Maid of Orleans, he must come to Berlin. The splendor of the *mise en scène* is more than imperial ; in the fourth act, the number of the *dramatis personæ* amounts to more than eight hundred ; music and all included, the whole produces such an eclatant effect, that every representation puts the audience in extasies. The cathedral, together with the whole decoration, consisting of a long colonnade, through which the procession enters into the church, are in the Gothic style." Schiller, however, agreed with Tieck in the opinion, that such an extraordinary expenditure of pompous magnificence in scenery and costume only tended to divert the spectator from the intrinsic excellencies of the piece, which such a giddy spectacle would inevitably throw into the shade.

III. THE CHARACTER OF JOANNA AS DELINEATED BY THE POET.

" In his Ghost-seer Schiller had exhibited a series of miraculous events, as the result of natural magic, the machinations of a deluding imposture—a construction which the rationalizing tendencies of the 18th century had been disposed to put on all the extraordinary phenomena of history and nature. Here, however, he restores for the behoof of piety and art the miracle again to the place it held in a remoter time of unconditional belief. The spirit world and the natural, heaven, earth and hell, the demon and the human element stand here in manifest connection, and supernatural beings exercise an immediate control over human events. The manner in which both these worlds of wonder and of nature are blended, are proofs of the preëminent skill of the artist. Whilst by means of a strong representation of wonderful agencies he annuls, as it were, the ordinary laws of physical nature on the one hand, and unfolds to the anticipating vision of the soul a midrealm of spirits, over and above the world of sense, wherein beings good and bad mysteriously move, so on the other hand he knows how to inspire us with faith in the miraculous itself, by causing it to spring only from a soil previously and duly prepared, by extinguishing the transitions from the natural to the supernatural, and by carrying out the causal nexus, which he sometimes jumps in the *subject* of the history, with a more rigorous consistency in the *form* of the representation. It is thus that he prevents the Fabulous from degenerating into the Phantastical. With the same artistic tact, the genius of Schiller has known how to convert the wonderful appearance of Joanna into a tragic form of flesh and bone. Strictly speaking, the Marquis of Posa, queen Elizabeth in Don Carlos, Max, Thekla, are greater wonders than the miraculous Maid of Orleans; for in the case of the former the element of the wonderful resides in their inner nature, and has the appearance of inconsistency; here however it lies in the relation to the Invisible, which by its very nature is incomprehensible. How did those characters in an age and in circumstances like their own attain to their ideas of life, to their heavenly purity of mind? As an off-set to these, the character and the whole grand mission of Joanna are sustained by the best poetical motives, and while nearly all the earlier ideal creations of the poet are thoroughly subjective and lyrical, he here has succeeded, in a surprising manner, in giving a firm and substantially objective form to a being that seems to move beyond the sphere of ordinary realities.

The father of the Maid is an honest, affectionate, and by no means an ignoble man, who does not refuse his daughter Louison to her suitor on account of his poverty. As an uncultured man, however, he is affected by the cheerless religious tenets of his times, and being of a subtilizing melancholy temperament, he always presupposes the worst in others, even in his daughter. His own belief in evil spirits was destined to develop itself in the more nobly organized soul of Joanna into a revelation-faith of a higher order. The religious enthusiasm of the times, the mysticism of the church, the simple occupation of pastoral life fostered the bud, until with the increasing distress of France, it burst forth into blossoms. By making the heroine a shepherdess, in violation of historic evidence, the poet has gained the advantage of a psychological ground for her mode of thinking and feeling. Emphatic and repeated mention is moreover made of an ancient enchanted tree, in order that it might be seen, that the legends which tradition had gathered around it, constituted the chief ingredient in the educational history of Joanna, and Dom Remy, where she had hitherto lived, is represented as a place of pilgrimage, which must have inspired her soul from childhood up with thoughts and presentiments of a religious order.*

* A psychological exposition of the so-called miraculous element in the character of Joanna and of the nature of her visions has been attempted by an eminent critic of the poetry of Schiller, from which we give the following extract:

"Our consciousness passes directly over into the nature of things. When in unity with nature, it is feeling, when in contradistinction from nature, the latter becomes objective through the medium of the senses. Joanna has both of these alternately for her Pathos, and has, moreover, the consciousness of it. It is thus that she sees and feels objects by immediate intuition. If a lamb has been lost, she discovers it in a dream, when she sleeps in the shade of the sacred oak. She herself says, that whilst others, like Raymond see only the natural side of things, she beholds the immortal. Her consciousness in the shape of feeling becomes one with the outward object, it becomes the intuitive soul of nature. Hence, having immediate converse with the object of nature, she is familiar with every herb, knows the course of the stars, the movement of the clouds, and hears the roarings of the secret powers of nature. She is, moreover, a prophetess, she sees things afar off both in time and space, and is by intuition herself the unity of whatever is directly or remotely connected with her pathos. It is thus, that she sees the king, where no one saw him but his Maker, sees the sword by which her victories are to be achieved lying in a distant city in an ancient vault of St. Catherine's churchyard. She informs the herald of the enemy who had been sent on the same morning by his general, that the latter had mean while fallen in battle. She is, moreover, a prophetess, and beholds futurity. But she prophesies not simply to others, as to the King and to Burgundy, but she likewise knows her own fate beforehand and is aware, that it is of no earthly nature. Her pathos is no earthly happiness, like that of Wallenstein, but the heavenly beatitude of love.

Hence Joanna is not simply in immediate unity with nature, but also in unity with the spirit. Though at first, and in their immediate form she receives the divine mandate and commission from the boughs of the sacred oak, yet the emotion of her mind is no longer a simple matter of feeling, but

The sequestered hamlet is now visited by rumors of the victories and success of the English, whose aim was to obtrude on France a master born on alien soil, "who does not love the people." The poet thought that he had carried a characteristic trait of woman's nature in representing Joanna, who was incapable of seizing the abstract idea of monarchy, as ever proposing to herself the kind and amiable king as the ultimate aim of all her exertions. The prophet Posa could only glow for a universal monarchy; the prophetess Joanna, unless she transcended the limits of her sex, or at any rate those of her times, could only aim at the restoration of a previous state of things, nor could she link her vocation to the concrete idea of the state, but in childlike, patriarchal wise, only to a venerated person. It will be perceived, that at the very outset a motive was thus presented to the poet for portraying king Charles VII. as an estimable kindly man, a friend of the people, and that a certain exaltation of royalty, foreign to all the previous pieces of Schiller, became a necessary appendage to the principal character of the tragedy.

It is this popular king, in behalf of whose preservation the rural maiden addresses a fervent prayer to the Divine Mother (Act I., Scene 10). And why so? was it not she, the spotless maid, who bore the Lord, and who herself was raised to heavenly splendor? The catholic church cherishes the conviction, that pure virginity can accomplish all that is grand and glorious on

belongs to the believing consciousness; the spirit alone can really become an object of cognition. In religion, however, and by faith it is the subject of immediate feeling, and this universal spiritual emotion is love. In the catholic church this love is symbolized most beautifully in the pure love of the Virgin. This is what Joanna feels in her heart. Though still sitting under the Druid oak, she yet no longer sleeps or dreams beneath its shade; she dispels her drowsiness by pious devotion and keeps awake. Her feeling being of a conscious description gradually elevates itself into a conception, an intuition. It is for this reason that the heavenly Virgin descends to her, clad like herself in the habiliments of a shepherdess. All that the heavenly one says to her, is her own feeling, her own conception; she is humble and a pure maiden, filled with heavenly love. By symbolizing her feeling into an intuition, the latter assumes the form of the holy mother with the beautiful Jesus-boy. The image becomes the symbol of faith; it represents the Queen of heaven hovering over a globe. It is thus that in the hands of Joanna, who in all these visions sees but the reflex of her own mind, the symbol of the spirit, the image of faith is converted into the ensign of war and victory."—HINRICHS.

earth. In the midst of this devout and elevated tone of mind,
the Queen of heaven appears to her beneath the magic tree and
summons her to crown the king at Rheims. It is thus that the
poet paves the way for the supersensuous, before it becomes
effectual in the life of the maiden. The divinely inspired one
is now conscious of her higher vocation, which, however, she
keeps silently locked up in her heart, until the decisive hour
strikes. A helmet, which a Gipsy woman urges upon the rustic
Bertrand, becomes to her the expected signal of her mission.
It is now that the spirit moves her to the duty of delivering
Orleans from the siege of the enemy. She feels herself irre-
sistibly drawn away from her home, driven out into the popu-
lous field of contest.

All this the poet represents in the prologue, which, as it is
not simply the exposition, but at the same time the beginning
of the action, may fitly be considered the first act of the piece.
In this prelude Joanna already appears as a being of a superior nature, as she subsequently proves herself to be. The
habit, for which her father upbraids her, of leaving her couch
at midnight and before daybreak, and of sitting for whole hours
under the Druid-tree is substantially corroborated by her subsequent narrative before the king. It is to give ear to the inward prophetic voice, that she separates herself from the shepherd maidens of the valley, that she feels herself a stranger in
her father's house, although she joyfully serves her elder sisters, and with a quiet obedience, practices the most difficult
of duties. Not a vestige of loving devotion makes as yet its
appearance, and her suitor Raymond rather venerates than loves
her; she appears to him to have some higher signification, to
have her origin in other times. To such an extent does the demon
element control the purely human emotions enchained in her bosom,
and she stands in contradiction both with her youth, and with the
nature of her sex. In the prologue she speaks not a single
word either to her sisters or to her father, and would appear
entirely closed to all softer emotions, unless the poet had neutralized this indifference towards men by the admixture of a touching
susceptibility for *nature*, which expresses itself at the close of the
prologue.

It is, however, not so much by her mysterious silence in the prologue, as it is by the doubtful light in which she at first is made to
appear, that the poet adds point to our curiosity in behalf of this

extraordinary being. And here it must be observed at the outset, that the spirit world, which wonderfully blends and interferes with the natural, is in the sense of mediæval belief, in itself divided and dualized, so that men are on the one hand guided by the kindly powers of heaven, and on the other deluded by the crafty wiles of hell. Under which of these contending influences does the mysterious maiden stand? The words of her father ("Stay not alone, and do not delve for roots"), by which he characterizes her daily occupation, already excite our apprehension. For, how could Thibaut ever think of making charges of such a special and peculiar nature, unless there was some ground for them? Is the silence of the accused a proof of her consciousness of guilt? The mystical enchanted oak, moreover, makes us equally doubtful and the signal chosen by the poet to indicate to Joanna, that the hour for action was at hand, produces an equally uneasy impression. Could *Heaven* for the purpose of sending her this signal, make use of a Gipsy woman, a person of that class of men, from which, according to popular belief, Hell not unfrequently selects its instruments?—Yet all our doubts vanish at the close of the prologue before the highly animated and enthusiastic words of the maiden, and it is here that she steps forth from the dubious twilight, in her own peculiar and proper form, like the sun from piles of heavy clouds.

Much as Joanna has raised our expectations by the enthusiastic valedictory, her reappearance in the camp of the King even exceeds them, where the moment and the manner, in which she enters into the action are so decisive and so full of grandeur. The Constable has declined to serve his unwarlike prince any longer, the treasury of Charles is exhausted, Orleans at the point of surrendering, the best of the troops, the Highlanders, are threatening to leave, a decision of Parliamant has declared, that the King and his descendants had forfeited their claim to the throne, young Henry VI. of England has been crowned at St. Denis, Philip of Burgundy and Charles' own mother have conspired to ruin him, the King himself is so disheartened by all this, that he is at the point of retreating beyond the Loire, and his most faithful friends are ready to forsake him.

It is here, where all earthly hope has vanished, that Joanna suddenly brings unexpected help from heaven. She comes not, as does the historic maiden, to *promise* help, she has already holpen, when she makes her appearance before the Dauphin; the enemy is defeated! And as the prophetess had proved the verity of her mission even before her arrival by her achievements, so she repeats the proof by what she says immediately after she enters. She distinguishes the king, whom she had never seen before, among the crowd of his attendants, and reveals to him the contents of his most secret prayers. To remove all scruples of a religious nature, the Archbishop imparts to her endeavors the sanction of the church. It is his peculiar function in the tragedy, to symbolize the religious point of view, in which the whole is to be conceived. The maid speedily wins the confidence of all, the people behind the scene has hailed in her its heaven-sent deliverer, the king is convinced of the divinity of her mission, two distinguished officers desire the chief command of the army to be entrusted to her, the chevaliers present applaud the appointment by the clashing of arms. A herald now entering from the earl of Salisbury, offers a compromise, before the storming of Orleans. She refuses to accept, and after revealing to him the death of his general, she hurries off with her warriors to rescue the beleaguered city.

At the commencement of the second act, we see every thing accomplished, what Joanna had promised at the close of the first. Orleans is redeemed, the English are beaten, they again rally in a camp, in order to renew the contest on the following day. But before they have been refreshed by slumber, the rampart is scaled, Joanna is in the midst of the camp, and the surprised enemy seeks his safety in disordered flight. The hostile camp is committed to the flames, the maiden kills the Welshman Montgomery, and conciliates the duke of Burgundy on the place of combat.

The episode with Montgomery, has been reprehended, partly on account of its epic prolixity (see the note to Scene 7, Act II), partly because the poet in contradiction with history makes the heroine shed blood before our eyes, thus suffering the pious innocence of her nature to degenerate into inhumanity and murderous delight. The character of Joanna cannot however, be considered in any other light but that of militant action, and as her patriotic ardor is personal throughout, so is her hatred towards the English; she pursues *each individual* enemy, and and her religiously patriotic enthusiasm enhances her national hate to such a degree, that she weens it her vocation to slay every Englishman that falls into her hands. In this scene she falls into a contradiction with the celestial purity of her nature, as it is exhibited by her history. In the following scene, however, she is wholly herself again, and the poet appears to have intentionally contrasted in two contiguous scenes that which she believed to be her duty to do, in obedience to a higher stern command, with that wherein she listens to the impulse of her human heart.

It is here that she interposes as an angel of peace between the combatants; by her fair humanity the wrath of Burgundy is melted, the might of her conviction bends his haughty soul, her soft insinuating suasion draws him completely over to her own pure patriotic side. It is the *childlike* element of her nature that accomplishes this conquest. Joanna is a great political character, but inasmuch as she acts without self-consciousness, she is wholly a woman, a shepherdess, a child. Without any consciousness or will of her own, she suffers herself to be guided unconditionally by the voice of the spirit that commands her. It is this kindly beautiful side of her character, which has here made its appearance after and beside the terribly sublime, that the poet now proceeds to expand more completely in the following act. Joanna as veritable goddess of peace, her head crowned with a chaplet, completes the reconciliation which she had already commenced, by prevailing upon Burgundy to pardon Du Chatêl, the murderer of his father. It is here, that two redoubted heroes, Dunois and La Hire, offer her their hand, but neither this fact nor the elevation of herself and family to noble rank can lead her astray. Against the gentle persuasions of the king, who wishes to inspire her with love's sweet longing sentiment, she rises with all the majesty of her greatness: "*Dauphin, art thou already weary of the epiphany divine?*" &c. But this very impetuosity with which she repels the suggestions of earthly affection, evinces that she is not wholly inaccessible to the feelings, to which surrounding circumstances, and even the Archbishop himself, conspire to invite her. Such a state of mind is, moreover, indicated by the words: "*This armistice it irks and wearies me,*" and by her exclamation, when the report of the enemy's passage of the Marne had arrived: "*Battle and combat! 'Tis now the soul is from her fetters free!*" It is thus that the poet prepares the reader for the following scene, and Joanna hastens to meet the very fate, which, by leaving the effeminate arms of peace, she vainly endeavoured to escape.

2

In Scene 6, Act III. we are again transported to the battle-field.
Already Talbot is mortally wounded, the redoubt has been taken
by storm, and the French have carried the day. But Joanna is
lured away from the battle-scene by a ghost in the shape of a
black Knight, to a deserted region. The poet has only given us
a distant hint as to the real character of this Knight. He did not
wish to weaken the sublime impression which the Indefinite and
the Mysterious always enhances, by a more perfect outline of
this terrific figure. Talbot, who having shortly before died an
atheist, is, in accordance with the belief of the times, made to
wander about the earth, as a tormented demon, and makes his
appearance here to give a practical refutation of that word of
unbelief, which after life, would leave of man but a hand-full
of dissipating dust.* By a simulated flight the Ghost diverts the
Maiden from the field of combat, and thereby rescues many
Britons from the perils of death. But the crafty demon has yet
another aim. He exhorts the heroine to stop short in the midst
of her career of victory. He warns her, not for the purpose
of saving, but merely to perplex her. This puzzling phantom is,
as it were, a sensuous personification of the inward contradiction
of her own mind ; it merely gives language to the misgivings
of her own heart, and acts as a precursor of the calamity predicted to herself by her own prophetic spirit. The drift of the whole
scene is, to fill the mind of the spectator with bodeful apprehensions ; it is a prelude and introduction to the approaching fall
of Joanna. "*Slay what is mortal*," had been the language of the
Knight just before his sudden disappearance. But as she looks
now into the face of Lionel, the only surviving general of the

* " The black Knight is to subserve the purpose of linking us with an additional tie to the romantic world of spirits, since in this piece two worlds are in
constant interference with each other. Can any one, who has paid some little
attention to the course of the action, for a moment doubt, but that the ghost of
Talbot is meant thereby, who having shortly before died an atheist, had found
his place among the damned of hell? Ever are men, when they have reached
the highest point of their ambition, nearest to their fall. This is the experience
of Joanna in this scene. The maid who had offended the Nemesis by the
haughty and boastful words, that she would not lay aside the sword, until
proud England had perished, and who in her desire to combat spirits even, had
transgressed the limits of a pious reverence, must now be punished for her insolence. A single touch by the spirit paralizes her power. More than this I
did not wish to express, nor did I intend to make it the motive for any thing
that follows."—SCHILLER.

enemy, she becomes incapable even of killing that which is mortal. She violates her vow, and henceforth she herself is changed, though the state of her mission remains the same. This passage is properly the point where the tragedy commences. The fact that the heaven-sent maid, with unalloyed enthusiasm, surmounting every difficulty, was thus far speeding her way triumphantly, towards the lofty goal, gave to all that precedes the character of an exalted Epos. We look upon her victorious career with every other emotion but that of fear and compassion. It is but softly and imperceptibly, that we behold a powerful enemy to her divine mission springing up in the very heart of the maiden herself; and in the present scene a fearfully tragic conflict suddenly arises between the Divine and the Human, between the Heroic and the Womanlike. Two worlds enter into a hostile collision with each other. This contradiction is not a fancied or an artificial one, but is deeply rooted in our human nature. It is perceptible in the whole of Schiller's own biography, and may be termed the heroism of liberty, the humanity of the heart. The struggle between duty and love, as exhibited in the character of Max in the poet's Wallenstein, furnishes us a striking illustration of it.

The most humane, the most womanly impulse of our nature gains the ascendancy over Joanna at the very moment, when, in obedience to a mistaken divine mandate of duty, she is about to perpetrate the most unwomanlike, the most inhuman act,—that of killing the vanquished enemy. With admirable skill, the poet has here linked together the most incompatible extremes. At the very moment, in which the most frightful act was to be committed in the name of heaven, *human* nature suddenly awakening in its omnipotence, asserts its eternal rights, and her heart breaks forth in its first and glowing love for him she was to murder. 'Twas not until Joanna had arrived at the utmost extremity of this one ground, that she could suddenly be transferred upon the other.— Still it must be taken into consideration, that this change of mind, as was intimated before, had already been inwardly prepared.— It is from this moment, that Joanna belongs to our species, belongs to her sex. Her armor now conceals a feeling heart. We suffer with the sufferer. The immediate consequence of this inward division of Joanna's nature is a corresponding external contradiction with the world, both of which the poet has so skilfully de-

lineated in the rhythmically lyrical monologue at the beginning
of Act IV."*

The cause of her monarch had been victorious, and the whole
nation was hastening in joyous throngs to Rheims, to testify with
jubilant exclamations, its loyal devotion to its chosen lord, who
was to be anointed with the sacred oil, whose head was to receive
the ancient crown of Dagobert.   Joanna alone is mournful.   Her
inmost soul is lacerated by the torments of a seditious conscience;
and while *one* thought, *one* high sentiment of joy and gratitude
was beating in every Frenchman's breast, she, who had brought
about this glorious occasion alone remains unmoved by it.   But
why should an act of commiseration be attended with such bane-
ful consequences?   And if it was not pity, but another feeling
equally human, could that be so fearfully guilty?   If heaven demands a blind, a passive instrument for the accomplishment of its
high purposes, why did it not selecting send one of those pure
Immortals who do not feel, who never weep?   Why should
she, frail mortal child, have ever exchanged the humble shepherd's staff for the sword?   Why had she ever heard the
hurtlings of the sacred oak, or seen the Queen of heaven?
But all this was not her choice.   A higher will had called
her away from her rural peaceful home, had hurried her into
life's rude conflicts, had elevated her to walk with monarchs
in proud regal halls, and it too had permitted her now mournfully
to fall!   It is thus that the new strange feeling of love and the
terrors of conscience are struggling for preëminence in the unhappy bosom of Joanna, whose accusations of the Queen of heaven
occasionally border on irreverence.

In the next scene Joanna's lacerated state of mind appears
still greater, when held in contrast with the serenity of Sorel's
ever-loving nature.   She envies her repose; she calls on her,
who could be *one* with the universal jubilee, who could love
the source of all delight, the sun, to whom all nature was but
the reflection of her own love, to pity her, to weep over the
anguish of her forlorn condition.   It is this very contemplation
of Sorel's perfect happiness, which now for the first time she
is able to comprehend, that causes her to shrink with terror
from the disorders of her own bosom.   It is with reluctance

* Thus far we have followed Karl Hoffmeister's spirited outline of Joanna's
character, from which the preceding, (from page 18 seq.) is somewhat freely
translated.

that she accepts the banner, which she herself had borne victoriously in so many a strife, from the hands of Dunois and La Hire, who had been commissioned to conduct her as victor prophetess to her proper place beside the king. She calls herself a traitress, an enemy of her country, to whom the Oriflamme had ever been a signal of consternation and of terror. She is deeply moved at the sight of her true-hearted kindred, whom the rumors of her greatness had drawn to Rheims among the eager crowd of visitors, who came to see the festive sight. The sudden change produced by this cordial recognition adds new fuel to her stupefaction, and she would fain have persuaded herself into the belief, that these kings, these battles and heroic deeds were but dreamy shadows, flitting ghosts, she once had seen beneath the enchanted tree—as in fact they were but realizations of her former visions,—and that she was still in her own loved native Dom Remy, surrounded by familiar friendly faces, safe and quiet. Her love for Lionel had now unlocked her heart, so stern and pitiless before, to the emotions of natural affection. She rues the day when she left her home and loving sisters, is ready to resign the pomp her heart now loathes; would wish to be a shepherdess again, and is resolved to atone with the severest penitence, that ever she had vainly thought herself above her kin. It was with faltering steps, with pale and perturbated countenance that she had entered the decorated sanctuary, for the purpose of performing the crowning office of her loyal devotion, and to receive herself the adorations of a grateful people. But, here at the summit of her hope—which her confident persuasion had made a certainty from the beginning—here at the goal of her whole race, the anguish of her inward contradiction becomes only the more acute, at the sight of what to her seems now a mockery. The music of the organ assumes the angry voice of thunder, the dome's high arching canopy seems ready to fall down upon her guilty head, the image of the Virgin flashes anger, and spirits chase her out from their pure presence.

In this consternation she flees precipitately from the church, leaving behind the banner, which she resolves henceforward never more to touch. The judgment of heaven had brought her father to the scene, who witnessing her inward struggle, regards it as new evidence of her guilt, and is resolved to rescue his child from the unhappy grasp of the arch-enemy, to lead her back to duty and to God, whom in the vain delusion of her high estate, she had in his opinion, impiously renounced. His gloomy sub-tilizing bigotry had never seen aught but perversity in the nature of Joanna; and he makes the unamiable attempt to surprise her publicly with an aggravated exposition of all the charges he had virtually made in the prologue. He tells the prince and all the assembled multitude that they had been grossly deluded, and that the arts of hell and not the hand of heaven had wrought out their deliverance. Her silence at the sight of such unnatural conduct and at the mandate to "answer in the name of the Triune, whether she was of the Holy and the Pure" only serve to heighten the frantic invectives of her parent, whose mad violence inspires the bystanding warriors even with terror. But neither the gentle exhortations of Sorel, nor the solicitations of La Hire and of the Bishop, urging her to assert her innocence and to repel the foul accusation of having "sold her immortal part to the arch-enemy of souls on cursed ground," nor yet the confident per-suasions of Dunois, who stakes his knightly honor for her inno-cence can rouse her from her speechless reverie ; and the peals of thunder following Dunois' challenge and Thibaut's final insult, while they increase the terror and confusion of the scene, are as heaven-sent auguries presumptive confirmation of the charges, which she tacitly admits. Dunois' concluding, affectionate effort even proves a fruitless one. A cloud of darkness, impenetrable, endless and eternal shrouds her mind, and makes the scene before her an unreality, a dream, a phantom. "This motionless reticence in opposition to such questions and incriminations has justly been called one of the grandest features of the piece, a silence that borders on sublimity.* She voluntarily takes upon

---

* This scene has also been the subject of many attacks. To these Schiller replies in his own defense : "The stubborn silence of Joanna, at the moment when in the presence of a large concourse of people she is accused of sorcery by her own father, is in perfect consistency with the visionary enthusiasm of her character. Add to this the impression, that from motives of filial duty she was not permitted to contradict her father, a motive that would likewise ex-plain her previous silence in the second scene of the prologue. Besides being governed by the superstitious prejudice of an enchanted world, so universally current in the Middle Ages, and fostered so long by priestcraft and selfishness, the father was, moreover, one of those common natures, who in their attempts to explain extraordinary phenomena rather recur to an evil superhuman prin-ciple, than to a good one, and who habitually ascribe a bad motive to every action. In addition to this, Thibaut is an atrabilarian, with whom at the very

herself, since heaven wishes it, the load of the most heinous
crime, in order to atone for an insignificant offence. She stands
there humbly in blind submission, and confutes the frightful accusation of her father by no word, no look, no movement of her
hand."

This mute penitence of hers, which has fitly been termed the
third and last phase of her inward life, was continued during her
self-caused banishment in solitude and misery. Forsaken as a
reprobate by all her previous admirers, by the valiant Dunois even,
dejected, humbled to the dust, she now wanders for three days in
the midst of the most terrible commotion of the elements, hap-
hazard through the impenetrable forests of the Ardennes. *Raymond*, her early still faithful lover, is her only companion in this
lonely pilgrimage, the voluntary sharer of her captivity and sufferings. It was his reappearance at the moment of her utter
abandonment, that had first broken the spell of her motionless
silence, that had elicited the first returning symptoms of emotion. But he even is not free from painful presumptions of her
guilt, though he guides her steps with faithful devotion, though
he soothes her discouragement by words of hope and conso-
lation. The rudeness of the collier-boy, who on discovering the
"Witch of Orleans," dashes the reviving cup from her lips, and
the consternate flight of the collier and his wife, who had en-
tertained her unawares, give rise to the utterance of her first
word: "Thou seest, the curse pursues me and all flee my presence; care for thyself alone and leave me likewise now." In
the ensuing conversation, to which these her first words were
preliminary, she finds to her surprise, that Raymond even is
infected with unhappy suspicions. He beseeches her to repent
and to return to the bosom of the Holy Church. This pains
her more than all, and she proceeds now to vindicate her innocence before one human judge at least. Raymond cannot
comprehend her former silence, and could scarcely have com-
prehended her real error, which she, therefore, prudently for-

outset, Joanna never exchanges a word. Still she is his daughter, and it
would be psychologically true, that just such a man should be the progenitor of
just such a prophetess.—Heaven acquits the Maid by precisely the same sign,
by which it had previously confirmed her guilt. As soon as she perceives it,
she regards herself at once absolved and pardoned. The fact that thunder
was ever the favorite augury of the uncultured intelligence, has hardly as yet
been sufficiently considered "

bears to touch, while she firmly repels the common charge of sorcery : "Her wondrous acts had been accomplished by the power of God and of his Saints, and by no evil influences; the accusations of her father she had mutely born from a desire to submit to what a higher power had decreed should happen to her." ᴗShe, moreover, assures him, that her banishment was no misfortune to her. It was the solitude of her exile, that had taught her to know herself again. While surrounded by the nimbus of exalted honor, her heart was rife with wretchedest division, and outwardly envied by all the world, she inwardly was most unhappy. Her sharp sufferings, her sore trials had exercised a sanatory power. The frightful mutiny of the elements, which had menaced nature herself with ruin, had been her friend. The purification of the world by its own self-restoring process had proved her own too ; and in her soul was peace. Her consciousness was rid now of the last vestige of contradiction and of weakness. The day will come, when those who have rejected and condemned her, will discover their delusion, and tears will flow at the rehearsal of her fate ! It is thus, that her soul has risen superior to her sharp vicissitudes, and her virtue at first impulsive and untried, is after these severest tests fitted to receive the canonizing palm.

Her outward struggle, however, is not yet over. Delivered into the hands of the enemy, she is again subjected to the importunities of Lionel (whom she now discovers to have been her enemy), and to the scoffing derisions of the unbelieving raven Isabeau. Surcharged at her command with heavy fetters, she is now forced to be a passive witness to the new contest on the battle-field, in which her people is in danger of a disgraceful defeat. Eagerly devouring every word of the scout, who is watching the movement of the doubtful encountᴎr, she now can suffer the pain of inactivity no longer. The report of her monarch's danger rouses her to a complete recovery of her former self. Invoking the aid of heaven in a fervent prayer, she Samson-like now bursts the chains of her imprisonment and flies to the rescue of her countrymen. Her heroic courage is at this time too attended with accustomed victory. The king is saved, but at her expense. The wound she has received is mortal, and the occasion of her end.

IV. THE REMAINING CHARACTERS OF THE DRAMA, DUNOIS, KING CHARLES, AGNES SOREL, ISABEAU, BURGUNDY, TALBOT.

Joanna's character occupies nearly the whole field of the tragedy. The development of the consecutive phases of her mysterious nature constitutes the final cause, the animating principle of the action. The subordinate personages are all carefully selected and portrayed with reference to the main, compared with which they are more of standing figures, who by similarity and contrast subserve the purpose of bringing out in bolder, but still harmonious relief the hidden powers of the heroine's exalted dignity. It now remains to add a brief outline of the peculiarities of the most prominent of them.

Dunois is wholly devoted to his monarch and to the cause for which he fights so valiantly. The noble anger of the hero at the indecision of Charles, whom the repeated blows of fortune had disheartened, and who was more fit to rule in peaceful times as *Prince d'amour* mid Troubadours and festal splendor, than to fight for his possessions in the field, command at once our respect and admiration. With manly protestations and bitter irony he opposes this supine inaction of the king and urges him to resolute and earnest effort, to save his crown from the enemy's impending grasp. To him the *Jongleurs*, the *Minstrels* and gallant festivals are, for the present at least, as odious as they were unseasonable. It is true, he too had read in tales of yore, "that Love was always paired with high chivalric deeds," but he had likewise been taught, that "Heroes and not shepherds sat about the Table's Round," and that "he who cannot bravely fight for Beauty's safety, is undeserving of its golden prize." He exhorts him, therefore, first to defend with knightly sword his own inheritance and noble woman's honor, and this accomplished, he might then at his leisure attend to "princely coronations with love's myrtles." The arguments, which he in his fiery vehemence employs, are as forcible as they are characteristic :—

> The meanest of thy people risks his goods and blood
> For his opinion, his hate and love,
> And All is party, when the bloody sign
> Of civil war is hung up in the street

2*

To him it strangely seems to be the world's high destiny and law, that the people should sacrifice themselves for their country and its sovereign; and worthless is in his opinion the nation, that does not with alacrity risk its all in the defence of its honor.   The sharp reproof he utters on finding his rhetoric vainly expended, his angry determination to take the cause of the deputation of Orleans into his own hand, and the offensive words addressed in his passion to the Dauphin (whom he accuses of being born a coward), make the loving interposition of Sorel necessary, to prevent a remediless rupture.   Nor does his subsequent conduct destroy the impression, which his first appearance in Act III. leaves on our minds.   His bravery, his decisive energy are ever in happy contrast with the indolent compliance of the king, whose cause without his (and Joanna's) aid, would have been lost repeatedly.   The predilection for Joanna, which he professes after witnessing her high career appears as honorable and as true, as it was chivalric.   It is in consonance with the sentiments, which on a previous occasion he had expressed on this subject.   His title to the prize of affection had been won by manly and heroic deeds.   When all her noble friends had deserted Joanna amid the sore trial she underwent in consequence of her father's accusations, Dunois alone remaining makes the last attempt to move her to self-defence, assuring her that he believed her more than all those auguries, than "e'en the thunder's voice that speaks above."

On the delineation of the King's character, the poet has evidently expended much care.   "My piece leads me back to the time of the Troubadours, and I must court the friendship of the Minnesingers, in order to get into the proper tone of it," was the confession he made to Goethe at the time, when he commenced the task.   It had been his original plan to make a dramatical trilogy of the subject, in order to be enabled to furnish a complete and faithful picture of the manners of the times, and of the extravagances of the voluptuous court of the Dauphin, as contrasted with the martial spirit of the English and the resolute enthusiasm of the Maid.   The subsequent abandonment of this plan resulted not only in a change of the general arrangement of the play, but also in a serious modification of the character of the king.   He is, therefore, represented as a weak, procrastinating prince, who in the stormy commotions of his times exhibited a remarkable lack of decision.   In compensation for this defect, however, the

poet makes him a man of many amiable qualities, of an affectionate, tender heart, susceptible of love and friendship, inspired
for all that is beautiful and noble. Though by no means destitute of personal courage, and willing even to fight on terms of
chivalric honor for his crown, he is still too indolently fond of
peace to carry on the war successfully. He rather seeks to forget the "rough barbarian reality" in the midst of his sweet
dreams of love, which the poet decks out with all the adornment
of Romantic ideality. He is the very soul of sentiment and
knightly courtliness ; he fain would, like king René, institute his
cours d'amour, were he not in imminent danger of losing his real
court and crown by the approaching enemy. He might have made
a peaceful people happy, but is unable to curb one in a state of
mutiny, nor does he wish to open with the sword the hearts that
are estranged and shut with hatred. This is his own confession.
Moreover, "to live upon the favor of haughty and self-willed vassals and to be lorded by them, is harder for a noble heart and
bitterer, than to succomb to destiny."

A very father to his people, he even prays in secret, that heaven
might accept *him* as an offering for his nation, and thus redeem
it from impending ruin. When the news reaches him, that his
Parliament and the Capital had rejected him, that those who were
nearest allied to him by ties of consanguinity had forsaken and
betrayed him, and that his own unnatural mother was nourishing
"the alien brood of enemies" at her breast, he falls into a melancholy reverie. His father's long insanity, the sudden death of
his elder brother, both causes of unhappy feuds, added to the calamities already mentioned, lead him to conclude that Heaven's
resistless hand is against him, and that with him the ill-fated
house of Valois is doomed to ruin. He, therefore, would rather
resign his claim than continue the destructive quarrel. Enough
of blood had already been shed in his opinion. We have already
seen, how this indecision of despair was counterbalanced by the
fiery ardor of Dunois.—He is never elated by the subsequent unexpected success of his arms, but ever ready to give heaven and
the Maid the honor of it. His dignity and repose, his loving and
conciliating nature, ever ready to forgive and pardon, are every
where apparent. The words he utters over the corpse of Talbot
exhibit a sense of chivalric honor worthy of a king.

Towards Joanna he is truely grateful. He crowns her victory
over the stubborn resistance of Burgundy, by elevating her to

equal rank with all his vassals, and paternally proposes to wed
her to a noble husband. The sentiments with which Joanna's
character and career inspired his mind, are best conveyed by the
words he utters after the coronation-ceremony :—

> If thou the rays of heavenly nature dost
> Conceal within this virgin body, then
> O take the bandage off from our senses,
> And let us see thee in thy form of light,
> As heaven doth see thee, that in dust we may,
> And prostrate, do thee homage.

AGNES SOREL is a character that appears in double contrast
with the severer beauty of the maiden on the one hand, and with the
fiendlike monstrosity of Isabeau on the other. Her whole nature
is disinterestedness, tenderness, affection. As she stands amazed
at the lofty dignity, the heroic firmness of Joanna, so she clings
with entire devotion to her royal lover, whose cares she shares,
whose anxiety she allays with ever ready suasion, and in whose
behalf she readily would sacrifice her treasures. It is she that
calls the angry Dunois back to loyalty and duty, when indignantly
he threatens to forsake the cause, he could no longer honorably
serve ; and when Charles proposes to pass the Loire, " to yield to
Heaven's all-powerful hand, that manifestly is in favor of the
English," she raises his dejected mind to nobler sentiments, at
the same time apologizing for the unbecoming weakness exhibited
by the king in the presence of his nobles by saying : " Such word
did ne'er escape thy valiant breast, The mother's deed unnatural
and rude, Hath broke my monarch's firm heroic heart;" and
when he still further indulges in gloomy reflections on the malignant star that seemed to preside over the destinies of his
house, she urges him to reliance on his own self by depicting to
him the prospects of the future happiness and tranquillity of his
realm. The serene confidence of her hope is here, as elsewhere,
both the mirror and the remedy of the king's irresolute timidity :—

> My faith extends its trusting hand to heaven ;
> So many pledges of its favor had
> It ne'er imparted, were our end to mourn.

The contrast between Sorel and the Maid, in so far as they are
both women, is by no means striking. Agnes is such a loving,
mild and generous nature, her happiness and every pleasure is so
closely identified with that of him she clings to, that there are

scenes, wherein her loveliness almost throws the heroine into the
shade, had not the artist's skillful hand removed the superhuman
greatness of the latter forever Virgin-like beyond the reach of all
comparison. The opposite of all this is the king's mother Isabeau. Her profligate life, her intriguing ambition had been the
cause of her banishment from the court even during the lifetime
of her unfortunate husband; on which account she now breathes
hatred and revenge. She has actively espoused the cause of
Burgundy and of the English, not from any special attachment
to the interests of either, but simply to give unlicensed course to
the dark passions that rage in her bosom. She is fully aware of
the mischief of her career: "All England, were it even to pour
its burghers all on our shore, could ne'er subdue this land, as long
as concord rules it; 'tis France alone, that France can overcome." In the scene wherein she strangely assumes the office of
mediatrix between Talbot and Burgundy, her character is mirrored both in her own language and in the opinion of her allies
of both nations: "I care naught either for Burgundians or the
English." The latter are in her eyes invading pirates, that audaciously stretch out their hands to seize that which never can right-
fully be their own; and Burgundy is basely vending what every
patriotic heart holds dear. Whilst she thus deals out abuse and
scorn to enemy and friend, she at the same time justifies her own
voluptuous profligacy of life by laying the blame to the evil
destiny, that had malignantly linked her youthful buoyant heart to
such a crazy consort. In regard to Joanna, she derides both the
faith and the credulity of others, and altogether rejects, as does
the inflexible Talbot, every higher influence either of heaven or
of hell in her case. But her boastfully scornful words: "*I* will
conduct you, *I* will be to you a maiden and a prophetess divine!"
find no response among her companions in arms, to whom her
presence even now is onerous. The curses, which she so pro-
fusely heaps upon the head of her own son, inspire the hardy
veteran Talbot even with terror: "Your course towards the Dauphin will neither meet with the approbation of men, nor with the
sanction of heaven." By placing the English king upon the throne
of France, she had intended to conciliate Burgundy with the
English, but "in the peace a Fury makes, there can be neither
permanence nor safety." Her presence in the camp had been the
source of ruinous confusion; the soldier drops his courage,
when he thinks the cause is hers. Her obdurate heart is stag-

gered by the sight, when Joanna, recovering her strength, now
bursts the heavy chains, with which by her own order she had
been surcharged, and the " ghost chimerical, at which the army
trembled " now for the first time puzzles her incredulity. Isabeau remains consistent with herself to the last ; to La Hire's
offer to conduct her where her pleasure prompted, she replies,
surrendering the sword :—

> To any place, 'tis all indifferent,
> So I may not encounter the Dauphin.

BURGUNDY is far less determined in his hate ; and although
he, together with Isabeau, represent the division of the royal
house and of the nation, yet his unpatriotic course is partly
the defence of his own just cause, and in the code of honor
prevalent in his day a filial duty even.   Still he is vacillating
at the very outset; so that Lionel in his passion ventures even
to lay their disgraceful catastrophe at Orleans to his charge.
But in the sharp altercation that ensues, Burgundy, repelling
the arrogance of his alien allies, bluntly tells their leader, that
they would never have reached the walls of Orleans, nor " e'er
beheld the smoke arising from a Frenchman's chimney," had
not his own strong arm prepared the way for them.   His reconciliation with the king and the reluctantly granted pardon
of Du Chatêl, are among the wonders accomplished by the
resistless magic of the Maid, who in consecrating the newly
established unity of France, as veritable Pythoness, predicts to
Burgundy on this occasion the future splendor of his house, as
his reward (Cf. Act III., Scene fourth, Note).

The touches that delineate TALBOT's indomitable soul are
few, but expressive.   The mysterious cause of the sudden panic,
that had seized his soldiers, who ere this had stood so bravely
around his own inexorable valor in so many a successful fight,
afflicts him sorely.   " As if Hell had belched out all its legions
of damned spirits, a dizzy spell is sweeping both the brave
and coward brainlessly along," and he the only sober man
amid the universal fever's rage !   But when madness conquers,
and the day of destiny is come, it is idle to resist.   Stupidity
can baffle the very Gods !   Had we as brave men been conquered by others likewise brave, the thought of a common
ever-fickle fortune might have been our solace, says he lamentingly, but to be foiled by such base jugglery !—It is this that

makes him inconsolable to the very last, and he breathes out
his soul into the everlasting sun, with the conviction of life's
nothingness and deep disdain of all that sorry stuff, he once
had deemed sublime and worth desiring. Talbot's valor is so
heroic, his indignation so characteristic, that his defeat enlists
our warmest sympathy, and we believe him worthy of a better
fate. The sight of the dreaded warrior, stern, unconquerable
once, but now laid low, commands the respect of the enemy even.
Dunois is deeply moved by it, and Charles himself exclaims :—

> A higher hand hath conquered him, not we !
> Here on the soil of France he lies, as does
> A hero on the shield he would not quit.
> Bring him away !
> (*Soldiers are raising the corpse and bearing it away.*)
> And peace be with his dust !
> * * * * * *
> His epitaph shall be the place he fell on.

It has hardly been just to find defects in the character of Talbot, nor does it appear that Schiller in this noble and powerful
delineation has fallen below his model Shakspeare.

V. GENERAL ARRANGEMENT AND EXECUTION, VERSIFICA-TION, LANGUAGE, PATHOS, CONCLUSION.

In regard to the execution of the plot, this tragedy has been
considered superior to any of Schiller's previous productions.
The action contains not a single inconsistency, not even one of
those blemishes which are perceptible in the poet's earlier creations. All the variations and collisions are sustained by suitable
motives, there is no vagueness of characterization, no harshness
of contrast (as e. g. in Don Carlos, &c.), no defect of any kind.
The natural and strictly consequential development of the action
imparts to the entire play such a degree of probability, that our
poetic faith is never in the least offended by the miracles even.
The soil from which they spring is that of Nature, Romance,
Chivalry, Religion, Love. This constitutes the essence of Romanticism, a term by which the poet himself has designated the
piece, and which is the animating principle of the subject, the
characters, as well as of the outward form. Whilst the Ancient
drama moves within a limited cyclus of subjects and ideas, and
in point of form is likewise limited to an established middle-

ground between the Epic and the Lyric elements, which it
balances in fair but rigorous proportions, the Modern and Romantic drama on the other hand not only opens to us a wider and
richer world of sentiment, character, passion, humor even, but
the outward reality, with which these are connected, and of
which they are the blossoms, is likewise more varied and extensive, and the form admits of wider, less definite proportions.
The chain of the Unities is broken; that of the action even
—the most essential of the three—is not always preserved with
strict consistency. Its very essence is freedom from established
rules, its region preeminently that of the imagination and the
fancy. Hence the epic profuseness of many of Shakspeare's
productions; hence the capricious and intricate confusion of
his Tempest and Mid-Summer-Night's-Dream. The same is
essentially the case with Schiller's drama under consideration.
The spirit of Romanticism pervades the whole, expresses itself
in all the rich profusion of its leading elements in every one
of the leading characters. The Place is changed no less than
thirteen times; the unity of Time is only observed within the
limits of the several acts. The action is divided into certain
stations, each terminating with the close of every act and beginning anew at the commencement of the next. The pathos,
which has risen at the end of every act to its highest point,
and which in every successive act has increased in intensity,
resumes at the close of the piece the force and interest of all
that preceded; and the whole ends majestically in a glorious
transfiguration-scene, an apotheosis, wherein the Maid, now purified and completely victorious, divests herself of mortal frailty,
and Herakles-like rises aloft to purer spheres above.

But what is particularly remarkable, is the frequent employ-
ment of metrical forms of the most varied description, by which
the poet gives fit utterance to the lyrical effusions, that are
interspersed throughout the piece. As we occasionally fall in
with verses, that approximate the negligence of Prose, so we
likewise find here and there a passage, wherein the Iambics
terminate in Rhyme, sometimes even an assemblage of-rhymed
verses, where there is an evident parallelism between the metrical movement of the rhythm and the thoughts and images
conveyed by the language. The first monologue of Joanna
(fourth Scene, Prologue) is in Ottave Rime, a measure admirably adapted for the expression of the highly animated senti-

ments, to which Joanna gives utterance on bidding farewell to the familiar scenes of home. In the second Monologue (Act fourth) the epic recitations are likewise clothed in the majestic movement of the same measure, whilst the abrupt and varied effusions of feeling flow on in a corresponding number of rhymed strophes of shorter lines, in which the Trochaic measure preponderates. The music behind the scene at once supports and harmonizes the conflicting emotions, into which Joanna's heart is now dissolved; and here, as elsewhere, its application is productive of the happiest effect. In the Montgomery Episode, the poet has, according to his own confession imitated the metrical form of the antique Trimeter, and piques himself with evident complaisance on his success. Whatever may be said of the propriety of that scene in the economy of the piece; whatever fault may be found with its epic prolixity, its Homeric latitude of detail,* it still remains as a whole in form and contents both an admirably

---

* Hegel remarks concerning the knight, "that his courage forsakes him entirely in the hour of danger, and still, pressed on the one hand by the infuriated Talbot, who punishes cowardice with death, and on the other by the Maid, who conquers even the most valiant, it is out of his power to flee. His pleadings are unmanly, so that the whole figure of the knight is neither suitable for the epos proper nor for tragedy, but is rather to be consigned to the sphere of the Comic (! ?). At the approach of Joanna he throws away shield and sword, and on his knees begs for his life. Moreover the arguments, which he produces at great length, in order to move her to pity, viz. his defenceless state, the opulence of his father, who would pay any ransom for his release, the gentleness of the sex, to which Joanna as a maiden belonged, the love of the sweet bride, who bathed in tears was anxiously awaiting the return of her beloved one, the distress of the parents he had left at home, the bitter lot of dying unwept in a foreign land—all these motives have on the one hand of themselves already reference to objective relations, that have both validity and worth, and on the other hand their calm and full exposition is of the Epic kind. In like manner the motive with which the poet justifies the circumstance, that Joanna *must listen* to the knight, is of an external nature, the defencelessness of the captive, namely; in strict dramatic consistency she would be bound to kill him at once and at first sight, having made her appearance from the first as the inexorable foe of all the English, and pronounced this direful hate with great expenditure of rhetoric, and even justified it by the fact, that a fearfully binding contract with the spirit-world compelled her to put every living thing in battle to the sword. If the question were merely, that Montgomery should not die unarmed, then he, who had already been listened to so long, would have in his own hands the best means of saving his life; he would only have to refrain from taking them up again. Yet upon her challenge to fight with her, who herself was mortal too, for life's sweet booty, he grasps the sword

executed *morçeau*, perfect in itself. It is by this free and almost
sportive use of rhythm, measure, rhyme, that the poet successfully maintains the wider sphere, in which the action of the tragedy moves. In this respect, as well as in the gorgeous array of
varied imagery and beauty of style, the piece is far beyond the
previous; if not of all the other productions of the artist. As it
regards the language, we observe natural clearness, perfect adaptation, varied elegance, often elevation of diction, which frequently
reminds us of Homeric simplicity, while in the speeches of Joanna
particularly, it not unfrequently rises to Biblical dignity, which
the poet from the nature of the subject found frequent occasion
to adopt with advantage. The naïve simplicity with which
Joanna depicts to the king the history of her mission, has justly
been the subject of special admiration in this respect.

The fact that her heart in opposition to her better conviction
loses itself in the mazes of contradictory aims and passions, which
makes it dramatically necessary for her either to recover the in-
tegrity of her nature both in itself and *ad extra*, or else of perishing
in consequence of it, has been deemed a blemish. To make the
subjective tragic pathos of purely internal collisions and struggles
the lever of the action was said to be something painful, sorry
and vexatious ; which the poet should seek to avoid, instead of
searching for it, or of making it the subject καr' ἐξοχὴν of his creations. This stricture, however, as applied to the drama in question,
does not hold good. Joanna is so completely identified with the
national movement, of which she is the chief representative, and
of part of which she is at once the creatrix and the leading guide,
that it becomes impossible to separate the person from the event,
or the latter from the former. This perfect identity of purpose
and of destiny makes it necessary for her to experience personally
and to feel not only a part, but the whole of the movement, of
which she is the chief exponent. Her own character must needs

again and perishes by her arm. This course of the Scene, without the broad epic
explications, would be more in consonance with dramatic propriety."—Schiller, however, himself justifies this part of his work. He says :—"Call the
Scene with the Welshman Montgomery an Epic Episode to your heart's con-
tent! It belongs to the breadth of an historical piece, that has burst the chain
of the Unities." He who is familar with his Homer will know what was my
aim. It was for the very sake of the Antique, that I selected the *Senarius* of the
ancient tragedy. The Cæsura makes this Verse extremely difficult, but at the
same time so beautiful and euphoneous, that I found it difficult to return to
the lame quinquepedal Iambics."

be tested by the ordeal of searching trials, before it can exhibit all the glories of its hidden excellence. Her country had long been sorely tried by jarring conflicts and internal divisions, and she too, its redemptrix, must necessarily undergo its anguish, before the restoration can become completed by her hand. Had the action found a happy termination in connection with the coronation-scene, had Joanna by her valor and her mediating reconciliations simply restored the harmony of the conflicting national elements, then her career of consecutive triumphs would have made the action an exalted Epopee; had she perished, as history represents her, by the hands of the enemy, in consequence of an unlucky turn of events, falsely accused of a heavy crime, and still asserting her innocence to the last, without the intervention of her friends, or of a *Deus ex machina* from heaven, her death, martyrlike and beautiful as it *might* had been painted, and as it actually was, would not have been grounded on a sufficient, not even on a justifiable motive in the construction of the plot, nor would the event, towards which alone her mission tended, and the end of her career have so happily and pathetically coincided, and the *dénouement* would consequently have been less poetical and less perfect. This is the very point, in regard to which the poet experienced no little difficulty, it having been originally his plan to end the piece historically and to have Joanna die at Rouen at the stake. It was not until after the completion of the third act, which he submitted to Goethe's judgment, that he at length decided to adopt the present mode of treatment, and to transfer (to use his own language) the entire *sujet* into the region of Romantic Possibility, to which Joanna's nature and history preëminently belong.

As it is, the rupture of her original inner Unity with nature, her righteous cause and heaven, besides unfolding to us a world of interesting, intensely pathetic emotions, by which the human side of her half-celestial character becomes unveiled, and besides giving rise to a multitude of thrilling scenes, appears, moreover, to have been the best if not the only dramatic method of a completely satisfactory solution of the problem, which the poet had proposed to himself. Without it there could hardly have been any *nodus*, consequently no proper solution. Her rosy death completes the great work of her life, which ends triumphantly together with the action; in dying she both seals her mission and her nation's redemption; and atoning for her error, which was after all but the semblance of one, and more of a heaven-permitted trial than of actual guilt, she rises again above all the impurities of earth, in tenfold splendor of her former purity, simplicity, humility, and grandeur!

National independence, both of state and of the church, is the soul of the grand historic movement, in which Joanna appears chief actor; it is the cause for which she fights and dies. It constitutes the Πάϑος of the action, the inner motive power of all the characters, of all the collisions, of all the reconciliations. The foreign enemy must be expelled, the land of Dagobert and St. Louis must have a monarch of its own, the people by which the power of the Saracens was broken, with whom the sacred war commenced, by whom Jerusalem was conquered, must maintain its independence, its religion, its traditions, its peculiar constitution. This is the substance of Joanna's own enthusiastic declaration in the Prologue. Her ideal was freedom in its concrete, real, popular form, and in the times in which she lived, the monarchical Monas was the only possible expression of it. The King defended the cause of the commons to shield himself against rebellious vassals, the people adhered to the King in the hope of escaping the tyranny of feudal oppression. Hence the national antagonism, the disruption of the Ideal and Reality within the state itself, hence too the lamentable encroachments on national independence *ab extra*, all of which are neutralized, restored to equilibrium by the grand historic poem, of which Joanna was chief acting Rhapsodist.* In a religious point of view, there is likewise a dualism of belief perceptible, which forms in fact one of the characteristic features of mediæval life in general. The creed and the traditions of the church on the one hand, a gloomy tendency to natural superstition among the ignorant, and the indifference of fatalism among the great, on the other. These incompatible elements give rise to numerous pathetic conflicts in the piece, which, however, are likewise completely reconciled in the end. Joanna's youthful reveries are *proved* to have been from above. Of her goodness, her piety, her purity of purpose as well as of her heroism and loyal devotion there remains no longer a shadow of doubt, and the belief in fatal destiny, with which not only Talbot, but the Bishop even seems to be infected, is supplanted by the manifest signs of a higher, a rational and a holy guidance of the affairs of life.

* " La jeune fille, à son insu, *creait*, pour ainsi parler, et *realisait* ses propres idées, elle en faisait des êtres, elle leur communiquait du trésor de sa vie virginale, une splendide et toute-puissante existence, à faire pâlir les misérables réalités de ce monde."—MICHELET.

Die Jungfrau von Orleans.

Eine romantische Tragödie

von

Schiller.

Perſonen.

Karl VII., König von Frankreich.
Königin Iſabeau, ſeine Mutter.
Agnes Sorel, ſeine Geliebte.
Philipp der Gute, Herzog von Burgund.
Graf Dunois, Baſtard von Orleans.
La Hire,
Du Chatel, } königliche Officiere.
Erzbiſchof von Rheims.
Chatillon, ein burgundiſcher Ritter.
Raoul, ein lothringiſcher Ritter.
Talbot, Feldherr der Engländer.
Lionel,
Faſtolf, } engliſche Anführer.
Montgomery, ein Walliſer.
Rathsherrn von Orleans.
Ein engliſcher Herold.
Thibaut d'Arc, ein reicher Landmann.
Margot,
Louiſon, } ſeine Töchter.
Johanna,
Etienne,
Claude Marie, } ihre Freier.
Raimond,
Bertrand, ein anderer Landmann.
Die Erſcheinung eines ſchwarzen Ritters.
Köhler und Köhlerweib.
Soldaten und Volk, königliche Kronbediente, Biſchöfe,
    Mönche, Marſchälle, Magiſtratsperſonen, Hofleute
    und andere ſtumme Perſonen im Gefolge des Krönungszuges.

46

Prolog.

Eine ländliche Gegend.

Vorn zur Rechten ein Heiligenbild in einer Kapelle; zur Linken eine hohe Eiche.

Erster Auftritt.

Thibaut d'Arc. Seine drei Töchter. Drei junge Schäfer, ihre Freier.

Thibaut.

Ja, liebe Nachbarn! Heute sind wir noch
Franzosen, freie Bürger noch und Herren
Des alten Bodens, den die Väter pflügten;
Wer weiß, wer morgen über uns befiehlt!
Denn aller Orten läßt der Engelländer
Sein sieghaft Banner fliegen; seine Rosse
Zerstampfen Frankreichs blühende Gefilde.
Paris hat ihn als Sieger schon empfangen,
Und mit der alten Krone Dagoberts
Schmückt es den Sprößling eines fremden Stamms.
Der Enkel unsrer Könige muß irren,
Enterbt und flüchtig, durch sein eignes Reich,
Und wider ihn im Heer der Feinde kämpft
Sein nächster Vetter und sein erster Pair,
Ja, seine Rabenmutter führt es an.
Rings brennen Dörfer, Städte. Näher stets
Und näher wälzt sich der Verheerung Rauch
An diese Thäler, die noch friedlich ruhn.
— Drum, liebe Nachbarn, hab' ich mich mit Gott
Entschlossen, weil ich's heute noch vermag,
Die Töchter zu versorgen; denn das Weib

47

Bedarf in Kriegesnöthen des Beschützers,
Und treue Lieb' hilft alle Lasten heben.

(Zu dem ersten Schäfer.)

— Kommt, Etienne! Ihr werbt um meine Margot.
Die Aecker grenzen nachbarlich zusammen,
Die Herzen stimmen überein — das stiftet
Ein gutes Ehband!

(Zu dem Zweiten.)

Claude Marie! Ihr schweigt,

Und meine Louison schlägt die Augen nieder?
Werd' ich zwei Herzen trennen, die sich fanden,
Weil ihr nicht Schätze mir zu bieten habt?
Wer hat jetzt Schätze? Haus und Scheune sind
Des nächsten Feindes oder Feuers Raub —
Die treue Brust des braven Manns allein
Ist ein sturmfestes Dach in diesen Zeiten.

Louison.

Mein Vater!

Claude Marie.

Meine Louison!

Louison (Johanna umarmend.)

Liebe Schwester!

Thibaut.

Ich gebe jeder dreißig Acker Landes
Und Stall und Hof und eine Heerde — Gott
Hat mich gesegnet, und so segn' er euch!

Margot (Johanna umarmend.)

Erfreue unsern Vater! Nimm ein Beispiel!
Laß diesen Tag drei frohe Bande schließen!

Thibaut.

Geht! Machet Anstalt! Morgen ist die Hochzeit;
Ich will, das ganze Dorf soll sie mit feiern.

(Die zwei Paare gehen, Arm in Arm geschlungen, ab.)

Zweiter Auftritt.

Thibaut. Raimond. Johanna.

Thibaut.

Jeanette, deine Schwestern machen Hochzeit,
Ich seh' sie glücklich, sie erfreu'n mein Alter;
Du, meine Jüngste, machst mir Gram und Schmerz.

Raimond.

Was fällt Euch ein! Was scheltet ihr die Tochter?

Thibaut.

Hier, dieser wackre Jüngling, dem sich keiner
Vergleicht im ganzen Dorf, der Treffliche,
Er hat dir seine Neigung zugewendet
Und wirbt um dich, schon ist's der dritte Herbst,
Mit stillem Wunsch, mit herzlichem Bemühn;
Du stößest ihn verschlossen, kalt zurück,
Noch sonst ein andrer von den Hirten allen
Mag dir ein gütig Lächeln abgewinnen.
— Ich sehe dich in Jugendfülle prangen,
Dein Lenz ist da, es ist die Zeit der Hoffnung,
Entfaltet ist die Blume deines Leibes;
Doch stets vergebens harr' ich, daß die Blume
Der zarten Lieb' aus ihrer Knospe breche
Und freudig reife zu der goldnen Frucht!
O, das gefällt mir nimmermehr und deutet
Auf eine schwere Irrung der Natur!
Das Herz gefällt mir nicht, das streng und kalt
Sich zuschließt in den Jahren des Gefühls.

Raimond.

Laßt's gut sein, Vater Arc! Laßt sie gewähren!
Die Liebe meiner trefflichen Johanna
Ist eine edle, zarte Himmelsfrucht,
Und still, allmählig reift das Köstliche!
Jetzt liebt sie noch zu wohnen auf den Bergen,
Und von der freien Heide fürchtet sie
Herabzusteigen in das niedre Dach

3

Der Menschen, wo die engen Sorgen wohnen.
Oft seh' ich ihr aus tiefem Thal mit stillem
Erstaunen zu, wenn sie auf hoher Trift
In Mitte ihrer Heerde ragend steht,
Mit edelm Leibe, und den ernsten Blick
Herabsenkt auf der Erde kleine Länder.
Da scheint sie mir was Höhres zu bedeuten,
Und dünkt mir's oft, sie stamm' aus andern Zeiten.

Thibaut.

Das ist es, was mir nicht gefallen will!
Sie flieht der Schwestern fröhliche Gemeinschaft,
Die öden Berge sucht sie auf, verlässet
Ihr nächtlich Lager vor dem Hahnenruf,
Und in der Schreckensstunde, wo der Mensch
Sich gern vertraulich an den Menschen schließt,
Schleicht sie, gleich dem einsiedlerischen Vogel,
Heraus ins graulich düstre Geisterreich
Der Nacht, tritt auf den Kreuzweg hin und pflegt
Geheime Zwiesprach mit der Luft des Berges.
Warum erwählt sie immer diesen Ort
Und treibt gerade hieher ihre Heerde?
Ich sehe sie zu ganzen Stunden sinnend
Dort unter dem Druidenbaume sitzen,
Den alle glücklichen Geschöpfe fliehn.
Denn nicht geheur ist's hier; ein böses Wesen
Hat seinen Wohnsitz unter diesem Baum
Schon seit der alten, grauen Heidenzeit.
Die Aeltesten im Dorf erzählen sich
Von diesem Baume schauerhafte Mähren;
Seltsamer Stimmen wundersamen Klang
Vernimmt man oft aus seinen düstern Zweigen.*

* The cultus of groves and of particular trees was in ancient times very extensively prevalent both among Germanic and Keltic nations, who regarded them either as the seat of their divinities or as in themselves divine. This is evident from numerous authorities both Pagan and Christian; e. g. Tacitus Germ. 9. *Lucos ac nemora consecrant, &c.*—C. 39. Stato tempore in *silvam auguriis patrum et prisca formidine sacram* omnes.... populi legationibus

Ich selbst, als mich in später Dämmrung einst
Der Weg an diesem Baum vorüberführte,
Hab' ein gespenstig Weib hier sitzen sehn.
Das streckte mir aus weit gefaltetem
Gewande langsam eine dürre Hand
Entgegen, gleich als winkt' es; doch ich eilte
Fürbaß, und Gott befahl ich meine Seele.

Raimond
(auf das Heiligenbild in der Kapelle zeigend).

Des Gnadenbildes segenreiche Nähe,
Das hier des Himmels Frieden um sich streut,
Nicht Satans Werk führt eure Tochter her.

Thibaut.

O nein, nein! Nicht vergebens zeigt sich's mir

coeunt. Id. pl. loc. al.—Vita St. Amandi, Acta Bened. sec. 2. p. 744 : Amandus audivit . . . . ut incoles terræ illius, relicto Deo, *arbores et ligna pro deo colerent, &c.*—Adam Bremens. speaking of the grove near Upsal says : *Is enim lucus tam sacer est* gentibus, ut *singulæ arbores* ejus ex morte vel tabo immolatorum *divinæ* credantur.—Dietmar p. 151 : Quam (sc. the temple at Riedegost) *undique silva ab incolis intacta et venerabilis* circumdat magna! Maximus Tyrius ed. Reiske 1, p. 142, says of the Kelts : ἄγαλμα δὲ Διὸς Κελτικὸν ὑψηλὴ δρῦς. In the sacred legends of the Eddas the *Yggdrasil* plays a conspicuous part both cosmologically and as one of the favorite resorts of the gods. The *Irminsûl* of the ancient Saxons was likewise an object of religious veneration. Notwithstanding the determined opposition of the earlier propagators of the purer religion (of which there are many accounts), the superstitions connected with these places of resort could not be entirely eradicated from the minds of the untutored masses, and traces of them can be found centuries after in popular legends. Thus in documents of a comparatively late period (e. g. A. D. 1000—1100) the names "hillige holt," "heilig forst"= *sacra silva* are not unfrequent; and in the Christian poetry of the Middle Ages occasional allusion is still made to certain trees, which, though they had long ceased to be objects of a religious cultus, were yet enveloped with the mist of sombre traditions and regarded with awe as the seat of supernatural beings; and as the simple-minded and illiterate still confounded national and sacred legends, these beings were sometimes of a good and sometimes of a wicked order. Schiller is therefore neither guilty of an anachronism nor of inconsistency, when he makes the same place the doubtful seat of good or evil influences, and the anxious apprehensions on the part of Thibaut, as well as the good assurance of Raymond and the Maiden are, aside from their dramatic design, in perfect keeping with the character of the times and of the social station of the persons to whom they are attributed. See Joanna's own account before the Archbishop, p. 88. Cf. Grimm. Deutsch. Myth. p. 39 seqq.

In Träumen an und ängstlichen Gesichten.
Zu dreien Malen hab' ich sie gesehn
Zu Rheims auf unsrer Könige Stuhle sitzen,
Ein funkelnd Diadem von sieben Sternen
Auf ihrem Haupt, das Scepter in der Hand,
Aus dem drei weiße Lilien entsprangen,
Und ich, ihr Vater, ihre beiden Schwestern
Und alle Fürsten, Grafen, Erzbischöfe,
Der König selber neigten sich vor ihr.
Wie kommt mir solcher Glanz in meine Hütte?
O, das bedeutet einen tiefen Fall!
Sinnbildlich stellt mir dieser Warnungstraum
Das eitle Trachten ihres Herzens dar.
Sie schämt sich ihrer Niedrigkeit — weil Gott
Mit reicher Schönheit ihren Leib geschmückt,
Mit hohen Wundergaben sie gesegnet
Vor allen Hirtenmädchen dieses Thals,
So nährt sie sünd'gen Hochmuth in dem Herzen,
Und Hochmuth ist's, wodurch die Engel fielen,
Woran der Höllengeist den Menschen faßt.

Raimond.

Wer hegt bescheidnern, tugendlichern Sinn,
Als eure fromme Tochter! Ist sie's nicht,
Die ihren ältern Schwestern freudig dient?
Sie ist die hochbegabteste von allen;
Doch seht ihr sie, wie eine niedre Magd,
Die schwersten Pflichten still gehorsam üben,
Und unter ihren Händen wunderbar
Gedeihen euch die Heerden und die Saaten;
Um Alles, was sie schafft, ergießet sich
Ein unbegreiflich, überschwänglich Glück.

Thibaut.

Ja wohl! Ein unbegreiflich Glück — Mir kommt
Ein eigen Grauen an bei diesem Segen!
— Nichts mehr davon. Ich schweige. Ich will schweigen:
Soll ich mein eigen theures Kind anklagen?

Ich kann nichts thun, als warnen, für sie beten!
Doch warnen muß ich — Fliehe diesen Baum,
Bleib nicht allein und grabe keine Wurzeln
Um Mitternacht, bereite keine Tränke
Und schreibe keine Zeichen in den Sand —
Leicht aufzuritzen ist das Reich der Geister,
Sie liegen wartend unter dünner Decke,
Und leise hörend, stürmen sie herauf.
Bleib nicht allein; denn in der Wüste trat
Der Satansengel selbst zum Herrn des Himmels.

Dritter Auftritt.

Bertrand tritt auf, einen Helm in der Hand. **Thibaut. Raimond.**
Johanna.

Raimond.

Still! Da kommt Bertrand aus der Stadt zurück.
Sieh, was er trägt!

Bertrand.

    Ihr staunt mich an, ihr seid
Verwundert ob des seltsamen Geräthes
In meiner Hand.

Thibaut.

    Das sind wir. Saget an,
Wie kamt ihr zu dem Helm, was bringt ihr uns
Das böse Zeichen in die Friedensgegend?

(Johanna, welche in beiden vorigen Scenen still und ohne Antheil auf der Seite
gestanden, wird aufmerksam und tritt näher.)

Bertrand.

Kaum weiß ich selbst zu sagen, wie das Ding
Mir in die Hand gerieth. Ich hatte eisernes
Geräth mir eingekauft zu Vaucouleurs;
Ein großes Drängen fand ich auf dem Markt,
Denn flücht'ges Volk war eben angelangt
Von Orleans mit böser Kriegespost.
Im Aufruhr lief die ganze Stadt zusammen,
Und als ich Bahn mir machte durchs Gewühl,

Da tritt ein braun Bohemerweib mich an
Mit diesem Helm, faßt mich ins Auge scharf
Und spricht: Gesell, ihr suchet einen Helm,
Ich weiß, ihr suchet einen. Da! Nehmt hin!
Um ein Geringes steht er euch zu Kaufe.
— Geht zu den Lanzenknechten, sagt' ich ihr,
Ich bin ein Landmann, brauche nicht des Helmes.
Sie aber ließ nicht ab und sagte ferner:
Kein Mensch vermag zu sagen, ob er nicht
Des Helmes braucht. Ein stählern Dach fürs Haupt
Ist jetzo mehr werth als ein steinern Haus.
So trieb sie mich durch alle Gaffen, mir
Den Helm aufnöthigend, den ich nicht wollte.
Ich sah den Helm, daß er so blank und schön
Und würdig eines ritterlichen Haupts,
Und da ich zweifelnd in der Hand ihn wog,
Des Abenteuers Seltsamkeit bedenkend,
Da war das Weib mir aus den Augen, schnell,
Hinweggerissen hatte sie der Strom
Des Volkes, und der Helm blieb mir in Händen.

   Johanna (rasch und begierig darnach greifend).
Gebt mir den Helm!

     Bertrand.
     Was frommt euch dies Geräthe?
Das ist kein Schmuck für ein jungfräulich Haupt.

   Johanna (entreißt ihm den Helm).
Mein ist der Helm, und mir gehört er zu.

     Thibaut.
Was fällt dem Mädchen ein?

     Raimond.
       Laßt ihr den Willen!
Wohl ziemt ihr dieser kriegerische Schmuck,
Denn ihre Brust verschließt ein männlich Herz.
Denkt nach, wie sie den Tigerwolf bezwang,
Das grimmig wilde Thier, das unsre Heerden
Verwüstete, den Schrecken aller Hirten.

Sie ganz allein, die löwenherz'ge Jungfrau,
Stritt mit dem Wolf und rang das Lamm ihm ab,
Das er im blut'gen Rachen schon davon trug.
Welch tapfres Haupt auch dieser Helm bedeckt,
Er kann kein würdigeres zieren!

Thibaut (zu Bertrand).

Sprecht!
Welch neues Kriegesunglück ist geschehn?
Was brachten jene Flüchtigen?

Bertrand.

Gott helfe
Dem König und erbarme sich des Landes!
Geschlagen sind wir in zwei großen Schlachten,
Mitten in Frankreich steht der Feind, verloren
Sind alle Länder bis an die Loire —
Jetzt hat er seine ganz Macht zusammen
Geführt, womit er Orleans belagert.

Thibaut.

Gott schütze den König!

Bertrand.

Unermeßliches
Geschütz ist aufgebracht von allen Enden,
Und wie der Bienen dunkelnde Geschwader
Den Korb umschwärmen in des Sommers Tagen,
Wie aus geschwärzter Luft die Heuschreckwolke
Herunterfällt und meilenlang die Felder
Bedeckt in unabsehbarem Gewimmel,
So goß sich eine Kriegeswolke aus
Von Völkern über Orleans Gefilde,
Und von der Sprache unverständlichem
Gemisch verworren, dumpf erbraust's das Lager.
Denn auch der mächtige Burgund, der Länder=
Gewaltige hat seine Mannen alle
Herbeigeführt, die Lütticher, Luxemburger,
Die Hennegauer, die vom Lande Namur
Und die das glückliche Brabant bewohnen,

Die üpp'gen Genter, die in Sammt und Seide
Stolziren, die von Seeland, deren Städte
Sich reinlich aus dem Meereswasser heben,
Die heerdenmelkenden Holländer, die
Von Utrecht, ja vom äußersten Westfriesland,
Die nach dem Eispol schaun — sie folgen Alle
Dem Heerbann des gewaltig herrschenden
Burgund und wollen Orleans bezwingen.

Thibaut.

O des unselig jammervollen Zwistes,
Der Frankreichs Waffen wider Frankreich wendet!

Bertrand.

Auch sie, die alte Königin, sieht man,
Die stolze Isabeau, die Bayerfürstin,
In Stahl gekleidet durch das Lager reiten,
Mit gift'gen Stachelworten alle Völker
Zur Wuth aufregen wider ihren Sohn,
Den sie in ihrem Mutterschooß getragen!

Thibaut.

Fluch treffe sie, und möge Gott sie einst,
Wie jene stolze Jesabel, verderben!

Bertrand.

Der fürchterliche Sal'sbury, der Mauern=
Zertrümmerer, führt die Belagrung an,
Mit ihm des Löwen Bruder Lionel
Und Talbot, der mit mörderischem Schwert
Die Völker niedermähet in den Schlachten.
In frechem Muthe haben sie geschworen,
Der Schmach zu weihen alle Jungfrauen,
Und, was das Schwert geführt, dem Schwert zu opfern.
Vier hohe Warten haben sie erbaut,
Die Stadt zu überragen; oben späht
Graf Sal'sbury mit mordbegier'gem Blick
Und zählt den schnellen Wandrer auf den Gassen.
Viel tausend Kugeln schon von Centners Last
Sind in die Stadt geschleudert, Kirchen liegen

Zertrümmert, und der königliche Thurm
Von Notre Dame bengt sein erhabnes Haupt.
Auch Pulvergänge haben sie gegraben,
Und über einem Höllenreiche steht
Die bange Stadt, gewärtig jede Stunde,
Daß es mit Donners Krachen sich entzünde.

(Johanna horcht mit gespannter Aufmerksamkeit und setzt sich den Helm auf.)

Thibaut.

Wo aber waren denn die tapfern Degen
Saintrailles, La Hire und Frankreichs Brustwehr,
Der heldenmüth'ge Bastard, daß der Feind
So allgewaltig reißend vorwärts drang?
Wo ist der König selbst? und sieht er müßig
Des Reiches Noth und seiner Städte Fall?

Bertrand.

Zu Chinon hält der König seinen Hof;
Es fehlt an Volk, er kann das Feld nicht halten.
Was nützt der Führer Muth, der Helden Arm,
Wenn bleiche Furcht die Heere lähmt?
Ein Schrecken, wie von Gott herabgesandt,
Hat auch die Brust der Tapfersten ergriffen.
Umsonst erschallt der Fürsten Aufgebot.
Wie sich die Schafe bang zusammendrängen,
Wenn sich des Wolfes Heulen hören läßt,
So sucht der Franke, seines alten Ruhms
Vergessend, nur die Sicherheit der Burgen.
Ein einz'ger Ritter nur, hört' ich erzählen,
Hab' eine schwache Mannschaft aufgebracht
Und zieh' dem König zu mit sechzehn Fahnen.

Johanna (schnell).

Wie heißt der Ritter?

Bertrand.

Baudricour.   Doch schwerlich
Möcht' er des Feindes Kundschaft hintergehn,
Der mit zwei Heeren seinen Fersen folgt.

3*

Johanna.

Wo hält der Ritter? Sagt mir's, wenn ihr's wiffet.

Bertrand.

Er steht kaum eine Tagereise weit
Von Vaucouleurs.

Thibout (zu Johanna).

Was kümmert's dich! Du fragst
Nach Dingen, Mädchen, die dir nicht geziemen.

Bertrand.

Weil nun der Feind so mächtig, und kein Schutz
Vom König mehr zu hoffen, haben sie
Zu Vaucouleurs einmüthig den Beschluß
Gefaßt, sich dem Burgund zu übergeben,
So tragen wir nicht fremdes Joch und bleiben
Beim alten Königsstamme — ja, vielleicht
Zur alten Krone fallen wir zurück,
Wenn einst Burgund und Frankreich sich versöhnen.

Johanna (in Begeisterung.)

Nichts von Verträgen! Nichts von Uebergabe!
Der Retter naht, er rüstet sich zum Kampf.
Vor Orleans soll das Glück des Feindes scheitern!
Sein Maß ist voll, er ist zur Ernte reif.
Mit ihrer Sichel wird die Jungfrau kommen
Und seines Stolzes Saaten niedermähn;
Herab vom Himmel reißt sie seinen Ruhm,
Den er hoch an den Sternen aufgehangen.
Verzagt nicht! Fliehet nicht! Denn eh' der Roggen
Gelb wird, eh sich die Mondesscheibe füllt,
Wird kein engländisch Roß mehr aus den Wellen
Der prächtig strömenden Loire trinken.

Bertrand.

Ach, es geschehen keine Wunder mehr!

Johanna.

Es geschehn noch Wunder — Eine weiße Taube
Wird fliegen und mit Adlerskühnheit diese Geier
Anfallen, die das Vaterland zerreißen.

Darniederkämpfen wird sie diesen stolzen
Burgund, den Reichsverräther, diesen Talbot,
Den himmelstürmend hunderthändigen,
Und diesen Sal'sbury, den Tempelschänder,
Und diese Inselwohner alle
Wie eine Heerde Lämmer vor sich jagen.
Der Herr wird mit ihr seyn, der Schlachten Gott.
Sein zitterndes Geschöpf wird er erwählen,
Durch eine zarte Jungfrau wird er sich
Verherrlichen, denn er ist der Allmächt'ge!

Thibaut.

Was für ein Geist ergreift die Dirn'?

Raimond.

Es ist
Der Helm, der sie so kriegerisch beseelt.
Seht eure Tochter an. Ihr Auge blitzt,
Und glühend Feuer sprühen ihre Wangen!

Johanna.

Dieß Reich soll fallen? Dieses Land des Ruhms,
Das schönste, das die ew'ge Sonne sieht
In ihrem Lauf, das Paradies der Länder,
Das Gott liebt, wie den Apfel seines Auges,
Die Fesseln tragen eines fremden Volks!
— Hier scheiterte der Heiden Macht. Hier war
Das erste Kreuz, das Gnadenbild erhöht;
Hier ruht der Staub des heil'gen Ludewig!
Von hier aus ward Jerusalem erobert.

Bertrand (erstaunt).

Hört ihre Rede! Woher schöpfte sie
Die hohe Offenbarung? — Vater Arc!
Euch gab Gott eine wundervolle Tochter!

Johanna.

Wir sollen keine eignen Könige
Mehr haben, keinen eingebornen Herrn —
Der König, der nie stirbt, soll aus der Welt
Verschwinden — der den heil'gen Pflug beschützt,

Der die Trift beschützt und fruchtbar macht die Erde —
Der die Leibeignen in die Freiheit führt,
Der die Städte freudig stellt um seinen Thron —
Der dem Schwachen beisteht und den Bösen schreckt,
Der den Neid nicht kennet — denn er ist der Größte —
Der ein Mensch ist und ein Engel der Erbarmung
Auf der feindsel'gen Erde — Denn der Thron
Der Könige, der von Golde schimmert, ist
Das Obdach der Verlassenen — hier steht
Die Macht und die Barmherzigkeit — es zittert
Der Schuldige, vertrauend naht sich der Gerechte
Und scherzet mit den Löwen um den Thron!
Der fremde König, der von Außen kommt,
Dem keines Ahnherrn heilige Gebeine
In diesem Lande ruhn, kann er es lieben?
Der nicht jung war mit unsern Jünglingen,
Dem unsre Worte nicht zum Herzen tönen,
Kann er ein Vater seyn zu seinen Söhnen?

Thibaut.

Gott schütze Frankreich und den König! Wir
Sind friedliche Landleute, wissen nicht
Das Schwert zu führen, und das kriegerische Roß
Zu tummeln — Laßt uns still gehorchend harren,
Wen uns der Sieg zum König geben wird.
Das Glück der Schlachten ist das Urtheil Gottes,
Und unser Herr ist, wer die heil'ge Oelung
Empfängt und sich die Kron' aufsetzt zu Rheims.
— Kommt an die Arbeit! Kommt! Und denke Jeder
Nur an das Nächste! Lassen wir die Großen,
Der Erde Fürsten um die Erde loosen;
Wir können ruhig die Zerstörung schauen,
Denn sturmfest steht der Boden, den wir bauen.
Die Flamme brenne unsre Dörfer nieder,
Die Saat zerstampfe ihrer Rosse Tritt,
Der neue Lenz bringt neue Saaten mit,
Und schnell erstehn die leichten Hütten wieder!

(Alle außer der Jungfrau gehen ab.)

Vierter Auftritt.
Johanna (allein).

Lebt wohl, ihr Berge, ihr geliebten Triften,
Ihr traulich stillen Thäler, lebet wohl!
Johanna wird nun nicht mehr auf euch wandeln,
Johanna sagt euch ewig Lebewohl!
Ihr Wiesen, die ich wässerte, ihr Bäume,
Die ich gepflanzet, grünet fröhlich fort!
Lebt wohl, ihr Grotten und ihr kühlen Brunnen!
Du Echo, holde Stimme dieses Thals,
Die oft mir Antwort gab auf meine Lieder,
Johanna geht, und nimmer kehrt sie wieder!

Ihre Plätze alle meiner stillen Freuden,
Euch laß' ich hinter mir auf immerdar!
Zerstreuet euch, ihr Lämmer, auf der Heiden!
Ihr seyd jetzt eine hirtenlose Schaar!
Denn eine andre Heerde muß ich weiden
Dort auf dem blut'gen Felde der Gefahr.
So ist des Geistes Ruf an mich ergangen;
Mich treibt nicht eitles, irdisches Verlangen.

Denn der zu Mosen auf des Horebs Höhen
Im feur'gen Busch sich flammend niederließ
Und ihm befahl, vor Pharao zu stehen,
Der einst den frommen Knaben Isai's,
Den Hirten, sich zum Streiter ausersehen,
Der stets den Hirten gnädig sich bewies,
Er sprach zu mir aus dieses Baumes Zweigen:
„Geh hin! Du sollst auf Erden für mich zeugen."

„In rauhes Erz sollst du die Glieder schnüren,
Mit Stahl bedecken deine zarte Brust!
Nicht Männerliebe darf dein Herz berühren
Mit sünd'gen Flammen eitler Erdenlust.
Nie wird der Brautkranz deine Locke zieren,
Dir blüht kein lieblich Kind an deiner Brust;
Doch werd' ich dich mit kriegerischen Ehren,
Vor allen Erdenfrauen dich verklären."

„Denn, wenn im Kampf die Muthigsten verzagen,
Wenn Frankreichs letztes Schicksal nun sich naht,
Dann wirst du meine Oriflamme* tragen
Und, wie die rasche Schnitterin die Saat,
Den stolzen Ueberwinder niederschlagen;
Umwälzen wirst du seines Glückes Rad,
Errettung bringen Frankreichs Heldensöhnen,
Und Rheims befrein und deinen König krönen!"

Ein Zeichen hat der Himmel mir verheißen:
Er sendet mir den Helm, er kommt von ihm,
Mit Götterkraft berühret mich sein Eisen,
Und mich durchflammt der Muth der Cherubim;
Ins Kriegsgewühl hinein will es mich reißen,
Es treibt mich fort mit Sturmes Ungestüm,
Den Feldruf hör' ich mächtig zu mir dringen,
Das Schlachtroß steigt, und die Trompeten klingen.

(Sie geht ab.)

---

* The Oriflamme (deriv. *aurea flamma*, or quasi *auri flamma?*) was the ancient royal standard of France, consisting of a golden lance, to which was attached a strip of red cloth, the pretended winding-sheet of St. Dennis, cut in the shape of a banner, the lower extremity of which was adorned with five tufts of green silk. It was originally the banner of the Abbey of St. Dennis, and was solemnly presented by the Abbot to the Lord Protector of the Convent, whenever the latter was called into the field in its behalf. The first protectors were the counts of Vexin and Pontoise; and when subsequently the county of Vexin was incorporated into the domain of the crown by Philip I., the protectorate of the Convent passed into the hands of the King in consequence of that act. Since that time the Oriflamme was borne by the army, until finally it became the chief standard of the monarchy. After the time of Charles VII., however, it never was displayed in the field again. Others affirm that it was lost at the battle of Agincourt. One authority, however, states, that in 1535 it was still to be seen in an Abbey, much injured by time.

Erster Aufzug.

Hoflager König Karls zu Chinon.

Erster Auftritt.

Dunois und Du Chatel.

Dunois.

Nein, ich ertrag' es länger nicht. Ich sage
Mich los von diesem König, der unrühmlich
Sich selbst verläßt. Mir blutet in der Brust
Das tapfre Herz, und glüh'nde Thränen möcht' ich weinen,
Daß Räuber in das königliche Frankreich
Sich theilen mit dem Schwert, die edeln Städte
Die mit der Monarchie gealtert sind,
Dem Feind die rost'gen Schlüssel überliefern,
Indeß wir hier in thatenloser Ruh
Die köstlich edle Rettungszeit verschwenden.
— Ich höre Orleans bedroht, ich fliege
Herbei aus der entlegnen Normandie,
Den König denk' ich kriegerisch gerüstet
An seines Heeres Spitze schon zu finden
Und find' ihn — hier! umringt von Gaukelspielern
Und Troubadours, spitzfind'ge Räthsel lösend
Und der Sorel galante Feste gebend
Als waltete im Reich der tiefste Friede!
— Der Connetable geht, er kann den Gräul
Nicht länger ansehn. — Ich verlaß' ihn auch
Und übergeb' ihn seinem bösen Schicksal.

Du Chatel.

Da kommt der König.

Zweiter Auftritt.

König Karl zu den Vorigen.

Karl.

Der Connetable * schickt sein Schwert zurück
Und sagt den Dienst mir auf. — In Gottes Namen!
So sind wir eines mürr'schen Mannes los,
Der unverträglich uns nur meistern wollte.

Dunois.

Ein Mann ist viel werth in so theurer Zeit;
Ich möcht' ihn nicht mit leichtem Sinn verlieren.

Karl.

Das sagst du nur aus Lust des Widerspruchs;
So lang er da war, warst du nie sein Freund.

Dunois.

Er war ein stolz verdrießlich schwerer Narr
Und wußte nie zu enden — diesmal aber
Weiß er's. Er weiß zu rechter Zeit zu gehn,
Wo keine Ehre mehr zu holen ist.

Karl.

Du bist in deiner angenehmen Laune;
Ich will dich nicht drin stören. — Du Chatel!
Es sind Gesandte da vom alten König
René, † belobte Meister im Gesang

---

* The term "Connetable" was, together with the office designated by it
(*comes stabuli* = equerry, master of the horse), originally borrowed, as were
many other titles and dignities, from the Roman Empire, which the earlier
Frankish Kings imitated in the organization of their own courts. At first there
were several of these *Cuenstables* as they were termed, and their office was
confined to the internal administration of the palace. At a later period, however, they held the highest offices in the gift of the king; and in the 11th
century that office was the first in the kingdom; the connetable of France
being commander-in-chief of all the royal troops, and at times possessed of a
power that almost equalled that of a Roman Dictator. It was abolished by
an edict of Louis XIII. in 1627.

† Anmerkung in der ersten Ausgabe. René der Gute, Graf
von Provence, aus dem Hause Anjou; sein Vater und Bruder waren Könige
von Neapel, und er selbst machte nach seines Bruders Tode Anspruch auf dieses

Und weit berühmt. — Man muß sie wohl bewirthen
Und jedem eine goldne Kette reichen.
(Zum Bastard.)
Worüber lachst du?

Dunois.
Daß du goldne Ketten
Aus deinem Munde schüttelst.

Du Chatel.
Sire! Es ist
Kein Geld in deinem Schatze mehr vorhanden.

Karl.
So schaffe welches. — Edle Sänger dürfen
Nicht ungeehrt von meinem Hofe ziehn,
Sie machen uns den dürren Scepter blühn,
Sie flechten den unsterblich grünen Zweig
Des Lebens in die unfruchtbare Krone,
Sie stellen herrschend sich den Herrschern gleich,
Aus leichten Wünschen bauen sie sich Throne,
Und nicht im Raume liegt ihr harmlos Reich;
Drum soll der Sänger mit dem König gehen;
Sie beide wohnen auf der Menschheit Höhen!

Du Chatel.
Mein königlicher Herr! Ich hab' dein Ohr
Verschont, so lang noch Rath und Hülfe war;
Doch endlich löst die Nothdurft mir die Zunge.
— Du hast nichts mehr zu schenken, ach, du hast
Nicht mehr, wovon du morgen könntest leben!
Die hohe Flut des Reichthums ist zerflossen,
Und tiefe Ebbe ist in deinem Schatz.
Den Truppen ist der Sold noch nicht bezahlt;
Sie drohen murrend abzuziehn — Kaum weiß
Ich Rath, dein eignes königliches Haus
Nothdürftig nur, nicht fürstlich, zu erhalten.

Reich, scheiterte aber in der Unternehmung. Er suchte die alte provençalische Poesie und die Cour d'amour wieder herzustellen und setzte einen Prince d'amour ein als höchsten Richter in Sachen der Galanterie und Liebe. In demselben romantischen Geist machte er sich mit seiner Gemahlin zum Schäfer.

Karl.

Verpfände meine königlichen Zölle,
— Und laß dir Geld darleihn von den Lombarden.

Du Chatel.

Sire, deine Kroneinkünfte, deine Zölle
Sind auf drei Jahre schon voraus verpfändet.

Dunois.

Und unterdeß geht Pfand und Land verloren.

Karl.

Uns bleiben noch viel reiche schöne Länder.

Dunois.

So lang es Gott gefällt und Talbots Schwert!
Wenn Orleans genommen ist, magst du
Mit deinem König René Schafe hüten.

Karl.

Stets übst du deinen Witz an diesem König;
Doch ist es dieser länderlose Fürst,
Der eben heut mich königlich beschenkte.

Dunois.

Nur nicht mit seiner Krone von Neapel,
Um Gottes willen nicht! Denn die ist feil,
Hab' ich gehört, seitdem er Schafe weidet.

Karl.

Das ist ein Scherz, ein heitres Spiel, ein Fest,
Das er sich selbst und seinem Herzen gibt,
Sich eine schuldlos reine Welt zu gründen
In dieser rauh barbar'schen Wirklichkeit.
Doch was er Großes, Königliches will —
Er will die alten Zeiten wieder bringen,
Wo zarte Minne herrschte, wo die Liebe
Der Ritter große Heldenherzen hob,
Und edle Frauen zu Gerichte saßen,
Mit zartem Sinne alles Feine schlichtend.
In jenen Zeiten wohnt der heitre Greis,
Und wie sie noch in alten Liedern leben,
So will er sie, wie eine Himmelsstadt

In goldnen Wolken, auf die Erde setzen —
Gegründet hat er einen Liebeshof,
Wohin die edlen Ritter sollen wallen,
Wo keusche Frauen herrlich sollen thronen,
Wo reine Minne wiederkehren soll,
Und mich hat er erwählt zum Fürst der Liebe.

Dunois
(nach einigem Stillschweigen).

Ich bin so sehr nicht aus der Art geschlagen,
Daß ich der Liebe Herrschaft sollte schmähn.
Ich nenne mich nach ihr, ich bin ihr Sohn,
Und all' mein Erbe liegt in ihrem Reich.
Mein Vater war der Prinz von Orleans,
Ihm war kein weiblich Herz unüberwindlich,
Doch auch kein feindlich Schloß war ihm zu fest.
Willst du der Liebe Fürst dich würdig nennen,
So sei der Tapfern Tapferster! — Wie ich
Aus jenen alten Büchern mir gelesen,
War Liebe stets mit hoher Ritterthat
Gepaart, und Helden, hat man mich gelehrt,
Nicht Schäfer saßen an der Tafelrunde.
Wer nicht die Schönheit tapfer kann beschützen,
Verdient nicht ihren goldnen Preis. — Hier ist
Der Fechtplatz! Kämpf' um deiner Väter Krone!
Vertheidige mit ritterlichem Schwert
Dein Eigenthum und edler Frauen Ehre —
Und hast du dir aus Strömen Feindesbluts
Die angestammte Krone kühn erobert,
Dann ist es Zeit und steht dir fürstlich an,
Dich mit der Liebe Myrthen zu bekrönen.

Karl
(zu einem Edelknecht, der hereintritt).

Was gibt's?

Edelknecht.
Rathsherren von Orleans flehen um Gehör.

Karl.

Führ' sie herein!

(Edelknecht geht ab).
Sie werden Hülfe fordern;
Was kann ich thun, der selber hülflos ist!

Dritter Auftritt.

Drei Rathsherren zu den Vorigen.

Karl.

Willkommen, meine vielgetreuen Bürger
Aus Orleans! Wie steht's um meine gute Stadt?
Fährt sie noch fort, mit dem gewohnten Muth
Dem Feind zu widerstehn, der sie belagert?

Rathsherr.

Ach, Sire! Es drängt die höchste Noth, und stündlich wach=
                                                    send
Schwillt das Verderben an die Stadt heran.
Die äußern Werke sind zerstört, der Feind
Gewinnt mit jedem Sturme neuen Boden.
Entblößt sind von Vertheidigern die Mauern,
Denn rastlos fechtend fällt die Mannschaft aus;
Doch Wen'ge sehn die Heimatpforte wieder,
Und auch des Hungers Plage droht der Stadt.
Drum hat der edle Graf von Rochepierre,
Der drin befiehlt, in dieser höchsten Noth
Vertragen mit dem Feind, nach altem Brauch,
Sich zu ergeben auf den zwölften Tag,
Wenn binnen dieser Zeit kein Heer im Feld
Erschien, zahlreich genug, die Stadt zu retten.
(Dunois macht eine heftige Bewegung des Zorns.)

Karl.

Die Frist ist kurz.

Rathsherr.

Und jetzo sind wir hier
Mit Feinds Geleit, daß wir dein fürstlich Herz
Anflehen, deiner Stadt dich zu erbarmen
Und Hülf' zu senden binnen dieser Frist,
Sonst übergibt er sie am zwölften Tage.

Dunois.

Saintrailles konnte seine Stimme geben
Zu solchem schimpflichen Vertrag?

Rathsherr.

Nein, Herr!
Solang der Tapfre lebte, durfte nie
Die Rede seyn von Fried' und Uebergabe.

Dunois.

So ist er todt?

Rathsherr.

An unfern Mauern sank
Der edle Held für seines Königs Sache.

Karl.

Saintrailles todt! O, in dem einz'gen Mann
Sinkt mir ein Heer!

(Ein Ritter kommt und spricht einige Worte leise mit dem Bastard, welcher betroffen auffährt.)

Dunois.

Auch das noch!

Karl.

Nun! Was gibt's?

Dunois.

Graf Douglas sendet her. Die schott'schen Völker
Empören sich und drohen abzuziehn,
Wenn sie nicht heut den Rückstand noch erhalten.

Karl.

Du Chatel!

Du Chatel (zuckt die Achseln.)
Sire! Ich weiß nicht Rath.

Karl.

Versprich,
Verpfände, was du hast, mein halbes Reich —

Du Chatel.

Hilft nichts! Sie sind zu oft vertröstet worden!

Karl.

Es sind die besten Truppen meines Heers!
Sie sollen mich jetzt nicht, nicht jetzt verlassen.

Rathsherr (mit einem Fußfall).

O König, hilf uns! Unsrer Noth gedenke!

Karl (verzweiflungsvoll).

Kann ich Armeen aus der Erde stampfen?
Wächs't mir ein Kornfeld in der flachen Hand?
Reißt mich in Stücken, reißt das Herz mir aus,
Und münzet es statt Goldes! Blut hab' ich
Für euch, nicht Silber hab' ich, noch Soldaten!

(Er sieht die Sorel hereintreten und eilt ihr mit ausgebreiteten Armen entgegen.)

Vierter Auftritt.

Agnes Sorel, ein Kästchen in der Hand, zu den Vorigen.

Karl.

O meine Agnes! Mein geliebtes Leben!
Du kommst, mich der Verzweiflung zu entreißen!
Ich habe dich, ich flieh an deine Brust,
Nichts ist verloren, denn du bist noch mein.

Sorel.

Mein theurer König!

(Mit ängstlich fragendem Blick umherschauend.)

Dunois! ist's wahr?
Du Chatel?

Du Chatel.

Leider!

Sorel.

Ist die Noth so groß?
Es fehlt an Gold? Die Truppen wollen abziehn?

Du Chatel.

Ja, leider ist es so!

Sorel (ihm das Kästchen aufdringend).

Hier, hier ist Gold,
Hier sind Juwelen — Schmelzt mein Silber ein —

Verkauft, verpfändet meine Schlösser — Leihet
Auf meine Güter in Provence — Macht Alles
Zu Gelde und befriediget die Truppen!
Fort! Keine Zeit verloren! (Treibt ihn fort.)

Karl.

Nun, Dunois? Nun, Du Chatel? Bin ich euch
Noch arm, da ich die Krone aller Frauen
Besitze? — Sie ist edel, wie ich selbst,
Geboren; selbst das königliche Blut
Der Valois ist nicht reiner; zieren würde sie
Den ersten Thron der Welt — doch sie verschmäht ihn,
Nur meine Liebe will sie seyn und heißen.
Erlaubte sie mir jemals ein Geschenk
Von höherm Werth, als eine frühe Blume
Im Winter oder seltne Frucht? Von mir
Nimmt sie kein Opfer an und bringt mir alle!
Wagt ihren ganzen Reichthum und Besitz
Großmüthig an mein untersinkend Glück.

Dunois.

Ja, sie ist eine Rasende, wie du,
Und wirft ihr Alles in ein brennend Haus
Und schöpft in's lecke Faß der Danaiden.
Dich wird sie nicht erretten, nur sich selbst
Wird sie mit dir verderben —

Sorel.

Glaub' ihm nicht!
Er hat sein Leben zehenmal für dich
Gewagt und zürnt, daß ich mein Gold jetzt wage.
Wie? Hab' ich dir nicht Alles froh geopfert,
Was mehr geachtet wird, als Gold und Perlen,
Und sollte jetzt mein Glück für mich behalten?
Komm! Laß uns allen überflüss'gen Schmuck
Des Lebens von uns werfen! Laß mich dir
Ein edles Beispiel der Entsagung geben!
Verwandle deinen Hofstaat in Soldaten,
Dein Gold in Eisen! Alles, was du hast,
Wirf es entschlossen hin nach deiner Krone!

Komm! Komm! Wir theilen Mangel und Gefahr!
Das kriegerische Roß laß uns besteigen,
Den zarten Leib dem glühnden Pfeil der Sonne
Preisgeben, die Gewölke über uns
Zur Decke nehmen und den Stein zum Pfühl.
Der rauhe Krieger wird sein eignes Weh'
Geduldig tragen, sieht er seinen König
Dem Aermsten gleich, ausdauern und entbehren!

Karl (lächelnd).

Ja, nun erfüllt sich mir ein altes Wort
Der Weissagung, das eine Nonne mir
Zu Clermont in prophet'schem Geiste sprach.
Ein Weib, verhieß die Nonne, würde mich
Zum Sieger machen über alle Feinde
Und meiner Väter Krone mir erkämpfen.
Fern sucht' ich sie im Feindeslager auf,
Das Herz der Mutter hofft' ich zu versöhnen;
Hier steht die Heldin, die nach Rheims mich führt:
Durch meiner Agnes Liebe werd' ich siegen!

Sorel.

Du wirst's durch deiner Freunde tapfres Schwert.

Karl.

Auch von der Feinde Zwietracht hoff' ich viel —
Denn mir ist sichre Kunde zugekommen,
Daß zwischen diesen stolzen Lords von England
Und meinem Vetter von Burgund nicht Alles mehr
So steht wie sonst — Drum hab' ich den La Hire
Mit Botschaft an den Herzog abgefertigt,
Ob mir's gelänge, den erzürnten Pair
Zur alten Pflicht und Treu' zurückzuführen. —
Mit jeder Stunde wart' ich seiner Ankunft.

Du Chatel (am Fenster).

Der Ritter sprengt so eben in den Hof.

Karl.

Willkommner Bote! Nun, so werden wir
Bald wissen, ob wir weichen oder siegen.

Fünfter Auftritt.

La Hire zu den Vorigen.

Karl (geht ihm entgegen).

La Hire! Bringst du uns Hoffnung oder keine?
Erklär' dich kurz. Was hab' ich zu erwarten?

La Hire.

Erwarte nichts mehr, als von deinem Schwert.

Karl.

Der stolze Herzog läßt sich nicht versöhnen?
O, sprich! Wie nahm er meine Botschaft auf?

La Hire.

Vor allen Dingen, und bevor er noch
Ein Ohr dir könne leihen, fordert er,
Daß ihm Du Chatel ausgeliefert werde,
Den er den Mörder seines Vaters nennt.

Karl.

Und, weigern wir uns dieser Schmachbedingung?

La Hire.

Dann sey der Bund zertrennt, noch eh' er anfing.

Karl.

Hast du ihn drauf, wie ich dir anbefahl,
Zum Kampf mit mir gefordert auf der Brücke
Zu Montereau, allwo sein Vater fiel?

La Hire.

Ich warf ihm deinen Handschuh hin und sprach:
Du wolltest deiner Hoheit dich begeben
Und als ein Ritter kämpfen um dein Reich.
Doch er versetzte: nimmer thät's ihm Noth,
Um das zu fechten, was er schou besitze.
Doch wenn dich so nach Kämpfen lüstete,
So würdest du vor Orleans ihn finden,
Wohin er morgen Willens sey zu gehn.
Und damit kehrt' er lachend mir den Rücken.

4

Karl.

Erhob sich nicht in meinem Parlamente
Die reine Stimme der Gerechtigkeit?

La Hire.

Sie ist verstummt vor der Parteien Wuth.
Ein Schluß des Parlaments erklärte dich
Des Throns verlustig, dich und dein Geschlecht.

Dunois.

Ha, frecher Stolz des herrgewordnen Bürgers!

Karl.

Hast du bei meiner Mutter nichts versucht?

La Hire.

Bei deiner Mutter?

Karl.

Ja! Wie ließ sie sich vernehmen?

La Hire
(nachdem er einige Augenblicke sich bedacht).

Es war gerad das Fest der Königskrönung,
Als ich zu Saint Denis eintrat. Geschmückt,
Wie zum Triumphe, waren die Pariser;
In jeder Gasse stiegen Ehrenbogen,
Durch die der engelländ'sche König zog.
Bestreut mit Blumen war der Weg, und jauchzend,
Als hätte Frankreich seinen schönsten Sieg
Erfochten, sprang der Pöbel um den Wagen.

Sorel.

Sie jauchzten — jauchzten, daß sie auf das Herz
Des liebevollen, sanften Königs traten!

La Hire.

Ich sah den jungen Harry Lancaster,
Den Knaben auf dem königlichen Stuhl
Sanct Ludwigs sitzen; feine stolzen Oehme
Bedford und Gloster standen neben ihm,
Und Herzog Philipp kniet' am Throne nieder
Und leistete den Eid für feine Länder.

Karl.

O ehrvergeff'ner Pair! Unwürd'ger Vetter!

La Hire.

Das Kind war bang und strauchelte, da es
Die hohen Stufen an dem Thron hinan stieg.
Ein böses Omen! murmelte das Volk,
Und es erhub sich schallendes Gelächter.
Da trat die alte Königin, deine Mutter,
Hinzu, und — mich entrüstet es, zu sagen!

Karl.

Nun?

La Hire.

    In die Arme faßte sie den Knaben
Und setzt' ihn selbst auf deines Vaters Stuhl.

Karl.

O Mutter! Mutter!

La Hire.

        Selbst die wüthenden
Burgundier, die mordgewohnten Banden,
Erglüheten vor Scham bei diesem Anblick.
Sie nahm es wahr, und an das Volk gewendet
Rief sie mit lauter Stimm': Dankt mir's, Franzosen,
Daß ich den kranken Stamm mit reinem Zweig
Veredle, euch bewahre vor dem miß=
Gebornen Sohn des hirnverrückten Vaters!

(Der König verhüllt sich, Agnes eilt auf ihn zu und schließt ihn in die Arme, alle
Umstehenden drücken ihren Abscheu, ihr Entsetzen aus.)

Dunois.

Die Wölfin! die wuthschnaubende Megäre!

Karl
(nach einer Pause zu den Rathsherren).

Ihr habt gehört, wie hier die Sachen stehn.
Verweilt nicht länger, geht nach Orleans
Zurück und meldet meiner treuen Stadt:
Des Eides gegen mich entlaff' ich sie.
Sie mag ihr Heil beherzigen und sich

Der Gnade des Burgundiers ergeben;
Er heißt der Gute, er wird menschlich sein.

Dunois.

Wie, Sire? Du wolltest Orleans verlassen!

Rathsherr (kniet nieder).

Mein königlicher Herr! Zieh deine Hand
Nicht von uns ab! Gib deine treue Stadt
Nicht unter Englands harte Herrschaft hin.
Sie ist ein edler Stein in deiner Krone,
Und keine hat den Königen, deinen Ahnherrn,
Die Treue heiliger bewahrt.

Dunois.

         Sind wir
Geschlagen? Ist's erlaubt, das Feld zu räumen,
Eh noch ein Schwertstreich um die Stadt geschehn?
Mit einem leichten Wörtlein, ehe Blut
Geflossen ist, denkst du die beste Stadt
Aus Frankreichs Herzen weg zu geben?

Karl.

                Gnug
Des Blutes ist geflossen und vergebens!
Des Himmels schwere Hand ist gegen mich:
Geschlagen wird mein Heer in allen Schlachten,
Mein Parlament verwirft mich, meine Hauptstadt,
Mein Volk nimmt meine Gegner jauchzend auf,
Die mir die Nächsten sind am Blut, verlassen,
Verrathen mich — die eigne Mutter nährt
Die fremde Feindesbrut an ihren Brüsten.
— Wir wollen jenseits der Loire uns ziehn
Und der gewalt'gen Hand des Himmels weichen,
Der mit dem Engelländer ist.

Sorel.

Das wolle Gott nicht, daß wir, an uns selbst
Verzweifelnd, diesem Reich den Rücken wenden!
Dies Wort kam nicht aus deiner tapfern Brust.
Der Mutter unnatürlich rohe That

Hat meines Königs Heldenherz gebrochen!
Du wirst dich wieder finden, männlich fassen,
Mit edlem Muth dem Schicksal widerstehen,
Das grimmig dir entgegen kämpft.

Karl
(in düstres Sinnen verloren).

Ist es nicht wahr?
Ein finster furchtbares Verhängniß waltet
Durch Valois Geschlecht; es ist verworfen
Von Gott; der Mutter Lasterthaten führten
Die Furien herein in dieses Haus.
Mein Vater lag im Wahnsinn zwanzig Jahre,
Drei ältre Brüder hat der Tod vor mir
Hinweggemäht, es ist des Himmels Schluß,
Das Haus des sechsten Karls soll untergehn.

Sorel.

In dir wird es sich neu verjüngt erheben!
Hab' Glauben an dich selbst. — O! nicht umsonst
Hat dich ein gnädig Schicksal aufgespart,
Von deinen Brüdern allen dich, den jüngsten,
Gerufen auf den ungehofften Thron.
In deiner sanften Seele hat der Himmel
Den Arzt für alle Wunden sich bereitet,
Die der Parteien Wuth dem Lande schlng.
Des Bürgerkrieges Flammen wirst du löschen,
Mir sagt's das Herz, den Frieden wirst du pflanzen,
Des Frankenreiches neuer Stifter sein.

Karl.

Nicht ich. Die rauhe, sturmbewegte Zeit
Heischt einen kraftbegabtern Steuermann.
Ich hätt' ein friedlich Volk beglücken können,
Ein wild empörtes kann ich nicht bezähmen,
Nicht mir die Herzen öffnen mit dem Schwert,
Die sich entfremdet mir in Haß verschließen.

Sorel.

Verblendet ist das Volk, ein Wahn betäubt es,
Doch dieser Taumel wird vorübergehn;

Erwachen wird, nicht fern mehr ist der Tag,
Die Liebe zu dem angestammten König,
Die tief gepflanzt ist in des Franken Brust,
Der alte Haß, die Eifersucht erwachen,
Die beide Völker ewig feindlich trennt;
Den stolzen Sieger stürzt sein eignes Glück.
Darum verlasse nicht mit Uebereilung
Den Kampfplatz, ring' um jeden Fußbreit Erde,
Wie deine eigne Brust vertheidige
Dies Orleans! Laß alle Fähren lieber
Versenken, alle Brücken niederbrennen,
Die über diese Scheide deines Reichs,
Das styg'sche Wasser der Loire, dich führen.

Karl.

Was ich vermocht', hab ich gethan. Ich habe
Mich dargestellt zum ritterlichen Kampf
Um meine Krone. — Man verweigert ihn.
Umsonst verschwend' ich meines Volkes Leben,
Und meine Städte sinken in den Staub.
Soll ich, gleich jener unnatürlichen Mutter,
Mein Kind zertheilen lassen mit dem Schwert?
Nein, daß es lebe, will ich ihm entsagen.

Dunois.

Wie, Sire, ist das die Sprache eines Königs?
Gibt man so eine Krone auf? Es setzt
Der Schlechtste deines Volkes Gut und Blut
An seine Meinung, seinen Haß und Liebe;
Partei wird Alles, wenn das blut'ge Zeichen
Des Bürgerkrieges ausgehangen ist.
Der Ackersmann verläßt den Pflug, das Weib
Den Rocken, Kinder, Greise waffnen sich,
Der Bürger zündet seine Stadt, der Landmann
Mit eignen Händen seine Saaten an,
Um dir zu schaden oder wohl zu thun
Und seines Herzens Wollen zu behaupten.
Nichts schont er selber und erwartet sich

Nicht Schonung, wenn die Ehre ruft, wenn er
Für seine Götter oder Götzen kämpft.
Drum weg mit diesem weichlichen Mitleiden,
Das einer Königsbrust nicht ziemt. — Laß du
Den Krieg ausrasen, wie er angefangen.
Du hast ihn nicht leichtsinnig selbst entflammt.
Für seinen König muß das Volk sich opfern,
Das ist das Schicksal und Gesetz der Welt.
Der Franke weiß es nicht und will's nicht anders.
Nichtswürdig ist die Nation, die nicht
Ihr Alles freudig setzt an ihre Ehre.

Karl (zu den Rathsherren).

Erwartet keinen anderen Bescheid.
Gott schütz' euch. Ich kann nicht mehr.

Dunois.

Nun, so kehre

Der Siegesgott auf ewig dir den Rücken,
Wie du dem väterlichen Reich. Du hast
Dich selbst verlassen: so verlaß ich dich.
Nicht Englands und Burgunds vereinte Macht,
Dich stürzt der eigne Kleinmuth von dem Thron.
Die Könige Frankreichs sind geborne Helden;
Du aber bist unkriegerisch gezeugt.

(Zu den Rathsherren.)

Der König gibt euch auf. Ich aber will
In Orleans, meines Vaters Stadt, mich werfen
Und unter ihren Trümmern mich begraben.

(Er will gehen, Agnes Sorel hält ihn auf.)

Sorel (zum König).

O, laß ihn nicht im Zorne von dir gehn!
Sein Mund spricht rauhe Worte, doch sein Herz
Ist treu, wie Gold; es ist derselbe doch,
Der warm dich liebt und oft für dich geblutet.
Kommt, Dunois! Gesteht, daß euch die Hitze
Des edeln Zorns zu weit geführt —Du aber
Verzeih' dem treuen Freund die heft'ge Rede!
O, kommt, kommt! Laßt mich eure Herzen schnell

Vereinigen, eh sich der rasche Zorn
Unlöschbar, der verderbliche, entflammt!
(Dunois fixirt den König und scheint eine Antwort zu erwarten.)

Karl (zu Du Chatel).

Wir gehen über die Loire.   Laß mein
Geräth zu Schiffe bringen!

Dunois (schnell zu Sorel).

Lebet wohl!
(Wendet sich schnell und geht, Rathsherren folgen.)

Sorel
(ringt verzweiflungsvoll die Hände).

O, wenn er geht, so sind wir ganz verlassen!
Folgt ihm, La Hire.   O, sucht ihn zu begüt'gen.
(La Hire geht ab.)

Sechster Auftritt.
Karl. Sorel. Du Chatel.

Karl.

Ist denn die Krone ein so einzig Gut?
Ist es so bitter schwer, davon zu scheiden?
Ich kenne, was noch schwerer sich erträgt.
Von diesen trotzig herrischen Gemüthern
Sich meistern lassen, von der Gnade leben
Hochsinnig eigenwilliger Vasallen,
Das ist das Harte für ein edles Herz
Und bittrer, als dem Schicksal unterliegen!
(Zu Du Chatel, der noch zaudert.)
Thu', was ich dir befohlen!

Du Chatel (wirft sich zu seinen Füßen).

O mein König!

Karl.

Es ist beschlossen.   Keine Worte weiter!

Du Chatel.

Mach' Frieden mit dem Herzog von Burgund!
Sonst seh' ich keine Rettung mehr für dich.

Karl.

Du räthſt mir dieſes, und dein Blut iſt es,
Womit ich dieſen Frieden ſoll verſiegeln?

Du Chatel.

Hier iſt mein Haupt. Ich hab' es oft für dich
Gewagt in Schlachten, und ich leg' es jetzt
Für dich mit Freuden auf das Blutgerüſte.
Befriedige den Herzog! Ueberliefre mich
Der ganzen Strenge ſeines Zorns und laß
Mein fließend Blut den alten Haß verſöhnen!

Karl

(blickt ihn eine Zeit lang gerührt und ſchweigend an).

Iſt es denn wahr? Steht es ſo ſchlimm mit mir,
Daß meine Freunde, die mein Herz durchſchauen,
Den Weg der Schande mir zur Rettung zeigen?
Ja, jetzt erkenn' ich meinen tiefen Fall;
Denn das Vertraun iſt hin auf meine Ehre.

Du Chatel.

Bedenk' —

Karl.

     Kein Wort mehr! Bringe mich nicht auf!
Müßt' ich zehn Reiche mit dem Rücken ſchauen,
Ich rette mich nicht mit des Freundes Leben.
— Thu', was ich dir befohlen. Geh' und laß
Mein Heergeräth einſchiffen.

Du Chatel.

        Es wird ſchnell
Gethan ſein.

(Steht auf und geht, Agnes Sorel weint heftig.)

Siebenter Auftritt.

Karl und Sorel.

Karl (ihre Hand faſſend).

Sei nicht traurig, meine Agnes!
Auch jenſeits der Loire liegt noch ein Frankreich,

4*

Wir gehen in ein glücklicheres Land.
Da lacht ein milder, nie bewölkter Himmel,
Und leichtre Lüfte wehn, und sanftre Sitten
Empfangen uns; da wohnen die Gesänge,
Und schöner blüht das Leben und die Liebe.

Sorel.

O, muß ich diesen Tag des Jammers schauen!
Der König muß in die Verbannung gehn,
Der Sohn auswandern aus des Vaters Hause
Und seine Wiege mit dem Rücken schauen.
O angenehmes Land, das wir verlassen,
Nie werden wir dich freudig mehr betreten!

Achter Auftritt.

La Hire kommt zurück. Karl und Sorel.

Sorel.

Ihr kommt allein. Ihr bringt ihn nicht zurück?
(Indem sie ihn näher ansieht.)
La Hire! Was gibt's? Was sagt mir euer Blick?
Ein neues Unglück ist geschehn?

La Hire.

                              Das Unglück
Hat sich erschöpft, und Sonnenschein ist wieder!

Sorel.

Was ist's? Ich bitt' euch.

La Hire (zum König).

                    Ruf' die Abgesandten
Von Orleans zurück!

Karl.

            Warum? Was gibt's?

La Hire.

Ruf' sie zurück! Dein Glück hat sich gewendet,
Ein Treffen ist geschehn, du hast gesiegt.

Sorel.

Gesiegt! O himmlische Musik des Wortes!

Karl.

La Hire!   Dich täuscht ein fabelhaft Gerücht.
Gesiegt!   Ich glaub' an keine Siege mehr.

La Hire.

O, du wirst bald noch größre Wunder glauben.
— Da kommt der Erzbischof.   Er führt den Bastard
In deinen Arm zurück —

Sorel.

O schöne Blume
Des Siegs, die gleich die edeln Himmelsfrüchte,
Fried' und Versöhnung trägt!

Neunter Auftritt.

**Erzbischof von Rheims. Dunois. Du Chatel mit
Raoul, einem geharnischten Ritter, zu den Vorigen.**

Erzbischof
(führt den Bastard zu dem König und legt ihre Hände in einander).

Umarmt euch, Prinzen!
Laßt allen Groll und Hader jetzo schwinden,
Da sich der Himmel selbst für uns erklärt.
(Dunois umarmt den König.)

Karl.

Reißt mich aus meinem Zweifel und Erstaunen.
Was kündigt dieser feierliche Ernst mir an?
Was wirkte diesen schnellen Wechsel?

Erzbischof
(führt den Ritter hervor und stellt ihn vor den König).

Redet!

Raoul.

Wir hatten sechzehn Fähnlein aufgebracht,
Lothringisch Volk, zu deinem Heer zu stoßen,
Und Ritter Baudricour aus Vaucouleurs
War unser Führer.   Als wir nun die Höhen
Bei Vermanton erreicht und in das Thal,
Das die Yonne durchströmt, herunter stiegen,
Da stand in weiter Ebene vor uns der Feind,

Und Waffen blitzten, da wir rückwärts sahn.
Umrungen sahn wir uns von beiden Heeren,
Nicht Hoffnung war zu siegen noch zu fliehn;
Da sank dem Tapfersten das Herz, und Alles,
Verzweiflungsvoll, will schon die Waffen strecken.
Als nun die Führer mit einander noch
Rath suchten und nicht fanden — sieh, da stellte sich
Ein seltsam Wunder unfern Augen dar!
Denn aus der Tiefe des Gehölzes plötzlich
Trat eine Jungfrau mit behelmtem Haupt
Wie eine Kriegesgöttin, schön zugleich
Und schrecklich anzusehn; um ihren Nacken
In dunkeln Ringen fiel das Haar; ein Glanz
Vom Himmel schien die Hohe zu umleuchten,
Als sie die Stimm' erhub und also sprach:
Was zagt ihr, tapfre Franken! Auf den Feind!
Und wären sein mehr denn des Sands im Meere,
Gott und die heil'ge Jungfrau führt euch an!
Und schnell dem Fahnenträger aus der Hand
Riß sie die Fahn' und vor dem Zuge her
Mit kühnem Anstand schritt die Mächtige.
Wir, stumm vor Staunen, selbst nicht wollend, folgen
Der hohen Fahn' und ihrer Trägerin,
Und auf den Feind gerad' an stürmen wir.
Der, hochbetroffen, steht bewegungslos,
Mit weit geöffnet starrem Blick das Wunder
Anstaunend, das sich seinen Augen zeigt —
Doch schnell, als hätten Gottes Schrecken ihn
Ergriffen, wendet er sich um
Zur Flucht, und, Wehr und Waffen von sich werfend,
Entschaart das ganze Heer sich im Gefilde;
Da hilft kein Machtwort, keines Führers Ruf;
Vor Schrecken sinnlos, ohne rückzuschau'n,
Stürzt Mann und Roß sich in des Flusses Bette,
Und läßt sich würgen ohne Widerstand;
Ein Schlachten war's, nicht eine Schlacht, zu nennen!
Zweitausend Feinde deckten das Gefild',

Die nicht gerechnet, die der Fluß verschlang,
Und von den Unfern ward kein Mann vermißt.

Karl.

Seltsam, bei Gott! höchst wunderbar und seltsam!

Sorel.

Und eine Jungfrau wirkte dieses Wunder?
Wo kam sie her?   Wer ist sie?

Raoul.

                              Wer sie sey,
Will sie allein dem König offenbaren.
Sie nennt sich eine Seherin und gott=
Gesendete Prophetin und verspricht,
Orleans zu retten, eh der Mond noch wechselt.
Ihr glaubt das Volk und dürstet nach Gefechten.
Sie folgt dem Heer, gleich wird sie selbst hier seyn.

(Man hört Glocken und ein Geklirr von Waffen, die aneinander geschlagen werden.)

Hört ihr den Auflauf? das Geläut' der Glocken?
Sie ist's, das Volk begrüßt die Gottgesandte.

Karl (zu Du Chatel).

Führt sie herein —

(Zum Erzbischof.)

                    Was soll ich davon denken?
Ein Mädchen bringt mir Sieg und eben jetzt,
Da nur ein Götterarm mich retten kann!
Das ist nicht in dem Laufe der Natur,
Und darf ich — Bischof, darf ich Wunder glauben?

Viele Stimmen (hinter der Scene).

Heil!   Heil der Jungfrau, der Erretterin!

Karl.

Sie kommt!

(Zu Dunois.)

              Nehmt meinen Platz ein, Dunois!
Wir wollen dieses Wundermädchen prüfen.
Ist sie begeistert und von Gott gesandt,
Wird sie den König zu entdecken wissen.

(Dunois setzt sich, der König steht zu seiner Rechten, neben ihm Agnes Sorel, der Erzbischof mit den Uebrigen gegenüber, daß der mittlere Raum leer bleibt.)

Zehnter Auftritt.

Die Vorigen. Johanna, begleitet von den **Rathsherren**
nb vielen **Rittern,** welche den Hintergrund der Scene anfüllen; mit edlem
Anstande tritt sie vorwärts und schaut die Umstehenden der Reihe nach an.

Dunois (nach einer tiefen feierlichen Stille).

Bist du es, wunderbares Mädchen —

Johanna

(unterbricht ihn, mit Klarheit und Hoheit ihn anschauend).

Bastard von Orleans! Du willst Gott versuchen!
Steh' auf von diesem Platz, der dir nicht ziemt!
An diesen Größeren bin ich gesendet.

(Sie geht mit entschiedenem Schritt auf den König zu, beugt ein Knie vor ihm und
steht sogleich wieder auf, zurücktretend. Alle Anwesenden drücken ihr Erstaunen
aus. Dunois verläßt seinen Sitz, und es wird Raum vor dem König.)

Karl.

Du siehst mein Antlitz heut' zum erstenmal;
Von wannen kommt dir diese Wissenschaft?

Johanna.

Ich sah dich, wo dich Niemand sah, als Gott.

(Sie nähert sich dem König und spricht geheimnißvoll.)

In jüngst verwichner Nacht, besinne dich!
Als Alles um dich her in tiefem Schlaf
Begraben lag, da standst du auf von deinem Lager
Und thatst ein brünstiges Gebet zu Gott.
Laß die hinausgehn, und ich nenne dir
Den Inhalt des Gebets.

Karl.

Was ich dem Himmel
Vertraut, brauch' ich vor Menschen nicht zu bergen.
Entdecke mir den Inhalt meines Flehns,
So zweifl' ich nicht mehr, daß dich Gott begeistert.

Johanna.

Es waren drei Gebete, die du thatst;
Gib wohl Acht, Dauphin, ob ich dir sie nenne!
Zum Ersten flehtest du den Himmel an,
Wenn unrecht Gut an dieser Krone hafte,
Wenn eine andre schwere Schuld, noch nicht
Gebüßt, von deiner Väter Zeiten her,

Diesen thränenvollen Krieg herbeigerufen,
Dich zum Opfer anzunehmen für dein Volk
Und auszugießen auf dein einzig Haupt
Die ganze Schale seines Zorns.

Karl (tritt mit Schrecken zurück).

Wer bist du, mächtig Wesen?   Woher kommst du?
(Alle zeigen ihr Erstaunen.)

Johanna.

Du thatst dem Himmel diese zweite Bitte:
Wenn es sein hoher Schluß und Wille sey,
Das Scepter deinem Stamme zu entwinden,
Dir Alles zu entziehn, was deine Väter,
Die Könige in deinem Reich, besaßen —
Drei einz'ge Güter flehtest du ihn an
Dir zu bewahren: die zufriedne Brust,
Des Freundes Herz und deiner Agnes Liebe.

(Der König verbirgt das Gesicht, heftig weinend; große Bewegung des Erstaunens
unter den Anwesenden.   Nach einer Pause.)

Soll ich dein dritt' Gebet dir nun noch nennen?

Karl.

Genug! Ich glaube dir!   So viel vermag
Kein Mensch!   Dich hat der höchste Gott gesendet.

Erzbischof.

Wer bist du, heilig wunderbares Mädchen?
Welch glücklich Land gebar dich?   Sprich!   Wer sind
Die gottgeliebten Eltern, die dich zeugten?

Johanna.

Ehrwürd'ger Herr, Johanna nennt man mich.
Ich bin nur eines Hirten niedre Tochter
Aus meines Königs Flecken Dom Remi,
Der in dem Kirchensprengel liegt von Toul,
Und hütete die Schafe meines Vaters
Von Kind auf — Und ich hörte viel und oft
Erzählen von dem fremden Inselvolk,
Das über Meer gekommen, uns zu Knechten
Zu machen und den fremdgebornen Herrn
Uns aufzuzwingen, der das Volk nicht liebt,

Und daß sie schon die große Stadt Paris
Inn' hätten und des Reiches sich ermächtigt.
Da rief ich flehend Gottes Mutter an,
Von uns zu wenden fremder Ketten Schmach,
Uns den einheim'schen König zu bewahren.*
Und vor dem Dorf, wo ich geboren, steht
Ein uralt Muttergottesbild, zu dem
Der frommen Pilgerfahrten viel geschah'n,
Und eine heil'ge Eiche steht daneben,
Durch vieler Wunder Segenskraft berühmt.
Und in der Eiche Schatten saß ich gern,
Die Heerde weidend, denn mich zog das Herz.
Und ging ein Lamm mir in den wüsten Bergen
Verloren, immer zeigte mir's der Traum,
Wenn ich im Schatten dieser Eiche schlief.
— Und einsmals, als ich eine lange Nacht
In frommer Andacht unter diesem Baum
Gesessen und dem Schlafe widerstand,
Da trat die Heilige zu mir, ein Schwert
Und Fahne tragend, aber sonst, wie ich,
Als Schäferin gekleidet, und sie sprach zu mir:
„Ich bin's. Steh' auf, Johanna! Laß die Heerde.
„Dich ruft der Herr zu einem anderen Geschäft!
„Nimm diese Fahne! Dieses Schwert umgürte dir!
„Damit vertilge meines Volkes Feinde,
„Und führe deines Herren Sohn nach Rheims,
„Und krön' ihn mit der königlichen Krone!"
Ich aber sprach: Wie kann ich solcher That
Mich unterwinden, eine zarte Magd,
Unkundig des verderblichen Gefechts!
Und sie versetzte: „Eine reine Jungfrau
„Vollbringt jedwedes Herrliche auf Erden,
„Wenn sie der ird'schen Liebe widersteht.
„Sieh' mich an! Eine keusche Magd, wie du,
„Hab' ich den Herrn, den göttlichen, geboren,
„Und göttlich bin ich selbst!" — Und sie berührte

---

* Cf. Thibaut's account in the Prologue, p. 9, 10, seq.

Mein Augenlied, und als ich aufwärts sah,
Da war der Himmel voll von Engelknaben,
Die trugen weiße Lilien in der Hand,
Und süßer Ton verschwebte in den Lüften.
— Und so drei Nächte nach einander ließ
Die Heilige sich sehn und rief: „Steh' auf, Johanna!
„Dich ruft der Herr zu einem anderen Geschäft."
Und als sie in der dritten Nacht erschien,
Da zürnte sie, und scheltend sprach sie dieses Wort:
„Gehorsam ist des Weibes Pflicht auf Erden,
„Das harte Dulden ist ihr schweres Loos;
„Durch strengen Dienst muß sie geläutert werden;
„Die hier gedienet, ist dort oben groß."
Und also sprechend ließ sie das Gewand
Der Hirtin fallen, und als Königin
Der Himmel stand sie da im Glanz der Sonnen,
Und goldne Wolken trugen sie hinauf,
Langsam verschwindend, in das Land der Wonnen.
(Alle sind gerührt, Agnes Sorel, heftig weinend, verbirgt ihr Gesicht an des Königs
Brust.)

Erzbischof (nach einem langen Stillschweigen.)
Vor solcher göttlichen Beglaubigung
Muß jeder Zweifel ird'scher Klugheit schweigen.
Die That bewährt es, daß sie Wahrheit spricht;
Nur Gott allein kann solche Wunder wirken.

Dunois.
Nicht ihren Wundern, ihrem Auge glaub' ich,
Der reinen Unschuld ihres Angesichts.

Karl.
Und bin ich Sünd'ger solcher Gnade werth?
Untrüglich allerforschend Aug', du siehst
Mein Innerstes und kennest meine Demuth!

Johanna.
Der Hohen Demuth leuchtet hell dort oben;
Du beugtest dich, drum hat er dich erhoben.

Karl.
So werd' ich meinen Feinden widerstehn?

Johanna.

Bezwungen leg' ich Frankreich dir zu Füßen!

Karl.

Und Orleans, sagst du, wird nicht übergehn?

Johanna.

Eh' siehst du die Loire zurücke fließen.

Karl.

Werd ich nach Rheims als Ueberwinder ziehn?

Johanna.

Durch tausend Feinde führ' ich dich dahin.

(Alle anwesenden Ritter erregen ein Getöse mit ihren Lanzen und Schilden und geben Zeichen des Muths.)

Dunois.

Stell' uns die Jungfrau an des Heeres Spitze,
Wir folgen blind, wohin die Göttliche
Uns führt!   Ihr Seherauge soll uns leiten,
Und schützen soll sie dieses tapfre Schwert!

La Hire.

Nicht eine Welt in Waffen fürchten wir,
Wenn sie einher vor unsern Schaaren zieht.
Der Gott des Sieges wandelt ihr zur Seite;
Sie führ' uns an, die Mächtige, im Streite!

(Die Ritter erregen ein großes Waffengetös' und treten vorwärts.)

Karl.

Ja, heilig Mädchen, führe du mein Heer,
Und seine Fürsten sollen dir gehorchen.
Dies Schwert der höchsten Kriegsgewalt, das uns
Der Kronfeldherr im Zorn zurückgesendet,
Hat eine würdigere Hand gefunden.
Empfange du es, heilige Prophetin,
Und sey fortan —

Johanna.

        Nicht also, edler Dauphin!
Nicht durch dies Werkzeug irdischer Gewalt
Ist meinem Herrn der Sieg verliehn.   Ich weiß
Ein ander Schwert, durch das ich siegen werde.

Ich will es dir bezeichnen, wie's der Geist
Mich lehrte; sende hin und laß es holen.

Karl.

Nenn' es, Johanna.

Johanna.

Sende nach der alten Stadt
Fierboys, dort, auf Sanct Kathrinens Kirchhof
Ist ein Gewölb, wo vieles Eisen liegt,
Von alter Siegesbeute aufgehäuft.
Das Schwert ist drunter, das mir dienen soll.
An dreien goldnen Lilien ist's zu kennen,
Die auf der Klinge eingeschlagen sind.
Dies Schwert laß holen, denn durch dieses wirst du siegen.

Karl.

Man sende hin und thue, wie sie sagt.

Johanna.

Und eine weiße Fahne laß mich tragen,
Mit einem Saum von Purpur eingefaßt.
Auf dieser Fahne sey die Himmelskönigin
Zu sehen mit dem schönen Jesusknaben,
Die über einer Erdenkugel schwebt,
Denn also zeigte mir's die heil'ge Mutter.

Karl.

Es sey so, wie du sagst.

Johanna (zum Erzbischof.)

Ehrwürd'ger Bischof,
Legt eure priesterliche Hand auf mich
Und sprecht den Segen über enre Tochter!
(Kniet nieder.)

Erzbischof.

Du bist gekommen, Segen auszutheilen,
Nicht zu empfangen — Geh' mit Gottes Kraft!
Wir aber sind Unwürdige und Sünder.
(Sie stehet auf.)

Edelknecht.

Ein Herold kommt vom engelländ'schen Feldherrn.

Johanna.

Laßt ihn eintreten, denn ihn sendet Gott!

(Der König winkt dem Edelknecht, der hinausgeht.)

Eilfter Auftritt.

Der Herold zu den Vorigen.

Karl.

Was bringst du, Herold? Sage deinen Auftrag!

Herold.

Wer ist es, der für Karl von Valois,
Den Grafen von Ponthieu, das Wort hier führt?

Dunois.

Nichtswürd'ger Herold! Niederträcht'ger Bube!
Erfrechst du dich, den König der Franzosen
Auf seinem eignen Boden zu verläugnen?
Dich schützt dein Wappenrock, sonst solltest du —

Herold.

Frankreich erkennt nur einen einz'gen König,
Und dieser lebt im engelländischen Lager.

Karl.

Seyd ruhig, Vetter! Deinen Auftrag, Herold!

Herold.

Mein edler Feldherr, den des Blutes jammert,
Daß schon geflossen und noch fließen soll,
Hält seiner Krieger Schwert noch in der Scheide,
Und ehe Orleans im Sturme fällt,
Läßt er noch gütlichen Vergleich dir bieten.

Karl.

Laß hören!

Johanna (tritt hervor.)

Sire! Laß mich an deiner Statt
Mit diesem Herold reden.

Karl.

Thu' das, Mädchen!

Entscheide du, ob Krieg sey oder Friede.

Johanna (zum Herold.)
Wer sendet dich und spricht durch deinen Mund?

Herold.
Der Britten Feldherr, Graf von Sal'sbury.

Johanna.
Herold, du lügst! Der Lord spricht nicht durch dich.
Nur die Lebend'gen sprechen, nicht die Todten.

Herold.
Mein Feldherr lebt in Fülle der Gesundheit
Und Kraft, und lebt euch allen zum Verderben.

Johanna.
Er lebte, da du abgingst. Diesen Morgen
Streckt' ihn ein Schuß aus Orleans zu Boden,
Als er vom Thurm La Tournelle niedersah.
— Du lachst, weil ich Entferntes dir verkünde?
Nicht meiner Rede, deinen Augen glaube!
Begegnen wird dir seiner Leiche Zug,
Wenn deine Füße dich zurücke tragen!
Jetzt, Herold, sprich und sage deinen Auftrag.

Herold.
Wenn du Verborgnes zu enthüllen weißt,
So kennst du ihn, noch eh' ich dir ihn sage.

Johanna.
Ich brauch' ihn nicht zu wissen, aber du
Vernimm den meinen jetzt! und diese Worte
Verkündige den Fürsten, die dich sandten!
— König von England und ihr Herzoge,
Bedford und Gloster, die das Reich verwesen!
Gebt Rechenschaft dem Könige des Himmels
Von wegen des vergoss'nen Blutes! Gebt
Heraus die Schlüssel alle von den Städten,
Die ihr bezwungen wider göttlich Recht!
Die Jungfrau kommt vom Könige des Himmels
Euch Frieden zu bieten oder blut'gen Krieg.
Wählt! Denn das sag' ich euch, damit ihr's wisset:
Euch ist das schöne Frankreich nicht beschieden

Vom Sohne der Maria — sondern Karl,
Mein Herr und Dauphin, dem es Gott gegeben,
Wird königlich einziehen zu Paris,
Von allen Großen seines Reichs begleitet.
— Jetzt, Herold, geh' und mach' dich eilends fort,
Denn eh du noch das Lager magst erreichen
Und Botschaft bringen, ist die Jungfrau dort
Und pflanzt in Orleans das Siegeszeichen.

(Sie geht, Alles setzt sich in Bewegung, der Vorhang fällt.)

Zweiter Aufzug.

Gegend, von Felsen begrenzt.

Erster Auftritt.

Talbot und Lionel, englische Heerführer. Philipp, Herzog von
Burgund. Ritter Fastolf und Chatillon mit Soldaten
und Fahnen.

Talbot.

Hier unter diesen Felsen lasset uns
Halt machen und ein festes Lager schlagen,
Ob wir vielleicht die flücht'gen Völker wieder sammeln,
Die in dem ersten Schrecken sich zerstreut.
Stellt gute Wachen aus, besetzt die Höhn!
Zwar sichert uns die Nacht vor der Verfolgung,
Und wenn der Gegner nicht auch Flügel hat,
So fürcht' ich keinen Ueberfall. — Dennoch
Bedarf's der Vorsicht; denn wir haben es
Mit einem kecken Feind und sind geschlagen.
(Ritter Fastolf geht ab mit den Soldaten).

Lionel.

Geschlagen! Feldherr, nennt das Wort nicht mehr.
Ich darf es mir nicht denken, daß der Franke
Des Engelländers Rücken heut' gesehn.
— O Orleans! Orleans! Grab unsers Ruhms!
Auf deinen Feldern liegt die Ehre Englands.
Beschimpfend lächerliche Niederlage!
Wer wird es glauben in der künft'gen Zeit!
Die Sieger bei Poitiers, Crequi
Und Azincourt gejagt von einem Weibe!

95

Burgund.

Das muß uns trösten.   Wir sind nicht von Menschen
Besiegt, wir sind vom Teufel überwunden.

Talbot.

Vom Teufel unsrer Narrheit — Wie Burgund?
Schreckt dies Gespenst des Pöbels auch die Fürsten?
Der Aberglaube ist ein schlechter Mantel
Für eure Feigheit — Eure Völker flohn zuerst.

Burgund.

Niemand hielt Stand.   Das Fliehn war allgemein.

Talbot.

Nein, Herr!   Auf eurem Flügel fing' es an.
Ihr stürztet euch in unser Lager, schreiend:
Die Höll' ist los, der Satan kämpft für Frankreich!
Und brachtet so die Unsern in Verwirrung.

Lionel.

Ihr könnt's nicht läugnen.   Euer Flügel wich
Zuerst.

Burgund.

     Weil dort der erste Angriff war.

Talbot.

Das Mädchen kannte unsers Lagers Blöße;
Sie wußte, wo die Furcht zu finden war.

Burgund.

Wie?   Soll Burgund die Schuld des Unglücks tragen?

Lionel.

Wir Engelländer, waren wir allein,
Bei Gott, wir hätten Orleans nicht verloren!

Burgund.

Nein — denn ihr hättet Orleans nie gesehen!
Wer bahnte euch den Weg in dieses Reich,
Reicht' euch die treue Freundeshand, als ihr
An diese feindlich fremde Küste stieget?
Wer krönte euren Heinrich zu Paris
Und unterwarf ihm der Franzosen Herzen?
Bei Gott! wenn dieser starke Arm euch nicht

Herein geführt, ihr fahet nie den Rauch
Von einem fränkischen Kamine steigen.

Lionel.

Wenn es die großen Worte thäten, Herzog,
So hättet ihr allein Frankreich erobert.

Burgund.

Ihr seyd unlustig, weil euch Orleans
Entging, und laßt nun eures Zornes Galle
An mir, dem Bundsfreund, aus. Warum entging
Uns Orleans, als eurer Habsucht wegen?
Es war bereit, sich mir zu übergeben,
Ihr, euer Neid allein hat es verhindert.

Talbot.

Nicht euretwegen haben wir's belagert.

Burgund.

Wie stünd's um euch, zög' ich mein Heer zurück?

Lionel.

Nicht schlimmer, glaubt mir, als bei Azincourt,
Wo wir mit euch und mit ganz Frankreich fertig wurden.

Burgund.

Doch that's euch sehr um unsre Freundschaft Noth,
Und theuer kaufte sie der Reichsverweser.

Talbot.

Ja, theuer, theuer haben wir sie heut
Vor Orleans bezahlt mit unsrer Ehre.

Burgund.

Treibt es nicht weiter, Lord, es könnt' euch reuen!
Verließ ich meines Herrn gerechte Fahnen,
Lud auf mein Haupt den Namen des Verräthers,
Um von dem Fremdling Solches zu ertragen?
Was thu' ich hier und fechte gegen Frankreich?
Wenn ich dem Undankbaren dienen soll,
So will ich's meinem angebornen König.

Talbot.

Ihr steht in Unterhandlung mit dem Dauphin,
5

Wir wissen's; doch wir werden Mittel finden,
Uns vor Verrath zu schützen.

Burgund.

Tod und Hölle!
Begegnet man mir so? — Chatillon!
Laß meine Völker sich zum Aufbruch rüsten;
Wir gehn in unser Land zurück.

(Chatillon geht ab.)

Lionel.

Glück auf den Weg!
Nie war der Ruhm der Britten glänzender,
Als da er, seinem guten Schwert allein
Vertrauend, ohne Helfershelfer focht.
Es kämpfe Jeder seine Schlacht allein;
Denn ewig bleibt es wahr: Französisch Blut
Und englisch kann sich redlich nie vermischen.

Zweiter Auftritt.

Königin Isabeau, von einem Pagen begleitet, zu den **Vorigen.**

Isabeau.

Was muß ich hören, Feldherrn! Haltet ein!
Was für ein hirnverrückender Planet
Verwirrt euch also die gesunden Sinne?
Jetzt, da euch Eintracht nur erhalten kann,
Wollt ihr in Haß euch trennen und euch selbst
Befehdend euren Untergang bereiten?
— Ich bitt' euch, edler Herzog, ruft den raschen
Befehl zurück. Und ihr, ruhmvoller Talbot,
Besänftiget den aufgebrachten Freund!
Kommt, Lionel, helft mir die stolzen Geister
Zufrieden sprechen und Versöhnung stiften.

Lionel.

Ich nicht, Mylady. Mir ist Alles gleich.
Ich denke so: Was nicht zusammen kann
Bestehen, thut am besten, sich zu lösen.

Isabeau.

Wie? Wirkt der Hölle Gaukelkunst, die uns
Im Treffen so verderblich war, auch hier
Noch fort, uns sinnverwirrend zu bethören?
Wer fing den Zank an? Redet! — Edler Lord!

(Zu Talbot.).

Seyd ihr's, der seines Vortheils so vergaß,
Den werthen Bundsgenossen zu verletzen?
Was wollt ihr schaffen ohne diesen Arm?
Er baute eurem König seinen Thron;
Er hält ihn noch und stürzt ihn, wenn er will;
Sein Heer verstärkt euch und noch mehr sein Name.
Ganz England, strömt' es alle seine Bürger
Auf unsre Küsten aus, vermöchte nicht
Dies Reich zu zwingen, wenn es einig ist.
Nur Frankreich konnte Frankreich überwinden.

Talbot.

Wir wissen den getreuen Freund zu ehren.
Dem falschen wehren, ist der Klugheit Pflicht.

Burgund.

Wer treulos sich des Dankes will entschlagen,
Dem fehlt des Lügners freche Stirne nicht.

Isabeau.

Wie, edler Herzog? Könntet ihr so sehr
Der Scham absagen und der Fürstenehre,
In jene Hand, die euren Vater mordete,
Die eurige zu legen? Wärt ihr rasend
Genug, an eine redliche Versöhnung
Zu glauben mit dem Dauphin, den ihr selbst
An des Verderbens Rand geschleudert habt?
So nah dem Falle wolltet ihr ihn halten
Und euer Werk wahnsinnig selbst zerstören?
H i e r stehen enre Freunde. Euer Heil
Ruht in dem festen Bunde nur mit England.

Burgund.

Fern ist mein Sinn vom Frieden mit dem Dauphin;

Doch die Verachtung und den Uebermuth
Des stolzen Englands kann ich nicht ertragen.

Isabeau.

Kommt! Haltet ihm ein rasches Wort zu gut.
Schwer ist der Kummer, der den Feldherrn drückt,
Und ungerecht, ihr wißt es, macht das Unglück.
Kommt! Kommt! Umarmt euch, laßt mich diesen Riß
Schnell heilend schließen, eh' er ewig wird.

Talbot.

Was dünket euch, Burgund?   Ein edles Herz
Bekennt sich gern von der Vernunft besiegt.
. Die Königin hat ein kluges Wort geredet;
Laßt diesen Händedruck die Wunde heilen,
Die meine Zunge übereilend schlug.

Burgund.

Madame sprach ein verständig Wort, und mein
Gerechter Zorn weicht der Nothwendigkeit.

Isabeau.

Wohl! So besiegelt den erneuten Bund
Mit einem brüderlichen Kuß, und mögen
Die Winde das Gesprochene verwehn.

(Burgund und Talbot umarmen sich.)

Lionel (betrachtet die Gruppe, für sich.)

Glück zu dem Frieden, den die Furie stiftet!

Isabeau.

Wir haben eine Schlacht verloren, Feldherrn,
Das Glück war uns zuwider; darum aber
Entsink' euch nicht der edle Muth.   Der Dauphin
Verzweifelt an des Himmels Schutz und ruft
Des Satans Kunst zu Hülfe; doch er habe
Umsonst sich der Verdammniß übergeben,
Und seine Hölle selbst errett' ihn nicht.
Ein sieghaft Mädchen führt des Feindes Heer;
Ich will das eure führen, ich will euch
Statt einer Jungfrau und Prophetin seyn.

Lionel.

Madame, geht nach Paris zurück! Wir wollen
Mit guten Waffen, nicht mit Weibern siegen.

Talbot.

Geht, geht! Seit ihr im Lager seyd, geht Alles
Zurück, kein Segen ist mehr in unsern Waffen.

Burgund.

Geht! Eure Gegenwart schafft hier nichts Gutes;
Der Krieger nimmt ein Aergerniß an euch.

Isabeau
(sieht Einen um den Andern erstaunt an.)

Ihr auch, Burgund? Ihr nehmet wider mich
Partei mit diesen undankbaren Lords?

Burgund.

Geht! Der Soldat verliert den guten Muth,
Wenn er für eure Sache glaubt zu fechten.

Isabeau.

Ich hab' kaum Frieden zwischen euch gestiftet,
So macht ihr schon ein Bündniß wider mich?

Talbot.

Geht, geht mit Gott, Madame! Wir fürchten uns
Vor keinem Teufel mehr, sobald ihr weg seyd.

Isabeau.

Bin ich nicht eure treue Bundsgenossin?
Ist eure Sache nicht die meinige?

Talbot.

Doch eure nicht die unsrige. Wir sind
In einem ehrlich guten Streit begriffen.

Burgund.

Ich räche eines Vaters blut'gen Mord;
Die fromme Sohnspflicht heiligt meine Waffen.

Talbot.

Doch, grad heraus, was ihr am Dauphin thut,
Ist weder menschlich gut, noch göttlich recht.

Isabeau.
Fluch soll ihn treffen bis ins zehnte Glied!
Er hat gefrevelt an dem Haupt der Mutter.

Burgund.
Er rächte einen Vater und Gemahl.

Isabeau.
Er warf sich auf zum Richter meiner Sitten!

Lionel.
Das war unehrerbietig von dem Sohn!

Isabeau.
In die Verbannung hat er mich geschickt.

Talbot.
Die öffentliche Stimme zu vollziehn.

Isabeau.
Fluch treffe mich, wenn ich ihm je vergebe!
Und eh' er herrscht in seines Vaters Reich —

Talbot.
Eh' opfert ihr die Ehre seiner Mutter!

Isabeau.
Ihr wißt nicht, schwache Seelen,
Was ein beleidigt Mutterherz vermag.
Ich liebe, wer mir Gutes thut, und hasse,
Wer mich verletzt, und ist's der eigne Sohn,
Den ich geboren, desto hassenswerther.
Dem ich das Daseyn gab, will ich es rauben,
Wenn er mit ruchlos frechem Uebermuth
Den eignen Schooß verletzt, der ihn getragen.
Ihr, die ihr Krieg führt gegen meinen Sohn,
Ihr habt nicht Recht, noch Grund, ihn zu berauben.
Was hat der Dauphin Schweres gegen euch
Verschuldet? Welche Pflichten brach er euch?
Euch treibt die Ehrsucht, der gemeine Neid;
Ich darf ihn hassen. ich hab' ihn geboren.

Talbot.
Wohl, an der Rache fühlt er seine Mutter!

Isabeau.

Armsel'ge Gleißner, wie veracht' ich euch,
Die ihr euch selbst, so wie die Welt, belügt!
Ihr Engelländer streckt die Räuberhände
Nach diesem Frankreich aus, wo ihr nicht Recht
Noch gült'gen Anspruch habt auf so viel Erde,
Als eines Pferdes Huf bedeckt. — Und dieser Herzog,
Der sich den Guten schelten läßt, verkauft
Sein Vaterland, das Erbreich seiner Ahnen,
Dem Reichsfeind und dem fremden Herrn. — Gleichwohl
Ist euch das dritte Wort Gerechtigkeit.
— Die Heuchelei veracht' ich. Wie ich bin,
So sehe mich das Aug' der Welt.

Burgund.

Wahr ist's!
Den Ruhm habt ihr mit starkem Geist behauptet.

Isabeau.

Ich habe Leidenschaften, warmes Blut,
Wie eine Andre, und ich kam als Königin
In dieses Land, zu leben, nicht zu scheinen.
Sollt' ich der Freud' absterben, weil der Fluch
Des Schicksals meine lebensfrohe Jugend
Zu dem wahnsinn'gen Gatten hat gesellt?
Mehr als das Leben lieb' ich meine Freiheit,
Und wer mich hier verwundet — Doch warum
Mit euch mich streiten über meine Rechte?
Schwer fließt das dicke Blut in euren Adern;
Ihr kennt nicht das Vergnügen, nur die Wuth!
Und dieser Herzog, der sein Leben lang
Geschwankt hat zwischen Bös und Gut, kann nicht
Von Herzen hassen, noch von Herzen lieben.
— Ich geh' nach Melun. Gebt mir diesen da,
(auf Lionel zeigend)
Der mir gefällt, zur Kurzweil und Gesellschaft,
Und dann macht, was ihr wollt! Ich frage nichts
Nach den Burgundern noch den Engelländern.
(Sie winkt ihrem Pagen und will gehen).

Lionel.

Verlaßt euch drauf. Die schönsten Frankenknaben,
Die wir erbeuten, schicken wir nach Melun.

Isabeau (zurückkommend.)

Wohl taugt ihr, mit dem Schwerte drein zu schlagen,
Der Franke nur weiß Zierliches zu sagen.

(Sie geht ab.)

Dritter Auftritt.

Talbot. Burgund. Lionel.

Talbot.

Was für ein Weib!

Lionel.

Nun eure Meinung, Feldherrn!
Fliehn wir noch weiter oder wenden uns
Zurück, durch einen schnellen, kühnen Streich
Den Schimpf des heut'gen Tages auszulöschen?

Burgund.

Wir sind zu schwach, die Völker sind zerstreut,
Zu neu ist noch der Schrecken in dem Heer.

Talbot.

Ein blinder Schrecken nur hat uns besiegt,
Der schnelle Eindruck eines Augenblicks.
Dies Furchtbild der erschreckten Einbildung
Wird, näher angesehn, in nichts verschwinden.
Drum ist mein Rath, wir führen die Armee
Mit Tagesanbruch über'n Strom zurück,
Dem Feind entgegen.

Burgund.
Ueberlegt —

Lionel.
Mit eurer
Erlaubniß. Hier ist nichts zu überlegen.
Wir müssen das Verlorne schleunig wieder
Gewinnen oder sind beschimpft auf ewig.

Talbot.

Es ist beschlossen.   Morgen schlagen wir.
Und dies Phantom des Schreckens zu zerstören,
Das unsre Völker blendet und entmannt,
Laßt uns mit diesem jungfräulichen Teufel
Uns messen in persönlichem Gefecht.
Stellt sie sich unserm tapfern Schwert, nun dann,
So hat sie uns zum letztenmal geschadet;
Stellt sie sich nicht — und seyd gewiß, sie meidet
Den ernsten Kampf — so ist das Heer entzaubert.

Lionel.

So sey's!   Und mir, mein Feldherr, überlasset
Dies leichte Kampfspiel, wo kein Blut soll fließen.
Denn lebend denk' ich das Gespenst zu fangen,
Und vor des Bastards Augen, ihres Buhlen,
Trag' ich auf diesen Armen sie herüber,
Zur Lust des Heers, in das britann'sche Lager.

Burgund.

Versprechet nicht zu viel.

Talbot.

                    Erreich' ich sie,
Ich denke sie so sanft nicht zu umarmen.
Kommt jetzo, die ermüdete Natur
Durch einen leichten Schlummer zu erquicken,
Und dann zum Aufbruch mit der Morgenröthe.

                              (Sie gehen ab.)

Vierter Auftritt.

Johanna mit der Fahne, im Helm und Brustharnisch, sonst aber weiblich
gekleidet.   Dunois, La Hire, Ritter und Soldaten
zeigen sich oben auf dem Felsenweg, ziehen still darüber hinweg und
erscheinen gleich darauf auf der Scene.

Johanna

(zu den Rittern, die sie umgeben, indem der Zug oben immer noch fortfährt).

Erstiegen ist der Wall, wir sind im Lager!
Jetzt werft die Hülle der verschwiegnen Nacht
Von euch, die euren stillen Zug verhehlte,

5*

Und macht dem Feinde eure Schreckensnähe
Durch lauten Schlachtruf kund — Gott und die Jungfrau!

Alle (rufen laut unter wildem Waffengetöse).

Gott und die Jungfrau!
(Trommeln und Trompeten.)

Schildwache (hinter der Scene).

Feinde! Feinde! Feinde!

Johanna.

Jetzt Fackeln her! Werft Feuer in die Zelte!
Der Flammen Wuth vermehre das Entsetzen,
Und drohend rings umfange sie der Tod!
(Soldaten eilen fort, sie will folgen.)

Dunois (hält sie zurück).

Du hast das Deine nun erfüllt, Johanna!
Mitten ins Lager hast du uns geführt,
Den Feind hast du in unsre Hand gegeben.
Jetzt aber bleibe von dem Kampf zurück,
Uns überlaß die blutige Entscheidung!

La Hire.

Den Weg des Siegs bezeichne du dem Heer,
Die Fahne trag' uns vor in reiner Hand;
Doch nimm das Schwert, das tödtliche, nicht selbst,
Versuche nicht den falschen Gott der Schlachten;
Denn blind und ohne Schonung waltet er.

Johanna.

Wer darf mir Halt gebieten? Wer dem Geist
Vorschreiben, der mich führt? Der Pfeil muß fliegen,
Wohin die Hand ihn seines Schützen treibt.
Wo die Gefahr ist, muß Johanna seyn;
Nicht heut', nicht hier ist mir bestimmt zu fallen;
Die Krone muß ich sehn auf meines Königs Haupt.
Dies Leben wird kein Gegner mir entreißen,
Bis ich vollendet, was mir Gott geheißen. (Sie geht ab.)

La Hire.

Kommt, Dunois! Laßt uns der Heldin folgen
Und ihr die tapfre Brust zum Schilde leihn!
(Gehen ab.)

Fünfter Auftritt.

Englische Soldaten fliehen über die Bühne; hierauf **Talbot**.

Erster.

Das Mädchen! Mitten im Lager!

Zweiter.

Nicht möglich! Nimmermehr! Wie kam sie in das Lager?

Dritter.

Durch die Luft! Der Teufel hilft ihr!

Vierter und Fünfter.

Flieht! Flieht! Wir sind Alle des Todes!

(Gehen ab.)

Talbot (kommt).

Sie hören nicht — Sie wollen mir nicht stehn!
Gelöst sind alle Bande des Gehorsams!
Als ob die Hölle ihre Legionen
Verdammter Geister ausgespien, reißt
Ein Taumelwahn den Tapfern und den Feigen
Gehirnlos fort; nicht eine kleine Schaar
Kann ich der Feinde Flut entgegenstellen,
Die wachsend, wogend in das Lager dringt!
— Bin ich der einzig Nüchterne, und Alles
Muß um mich her in Fiebers Hitze rasen?
Vor diesen fränk'schen Weichlingen zu fliehn,
Die wir in zwanzig Schlachten überwunden! —
Wer ist sie denn, die Unbezwingliche,
Die Schreckensgöttin, die der Schlachten Glück
Auf einmal wendet und ein schüchtern Heer
Von feigen Reh'n in Löwen umgewandelt?
Eine Gauklerin, die die gelernte Rolle
Der Heldin spielt, soll wahre Helden schrecken?
Ein Weib entriß mir allen Siegesruhm?

Soldat (stürzt herein).

Das Mädchen! Flieh! Flieh, Feldherr!

Talbot (stößt ihn nieder).

Flieh zur Hölle
Du selbst! Den soll dies Schwert durchbohren,
Der mir von Furcht spricht und von feiger Flucht!

(Er geht ab.)

Sechster Auftritt.

Der Prospect öffnet sich. Man sieht das englische Lager in vollen Flammen stehen.
Trommeln, Flucht und Verfolgung. Nach einer Weile kommt
Montgomery.

Montgomery (allein).

Wo soll ich hinfliehn? Feinde rings umher und Tod!
Hier der ergrimmte Feldherr, der, mit droh'ndem Schwert
Die Flucht versperrend, uns dem Tod entgegentreibt.
Dort die Fürchterliche, die verderblich um sich her
Wie die Brunst des Feuers raset — und ringsum kein Busch
Der mich verbärge, keiner Höhle sich'rer Raum!
O, wär' ich nimmer über Meer hieher geschifft,
Ich Unglücksel'ger! Eitler Wahn bethörte mich,
Wohlfeilen Ruhm zu suchen in dem Frankenkrieg,
Und jetzo führt mich das verderbliche Geschick
In diese blut'ge Mordschlacht. — Wär' ich weit von hier
Daheim noch an der Savern' blühendem Gestad',
Ich sichern Vaterhause, wo die Mutter mir
Im Gram zurück blieb und die zarte, süße Braut.

(Johanna zeigt sich in der Ferne.)

Weh mir! Was seh' ich! Dort erscheint die Schreckliche!
Aus Brandes Flammen, düster leuchtend, hebt sie sich,
Wie aus der Hölle Rachen ein Gespenst der Nacht,
Hervor. — Wohin entrinn' ich! Schon ergreift sie mich
Mit ihren Feueraugen, wirft von fern
Der Blicke Schlingen nimmer fehlend nach mir aus.
Um meine Füße, fest und fester, wirret sich
Das Zauberknäul, daß sie gefesselt mir die Flucht
Versagen! Hinsehn muß ich, wie das Herz mir auch
Dagegen kämpfe, nach der tödtlichen Gestalt!

(Johanna thut einige Schritte ihm entgegen und bleibt wieder stehen.)

Sie naht! Ich will nicht warten, bis die Grimmige
Zuerst mich anfällt! Bittend will ich ihre Knie
Umfassen, um mein Leben flehn — sie ist ein Weib —
Ob ich vielleicht durch Thränen sie erweichen kann!

(Indem er auf sie zugehen will, tritt sie ihm rasch entgegen.)

Siebenter Auftritt.

Johanna. Montgomery.

Johanna.

Du bist des Todes!   Eine britt'sche Mutter zengte dich.

Montgomery (fällt ihr zu Füßen).

Halt' ein, Furchtbare!   Nicht den Unvertheidigten
Durchbohre! Weggeworfen hab' ich Schwert und Schild,
Zu deinen Füßen sink' ich wehrlos, flehend hin.
Laß mir das Licht des Lebens, nimm mein Lösegeld!
Reich an Besitzthum wohnt der Vater mir daheim
Im schönen Lande Wallis, wo die schlängelnde
Savern' durch grüne Auen rollt den Silberstrom,
Und fünfzig Dörfer kennen seine Herrschaft an.
Mit reichem Golde löf't er den geliebten Sohn,
Wenn er mich im Frankenlager lebend noch vernimmt.

Johanna.

Betrogner Thor! Verlorner! In der Jungfrau Hand
Bist du gefallen, die verderbliche, woraus
Nicht Rettung noch Erlösung mehr zu hoffen ist.
Wenn dich das Unglück in des Krokodils Gewalt
Gegeben oder des gefleckten Tigers Klau'n,
Wenn du der Löwenmutter junge Brut geraubt,
Du könntest Mitleid finden und Barmherzigkeit,
Doch tödtlich ist's der Jungfrau zu begegnen.
Denn dem Geisterreich, dem strengen, unverletzlichen,
Verpflichtet mich der furchtbar bindende Vertrag,
Mit dem Schwert zu tödten alles Lebende, das mir
Der Schlachtengott verhängnißvoll entgegenschickt.*

---

* Throughout this scene there is perceptible an evident imitation of similar
situations in different parts of the Iliad; e. g. B. 21, v. 34, seq. where Lycaon, the
son of Priam, prostrates himself before Achilles, beseeching him to spare his
life, but the latter remains inexorable and assigns his own fated end as the motive of his conduct. B. 6, v. 45, Adrastos embracing the knees of Menelaos
offers him a rich ransom for his life, both of useful and of precious metals, that,
according to his account, are stored in profusion in the vaults of his father's
house. B. 11, v. 221, seq. Iphidamas, who subdued by the hand of Agamem-

Montgomery.

Furchtbar ist deine Rede, doch dein Blick ist sanft,
Nicht schrecklich bist du in der Nähe anzuschaun;
Es zieht das Herz mich zu der lieblichen Gestalt.
O, bei der Milde deines zärtlichen Geschlechts
Fleh' ich dich an. Erbarme meiner Jugend dich!

Johanna.

Nicht mein Geschlecht beschwöre! nenne mich nicht Weib!
Gleichwie die körperlosen Geister, die nicht frein
Auf irb'sche Weise, schließ' ich mich an kein Geschlecht
Der Menschen an, und dieser Panzer deckt kein Herz.

Montgomery.

O, bei der Liebe heilig waltendem Gesetz,
Dem alle Herzen huldigen, beschwör' ich dich!
Daheim gelassen hab' ich eine holde Braut,
Schön, wie du selbst bist, in der Jugend Reiz.
Sie harret weinend des Geliebten Wiederkunft.
O, wenn du selber je zu lieben hoffst und hoffst
Beglückt zu seyn durch Liebe, trenne grausam nicht
Zwei Herzen, die der Liebe heilig Bündniß knüpft!

Johanna.

Du rufest lauter irdisch fremde Götter an,
Die mir nicht heilig noch verehrlich sind. Ich weiß
Nichts von der Liebe Bündniß, das du mir beschwörst,
Und nimmer kennen werd' ich ihren eiteln Dienst;
Vertheidige dein Leben, denn dir ruft der Tod.

Montgomery.

O, so erbarme meiner jammervollen Eltern dich,
Die ich zu Haus verlassen. Ja, gewiß auch du
Verließest Eltern, die die Sorge quält um dich. *

non falls "ov'rtaken by the brazen sleep", at a distance from his tender
spouse, before he had enjoyed her love :—

...... πεσὼν κοιμήσατο χάλκεον ὕπνον,
οἰκτρός, ἀπὸ μνηστῆς ἀλόχου, ἀστοῖσιν ἀρήγων,
κουριδίης, ἧς οὔτι χάριν ἴδε ....

* Again an allusion to Homer, to the much more extended and far more
affecting appeal of Priam to Achilles :—

Μνῆσαι πατρὸς σεῖο, θεοῖς ἐπιεικελ' Ἀχιλλεῦ, τηλίκου, ὥσπερ ἐγὼν, ὀλοῷ
ἐπὶ γήραος οὐδῷ. κ. τ. λ. κ. τ. λ. Il 24, v. 485—512.

Johanna.

Unglücklicher! Und du erinnerst mich daran,
Wie viele Mütter dieses Landes kinderlos
Wie viele zarte Kinder vaterlos, wie viel
Verlobte Bräute Wittwen worden sind durch euch!
Auch Englands Mütter mögen die Verzweiflung nun
Erfahren, und die Thränen kennen lernen,
Die Frankreichs jammervolle Gattinnen geweint.

Montgomery.

O, schwer ist's, in der Fremde sterben unbeweint.

Johanna.

Wer rief euch in das fremde Land, den blüh'nden Fleiß
Der Felder zu verwüsten, von dem heim'schen Herd
Uns zu verjagen und des Krieges Feuerbrand
Zu werfen in der Städte friedlich Heiligthum?
Ihr träumtet schon in eures Herzens eitelm Wahn,
Den freigebornen Franken in der Knechtschaft Schmach
Zu stürzen und dies große Land, gleichwie ein Boot,
An euer stolzes Meerschiff zu befestigen!
Ihr Thoren! Frankreichs königliches Wappen hängt
Am Throne Gottes. Eher riff't ihr einen Stern
Vom Himmelswagen, als ein Dorf aus diesem Reich,
Dem unzertrennlich ewig einigen! — Der Tag
Der Rache ist gekommen; nicht lebendig mehr
Zurücke messen werdet ihr das heil'ge Meer,
Das Gott zur Länderscheide zwischen euch und uns
Gesetzt, und das ihr frevelnd überschritten habt.

Montgomery (läßt ihre Hand los).

O, ich muß sterben! Grausend faßt mich schon der Tod.

Johanna.

Stirb, Freund! Warum so zaghaft zittern vor dem Tod,
Dem unentfliehbaren Geschick? — Sieh mich an! Sieh.
Ich bin nur eine Jungfrau, eine Schäferin
Geboren; nicht des Schwerts gewohnt ist diese Hand,
Die den unschuldig frommen Hirtenstab geführt.
Doch, weggerissen von der heimathlichen Flur,

Von Vaters Busen, von der Schwester lieber Brust,
Muß ich hier, ich muß — Mich treibt die Götterstimme,
                                                    nicht
Eignes Gelüsten — euch zu bitterm Harm, mir nicht
Zur Freude, ein Gespenst des Schreckens, würgend gehn,
Den Tod verbreiten und sein Opfer seyn zuletzt!
Denn nicht den Tag der frohen Heimkehr werd' ich sehn.
Noch Vielen von den Euren werd' ich tödtlich seyn,
Noch viele Wittwen machen, aber endlich werd'
Ich selbst umkommen und erfüllen mein Geschick.
— Erfülle du auch deines. Greife frisch zum Schwert,
Und um des Lebens süße Beute kämpfen wir.

         Montgomery (steht auf).
Nun, wenn du sterblich bist, wie ich, und Waffen dich
Verwunden, kann's auch meinem Arm beschieden seyn,
Zur Höll' dich sendend, Englands Noth zu endigen.
In Gottes gnäd'ge Hände leg' ich mein Geschick.
Ruf du, Verdammte, deine Höllengeister an,
Dir beizustehen! Wehre deines Lebens dich!
(Er ergreift Schild und Schwert und bringt auf sie ein; kriegerische Musik erschallt
in der Ferne, nach einem kurzen Gefechte fällt Montgomery.)

Achter Auftritt.

Johanna allein.

Dich trug dein Fuß zum Tode — Fahre hin!
(Sie tritt von ihm weg und bleibt gedankenvoll stehen.)
Erhabne Jungfrau, du wirkst Mächtiges in mir!
Du rüstest den unkriegerischen Arm mit Kraft,
Dies Herz mit Unerbittlichkeit bewaffnest du.
In Mitleid schmilzt die Seele, und die Hand erbebt,
Als bräche sie in eines Tempels heil'gen Bau,
Den blühnden Leib des Gegners zu verletzen,
Schon vor des Eisens blanker Schneide schaudert mir,
Doch, wenn es Noth thut, alsbald ist die Kraft mir da,
Und nimmer irrend in der zitternden Hand, regiert
Das Schwert sich selbst, als wär' es ein lebend'ger Geist.

Neunter Auftritt.

Ein Ritter mit geschlossenem Visir. **Johanna.**

Ritter.

Verfluchte! Deine Stunde ist gekommen,
Dich sucht' ich auf dem ganzen Feld der Schlacht,
Verderblich Blendwerk! Fahre zu der Hölle
Zurück, aus der du aufgestiegen bist.

Johanna.

Wer bist du, den ein böser Engel mir
Entgegen schickt? Gleich eines Fürsten ist
Dein Anstand; auch kein Britte scheinst du mir;
Denn dich bezeichnet die burgund'sche Binde,
Vor der sich meines Schwertes Spitze neigt.

Ritter.

Verworfne, du verdientest nicht zu fallen
Von eines Fürsten edler Hand. Das Beil
Des Henkers sollte dein verdammtes Haupt
Vom Rumpfe trennen, nicht der tapfre Degen
Des königlichen Herzogs von Burgund.

Johanna.

So bist du dieser edle Herzog selbst?

Ritter (schlägt das Visir auf).

Ich bin's. Elende, zittre und verzweifle!
Die Satanskünste schützen dich nicht mehr.
Du hast bis jetzt nur Schwächlinge bezwungen;
Ein Mann steht vor dir.

Zehnter Auftritt.

Dunois und **La Hire** zu den **Vorigen.**

Dunois.

Wende dich, Burgund!
Mit Männern kämpfe, nicht mit Jungfrauen.

La Hire.

Wir schützen der Prophetin heilig Haupt;
Erst muß dein Degen diese Brust durchbohren —

Burgund.

Nicht diese buhlerische Circe fürcht' ich,
Noch euch, die sie so schimpflich hat verwandelt.
Erröthe, Bastard, Schande dir, La Hire,
Daß du die alte Tapferkeit zu Künsten
Der Höll' erniedrigst, den verächtlichen
Schildknappen einer Teufelsdirne machst.
Kommt her! euch Allen biet' ich's! Der verzweifelt
An Gottes Schutz, der zu dem Teufel flieht.

(Sie bereiten sich zum Kampfe, Johanna tritt dazwischen).

Johanna.

Haltet inne!

Burgund.

Zitterst du für deinen Buhlen?
Vor deinen Augen soll er —

(Dringt auf Dunois ein.)

Johanna.

Haltet inne!

Trennt sie, La Hire — Kein französisch Blut soll fließen!
Nicht Schwerter sollen diesen Streit entscheiden.
Ein Andres ist beschlossen in den Sternen —
Aus einander, sag' ich — Höret und verehrt
Den Geist, der mich ergreift, der aus mir redet!

Dunois.

Was hältst du meinen aufgehobnen Arm
Und hemmst des Schwertes blutige Entscheidung?
Das Eisen ist gezückt, es fällt der Streich,
Der Frankreich rächen und versöhnen soll.

Johanna

(stellt sich in die Mitte und trennt beide Theile durch einen weiten Zwischenraum; zum Bastard).

Tritt auf die Seite!

(Zu La Hire.)

Bleib gefesselt stehen!
Ich habe mit dem Herzoge zu reden.

(Nachdem Alles ruhig ist.)

Was willst du thun, Burgund? Wer ist der Feind,

Den deine Blicke mordbegierig suchen?
Dieser edle Prinz ist Frankreichs Sohn, wie du;
Dieser Tapfre ist dein Waffenfreund und Landsmann;
Ich selbst bin deines Vaterlandes Tochter.
Wir Alle, die du zu vertilgen strebst,
Gehören zu den Deinen — unsre Arme
Sind aufgethan, dich zu empfangen, unsre Knie
Bereit, dich zu verehren — unser Schwert
Hat keine Spitze gegen dich.   Ehrwürdig
Ist uns das Antlitz, selbst im Feindeshelm,
Das unsers Königs theure Züge trägt.

Burgund.

Mit süßer Rede schmeichlerischem Ton
Willst du, Sirene! deine Opfer locken.
Arglist'ge, mich bethörst du nicht.   Verwahrt
Ist mir das Ohr vor deiner Rede Schlingen,
Und deines Auges Feuerpfeile gleiten
Am guten Harnisch meines Busens ab.
Zu den Waffen, Dunois!
Mit Streichen, nicht mit Worten laß uns fechten.

Dunois.

Erst Worte und dann Streiche.   Fürchtest du
Vor Worten dich? Auch das ist Feigheit
Und der Verräther einer bösen Sache.

Johanna.

Uns treibt nicht die gebieterische Noth
Zu deinen Füßen; nicht als Flehende
Erscheinen wir vor dir. — Blick um dich her!
In Asche liegt das engelländ'sche Lager,
Und eure Todten decken das Gefild.
Du hörst der Franken Kriegsdrommete tönen;
Gott hat entschieden, unser ist der Sieg.
Des schönen Lorbeers frisch gebrochnen Zweig
Sind wir bereit mit unserm Freund zu theilen.
— O komm herüber! Edler Flüchtling, komm!
Herüber, wo das Recht ist und der Sieg.

Ich selbst, die Gottgesandte, reiche dir
Die schwesterliche Hand.   Ich will dich rettend
Herüberziehn auf unsre reine Seite. —
Der Himmel ist für Frankreich.   Seine Engel —
Du siehst sie nicht — sie fechten für den König;
Sie alle sind mit Lilien geschmückt.
Lichtweiß, wie diese Fahn', ist unsre Sache;
Die reine Jungfrau ist ihr keusches Sinnbild.

Burgund.

Verstrickend ist der Lüge trüglich Wort,
Doch ihre Rede ist wie eines Kindes.
Wenn böse Geister ihr die Worte leihn,
So ahmen sie die Unschuld siegreich nach.
Ich will nicht weiter hören.   Zu den Waffen!
Mein Ohr, ich fühl's, ist schwächer, als mein Arm.

Johanna.

Du nennst mich eine Zauberin, gibst mir Künste
Der Hölle Schuld — Ist Frieden stiften, Haß
Versöhnen ein Geschäft der Hölle? Kommt
Die Eintracht aus dem ew'gen Pfuhl hervor?
Was ist unschuldig, heilig, menschlich gut,
Wenn es der Kampf nicht ist um's Vaterland?
Seit wann ist die Natur so mit sich selbst
Im Streite, daß der Himmel die gerechte Sache
Verläßt, und daß die Teufel sie beschützen?
Ist aber das, was ich dir sage, gut,
Wo anders als von oben konnt' ich's schöpfen?
Wer hätte sich auf meiner Schäfertrift
Zu mir gesellt, das kind'sche Hirtenmädchen
In königlichen Dingen einzuweih'n?
Ich bin vor hohen Fürsten nie gestanden,
Die Kunst der Rede ist dem Munde fremd.
Doch jetzt, da ich's bedarf, dich zu bewegen,
Besitz' ich Einsicht, hoher Dinge Kunde,
Der Länder und der Könige Geschick

Liegt sonnenhell vor meinem Kindesblick,
Und einen Donnerkeil führ' ich im Munde.

Burgund

(lebhaft bewegt, schlägt die Augen zu ihr auf und betrachtet sie mit Erstaunen und
Rührung.)

Wie wird mir? Wie geschieht mir? Ist's ein Gott,
Der mir das Herz im tiefsten Busen wendet!
— Sie trügt nicht, diese rührende Gestalt!
Nein, nein! Bin ich durch Zaubers Macht geblendet,
So ist's durch eine himmlische Gewalt;
Mir sagt's das Herz, sie ist von Gott gesendet.

Johanna.

Er ist gerührt, er ist's! Ich habe nicht
Umsonst gefleht; des Zornes Donnerwolke schmilzt
Von seiner Stirne thränenthauend hin,
Und aus den Augen, friedestrahlend, bricht
Die goldne Sonne des Gefühls hervor.
— Weg mit den Waffen — drücket Herz an Herz —
Er weint, er ist bezwungen, er ist unser!

(Schwert und Fahne entsinken ihr, sie eilt auf ihn zu mit ausgebreiteten Armen und
umschlingt ihn mit leidenschaftlichem Ungestüm. La Hire und Dunois
lassen die Schwerter fallen und eilen ihn zu umarmen.)

Dritter Aufzug.

Hoflager des Königs zu Chalons an der Marne.

Erster Auftritt.

Dunois und La Hire.

Dunois.

Wir waren Herzensfreunde, Waffenbrüder,
Für eine Sache hoben wir den Arm
Und hielten fest in Noth und Tod zusammen.
Laßt Weiberliebe nicht das Band zertrennen,
Das jeden Schicksalswechsel ausgehalten!

La Hire.

Prinz, hört mich an!

Dunois.

   Ihr liebt das wunderbare Mädchen,
Und mir ist wohl bekannt, worauf ihr sinnt.
Zum König denkt ihr steh'nden Fußes jetzt
Zu gehen und die Jungfrau zum Geschenk
Euch zu erbitten — Eurer Tapferkeit
Kann er den wohlverdienten Preis nicht weigern.
Doch wißt — eh' ich in eines Andern Arm
Sie sehe —

La Hire.

  Hört mich, Prinz!

Dunois.

    Es zieht mich nicht
Der Augen flüchtig schnelle Lust zu ihr.
Den unbezwungnen Sinn hat nie ein Weib
Gerührt, bis ich die Wunderbare sah,
Die eines Gottes Schickung diesem Reich

Zur Retterin bestimmt und mir zum Weibe,
Und in dem Augenblick gelobt' ich mir
Mit heil'gem Schwur, als Braut sie heimzuführen.
Denn nur die Starke kann die Freundin seyn
Des starken Mannes, und dies glüh'nde Herz
Sehnt sich, an einer gleichen Brust zu ruhu,
Die seine Kraft kann fassen und ertragen.

La Hire.

Wie könnt' ich's wagen, Prinz, mein schwach Verdienst
Mit eures Namens Heldenruhm zu messen!
Wo sich Graf Dunois in die Schranken stellt,
Muß jeder andre Mitbewerber weichen.
Doch eine niedre Schäferin kann nicht
Als Gattin würdig euch zur Seite stehn.
Das königliche Blut, das eure Adern
Durchrinnt, verschmäht so niedrige Vermischung.

Dunois.

Sie ist das Götterkind der heiligen
Natur, wie ich, und ist mir ebenbürtig.
Sie sollte eines Fürsten Hand entehren,
Die eine Braut der reinen Engel ist,
Die sich das Haupt mit einem Götterschein
Umgibt, der heller strahlt, als ird'sche Kronen,
Die jedes Größte, Höchste dieser Erden
Klein unter ihren Füßen liegen sieht?
Denn alle Fürstenthronen, auf einander
Gestellt, bis zu den Sternen fortgebaut,
Erreichten nicht die Höhe, wo sie steht
In ihrer Engelsmajestät!

La Hire.

Der König mag entscheiden.

Dunois.

Nein, sie selbst
Entscheide! Sie hat Frankreich frei gemacht,
Und selber frei muß sie ihr Herz verschenken.

La Hire.

Da kommt der König!

Zweiter Auftritt.

Karl. Agnes Sorel. Du Chatel und Chatillon zu den
Vorigen.

Karl (zu Chatillon).

Er kommt? Er will als seinen König mich
Erkennen, sagt ihr, und mir huldigen?

Chatillon.

Hier, Sire, in deiner königlichen Stadt
Chalons, will sich der Herzog, mein Gebieter,
Zu deinen Füßen werfen. — Mir befahl er,
Als meinen Herrn und König dich zu grüßen.
Er folgt mir auf dem Fuß, gleich naht er selbst.

Sorel.

Er kommt! O schöne Sonne dieses Tags,
Der Freude bringt und Frieden und Versöhnung.

Chatillon.

Mein Herr wird kommen mit zweihundert Rittern,
Er wird zu deinen Füßen niederknien;
Doch er erwartet, daß du es n i c h t duldest,
Als deinen Vetter freundlich ihn umarmest.

Karl.

Mein Herz glüht, an dem seinigen zu schlagen.

Chatillon.

Der Herzog bittet, daß des alten Streits
Beim ersten Wiedersehn mit keinem Worte
Meldung gescheh'.

Karl.

Versenkt im Lethe sey
Auf ewig das Vergangene.   Wir wollen
Nur in der Zukunft heitre Tage sehn.

Chatillon.

Die für Burgund gefochten, Alle sollen
In die Versöhnung aufgenommen seyn.

Karl.

Ich werde so mein Königreich verdoppeln!

Chatillon.

Die Königin Isabeau soll in dem Frieden
Mit eingeschlossen seyn, wenn sie ihn annimmt.

Karl.

Sie führet Krieg mit mir, nicht ich mit ihr.
Unser Streit ist aus, sobald sie selbst ihn endigt.

Chatillon.

Zwölf Ritter sollen bürgen für dein Wort.

Karl.

Mein Wort ist heilig.

Chatillon.

Und der Erzbischof
Soll eine Hostie theilen zwischen dir und ihm
Zum Pfand und Siegel redlicher Versöhnung.

Karl.

So sey mein Antheil an dem ew'gen Heil,
Als Herz und Handschlag bei mir einig sind.
Welch andres Pfand verlangt der Herzog noch?

Chatillon.

(mit einem Blick auf Du Chatel).

Hier seh' ich Einen, dessen Gegenwart
Den ersten Gruß vergiften könnte.

(Du Chatel geht schweigend.)

Karl.

Geh,
Du Chatel! Bis der Herzog deinen Anblick
Ertragen kann, magst du verborgen bleiben!
(Er folgt ihm mit den Augen, dann eilt er ihm nach und umarmt ihn.)
Rechtschaffner Freund! Du wolltest mehr als dies
Für meine Ruhe thun!

(Du Chatel geht ab.)

Chatillon.

Die andern Punkte nennt dies Instrument.

Karl (zum Erzbischof).

Bringt es in Ordnung. Wir genehm'gen Alles;
Für einen Freund ist uns kein Preis zu hoch.
Geht, Dunois! Nehmt hundert edle Ritter

6

Mit euch und holt den Herzog freundlich ein.
Die Truppen alle sollen sich mit Zweigen
Bekränzen, ihre Brüder zu empfangen.
Zum Feste schmücke sich die ganze Stadt,
Und alle Glocken sollen es verkünden,
Daß Frankreich und Burgund sich neu verbünden.
(Ein Edelknecht kommt. Man hört Trompeten.)
Horch! was bedeutet der Trompeten Ruf?

Edelknecht.

Der Herzog von Burgund hält seinen Einzug.

(Geht ab.)

Dunois.
(geht mit La Hire und Chatillon).
Auf, ihm entgegen!

Karl (zur Sorel).

Agnes, du weinst? Beinah gebricht auch mir
Die Stärke, diesen Auftritt zu ertragen.
Wie viele Todesopfer mußten fallen,
Bis wir uns friedlich konnten wiedersehn!
Doch endlich legt sich jedes Sturmes Wuth,
Tag wird es auf die dickste Nacht, und, kommt
Die Zeit, so reifen auch die spät'sten Früchte!

Erzbischof (am Fenster).

Der Herzog kann sich des Gedränges kaum
Erledigen. Sie heben ihn vom Pferd,
Sie küssen seinen Mantel, seine Sporen.

Karl.

Es ist ein gutes Volk in seiner Liebe
Raschlodernd, wie in seinem Zorn. — Wie schnell
Vergessen ist's, daß eben dieser Herzog
Die Väter ihnen und die Söhne schlug;
Der Augenblick verschlingt ein ganzes Leben!
— Faß dich, Sorel! Auch deine heft'ge Freude
Möcht' ihm ein Stachel in die Seele seyn!
Nichts soll ihn hier beschämen, noch betrüben.

Dritter Auftritt.

Herzog von Burgund. Dunois. La Hire. Chatillon und noch zwei andere Ritter von des Herzogs Gefolge. Der Herzog bleibt am Eingang stehen; der **König** bewegt sich gegen ihn, sogleich nähert sich Burgund, und in dem Augenblick, wo er sich auf ein Knie will niederlassen, empfängt ihn der König in seinen Armen.

Karl.

Ihr habt uns überrascht — euch einzuholen
Gedachten wir — Doch ihr habt schnelle Pferde.

Burgund.

Sie trugen mich zu meiner Pflicht.

(Er umarmt die Sorel und küßt sie auf die Stirne.)

Mit eurer

Erlaubniß, Base! Das ist unser Herrenrecht
Zu Arras, und kein schönes Weib darf sich
Der Sitte weigern.

Karl.

Eure Hofstatt ist
Der Sitz der Minne, sagt man, und der Markt,
Wo alles Schöne muß den Stapel halten.

Burgund.

Wir sind ein handeltreibend Volk, mein König!
Was köstlich wächst in allen Himmelsstrichen,
Wird ausgestellt zur Schau und zum Genuß
Auf unserm Markt zu Brügg; das höchste aber
Von allen Gütern ist der Frauen Schönheit.

Sorel

Der Frauen Treue gilt noch höhern Preis;
Doch auf dem Markte wird sie nicht gesehn.

Karl.

Ihr steht in bösem Ruf und Leumund, Vetter,
Daß ihr der Frauen schönste Tugend schmäht.

Burgund.

Die Ketzerei straft sich am schwersten selbst.
Wohl euch, mein König! Früh hat euch das Herz,
Was mich ein wildes Leben spät, gelehrt!

(Er bemerkt den Erzbischof und reicht ihm die Hand.)

Ehrwürdiger Mann Gottes, euren Segen!
Euch trifft man immer auf dem rechten Platz:
Wer euch will finden, muß im Guten wandeln.

Erzbischof.

Mein Meister rufe, wann er will, dies Herz
Ist freudensatt, und ich kann fröhlich scheiden,
Da meine Augen diesen Tag gesehn!

Burgund (zur Sorel).

Man spricht, ihr habt euch eurer edeln Steine
Beraubt, um Waffen gegen mich daraus
Zu schmieden? Wie? Seyd ihr so kriegerisch
Gesinnt? War's euch so ernst, mich zu verderben?
Doch unser Streit ist nun vorbei, es findet
Sich Alles wieder, was verloren war.
Auch euer Schmuck hat sich zurück gefunden;
Zum Kriege wider mich war er bestimmt:
Nehmt ihn aus meiner Hand zum Friedenszeichen.

(Er empfängt von einem seiner Begleiter das Schmuckkästchen und überreicht es ihr
geöffnet. Agnes Sorel sieht den König betroffen an.)

Karl.

Nimm das Geschenk, es ist ein zweifach theures Pfand
Der schönen Liebe mir und der Versöhnung.

Burgund

(indem er eine brillantne Rose in ihre Haare steckt).

Warum ist es nicht Frankreichs Königskrone?
Ich würde sie mit gleich geneigtem Herzen
Auf diesem schönen Haupt befestigen.

(Ihre Hand bedeutend fassend.)

Und — zählt auf mich, wenn ihr dereinst des Freundes
Bedürfen solltet!

(Agnes Sorel, in Thränen ausbrechend, tritt auf die Seite, auch der König bekämpft
eine große Bewegung, alle Umstehenden blicken gerührt auf beide Fürsten.)

Burgund

(nachdem er Alle der Reihe nach angesehen, wirft er sich in die Arme des Königs).

O, mein König!

(In demselben Augenblick eilen die drei burgundischen Ritter auf Dunois, La Hire
und den Erzbischof zu und umarmen einander. Beide Fürsten liegen eine Zeitlang
einander sprachlos in den Armen.)

Euch konnt' ich haffen! Euch konnt' ich entfagen!

Karl.

Still, ftill! Nicht weiter!

Burgund.

Diefen Engelländer
Konnt' ich krönen! Diefem Frembling Treue fchwören!
Euch, meinen König, ins Verberben ftürzen!

Karl.

Vergeßt es! Alles ift verziehen. Alles
Tilgt diefer einz'ge Augenblick. Es war
Ein Schicffal, ein unglückliches Geftirn!

Burgund (faßt feine Hand).

Ich will gut machen! Glaubet mir, ich will's.
Alle Leiden follen euch erftattet werden.
Euer ganzes Königreich follt ihr zurück
Empfangen — nicht ein Dorf foll daran fehlen!

Karl.

Wir find vereint. Ich fürchte keinen Feind mehr.

Burgund.

Glaubt mir, ich führte nicht mit frohem Herzen
Die Waffen wider euch. O, wüßtet ihr —
Warum habt ihr mir d i e f e nicht gefchickt?

(Auf die Sorel zeigend.)

Nicht widerftanden hätt' ich ihren Thränen.
Nun foll uns keine Macht der Hölle mehr
Entzweien, da wir Bruft an Bruft gefchloffen!
Jetzt hab' ich meinen wahren Ort gefunden,
An diefem Herzen endet meine Irrfahrt.

Erzbifchof (tritt zwifchen beide).

Ihr feid vereinigt, Fürften! Frankreich fteigt,
Ein neu verjüngter Phönix, aus der Afche;
Uns lächelt eine fchöne Zukunft an.
Des Landes tiefe Wunden werden heilen,
Die Dörfer, die verwüfteten, die Städte
Aus ihrem Schutt fich prangender erheben,
Die Felder decken fich mit neuem Grün —

Doch, die das Opfer eures Zwists gefallen,
Die Todten stehen nicht mehr auf; die Thränen,
Die eurem Streit geflossen, sind und bleiben
Geweint! Das kommende Geschlecht wird blühen;
Doch das vergangne war des Elends Raub,
Der Enkel Glück erweckt nicht mehr die Väter.
Das sind die Früchte eures Bruderzwists!
Laßt's euch zur Lehre dienen! Fürchtet die Gottheit
Des Schwerts, eh' ihr's der Scheid' entreißt. Loslassen
Kann der Gewaltige den Krieg, doch nicht
Gelehrig, wie der Falk sich aus den Lüften
Zurückschwingt auf des Jägers Hand, gehorcht
Der wilde Gott dem Ruf der Menschenstimme.
Nicht zweimal kommt im rechten Augenblick,
Wie heut, die Hand des Retters aus den Wolken.

Burgund.

O Sire! Euch wohnt ein Engel an der Seite.
— Wo ist sie? Warum seh' ich sie nicht hier?

Karl.

Wo ist Johanna? Warum fehlt sie uns
In diesem festlich schönen Augenblick,
Den sie uns schenkte?

Erzbischof.

Sire! Das heil'ge Mädchen
Liebt nicht die Ruhe eines müß'gen Hofs,
Und ruft sie nicht der göttliche Befehl
Ans Licht der Welt hervor, so meidet sie
Verschämt den eiteln Blick gemeiner Augen.
Gewiß bespricht sie sich mit Gott, wenn sie
Für Frankreichs Wohlfahrt nicht geschäftig ist;
Denn allen ihren Schritten folgt der Segen.

Vierter Auftritt.

Johanna zu den Vorigen.

Sie ist im Harnisch, aber ohne Helm, und trägt einen Kranz in den Haaren.

Karl.

Du kommst als Priesterin geschmückt, Johanna,
Den Bund, den du gestiftet, einzuweihn!

Burgund.

Wie schrecklich war die Jungfrau in der Schlacht,
Und wie umstrahlt mit Anmuth sie der Friede!
— Hab' ich mein Wort gelös't, Johanna? Bist du
Befriedigt, und verdien' ich deinen Beifall?

Johanna.

Dir selbst hast du die größte Gunst erzeigt.
Jetzt schimmerst du in segenvollem Licht,
Da du vorhin in blutroth düsterm Schein,
Ein Schreckensmond, an diesem Himmel hingst.

(Sich umschauend.)

Viel edle Ritter find' ich hier versammelt,
Und alle Augen glänzen freudenhell;
Nur einem Traurigen hab' ich begegnet,
Der sich verbergen muß, wo Alles jauchzt.

Burgund.

Und wer ist sich so schwerer Schuld bewußt,
Daß er an unsrer Huld verzweifeln müßte?

Johanna.

Darf er sich nahn? O, sage, daß er's darf!
Mach' dein Verdienst vollkommen. Eine Versöhnung
Ist keine, die das Herz nicht ganz befreit.
Ein Tropfen Haß, der in dem Freudenbecher
Zurückbleibt, macht den Segenstrank zum Gift.
— Kein Unrecht sey so blutig, daß Burgund
An diesem Freudentag es nicht vergebe!

Burgund.

Ha, ich verstehe dich!

Johanna.

Und willst verzeihn?
Du willst es, Herzog? — Komm herein, Du Chatel!
(Sie öffnet die Thür und führt Du Chatel herein; dieser bleibt in der Entfernung
stehen.)
Der Herzog ist mit seinen Feinden allen
Versöhnt, er ist es auch mit dir.
(Du Chatel tritt einige Schritte näher und sucht in den Augen des Herzogs zu
lesen.)

Burgund.

Was machst du
Aus mir, Johanna?   Weißt du, was du forderst?

Johanna.

Ein güt'ger Herr thut seine Pforten auf
Für alle Gäste, keinen schließt er aus:
Frei, wie das Firmament die Welt umspannt,
So muß die Gnade Freund und Feind umschließen;
Es schickt die Sonne ihre Strahlen gleich
Nach allen Räumen der Unendlichkeit;
Gleichmessend gießt der Himmel seinen Thau
Auf alle durstenden Gewächse aus;
Was irgend gut ist und von oben kommt,
Ist allgemein und ohne Vorbehalt;
Doch in den Falten wohnt die Finsterniß!

Burgund.

O, sie kann mit mir schalten, wie sie will;
Mein Herz ist weiches Wachs in ihrer Hand.
— Umarmet mich, Du Chatel!   Ich vergeb' euch.
Geist meines Vaters, zürne nicht, wenn ich
Die Hand, die dich getödtet, freundlich fasse!
Ihr Todesgötter, rechnet mir's nicht zu,
Daß ich mein schrecklich Rachgelübde breche!
Bei euch dort unten in der ew'gen Nacht,
Da schlägt kein Herz mehr, da ist Alles ewig,
Steht Alles unbeweglich fest — doch anders
Ist es hier oben in der Sonne Licht.

Der Mensch ist, der lebendig fühlende,
Der leichte Raub des mächt'gen Augenblicks.

Karl (zu Johanna).

Was dank' ich dir nicht Alles, hohe Jungfrau!
Wie schön hast du dein Wort gelös't!
Wie schnell mein ganzes Schicksal umgewandelt!
Die Freunde hast du mir versöhnt, die Feinde
Mir in den Staub gestürzt und meine Städte
Dem fremden Joch entrissen. — Du allein
Vollbrachtest Alles. — Sprich, wie lohn' ich dir!

Johanna.

Sey immer menschlich, Herr, im Glück, wie du's
Im Unglück warst — und auf der Größe Gipfel
Vergiß nicht, was ein Freund wiegt in der Noth:
Du hast's in der Erniedrigung erfahren.
Verweigre nicht Gerechtigkeit und Gnade
Dem Letzten deines Volks: denn von der Heerde
Berief dir Gott die Retterin — Du wirst
Ganz Frankreich sammeln unter deinen Scepter,
Der Ahn= und Stammherr großer Fürsten seyn;
Die nach dir kommen, werden heller leuchten,
Als die dir auf dem Thron vorangegangen.
Dein Stamm wird blühn, solang er sich die Liebe
Bewahrt im Herzen seines Volks.
Der Hochmuth nur kann ihn zum Falle führen,
Und von den niedern Hütten, wo dir jetzt
Der Retter ausging, droht geheimnißvoll
Den schuldbefleckten Enkeln das Verderben!

Burgund.

Erleuchtet Mädchen, das der Geist beseelt!
Wenn deine Augen in die Zukunft dringen,
So sprich mir auch von meinem Stamm! Wird er
Sich herrlich breiten, wie er angefangen?

Johanna.

Burgund! Hoch bis zur Throneshöhe hast
Du deinen Stuhl gesetzt, und höher strebt
Das stolze Herz, es hebt bis in die Wolken

6*

Den kühnen Bau. — Doch eine Hand von oben
Wird seinem Wachsthum schleunig Halt gebieten.
Doch fürchte drum nicht deines Hauses Fall!
In einer Jungfrau lebt es glänzend fort,
Und sceptertragende Monarchen, Hirten
Der Völker, werden ihrem Schooß entblühn.
Sie werden herrschen auf zwei großen Thronen,
Gesetze schreiben der bekannten Welt
Und einer neuen, welche Gottes Hand
Noch zudeckt hinter unbeschifften Meeren.*

* To understand this passage, as well as several others of this scene, properly, it is necessary to recur to some of the historical events on which they are
based. Philip the Good, the duke of the drama, was a scion of the Modern
house of Burgundy, of which Philip the Bold was the founder, and author of
the most brilliant period of its history. After having extended his power by
the acquisition of a number of valuable districts and cities, he was chosen Regent of France during part of the period of the mental derangement of Charles
VI., husband of Isabeau. This elevation drew on him the hatred of Louis,
duke of Orleans, brother to the king, who, having been a rival candidate for
the Regency, could not idly devour the chagrin of his disappointment. After
the death of Philip (1404), John the Intrepid inherited the debts and enemies of his father. The duke of Orleans had now won the object of his am-
bitiou, and preparations were already made on both sides to settle the hereditary quarrel by force of arms, when contrary to all expectations a public and
solemn reconciliation took place in the presence of both armies, under the walls
of Montfaucon. Soon after, however, the duke was publicly attacked and as-
sassinated, and John confessed himself the author of the treacherous deed,
which remotely became the cause of all the subsequent troubles in France. He
managed, however, to obtain the pardon of the king; and was even about to
repeat the scene of a public reconciliation with the Dauphin, when he was
visited by a retributive Nemesis, and murdered by the followers of the former,
after the first exchange of salutations, on the bridge of Monterau. (The poet
makes Du Chatêl the author of the crime). His son and successor, Philip the
Good, (the Burgundy of the Drama), in revenge of the murder of his sire, first
brought about the exclusion of the Dauphin from the peace concluded between
France and England (1420), and in the struggle, of which the drama exhibits
so vivid a picture, he exposed the cause of a foreign enemy for the purpose of
defending his own. The complete adjustment of the difficulty, which the poet
accomplishes, with so much dramatic effect, through the mediation of the
Maiden, and evidently for the purpose of exalting the character of the latter,
was brought about by the peace of Arras (1435); greatly to the advantage of
the Duke, who, besides extorting from Charles VII. a formal apology for the
murder of Duke John, obtained for himself and heirs a large number of valuable districts (among which were the county of Boulogne and the dukedom

Karl.

O, sprich, wenn es der Geist dir offenbaret,
Wird dieses Freundesbündniß, das wir jetzt
Erneut, auch noch die späten Enkelsöhne
Vereinigen?

Johanna
(nach einigem Stillschweigen.)

Ihr Könige und Herrscher!
Fürchtet die Zwietracht! wecket nicht den Streit
Aus seiner Höhle, wo er schläft: denn, einmal
Erwacht, bezähmt er spät sich wieder! Enkel
Erzeugt er sich, ein eisernes Geschlecht,
Fortzündet an dem Brande sich der Brand.
— Verlangt nicht mehr zu wissen! Freuet euch
Der Gegenwart. Laßt mich die Zukunft still
Bedecken!

Sorel.

Heilig Mädchen, du erforscheft
Mein Herz, du weißt, ob es nach Größe eitel strebt:
Auch mir gib ein erfreuliches Orakel.

Johanna.

Mir zeigt der Geist nur große Weltgeschicke;
Dein Schicksal ruht in deiner eignen Brust!

Dunois.

Was aber wird dein eigen Schicksal seyn,
Erhabnes Mädchen, das der Himmel liebt?
Dir blüht gewiß das schönste Glück der Erden,
Da du so fromm und heilig bist.

---

of Luxemburg) from the domain of the crown. The splendor of the house of Burgundy became still greater during the reign of *Charles the Bold*, only surviving son of Philip, who in his day was one of the most powerful princes of Europe. The virgin, to whom the Maid here in prophetic exaltation alludes, as the redemptrix of the house and harbinger of its future greatness, was Mary of Burgundy, the only child of Charles and heiress to his immense estates. Of the seven princes that were the rival suitors for her hand, the chivalric and handsome Maximilian of Austria was the successful one. The sceptre-bearing monarchs, shepherds of people, of the passage were Emperor Charles V. and Philip II. of Spain, lineal descendants of Mary. The empire of these extended over both hemispheres. Cf. the preceding Scene, and the conclusion of Act second.

Johanna.

Das Glück
Wohnt droben in dem Schooß des ew'gen Vaters.

Karl.

Dein Glück sey fortan deines Königs Sorge!
Denn deinen Namen will ich herrlich machen
In Frankreich; selig preisen sollen dich
Die spätesten Geschlechter — und gleich jetzt
Erfüll' ich es. — Knie nieder!

(Er zieht das Schwert und berührt sie mit demselben.)

Und steh' auf
Als eine Edle! Ich erhebe dich,
Dein König, aus dem Staube deiner dunkeln
Geburt — Im Grabe adl' ich deine Väter —
Du sollst die Lilie im Wappen tragen,
Den Besten sollst du ebenbürtig seyn
In Frankreich; nur das königliche Blut
Von Valois sey edler, als das deine!
Der Größte meiner Großen fühle sich
Durch deine Hand geehrt; mein sey die Sorge,
Dich einem edlen Gatten zu vermählen.

Dunois (tritt vor).

Mein Herz erkor sie, da sie niedrig war:
Die neue Ehre, die ihr Haupt umglänzt,
Erhöht nicht ihr Verdienst, noch meine Liebe.
Hier in dem Angesichte meines Königs
Und dieses heiligen Bischofs reich' ich ihr
Die Hand als meiner fürstlichen Gemahlin,
Wenn sie mich würdig hält, sie zu empfangen.

Karl.

Unwiderstehlich Mädchen, du häufst Wunder
Auf Wunder! Ja, nun glaub' ich, daß dir nichts
Unmöglich ist. Du hast dies stolze Herz
Bezwungen, das der Liebe Allgewalt
Hohn sprach bis jetzt.

La Hire (tritt vor).

Johanna's schönster Schmuck,
Kenn' ich sie recht, ist ihr bescheidnes Herz.
Der Huldigung des Größten ist sie werth,
Doch nie wird sie den Wunsch so hoch erheben,
Sie strebt nicht schwindelnd eitler Hoheit nach;
Die treue Neigung eines redlichen
Gemüths genügt ihr und das stille Loos,
Das ich mit dieser Hand ihr anerbiete.

Karl.

Auch du, La Hire? Zwei treffliche Bewerber,
An Heldentugend gleich und Kriegesruhm!
— Willst du, die meine Feinde mir versöhnt,
Mein Reich vereinigt, mir die liebsten Freunde
Entzwein? Es kann sie Einer nur besitzen,
Und Jeden acht' ich solches Preises werth.
So rede du, dein Herz muß hier entscheiden.

Sorel (tritt näher).

Die edle Jungfrau seh' ich überrascht,
Und ihre Wangen färbt die zücht'ge Scham.
Man geb' ihr Zeit, ihr Herz zu fragen, sich
Der Freundin zu vertrauen und das Siegel
Zu lösen von der festverschloßnen Brust.
Jetzt ist der Augenblick gekommen, wo
Auch ich der strengen Jungfrau schwesterlich
Mich nahen, ihr den treu verschwiegnen Busen
Darbieten darf.—Man laß uns weiblich erst
Das Weibliche bedenken und erwarte,
Was wir beschließen werden.

Karl (im Begriff zu gehen).
Also sey's!

Johanna.

Nicht also, Sire! Was meine Wangen färbte,
War die Verwirrung nicht der blöden Scham.
Ich habe dieser edeln Frau nichts zu vertraun,
Deß ich vor Männern mich zu schämen hätte.

Hoch ehrt mich dieser edeln Ritter Wahl;
Doch nicht verließ ich meine Schäfertrift,
Um weltlich eitle Hoheit zu erjagen,
Noch mir den Brautkranz in das Haar zu flechten,
Legt' ich die ehrne Waffenrüstung an.
Berufen bin ich zu ganz anderm Werk,
Die reine Jungfrau nur kann es vollenden.
Ich bin die Kriegerin des höchsten Gottes,
Und keinem Manne kann ich Gattin seyn.

Erzbischof.

Dem Mann zur liebenden Gefährtin ist
Das Weib geboren — wenn sie der Natur
Gehorcht, dient sie am würdigsten dem Himmel!
Und hast du dem Befehle deines Gottes,
Der in das Feld dich rief, genug gethan,
So wirst du deine Waffen von dir legen
Und wiederkehren zu dem sanfteren
Geschlecht, das du verläugnet hast, das nicht
Berufen ist zum blut'gen Werk der Waffen.

Johanna.

Ehrwürd'ger Herr, ich weiß noch nicht zu sagen,
Was mir der Geist gebieten wird zu thun;
Doch wenn die Zeit kommt, wird mir seine Stimme
Nicht schweigen, und gehorchen werd' ich ihr.
Jetzt aber heißt er mich mein Werk vollenden.
Die Stirne meines Herren ist noch nicht
Gekrönt, das heil'ge Oel hat seine Scheitel
Noch nicht benetzt, noch heißt mein Herr nicht König.

Karl.

Wir sind begriffen auf dem Weg nach Rheims.

Johanna.

Laß uns nicht still stehn, denn geschäftig sind
Die Feinde rings, den Weg dir zu verschließen.
Doch mitten durch sie Alle führ' ich dich!

Dunois.

Wenn aber Alles wird vollendet seyn,

Wenn wir zu Rheims nun siegend eingezogen,
Wirst du mir dann vergönnen, heilig Mädchen —

Johanna.

Will es der Himmel, daß ich sieggekrönt
Aus diesem Kampf des Todes wiederkehre,
So ist mein Werk vollendet — und die Hirtin
Hat kein Geschäft mehr in des Königs Hause.

Karl (ihre Hand fassend).

Dich treibt des Geistes Stimme jetzt, es schweigt
Die Liebe in dem gotterfüllten Busen;
Sie wird nicht immer schweigen, glaube mir!
Die Waffen werden ruhn, es führt der Sieg
Den Frieden an der Hand; dann kehrt die Freude
In jeden Busen ein, und sanftere
Gefühle wachen auf in allen Herzen —
Sie werden auch in deiner Brust erwachen,
Und Thränen süßer Sehnsucht wirst du weinen,
Wie sie dein Auge nie vergoß — dies Herz,
Das jetzt der Himmel ganz erfüllt, wird sich
Zu einem ird'schen Freunde liebend wenden —
Jetzt hast du rettend Tausende beglückt,
Und, Einen zu beglücken, wirst du enden!

Johanna.

Dauphin! Bist du der göttlichen Erscheinung
Schon müde, daß du ihr Gefäß zerstören,
Die reine Jungfrau, die dir Gott gesendet,
Herab willst ziehn in den gemeinen Staub?
Ihr blinden Herzen! Ihr Kleingläubigen!
Des Himmels Herrlichkeit umleuchtet euch,
Vor eurem Aug' enthüllt er seine Wunder,
Und ihr erblickt in mir nichts als ein Weib!
Darf sich ein Weib mit kriegerischem Erz
Umgeben, in die Männerschlacht sich mischen?
Weh mir, wenn ich das Rachschwert meines Gottes
In Händen führte und im eiteln Herzen
Die Neigung trüge zu dem ird'schen Mann!

Mir wäre beffer, ich wär' nie geboren!
Kein folches Wort mehr, fag' ich euch, wenn ihr
Den Geift in mir nicht zürnend wollt entrüften!
Der Männer Auge fchon, das mich begehrt,
Ift mir ein Grauen und Entheiligung.

Karl.

Brecht ab.   Es ift umfonft, fie zu bewegen.

Johanna.

Befiehl, daß man die Kriegsdrommete blafe!
Mich preßt und ängftigt diefe Waffenftille!
Es jagt mich auf aus diefer müß'gen Ruh
Und treibt mich fort, daß ich mein Werk erfülle,
Gebieterifch mahnend meinem Schickfal zu.

Fünfter Auftritt.

Ein Ritter eilfertig.

Karl.

Was ift's?

Ritter.

Der Feind ift über die Marne gegangen
Und ftellt fein Heer zum Treffen.

Johanna (begeiftert).

Schlacht und Kampf!
Jetzt ift die Seele ihrer Bande frei.
Bewaffnet euch, ich ordn' indeß die Schaaren.

(Sie eilt hinaus.)

Karl.

Folgt ihr, La Hire — Sie wollen uns am Thore
Von Rheims noch um die Krone kämpfen laffen!

Dunois.

Sie treibt nicht wahrer Muth.   Es ift der letzte
Verfuch ohnmächtig wüthender Verzweiflung.

Karl.

Burgund, euch fporn' ich nicht.   Heut' ift der Tag,
Um viele böfe Tage zu vergüten.

Burgund.

Ihr sollt mit mir zufrieden seyn.

Karl.

Ich selbst
Will euch vorangehn auf dem Weg des Ruhms,
Und in dem Angesicht der Krönungsstadt
Die Krone mir erfechten. — Meine Agnes,
Dein Ritter sagt dir Lebewohl!

Agnes (umarmt ihn).

Ich weine nicht, ich zittre nicht für dich,
Mein Glaube greift vertrauend in die Wolken.
So viele Pfänder seiner Gnade gab
Der Himmel nicht, daß wir am Ende trauern.
Vom Sieg' gekrönt umarm' ich meinen Herrn,
Mir sagt's das Herz, in Rheims bezwungnen Mauern.

(Trompeten erschallen mit muthigem Ton und gehen, während daß verwandelt
wird, in ein wildes Kriegsgetümmel über; das Orchester fällt ein bei offener Scene
und wird von kriegerischen Instrumenten hinter der Scene begleitet.)

———

Der Schauplatz verwandelt sich in eine freie Gegend, die von Bäumen begränzt
wird. Man sieht während der Musik Soldaten über den Hintergrund schnell
wegziehen.

Sechster Auftritt.

Talbot, auf **Fastolf** gestützt und von **Soldaten** begleitet. Gleich
darauf **Lionel.**

Talbot.

Hier unter diesen Bäumen setzt mich nieder,
Und ihr begebt euch in die Schlacht zurück;
Ich brauche keines Beistands, um zu sterben.

Fastolf.

O unglückselig jammervoller Tag!

(Lionel tritt auf.)

Zu welchem Anblick kommt ihr, Lionel!
Hier liegt der Feldherr auf den Tod verwundet.

Lionel.

Das wolle Gott nicht! Edler Lord, steht auf!
Jetzt ist's nicht Zeit, ermattet hinzusinken.

Weicht nicht dem Tod, gebietet der Natur
Mit eurem mächt'gen Willen, daß sie lebe.

Talbot.

Umsonst! Der Tag des Schicksals ist gekommen,
Der unsern Thron in Frankreich stürzen soll.
Vergebens in verzweiflungsvollem Kampf
Wagt' ich das Letzte noch, ihn abzuwenden.
Vom Strahl dahingeschmettert lieg' ich hier,
Um nicht mehr aufzustehn.— Rheims ist verloren.
So eilt, Paris zu retten.

Lionel.

'Paris hat sich vertragen mit dem Dauphin:
So eben bringt ein Eilbot uns die Nachricht.

Talbot (reißt den Verband auf.)

So strömet hin, ihr Bäche meines Bluts,
Denn überdrüssig bin ich dieser Sonne!

Lionel.

Ich kann nicht bleiben. — Fastolf, bringt den Feldherrn
An einen sichern Ort: wir können uns
Nicht lange mehr auf diesem Posten halten.
Die Unsern fliehen schon von allen Seiten;
Unwiderstehlich dringt das Mädchen vor —

Talbot.

Unsinn, du siegst, und ich muß untergehn;
Mit der Dummheit kämpfen Götter selbst vergebens.
Erhabene Vernunft, lichthelle Tochter
Des göttlichen Hauptes, weise Gründerin
Des Weltgebäudes, Führerin der Sterne,
Wer bist du denn, wenn du, dem tollen Roß
Des Aberwitzes an den Schweif gebunden,
Ohnmächtig rufend, mit dem Trunkenen
Dich sehend in den Abgrund stürzen mußt!
Verflucht sey, wer sein Leben an das Große
Und Würd'ge wendet und bedachte Pläne
Mit weisem Geist entwirft! Dem Narrenkönig
Gehört die Welt —

Lionel.

Mylord! Ihr habt nur noch
Für wenige Augenblicke Leben — Denkt
An euren Schöpfer!

Talbot.

Wären wir als Tapfere
Durch andre Tapfere besiegt, wir könnten
Uns trösten mit dem allgemeinen Schicksal,
Das immer wechselnd seine Kugel dreht —
Doch solchem groben Gaukelspiel erliegen!
War unser ernstes arbeitvolles Leben
Keines ernsthaftern Ausgangs werth?

Lionel (reicht ihm die Hand).

Mylord, fahrt wohl! Der Thränen schuldigen Zoll
Will ich euch redlich nach der Schlacht entrichten,
Wenn ich alsdann noch übrig bin. Jetzt aber
Ruft das Geschick mich fort, das auf dem Schlachtfeld
Noch richtend sitzt und seine Loose schüttelt;
Auf Wiedersehn in einer andern Welt!
Kurz ist der Abschied für die lange Freundschaft.

(Geht ab.)

Talbot.

Bald ist's vorüber, und der Erde geb' ich,
Der ew'gen Sonne die Atome wieder,
Die sich zu Schmerz und Lust in mir gefügt —
Und von dem mächt'gen Talbot, der die Welt
Mit seinem Kriegsruhm füllte, bleibt nichts übrig,
Als eine Handvoll leichten Staubs. — So geht
Der Mensch zu Ende — und die einzige
Ausbeute, die wir aus dem Kampf des Lebens
Wegtragen, ist die Einsicht in das Nichts
Und herzliche Verachtung alles dessen,
Was uns erhaben schien und wünschenswerth. —

Siebenter Auftritt.

Karl. Burgund. Dunois. Du Chatel und Soldaten
treten auf.

Burgund.

Die Schanze ist erstürmt.

Dunois.

Der Tag ist unser.

Karl (Talbot bemerkend).

Seht, wer es ist, der dort vom Licht der Sonne
Den unfreiwillig schweren Abschied nimmt?
Die Rüstung zeigt mir keinen schlechten Mann,
Geht, springt ihm bei, wenn ihm noch Hülfe frommt.

(Soldaten aus des Königs Gefolge treten hinzu.)

Fastolf.

Zurück! Bleibt fern! Habt Achtung vor dem Todten,
Dem ihr im Leben nie zu nah'n gewünscht!

Burgund.

Was seh' ich! Talbot liegt in seinem Blut!

(Er geht auf ihn zu. Talbot blickt ihn starr an und stirbt.)

Fastolf.

Hinweg, Burgund! Den letzten Blick des Helden
Vergifte nicht der Anblick des Verräthers!

Dunois.

Furchtbarer Talbot! Unbezwinglicher!
Nimmst du vorlieb mit so geringem Raum,
Und Frankreichs weite Erde konnte nicht
Dem Streben deines Riesengeistes gnügen.
— Erst jetzo, Sire, begrüß' ich euch als König:
Die Krone zitterte auf eurem Haupt,
Solang ein Geist in diesem Körper lebte.

Karl
(nachdem er den Todten stillschweigend betrachtet).

Ihn hat ein Höherer besiegt, nicht wir!
Er liegt auf Frankreichs Erde, wie der Held
Auf seinem Schild, den er nicht lassen wollte.
Bringt ihn hinweg!

(Soldaten heben den Todten auf und tragen ihn fort.)

Fried' sey mit seinem Staube!
Ihm soll ein ehrenvolles Denkmal werden.
Mitten in Frankreich, wo er seinen Lauf
Als Held geendet, ruhe sein Gebein!
So weit, als er, drang noch kein feindlich Schwert,
Seine Grabschrift sey der Ort, wo man ihn findet.

Fastolf (gibt sein Schwert ab).

Herr, ich bin dein Gefangener.

Karl
(gibt ihm sein Schwert zurück).

· Nicht also!
Die fromme Pflicht ehrt auch der rohe Krieg,
Frei sollt ihr eurem Herrn zu Grabe folgen.
Jetzt eilt, Du Chatel — Meine Agnes zittert —
Entreißt sie ihrer Angst um uns — bringt ihr
Die Botschaft, daß wir leben, daß wir siegten,
Und führt sie im Triumph nach Rheims!

(Du Chatel geht ab.)

Achter Auftritt.
La Hire zu den Vorigen.

Dunois.

La Hire,
Wo ist die Jungfrau?

La Hire.
Wie? Das frag' ich euch.
An eurer Seite fechtend ließ ich sie.

Dunois.
Von eurem Arme glaubt' ich sie beschützt,
Als ich dem König beizuspringen eilte.

Burgund.
Im dichtsten Feindeshaufen sah ich noch
Vor Kurzem ihre weiße Fahne wehn.

Dunois.
Weh' uns, wo ist sie? Böses ahnet mir!
Kommt, eilen wir, sie zu befrein. — Ich fürchte,

Sie hat der kühne Muth zu weit geführt,
Umringt von Feinden, kämpft sie ganz allein
Und hülflos unterliegt sie jetzt der Menge.

Karl.

Eilt, rettet sie!

La Hire.

Ich folg' euch, kommt!

Burgund.

Wir alle!

(Sie eilen fort.)

Eine andere öde Gegend des Schlachtfeldes.

Man sieht die Thürme von Rheims in der Ferne von der Sonne beleuchtet.

Neunter Auftritt.

Ein Ritter in ganz schwarzer Rüstung, mit geschlossenem Visir. Johanna verfolgt ihn bis auf die vordere Bühne, wo er stille steht und sie erwartet.

Johanna.

Arglist'ger! Jetzt erkenn' ich deine Tücke!
Du hast mich trüglich durch verstellte Flucht
Vom Schlachtfeld weggelockt und Tod und Schicksal
Von vieler Brittensöhne Haupt entfernt.
Doch jetzt ereilt dich selber das Verderben.

Schwarzer Ritter.

Warum verfolgst du mich und heftest dich
So wuthentbrannt an meine Fersen? Mir
Ist nicht bestimmt, von deiner Hand zu fallen.

Johanna.

Verhaßt in tiefster Seele bist du mir,
Gleichwie die Nacht, die deine Farbe ist.
Dich weg zu tilgen von dem Licht des Tags,
Treibt mich die unbezwingliche Begier.
Wer bist du? Oeffne dein Visir. — Hätt' ich
Den kriegerischen Talbot in der Schlacht
Nicht fallen sehn, so sagt' ich, du wärst Talbot.

Schwarzer Ritter.

Schweigt dir die Stimme des Prophetengeistes?

Johanna.

Sie redet laut in meiner tiefsten Brust,
Daß mir das Unglück an der Seite steht.

Schwarzer Ritter.

Johanna d'Arc! Bis an die Thore Rheims
Bist du gedrungen auf des Sieges Flügeln.
Dir gnüge der erworbne Ruhm. Entlasse
Das Glück, das dir als Sklave hat gedient,
Eh' es sich zürnend selbst befreit; es haßt
Die Treu', und keinem dient es bis ans Ende.

Johanna.

Was heißest du in Mitte meines Laufs
Mich stille stehen und mein Werk verlassen?
Ich führ' es aus und löse mein Gelübde!

Schwarzer Ritter.

Nichts kann dir, du Gewalt'ge, widerstehn,
In jedem Kampfe siegst du. — Aber gehe
In keinen Kampf mehr. Höre meine Warnung!

Johanna.

Nicht aus den Händen leg' ich dieses Schwert,
Als bis das stolze England niederliegt.

Schwarzer Ritter.

Schau hin! Dort hebt sich Rheims mit seinen Thürmen,
Das Ziel und Ende deiner Fahrt — die Kuppel
Der hohen Kathedrale siehst du leuchten,
Dort wirst du einziehn im Triumphgepräng,
Deinen König krönen, dein Gelübde lösen.
— Geh' nicht hinein! Kehr' um! Hör' meine Warnung!

Johanna.

Wer bist du, doppelzüngig falsches Wesen,
Das mich erschrecken und verwirren will?
Was maßest du dir an, mir falsch Orakel
Betrüglich zu verkündigen!

(Der schwarze Ritter will abgehen, sie tritt ihm in den Weg).

Nein, du stehst
Mir Rede oder stirbst von meinen Händen!

(Sie will einen Streich auf ihn führen.)

Schwarzer Ritter.
(berührt sie mit der Hand, sie bleibt unbeweglich stehen.)
Tödte, was sterblich ist!
(Nacht, Blitz und Donnerschlag.   Der Ritter versinkt.)

Johanna
(steht anfangs erstaunt, faßt sich aber bald wieder).
Es war nichts Lebendes.   Ein trüglich Bild
Der Hölle war's, ein widerspenst'ger Geist,
Heraufgestiegen aus dem Feuerpfuhl,
Mein edles Herz im Busen zu erschüttern.
Wen fürcht' ich mit dem Schwerte meines Gottes?
Siegreich vollenden will ich meine Bahn,
Und käm' die Hölle selber in die Schranken,
Mir soll der Muth nicht weichen und nicht wanken!
(Sie will abgehen.)

Zehnter Auftritt.
Lionel. Johanna.

Lionel.
Verfluchte! rüste dich zum Kampf — Nicht Beide
Verlassen wir lebendig diesen Platz.
Du hast die Besten meines Volks getödtet;
Der edle Talbot hat die große Seele
In meinen Busen ausgehaucht. — Ich räche
Den Tapfern oder theile sein Geschick.
Und daß du wissest, wer dir Ruhm verleiht,
Er sterbe oder siege — Ich bin Lionel,
Der letzte von den Fürsten unsers Heers,
Und unbezwungen ist noch dieser Arm.
(Er bringt auf sie ein; nach einem kurzen Gefechte schlägt sie ihm das Schwert aus der Hand.)
Treuloses Glück!
(Er ringt mit ihr.)

Johanna
(ergreift ihn von hinten zu am Helmbusch und reißt ihm den Helm gewaltsam herunter, daß sein Gesicht entblößt wird, zugleich zuckt sie das Schwert mit der Rechten.)
Erleide, was du suchtest!
Die heil'ge Jungfrau opfert dich durch mich!
(In diesem Augenblick sieht sie ihm ins Gesicht; sein Anblick ergreift sie, sie bleibt unbeweglich stehen und läßt dann langsam den Arm sinken.)

Lionel.

Was zauderst du und hemmst den Todesstreich?
Nimm mir das Leben auch, du nahmst den Ruhm;
Ich bin in deiner Hand, ich will nicht Schonung.

(Sie gibt ihm ein Zeichen mit der Hand, sich zu entfernen.)

Entfliehen soll ich? Dir soll ich mein Leben
Verdanken? — Eher sterben!

Johanna (mit abgewandtem Gesicht.)

Ich will nichts davon wissen, daß dein Leben
In meine Macht gegeben war.

Lionel.

Ich hasse dich und dein Geschenk — Ich will
Nicht Schonung — Tödte deinen Feind, der dich
Verabscheut, der dich tödten wollte.

Johanna.

Tödte mich

— Und fliehe!

Lionel.

Ha! Was ist das?

Johanna (verbirgt das Gesicht.)

Wehe mir!

Lionel (tritt ihr näher).

Du tödtest, sagt man, alle Engelländer,
Die du im Kampf bezwingst — Warum nur mich
Verschonen?

Johanna

(erhebt das Schwert mit einer raschen Bewegung gegen ihn, läßt es aber, wie sie
ihn ins Gesicht faßt, schnell wieder sinken.)

Heil'ge Jungfrau!

Lionel.

Warum nennst du
Die Heil'ge? Sie weiß nichts von dir; der Himmel
Hat keinen Theil an dir.

Johanna (in der heftigsten Beängstigung)

Was hab' ich
Gethan! Gebrochen hab' ich mein Gelübde!

(Sie ringt verzweifelnd die Hände.)

7

Lionel

(betrachtet sie mit Theilnahme und tritt ihr näher.)

Unglücklich Mädchen! Ich beklage dich.
Du rührst mich; du hast Großmuth ausgeübt
An mir allein; ich fühle, daß mein Haß
Verschwindet, ich muß Antheil an dir nehmen!
— Wer bist du? Woher kommst du?

Johanna.

Fort! Entfliehe!

Lionel.

Mich jammert deine Jugend, deine Schönheit!
Dein Anblick dringt mir an das Herz. Ich möchte
Dich gerne retten — Sage mir, wie kann ich's?
Komm! Komm! Entsage dieser gräßlichen
Verbindung — Wirf sie von dir, diese Waffen!

Johanna.

Ich bin unwürdig, sie zu führen!

Lionel.

Wirf
Sie von dir, schnell, und folge mir!

Johanna (mit Entsetzen.)

Dir folgen!

Lionel.

Du kannst gerettet werden. Folge mir,
Ich will dich retten, aber säume nicht.
Mich faßt ein ungeheurer Schmerz um dich
Und ein unnennbar Sehnen, dich zu retten —

(Bemächtigt sich ihres Arms.)

Johanna.

Der Bastard naht! Sie sind's! Sie suchen mich!
Wenn sie dich finden —

Lionel.

Ich beschütze dich!

Johanna.

Ich sterbe, wenn du fällst von ihren Händen!

Lionel.

Bin ich dir theuer?

Johanna.

Heilige des Himmels!

Lionel.

Werd' ich dich wiedersehen? von dir hören?

Johanna.

Nie! Niemals!

Lionel.

Dieses Schwert zum Pfand, daß ich
Dich wiedersehe!

(Er entreißt ihr das Schwert.)

Johanna.

Rasender, du wagst es?

Lionel.

Jetzt weich' ich der Gewalt, ich seh' dich wieder!

(Er geht ab.)

Eilfter Auftritt.

Dunois und La Hire. Johanna.

La Hire.

Sie lebt! Sie ist's!

Dunois.

Johanna, fürchte nichts!
Die Freunde stehen mächtig dir zur Seite.

La Hire.

Flieht dort nicht Lionel?

Dunois.

Laßt ihn entfliehn!
Johanna, die gerechte Sache siegt.
Rheims öffnet seine Thore; alles Volk
Strömt jauchzend seinem Könige entgegen —

La Hire.

Was ist der Jungfrau? Sie erbleicht, sie sinkt!
(Johanna schwindelt und will sinken.)

Dunois.

Sie ist verwundet — Reißt den Panzer auf —
Es ist der Arm und leicht ist die Verletzung.

La Hire.

Ihr Blut entfließt!

Johanna.
Laß es mit meinem Leben

Hinströmen!
(Sie liegt ohnmächtig in La Hire's Armen.)

Vierter Aufzug.

Ein festlich geschmückter Saal.

Die Säulen sind mit Festons umwunden; hinter der Scene Flöten und Hoboen.

Erster Auftritt.

Johanna.

Die Waffen ruhn, des Krieges Stürme schweigen,
Auf blut'ge Schlachten folgt Gesang und Tanz,
Durch alle Straßen tönt der muntre Reigen,
Altar und Kirche prangt in Festesglanz,
Und Pforten bauen sich aus grünen Zweigen,
Und um die Säule windet sich der Kranz;
Das weite Rheims faßt nicht die Zahl der Gäste,
Die wallend strömen zu dem Völkerfeste.

Und einer Freude Hochgefühl entbrennet,
Und ein Gedanke schlägt in jeder Brust,
Was sich noch jüngst in blut'gem Haß getrennet,
Das theilt entzückt die allgemeine Lust.
Wer nur zum Stamm der Franken sich bekennet,
Der ist des Namens stolzer sich bewußt:
Erneuert ist der Glanz der alten Krone,
Und Frankreich huldigt seinem Königssohne.

Doch mich, die all dies Herrliche vollendet,
Mich rührt es nicht, das allgemeine Glück;
Mir ist das Herz verwandelt und gewendet,
Es flieht von dieser Festlichkeit zurück,
Ins britt'sche Lager ist es hingewendet,
Hinüber zu dem Feinde schweift der Blick,

149

Und aus der Freude Kreis muß ich mich stehlen,
Die schwere Schuld des Busens zu verhehlen.

    Wer? Ich? Ich eines Mannes Bild
In meinem reinen Busen tragen?
Dies Herz von Himmelsglanz erfüllt,
Darf einer ird'schen Liebe schlagen?
Ich, meines Landes Retterin,
Des höchsten Gottes Kriegerin,
Für meines Landes Feind entbrennen?
Darf ich's der keuschen Sonne nennen,
Und mich vernichtet nicht die Scham?

(Die Musik hinter der Scene geht in eine weiche, schmelzende Melodie über.)

    Wehe! Weh' mir! Welche Töne!
Wie verführen sie mein Ohr!
Jeder ruft mir seine Stimme,
Zaubert mir sein Bild hervor!

    Daß der Sturm der Schlacht mich faßte,
Speere sausend mich umtönten,
In des heißen Streites Wuth!
Wieder fänd' ich meinen Muth!

    Diese Stimmen, diese Töne,
Wie umstricken sie mein Herz!
Jede Kraft in meinem Busen
Lösen sie in weichem Sehnen,
Schmelzen sie in Wehmuths=Thränen!

(Nach einer Pause lebhafter.)

Sollt' ich ihn tödten? Konnt' ich's, da ich ihm
Ins Auge sah? Ihn tödten! Eher hätt' ich
Den Mordstahl auf die eigne Brust gezückt!
Und bin ich strafbar, weil ich menschlich war?
Ist Mitleid Sünde? — Mitleid! Hörtest du
Des Mitleids Stimme und der Menschlichkeit
Auch bei den Andern, die dein Schwert geopfert?
Warum verstummte sie, als der Walliser dich,
Der zarte Jüngling, um sein Leben flehte?

Arglistig Herz! du lügst dem ew'gen Licht,
Dich trieb des Mitleids fromme Stimme nicht!

Warum mußt' ich ihm in die Augen sehn!
Die Züge schaun des edeln Angesichts!
Mit deinem Blick fing dein Verbrechen an,
Unglückliche! Ein blindes Werkzeug fordert Gott;
Mit blinden Augen mußtest du's vollbringen?
Sobald du sahst, verließ dich Gottes Schild,
Ergriffen dich der Hölle Schlingen!

(Die Flöten wiederholen, sie versinkt in eine stille Wehmuth.)

 Frommer Stab! O, hätt' ich nimmer
Mit dem Schwerte dich vertauscht!
Hätt' es nie in deinen Zweigen,
Heil'ge Eiche, mir gerauscht!
Wärst du nimmer mir erschienen,
Hohe Himmelskönigin!
Nimm, ich kann sie nicht verdienen,
Deine Krone, nimm sie hin!

 Ach, ich sah den Himmel offen
Und der Sel'gen Angesicht!
Doch auf Erden ist mein Hoffen!
Und im Himmel ist es nicht!
Mußtest du ihn auf mich laden,
Diesen furchtbaren Beruf!
Konnt' ich dieses Herz verhärten,
Das der Himmel fühlend schuf!

 Willst du deine Macht verkünden,
Wähle sie, die frei von Sünden,
Stehn in deinem ew'gen Haus;
Deine Geister sende aus,
Die Unsterblichen, die Reinen,
Die nicht fühlen, die nicht weinen!
Nicht die zarte Jungfrau wähle,
Nicht der Hirtin weiche Seele!

Kümmert mich das Loos der Schlachten,
Mich der Zwist der Könige?
Schuldlos trieb ich meine Lämmer
Auf des stillen Berges Höh'.
Doch du rissest mich ins Leben,
In den stolzen Fürstensaal,
Mich der Schuld dahin zu geben,
Ach, es war nicht meine Wahl!

Zweiter Auftritt.

Agnes Sorel. Johanna.

Sorel

(kommt in lebhafter Rührung; wie sie die Jungfrau erblickt, eilt sie auf sie zu und fällt ihr um den Hals; plötzlich besinnt sie sich, läßt sie los und fällt vor ihr nieder.)

Nein! Nicht so! Hier im Staub vor dir —

Johanna (will sie aufheben).

Steh' auf!

Was ist dir? Du vergissest dich und mich.

Sorel.

Laß mich, es ist der Freude Drang, der mich
Zu deinen Füßen niederwirft — ich muß
Mein überwallend Herz vor Gott ergießen,
Den Unsichtbaren bet' ich an in dir.
Du bist der Engel, der mir meinen Herrn
Nach Rheims geführt und mit der Krone schmückt.
Was ich zu sehen nie geträumt, es ist
Erfüllt! Der Krönungszug bereitet sich,
Der König steht im festlichen Ornat,
Versammelt sind die Pairs, die Mächtigen
Der Krone, die Insignien zu tragen,
Zur Kathedrale wallend strömt das Volk,
Es schallt der Reigen, und die Glocken tönen.
O, dieses Glückes Fülle trag' ich nicht!

(Johanna hebt sie sanft in die Höhe. Agnes Sorel hält einen Augenblick inne, indem sie der Jungfrau näher ins Auge sieht.)

Doch du bleibst immer ernst und streng; du kannst
Das Glück erschaffen, doch du theilst es nicht.
Dein Herz ist kalt, du fühlst nicht unsre Freuden,
Du hast der Himmel Herrlichkeit gesehn,
Die reine Brust bewegt kein irdisch Glück.

(Johanna ergreift ihre Hand mit Heftigkeit, läßt sie aber schnell wieder fahren.)

O, könntest du ein Weib seyn und empfinden!
Leg' diese Rüstung ab, kein Krieg ist mehr,
Bekenne dich zum sanfteren Geschlechte!
Mein liebend Herz flieht scheu vor dir zurück,
Solange du der strengen Pallas gleichst.

Johanna.

Was forderst du von mir!

Sorel.

Entwaffne dich!
Leg' diese Rüstung ab!   Die Liebe fürchtet,
Sich dieser stahlbedeckten Brust zu nahn.
O, sey ein Weib, und du wirst Liebe fühlen!

Johanna.

Jetzt soll ich mich entwaffnen!   Jetzt!   Dem Tod
Will ich die Brust entblößen in der Schlacht!
Jetzt nicht — o, möchte siebenfaches Erz
Vor euren Festen, vor mir selbst mich schützen!

Sorel.

Dich liebt Graf Dunois.   Sein edles Herz,
Dem Ruhm nur offen und der Heldentugend,
Es glüht für dich in heiligem Gefühl.
O, es ist schön, von einem Helden sich geliebt
Zu sehn — es ist noch schöner, ihn zu lieben!

(Johanna wendet sich mit Abscheu hinweg.)

Du hassest ihn! — Nein, nein, du kannst ihn nur
Nicht lieben — Doch, wie solltest du ihn hassen!
Man haßt nur den, der den Geliebten uns
Entreißt; doch dir ist Keiner der Geliebte!
Dein Herz ist ruhig — Wenn es fühlen könnte —

7*

Johanna.

Beklage mich! Beweine mein Geschick!

Sorel.

Was könnte dir zu deinem Glücke mangeln?
Du hast dein Wort gelös't, Frankreich ist frei,
Bis in die Krönungsstadt hast du den König
Siegreich geführt und hohen Ruhm erstritten;
Dir huldiget, dich preis't ein glücklich Volk;
Von allen Zungen überströmend fließt
Dein Lob; du bist die Göttin dieses Festes;
Der König selbst mit seiner Krone strahlt
Nicht herrlicher, als du.

Johanna.

O, könnt' ich mich
Verbergen in den tiefsten Schooß der Erde!

Sorel.

Was ist dir? Welche seltsame Bewegung!
Wer dürfte frei aufschaun an diesem Tage,
Wenn du die Blicke niederschlagen sollst?
Mich laß erröthen, mich, die neben dir
So klein sich fühlt, zu deiner Heldenstärke sich,
Zu deiner Hoheit nicht erheben kann!
Denn soll ich meine ganze Schwäche dir
Gestehen? Nicht der Ruhm des Vaterlandes,
Nicht der erneute Glanz des Thrones, nicht
Der Völker Hochgefühl und Siegesfreude
Beschäftigt dieses schwache Herz. Es ist
Nur Einer, der es ganz erfüllt; es hat
Nur Raum für dieses einzige Gefühl:
Er ist der Angebetete, ihm jauchzt das Volk,
Ihn segnet es, ihm streut es diese Blumen,
Er ist der Meine, der Geliebte ist's.

Johanna.

O, du bist glücklich! Selig preise dich!
Du liebst, wo Alles liebt! Du darfst dein Herz
Aufschließen, laut aussprechen dein Entzücken

Und offen tragen vor der Menschen Blicken!
Dies Fest des Reichs ist deiner Liebe Fest.
Die Völker alle, die unendlichen,
Die sich in diesen Mauern flutend drängen,
Sie theilen dein Gefühl, sie heil'gen es;
Dir jauchzen sie, dir flechten sie den Kranz,
Eins bist du mit der allgemeinen Wonne,
Du liebst das Allerfreuende, die Sonne,
Und was du siehst, ist deiner Liebe Glanz!

Sorel (ihr um den Hals fallend).

O, du entzückst mich, du verstehst mich ganz!
Ja, ich verkannte dich, du kennst die Liebe,
Und was ich fühle, sprichst du mächtig aus.
Von seiner Furcht und Scheue löf't sich mir
Das Herz, es wallt vertrauend dir entgegen —

Johanna
(entreißt sich mit Heftigkeit ihren Armen).

Verlaß mich! Wende dich von mir! Beflecke
Dich nicht mit meiner pesterfüllten Nähe!
Sey glücklich, geh'! Mich laß in tiefster Nacht
Mein Unglück, meine Schande, mein Entsetzen
Verbergen —

Sorel.

Du erschreckst mich, ich begreife
Dich nicht; doch ich begriff dich nie — und stets
Verhüllt war mir dein dunkel tiefes Wesen.
Wer möcht' es fassen, was dein heilig Herz,
Der reinen Seele Zartgefühl erschreckt!

Johanna.

Du bist die Heilige! Du bist die Reine!
Sähst du mein Innerstes, du stießest schaudernd
Die Feindin von dir, die Verrätherin!

Dritter Auftritt.

Dunois. Du Chatel und **La Hire** mit der Fahne der Johanna.

Dunois.

Dich suchen wir, Johanna. Alles ist
Bereit; der König sendet uns, er will,
Daß du vor ihm die heil'ge Fahne tragest.
Du sollst dich schließen an der Fürsten Reih'n,
Die Nächste an ihm selber sollst du gehn;
Denn er verläugnet's nicht, und alle Welt
Soll es bezeugen, daß er dir allein
Die Ehre dieses Tages zuerkennt.

La Hire.

Hier ist die Fahne. Nimm sie, edle Jungfrau!
Die Fürsten warten, und es harrt das Volk.

Johanna.

Ich vor ihm herziehn? Ich die Fahne tragen?

Dunois.

Wem anders ziemt' es! Welche andre Hand
Ist rein genug, das Heiligthum zu tragen!
Du schwangst sie im Gefechte: trage sie
Zur Zierde nun auf diesem Weg der Freude.

(La Hire will ihr die Fahne überreichen, sie bebt schaudernd davor zurück.)

Johanna.

Hinweg! Hinweg!

La Hire.

   Was ist dir? Du erschrickst
Vor deiner eignen Fahne! — Sieh sie an!

   (Er rollt die Fahne auseinander.)

Es ist dieselbe, die du siegend schwangst.
Die Himmelskönigin ist drauf gebildet,
Die über einer Erdenkugel schwebt;
Denn also lehrte dich's die heil'ge Mutter.

Johanna (mit Entsetzen hinschauend).

Sie ist's! Sie selbst! Ganz so erschien sie mir.
Seht, wie sie herblickt und die Stirne faltet,
Zornglühend aus den finstern Wimpern schaut!

Sorel.

O, ſie iſt außer ſich! Komm zu dir ſelbſt!
Erkenne dich! Du ſiehſt nichts Wirkliches!
Das iſt ihr irdiſch nachgeahmtes Bild,
Sie ſelber wandelt in des Himmels Chören!

Johanna.

Furchtbare, kommſt du, dein Geſchöpf zu ſtrafen?
Verderbe, ſtrafe mich, nimm deine Blitze,
Und laß ſie fallen auf mein ſchuldig Haupt.
Gebrochen hab' ich meinen Bund, entweiht,
Geläſtert hab' ich deinen heil'gen Namen!

Dunois.

Weh uns! Was iſt das? Welch' unſel'ge Reden!

La Hire (erſtaunt zu Du Chatel).

Begreift ihr dieſe ſeltſame Bewegung?

Du Chatel.

Ich ſehe, was ich ſeh'. Ich hab' es längſt
Gefürchtet.

Dunois.

Wie? Was ſagt ihr?

Du Chatel.

Was ich denke,
Darf ich nicht ſagen. Wollte Gott, es wäre
Vorüber, und der König wär' gekrönt!

La Hire.

Wie? Hat der Schrecken, der von dieſer Fahne
Ausging, ſich auf dich ſelbſt zurück gewendet?
Den Britten laß vor dieſen Zeichen zittern,
Den Feinden Frankreichs iſt es fürchterlich,
Doch ſeinen treuen Bürgern iſt es gnädig.

Johanna.

Ja, du ſagſt recht; den Freunden iſt es hold,
Und auf die Feinde ſendet es Entſetzen!
(Man hört den Krönungsmarſch.)

Dunois.

So nimm die Fahne! Nimm sie! Sie beginnen
Den Zug, kein Augenblick ist zu verlieren!
(Sie bringen ihr die Fahne auf, sie ergreift sie mit heftigem Widerstreben und geht
ab, die Andern folgen.)

Die Scene verwandelt sich in einen freien Platz vor der Kathedralkirche.

Vierter Auftritt.

Zuschauer erfüllen den Hintergrund, aus ihnen heraus treten **Bertrand**,
Claude Marie und **Etienne** und kommen vorwärts; in der Folge
auch **Margot** und **Louison**. Der Krönungsmarsch erschallt gedämpft
aus der Ferne.

Bertrand.

Hört die Musik! Sie sind's! Sie nahen schon!
Was ist das Beste? Steigen wir hinauf
Auf die Platforme oder drängen uns
Durchs Volk, daß wir vom Aufzug nichts verlieren?

Etienne.

Es ist nicht durchzukommen. Alle Straßen sind
Von Menschen vollgedrängt zu Roß und Wagen.
Laßt uns hieher an diese Häuser treten:
Hier können wir den Zug gemächlich sehen,
Wenn er vorüber kommt.

Claude Marie.

Ist's doch, als ob
Halb Frankreich sich zusammen hier gefunden;
So allgewaltig ist die Flut, daß sie
Auch uns im fernen lothringischen Land
Hat aufgehoben und hieher gespült!

Bertrand.

Wer wird
In seinem Winkel müßig sitzen, wenn
Das Große sich begibt im Vaterland!
Es hat auch Schweiß und Blut genug gekostet,
Bis daß die Krone kam aufs rechte Haupt!
Und unser König, der der wahre ist,

Dem wir die Kron' itzt geben, soll nicht schlechter
Begleitet seyn, als der Pariser ihrer,
Den sie zu Saint Denis gekrönt! Der ist
Kein Wohlgesinnter, der von diesem Fest
Wegbleibt und nicht mitruft: Es lebe der König!

Fünfter Auftritt.

Margot und **Louison** treten zu ihnen.

Louison.

Wir werden unsre Schwester sehen, Margot!
Mir pocht das Herz.

Margot.

   Wir werden sie im Glanz
Und in der Hoheit sehn und zu uns sagen:
Es ist Johanna, es ist unsre Schwester!

Louison.

Ich kann's nicht glauben, bis ich sie mit Augen
Gesehn, daß diese Mächtige, die man
Die Jungfrau nennt von Orleans, unsre Schwester
Johanna ist, die uns verloren ging.

(Der Marsch kommt immer näher.)

Margot.

Du zweifelst noch? Du wirst's mit Augen sehn!

Bertrand.

Gebt acht! Sie kommen!

Sechster Auftritt.

Flötenspieler und **Hoboisten** eröffnen den Zug; **Kinder** folgen
weiß gekleidet, mit Zweigen in der Hand; hinter diesen zwei **Herolde**; darauf ein Zug von **Hellebardierern**, **Magistratspersonen** in
der Robe folgen; hierauf zwei **Marschälle** mit dem Stabe, **Herzog
von Burgund**, das Schwert tragend, **Dunois** mit dem Scepter, andere
Große mit der Krone, dem Reichsapfel und dem Gerichtsstabe, andere mit
Opfergaben; hinter diesen **Ritter** in ihrem Ordensschmuck; **Chorknaben** mit dem Rauchfaß, dann zwei **Bischöfe** mit der Ste. Ampoule, **Erzbischof** mit dem Crucifix; ihm folgt **Johanna** mit der Fahne. Sie geht

mit gesenktem Haupt und ungewissen Schritten, die Schwestern geben bei ihrem Anblick Zeichen des Erstaunens und der Freude.   Hinter ihr kommt der **König** unter einem Thronhimmel, welchen vier **Barone** tragen, Hofleute folgen, **Soldaten** schließen.   Wenn der Zug in die Kirche hinein ist, schweigt der Marsch.

Siebenter Auftritt.

**Louison. Margot. Claude Marie. Etienne.
Bertrand.**

Margot.

Sahst du die Schwester?

Claude Marie.

                    Die im goldnen Harnisch,
Die vor dem König herging mit der Fahne?

Margot.

Sie war's.   Es war Johanna, unsre Schwester!

Louison.

Und sie erkannt' uns nicht!   Sie ahnete
Die Nähe nicht der schwesterlichen Brust.
Sie sah zur Erde und erschien so blaß,
Und unter ihrer Fahne ging sie zitternd —
Ich konnte mich nicht freun, da ich sie sah.

Margot.

So hab' ich unsre Schwester nun im Glanz
Und in der Herrlichkeit gesehn. — Wer hätte
Auch nur im Traum geahnet und gedacht,
Da sie die Heerde trieb auf unsern Bergen,
Daß wir in solcher Pracht sie würden schaun.

Louison.

Der Traum des Vaters ist erfüllt, daß wir
Zu Rheims uns vor der Schwester würden neigen.
Das ist die Kirche, die der Vater sah
Im Traum, und Alles hat sich nun erfüllt.
Doch der Vater sah auch traurige Gesichte!
Ach, mich bekümmert's, sie so groß zu sehn!

Bertrand.

Was stehn wir müßig hier?   Kommt in die Kirche,
Die heil'ge Handlung anzusehn!

Margot.

Ja, kommt!
Vielleicht, daß wir der Schwester dort begegnen.

Louison.

Wir haben sie gesehen. Kehren wir
In unser Dorf zurück.

Margot.

Was? Eh' wir sie
Begrüßt und angeredet?

Louison.

Sie gehört
Uns nicht mehr an; bei Fürsten ist ihr Platz
Und Königen — Wer sind wir, daß wir uns
Zu ihrem Glanze rühmend eitel drängen?
Sie war uns fremd, da sie noch unser war!

Margot.

Wird sie sich unser schämen, uns verachten?

Bertrand.

Der König selber schämt sich unser nicht!
Er grüßte freundlich auch den Niedrigsten.
Sey sie so hoch gestiegen, als sie will,
Der König ist doch größer!

(Trompeten und Pauken erschallen aus der Kirche.)

Claude Marie.

Kommt zur Kirche!

(Sie eilen nach dem Hintergrunde, wo sie sich unter dem Volke verlieren.)

Achter Auftritt.

Thibaut kommt, schwarz gekleidet. Raimond folgt ihm und will ihn
zurücke halten.

Raimond.

Bleibt, Vater Thibaut, bleibt aus dem Gedränge
Zurück! Hier seht ihr lauter frohe Menschen,
Und euer Gram beleidigt dieses Fest.
Kommt! Fliehn wir aus der Stadt mit eil'gen Schritten.

Thibaut.

Sahst du mein unglückselig Kind? Hast du
Sie recht betrachtet?

Raimond.

O, ich bitt euch, flieht!

Thibaut.

Bemerkteft du, wie ihre Schritte wankten,
Wie bleich und wie verstört ihr Antlitz war!
Die Unglückselige fühlt ihren Zustand;
Das ist der Augenblick, mein Kind zu retten,
Ich will ihn nutzen.

(Er will gehen.)

Raimond.

Bleibt! Was wollt ihr thun?

Thibaut.

Ich will sie überraschen, will sie stürzen
Von ihrem eiteln Glück; ja, mit Gewalt
Will ich zu ihrem Gott, dem sie entsagt,
Zurück sie führen.

Raimond.

Ach, erwägt es wohl!
Stürzt euer eigen Kind nicht ins Verderben!

Thibaut.

Lebt ihre Seele nur, ihr Leib mag sterben.

Johanna stürzt aus der Kirche heraus ohne ihre Fahne; Volk dringt zu, adorirt sie
und küßt ihre Kleider, sie wird durch das Gedränge im Hintergrund aufgehalten.)

Sie kommt! Sie ist's! Bleich stürzt sie aus der Kirche,
Es treibt die Angst sie aus dem Heiligthum.
Das ist das göttliche Gericht, das sich
An ihr verkündiget!

Raimond.

Lebt wohl!
Verlangt nicht, daß ich länger euch begleite!
Ich kam voll Hoffnung und ich geh' voll Schmerz.
Ich habe eure Tochter wieder gesehn
Und fühle, daß ich sie auf's neu verliere.

(Er geht ab, Thibaut entfernt sich auf der entgegengesetzten Seite.)

Neunter Auftritt.

Johanna. Volk. Hernach ihre Schwestern.

Johanna

(hat sich des Volkes erwehrt und kommt vorwärts.)

Ich kann nicht bleiben — Geister jagen mich,
Wie Donner schallen mir der Orgel Töne,
Des Doms Gewölbe stürzen auf mich ein,
Des freien Himmels Weite muß ich suchen!
Die Fahne ließ ich in dem Heiligthum,
Nie, nie soll diese Hand sie mehr berühren!
Mir war's, als hätt' ich die geliebten Schwestern,
Margot und Louison, gleich einem Traum
An mir vorüber gleiten sehen. — Ach!
Es war nur eine täuschende Erscheinung!
Fern sind sie, fern und unerreichbar weit,
Wie meiner Kindheit, meiner Unschuld Glück!

Margot (hervortretend).

Sie ist's! Johanna ist's!

Louison (eilt ihr entgegen).

O, meine Schwester!

Johanna.

So war's kein Wahn — Ihr seyd es — Ich umfass' euch,
Dich, meine Louison! dich, meine Margot!
Hier in der fremden, menschenreichen Oede
Umfang' ich die vertraute Schwesterbrust!

Margot.

Sie kennt uns noch, ist noch die gute Schwester.

Johanna.

Und eure Liebe führt euch zu mir her
So weit, so weit! Ihr zürnt der Schwester nicht,
Die lieblos ohne Abschied euch verließ!

Louison.

Dich führte Gottes dunkle Schickung fort.

Margot.

Der Ruf von dir, der alle Welt bewegt,

Der deinen Namen trägt auf allen Zungen
Hat uns erweckt in unserm stillen Dorf
Und hergeführt zu dieses Festes Feier.
Wir kommen deine Herrlichkeit zu sehn,
Und wir sind nicht allein!

Johanna (schnell).

     Der Vater ist mit euch!
Wo, wo ist er? Warum verbirgt er sich?

Margot.

Der Vater ist nicht mit uns.

Johanna.

     Nicht? Er will sein Kind
Nicht sehn? Ihr bringt mir seinen Segen nicht?

Louison.

Er weiß nicht, daß wir hier sind.

Johanna.

     Weiß es nicht!
Warum nicht? — Ihr verwirret euch? Ihr schweigt
Und seht zur Erde! Sagt, wo ist der Vater?

Margot.

Seitdem du weg bist —

Louison (winkt ihr).

     Margot!

Margot.

     Ist der Vater
Schwermüthig worden.

Johanna.

     Schwermüthig!

Louison.

     Tröste dich!
Du kennst des Vaters ahnungsvolle Seele!
Er wird sich fassen, sich zufrieden geben,
Wenn wir ihm sagen, daß du glücklich bist.

Margot.

Du bist doch glücklich? Ja, du mußt es seyn,
Da du so groß bist und geehrt!

Johanna.

Ich bin's,
Da ich euch wieder sehe, eure Stimme
Vernehme, den geliebten Ton, mich heim
Erinnre an die väterliche Flur.
Da ich die Heerde trieb auf unsern Höhen,
Da war ich glücklich, wie im Paradies —
Kann ich's nicht wieder seyn, nicht wieder werden?

Sie verbirgt ihr Gesicht an Louisons Brust. (Claude Marie, Etienne und Bertrand zeigen sich und bleiben schüchtern in der Ferne stehen.)

Margot.

Kommt, Etienne! Bertrand! Claude Marie!
Die Schwester ist nicht stolz; sie ist so sanft
Und spricht so freundlich, als sie nie gethan,
Da sie noch in dem Dorf mit uns gelebt.

(Jene treten näher und wollen ihr die Hand reichen; Johanna sieht sie mit starren Blicken an und fällt in ein tiefes Staunen.)

Johanna.

Wo war ich? Sagt mir, war das Alles nur
Ein langer Traum, und ich bin aufgewacht?
Bin ich hinweg aus Dom Remi? Nicht wahr?
Ich war entschlafen unter'm Zauberbaum
Und bin erwacht, und ihr steht um mich her,
Die wohlbekannten traulichen Gestalten?
Mir hat von diesen Königen und Schlachten
Und Kriegesthaten nur geträumt — Es waren
Nur Schatten, die an mir vorüber gingen:
Denn lebhaft träumt sich's unter diesem Baum. —
Wie kämet ihr nach Rheims? Wie käm' ich selbst
Hieher? Nie, nie verließ ich Dom Remi!
Gesteht mir's offen und erfreut mein Herz.

Louison.

Wir sind zu Rheims. Dir hat von diesen Thaten
Nicht bloß geträumt; du hast sie alle wirklich
Vollbracht. — Erkenne dich, blick' um dich her.
Befühle deine glänzend goldne Rüstung!

(Johanna fährt mit der Hand nach der Brust, besinnt sich und erschrickt.)

Bertrand.
Aus meiner Hand empfangt ihr diesen Helm.

Claude Marie.
Es ist kein Wunder, daß ihr denkt zu träumen:
Denn was ihr ausgerichtet und gethan,
Kann sich im Traum nicht wunderbarer fügen.

Johanna (schnell).
Kommt, laßt uns fliehn! Ich geh' mit euch, ich kehre
In unser Dorf, in Vaters Schooß zurück.

Louison.
O, komm, komm mit uns!

Johanna.
Diese Menschen alle
Erheben mich weit über mein Verdienst!
Ihr habt mich kindisch, klein und schwach gesehn;
Ihr liebt mich, doch ihr betet mich nicht an!

Margot.
Du wolltest allen diesen Glanz verlassen?

Johanna.
Ich werf' ihn von mir, den verhaßten Schmuck,
Der euer Herz von meinem trennt,
Und eine Hirtin will ich wieder werden.
Wie eine niedere Magd will ich euch dienen,
Und büßen will ich's mit der strengsten Buße,
Daß ich mich eitel über euch erhob!
(Trompeten erschallen.)

Zehnter Auftritt.

Der König tritt aus der Kirche; er ist im Krönungsornat. Agnes
Sorel, Erzbischof, Burgund, Dunois, La Hire, Du
Chatel, Ritter, Hofleute und Volk.

Alle Stimmen
(rufen wiederholt, während der König vorwärts kommt.)
Es lebe der König, Karl der Siebente!
(Trompeten fallen ein. Auf ein Zeichen, das der König giebt, gebieten die Herolde
mit erhobenem Stabe Stillschweigen.)

König.

Mein gutes Volk, habt Dank für eure Liebe!
Die Krone, die uns Gott auf's Haupt gesetzt,
Durchs Schwert ward sie gewonnen und erobert,
Mit edlem Bürgerblut ist sie benetzt;
Doch friedlich soll der Oelzweig sie umgrünen.
Gedankt sey Allen, die für uns gefochten,
Und Allen, die uns widerstanden, sey
Verziehn, denn Gnade hat uns Gott erzeigt,
Und unser erstes Königswort sey — Gnade!

Volk.

Es lebe der König, Karl der Gütige!

König.

Von Gott allein, dem höchsten Herrschenden,
Empfangen Frankreichs Könige die Krone.
Wir aber haben sie sichtbarer Weise
Aus seiner Hand empfangen.

(Zur Jungfrau sich wendend.)

Hier steht die Gottgesendete, die euch
Den angestammten König wieder gab,
Das Joch der fremden Tyrannei zerbrochen!
Ihr Name soll dem heiligen Denis
Gleich seyn, der dieses Landes Schützer ist,
Und ein Altar sich ihrem Ruhm erheben!

Volk.

Heil, Heil der Jungfrau, der Erretterin!

(Trompeten.)

König (zur Johanna.)

Wenn du von Menschen bist gezeugt, wie wir,
So sage, welches Glück dich kann erfreuen?
Doch, wenn dein Vaterland dort oben ist,
Wenn du die Strahlen himmlischer Natur
In diesem jungfräulichen Leib verhüllst,
So nimm das Band hinweg von unsern Sinnen
Und laß dich sehn in deiner Lichtgestalt,

Wie dich der Himmel sieht, daß wir anbetend
Im Staube dich verehren.

(Ein allgemeines Stillschweigen; jedes Auge ist auf die Jungfrau gerichtet.)

Johanna (plötzlich aufschreiend.)

Gott! Mein Vater!

Eilfter Auftritt.

Thibaut tritt aus der Menge und steht ihr gerade gegenüber.

Mehrere Stimmen.

Ihr Vater!

Thibaut.

Ja, ihr jammervoller Vater,
Der die Unglückliche gezeugt, den Gottes
Gericht hertreibt, die eigne Tochter anzuklagen.

Burgund.

Ha! Was ist das!

Du Chatel.

Jetzt wird es schrecklich tagen!

Thibaut (zum König.)

Gerettet glaubst du dich durch Gottes Macht?
Betrogner Fürst! Verblendet Volk der Franken!
Du bist gerettet durch des Teufels Kunst.

(Alle treten mit Entsetzen zurück.)

Dunois.

Ras't dieser Mensch?

Thibaut.

Nicht ich, du aber rasest,
Und diese hier, und dieser weise Bischof,
Die glauben, daß der Herr der Himmel sich
Durch eine schlechte Magd verkünden werde.
Laß sehn, ob sie auch in des Vaters Stirn
Der dreisten Lüge Gaukelspiel behauptet,
Womit sie Volk und König hinterging.
Antworte mir im Namen des Dreieinen:
Gehörst du zu den Heiligen und Reinen?

(Allgemeine Stille; alle Blicke sind auf sie gespannt; sie steht unbeweglich.)

Sorel.

Gott, sie verstummt!

Thibaut.

Das muß sie vor dem furchtbarn Namen,
Der in der Hölle Tiefen selbst
Gefürchtet wird! — Sie eine Heilige,
Von Gott gesendet? — An verfluchter Stätte
Ward es ersonnen, unterm Zauberbaum,
Wo schon von Alters her die bösen Geister
Den Sabbath halten — Hier verkaufte sie
Dem Feind der Menschen ihr unsterblich Theil,
Daß er mit kurzem Weltruhm sie verherrliche.
Laßt sie den Arm aufstreifen, seht die Punkte,
Womit die Hölle sie gezeichnet hat!

Burgund.

Entsetzlich! — Doch dem Vater muß man glauben,
Der wider seine eigne Tochter zeugt.

Dunois.

Nein, nicht zu glauben ist dem Rasenden,
Der in dem eignen Kind sich selber schändet.

Sorel (zur Johanna.)

O, rede! Brich dies unglückfel'ge Schweigen!
Wir glauben dir! Wir trauen fest auf dich!
Ein Wort aus deinem Mund, ein einzig Wort
Soll uns genügen — Aber sprich! Vernichte
Die gräßliche Beschuldigung — Erkläre,
Du seyst unschuldig, und wir glauben dir.

(Johanna steht unbeweglich; Agnes Sorel tritt mit Entsetzen von ihr hinweg.)

La Hire.

Sie ist erschreckt. Erstaunen und Entsetzen
Schließt ihr den Mund. — Vor solcher gräßlichen
Anklage muß die Unschuld selbst erbeben.

(Er nähert sich ihr.)

Faß dich, Johanna. Fühle dich. Die Unschuld
Hat eine Sprache, einen Siegerblick,
Der die Verleumdung mächtig niederblitzt!
In edelm Zorn erhebe dich, blick auf,

8

Beschäme, strafe den unwürdigen Zweifel,
Der deine heil'ge Tugend schmäht.

<small>Janna steht unbeweglich. La Hire tritt entsetzt zurück; die Bewegung vermehrt
sich.)</small>

Dunois.

Was zagt das Volk? Was zittern selbst die Fürsten?
Sie ist unschuldig — Ich verbürge mich,
Ich selbst für sie mit meiner Fürstenehre.
Hier werf' ich meinen Ritterhandschuh hin;
Wer wagt's, sie eine Schuldige zu nennen?

<small>(Ein heftiger Donnerschlag; Alle stehen entsetzt.)</small>

Thibaut.

Antworte bei dem Gott, der droben donnert!
Sprich, du seyst schuldlos. Läugn' es, daß der Feind
In deinem Herzen ist, und straf' mich Lügen!

<small>(Ein zweiter stärkerer Schlag; das Volk entflieht zu allen Seiten.)</small>

Burgund.

Gott schütz' uns! Welche fürchterliche Zeichen!

Du Chatel <small>(zum König.)</small>

Kommt, kommt, mein König! Fliehet diesen Ort!

Erzbischof <small>(zu Johanna.)</small>

Im Namen Gottes frag' ich dich: Schweigst du
Aus dem Gefühl der Unschuld oder Schuld?
Wenn dieses Donners Stimme für dich zeugt,
So fasse dieses Kreuz und gib ein Zeichen!

<small>(Johanna bleibt unbeweglich. Neue heftige Donnerschläge. Der König, Agnes
Sorel, Erzbischof, Burgund, La Hire und Du Chatel gehen ab.)</small>

Zwölfter Auftritt.

<small>Dunois. Johanna.</small>

Dunois.

Du bist mein Weib — Ich hab' an dich geglaubt
Beim ersten Blick, und also denk' ich noch.
Dir glaub' ich mehr, als diesen Zeichen allen,
Als diesem Donner selbst, der droben spricht.
Du schweigst in edelm Zorn, verachtest es,

In deine heil'ge Unschuld eingehüllt,
So schändlichen Verdacht zu widerlegen.
— Veracht' es, aber mir vertraue dich:
An deiner Unschuld hab' ich nie gezweifelt.
Sag' mir kein Wort; die Hand nur reiche mir
Zum Pfand und Zeichen, daß du meinem Arme
Getrost vertraust und deiner guten Sache.

(Er reicht ihr die Hand hin, sie wendet sich mit einer zuckenden Bewegung von ihm hinweg; er bleibt in starrem Entsetzen stehen.)

Dreizehnter Auftritt.

Johanna. Du Chatel. Dunois. Zuletzt Raimond.

Du Chatel (zurückkommend).

Johanna d'Arc, der König will erlauben,
Daß ihr die Stadt verlasset ungekränkt.
Die Thore stehn euch offen. Fürchtet keine
Beleidigung. Euch schützt des Königs Frieden —
Folgt mir, Graf Dunois — Ihr habt nicht Ehre,
Hier länger zu verweilen. — Welch ein Ausgang!

(Er geht. Dunois fährt aus seiner Erstarrung auf, wirft noch einen Blick auf Johanna und geht ab. Diese steht einen Augenblick ganz allein. Endlich erscheint Raimond, bleibt eine Weile in der Ferne stehen und betrachtet sie mit stillem Schmerz. Dann tritt er auf sie zu und faßt sie bei der Hand.)

Raimond.

Ergreift den Augenblick! Die Straßen
Sind leer. Gebt mir die Hand! Ich will euch führen.

(Bei seinem Anblick gibt sie das erste Zeichen der Empfindung, sieht ihn starr an und blickt zum Himmel; dann ergreift sie ihn heftig bei der Hand und geht ab.)

Fünfter Aufzug.

Ein wilder Wald.

In der Ferne Köhlerhütten. Es ist ganz dunkel. Heftiges Donnern und Blitzen, dazwischen Schießen.

Erster Auftritt.

Köhler und Köhlerweib.

Köhler.

Das ist ein grausam mördrisch Ungewitter,
Der Himmel droht in Feuerbächen sich
Herabzugießen und am hellen Tag
Ist's Nacht, daß man die Sterne könnte sehn.
Wie eine losgelaff'ne Hölle tobt
Der Sturm, die Erde bebt, und krachend beugen
Die alt verjährten Eschen ihre Krone.
Und dieser fürchterliche Krieg dort oben,
Der auch die wilden Thiere Sanftmuth lehrt,
Daß sie sich zahm in ihre Gruben bergen,
Kann unter Menschen keinen Frieden stiften —
Aus dem Geheul der Winde und des Sturms
Heraus hört ihr das Knallen des Geschützes;
Die beiden Heere stehen sich so nah,
Daß nur der Wald sie trennt, und jede Stunde
Kann es sich blutig, fürchterlich entladen.

Köhlerweib.

Gott steh' uns bei! Die Feinde waren ja
Schon ganz aufs Haupt geschlagen und zerstreut.
Wie kommt's, daß sie aufs Neu' uns ängstigen?

Köhler.

Das macht, weil sie den König nicht mehr fürchten.
Seitdem das Mädchen eine Hexe ward

172

Zu Rheims, der böse Feind uns nicht mehr hilft,
Geht Alles rückwärts.

Köhlerweib.
Horch! Wer naht sich da?

Zweiter Auftritt.
Raimond und Johanna zu den Vorigen.

Raimond.
Hier seh' ich Hütten. Kommt, hier finden wir
Ein Obdach vor dem wüth'gen Sturm. Ihr haltet's
Nicht länger aus, drei Tage schon seyd ihr
Herumgeirrt, der Menschen Auge fliehend,
Und wilde Wurzeln waren eure Speise.

(Der Sturm legt sich, es wird hell und heiter.)

Es sind mitleid'ge Köhler. Kommt herein!

Köhler.
Ihr scheint der Ruhe zu bedürfen. Kommt!
Was unser schlechtes Dach vermag, ist euer.

Köhlerweib.
Was will die zarte Jungfrau unter Waffen?
Doch freilich! Jetzt ist eine schwere Zeit,
Wo auch das Weib sich in den Panzer steckt!
Die Königin selbst, Frau Isabeau, sagt man,
Läßt sich gewaffnet sehn in Feindes Lager,
Und eine Jungfrau, eines Schäfers Dirn',
Hat für den König unsern Herrn gefochten.

Köhler.
Was redet ihr? Geht in die Hütte, bringt
Der Jungfrau einen Becher zur Erquickung.

(Köhlerweib geht nach der Hütte.)

Raimond (zur Johanna).
Ihr seht, es sind nicht alle Menschen grausam;
Auch in der Wildniß wohnen sanfte Herzen.
Erheitert euch! Der Sturm hat ausgetobt,
Und friedlich strahlend geht die Sonne nieder.

Köhler.

Ich denk', ihr wollt zu unsers Königs Heer,
Weil ihr in Waffen reiset — Seht euch vor!
Die Engelländer stehen nah gelagert,
Und ihre Schaaren streifen durch den Wald.

Raimond.

Weh' uns!   Wo ist da zu entkommen?

Köhler.

Bleibt,
Bis daß mein Bub zurück ist aus der Stadt,
Der soll euch auf verborgnen Pfaden führen,
Daß ihr nichts zu befürchten habt.   Wir kennen
Die Schliche.

Raimond (zur Johanna).

Legt den Helm ab und die Rüstung;
Sie macht euch kenntlich und beschützt euch nicht.
(Johanna schüttelt den Kopf.)

Köhler.

Die Jungfrau ist sehr traurig — Still! Wer kommt da?

Dritter Auftritt.

Köhlerweib kommt aus der Hütte mit einem Becher. Köhlerbub.

Köhlerweib.

Es ist der Bub, den wir zurück erwarten.
(Zur Johanna.)
Trinkt, edle Jungfrau!   Mög's euch Gott gesegnen!

Köhler (zu seinem Sohn).

Kommst du, Anet?   Was bringst du?

Köhlerbub

(hat die Jungfrau ins Auge gefaßt, welche eben den Becher an den Mund setzt; er
erkennt sie, tritt auf sie zu und reißt ihr den Becher vom Munde).

Mutter! Mutter!
Was macht ihr? Wen bewirthet ihr? Das ist die Hexe
Von Orleans!

Köhler und Köhlerweib.

Gott sey uns gnädig!
(Bekreuzen sich und entfliehen.)

Vierter Auftritt.

Raimond. Johanna.

Johanna (gefaßt und sanft).

Du siehst, mir folgt der Fluch, und Alles flieht mich:
Sorg' für dich selber und verlaß mich auch.

Raimond.

Ich euch verlassen! jetzt! Und wer soll euer
Begleiter seyn?

Johanna.

Ich bin nicht unbegleitet.
Du hast den Donner über mir gehört.
Mein Schicksal führt mich. Sorge nicht, ich werde
An's Ziel gelangen, ohne daß ich's suche.

Raimond.

Wo wollt ihr hin? Hier stehn die Engelländer,
Die euch die grimmig blut'ge Rache schwuren —
Dort stehn die Unsern, die euch ausgestoßen,
Verbannt —

Johanna.

Mich wird nichts treffen, als was seyn muß.

Raimond.

Wer soll euch Nahrung suchen? Wer euch schützen
Vor wilden Thieren und noch wildern Menschen?
Euch pflegen, wenn ihr krank und elend werdet?

Johanna.

Ich kenne alle Kräuter, alle Wurzeln;
Von meinen Schafen lernt' ich das Gesunde
Vom Gift'gen unterscheiden — Ich verstehe
Den Lauf der Sterne und der Wolken Zug,
Und die verborg'nen Quellen hör' ich rauschen.
Der Mensch braucht wenig, und an Leben reich
Ist die Natur.

Raimond (faßt sie bei der Hand).

Wollt ihr nicht in euch gehn?

Euch nicht mit Gott versöhnen — in den Schooß
Der heil'gen Kirche reuend wiederkehren?

Johanna.

Auch du hältst mich der schweren Sünde schuldig?

Raimond.

Muß ich nicht? Euer schweigendes Geständniß —

Johanna.

Du, der mir in das Elend nachgefolgt,
Das einz'ge Wesen, das mir treu geblieben,
Sich an mich kettet, da mich alle Welt
Ausstieß, du hältst mich auch für die Verworfne,
Die ihrem Gott entsagt —

(Raimond schweigt.)

O, das ist hart!

Raimond (erstaunt).

Ihr wäret wirklich keine Zauberin?

Johanna.

Ich eine Zauberin!

Raimond.

Und diese Wunder,
Ihr hättet sie vollbracht mit Gottes Kraft
Und seiner Heiligen?

Johanna.

Mit welcher sonst?

Raimond.

Und ihr verstummtet auf die gräßliche
Beschuldigung? Ihr redet jetzt, und vor dem König,
Wo es zu reden galt, verstummtet ihr?

Johanna.

Ich unterwarf mich schweigend dem Geschick,
Das Gott, mein Meister, über mich verhängte.

Raimond.

Ihr konntet eurem Vater nichts erwiedern?

Johanna.

Weil es vom Vater kam, so kam's von Gott,
Und väterlich wird auch die Prüfung seyn.

Raimond.

Der Himmel selbst bezeugte eure Schuld!

Johanna.

Der Himmel sprach: drum schwieg ich.

Raimond.

Wie? Ihr konntet
Mit einem Wort euch reinigen, und ließt
Die Welt in diesem unglücksel'gen Irrthum?

Johanna.

Es war kein Irrthum, eine Schickung war's.

Raimond.

Ihr littet alle diese Schmach unschuldig,
Und keine Klage kam von euren Lippen!
— Ich staune über euch, ich steh' erschüttert;
Im tiefsten Busen kehrt sich mir das Herz!
O, gerne nehm' ich euer Wort für Wahrheit,
Denn schwer ward mir's, an eure Schuld zu glauben.
Doch konnt' ich träumen, daß ein menschlich Herz
Das Ungeheure schweigend würde tragen!

Johanna.

Verdient' ich's, die Gesendete zu seyn,
Wenn ich nicht blind des Meisters Willen ehrte?
Und ich bin nicht so elend, als du glaubst.
Ich leide Mangel, doch das ist kein Unglück
Für meinen Stand; ich bin verbannt und flüchtig,
Doch in der Oede lernt' ich mich erkennen.
Da, als der Ehre Schimmer mich umgab,
Da war der Streit in meiner Brust; ich war
Die Unglückseligste, da ich der Welt
Am meisten zu beneiden schien — Jetzt bin ich
Geheilt, und dieser Sturm in der Natur,
Der ihr das Ende drohte, war mein Freund:
Er hat die Welt gereinigt und auch mich.
In mir ist Friede — Komme, was da will,
Ich bin mir keiner Schwachheit mehr bewußt!

8*

Raimond.

O, kommt, kommt, laßt uns eilen, eure Unschuld
Laut, laut vor aller Welt zu offenbaren!

Johanna.

Der die Verwirrung sandte, wird sie lösen!
Nur, wenn sie reif ist, fällt des Schicksals Frucht!
Ein Tag wird kommen, der mich reiniget,
Und die mich jetzt verworfen und verdammt,
Sie werden ihres Wahnes inne werden,
Und Thränen werden meinem Schicksal fließen.

Raimond.

Ich sollte schweigend dulden, bis der Zufall —

Johanna (ihn sanft bei der Hand fassend).

Du siehst nur das Natürliche der Dinge,
Denn deinen Blick umhüllt das irb'sche Band.
Ich habe das Unsterbliche mit Augen
Gesehen — Ohne Götter fällt kein Haar
Vom Haupt des Menschen — Siehst du dort die Sonne
Am Himmel niedergehen — So gewiß
Sie morgen wiederkehrt in ihrer Klarheit,
So unausbleiblich kommt der Tag der Wahrheit!

Fünfter Auftritt.

Königin Isabeau mit **Soldaten** erscheint im Hintergrunde.

Isabeau (noch hinter der Scene).

Dies ist der Weg ins engelländ'sche Lager!

Raimond.

Weh' uns! Die Feinde!
(Soldaten treten auf, bemerken im Hervorkommen die Johanna und taumeln er=
schrocken zurück.)

Isabeau.

Nun! Was hält der Zug!

Soldaten.

Gott steh' uns bei!

Isabeau.

Erschreckt euch ein Gespenst?

Seyd ihr Soldaten? Memmen seyd ihr! Wie?
(Sie drängt sich durch die Andern, tritt hervor und fährt zurück, wie sie die Jungfrau erblickt.)

Was seh' ich! Ha!
(Schnell faßt sie sich und tritt ihr entgegen.)
Ergib dich! Du bist meine

Gefangene!

Johanna.

Ich bin's.
(Raimond entflieht mit Zeichen der Verzweiflung.)

Isabeau (zu den Soldaten).
Legt sie in Ketten!
Die Soldaten nahen sich der Jungfrau schüchtern; sie reicht den Arm hin und wird
gefesselt.)

Ist das die Mächtige, Gefürchtete,
Die eure Schaaren wie die Lämmer scheuchte,
Die jetzt sich selber nicht beschützen kann?
Thut sie nur Wunder, wo man Glauben hat,
Und wird zum Weib, wenn ihr ein Mann begegnet?
(Zur Jungfrau.)
Warum verließest du dein Heer? Wo bleibt
Graf Dunois, dein Ritter und Beschützer?

Johanna.

Ich bin verbannt.

Isabeau (erstaunt zurücktretend).
Was? Wie? Du bist verbannt?

Verbannt vom Dauphin?

Johanna.
Frage nicht! Ich bin
In deiner Macht, bestimme mein Geschick.

Isabeau.
Verbannt, weil du vom Abgrund ihn gerettet,
Die Krone ihm hast aufgesetzt zu Rheims,
Zum König über Frankreich ihn gemacht?
Verbannt! Daran erkenn' ich meinen Sohn!
— Führt sie ins Lager. Zeiget der Armee
Das Furchtgespenst, vor dem sie so gezittert!
Sie eine Zauberin? Ihr ganzer Zauber

Ist euer Wahn und euer feiges Herz!
Eine Närrin ist sie, die für ihren König
Sich opferte und jetzt den Königslohn
Dafür empfängt — Bringt sie zu Lionel —
Das Glück der Franken send' ich ihm gebunden;
Gleich folg' ich selbst.

Johanna.

Zu Lionel? Ermorde mich
Gleich hier, eh' du zu Lionel mich sendest.

Isabeau (zu den Soldaten).

Gehorchet dem Befehle! Fort mit ihr!

(Geht ab.)

Sechster Auftritt.

Johanna. Soldaten.

Johanna (zu den Soldaten).

Engländer! Duldet nicht, daß ich lebendig
Aus eurer Hand entkomme! Rächet euch!
Zieht eure Schwerter, taucht sie mir ins Herz,
Reißt mich entseelt zu eures Feldherrn Füßen!
Denkt, daß ich's war, die eure Trefflichsten
Getödtet, die kein Mitleid mit euch trug,
Die ganze Ströme engelländ'schen Bluts
Vergossen, euren Tapfern Heldensöhnen
Den Tag der frohen Wiederkehr geraubt!
Nehmt eine blut'ge Rache! Tödtet mich!
Ihr habt mich jetzt; nicht immer möchtet ihr
So schwach mich sehn —

Anführer der Soldaten.

Thut, was die Königin befahl!

Johanna.

Sollt' ich
Noch unglücksel'ger werden, als ich war!
Furchtbare Heil'ge! Deine Hand ist schwer!
Hast du mich ganz aus deiner Huld verstoßen?

Kein Gott erſcheint, kein Engel zeigt ſich mehr,
Die Wunder ruhn, der Himmel iſt verſchloſſen.
(Sie folgt den Soldaten.)

Das franzöſiſche Lager.

Siebenter Auftritt.

Dunois zwiſchen dem Erzbiſchof und Du Chatel.

Erzbiſchof.

Bezwinget euern finſtern Unmuth, Prinz!
Kommt mit uns! Kehrt zurück zu euerm König!
Verlaſſet nicht die allgemeine Sache
In dieſem Augenblick, da wir, aufs neu'
Bedränget, eures Heldenarms bedürfen.

Dunois.

Warum ſind wir bedrängt, warum erhebt
Der Feind ſich wieder? Alles war gethan,
Frankreich war ſiegend, und der Krieg geendigt.
Die Retterin habt ihr verbannt: nun rettet
Euch ſelbſt! Ich aber will das Lager
Nicht wieder ſehen, wo ſie nicht mehr iſt.

Du Chatel.

Nehmt beſſern Rath an, Prinz! Entlaßt uns nicht
Mit einer ſolchen Antwort!

Dunois.

       Schweigt, Du Chatel!
Ich haſſe euch, von euch will ich nichts hören:
Ihr ſeyd es, der zuerſt an ihr gezweifelt.

Erzbiſchof.

Wer ward nicht irr' an ihr und hätte nicht
Gewankt an dieſem unglückſel'gen Tage,
Da alle Zeichen gegen ſie bewieſen!
Wir waren überraſcht, betäubt; der Schlag
Traf zu erſchütternd unſer Herz — Wer konnte
In dieſer Schreckensſtunde prüfend wägen?
Jetzt kehrt uns die Beſonnenheit zurück:

Wir sehn sie, wie sie unter uns gewandelt,
Und keinen Tadel finden wir an ihr.
Wir sind verwirrt — Wir fürchten, schweres Unrecht
Gethan zu haben. — Reue fühlt der König,
Der Herzog klagt sich an, La Hire ist trostlos,
Und jedes Herz hüllt sich in Trauer ein.

Dunois.

Sie eine Lügnerin? Wenn sich die Wahrheit
Verkörpern will in sichtbarer Gestalt,
So muß sie ihre Züge an sich tragen!
Wenn Unschuld, Treue, Herzensreinigkeit
Auf Erden irgend wohnt — auf ihren Lippen,
In ihren klaren Augen muß sie wohnen!

Erzbischof.

Der Himmel schlage durch ein Wunder sich
Ins Mittel und erleuchte dies Geheimniß,
Das unser sterblich Auge nicht durchdringt —
Doch, wie sich's auch entwirren mag und lösen,
Eins von den Beiden haben wir verschuldet:
Wir haben uns mit höll'schen Zauberwaffen
Vertheidigt oder eine Heilige verbannt;
Und beides ruft des Himmels Zorn und Strafen
Herab auf dieses unglücksel'ge Land!

Achter Auftritt.

Ein Edelmann zu den Vorigen, hernach **Raimond.**

Edelmann.

Ein junger Schäfer fragt nach deiner Hoheit,
Er fordert dringend, mit dir selbst zu reden,
Er komme, sagt er, von der Jungfrau —

Dunois.

Eile!
Bring' ihn herein! Er kommt von ihr!
(Edelmann öffnet dem Raimond die Thür. Dunois eilt ihm entgegen.)
Wo ist sie?
Wo ist die Jungfrau?

Raimond.

Heil euch, edler Prinz!
Und Heil mir, daß ich diesen frommen Bischof,
Den heil'gen Mann, den Schirm der Unterdrückten,
Den Vater der Verlaff'nen bei euch finde!

Dunois.

Wo ist die Jungfrau?

Erzbischof.

Sag' es uns, mein Sohn!

Raimond.

Herr, sie ist keine schwarze Zauberin!
Bei Gott und allen Heiligen bezeug' ich's.
Im Irrthum ist das Volk. Ihr habt die Unschuld
Verbannt, die Gottgesendete verstoßen!

Dunois.

Wo ist sie? Sage!

Raimond.

Ihr Gefährte war ich
Auf ihrer Flucht in dem Ardennerwald;
Mir hat sie dort ihr Innerstes gebeichtet.
In Martern will ich sterben, meine Seele
Hab' keinen Antheil an dem ew'gen Heil,
Wenn sie nicht rein ist, Herr, von aller Schuld!

Dunois.

Die Sonne selbst am Himmel ist nicht reiner!
Wo ist sie? Sprich!

Raimond.

O, wenn euch Gott das Herz
Gewendet hat — so eilt, so rettet sie!
Sie ist gefangen bei den Engelländern.

Dunois.

Gefangen? Was?

Erzbischof.

Die Unglückselige!

Raimond.

In den Ardennen, wo wir Obdach suchten,
Ward sie ergriffen von der Königin
Und in der Engelländer Hand geliefert.
O, rettet sie, die euch gerettet hat,
Von einem grausenvollen Tode!

Dunois.

Zu den Waffen! Auf! Schlagt Lärmen! Rührt die
Trommeln!
Führt alle Völker ins Gefecht! Ganz Frankreich
Bewaffne sich! Die Ehre ist verpfändet,
Die Krone, das Palladium entwendet.
Setzt alles Blut, setzt euer Leben ein!
Frei muß sie seyn, noch eh' der Tag sich endet!

(Gehen ab.)

Ein Wartthurm, oben eine Oeffnung.

Neunter Auftritt.

Johanna und Lionel.

Fastolf (eilig hereintretend).

Das Volk ist länger nicht zu bändigen.
Sie fordern wüthend, daß die Jungfrau sterbe.
Ihr widersteht vergebens. Tödtet sie
Und werft ihr Haupt von dieses Thurmes Zinnen.
Ihr fließend Blut allein versöhnt das Heer.

Isabeau (kommt).

Sie setzen Leitern an, sie laufen Sturm!
Befriediget das Volk. Wollt ihr erwarten,
Bis sie den ganzen Thurm in blinder Wuth
Umkehren, und wir Alle mit verderben?
Ihr könnt sie nicht beschützen. Gebt sie hin.

Lionel.

Laßt sie anstürmen! Laßt sie wüthend toben!
Dies Schloß ist fest, und unter seinen Trümmern
Begrab' ich mich, eh' mich ihr Wille zwingt.

— Antworte mir, Johanna! Sey die Meine,
Und gegen eine Welt beschütz' ich dich.

Isabeau.

Seyd ihr ein Mann?

Lionel.

Verstoßen haben dich
Die Deinen: aller Pflichten bist du ledig
Für dein unwürdig Vaterland. Die Feigen,
Die um dich warben, sie verließen dich;
Sie wagten nicht den Kampf um deine Ehre.
Ich aber, gegen mein Volk und das deine
Behaupt' ich dich. — Einst ließest du mich glauben,
Daß dir mein Leben theuer sey! Und damals
Stand ich im Kampf als Feind dir gegenüber;
Jetzt hast du keinen Freund, als mich!

Johanna.

Du bist
Der Feind mir, der verhaßte, meines Volks.
Nichts kann gemein seyn zwischen dir und mir.
Nicht lieben kann ich dich; doch wenn dein Herz
Sich zu mir neigt, so laßt es Segen bringen
Für unsre Völker. — Führe deine Heere
Hinweg von meines Vaterlandes Boden,
Die Schlüssel aller Städte gib heraus,
Die ihr bezwungen, allen Raub vergüte,
Gib die Gefangnen ledig, sende Geiseln
Des heiligen Vertrags, so biet' ich dir
Den Frieden an in meines Königs Namen.

Isabeau.

Willst du in Banden uns Gesetze geben?

Johanna.

Thu' es bei Zeiten, denn du mußt es doch.
Frankreich wird nimmer Englands Fesseln tragen.
Nie, nie wird das geschehen! Eher wird es
Ein weites Grab für eure Heere seyn.
Gefallen sind euch eure Besten, denkt

Auf eine ſichre Rückkehr; euer Ruhm
Iſt doch verloren, eure Macht iſt hin.

Iſabeau.

Könnt ihr den Trotz der Raſenden ertragen?

Zehnter Auftritt.

Ein Hauptmann kommt eilig.

Hauptmann.

Eilt, Feldherr, eilt, das Heer zur Schlacht zu ſtellen!
Die Franken rücken an mit fliegenden Fahnen;
Von ihren Waffen blitzt das ganze Thal.

Johanna (begeiſtert).

Die Franken rücken an! Jetzt, ſtolzes England,
Heraus ins Feld! Jetzt gilt es, friſch zu fechten!

Faſtolf.

Unſinnige, bezähme deine Freude!
Du wirſt das Ende dieſes Tags nicht ſehn.

Johanna.

Mein Volk wird ſiegen und ich werde ſterben!
Die Tapfern brauchen meines Arms nicht mehr.

Lionel.

Ich ſpotte dieſer Weichlinge. Wir haben
Sie vor uns hergeſcheucht in zwanzig Schlachten,
Eh' dieſes Heldenmädchen für ſie ſtritt!
Das ganze Volk veracht' ich bis auf Eine,
Und dieſe haben ſie verbannt. — Kommt, Faſtolf,
Wir wollen ihnen einen zweiten Tag
Bei Crequi und Poitiers bereiten.
Ihr, Königin, bleibt in dieſem Thurm, bewacht
Die Jungfrau, bis das Treffen ſich entſchieden;
Ich laſſ' euch fünfzig Ritter zur Bedeckung.

Faſtolf.

Was? Sollen wir dem Feind entgegen gehn,
Und dieſe Wüthende im Rücken laſſen?

Johanna.

Erschreckt dich ein gefesselt Weib?

Lionel.

Gib mir

Dein Wort, Johanna, dich nicht zu befreien!

Johanna.

Mich zu befreien ist mein einz'ger Wunsch.

Isabeau.

Legt ihr dreifache Fesseln an! Mein Leben
Verbürg' ich, daß sie nicht entkommen soll.

(Sie wird mit schweren Ketten um den Leib und um die Arme gefesselt.)

Lionel (zur Johanna).

Du willst es so! Du zwingst uns! Noch steht's bei dir!
Entsage Frankreich, trage Englands Fahne,
Und du bist frei, und diese Wüthenden,
Die jetzt dein Blut verlangen, dienen dir.

Fastolf (dringend).

Fort, fort, mein Feldherr!

Johanna.

Spare deine Worte!

Die Franken rücken an. Vertheid'ge dich!

(Trompeten ertönen. Lionel eilt fort.)

Fastolf.

Ihr wißt, was ihr zu thun habt, Königin!
Erklärt das Glück sich gegen uns, seht ihr,
Daß unsre Völker fliehen —

Isabeau (einen Dolch ziehend).

Sorget nicht,

Sie soll nicht leben, unsern Fall zu sehn.

Fastolf (zur Johanna).

Du weißt, was dich erwartet. Jetzt erflehe
Glück für die Waffen deines Volks!

(Er geht ab.)

Eilfter Auftritt.

Isabeau. Johanna. Soldaten.

Johanna.

Das will ich!
Daran soll Niemand mich verhindern — Horch!
Das ist der Kriegsmarsch meines Volks! Wie muthig
Er in das Herz mir schallt und siegverkündend!
Verderben über England! Sieg den Franken!
Auf, meine Tapfern! Auf! Die Jungfrau ist
Euch nah: sie kann nicht vor euch her, wie sonst,
Die Fahne tragen — schwere Bande fesseln sie;
Doch frei aus ihrem Kerker schwingt die Seele
Sich auf den Flügeln eures Kriegsgesangs.

Isabeau (zu einem Soldaten).

Steig' auf die Warte dort, die nach dem Feld
Hin sieht, und sag' uns, wie die Schlacht sich wendet.

(Soldat steigt hinauf.)

Johanna.

Muth, Muth, mein Volk! Es ist der letzte Kampf!
Den einen Sieg noch und der Feind liegt nieder!

Isabeau.

Was siehest du?

Soldat.

Schon sind sie an einander.
Ein Wüthender auf einem Barberroß,
Im Tigerfell, sprengt vor mit den Gensdarmen.

Johanna.

Das ist Graf Dunois! Frisch, wackrer Streiter!
Der Sieg ist mit dir!

Soldat.

Der Burgunder greift
Die Brücke an.

Isabeau.

Daß zehen Lanzen ihm
Ins falsche Herz eindrängen, dem Verräther!

Soldat.

Lord Fastolf thut ihm mannhaft Widerstand.
Sie sitzen ab, sie kämpfen Mann für Mann,
Des Herzogs Leute und die unsrigen.

Isabeau.

Siehst du den Dauphin nicht? Erkennst du nicht
Die königlichen Zeichen?

Soldat.

Alles ist
In Staub vermengt. Ich kann nichts unterscheiden.

Johanna.

Hätt' er mein Auge, oder stünd' ich oben,
Das Kleinste nicht entginge meinem Blick!
Das wilde Huhn kann ich im Fluge zählen,
Den Falk erkenn' ich in den höchsten Lüften.

Soldat.

Am Graben ist ein fürchterlich Gedräng;
Die Größten, scheint's, die Ersten kämpfen dort.

Isabeau.

Schwebt unsre Fahne noch?

Soldat.

Hoch flattert sie.

Johanna.

Könnt' ich nur durch der Mauer Ritze schauen,
Mit meinem Blick wollt' ich die Schlacht regieren!

Soldat.

Weh' mir, was seh' ich! Unser Feldherr ist
Umzingelt!

Isabeau (zuckt den Dolch auf Johanna).

Stirb, Unglückliche!

Soldat (schnell).

Er ist befreit.
Im Rücken faßt der tapfre Fastolf
Den Feind — er bricht in seine dichtsten Schaaren.

Isabeau (zieht den Dolch zurück).

Das sprach dein Engel!

Soldat.

Sieg! Sieg! Sie entfliehen!

Isabeau.

Wer flieht?

Soldat.

Die Franken, die Burgunder fliehn.
Bedeckt mit Flüchtigen ist das Gefilde.

Johanna.

Gott! Gott! So sehr wirst du mich nicht verlassen!

Soldat.

Ein schwer Verwundeter wird dort geführt.
Viel Volk springt ihm zu Hülf', es ist ein Fürst.

Isabeau.

Der Unsern Einer oder Fränkischen?

Soldat.

Sie lösen ihm den Helm; Graf Dunois ist's.

Johanna

(greift mit krampfhafter Anstrengung in ihre Ketten.)

Und ich bin nichts als ein gefesselt Weib!

Soldat.

Sieh! Halt! Wer trägt den himmelblauen Mantel,
Verbrämt mit Gold?

Johanna (lebhaft).

Das ist mein Herr, der König!

Soldat.

Sein Roß wird scheu — es überschlägt sich — stürzt —
Er windet schwer arbeitend sich hervor —

(Johanna begleitet diese Worte mit leidenschaftlichen Bewegungen.)

Die Unsern nahen schon in vollem Lauf —
Sie haben ihn erreicht — umringen ihn —

Johanna.

O, hat der Himmel keine Engel mehr?

Isabeau (hohnlachend).

Jetzt ist es Zeit! Jetzt, Retterin, errette!

Johanna
(stürzt auf die Knie, mit gewaltsam heftiger Stimme betend).

Höre mich, Gott, in meiner höchsten Noth!
Hinauf zu dir, in heißem Flehenswunsch,
In deine Himmel send' ich meine Seele.
Du kannst die Fäden eines Spinngewebs
Stark machen, wie die Taue eines Schiffs;
Leicht ist es deiner Allmacht, ehrne Bande
In dünnes Spinngewebe zu verwandeln —
Du willst, und diese Ketten fallen ab,
Und diese Thurmwand spaltet sich — Du halfst
Dem Simson, da er blind war und gefesselt
Und seiner stolzen Feinde bittern Spott
Erduldete. — Auf dich vertrauend faßt' er
Die Pfosten seines Kerkers mächtig an
Und neigte sich und stürzte das Gebäude —

Soldat.
Triumph! Triumph!

Isabeau.
Was ist's?

Soldat.
Der König ist
Gefangen!

Johanna (springt auf.)
So sey Gott mir gnädig!

(Sie hat ihre Ketten mit beiden Händen kraftvoll gefaßt und zerissen. In demselben Augenblick stürzt sie sich auf den nächststehenden Soldaten, entreißt ihm sein
Schwert und eilt hinaus. Alle sehen ihr mit starrem Erstaunen nach.)

Zwölfter Auftritt.
Vorige ohne Johanna.

Isabeau (nach einer langen Pause.)

Was war das? Träumte mir? Wo kam sie hin?
Wie brach sie diese zentnerschweren Bande?
Nicht glauben würd' ich's einer ganzen Welt,
Hätt' ich's nicht selbst gesehn mit meinen Augen.

Soldat (auf der Warte.)

Wie? Hat sie Flügel? Hat der Sturmwind sie
Hinabgeführt?

Isabeau.

Sprich, ist sie unten?

Soldat.

Mitten

Im Kampfe schreitet sie — Ihr Lauf ist schneller,
Als mein Gesicht — Jetzt ist sie hier — jetzt dort —
Ich sehe sie zugleich an vielen Orten!
— Sie theilt die Haufen — Alles weicht vor ihr;
Die Franken stehn, sie stellen sich aufs neu'!
— Weh mir! Was seh' ich! Unsre Völker werfen
Die Waffen von sich, unsre Fahnen sinken —

Isabeau.

Was? Will sie uns den sichern Sieg entreißen?

Soldat.

Grad' auf den König dringt sie an — Sie hat ihn
Erreicht — Sie reißt ihn mächtig aus dem Kampf.
— Lord Fastolf stürzt — Der Feldherr ist gefangen.

Isabeau.

Ich will nicht weiter hören. Komm herab!

Soldat.

Flieht, Königin! Ihr werdet überfallen.
Gewaffnet Volk dringt an den Thurm heran.

(Er steigt herunter.)

Isabeau (das Schwert ziehend.)

So fechtet, Memmen!

Dreizehnter Auftritt.

La Hire mit Soldaten kommt. Bei seinem Eintritt streckt das Volk
der Königin die Waffen.

La Hire (naht ihr ehrerbietig.)

Königin, unterwerft euch
Der Allmacht — Eure Ritter haben sich

Ergeben, aller Widerstand ist unnütz!
— Nehmt meine Dienste an.   Befehlt, wohin
Ihr wollt begleitet seyn.

Isabeau.
Jedweder Ort
Gilt gleich, wo ich dem Dauphin nicht begegne.
(Gibt ihr Schwert ab und folgt ihm mit den Soldaten).

Die Scene verwandelt sich in das Schlachtfeld.

Vierzehnter Auftritt.

Soldaten mit fliegenden Fahnen erfüllen den Hintergrund.   Vor ihnen der **König** und der **Herzog von Burgund**; in den Armen beider Fürsten liegt **Johanna**, tödlich verwundet, ohne Zeichen des Lebens.   Sie treten langsam vorwärts. **Agnes Sorel** stürzt herein.

Sorel (wirft sich an des Königs Brust.)
Ihr seyd befreit — Ihr lebt — Ich hab' euch wieder!

König.
Ich bin befreit — Ich bin's um diesen Preis!
(Zeigt auf Johanna.)

Sorel.
Johanna! Gott! Sie stirbt!

Burgund.
Sie hat geendet!
Seht einen Engel scheiden!   Seht, wie sie daliegt,
Schmerzlos und ruhig, wie ein schlafend Kind!
Des Himmels Friede spielt um ihre Züge;
Kein Athem hebt den Busen mehr, doch Leben
Ist noch zu spüren in der warmen Hand.

König.
Sie ist dahin — Sie wird nicht mehr erwachen,
Ihr Auge wird das Ird'sche nicht mehr schauen.
Schon schwebt sie droben, ein verklärter Geist,
Sieht unsern Schmerz nicht mehr und unsre Reue.

Sorel.
Sie schlägt die Augen auf, sie lebt!
9

Burgund (erstaunt.)

Kehrt sie

Uns aus dem Grab zurück? Zwingt sie den Tod?
Sie richtet sich empor! Sie steht!

Johanna
(steht ganz aufgerichtet und schaut umher.)

Wo bin ich?

Burgund.

Bei deinem Volk, Johanna, bei den Deinen!

König.

In deiner Freunde, deines Königs Armen!

Johanna
(nachdem sie ihn lange starr angesehen.)

Nein, ich bin keine Zauberin! Gewiß,
Ich bin's nicht.

König.

Du bist heilig, wie ein Engel;
Doch unser Auge war mit Nacht bedeckt.

Johanna (sieht lächelnd umher.)

Und ich bin wirklich unter meinem Volk
Und bin nicht mehr verachtet und verstoßen?
Man flucht mir nicht, man sieht mich gütig an?
— Ja, jetzt erkenn' ich deutlich Alles wieder!
Das ist mein König! Das sind Frankreichs Fahnen!
Doch meine Fahne seh' ich nicht — Wo ist sie?
Nicht ohne meine Fahne darf ich kommen;
Von meinem Meister ward sie mir vertraut,
Vor seinem Thron muß ich sie niederlegen;
Ich darf sie zeigen, denn ich trug sie treu.

König (mit abgewandtem Gesicht.)

Gebt ihr die Fahne!
(Man reicht sie ihr. Sie steht ganz frei aufgerichtet, die Fahne in der Hand. —
Der Himmel ist von einem rosigten Scheine beleuchtet.)

Johanna.

Seht ihr den Regenbogen in der Luft?
Der Himmel öffnet seine goldnen Thore,
Im Chor der Engel steht sie glänzend da,

Sie hält den ew'gen Sohn an ihrer Brust,
Die Arme streckt sie lächelnd mir entgegen.
Wie wird mir? — Leichte Wolken heben mich —
Der schwere Panzer wird zum Flügelkleide.
Hinauf — hinauf — die Erde flieht zurück —
Kurz ist der Schmerz, und ewig ist die Freude!

(Die Fahne entfällt ihr, sie sinkt todt darauf nieder. — Alle stehen lange in sprach-
loser Rührung. — Auf einen leisen Wink des Königs werden alle Fahnen auf sie
niedergelassen, daß sie ganz davon bedeckt wird.)

ADDITIONAL NOTES ON THE MAID OF ORLEANS.

Page 47. The foreign (proper) names are generally to be pronounced, as they are in the original languages, and have the same number of syllables: e. g. Thibaut (´) ; La Hire (ᴗ -´); Dauphin (-´ ᴗ); Maire (-´); Sire (-´), p. 68. v. 7; Etienne (-´ ᴗ -) p. 48, v. 3; Orleans (-´ ᴗ -); Connetable (-´ ᴗ -ᴗ) p. 63; Saint Denis (-´ ᴗ -) p. 74. v. 10; Claude Marie (- ᴗ -´) p. 48, v. 6, &c. &c.—In some words the poet, however, has germanized the pronunciation, for the sake of the measure: e. g. Loire (ᴗ -´) p. 78, v. 13; p. 80, v. 3; Dulois (-´ ᴗ -) p. 77. v. 6; Dunois (-´ ᴗ -) p. 79, v. 28; p. 179, v. 10; Jeanette (ᴗ -´ ᴗ) p. 49, v. 1; Oriflamme (-´ ᴗ -ᴗ) p. 62, v. 3.—The name Du Chatel is (-´ ᴗ -) on page 64, v. 14. and (ᴗ -´ ᴗ) on pp. 72, v. 12; 121, v. 14; 128, v. 2. The name of the river Yonne on page 83, v. 18 is a dissyllable (ᴗ -´).—In general, the course of the metrical line will be the best guide to the reader.—In regard to the family-name of the Maid, Michelet maintains that its original form was *Darc* and not *d'Arc.*

P. 47, v. 5. The form Engelländer is prolonged for the sake of the measure and = Engländer. For the same reason Engelland for England; engelländisch and engländisch for englisch in other passages.—On the adverbial genitive aller Arten (in all places, every where) which occurs often in the drama, see Gram. § 51.—On the frequent elision of the (e) in infinitive and plural terminations, e. g. sehn, Höhn, for sehen, Höhen, and on other euphonic omissions of that vowel, cf. Gram. § 141, Rem. 3 & 4 ; § 60, § 64, § 94. In regard to the entire omission of the adjective-termination (equally frequent), e. g. sieghaft(es) Banner, unbegreiflich(es) Glück ꝛc., see Gram. § 60, Obs. 2d, case 2d

Page 96, v. 17. Notice the syntactical peculiarity:— w a r e n wir allein, instead of w ä r e n wir allein g e w e s e n. The Imperf. Indic. is thus sometimes used in a conditional sense, instead of the plup. subj. when the conjunction is omitted. So in v. 1, p 97:—Ihr s a h e t nie den Rauch — — — aufsteigen, for Ihr h ä t t e t nie g e s e h n d. R. aufsteigen u s. w. And in another play:—Maria Stuart w a r (= wäre) heut noch frei, wenn ich es nicht verhindert (hätte). This is a latinizing construction, and in German perhaps only admissible in poetry. Thus *Longe utilius* fuit (= fuisset), *angustias aditus occupare* (Curtius). *Germanicus ferrum a latere deripuit, elatumque* deferebat *in pectus (would have plunged* it into his heart, had not, &c.), ni *proximi prensam dextram vi* attinuissent (Tacit. **Annal.** 1, 35). In Greek the preterite indicative with εἰ and ἂν is the regular conditional form in certain cases, e. g. εἰ τοῦτο ἔλεγες, ἡμάρτανες ἄν, si hoc diceres, errares. So also in the French *Si je* pouvais, *je le ferais bien.* Compare Heyse's Ausf. Lehrb. d. deutsch. Spr. p. 771; Zumpt's Lat. Gram § 519; Kühner's Ausführl. Griech. Gram. § 451

Page 69, *v.* 9. Die fchott'fchen Völfer, ꝛc.—These were the companies of archers, which Charles had hired with the hope of coping with English forces of that description, who in the battles of Cressy, Poitiers, Agincourt, Crevant and Verneuil had decided the contest. In all these engagements the French archers had been inferior to those of the enemy. Hence the present necessity for foreign mercenaries, and the subsequent organization of the *francs archers* (1448), a class of troops more carefully selected and better paid than the rest.

Page 113, *v.* 8. Die burgunbifche Binde. What distinctive badge (band or fillet) the poet here refers to, I have not been able to ascertain, unless he alludes to that of the order of the Golden Fleece, which was founded by this Duke in 1430, and of which he was the first Grand Master. The ordinary decoration (at a later period, however,) consisted of a red silk ribbon, to which the golden fleece was attached; the gala-decoration was a golden chain and fleece.

Page 159, *2d line from below.* Zwei Bifchöfe mit der St. Ampoule. This was the celebrated Ampulla Remensis, called by the French *la sainte ampoule* (the sacred ampulla or phial), which, according to the legendary account, was brought down from heaven by a dove at the coronation of Clovis I., which took place at Rheims in the year 496. With its neverfailing oil all the subsequent Kings of France were anointed down to Louis XVI. During the Revolution the vessel was broken. A fragment of it, however, together with a portion of the oil was saved by a believer and sent to the Archbishop of Rheims, who in the year 1825 again applied the virtuous unguent to the anointment of Charles X.

Page 188, *v.* 17. Sprengt vor mit den Gendarmen.—The term *gens d'armes* (= *gens armata*, men-at-arms) was originally used to designate the masses of armed men generally. In the 15th and 16th centuries (and in the passage) it was exclusively applied to the heavy cavalry, which being equipped with helmets, cuirasses, pistols, mailed horses, &c. constituted the main strength of the army. At the time of the Revolution this gendarmerie-corps was abolished and the term applied to a military police-corps (both horse and foot), charged with safety of the public roads, &c. This latter organization, together with the name, has also been adopted by several German states.

IPHIGENIA IN TAURIS:

A DRAMA

BY

GOETHE.

197

Κρόκου βαφὰς δ' ἐς πέδον χέουσα,
ἔβαλλ' ἕκαττον θυτήρων ἀπ' ὄμματος βέλει φιλοίκτῳ,
πρέπουσά 9' ὡς ἐν γραφαῖς, προσεννέπειν
9έλουσ', ἐπεὶ πολλάκις
πατρός κατ' ἀνδρῶνας εὐτραπέζους
ἔμελψεν · ἁγνὰ δ' ἀταύρωτος αὐδᾷ πατρὸς
φίλου τριτόσπονδον εὔποτμον
αἰῶνα φίλως ἐτίμα.

ÆSCHYLOS AGAMEMNON, (v. 216—223.)

TRANSLATION.—And as she poured the saffron's dye upon the ground, she smote each of her immolators with a pity-moving shaft from her bright eye: beautiful as the artistic figure of a picture, desiring yet to speak to them, as often she had done, when in the father's sumptuous banquet-halls she sung to them. For the sacred spotless maid was fond of celebrating with her voice the happy lot of her beloved parent, while Jupiter received the third libation

198

INTRODUCTION

TO

GOETHE'S IPHIGENIA IN TAURIS.

I. THE LEGEND OF IPHIGENIA.

IPHIGENIA was the daughter of Agamemnon and Klytemnestra.
A less generally received legend makes her the daughter of Theseus and Helen, adopted by Klytemnestra. (Cf. p. 207, Note †).
When the Grecian fleet had assembled at Aulis on its way to
Troy, it was detained by adverse winds sent by Diana, whom
Agamemnon had enraged by killing in the chase a stag sacred to
that goddess. In this embarrassment Kalchas declared, that the
anger of the goddess could only be appeased by the immolation of
the offender's daughter, and the impatient army, weary of the
long detention, loudly demanded the victim for the sacrifice, to
which Agamemnon himself at last reluctantly consented. Under
the pretence of desiring to wed her to Achilles, he sent for her to
Mycenæ; but when she had arrived at Aulis, he led her to the
altar. At the moment, however, when the sacrificial knife was
raised to pierce her bosom, she dissappeared all of a sudden, and
in her place appeared a hind, the blood of which now streamed
upon the altar. Diana being moved with pity towards the victim-
princess, translated her in a cloud to Tauris, where she made her
priestess in her temple. The inhuman custom of the Tauri to
sacrifice all strangers to Diana, made it the duty of the priestess
to consecrate the victims, and to initiate the sacrifice. Meanwhile Orestes, who was pursued by the furies of his mother,
arrived, with the intent of robbing the image of the goddess, as he
had been commanded to do by the oracle at Delphi, which had
made this act the condition of his liberation from the curses of
Klytemnestra. When Orestes and Pylades, his bosom-friend,
were led before the altar, Iphigenia, recognizing her brother, at

199

once embraced his offer to reconduct her to her native Hellas. They safely arrived, together with the image, at Brauron near Marathon, where Iphigenia died as priestess.) According to other accounts she did not die at all, but was changed into Hecate. By a third legend Diana endowed her with immortality and eternal youth; and under the name of Oreilochia, she became the consort of Achilles, on the isle of Leuke. (The story of Iphigenia in Tauris and of her subsequent cultus in Greece is post-homeric.)

Euripides has made the legend the subject of two dramas, and both his Iphigenia Aulica and his Iphigenia Taurica have come down to us entire. Among the modern poets Racine and Goethe, both with hellenizing purposes, and each with different success, have chosen, the one the former, the other the latter of these original plays, as the prototypes of their new dramatic treatment of the story. (To show how widely the work of Goethe differs from that of Euripides, not only in the *ensemble* of the action, but in so many of the incidents, collisions, motives and in the dénouement itself, the argument of both dramas is here submitted to the comparison of the reader.

II. PARALLELISM BETWEEN THE IPHIGENIA OF EURIPIDES AND THAT OF GOETHE.

EURIPIDES.

Act I. (v. 1—236.)

THE drama begins as usual, with a prologue, here in the form of a monologue, wherein Iphigenia gives a brief exposition of her origin, of her treacherous and cruel treatment at Aulis, of her wonderful deliverance from the hands of her immolators, and of her miraculous translation to Tauris, where now she serves as priestess in the temple of the goddess, to whom she is indebted for her preservation. But in her present situation she does not altogether feel at ease. The goddess takes delight in sacrifices and in festivals, of which the name alone is honorable,* and there are things, which out of reverence towards the deity she passes over in silence. By the strict order of the King she is bound to perpetuate the ancient barbarous custom of dooming to the altar every stranger of Grecian origin whom chance had landed on the inhospitable shore, and to initiate herself to the horrid sacrifice which her ministers complete within the temple. It is for these reasons, that her present lot afflicts her with a silent grief, for which she is resolved to find relief by informing the Æther of whatever new visions the present night might bring.† She has had, moreover, recently a dream, in which it seemed to her, that she had been released from her captivity, and that she dwelt again at Argos. As she was sleeping in the midst of her apartments (παρθενῶσι δ' ἐν μέσοις), a sudden concussion of the elements roused her from her slumber, and she fled in consternation, while she witnessed the palace falling to ruins. One column only of her paternal mansion was left standing, the capital of which seemed to her to be covered with a head of auburn hair, and to be endowed with the powers of human speech. This column she now proceeded to besprinkle with the sacred water and to consecrate for sacrifice, as she was wont to do to the stranger captives at Tauris, at the same time uttering loud lamentations. From this dream she infers, that Orestes is dead, and that she herself had initiated his sacrifice. The columns of the ruined house she

---

* "Οθεν νόμοισι τοῖσι ἥδεται θεὰ
"Αρτεμις ἑορτῆς, τοὔνομ' ἧς καλὸν μόνον.   v. 35.

† "Α καινὰ δ' ἥκει νὺξ φέρουσα φάσματα,
λέξω πρὸς αἰθέρ', εἴ τι δὴ τόδ' ἐστ' ἄκος.   v. 42.

Fuit ea Græcorum consuetudo; unde in Sophoclis Electra tanquam res usitata a Chrysothemide commemoratur.—MUSGRAVE.

interprets to be its male descendants. _ She is therefore resolved to bestow on her absent and departed brother the last external honors of affection,* and aided by her attendants, countrywomen of hers, she proceeds to prepare the solemn oblation.

Pylades and Orestes having landed on the shore of the Tauri, are now deliberating in what manner they may carry off the image of Diana, in obedience to the command of the oracular responses of Phœbus Apollo.

Orestes complains of the cruelty of that god, who after having himself incited him to the matricidal act, was now compelling him to undergo the sharpest vicissitudes of fortune, in order that he might get rid of the dire pursuit of the Furies. He urges to immediate flight, before the barbarous custom of the inhospitable Tauri should sieze them as victims for the altar. It is the opinion of Pylades, however, that they should hide themselves in some safe place, and deliberate about their affairs at their leisure by night. Orestes is pleased with the proposition.

Iphigenia laments the fate of her brother Orestes, whom from the admonitions of her dreams she considers dead, and makes preparations for the sacrifice which after the custom of her country she is bound to bring to his shades. In this she is joined by her countrywomen of the chorus.

She complains, moreover, of the fatal calamity of her ancestral house, and of her own hard lot, which compelled her, a Grecian woman, to reside among uncouth Barbarians, and to participate in their inhuman rites.

This long and sombre lament of the priestess, in which she is occasionally interrupted by the responses of the chorus, is in the form of a choral elegy, the abrupt and varied movements of which are in admirable correspondence with the tender emotions of sorrow and calm resignation to which her heart is giving vent.

Act II. (v. 237—456.)

A Scythian herdsman comes to announce to the priestess, that two Grecian youths had been captured on the sea-shore and brought before king Thoas, who according to custom had ordered them to be immolated to Diana; hence he reminds her of her duty to prepare the lustral water and to initiate the sacrifice. This, as we learn from Iphigenia's previous account, was not actually performed by her own hands, but by her ministers within the temple. At the request of the priestess, the

---

* Νῦν οὖν ἀδελφῷ βούλομαι δοῦναι χοὰς,
  παροῦσ' ἀπόντι. v. 61.

herdsman gives a circumstantial account of the manner in which the
two victims had attracted the attention of the natives, and how after an
obstinate defence they had at last been vanquished by a superior number, and not without great difficulty.   Orestes, who at first was discovered to be in a raving fit, and under the hallucinating impression,
that he was pursued by the furies of his mother, recovered the mas-
tery over his mind during the desperate struggle with the barbarous enemy.*

* The first discovery of the strangers was a source of no little perplexity to the
Tauric herdsmen.   One of the more devout of their number at once concluded that
they were divinities, and even began to address them in adoration as Kastor and
Pollux. His over-hasty simplicity, however, soon became a subject of ridicule on
the part of the rest, who were of a less reverential tone of mind.   They concluded
that the persons at a distance were shipwrecked mariners, whom they were bound
by custom to bring as captives to their King. The poet's description of the capture
and of the madness of Orestes is highly animated :—

<blockquote>
*   *   *   *   Of the stranger youths
One at this instant started from the rock ;
Awhile he stood, and wildly tossed his head
And groaned, his loose arms trembling all their length,
Convulsed with madness : as an hunter loud
Then cried, "Dost thou behold her, Pylades,
Dost thou not see this dragon fierce from hell
Rushing to kill me, and against me rousing
Her horrid vipers ?   See this other here,
Emitting fire and slaughter from her vests,
Sails on her wings, my mother in her arms
Bearing, to hurl this mass of rock upon me !
Ah, she will kill me ! Whither shall I fly ?"
His visage might we see no more the same,
And his voice varied, now the roars of bulls,
The howl of dogs now uttering, mimic sounds
Sent by the madd'ning Furies, as they say.
Together thronging, as of death assured,
We sit in silence ; but he drew his sword,
And like a lion rushing 'midst our herds
Plunged in their sides the weapon, weening thus
To drive the Furies, till the briny wave
Foamed with their blood. But when among our herds
We saw this havoc made, we all 'gan rouse
To arms, and blew our sounding shells t' alarm
The neighboring peasants ; for we thought in fight
Rude herdsmen to these youthful strangers, trained
To arms, ill matched ; and forthwith to our aid
Flocked numbers. But, his frenzy of its force
Abating, on the earth the stranger falls,
Foam bursting from his mouth ; but when we saw
Th' advantage, each adventured on, and hurled
What might annoy him fall'n : the other youth
Wiped off the foam, took of his person care,
</blockquote>

After the exit of the herdsman, Iphigenia under the impression that Orestes was now dead, is seized with a feeling of hatred towards her countrymen, to whose inhumanity all her misfortunes were to be ascribed. Heretofore her heart had always been tender (γαληνὸς) and smitten with sympathy at the sight of her stranger countrymen, on whose fate she had always bestowed a friendly tear ; * but now that death had broken the last endearing tie, that had linked her to her native land, the memory of all her wrongs comes back with reiterated force, and makes her mind inexorable. Hence she expresses the wish, that Helen or Menelaos might fall as victims by her order, so that by their death she might avenge the brother's imaginary slaughter. She complains, moreover, of the unnaturally cruel conduct of her father, who lured her from her home under the false pretense of desiring to wed her to Achilles, while his real purpose was to immolate her on the altar. It was Pluto, that was to be her spouse, and not Achilles, the son of Peleus, who had been promised her. Her nuptials were of a bloody,

> His fine-wrought robe spread over him, with heed
> The flying stones observing, warded off
> The wounds, and each kind office to his friend
> Attentively performed. His sense returned,
> The stranger started up, and soon perceived
> The tide of foes that rolled impetuous on,
> The danger and distress that closed them round:
> He heaved a sigh ; an unremitting storm
> Of stones we poured, and each incited each.
> Then we this dreadful exhortation heard :
> Pylades, we shall die ; but let us die
> With glory ; draw thy sword and follow me !
> But when we saw the enemies advance
> With brandished swords, the steep height crowned with wood
> We fill in flight ; but others, if one flies,
> Press on them ; if again they drive these back,
> What before fled turns, with a storm of stones
> Assaulting them ; but, what exceeds belief,
> Hurled by a thousand hands not one could hit
> The victims of the goddess ; scarce at length,
> Not by brave daring seized we them, but 'round
> We closed upon them, and their swords with stones
> Beat, wily, from their hands ; for on their knees
> They through fatigue had sunk upon the ground :
> We bare them to the monarch of this land, &c.
>
> POTTER.

* Ὦ καρδία τάλαινα, πρὶν μὲν εἰς ξένους
γαληνὸς ἦσθα, καὶ φιλοικτίρμων ἀεὶ,
εἰς τοὐμόφυλον ἀναμετρουμένη δάκρυ,
Ἕλληνας ἄνδρας ἡνίκ᾽ εἰς χέρας λάβοις.

κ. τ. λ. V. 345—348.

treacherous kind.* She reprobates the custom of the Tauri, by which the stranger was made to bleed, nor can she believe, that those whose hands had been defiled, should be driven away as impious from the altar of her, who herself was reputed to take delight in human sacrifices : "The spouse of Jove, Latona could never have brought forth so great absurdity. † She deems the banquet of Tantalos incredible ; and holds that all such abominations, which men have impiously attributed to the Gods, are but the reflex of their own corrupted nature. ‡

The chorus now begins to discuss the question, who the youthful prisoners might be, how they could have ever ventured to encounter the many perils of the Euxine sea, what business or what hope could ever have induced them to undergo a voyage fraught with so many hardships and such constant dangers, to arrive at a land, where a maiden sprinkles the altars and columns of temples with human gore. § The chorus then likewise expresses the wish, that Helen, the pest of universal Greece, might arrive among the Tauri, in order that by her death she might atone for the many woes, which on her account the Greeks had already suffered, and then concludes the act by praying for a release from foreign servitude, and a safe return to Greece. (It will be remembered, that the chorus is composed of Grecian women, attendants of Iphigenia.)

ACT III. (v. 457—725.)

In accordance with the command of the king, the new victims, Pylades and Orestes, are now ushered into the temple. The priestess orders her attendants to loosen the chains of the prisoners according to custom, and to make the necessary preparations for the sacrifice. Struck with the personal appearance of the captives, and recognizing them at once to be Greeks, Iphigenia proceeds to question them minutely

* — — — ἐν ἁρμάτων δ' ὄχοις
εἰς αἱματηρὸν γάμον ἐπόρθμευσας δόλῳ. V. 371.

† Οὐκ ἔσθ' ὅπως ἔτικτεν ἡ Διὸς δάμαρ,
Αητὼ, τοσαύτην ἀμαθίαν,
h. e. Jovis et Latonæ filia sapientior est,
quam ut tale quid admittat. V. 386.

‡ Τοὺς δ' ἐνθάδ', αὐτοὺς ὄντας ἀνθρωποκτόνους,
εἰς τὴν θεὸν τὸ φαῦλον ἀναφέρειν δοκῶ. V. 390.

§ — ἔνθα κύρα
διατέγγει βωμοὺς,
καὶ περὶ κίονας να-
ῶν αἷμα βρότειον. V. 404–407.

about their family, their country, the cause of their arrival on the inhospitable shore.   Moreover, the further history of the Trojan campaign,
the fate of the leading Grecian generals, and particularly the fortunes
of Agamennon and his house are made the subject of diligent inquiry,
until the priestess has elicited all the calamities that had befallen her
family since her absence from her home. Thus far the name of Pylades
(whom Iphigenia had never known in Greece) alone was known to her,
Orestes having managed from motives of policy to conceal his own.
The priestess proposes to spare one of the victims on the condition,
that he should become the bearer of a letter which had been written for
her on a former occasion, and which she is anxious to have conveyed to
her friends.   Orestes having been selected for this purpose, and Pylades
being thus doomed to the altar, the former pertinaciously refuses to
accept his own safety at the expense of his friend's, and prevails upon
Iphigenia to select Pylades for that mission.   Admiring these generous
sentiments of disinterested honor, and wishing her own absent brother
to be of an equally noble mind, the priestess promises the expostulating
victim a more honorable death and sepulture than usual ; his body shall
be anointed with the yellow olive-oil, and his pyre besprinkled with the
flower-distilled moisture of the yellow mountain-bee.*

The priestess having now absented herself for the purpose of prepar-
ing the promised letter, the memorable contest arises between the two
friends, as to which of the two should die for the other; whilst the
chorus in his interlocutions laments the fate of the one, and beatifies
the flattering prospects of the other.

Orestes having at length prevailed upon Pylades to acquiesce in his
choice, gives to the latter the necessary directions for his future conduct
at Argos, conjuring him to honor his memory with sepulchral rites and
a monument at home, and commending his sister Electra and all the
future interests of his house to his charge.   Pylades solemnly promises
to perform these last wishes of his friend, though he still trusts, in the
veracity of the oracular response, while Orestes at the sight of the
approaching priestess gives himself up to utter despair.

<hr>

ACT IV. (v. 726—1153.)

Iphigenia having now returned with the letter, demands of the bearer
to give oath for its certain delivery after his arrival at Argos, which

* Πολὺν τε γάρ σοι κόσμον ἐνθήσω τάφῳ,
ξανθῷ τ' ἐλαίᾳ σῶμα σὸν κατασβέσω·
καὶ τῆς ὀρείας ἀνθεμόῤῥυτον γάνος
ξουθῆς μελίσσης εἰς πυρὰν βαλῶ σέθεν.   V. 633—636.

Pylades readily grants her, claiming, however, exemption from the obligation of the oath, in case some unavoidable accident at sea should occasion the loss of the letter along with his effects. To guard against the unlucky results of such a contingency, *Iphigenia gives to Pylades a verbal exposition of the contents of her epistle, at the same time designating the name of the person to whom it was to be delivered.* This person was none other than Orestes, to whom she gives a brief account of her deliverance in Aulis, and of the miseries of her present situation, from which she beseeches him to rescue her. This unexpected disclosure leads to a recognition, which the priestess, however, is slow to admit, until she is fully convinced by unmistakeable evidence, that her brother is really before her.* The discovery is attended with mutual congratulations, with tears of joy and cordial embraces, to which the poet gives fit expression by the varied intricacies of the choral strophes. Iphigenia then proceeds to explain more fully, how Artemis, her goddess, rescued her from the hands of her immolators at Aulis by substituting a hind in her stead, and how she found herself alive at Tauris ; † Orestes

* Euripides makes Orestes produce the proofs of his identity by recalling to the memory of the priestess certain objects of hereditary and domestic interest, with which both had been familiar at their common home, viz.: the texture, woven by her own skilled hand, on which the quarrel of Atreus and Thyestes about the golden fleece, and another one, on which the revolutions of the sun were represented, and which her mother had given her as a wedding present (I follow Musgrave's emendation. who v. 819 reads κάλλος τ' ἐς Αὖλιν for καὶ λούτρ' ἐς Αὖλιν, which gives no sense), when she went to Aulis ; the locks of hair she sent her in return, when she expected to die before the altar. The spear, moreover, with which Pelops vanquished Œnomaos, when he courted Hippodamia, and which had been preserved as an ancestral relic in Iphigenia's chamber. V. 815—827. Goethe has introduced the discovery and recognition of brother and sister by entirely different motives (Act III, Scene first) ; his proofs of identity are also more forcible and more beautiful, and are moreover discovered by the priestess herself:—1) the natural spot on his right hand ; 2) the scar on one of his eye-brows ; 3) his resemblance to Agamemnon ; 4) the inward shoutings of the sister's heart (Act V. Scene sixth.)

† In regard to the fate of Iphigenia at Aulis, there were various and contradictory accounts among the Ancients themselves. Homer knows nothing whatever of the detention of the army, nor of the attempted sacrifice, nor of her residence in Scythia. In the ninth book of the Iliad (v. 142—147) he makes Agamemnon offer his daughter *Iphinassa* in marriage to the enraged Achilles, nearly ten years after the arrival of the Greeks at Troy ; and by her father's account she had meanwhile remained at home with her mother and sisters (of which he mentions two).—In the touchingly beautiful delineation of the events at Aulis, which is found in the Agamemnon of Æschylos (v. 166—223, ed. Klausen), the poet seems to convey the impression, that the blood of the unhappy victim actually flowed upon the altar of the inexorable Goddess (unless the disputed κρόκον βαφάς of v. 216 be referred to the color of the robe or fillet worn by the victim on that occasion, which I regard improbable ; her *shedding the saffron's dye,* i. e. her blood *upon the ground* is much more in accordance with the context of the graphic picture). Nor does Sophocles in his Electra (v. 517 et. a. l.) convey any other impression than that of the actual

in return gives an account of his adventures and of the mission, that brought him to the shore of the Barbarians. This was of such a nature, that Iphigenia could at once and with alacrity second the efforts of her brother to purloin the heaven-descended image of Diana, and thus prepare the way for the expiation and redemption of her ruined house. The plan for speedy flight is formed at once, and the promised favor of Phœbus, at whose command the perilous adventure had been undertaken, inspires the doubting hearts of all with the hope of a prosperous result. The act closes with a solemn choral hymn, in which the attendants of the priestess commemorate the ills of their long captivity, which the joyous prospect of their restoration is already beginning to relieve.

Act V. (v. 1154—1500.)

Thoas, the king of the Tauri, now enters for the purpose of inquiring into the progress of the sacrifice, but is surprised to find the priestess in the act of removing the image of the goddess from its seats immoveable (ἐξ ἀκινήτων βάθρων). Iphigenia justifies her conduct by informing the king, that the image had been contaminated by the presence

immolation of the princess ; and later poets, e. g. Lucretius in the elegant passage of the first Book De Rer. Nat. (v. 85—102), Horace (Satirarum Lib. II. Sat. 3, v. 199, seq.), Virgil (Æneid. Lib. II. v. 166) have likewise ignored the legend of a miraculous substitution, and treated the inhuman act as the lamentable result of a barbarous superstition. Euripides, on the other hand, in this drama as well as in the Iphigenia Aulica has either invented or adopted the more humane legend, according to which Artemis out of commiseration for the unhappy princess, substituted a hind in her place at the instant of the raising of the sacrificial knife, at the same time translating the intended victim to her own temple at Tauris ; and Ovid (Metam. Lib. XII.) has converted the miraculous translation into a metamorphosis. Pausanias (Corinth p. 125) makes mention of a third version of the legend, and as one which not only was adopted by many of the ancient lyric poets, e. g. by Stesichoros and others, but in his time universally believed in the country of Argos. According to this, the Iphigenia sacrificed at Aulis was not the daughter of Agamemnon, but the issue of a secret union between Theseus and Helen ; who by her vicarious death not only saved the life of the real princes, but also atoned in a measure for the unnumbered woes, which the vices of her mother had inflicted on the Greeks.—The discovery of this second Iphigenia was a source of no little self-congratulation to a distinguished modern poet (Racine), who in the economy of his tragedy, which bears the name of our heroine, represents this daughter of Helen, who as the captive of Achilles at first appears under the name of Eriphile, as the jealous and intriguing rival of Agamemnon's daughter for the hand of the Grecian hero, so that her discovery and immolation appears to some extent a merited punishment of her own conduct towards the amiable princess. This dénouement, he thought, would not only afford the spectator the pleasure of witnessing the unexpected deliverance of an innocent and charming being, but it would also save him from the horrors of a miracle (d'une Déesse et d'une machine), which the faint-hearted poetical faith of his enlightened contemporaries could no longer endure !

of the victims, he had sent her, their hands having been defiled by the crime parricide; on which account both the prisoners and the image needed a purifying ablution in the sea, before the goddess could accept the offering. The king, whose confidence in the priestess had thus far been unlimited, consents to all without any apparent suspicion; while the priestess proceeds to give the necessary directions for the consummation of her purpose. All the citizens, together with the king, were to be excluded from participation in the ceremony on the peril of contamination; the former were all to remain quiet in their own houses, the latter was to have the charge of the temple during the absence of the priestess. Only a small escort of the royal guards, which Iphigenia knew to be decidedly inferior to the Greeks awaiting their arrival in the ship, was to accompany the sacred procession. Whilst the latter is already slowly proceeding from the temple, the priestess, after having uttered the usual *procul* to all those who in the opinion of the Ancients were particularly liable to defilement by the sight, addresses a solemn prayer to the virgin goddess, whose habitation was to be purified by the ablution about to be performed, and concludes with the significant words:

"The rest, although I do not mention, to the gods, who know the more, and to thyself at least I indicate, O Goddess." *

The chorus then proceeds to chant the praises of Apollo, his birth, his victory over the serpent Pytho, and his oracular power, which in place of ancient Themis he had obtained from Jove. The advantages of the Delphic dispensation over the dreamy imposture of the old, form the concluding strain of the ode.

A messenger now arrives and gives to king Thoas a circumstantial account of the flight of Iphigenia and all her party, and of the robbery of the sacred image. The resistance of the deluded attendants had proved too late and ineffectual, to prevent the accomplishment of the unexpected deed. The king in his anger is already flinging about his orders to those around him, to pursue the fugitives by sea and land, threatening the severest punishment to the deceivers and to the tremulous chorus, which had been cognizant of their intent, *when Minerva suddenly interposing, checks his wrath, and unfolding to him the counsel of the Gods, in obedience to which Orestes had effected this escape, she commands him to acquiesce in the will of the supernal powers, which it would be folly for mortals to resist.* To Orestes and Iphigenia, whom though absent she yet makes hear, the *Dea ex machina* addresses particular directions both in regard to their own future conduct and the destiny that awaits them, as well as in behalf of the further disposition of the image, which was to become an object of special veneration among the

---

* ———— ———— τἄλλα δ' οὐ λεγουσ', ὅμως
τοῖς τὰ πλείον' εἰδόσιν θεοῖς, σοί τε σημαίνω, θεά. V. 1233.

Atheneans; while in conclusion she bids the ship-conducting breezes
to waft Agamemnon's children safely on towards her own Athens,
where she herself proposes to accompany them. The chorus concludes
the piece by a solemn hymn of praise to Pallas and to Niké.

GOETHE.

ACT I. (Scene 1—4.)

THE drama likewise begins with a monologue, spoken by Iphigenia,
in which the priestess gives utterance to the feelings that have agitated
her bosom ever since she entered the sacred grove of the sequestered
sanctuary. While she is perfectly resigned to the higher will that has
consigned her to her present lot, she still must ever feel herself a stranger in the place of her captivity, nor can her heart there ever feel at
home. The ancestral halls, where first the sun unsealed the heavens
to her admiring eyes, the charming scenery of her own fair native
Hellas, the happy days spent with the sporting comrades of her youth,
are ever again recurring to her busy memory, and appear in painful
contrast with the lonely days which far from parents and her kindred,
she is doomed to spend in the dreary solitude of Diana's temple.

But the billow's hollow-roaring din is the only answer she receives
in return for the sighs which she daily sends across the sea to her
fair native Argos, and she must ever learn again, that all her premature repinings against the dispensations of the higher powers are
of no avail. This leads her to lament the onerous barriers, that
circumscribe the sphere of woman's activity, especially when contrasted
with the wider scope of man's superior energies, which make him
rule both at home and in war, and to combat adversity in every form,
whilst woman's happiness consists in her submission. Her lot is ever
lamentable, but doubly wretched, if dire misfortune drives her to a distance. Hence she must feel her present condition to be a state of
servitude, which all the kindness of the noble king can but imperfectly
relieve, and she must blush to own, that her service of the deity of her
deliverance, who was entitled to perpetual gratitude, is performed
with secret murmurings and reluctance, whilst it ought to be the
offering of a willing heart. Still she can never cease to trust in
the Jove-born maid, who had received her, the outcast victim, into
her own gentle, sacred arms of love, and whom she now beseeches
to grant her safe return to her own kinsmen, to set her free from this
her present life, a second death!

Arkas, the royal messenger now entering announces to the priestess the near advent of the king and of his army, who are desirous of offering to the goddess their grateful sacrifices for recent signal victories, for which they held themselves indebted to her favor. When the priestess assures him, that Diana was waiting with gracious look, to receive the welcome gift from the hands of the King, the messenger takes occasion to open a conversation, by expressing the wish that her own look, at the gloom of which he had ever been forced to shudder, might also become brighter and more propitious to them all ; he complains that a mysterious grief had so long been shrouding the inmost soul of their dear and venerated priestess, and that for years they should have been waiting in vain for some word of friendly confidence to escape her breast. Iphigenia justifies her gloomy reserve, by pleading that she must ever feel herself an exile and an orphan in a foreign land, and that the ancient curse, which had rent the dearest ties of her early youth asunder, would never suffer fresh delight of life again to bloom in her ; and although she makes a grateful acknowledgment of the ever-constant kindness of the King and of the reverence of his people, yet she compares her present joyless life to that of the shades, who dwell in self forgetting silence on the banks of Lethe.

To relieve her from these gloomy reveries, Arkas begins to enumerate the many blessings which her beneficent presence had brought to the Taurians and to its valiant but grief-stricken King. He reminds her, how by cheering the gloomy mind of Thoas, she had induced him to ease for them the task of mute obedience, and to take delight in mild paternal sway ; how her gently stern persuasion had put a check upon the ancient ruthless custom of sacrificing every stranger on Diana's altar ; and how the goddess, instead of being offended by the want of the accustomed sacrifice, had showered down her favors in richer measure even than before, and made the priestess the eternal source of new prosperity to the entire people. But to all this Iphigenia has but one modest reply : " *To one who forward looks to what is left, the little done soon dwindles into nought,*" nor is she disposed to weigh her meritorious deeds too nicely.

Arkas now introduces another subject of his mission, from which the priestess shrinks with evident aversion. He appears in the character of suitor for the absent King. The recent loss of his only son had made the latter distrustful of nearly all his former vassals ; he saw with envy his realm's successor in every noble's son, and was in perpetual dread of bold insurrection, a helpless solitary age, and an early death. It is to provide against these contingencies, that the King is resolved to own the priestess as his wedded spouse, and Arkas is commissioned to renew the oft-repeated suit, which the King in the next scene again

prefers in person.   But while Iphigenia expresses herself ready to
receive her royal benefactor with due consideration, she shows an equal
determination to repel his courtship, as an evil from which her heart
recoils, and she even threatens, in case of need, to invoke the aid of all
the gods, and of the maiden goddess resolute, for her protection.

In the next (third) scene, Iphigenia explains at length to Thoas, the
cause of her shy and distrustful reserve, by which hitherto she had
wounded the generous heart of her royal friend, who had done all in
his power to make her situation as acceptable as possible.   She assures
him, that no unkind suspicion, but embarrassment and the fear of a
premature expulsion from his realm, had been the reason for her silence
in regard to her origin and family, which the King's kind encouragement now induces her at length to break.

The priestess then proceeds to give an account of the history and
fate of all her progenitors and of the frightful abominations, that had
entailed the fatal curses of the gods on all their descendants; of Tantalos, whose insolent demeanor thrust him down from Jove's abode to
ancient Tartaros; of the unhappy divisions in the family of Pelops,
of the revolting banquet of the revengeful Atreus, from which the sun
his countenance averted; of her own family and early recollections; of
the calamity and attempted immolation at Aulis, of her rescue and
miraculous translation to her present asylum in Tauris.

The King again takes occasion to urge his suit, more earnestly even
than before, but Iphigenia evades it by maintaining, that the goddess
has at present the only claim to her devoted life, nor does she abandon
the hope of finding yet a glad return to her own native land, and of solacing
the old age of her unhappy father.   Her conduct excites the indignation
of the King, who attributes her pertinacious refusal to ingratitude; and
in his anger he threatens to renew the long-intermitted custom of
dooming to the altar of Diana every stranger that arrived at Tauris.
Two such had recently been found concealed in caves along the shore,
and they were to be the next victims.

The act concludes with a monologue, which the priestess in the form
of a solemn prayer addresses to her patron goddess, beseeching her to
keep her hands pure from bloody guilt, and to prepare for her a happy
release from her present embarrassment.

ACT II. (Scene 1—2).

The two stranger-captives, to whom the king alluded at the close of
the previous Act, prove to be none other than Orestes and Pylades, the
brother and the cousin of the priestess.   They have already become acquainted with the fate, that was awaiting them.   Orestes, whose heart
had long been lacerated by the agonies of a guilty conscience, by the

terrible pursuit of the avenging Furies of his mother, gives himself up to a pensively gloomy resignation ; the expected death before the altar, inglorious as it is, yet seems to him to be preferable to the disgraceful end of his father, who had fallen in his own house by the hand of the assassin, and the equal fate of a languid night eternal, that awaited both himself and the hideous spectres which disturbed him here, held out to him the melancholy prospect of at least a partial repose. Hard as it is for any one to renounce the fair light of the sun forever, he still can do it without a single murmur, and his only grief is, that Pylades, the innocent companion of his curse, should unjustly share an equal lot so prematurely! Pylades exerts his utmost powers of persuasion to re-animate the sinking spirits of his unfortunate and gloomy friend. He reminds him of Apollo's pledge, that in his sister's temple, help, con-solation and a safe return was kept in store for them. His faith in the veracity of the god is to him a never-failing source of hope, to which he is resolved to cling, even after the priestess shall have raised the consecrating hand, to cut their locks. He therefore urges Orestes, who still persists in melancholy reveries about the fate of his unlucky house, to cherish reminiscences of the happier days, when they together revelled in the joyous sports of youth, which they both now proceed to depict in the most glowing terms, Orestes still maintaining, that his earlier mirth even was infused into his nature by his friend's, compared with whom, the particolored butterfly, he was even then the dark-hued flower. Pylades does not fail to strike every possible chord of hope. He tells his companion, that he himself was assuming the part of the Furies by his impatience and his unbelief; if they suc-ceeded in their purpose of carrying off Apollo's sister and of bringing her to Delphi, as they had been commissioned by the god, then the in-fernal sisters, who even now were kept off from the sacred grove, would be forever deprived of their power over their unhappy victim. Diana herself desired to depart from the unhallowed coast of barbarous tribes and from their bloody rites. *They* were elected for this noble mission, and who knows what other lofty purposes the gods may yet in future keep reserved for them? He exhorts, therefore, to united and resolute effort for the accomplishment of the design, that had brought them to that shore. As for himself, he had already acted; he had eli-cited from spies, that the foul law of the Barbarians, which now was threatening their safety, was held in prudent check by a stranger maiden, an angelic being, whom men believed to have descended from the race of the Amazons. This he deems an auspicious circumstance. On seeing her approach, he requests Orestes to step aside and to leave him to confer with her apart, nor does he think it prudent, that they should tell their names directly, or acquaint her with the object of their coming.

Pylades, on being released from his chains by the priestess, bursts

out into exclamations of enraptured delight at the discovery, that she is
a Grecian woman, speaking the language of his native land.) Her desire to receive some information in regard to the origin and the adventures of the captives he gratifies by *inventing a fictitious story* (*similar
in its leading features to the actual*), *calling himself Kephalos, his companion. Laodamas, and both sons of Adrastos from Krete.* His brother's
hands having been embrued in fratricidal blood, they had come to the
temple of Diana in obedience to the command of Apollo, for the purpose of seeking deliverance for the fury-driven criminal, in whose behalf the speaker solicits the commiseration of the priestess.   Pylades
having made an accidental allusion to the Trojan war, has now to
answer many questions with reference to it; until the inquisitive im-
portunity of the priestess has elicited from him all the particulars of that
event, the sacking of the long-beleaguered city, the fate of the leading
Grecian chiefs, including even the disgraceful end of the royal Agamemnon, which Klytemnestra, in revenge for the foul immolation of her
eldest daughter at Aulis, had treacherously prepared for the returning
king. The subsequent calamities of the royal house, however, are not yet
mentioned, Iphigenia being already too deeply moved by the unexpected
news.   The emotions betrayed by her lead Pylades to infer, that she
must have known the king herself, and from this circumstance he derives
new encouragement for the success of his plan.

ACT III. (Scene 1—3).

Iphigenia lamentingly performs the duty of loosening the chains of the
next prisoner, preparatory to his dedication for the sacrifice. But however much it may pain her to betray a countryman, it is a necessity from
which there is no escape. She embraces this opportunity of pursuing
her inquiries into the history of her family still further, and thus learns
the murder of her mother Klytemnestra by the hand of Orestes, who had
escaped the fate of his father by concealment in the house of his uncle
Strophios, where in intimate union with Pylades, his cousin, he had
grown up to be the avenger of his sire. Her eager inquiries into the
fate of the unhappy son, induce the prisoner to describe in the most
touching terms the agonies of the criminal, whom the Furies with their
hideous attendants, Doubt and Repentance, were driving about in a
giddy and wretched exile. *When the priestess expresses her pity for the
unfortunate captive, whom she had already learnt to be in equal plight, the
latter can maintain the deception no longer, and confesses himself to be*
Orestes, sinking towards the pit and longing for the end of his miserable
life. His torments are so terrible, that while he exhorts the priestess
to devise some plan of speedy flight for herself and his worthier com-

panion, in order that they might recommence a new and happy life in Greece, he himself desires alone and unattended to descend among the shades below. A lonely death disgraceful seems to him to be the only way of escape from the infernal escort, that is pursuing his path wherever he goes. He heeds not the loving gentle encouragement of the priestess, whom the discovery of her long lost brother has encircled with a sea of sweetest joy, *and repels her embrace, unwilling to believe that she is really his sister.* The most frightful convulsions now agitate his bosom with such intensity, that the whole hideous spectacle of his mother's death and of the advancing Furies, rises up again with all its terrible reality before his imagination, until the maniac sinks exhausted by the struggle, and the priestess rushes out to look for Pylades.

This temporary stupefaction of Orestes has had the effect of a partial mitigation of his sufferings. The terrible images which his reproductive imagination had before evoked, are now blended with softer visions of reconciliation and forgiveness, which in strange confusion are flitting through the dim twilight of his dreamlike reverie. The princely house of Tantalos, so fiercely divided here on earth, appears to him to move in peaceful harmony through festive halls beyond the night of death. His ancestors Atreus and Thyestes are walking together in converse intimate, and the boys who had been so foully served as viands at the hateful banquet, are running in joyful sports around their father. Klytemnestra has reached her hand to Agamemnon and is walking by his side. And why should not Orestes venture to approach? Should he alone be excluded from the universal reconciliation? They *do* bid him a welcome, they receive him too! The heroic breast of the ancestral Sire (Tantalos) alone remains rivetted fast to ruthless torments with brazen chains!

From these half terrible, half joyful reveries, their victim is aroused by the approach of Iphigenia and Pylades. The earnest and beautiful invocation addressed to the twin deities by the sister in his behalf, the exhortations of his friend, urging him to summon all his energies, to *notice* the sacred grove, the rosy light of day, to *feel* the sister's arm and friend's, dispel at last completely his dreamy delusion, that he was living in the land of shades. The recognition now becomes a complete, a *conscious* one. The sister's love, the friend's devotion awaken his gratitude towards the gods. He is completely cured. The curse is dissipating. He hears the dire Eumenides depart to ancient Tartaros, closing its brazen gates with far-off-thundering violence. The earth assumes a new, a more inviting form ; new joys of life and prospects of a loftier career are now before him. Pylades exhorts to immediate preparations for flight.

ACT IV. (Scene 1—5).

The Act again commences with a monologue, in which Iphigenia gratefully acknowledges the hand of a superior power in the events that had just transpired, at the same time invoking the blessing of the gods on Pylades and all his plans for their deliverance, whilst the latter, together with Orestes, are looking after their ship and hastening their preparations for speedy flight. In regard to her conduct towards the king, she had already received the minutest instruction; but the proposed deception, to which in every shape her heart had ever been a stranger, the possibility of a sudden relapse on the part of her brother, and the still greater possibility of detection, give rise to uneasy apprehensions, which the approach of armed warriors, is increasing still further.

To the message of Arkas, requesting her to dispatch the sacrifice, for which the king and the people were already waiting, the priestess replies, that the image of Diana had been polluted by the presence of the culprit victim, and that a lustration in the sea must needs precede the immolation. The messenger, however, insists on the necessity of obtaining first the consent of the king for such an unusual delay, to which the priestess much against her will has at last to submit. He chides her kindly for not having heeded his former advice in her deportment towards the king, which would have saved her from her present duty and embarrassment. He still expresses the hope, that the generous conduct of his monarch may induce her to relax her aversion towards his suit, and that she yet may be induced to reciprocate the deeply-rooted and sincere affection of her royal lover.

The priestess is very much disconcerted by the words of Arkas, and her heart, which the unexpected recovery of her brother and the prospect of the approaching return homeward had filled with ecstasies of joy, is now again the seat of anxiety and doubt. *She feels that those whom she deserts, are also men, and her deception seems doubly hateful by reason of its ingratitude.* Still she is convinced, that the solitude must now be left behind, and that the mountain wave must rock her towards her home !

Pylades arrives, transported with joy at the complete restoration of his long-afflicted friend, and at the prospect of immediate departure, for which all the preparations were now completed. He is already on the point of entering the temple for the purpose of seizing the darling object of their wishes, when to his astonishment he learns the new impediment from the hesitating and embarrassed priestess. It was his own advice, that had contrary to all expectations given rise to the present difficulty. While he himself proposes to hasten, to console the anxiously waiting comrades, he exhorts the priestess calmly to await the return of the messenger, and then to assert the right of her priestly office, which entitled her to exclude the king and other witnesses from participation in the lustral ceremony. The apprehensions of the king she was to dispel by assuring him, that both the victims were kept well guarded in the temple; and he himself promises to watch her orders from a neighboring thicket, so as to be ready for action at the decisive moment. He has, however, no little difficulty in combatting her scruples of conscience in regard to the ingratitude of the act, which obliges her to deceive and rob a noble man, who had been a second father to her; and although he respects her spotless purity of mind, which shrinks with pious horror from the violation of her duty, he nevertheless urges on her the necessity of the deed as an act of self-preservation, as well as the magnitude of their ulterior purpose, which was nothing less than the restoration of her ancient ruined house to all the glories of its pristine splendor.

In the monologue, that forms the conclusion of this act, the inward antagonism of Iphigenia's mind between fraternal affection and the loyalty of duty towards her benefactor again makes its appearance, and fills her soul with melancholy reflections. The long and fondly cherished hope of expiating the hereditary curse, of wiping off with undefiled hand the guilt of her ancestral house, which the miraculous cure of her lately found brother had already so happily initiated, can only be realized by the deception of the king, and by the robbery of the sacred image entrusted to her care by those to whom she owed her life and preservation! This double crime, however, is imposed on her by the iron hand of blind necessity, whilst the preservation of her brother and the expiation of her house is a duty, to which the Delphic god himself has promised his assistance. She, therefore, calls upon the gods to rescue her from this extremity, to save their sacred image in her soul! Her happiness is still submission to their will; and she beseeches them to preserve her from that rebellious opposition of heart, which in the history of her own family they had so fearfully punished, and of the consequences of which the song of the Parcæ, recited by her from her earliest recollections, exhibits so terrible and so sublime a picture!

Act V. (Scene 1—6.)

Arkas apprizes the king of the alarming rumor, flying about all of a sudden, that the ship, which had brought the aliens to their shore, was still secreted in a hidden inlet. Moreover, the phrensy of one of the strangers, the delay of the sacrifice, and the purifying rite, have now excited his suspicion, that either the prisoners or the priestess are pre-

paring for clandestine flight. The king in his alarm gives immediate
orders for sharp inquest both along the shore and in Diana's grove, and
for the apprehension of the fugitives, wherever they may be found, at
the same time dispatching a message to call the priestess to his presence
without delay.

The memory of his kind indulgence towards the captive priestess,
which he now finds requited by falsehood and base treachery, gives rise
to violent expressions of indignation, of self-reproaches and regret on
the part of the king.

The present appearance of Iphigenia exhibits her in a phase of character, that is entirely new ; and she now assumes an attitude of determined resistance to a command, from which the soft humanity of her
heart must ever recoil with dizzy horror. She boldly tells the king, that
by the delay of the sacrifice, the goddess had intended to grant him time
yet - for reflection, and that, if his breast was really hardened for this
barbarous resolve, he should rather not have come. She addresses him
no longer as his priestess, with deferential submission, but as Agamemnon's daughter, as a noble woman, conscious of the rights and powers
of her sex, and ready to defend them. The plea of the necessity of the
act, as based upon long-established and invariable usage, she repels by
asserting the stronger obligations of another law, more ancient still, the
law of hospitality, by which all strangers were inviolable. Moreover,
the memory of an equal fate is yet alive in her ; she sees herself in the
prisoners ; she too had trembled once before the altar, the knife was
raised already to pierce her throbbing bosom full of life ; her eyes grew
dim and—she awoke alive ! Her own preservation commands her to ren-
der to misfortune, what the gods had kindly granted to herself. But all
her attempts to defend the rights of her own bosom, all these arguments
in favor of the captives are unable to divert the pitiless heart of the monarch from his purpose, to which the vague uncertainty of his suspi-
sions, and still more the chagrin of his disappointed affection make him
cling with doubly obstinate tenacity. Her appeal to his sense of honor,
the shame of taking advantage of woman's frailty, which Agamemnon's
son, were he now present, would readily defend with valiant arm, are
equally incapable of moving him, and she is finally obliged to exclaim :
*Shall I invoke the goddess for a wonder ? Is there no power in my being's
depth ?*

It is here, where the pertinacious inquiries of Thoas in regard to the
strangers, in whose behalf her pleadings are so unusually earnest and
persevering, compel her *at last to resort to the desperate resolve of
making a frank confession of the whole,* at the risk of incurring the
keenest reproaches of her friends, in case her attempt should fail her.
Yes, they *had* been planning there clandestine fraud ; the captives had

gone in search of their secreted comrades, who with the ship were waiting on the shore ; the eldest of the intended victims was Orestes, her own brother, the other, Pylades his bosom-friend ; Apollo had sent them to the shore from Delphi with divine command to rob the statue of Diana, which was to purify the fury-driven criminal from guilt. It is the inward voice of truth and of humanity, which makes itself heard within the heart of every man of every clime, to which she now appeals in behalf of herself and brother—last remnant of the house of Tantalos, which she with spotless hand proposes now to purify from its long curse ; and she makes use of all the arguments that a pure affectionate heart, and the magnitude of her purpose can suggest to induce the re-luctant king to permit their peaceable departure. The heart of the latter, however, still revolts in angry heavings against the unreasonable-ness of the demand. In the following scene Orestes again makes his appearance, without at first perceiving the king, exhorting his followers to hold out bravely against the superior masses of the enemy and calling on his sister to follow him in instantaneous flight. His perception of the king threatens with a dangerous collision, which the speedy me-diation of the priestess, however, checks at once.

Pylades and Arkas arriving, announce, each with a different purpose, that the Greeks in spite of their desperate resistance were likely to be vanquished, being slowly driven back towards the sea ; and both return at the command of their superiors, to bid their warriors halt, until the conference was over.

Thoas being desirous of some proof, that he had truly Agamemnon's son, and brother of the maid before him, Orestes, besides exhibiting the sword with which his sire had slain the valiant men of Troy, desires the King to chose one of the noblest and the bravest of his followers as a match for him, in order that in single combat he might fight, not for their own freedom simply, but as the stranger-representative for the safety and freedom of all, who might visit their shore thereafter. His own fate was to decide the fate of all, and the whole nation was by imitation to sanction its ruler's generous deed. This exhibition of magnanimity excites the admiration and the pride of Thoas to such a degree, that he himself proposes in spite of his age to risk at once the chance of arms with him—an issue, which the immediate and earnest interposition of Iphigenia prevents. As for herself, she is firmly convinced, that the youth before them is her veritable brother. The natural mark (as of three stars) on his right hand, from which the priest had prognosticated heavy deeds, the scar on one of his eye-brows, occasioned by a fall from the arms of Electra, his sire's similitude, and still more the inward shoutings of her heart, are to her indubitable evidence of his identity.

When, in spite of all this, the King still deems a hostile exchange of arms necessary to settle their dispute about the image of the goddess, with which he expresses himself unwilling to part, Orestes makes the sudden discovery, that the ambiguous oracular response had thus far been improperly interpreted by them, *that the sister which was to be returned to Hellas, was not Apollo's Artemis, but his own dear Iphigenia,* and that consequently the statue which was the cause of their contention, might remain at Tauris. As for the promised cure of his insanity, and his deliverance from the Furies, both had already been accomplished. *The touch, the loving suasion of his sister had exercised a sanatory power, a regenerating influence on him.* The glorious counsel of Diana, had kept her undefiled and pure within the precincts of her temple's solitude, to prove a blessing to her friends and brother, to accomplish the purification and the restoration of her ancestral house.

The full accomplishment of this their purpose, depended now on the kind consent and reconciliation of one man only, which the earnest entreaties of both brother and sister conspire to obtain. The affectionate and dutiful Iphigenia, however, is not contented with his reluctantly granted " *Then go !* " She wishes to receive a parting word of love from him, whom she still desires to honor as her second father. A friendly hospitality was to subsist between the Taurian and the Greek. The gods themselves were to requite the King's kind deed and pure benignity ! The *"Farewell!"* of the priestess (and her right hand ?) is at last reciprocated by the King.

III. HISTORY OF THE COMPOSITION OF GOETHE'S IPHIGENIA, AND A CRITICAL EXAMINATION OF THE CONTENTS OF THE DRAMA.

The drama under consideration was first written in prose, and under circumstances of a peculiar nature, quite unusual in the history of the poet. The plan had already been conceived in the year 1776, and in 1779, while Goethe acted at " Pontifex Maximus " of road-inspection and street-sweeping, as his friend Herder humorously terms the office of the ducal functionary, and while he presided over the conscriptions of military recruitments, the leisure of his evenings and other intervals were dedicated to its execution. In the midst of this apparently uncongenial but health-invigorating occupation, the " Poeta ambulans " (as he calls himself), who at all times had understood the art of preserving a sacred inward serenity of mind even under the most heterogeneous outward circumstances, was not unvisited by the inspirations of his ever-active muse.

Even while travelling on the road or stopping at the inns he drew forth from the depths of his imagination the choicest treasures, and in favorable moments threw them out with customary genial expedition upon the stream of Time. It is thus, that his most perfect drama was composed at odd intervals, stolen from the duties of an active life.

The previous maturity of his plan may best be learned from the rapidity of its execution. An inscription on the Schwalbenstein near Ilmenau, bearing the date of March 19th, 1779, says with reference to the fourth Act: " *Sereno die, quieta mente, composed in one day after a choice of three years,*" and on the 28th of March the fifth and last Act was likewise finished. Though the drama in this its original form (in which it has been published since the death of the author, among his collected works), is in point of composition and general arrangement essentially the same as the present version, still the author afterwards strangely regarded it rather as an unfinished sketch, "written in poetic prose, occasionally losing itself in the Iambic rhythm and sometimes resembling other measures." The only material difference, however, consisted in the concluding scene, in which the poet had originally united all the *personages* of the piece into one group, while in the revised poetical edition, the leading characters alone make their appearance at the end. This elimination attests the skill of the artist, who thus concentrates the attention of the reader or spectator upon the persons, to whom the moral power of the pathos at the moment of separation preëminently, if not exclusively, belongs, and who in the final happy arrangement form the sole expression of it.

The precise nature of his poetical prose was likewise mistaken by the poet in his critical valuation of his work. The unintentional and instinctive transitions into the quinquepedal Iambics of the Ancient drama are by far more frequent than he himself had supposed, so that many passages needed but little change, to convert them into their present form. An equally instinctive approximation to the stern regularity of the antique form, makes itself apparent in the careful avoidance of the rhyme, in the rapidity of the dialogue at moments of intenser interest, and in the free play of a bolder rhythm in the pæonic, anapæstic and dactylic measures, which in several monologues give fit expression to the abrupter and profounder emotions of the empassioned characters.

But in spite of all these peculiarities it cannot be maintained,

that the Iphigenia either in regard to subject or to form belongs to the classical period of the poet's history; it had already been essentially completed, when that new and interesting phase of his life took its commencement. And yet it must be regarded as the anticipation of it. It is the first indication of the inward revolution, i. e. of the poetical regeneration, which a few years afterwards the poet experienced during his residence in Italy. Inasmuch as, however, during the whole of this important journey (of the years 1786—1787), the drama was the Vademecum of the poet, and its reproduction in a rigorously metrical form his main occupation, the words of a distinguished literary critic are still, and without any limitation, true of this remarkable production :—
" The Iphigenia is a symbolical poem, in which the poet, who had just passed beyond the period of his titanic restlessness, celebrates in the redemption of the ancient house of Tantalos, his own reconciliation, his own newly acquired clearness and serenity of mind." *

It was by his absentment from the court of Weimar, that Goethe brought about this change of mind. It was one of the objects of the newly undertaken journey, to put himself at a distance from some of his earlier friends, whose influences on his mode of thinking and on his productivity he felt to be pernicious. His faith in the English and Northern poetry of nature had recently experienced repeated shocks, his Homer and his Ariosto began to take their place by the side of his Shakespeare and his Ossian. The " titanic ideas of his youthful years appeared to him like airy, spectral images, that served as harbingers to a severer period." He now felt the importance of adding order, taste and the beauty of the Ideal to the truth and the freedom of Nature, which in life, in science and in art had thus far been his only aim and idol. The works of Ancient Art in Italy supplanted his predilection for Gothic Architecture and for the Mediæval Style in Painting. " In comparing the creations of Nature with those of Plastic Art, he found that the former, like an artist, seeks to realize her final causes and ideas, without ever fully accomplishing her purposes, and that here lies properly the point of departure for art. It is here, where Man comes to the assistance of Nature. His superior intellectual endowments enable him to come up to the highest requisitions of his art. He reproduces the works of Nature, im-

* Gervinus.

parts to them a purer, a nobler, an ideal reality." * Goethe now saw, that in the highest productions of Grecian Art there was a perfect reconciliation between Nature and Art, between the Actual and the Ideal; and that the same was the case with the Greek poets. Formerly he had always invested his Homer with a halo of hyperpoetical splendor, but now he read him again with different eyes in Sicily. He recognized in him the very same naturalness, which he himself had sought during the first period of his poetic career, but here it was in union with the ideality and purity, for which he strove in this his second period. It was now, that he longed for a closer communion with the spirit of antiquity, that he desired to have his whole soul interpenetrated by its silent influences. The study of the Antique in its every form, and his favorite study of nature were carried on simultaneously, and with unremitting assiduity. The beautiful, the noble, the ideal was to be developed and eliminated from the amorphous multiplicity of the actual and common. It is by this process, that the poet arrived at the classical stand-point of his subsequent poetical career; he had now found the canon, by which to judge all the productions of modern origin, and after which he ever after strove to realize his own.

It has already been intimated, that Goethe had resolved to make his Iphigenia the companion of his journey into the charming country, which for years before he had so anxiously desired once to visit. No sooner had he been fairly under way, than he singled out the poem from the package of books, which he had taken with him for his amusement. He writes from the Brenner: "The glorious images of the surrounding scenery will not, I hope, be detrimental to my poetic tone of mind, but with the health-invigorating influence of exercise and open air conspire to awaken and enliven it."

The first lines of the new metrical version were written at the lake of Garda, while at noontide a powerful breeze was lashing the shore with its swelling waves, and where the poet felt himself as much in solitude, as did erewhile his heroine on the strand of Tauris. The work was continued at Verona, Vicenza, Padua and Venice. A temporary interruption took place in consequence of a new plan for another drama, "Iphigenia at Delphi," † which

* Gervinus.

† The following is an outline of the principal features of the plan of this projected drama :—

on his way from Cento to Bologna had suddenly presented itself
to the reflections of the poet. The task, however, was resumed
again with energy at Rome, where he worked at it perseveringly,
until at last he could inform his friends, that two copies of the
drama, of nearly the same import, were now lying all completed
on his table (Jan. 6th, 1787).

In this translation of the poem into Iambics, the society and
the Prosody of Moritz were of great advantage to the poet.
Goethe had by an accident made the valuable acquaintance of
that " pure and excellent " man towards the end of November,
during his residence in Rome, and both were soon united with
the ties of the most intimate friendship. During their solitary
walks and conversations many points of praxis in the poetic art
were made the theme of mutual interest, and the poet readily
embraced and applied the theorist's doctrine that "in regard to
quantity there exists a certain order of gradation among syllables,
so that the more significant, when in connection with one less
significant, is long and makes the latter short ; and that, on the
other hand, this same long syllable can again become short in
the proximity of another one of greater intellectual weight."
It is by this principle, that Goethe corrected many a passage of

Electra in the confident assurance, that Orestes would bring the image of
the Tauric Diana to Delphi, makes her appearance in the temple of Apollo,
for the purpose of dedicating the ruthless axe, which had wrought so much
mischief in the house of Pelops, as the final votive-offering to the God. While
engaged in this act, she is joined by a countryman of hers, who relates to her
how he had accompanied Orestes and Pylades to Tauris, and how he had seen
both his friends conducted as victims to the altar—a fate from which he himself had been lucky enough to escape. This unexpected intelligence makes
Electra frantic, and she hardly knows, whether to make the Gods or men the
object of her revengeful rage. Meanwhile Iphigenia, Orestes and Pylades
have likewise arrived at Delphi ; Iphigenia's holy repose appears in wonderfully marked contrast with the dark and worldly passion of Electra, when
they both meet without knowing each other. The Grecian fugitive, on perceiving Iphigenia, recognizes the priestess, who had sacrificed his friends, and
acquaints Electra with the discovery. The latter is on the point of murdering
Iphigenia with the fatal hatchet, which she had again extorted from the
priest, when a fortunate turn of circumstances averts this last and frightful
evil from the sisters. Goethe thought, if this scene succeeded, that hardly
any thing more sublime and more touching could ever have been seen on the
stage. This plan, however, was unfortunately never realized ; partly, it is
supposed, because the poet had made a premature communication of it to his
friends.

his new work, which in perfection of form leaves all his previous productions far behind.

The first representation of the original piece had already taken place on the 6th of April, 1779; greatly to the satisfaction of the poet, who on that occasion had the pleasure of witnessing its powerful effect on "*men of purity of character and heart.*" He himself had assumed the part of actor, and made his appearance in the character of Orestes. The masterly histrionic perform-ance of the poet left a lasting impression on the minds of many of the spectators, and his physician Hufeland, who attended and described the poet's last illness, alludes to this event many years afterwards in terms of high encomium:—"Never shall I forget the impression, which Goethe, as Orestes in his Greek costume, made on me at the first representation of his Iphigenia; he looked like an Apollo. Never before did any one witness such a union of physical and intellectual perfection and beauty."

Nor was the subsequent approval of the poem in its more per-fect shape, both on the stage and in the wider circle of its readers less decided and auspicious than the first. In regard to its merits, there has been but one voice from the beginning, and a multitude of monographs, programmes and lectures on the subject have vied with each other in their attempts to bring out all the hidden excel-lencies of the piece. Schiller alone was disposed to detract from it (surely not from any base or envious motive). And yet, in spite of his many and singular exceptions, he acknowledges, "that at the moment of its origin it had been a veritable meteor, of which the age itself and the majority of voices cannot even now see all the grandeur. It is a production, which from its universal high poetic qualities, of which independently of its dramatic form it is pos-sessed, and considered simply as the work of the creative in-tellect, will remain invaluable for all coming ages."

Schiller had shortly before made the remark, that after a repeat-ed and careful perusal, he had found the piece so *astonishingly modern and ungreek,* that he could not comprehend how it ever could have been possible to compare it with any ancient classical production. He found in it an utter lack of sensuous power, of animation of movement, in short, of all that stamps a work with the genuine specific character of a dramatic composition. Of this misapprehension of the true nature of this play, hereafter. In regard to the classicality or rather hellenicity of the piece, however, Schiller is not the only one, who has experienced doubts

10*

on the subject; and this question, which has undergone repeated
and various discussion, can hardly be decided by a simple affir-
mation or negation.

The absence of the chorus, of that most essential moral ingredient in the ancient tragedy, is at once felt by the critic, nor do
the repeated and admirably executed monologues, by which the
poet seems to have intended to supply its place in the economy of
the piece, preserve in our estimation that fair and perfect counterpoise between passionate conflict and calm reflection, between
fatal necessity and sublime resignation, between the sprightly
movement of the dialogue and the retarding effusions of serener
sentiments, which among the Ancients constitutes the most essential principle of tragic composition. This important function of
the chorus in the interlacement of the plot, this calm mirror of the
violent conflicts of the action, this powerful lever of the pathos in
its climax, we miss far more sensibly, than we do the actual presence of the Eumenides. This is the second objection which
Schiller urges against the classicality of the piece :—"Without the
Furies there can be no Orestes; and now, as the cause of his condition does not fall within the limits of the senses, as it resides
wholly within the mind of the tormented victim, his state of tor-
ment appears too long and uniform without an object." How
greatly, however, Schiller has on this point too mistaken not
only the real character of Goethe's work but of the ancient tragedy
itself, it would not be difficult to prove. The Eumenides of Æschylos is the only drama, wherein the Furies (who constitute the
chorus) are actually present among the personages of the play,
and where, together with the ghost of Klytemnestra, they visibly
pursue the foot-steps of the unhappy culprit, and appear in all
their terror as his pitiless accusers in the presence of his judges.
But even there the terrific effect produced by the inexorable goddess of vengeance, whose name the Ancients themselves could
never pronounce without a shudder, and which the poets on that
account invested with a euphenism, is mitigated at the close by
the mediation of Minerva, whose promises and flatteries convert
the curses of the direful sisters into endless blessings; so that the
chorus changes its ground entirely. Euripides on the other hand,
so far from ever bringing the Furies actually unto the stage (for example in his Orestes, where they might have been expected), does
not even introduce the madness of the stranger captive directly.
A herdsman is made to give us a description of his ravings on

the shore, at the time of his capture, and the poet makes the terrible encounter with the alien enemy produce a temporary cure, so that Orestes, although not yet free from his calamity and curse, remains a sane and rational man in all the subsequent course of the action. Goethe has, moreover depicted the inward torments of the matricide in such a vivid and pathetic manner, that we surely can dispense with their outward personification; their presence, besides being likely to offend our poetical faith, could hardly increase the terror and the pathos of those parts in which the culprit's bosom agonizes beneath the crushing burden of his guilt, and where the gloomy visions of his phrenzied reveries, the spectral terrors of his own imagination surely make the real presence of their mythical personifications more than superfluous. With Goethe both the malady and its cure are of an inward, a subjective nature. In this respect it has been justly remarked,* "that a Hellenic poet *might bring* the Erinnyes before the eye of the spectator, in whose belief they had an actual existence, who honored them with special sanctuaries, who made their ancient sacred images the object of a religious cultus. For us, however, they have no longer any reality; it is only in the heart of man, that we can recognize this fearful discord, the ever-returning fermentations of this inner strife. By these we see the mind of Orestes violently seized, by these we see him sink exhausted."

There are however a number of other elements in the economy of the piece, which are decidedly modern in their character. The impatient suit of Thoas for the hand of the priestess, which is repeatedly urged, and which as the main motive of several collisions enters so largely into the mechanism of the entire action, could hardly have proceeded from the pen of an ancient dramatist; and in Euripides, at least, there is no vestige of such a motive for the renewal of the foul sacrifice, or of such an impediment to the departure of the priestess. The characters of Pylades and Orestes, and the sentimental type of their earlier intercourse so vividly delineated by the poet, are decidedly modern, nay romantic even. The Ancients were utter strangers to such dreamy phantasies about the past, such glowing and idealizing visions of the future, as the poet has put into the mouth of the youthful friends (cf. Act II., Scene I.). One of the fundamental conceptions of the drama bears the evident imprint of a christian type. The long accumulated crimes of a whole family are to be wiped away by the spotless

* By Jahn.

hand, the loving mediation of one of its members, whose heart has remained free from the contaminating influences of her kindred. The humanity of all the characters, lastly, of the Greeks as well as of the Scythians appears here in a more elevated form than it ever existed among the Ancients, who in spite of the refinement of their civilization were ever incapable of transcending the limits of national prejudice and of a painfully exclusive particularism. The separation of the Greek from the Barbarian, like that of the Jew from the Gentile, conventional and accidental as it was, was held to be a matter of necessity, nor did the most enlightened Grecian ever expect to find the voice of truth and of humanity in a Barbarian's heart, to which the priestess in her interview with Thoas so confidently and so successfully makes her appeal. It is this pure, this universal humanity, into the loftier sphere of which both Taurian and Grecian are here elevated, that makes the interposition of Minerva entirely superfluous in the final settlement of the dispute. The moral power of persuasion, which finds its echo in men of every clime "in whose unsullied breast life's fountain unimpeded flows," accomplishes this victory; and all the tragic conflicts and collisions of the piece as well as their solution, are transferred into the bosom of the characters themselves. The question, therefore may again be asked : What then can support the drama's claim to classicality ?. To this we may reply :— Its limitation, the symmetry of its composition, the simplicity of the plot, its perspicuity and elegance of diction, the variety and perfect adaptation of its versification, which makes us forget the absence of the chorus even, the complete interpenetration of form and contents, and above all the serene repose, the plastic transparency, which manifests itself in all the master-pieces of Antiquity.

It is this that gives to Milton's Samson Agonistes an undoubted claim to antique excellence, in spite even of the heterogeneous nature of the subject; and Goethe has himself somewhere pronounced that tragedy of the English Æschylos superior to all the unhellenic modern imitations of the Ancients. We need not, therefore, hesitate to assert, that by the work in question, by the *ensemble* of the fable and the form, as well as by the specialities of their detail, we are perpetually reminded of the lofty cothurnus of the Greeks. Not only does the entire subject move within the well-known cyclus of the ancient tragedy, but all the leading incidents, the legends, the manners and the customs are purely Grecian,

and constantly point us not only to the immediate source, from
which the poet borrowed the general conception, but to all the
three immortal coryphæi of the antique tragedy at once.

The essence of the Hellenic mind, the peculiar and distinctive
spirit of its Art, as it revealed itself to Goethe, both in his earlier
studies of its literature, and more especially during his residence
in Italy, appears diffused throughout the whole of this production,
and will forever secure it an undisputed place by the side of the
noblest creations of the Ancients.

In regard to the fundamental idea of the piece, it has been
justly observed,* that it is the power with which moral truth,
the profounder intensity and purity of woman's mind and nature
exercise a transforming, purifying and elevating influence on all
that come within the limits of its action. The presence of Iphigenia has a humanizing, an ennobling effect on Thoas and on all
his Scythians. The healing of Orestes and the removal of the
ancient curse, which rests on the house of Tantalos, are accomplished by her expiating mediation. Her conciliatory suasion
puts an end to the angry quarrel, which towards the close of the
piece is beginning to be kindled between Thoas and Orestes.

The restoration of Iphigenia from the land of the Barbarians,
in which she leads the life of involuntary captivity, to the house of
her ancestors constitutes, as we at once perceive, the action of the
play. The introductory monologue already points to this her return, as the object of her ardent wishes, and the subsequent course
of the drama indicates step by step the measures for its realization.
Schiller, indeed, puts this external contexture of the action in
rank and file with the ideal ground-work of the piece, and even
speaks of *two* actions. He says in a letter to Goethe: " I would
furthermore submit it to your consideration, whether it would not
contribute to the enlivenment of the dramatic interest, to make
earlier mention of Thoas and his Taurians, who during two acts
are entirely idle, in order to keep up with equal intensity *both
actions*, the one of which, as it now stands, remains too long in a
state of repose." † This, however, cannot be justified. The

* By Kieser.
† Hegel likewise complains of a lack of dramatic energy in the piece. He
says (Æsthet. vol 3, p. 506):—"Goethe's Iphigenia and Tasso are both of
them excellent, as regards the vitality of their characters, and still they are
defective in strictly dramatic energy and animation. Thus Schiller has already remarked in regard to the Iphigenia, *that the moral sentiments of the*

whole drama is based _on one action only_, the liberation of Iphigenia, her restoration from the land of the Tauri; and that which Schiller considers a second and more inward action, the mutual recognition of brother and sister, the expiation of Orestes and the inward struggle in the breast of Iphigenia—all this is made subservient to the movement of that one action, and most intimately interwoven with it. It is by this very union, that the action which of itself alone would hardly suffice to form a worthy theme for a tragedy, receives its full significance. The retrodution of a noble princess from the land of inhuman Barbarians, in which a mysterious dispensation of the Higher Powers had cast her lot, where she is held fast by the gentler ties of gratitude and of a repectful affection, to the land of her own fathers, which the double charm of a beautiful nature and of a generous, humane enlightenment conspire to adorn, such a theme is surely not poor in poetical motives ; but how much more significant does this return become, when it links itself to the expiation of an ancient curse, with which an august royal house has long been laden ; if the returning maid brings back the peace, the blessing from the Gods, the splendor of the ancient regal power beneath the roof of her paternal mansion !

Here, however, we at once perceive a difficulty in the problem, which the poet has proposed to solve. The peace, the salvation, which Iphigenia's return brings to her paternal house, lie beyond the limits of the piece in a nearer or remoter future, and could on that account not be directly presented to our eyes. And yet the spectator was to have a full assurance of these concomitant effects of her return, in order to be able to take a profounder interest in the course of the action. How much easier in this respect was Schiller's task in his Maid of Orleans ! He could make Joanna fulfil the whole of her mission before our eyes. At the time of

heart, its inner revolutions and changes are made the action of the piece, and thus outwardly unfolded to our view. And indeed the mere expression and delineation of the inner world of different characters in determinate situations is not enough, but the collision of their individual aims must make itself prominent, must urge and push the movement onward. It is on this account that Schiller finds too calm a course and too much retardation in the piece, which, if held up to the rigorous requirements of tragic composition, exhibits even, in his opinion a manifest encroachment on the domain of the Epopee. For, the efficient cause of all dramatic effect is the action as action, and not the mere exposition of character as such, and independently of a determinate aim, and its accomplishment."

her end, the power of England is already broken, and the crown
of his ancestors has already been placed upon the head of the
Dauphin. In the Tauric Iphigenia of Euripides the case is likewise different.: There the ultimate goal of the action was not so
much the return of the princess, but rather the abduction of the
image of Artemis, which an oracular response had made the condition of the propitiation of the divine wrath.

As soon as this condition was fulfilled, the believing Athenian
no longer doubted the completion of the divine promise. Our
poet could not presuppose the same believing disposition in his
public, and was therefore obliged to produce in some other way
the assurance, that Iphigenia would certainly accomplish the purification of her ancestral house. He justly thought, that he could
best effect such a conviction, by making his Iphigenia exercise a
purifying, conciliating and ennobling influence in all directions
within the limits of the piece itself. Hence the emphatic and
repeated allusions to the beneficent effects of this her influence on
Thoas and his Taurians; hence too the fact, that the cure of
Orestes is already completed within the limits of the drama,
sooner even, than the God himself had promised. For the same
reason, the representation of the moral element, the general development of the internal processes and changes occupies so wide
a space in comparison with the movement of the outward action.
The *soul*, as Schiller says, was to constitute the characteristic
excellence of the piece.*

Among the exceptions, that have been made against this piece
of Goethe, is the somewhat tedious prolongation of many of the
exposition-scenes and of the lyrical monologues. The retardation, to which these parts give rise, has been pronounced too
great, and in general the sluggish movement of the fable, the too
gradual development of the action has been regarded as a blemish.
But are not all these expositions necessary links in the mechanism
of the whole? Do they not all serve either as preparatory motives
for what follows, or as justifications of what precedes? Nay, in
the absence of a chorus, could they well be dispensed with in a
piece, where the moral, the psychical revolutions of the heart are
made to take the place of external incident, and where the pathos
of the characters does not transcend the limits of the mind? This
delineation both of the softest emotions, and of the intensest pas-

* Viehoff.

sions of the heart, as well as of the mysterious influences of one
human soul upon the diseased condition of another, constitutes, as
has already been intimated, the characteristic excellence of the
drama. In this respect the poet has been so admirably successful, he has so vividly unfolded to our view the most secret
moral powers of our nature, that in the whole range of dramatic
literature, we might perhaps in vain look for the rival of this
production. But by the very nature of the problem, the movement of the outward action must necessarily be slower, if not
subordinate to another purpose ; and there are scenes in which
the retardation can only be justified on that ground. In a drama
of the ordinary type, it would be as intolerably tedious, as it
would be out of place. The interest of the reader, however,
is admirably sustained throughout the whole. Even the long
account of Iphigenia relating to her personal history preceding
her arrival in Tauris (Act I. Scene 3), so far from becoming
wearisome, enlist the attention and the lively sympathy of the
spectator as much as it does that of the king. So does the somewhat lengthy exposition of the history of the Trojan war since
the detention of the army at Aulis, and the rehearsal of the fate
of the prominent chieftains of the war, including the calamities of Agamemnon's house, which the priestess elicits from the
victim-prisoners (Act II. Scene 2 ; Act III. Scene 1st). The
former of these prolonged dialogues contains at the same time
the motive for the renewal of the long-intermitted sacrifice,
the latter furnishes a natural occasion for the mutual recognition
of brother and sister. Pylades, unwilling to confess the crime
of his companion to its full extent, and still unable to conceal
it wholly, the latter being every moment liable to an attack of
his insanity, attempts to mitigate the criminality of Orestes by
inventing a fictitious story, similar in its leading features to
the real one, in which he converts the matricide into a fratri-
cide. This perversion of the truth, which Hermann and others
have censured as gratuitous, is wholly in keeping with the
character of the man, who professes to follow Ulysses as his
model of heroic exellence, who like his prototype, seeks every
where to gain his point by a temporizing caution, by a politic
concealment of his real purposes. The story, moreover, serves
as a preparation for the subsequent recognition-scene, which is
based on a far more poetical motive than that of Euripides.
Goethe has thus made the letter-scene of his predecessor en-

tirely superfluous, and the discovery results from the natural succession of the incidents themselves.

Equally important in the moral economy of the play is the introductory scene of the second Act, which has likewise been unjustly censured for its disproportionate length. The difficult nature of the subject accounts for the expansion. In that long interview Pylades makes the first attempt to rouse his gloomy friend from the melancholy reveries of his ever-active imagination, and to dispel his subtilizing reflections on his guilt by the brighter reminiscence of their earlier and more joyful days. He spares no effort, no argument to divert his mind from every recollection of the horrid deed, and to inspire him with courage for a new career of happier existence. The very failure of this attempt, so earnestly, so kindly and so perseveringly made, points us to the difficulty of the cure, to the deeply-rooted nature of the dangerous malady, which needs a far more powerful remedy for its complete removal. Pylades, being one of those sagacious and happy natures, who with all their practical insight and caution, are ever incapable of comprehending the profounder verities and wants of our inner nature, is utterly unable to accomplish the desired oblivion, in his friend. He stands in need of a better physician, of a purer, deeper and more affectionate heart, into which to pour the seething contents of his own. The whole of the third Act is devoted to this remarkable psychical cure which is one of the characteristic features of the play, and at the same time one of the prominent points of difference from the original. Euripides links the justification of the criminal to the future mercy of Apollo, which is dependent on the safe arrival of the statue, which the fugitives actually carry away with them. Æschylos, who has consecrated three dramas to the fate of Agamemnon and his son,* accomplishes the absolution of the latter

---

* This trilogy is commonly called the *Oresteia*, and consists of the Agamemnon, the Choëphoræ, and the Eumenides. An outline of these tragedies is given by Schlegel (Dramat. Liter. Lect. VI.), to which the reader is referred. On their moral and religious significance in the history of ancient civilization Welcker (Trilog. Æschyl. p. 447) has descanted, from whom the following:—

"In a philosophical point of view, there is hardly another trilogy, the Prometheus excepted, that has been more significant than this *Oresteia*. It treats of the most difficult problem, that can be propounded for the solution of mankind, next to that, which is treated in the Prometheus; nay the phases of human destiny have here even a more tragical and a more melancholy appearance than in the former. It was the duty of Orestes, as a son, to avenge

by the sublime machinery of a trial, before a tribunal instituted
his father and to protect his sister: it was his duty as a prince, to punish his
culprit-mother. Hence his deed, according to Odyssee I., 298; III., 196, was
not only considered just, but the ground of the highest renown. But, although
he had been instigated to perpetrate the deed by the Delphic Apollo himself,
from whom the Hellenic Laws derived their supreme sanction (Choëph. 255),
yet still the power of the maternal curses (γενέϑλιοι ἀραί Choëph. 849;
μητρὸς ἔγκοτοι κύνες 861, ἀραί and Ἐριννύες are equipollent. Eumen. 420) has
its ground and origin in nature itself, and the Erinnyes, who enforce the law
(v. 212), that no kindred blood is to be spilled, are members of the ancient
dynasty of Gods. The temporal and civil calamities, with which Apollo
threatens to visit Orestes (Choëph. 257 seqq.), in case he does not fulfil his
duty—a memorable remnant of the ancient custom of private vengeance—the
Erinnyes from the father's blood, the invisible anger of his sire, are in no respect inferior to those, which the Erinnyes of his mother actually inflict on
him; and hence they are so emphatically delineated in all their terrors, in
order that they may not fail to counterpoise the actual torments of the
sufferer, as represented in the play. The same demand is made of the unhappy man by the gentler members of the chorus even, as well as by Electra.
He knows the consequences, without recoiling from them (v. 399): "When
through the gods and through my arm she has atoned for the dishonor of my
sire, then I am ready to depart and perish." Still he hesitates the moment
before proceeding to the deed, v. 836: "Pylades, what am I doing, shall I
shun the mother's death?" And after all, it is not *he*, but the father's
avenging fate, that consigns her to destruction (v. 848). And even at the
moment where he already feels the preliminary symptoms of his phrenzy, he
yet appeals to his right (especially before the witnesses), and asserts his innocence from guilt (v. 958). The same before the tribunal of the Gods in the
Eumenides (Eumen. v. 446). The votes of the Areopagos, moreover, are
equally divided; for the conflict of these two ideas there is no solution, except
in a higher order of things, in a divine and gracious pardon of the involuntary
guilt. This is obtained by the mediation of the tribunal, expressly instituted
by Minerva, where the goddess herself procures his absolution by her casting-
vote, at the same time making a compact with the angrily protesting goddesses
(the Erinnyes), binding them henceforward to be expiable, and to assume the
euphemistic name (Eumenides), by which thereafter they were to be addressed
in prayer. This source of refuge, which Athens was proud to number among
its peculiar sanctuaries, was at the time of the transition from private vengeance
to public provisions for justice to be invested with a divine and mystic sanction.
This was so much the more essential, as the Ancients regarded the state as the
expression of humanity in a much wider sense than we do, and among them
there was a closer interpenetration of the spiritual of the secular order of
things. A crime, which nature itself or a natural destiny seemed to have de-
posited in individual men, could only be expiated by the provisions of a divine
institution. This morally religious problem and its solution constitute the
Unity of the pieces, and as all this is represented in the person of Orestes, the
trilogy has justly been called *the Oresteia*, after his name.

by Minerva, where the accusers, the defenders and the presiding judges are all gods.

As Goethe, however, had already transferred the Furies into the bosom of the culprit himself, so he effects his expiation and his cure without the special intervention of the higher powers. The sister-priestess, by whose spotless hand the whole ancestral house is to be purified, accomplishes herself successfully and completely, what Pylades had vainly aimed to do, and by the healing of her brother, initiates the grand work of her future mission. The sacredness of the family, which Orestes by his vengeful act had fearfully violated, under the questionable impulse of a filial duty, could only be restored by the loving mediation of one of its members, who had never been involved in any of its crimes. Electra, who had herself been accessory to the deed, could offer no consoling or forgiving word to the unhappy brother. The sister, whom a happier destiny had kept secreted in the temple's solitude was to receive the penitent confession, was to pronounce the healing absolution.

This was so much the more efficacious, as it came from one, who in the opinion of the Ancients, in her turn had now the right of exacting vengeance from the matricide, and of continuing the internecine quarrel of her ill-fated house, of which her own supposed immolation had been the unhappy cause. And well nigh had an evil destiny in its exorable blindness perpetuated the abomination, against her will and without her knowledge. The unknown culprit was already in her hands and she was dooming him unconsciously to certain death before the altar. His frank confession and the resulting discovery bring him unexpected deliverance from a fate, to which a righteous Nemesis would seem to have consigned him. The voice of the priestess too, at first stirs up the inmost depths of his soul, and her appearance resuscitates once more the frightful memory of his mother; and yet that voice is full of love, of reconciliation and forgiveness, which like some ray of heavenly light now seeks to penetrate and melt the icy midnight of his gloom.

It is this secret magic of her pure affectionate soul, that encourages him to take the first bold step for his recovery. By making a *full confession* of his crime, which like a heavy incubus had rested on his mind, which made him sink towards the pit and long for death, he fulfils the first condition of a complete removal of his inward agonies. The pure joy of the sis-

ter, her grateful and pious invocation of the gods, her kind encouragement, her loving benediction break at last the spell of
anguish, and convert the phrenzy of despair into the softer emotions of repentance and contrition. This whole conflict of re-
morseful anguish, of gloomy despondency and of contrite penitence is painted in all its phases and transitions with a power
and a truth, that show the artist's profoundest acquaintance with
the most secret workings of our moral nature.

The struggle of conflicting emotions reaches the acme of its
intensity at the close of the first scene of the third Act, and Orestes, exhausted by the terrible commotion, falls into a temporary
state of unconsciousness. A short sweet slumber heals to some
extent the wounds, which the boisterous storm of passions had
inflicted; and with the partial recovery of his conscious mind,
the first symptoms of convalescence make their appearance.
The call of affection, which resounded from Iphigenia's heart
into the midnight of his phrenzy, was not without its effect. The
short stupefaction is at first followed by a half conscious dreamlike reverie, wherein the imagination, still clinging to those terrible thoughts of death, which had filled his mind before, begins
now to mitigate their terror by blending them with softer images
of reconciliation and forgiveness.

"Orestes sees in a vision his ancestors Atreus and Thyestes
walking together in friendly conversation, and the boys that had
been sacrificed, sporting around them; Klytemnestra confidently
extends her hand to her forgiving consort, and he infers *that he too*
may expect the pardon of his mother. From this scene of universal reconciliation Tantalos alone appears excluded, who by his
haughty insolence had committed an unpardonable sin against
Higher Powers. The poet makes use of this figure to call Orestes back from the region of imaginary phantoms to the present
reality before him. The previous images were evoked by the
productive imagination, which is a purely creative faculty, but in
this conception, which is only a legendary reminiscence, the *reproductive* imagination is concerned; and by this transition Orestes
is brought one step nearer to reality. Pylades and Iphigenia now
make their appearance; Orestes recognizes them, but he still
believes himself together with them in the world of shades. This
last delusion is dispelled partly by Iphigenia's beautiful prayer to
Diana, partly and more especially by the exhortations of Pylades.
After the affection of the sister had quelled the tumultuous com-

motion of his mind, from which the clouds had risen, which had
obscured the understanding of Orestes, the call of Pylades completes the cure and the collection of his mind yet wandering in
the regions of its dreams, by making every effort to rivet his
attention to definite objects of reality:—*Dost thou not know us
and this sacred grove? &c.* He tries to paralyze the morbid
activity of his internal sense by offering a powerful stimulus to
the most important outward senses, to his sight, his touch, his
ear:—*Perceiv'st thou not?... Dost thou not feel?... Attend
to my word!* And he finally even appeals to the instinct of
self-preservation:—*Every moment now is precious, &c.*"*

The words which Orestes utters in the subsequent address to
Iphigenia (Act III., Scene third) exhibit the completeness of the
change. The joy at his recovery, which in the sister's arms and
on the bosom of his friend he hopes may be permanent, flows
out in unfeigned gratitude towards the Gods, who Iris-like had
parted the grey veil of the last cloud so benignantly. His heart
informs him of the dissipation of the curse; he hears the dire
Eumenides depart for Tartaros, closing its brazen gates with far-
off-thundering violence. The earth itself exhales fresh odors
sweet, invites him to its far-extending plains, new joys of life and
lofty deeds to seek!

With the close of the third Act the cure of Orestes is already
completed. If that had been the main object of the piece, the
remainder would appear too widely extended, if not entirely
superfluous. Hence the necessity of another moral collision of
great significance in the concluding acts of the drama.

Iphigenia had grown up in the sacred precincts of Diana's
temple to be a paragon of womanly excellence, the model of the
purest humanity, of the truest, the noblest refinement of character and heart. She has now imposed on her the important mission of delivering her family from the festering ruin of an in-
veterate curse. This her mission has already been successfully
commenced by the healing of her brother, who as the only surviving male member of her house had been the main object of the
divine vengeance. Him she has already completely rescued from
the grasp of the Erinnyes. It is here, however, where the course
of the action demands another dramatic opposition, another impediment, which the priestess is to overcome, another trial, to which
her virtue is to be subjected and over which it is at last to rise vic-

* Viehoff.

toriòus. This is the conflict in Iphigenia's own breast, in which
the advice of Pylades, to whose direction the future movements
of the party were entrusted, has involved her. She was to resort
to deception with reference to her flight and the intended seizure
of the image ; and this deception was to be practiced on a man
whom she was bound to venerate as her protector, whose kindness had endeared him as a second father ! On this account her
heart is painfully divided and vacillating between fraternal affection and the deeply rooted instinct of self-preservation on the one
hand, and the duty of gratitude towards her generous benefactor
on the other. In this last interior conflict, which the poet has so
beautifully portrayed, the noble nature of Iphigenia's heart becomes unveiled to us in all the richness of its loveliness, its tenderness, its spotless purity.

It is by throwing out the uncongenial hateful element of dissi-
mulation and of falsehood, which threatens to defile her soul, that
she brings about that beautiful solution of the nodus of the action,
which Euripides could not accomplish but by the interference of
a higher power. She makes the bold resolve of frankly con-
fessing the concerted robbery and fraud, even at the risk of frus-
trating entirely the plan of flight, which her friends had already
matured. It is by other weapons, however, that she thinks to
conquer, and the magnitude, the exalted nature of her mission
afford her an abundance of moral arguments, to which the mind
of Thoas is not wholly inaccessible, and by which his stubborn
heart is conquered in the end.

It is thus that we see the same moral power, by which before she had shed the lustre of a humanizing refinement on all
around her, triumphantly victorious in her own struggle against
a temptation, which threatens to destroy the inward peace and
purity of her mind. Her virtue, moreover, after this ordeal is
doubly deserving of our further confidence, and guarantees to
us the permanence of her work, the certainty of its accomplishment. The enemy of her heart being overcome, the remaining
outward impediments and difficulties of her path will likewise
vanish.

The concluding scenes of the piece in which the collision between Orestes and the king chiefly occupies the attention of the
reader, are full of dramatic interest and animation. To the settlement of the last remaining point of dispute, which the king proposes to decide by force of arms, the unexpected discovery of

Orestes, that by the sister Apollo meant the priestess herself, and not his own sister Artemis, is as happy as it is original. Perhaps it was suggested to the poet by the ancient legend, that Diana and Iphigenia were synonymous, and that the latter was the former deified or *vice versa*.

The final laconic "farewell" of Thoas, who finds himself completely vanquished by the resistless suasion of the priestess and her brother, is in perfect keeping with the character of the uncultured king of the Barbarians, who "accustomed only to command and act, had never learnt the art of conversation." The previous concluding speech of Iphigenia, who could not bear to abide by the indignantly reluctant " *Then go!* " of her noble friend, completely harmonizes the only remaining discord of this last collision. Her warm affection, her ingenuous gratitude, her earnest desire, that a friendly hospitality should ever thereafter subsist between the Scythian and the Greek, may be supposed to reconcile the king completely to his disappointment and his loss. All his objections are hushed by the earnestly eloquent appeals of Iphigenia and her brother; he acquesces in their departure and the reader may confidently supply the reciprocal exchange of the pledge of ancient friend ship, for which the priestess in conclusion expresses a desire This dénouement of the drama has justly been the subject of admiration. "The profounder mediation of the tragic conception does not consist in the mere juxtaposition or conversion of the extremes (of characters and collisions), but in their mutual obtusion and compensation. This mode of conception is peculiar to the modern drama. The Ancients had indeed already plays, which terminated in a similar manner, that is to say, none of the characters are sacrificed, but saved by an adjustment of the strife. The Eumenides of Æschylos, the Philoctetes of Sophocles and the Tauric Iphigenia of Euripides are examples of this kind. But in all these instances the reconciliation is accomplished *ab extra* by the interposition of the gods, &c., and has not its inward source in the characters themselves, while in the modern drama it is the contending parties themselves, who by the course of their own actions find themselves gradually brought to a voluntary cessation from their quarrel, and to a mutual reconciliation of their separate aims and characters." *

* Hegel.

This reconciliation is so complete in the piece before us,
that its close is invested with an evening-sky of calm serenity
and of godlike repose; and the reader cannot suppress the
wish, that favorable breezes may gently swell the sails of the
departing ones, and that the gods may smile on all their future
purposes!

Iphigenie auf Tauris.

Ein Schauspiel

von

Goethe.

241.—11.

Perſonen.

Iphigenie.

Thoas, König der Taurier.

Oreſt.

Pylades.

Arkas.

Schauplatz: Hain vor Dianens Tempel.

Erster Aufzug.

Erster Auftritt.

Iphigenie.

Heraus in eure Schatten, rege Wipfel
Des alten, heil'gen, dichtbelaubten Haines,
Wie in der Göttin stilles Heiligthum,
Tret' ich noch jetzt mit schauderndem Gefühl,
Als wenn ich sie zum Erstenmal beträte,
Und es gewöhnt sich nicht mein Geist hierher.
So manches Jahr bewahrt mich hier verborgen
Ein hoher Wille, dem ich mich ergebe;
Doch immer bin ich, wie im ersten, fremd:
Denn ach, mich trennt das Meer von den Geliebten,
Und an dem Ufer steh' ich lange Tage,
Das Land der Griechen mit der Seele suchend;
Und gegen meine Seufzer bringt die Welle
Nur dumpfe Töne brausend mir herüber.
Weh dem, der fern von Eltern und Geschwistern
Ein einsam Leben führt! Ihm zehrt der Gram
Das nächste Glück vor seinen Lippen weg;
Ihm schwärmen abwärts immer die Gedanken
Nach seines Vaters Hallen, wo die Sonne
Zuerst den Himmel vor ihm aufschloß, wo
Sich Mitgeborne spielend fest und fester
Mit sanften Banden an einander knüpften.
Ich rechte mit den Göttern nicht; allein
Der Frauen Zustand ist beklagenswerth.
Zu Hauf' und in dem Kriege herrscht der Mann
Und in der Fremde weiß er sich zu helfen.

243

Ihn freuet der Beſitz; ihn krönt der Sieg;
Ein ehrenvoller Tod iſt ihm bereitet.
Wie eng=gebunden iſt des Weibes Glück!
Schon einem rauhen Gatten zu gehorchen,
Iſt Pflicht und Troſt; wie elend, wenn ſie gar
Ein' feindlich Schickſal in die Ferne treibt!
So hält mich Thoas hier, ein edler Mann,
In ernſten, heil'gen Sklavenbanden feſt.
O wie beſchämt geſteh' ich, daß ich dir
Mit ſtillem Wiederwillen diene, Göttin,
Dir, meiner Retterin! Mein Leben ſollte
Zu freiem Dienſte dir gewidmet ſeyn.
Auch hab' ich ſtets auf dich gehofft und hoffe
Noch jetzt auf dich, Diana, die du mich,
Des größten Königes verſtoßne Tochter,
In deinen heil'gen, ſanften Arm genommen.
Ja, Tochter Zeus, wenn du den hohen Mann,
Den du, die Tochter fordernd, ängſtigteſt,
Wenn du den göttergleichen Agamemnon,
Der dir ſein Liebſtes zum Altare brachte,
Von Troja's umgewandten Mauern rühmlich
Nach ſeinem Vaterland' zurück begleitet,
Die Gattin ihm, Elektren und den Sohn,
Die ſchönen Schätze wohl erhalten haſt:
So gib auch mich den Meinen endlich wieder,
Und rette mich, die du vom Tod' errettet,
Auch von dem Leben hier, dem zweiten Tode!

Zweiter Auftritt.

Iphigenie. Arkas.

Arkas.

Der König ſendet mich hieher und beut
Der Prieſterin Dianens Gruß und Heil.
Dies iſt der Tag, da Tauris ſeiner Göttin
Für wunderbare neue Siege dankt.

Ich eile vor dem König und dem Heer,
Zu melden daß er kommt und daß es naht.

Iphigenie.

Wir sind bereit sie würdig zu empfangen,
Und unsre Göttin sieht willkommnem Opfer
Von Thoas Hand mit Gnadenblick entgegen.

Arkas.

O fänd' ich auch den Blick der Priesterin,
Der werthen, vielgeehrten, deinen Blick,
O heil'ge Jungfrau, heller, leuchtender,
Uns allen gutes Zeichen!   Noch bedeckt
Der Gram geheimnißvoll dein Innerstes;
Vergebens harren wir schon Jahre lang
Auf ein vertraulich Wort aus deiner Brust.
So lang' ich dich an dieser Stätte kenne,
Ist dies der Blick, vor dem ich immer schaudre;
Und wie mit Eisenbanden bleibt die Seele
Ins Innerste des Busens dir geschmiedet.

Iphigenie.

Wie's der Vertriebnen, der Verwais'ten ziemt.

Arkas.

Scheinst du dir hier vertrieben und verwais't?

Iphigenie.

Kann uns zum Vaterland' die Fremde werden?

Arkas.

Und dir ist fremd das Vaterland geworden.

Iphigenie.

Das ist's, warum mein blutend Herz nicht heilt.
In erster Jugend, da sich kaum die Seele
An Vater, Mutter und Geschwister band;
Die neuen Schößlinge, gesellt und lieblich,
Vom Fuß der alten Stämme himmelwärts
Zu dringen strebten; leider faßte da
Ein fremder Fluch mich an und trennte mich
Von den Geliebten, riß das schöne Band

Mit eh'rner Faust entzwei.   Sie war dahin,
Der Jugend beste Freude, das Gedeihn
Der ersten Jahre.   Selbst gerettet, war
Ich nur ein Schatten mir, und frische Lust
Des Lebens blüht in mir nicht wieder auf.

Arkas.

Wenn du dich so unglücklich nennen willst,
So darf ich dich auch wohl undankbar nennen.

Iphigenie.

Dank habt ihr stets.

Arkas.

            Doch nicht den reinen Dank,
Um dessentwillen man die Wohlthat thut;
Den frohen Blick, der ein zufriednes Leben
Und ein geneigtes Herz dem Wirthe zeigt.
Als dich ein tief=geheimnißvolles Schicksal
Vor so viel Jahren diesem Tempel brachte,
Kam Thoas dir, als einer Gottergeb'nen,
Mit Ehrfurcht und mit Neigung zu begegnen,
Und dieses Ufer ward dir hold und freundlich,
Das jedem Fremden sonst voll Grausens war,
Weil Niemand unser Reich vor dir betrat,
Der an Dianens heil'gen Stufen nicht,
Nach altem Brauch, ein blutig Opfer, fiel.

Iphigenie.

Frei athmen macht das Leben nicht allein.
Welch Leben ist's, das an der heil'gen Stätte,
Gleich einem Schatten um sein eigen Grab,
Ich nur vertrauern muß?   Und nenn' ich das
Ein fröhlich selbstbewußtes Leben, wenn
Uns jeder Tag, vergebens hingeträumt,
Zu jenen grauen Tagen vorbereitet,
Die an dem Ufer Lethe's, selbstvergessend,
Die Trauerschaar der Abgeschiednen feiert?
Ein unnütz Leben ist ein früher Tod;
Dies Frauenschicksal ist vor allen mein's.

Arkas.

Den edeln Stolz, daß du dir selbst nicht g'nügest,
Verzeih' ich dir, so sehr ich dich bedaure;
Er raubet den Genuß des Lebens dir.
Du hast hier nichts gethan seit deiner Ankunft?
Wer hat des Königs trüben Sinn erheitert?
Wer hat den alten grausamen Gebrauch,
Daß am Altar Dianens jeder Fremde
Sein Leben blutend läßt, von Jahr zu Jahr,
Mit sanfter Ueberredung aufgehalten,
Und die Gefangnen vom gewissen Tod'
Ins Vaterland so oft zurückgeschickt?
Hat nicht Diane, statt erzürnt zu seyn,
Daß sie der blut'gen alten Opfer mangelt,
Dein sanft Gebet in reichem Maß erhört?
Umschwebt mit frohem Fluge nicht der Sieg
Das Heer? und eilt er nicht sogar voraus?
Und fühlt nicht Jeglicher ein besser Loos,
Seitdem der König, der uns weis' und tapfer
So lang geführet, nun sich auch der Milde
In deiner Gegenwart erfreut und uns
Des schweigenden Gehorsams Pflicht erleichtert?
Das nennst du unnütz, wenn von deinem Wesen
Auf Tausende herab ein Balsam träufelt?
Wenn du dem Volke, dem ein Gott dich brachte,
Des neuen Glückes ew'ge Quelle wirst,
Und an dem unwirthbaren Todes-Ufer
Dem Fremden Heil und Rückkehr zubereitest?

Iphigenie.

Das Wenige verschwindet leicht dem Blick,
Der vorwärts sieht, wie viel noch übrig bleibt.

Arkas.

Doch lobst du den, der, was er thut, nicht schätzt?

Iphigenie.

Man tadelt den, der seine Thaten wägt.

Arkas.

Auch den, der wahren Werth zu stolz nicht achtet,
Wie den, der falschen Werth zu eitel hebt.
Glaub' mir und hör' auf eines Mannes Wort,
Der treu und redlich dir ergeben ist:
Wenn heut der König mit dir redet, so
Erleichtr' ihm, was er dir zu sagen denkt.

Iphigenie.

Du ängstest mich mit jedem guten Worte;
Oft wich ich seinem Antrag mühsam aus.

Arkas.

Bedenke, was du thust und was dir nützt.
Seitdem der König seinen Sohn verloren,
Vertraut er Wenigen der Seinen mehr,
Und diesen Wenigen nicht mehr wie sonst.
Mißgünstig sieht er jedes Edeln Sohn
Als seines Reiches Folger an; er fürchtet
Ein einsam hülflos Alter, ja vielleicht
Verwegnen Aufstand und frühzeit'gen Tod.
Der Scythe setzt in's Reden keinen Vorzug,
Am wenigsten der König. Er, der nur
Gewohnt ist zu befehlen und zu thun,
Kennt nicht die Kunst, von Weitem ein Gespräch
Nach seiner Absicht langsam fein zu lenken.
Erschwer's ihm nicht durch ein rückhaltend Weigern,
Durch ein vorsetzlich Mißverstehen. Geh'
Gefällig ihm den halben Weg entgegen.

Iphigenie.

Soll ich beschleunigen, was mich bedroht?

Arkas.

Willst du sein Werben eine Drohung nennen?

Iphigenie.

Es ist die schrecklichste von allen mir.

Arkas.

Gib ihm für seine Neigung nur Vertrau'n.

Iphigenie.

Wenn er von Furcht erst meine Seele lös't.

Arkas.

Warum verschweigst du deine Herkunft ihm?

Iphigenie.

Weil einer Priesterin Geheimniß ziemt.

Arkas.

Dem König sollte nichts Geheimniß seyn;
Und ob er's gleich nicht fordert, fühlt er's doch
Und fühlt es tief in seiner großen Seele,
Daß du sorgfältig dich vor ihm verwahrst.

Iphigenie.

Nährt er Verdruß und Unmuth gegen mich?

Arkas.

So scheint es fast. Zwar schweigt er auch von dir;
Doch haben hingeworfne Worte mich
Belehrt, daß seine Seele fest den Wunsch
Ergriffen hat, dich zu besitzen. Laß,
O überlaß ihn nicht sich selbst! damit
In seinem Busen nicht der Unmuth reife
Und dir Entsetzen bringe, du zu spät
An meinen treuen Rath mit Reue denkest.

Iphigenie.

Wie? Sinnt der König, was kein edler Mann,
Der seinen Namen liebt und dem Verehrung
Der Himmlischen den Busen bändiget,
Je denken sollte? Sinnt er vom Altar
Mich in sein Bette mit Gewalt zu ziehn?
So ruf' ich alle Götter und vor allen
Dianen, die entschloßne Göttin an,
Die ihren Schutz der Priesterin gewiß
Und Jungfrau einer Jungfrau gern gewährt.

Arkas.

Sey ruhig! Ein gewaltsam neues Blut
Treibt nicht den König, solche Jünglingsthat
Verwegen auszuüben. Wie er sinnt,

11*

Befürcht' ich andern harten Schluß von ihm,
Den unaufhaltbar er vollenden wird:
Denn seine Seel' ist fest und unbeweglich.
Drum bitt' ich dich), vertrau' ihm, sey ihm dankbar,
Wenn du ihm weiter nichts gewähren kannst.

Iphigenie.

O sage, was dir weiter noch bekannt ist.

Arkas.

Erfahr's von ihm. Ich seh' den König kommen;
Du ehrst ihn, und dich heißt dein eigen Herz,
Ihm freundlich und vertraulich zu begegnen.
Ein edler Mann wird durch ein gutes Wort
Der Frauen weit geführt.

Iphigenie (allein).

            Zwar seh' ich nicht,
Wie ich dem Rath des Treuen folgen soll.
Doch folg' ich gern der Pflicht, dem Könige
Für seine Wohlthat gutes Wort zu geben,
Und wünsche mir, daß ich dem Mächtigen,
Was ihm gefällt, mit Wahrheit sagen möge.

Dritter Auftritt.

Iphigenie. Thoas.

Iphigenie.

Mit königlichen Gütern segne dich
Die Göttin! Sie gewähre Sieg und Ruhm
Und Reichthum und das Wohl der Deinigen
Und jedes frommen Wunsches Fülle dir!
Daß, der du über Viele sorgend herrschest,
Du auch vor Vielen seltnes Glück genießest.

Thoas.

Zufrieden wär' ich, wenn mein Volk mich rühmte;
Was ich erwarb, genießen Andre mehr
Als ich. Der ist am glücklichsten, er sey
Ein König oder ein Geringer, dem

In seinem Hause Wohl bereitet ist.
Du nahmest Theil an meinem tiefen Schmerze,
Als mir das Schwert der Feinde meinen Sohn,
Den letzten, besten, von der Seite riß.
So lang' die Rache meinen Geist besaß,
Empfand ich nicht die Oede meiner Wohnung;
Doch jetzt, da ich befriedigt wiederkehre,
Ihr Reich zerstört, mein Sohn gerochen ist,
Bleibt mir zu Hause nichts, das mich ergötze.
Der fröhliche Gehorsam, den ich sonst
Aus einem jeden Auge blicken sah,
Ist nun von Sorg' und Unmuth still gedämpft.
Ein Jeder sinnt, was künftig werden wird,
Und folgt dem Kinderlosen, weil er muß.
Nun komm' ich heut in diesen Tempel, den
Ich oft betrat, um Sieg zu bitten und
Für Sieg zu danken.   Einen alten Wunsch
Trag' ich im Busen, der auch dir nicht fremd,
Noch unerwartet ist: ich hoffe, dich,
Zum Segen meines Volks und mir zum Segen,
Als Braut in meine Wohnung einzuführen.

Iphigenie.

Der Unbekannten bietest du zu viel,
O König, an.   Es steht die Flüchtige
Beschämt vor dir, die nichts an diesem Ufer
Als Schutz und Ruhe sucht, die du ihr gabst.

Thoas.

Daß du in das Geheimniß deiner Abkunft
Vor mir wie vor dem Letzten stets dich hüllest,
Wär' unter keinem Volke recht und gut.
Dies Ufer schreckt die Fremden: das Gesetz
Gebietet's und die Noth.   Allein von dir,
Die jedes frommen Rechts genießt, ein wohl
Von uns empfangner Gast, nach eignem Sinn
Und Willen, ihres Tages sich erfreut,
Von dir hofft' ich Vertrauen, das der Wirth
Für seine Treue wohl erwarten darf.

Iphigenie.

Verbarg ich meiner Eltern Namen und
Mein Haus, o König, war's Verlegenheit,
Nicht Mißtrau'n. Denn vielleicht, ach wüßtest du
Wer vor dir steht, und welch verwünschtes Haupt
Du nährst und schützest, ein Entsetzen faßte
Dein großes Herz mit seltnem Schauer an,
Und statt die Seite deines Thrones mir
Zu bieten, triebest du mich vor der Zeit
Aus deinem Reiche, stießest mich vielleicht,
Eh' zu den Meinen frohe Rückkehr mir
Und meiner Wandrung Ende zugedacht ist,
Dem Elend zu, das jeden Schweifenden,
Von seinem Hauf' Vertriebnen überall
Mit kalter fremder Schreckenshand erwartet.

Thoas.

Was auch der Rath der Götter mit dir sey,
Und was sie deinem Hauf' und dir gedenken;
So fehlt es doch, seitdem du bei uns wohnst
Und eines frommen Gastes Recht genießest,
An Segen nicht, der mir von oben kommt.
Ich möchte schwer zu überreden seyn,
Daß ich an dir ein schuldvoll Haupt beschütze.

Iphigenie.

Dir bringt die Wohlthat Segen, nicht der Gast.

Thoas.

Was man Verruchten thut, wird nicht gesegnet.
Drum endige dein Schweigen und dein Weigern;
Es fordert dies kein ungerechter Mann.
Die Göttin übergab dich meinen Händen;
Wie du ihr heilig warst, so warst du's mir.
Auch sey ihr Wink noch künftig mein Gesetz:
Wenn du nach Hause Rückkehr hoffen kannst,
So sprech' ich dich von aller Forderung los.
Doch ist der Weg auf ewig dir versperrt,
Und ist dein Stamm vertrieben, oder durch

Ein ungeheures Unheil ausgelöscht,
So bist du mein durch mehr als Ein Gesetz.
Sprich offen! und du weißt, ich halte Wort.

Iphigenie.

Vom alten Bande löset ungern sich
Die Zunge los, ein langverschwiegenes
Geheimniß endlich zu entdecken.   Denn
Einmal vertraut, verläßt es ohne Rückkehr
Des tiefen Herzens sichre Wohnung, schadet,
Wie es die Götter wollen, oder nützt.
Vernimm! Ich bin aus Tantalus Geschlecht.

Thoas.

Du sprichst ein großes Wort gelassen aus.
Nennst du Den deinen Ahnherrn, den die Welt
Als einen eh'mals Hochbegnadigten
Der Götter kennt? Ist's jener Tantalus,
Den Jupiter zu Rath und Tafel zog,
An dessen alterfahrnen, vielen Sinn
Verknüpfenden Gesprächen Götter selbst,
Wie an Orakelsprüchen, sich ergötzten?

Iphigenie.

Er ist es; aber Götter sollten nicht
Mit Menschen, wie mit Ihresgleichen, wandeln;
Das sterbliche Geschlecht ist viel zu schwach
In ungewohnter Höhe nicht zu schwindeln.
Unedel war er nicht und kein Verräther;
Allein zum Knecht zu groß, und zum Gesellen
Des großen Donn'rers nur ein Mensch.   So war
Auch sein Vergehen menschlich; ihr Gericht
War streng, und Dichter singen: Uebermuth
Und Untreu stürzten ihn von Jovis Tisch
Zur Schmach des alten Tartarus hinab.
Ach und sein ganz Geschlecht trug ihren Haß!

Thoas.

Trug es die Schuld des Ahnherrn oder eigne?

Iphigenie.

Zwar die gewalt'ge Brust und der Titanen
Kraftvolles Mark war seiner Söhn' und Enkel
Gewisses Erbtheil; doch es schmiedete
Der Gott um ihre Stirn ein ehern Band.
Rath, Mäßigung und Weisheit und Geduld
Verbarg er ihrem scheuen düstern Blick;
Zur Wuth ward ihnen jegliche Begier,
Und gränzenlos drang ihre Wuth umher.
Schon Pelops, der Gewaltig=wollende,
Des Tantalus geliebter Sohn, erwarb
Sich durch Verrath und Mord das schönste Weib,
Des Oenomaus Tochter, Hippodamien.
Sie bringt den Wünschen des Gemahls zwei Söhne,
Thyest und Atreus. Neidisch sehen sie
Des Vaters Liebe zu dem ersten Sohn
Aus einem andern Bette wachsend an.
Der Haß verbindet sie und heimlich wagt
Das Paar im Brudermord die erste That.
Der Vater wähnet Hippodamien
Die Mörderin, und grimmig fordert er
Von ihr den Sohn zurück, und sie entleibt
Sich selbst —

Thoas.

Du schweigest? Fahre fort zu reden!
Laß dein Vertrau'n dich nicht gereuen! Sprich!

Iphigenie.

Wohl dem, der seiner Väter gern gedenkt,
Der froh von ihren Thaten, ihrer Größe
Den Hörer unterhält und still sich freuend
Ans Ende dieser schönen Reihe sich
Geschlossen sieht! Denn es erzeugt nicht gleich
Ein Haus den Halbgott noch das Ungeheuer;
Erst eine Reihe Böser oder Guter
Bringt endlich das Entsetzen, bringt die Freude
Der Welt hervor. — Nach ihres Vaters Tode
Gebieten Atreus und Thyest der Stadt,

Gemeinsam=herrschend. Lange konnte nicht
Die Eintracht dauern. Bald entehrt Thyest
Des Bruders Bette. Rächend treibet Atreus
Ihn aus dem Reiche. Tückisch hatte schon
Thyest, auf schwere Thaten sinnend, lange
Dem Bruder einen Sohn entwandt und heimlich
Ihn als den seinen schmeichelnd auferzogen.
Dem füllet er die Brust mit Wuth und Rache
Und sendet ihn zur Königsstadt, daß er
Im Oheim seinen eignen Vater morde.
Des Jünglings Vorsatz wird entdeckt; der König
Straft grausam den gesandten Mörder, wähnend,
Er tödte seines Bruders Sohn. Zu spät
Erfährt er, wer vor seinen trunknen Augen
Gemartert stirbt; und die Begier der Rache
Aus seiner Brust zu tilgen, sinnt er still
Auf unerhörte That. Er scheint gelassen,
Gleichgültig und versöhnt, und lockt den Bruder
Mit seinen beiden Söhnen in das Reich
Zurück, ergreift die Knaben, schlachtet sie,
Und setzt die ekle schaudervolle Speise
Dem Vater bei dem ersten Mahle vor.
Und da Thyest an seinem Fleische sich
Gesättigt, eine Wehmuth ihn ergreift,
Er nach den Kindern fragt, den Tritt, die Stimme
Der Knaben an des Saales Thüre schon
Zu hören glaubt, wirft Atreus grinsend
Ihm Haupt und Füße der Erschlagnen hin. —
Du wendest schaudernd dein Gesicht, o König:
So wendete die Sonn' ihr Antlitz weg
Und ihren Wagen aus dem ew'gen Gleise!
Dieß sind die Ahnherrn deiner Priesterin;
Und viel unseliges Geschick der Männer,
Viel Thaten des verworrnen Sinnes deckt
Die Nacht mit schweren Fittigen und läßt
Uns nur die grauenvolle Dämmrung sehn.

Thoas.

Verbirg sie schweigend auch.   Es sey genug
Der Gräuel!   Sage nun, durch welch ein Wunder
Von diesem wilden Stamme Du entsprangst.

Iphigenie.

Des Atreus ältster Sohn war Agamemnon:
Er ist mein Vater.   Doch ich darf es sagen,
In ihm hab' ich seit meiner ersten Zeit
Ein Muster des vollkommnen Manns gesehn.
Ihm brachte Klytemnestra mich, den Erstling
Der Liebe, dann Elektren.   Ruhig herrschte
Der König, und es war dem Hause Tantal's
Die lang' entbehrte Rast gewährt.   Allein
Es mangelte dem Glück der Eltern noch
Ein Sohn, und kaum war dieser Wunsch erfüllt,
Daß zwischen beiden Schwestern nun Orest
Der Liebling wuchs, als neues Uebel schon
Dem sichern Hause zubereitet war.
Der Ruf des Krieges ist zu euch gekommen,
Der, um den Raub der schönsten Frau zu rächen,
Die ganze Macht der Fürsten Griechenlands
Um Trojens Mauern lagerte.   Ob sie
Die Stadt gewonnen, ihrer Rache Ziel
Erreicht, vernahm ich nicht.   Mein Vater führte
Der Griechen Heer.   In Aulis harrten sie
Auf günst'gen Wind vergebens: denn Diane,
Erzürnt auf ihren großen Führer, hielt
Die Eilenden zurück und forderte
Durch Kalchas Mund des Königs ältste Tochter.
Sie lockten mit der Mutter mich ins Lager;
Sie rissen mich vor den Altar und weihten
Der Göttin dieses Haupt. — Sie war versöhnt:
Sie wollte nicht mein Blut, und hüllte rettend
In eine Wolke mich; in diesem Tempel
Erkannt' ich mich zuerst vom Tode wieder.
Ich bin es selbst, bin Iphigenie,

Des Atreus Enkel, Agamemnon's Tochter,
Der Göttin Eigenthum, die mit dir spricht.

Thoas.

Mehr Vorzug und Vertrauen geb' ich nicht
Der Königstochter als der Unbekannten.
Ich wiederhole meinen ersten Antrag:
Komm, folge mir und theile, was ich habe.

Iphigenie.

Wie darf ich solchen Schritt, o König, wagen?
Hat nicht die Göttin, die mich rettete,
Allein das Recht auf mein geweihtes Leben?
Sie hat für mich den Schutzort ausgesucht,
Und sie bewahrt mich einem Vater, den
Sie durch den Schein genug gestraft, vielleicht
Zur schönsten Freude seines Alters hier.
Vielleicht ist mir die frohe Rückkehr nah;
Und ich, auf ihren Weg nicht achtend, hätte
Mich wider ihren Willen hier gefesselt?
Ein Zeichen bat ich, wenn ich bleiben sollte.

Thoas.

Das Zeichen ist, daß du noch hier verweilst.
Such' Ausflucht solcher Art nicht ängstlich auf.
Man spricht vergebens viel, um zu versagen;
Der Andre hört von Allem nur das Nein.

Iphigenie.

Nicht Worte sind es, die nur blenden sollen;
Ich habe dir mein tiefstes Herz entdeckt.
Und sagst du dir nicht selbst, wie ich dem Vater,
Der Mutter, den Geschwistern mich entgegen
Mit ängstlichen Gefühlen sehnen muß?
Daß in den alten Hallen, wo die Trauer
Noch manchmal stille meinen Namen lispelt,
Die Freude, wie um eine Neugeborne,
Den schönsten Kranz von Säul' an Säulen schlinge.
O sendetest du mich auf Schiffen hin!
Du gäbest mir und Allen neues Leben.

Thoas.

So kehr' zurück! Thu', was dein Herz dich heißt,
Und höre nicht die Stimme guten Raths
Und der Vernunft. Sey ganz ein Weib und gib
Dich hin dem Triebe, der dich zügellos
Ergreift und dahin oder dorthin reißt.
Wenn ihnen eine Lust im Busen brennt,
Hält vom Verräther sie kein heilig Band,
Der sie dem Vater oder dem Gemahl
Aus langbewährten, treuen Armen lockt;
Und schweigt in ihrer Brust die rasche Gluth,
So dringt auf sie vergebens treu und mächtig
Der Ueberredung goldne Zunge los.

Iphigenie.

Gedenk, o König, deines edeln Wortes!
Willst du mein Zutrau'n so erwiedern? Du
Schienst vorbereitet, Alles zu vernehmen.

Thoas.

Auf's Ungehoffte war ich nicht bereitet;
Doch sollt' ich's auch erwarten: wußt' ich nicht,
Daß ich mit einem Weibe handeln ging?

Iphigenie.

Schilt nicht, o König, unser arm Geschlecht.
Nicht herrlich wie die euern, aber nicht
Unedel sind die Waffen eines Weibes.
Glaub' es, darin bin ich dir vorzuziehn,
Daß ich dein Glück mehr als du selber kenne.
Du wähnest, unbekannt mit dir und mir,
Ein näher Band wird uns zum Glück vereinen,
Voll guten Muthes, wie voll guten Willens,
Dringst du in mich, daß ich mich fügen soll;
Und hier dank' ich den Göttern, daß sie mir
Die Festigkeit gegeben, dieses Bündniß
Nicht einzugehen, das sie nicht gebilligt.

Thoas.

Es spricht kein Gott; es spricht dein eignes Herz.

Iphigenie.

Sie reden nur durch unser Herz zu uns.

Thoas.

Und hab' Ich, sie zu hören, nicht das Recht?

Iphigenie.

Es überbraust der Sturm die zarte Stimme.

Thoas.

Die Priesterin vernimmt sie wohl allein?

Iphigenie.

Vor allen Andern merke sie der Fürst.

Thoas.

Dein heilig Amt und dein geerbtes Recht
An Jovis Tisch bringt dich den Göttern näher,
Als einen erdgebornen Wilden.

Iphigenie.

         So
Büß' ich nun das Vertrau'n, das du erzwangst.

Thoas.

Ich bin ein Mensch; und besser ist's, wir enden.
So bleibe denn mein Wort: Sey Priesterin
Der Göttin, wie sie dich erkoren hat;
Doch mir verzeih' Diane, daß ich ihr,
Bisher mit Unrecht und mit innerm Vorwurf,
Die alten Opfer vorenthalten habe.
Kein Fremder nahet glücklich unserm Ufer;
Von Alters her ist ihm der Tod gewiß.
Nur Du hast mich mit einer Freundlichkeit,
In der ich bald der zarten Tochter Liebe,
Bald stille Neigung einer Braut zu sehn
Mich tief erfreute, wie mit Zauberbanden
Gefesselt, daß ich meiner Pflicht vergaß.
Du hattest mir die Sinnen eingewiegt,
Das Murren meines Volks vernahm ich nicht;
Nun rufen sie die Schuld von meines Sohnes
Frühzeit'gem Tode lauter über mich.

Um deinetwillen halt' ich länger nicht
Die Menge, die das Opfer dringend fordert.

Iphigenie.

Um meinetwillen hab' ich's nie begehrt.
Der mißversteht die Himmlischen, der sie
Blutgierig wähnt; er dichtet ihnen nur
Die eignen grausamen Begierden an.
Entzog die Göttin mich nicht selbst dem Priester?
Ihr war mein Dienst willkommner, als mein Tod.

Thoas.

Es ziemt sich nicht für uns, den heiligen
Gebrauch mit leicht beweglicher Vernunft
Nach unserm Sinn zu deuten und zu lenken.
Thu' deine Pflicht, ich werde meine thun.
Zwei Fremde, die wir in des Ufers Höhlen
Versteckt gefunden, und die meinem Lande
Nichts Gutes bringen, sind in meiner Hand.
Mit diesen nehme deine Göttin wieder
Ihr erstes, rechtes, lang' entbehrtes Opfer!
Ich sende sie hieher; du weißt den Dienst.

Vierter Auftritt.

Iphigenie allein.

Du hast Wolken, gnädige Retterin,
Einzuhüllen unschuldig Verfolgte,
Und auf Winden dem ehrnen Geschick sie
Aus den Armen, über das Meer,
Ueber der Erde weiteste Strecken
Und wohin es dir gut dünkt, zu tragen.
Weise bist du und siehest das Künftige;
Nicht vorüber ist dir das Vergangne,
Und dein Blick ruht über den Deinen
Wie dein Licht, das Leben der Nächte,
Ueber der Erde ruhet und waltet.
O enthalte vom Blut meine Hände!
Nimmer bringt es Segen und Ruhe;

Und die Gestalt des zufällig Ermordeten
Wird auf des traurig-unwilligen Mörders
Böse Stunden lauern und schrecken.
Denn die Unsterblichen lieben der Menschen
Weit verbreitete gute Geschlechter,
Und sie fristen das flüchtige Leben
Gerne dem Sterblichen, wollen ihm gerne
Ihres eigenen, ewigen Himmels
Mitgenießendes fröhliches Anschau'n
Eine Weile gönnen und lassen.

Zweiter Aufzug.

***

Erster Auftritt.
Oreſt. Pylades.

Oreſt.

Es iſt der Weg des Todes, den wir treten:
Mit jedem Schritt wird meine Seele ſtiller.
Als ich Apollen bat, das gräßliche
Geleit der Rachegeiſter von der Seite
Mir abzunehmen, ſchien er Hülf' und Rettung
Im Tempel ſeiner vielgeliebten Schweſter,
Die über Tauris herrſcht, mit hoffnungsreichen
Gewiſſen Götterworten zu verſprechen;
Und nun erfüllet ſich's, daß alle Noth
Mit meinem Leben völlig enden ſoll.
Wie leicht wird's mir, dem eine Götterhand
Das Herz zuſammendrückt, den Sinn betäubt,
Dem ſchönen Licht der Sonne zu entſagen!
Und ſollen Atreus Enkel in der Schlacht
Ein ſiegbekröntes Ende nicht gewinnen;
Soll ich wie meine Ahnen, wie mein Vater,
Als Opferthier im Jammertode bluten:
So ſey es! Beſſer hier vor dem Altar,
Als im verworfnen Winkel, wo die Netze
Der nahverwandte Meuchelmörder ſtellt.
Laßt mir ſo lange Ruh', ihr Unterird'ſchen,
Die nach dem Blut' ihr, das von meinen Tritten
Hernieder träufelnd meinen Pfad bezeichnet,
Wie losgelaſſne Hunde ſpürend hetzt.

Laßt mich, ich komme bald zu euch hinab;
Das Licht des Tags soll euch nicht sehn, noch mich.
Der Erde schöner grüner Teppich soll
Kein Tummelplatz für Larven seyn.   Dort unten
Such' ich euch auf : dort bindet alle dann
Ein gleich Geschick in ew'ge matte Nacht.
Nur dich, mein Pylades, dich, meiner Schuld
Und meines Banns unschuldigen Genossen,
Wie ungern' nehm ich dich in jenes Trauerland
Frühzeitig mit! Dein Leben oder Tod
Gibt mir allein noch Hoffnung oder Furcht.

Pylades.

Ich bin noch nicht, Orest, wie du bereit,
In jenes Schattenreich hinabzugehn.
Ich sinne noch, durch die verworrnen Pfade
Die nach der schwarzen Nacht zu führen scheinen,
Uns zu dem Leben wieder aufzuwinden.
Ich denke nicht den Tod; ich sinn' und horche,
Ob nicht zu irgend einer frohen Flucht
Die Götter Rath und Wege zubereiten.
Der Tod, gefürchtet oder ungefürchtet,
Kommt unaufhaltsam.   Wenn die Priesterin
Schon, unsre Locken weihend abzuschneiden,
Die Hand erhebt, soll dein' und meine Rettung
Mein einziger Gedanke seyn.   Erhebe
Von diesem Unmuth deine Seele; zweifelnd
Beschleunigest du die Gefahr.   Apoll
Gab uns das Wort: im Heiligthum der Schwester
Sey Trost und Hülf' und Rückkehr dir bereitet.
Der Götter Worte sind nicht doppelsinnig,
Wie der Gedrückte sie im Unmuth wähnt.

Orest.

Des Lebens dunkle Decke breitete
Die Mutter mir schon um das zarte Haupt,
Und so wuchs ich herauf, ein Ebenbild
Des Vaters, und es war mein stummer Blick
Ein bittrer Vorwurf ihr und ihrem Buhlen.

Wie oft, wenn still Elektra, meine Schwester,
Am Feuer in der tiefen Halle saß,
Drängt' ich beklommen mich an ihren Schoß,
Und starrte, wie sie bitter weinte, sie
Mit großen Augen an. Dann sagte sie
Von unserm hohen Vater viel: wie sehr
Verlangt' ich ihn zu sehn, bei ihm zu seyn!
Mich wünscht' ich bald nach Troja, ihn bald her.
Es kam der Tag —

Pylades.
O laß von jener Stunde
Sich Höllengeister nächtlich unterhalten!
Uns gebe die Erinnrung schöner Zeit
Zu frischem Heldenlaufe neue Kraft.
Die Götter brauchen manchen guten Mann
Zu ihrem Dienst auf dieser weiten Erde.
Sie haben noch auf dich gezählt; sie gaben
Dich nicht dem Vater zum Geleite mit,
Da er unwillig nach dem Orcus ging.

Orest.
O wär' ich, seinen Saum ergreifend, ihm
Gefolgt!

Pylades.
So haben die, die dich erhielten,
Für mich gesorgt: denn was ich worden wäre,
Wenn du nicht lebtest, kann ich mir nicht denken;
Da ich mit dir und deinetwillen nur
Seit meiner Kindheit leb' und leben mag.

Orest.
Erinnre mich nicht jener schönen Tage,
Da mir dein Haus die freie Stätte gab,
Dein edler Vater klug und liebevoll
Die halberstarrte junge Blüthe pflegte;
Da du ein immer munterer Geselle,
Gleich einem leichten bunten Schmetterling
Um eine dunkle Blume, jeden Tag

Um mich mit neuem Leben gaukeltest,
Mir deine Lust in meine Seele spieltest,
Daß ich, vergessend meiner Noth, mit dir
In rascher Jugend hingerissen schwärmte.

Pylades.

Da fing mein Leben an, als ich dich liebte.

Orest.

Sag': meine Noth begann, und du sprichst wahr.
Das ist das Aengstliche von meinem Schicksal,
Daß ich, wie ein verpesteter Vertriebner,
Geheimen Schmerz und Tod im Busen trage;
Daß, wo ich den gesund'sten Ort betrete,
Gar bald um mich die blühenden Gesichter
Den Schmerzenszug langsamen Tod's verrathen.

Pylades.

Der Nächste wär' ich diesen Tod zu sterben,
Wenn je dein Hauch, Orest, vergiftete.
Bin ich nicht immer noch voll Muth und Lust?
Und Lust und Liebe sind die Fittige
Zu großen Thaten.

Orest.

Große Thaten? Ja,
Ich weiß die Zeit, da wir sie vor uns sahn!
Wenn wir zusammen oft dem Wilde nach
Durch Berg' und Thäler rannten, und dereinst
An Brust und Faust dem hohen Ahnherrn gleich
Mit Keul' und Schwert dem Ungeheuer so,
Dem Räuber auf der Spur zu jagen hofften;
Und dann wir Abends an der weiten See
Uns aneinander lehnend ruhig saßen,
Die Wellen bis zu unsern Füßen spielten,
Die Welt so weit, so offen vor uns lag;
Da fuhr wohl Einer manchmal nach dem Schwert,
Und künft'ge Thaten drangen wie die Sterne
Rings um uns her unzählig aus der Nacht!

12

Pylades.

Unendlich ist das Werk, das zu vollführen
Die Seele bringt. Wir möchten jede That
So groß gleich thun als wie sie wächst und wird,
Wenn Jahre lang durch Länder und Geschlechter
Der Mund der Dichter sie vermehrend wälzt.
Es klingt so schön, was unsre Väter thaten,
Wenn es, in stillen Abendschatten ruhend,
Der Jüngling mit dem Ton der Harfe schlürft;
Und was wir thun, ist, wie es ihnen war,
Voll Müh' und eitel Stückwerk!
So laufen wir nach dem, was vor uns flieht,
Und achten nicht des Weges, den wir treten,
Und sehen neben uns der Ahnherrn Tritte
Und ihres Erdenlebens Spuren kaum.
Wir eilen immer ihrem Schatten nach,
Der göttergleich in einer weiten Ferne
Der Berge Haupt auf goldnen Wolken krönt.
Ich halte nichts von dem, der von sich denkt,
Wie ihn das Volk vielleicht erheben möchte;
Allein, o Jüngling, danke du den Göttern,
Daß sie so früh durch dich so viel gethan!

Orest.

Wenn sie dem Menschen frohe That bescheren,
Daß er ein Unheil von den Seinen wendet,
Daß er sein Reich vermehrt, die Grenzen sichert,
Und alte Feinde fallen oder fliehn;
Dann mag er danken! denn ihm hat ein Gott
Des Lebens erste, letzte Lust gegönnt.
Mich haben sie zum Schlächter auserkoren,
Zum Mörder meiner doch verehrten Mutter,
Und eine Schandthat schändlich rächend, mich
Durch ihren Wink zu Grund' gerichtet. Glaube,
Sie haben es auf Tantal's Haus gerichtet,
Und ich, der Letzte, soll nicht schuldlos, soll
Nicht ehrenvoll vergehn.

Pylades.

Die Götter rächen
Der Väter Missethat nicht an dem Sohn!
Ein Jeglicher, gut oder böse, nimmt
Sich seinen Lohn mit seiner That hinweg;
Es erbt der Eltern Segen, nicht ihr Fluch.

Orest.

Uns führt ihr Segen, dünkt mich, nicht hierher.

Pylades.

Doch wenigstens der hohen Götter Wille.

Orest.

So ist's ihr Wille denn, der uns verderbt.

Pylades.

Thu', was sie dir gebieten und erwarte!
Bringst du die Schwester zu Apollen hin,
Und wohnen Beide dann vereint zu Delphi,
Verehrt von einem Volk, das edel denkt;
So wird für diese That das hohe Paar
Dir gnädig seyn, sie werden aus der Hand
Der Unterird'schen dich erretten. Schon
In diesen heil'gen Hain wagt keine sich.

Orest.

So hab' ich wenigstens geruh'gen Tod.

Pylades.

Ganz anders denk' ich, und nicht ungeschickt
Hab' ich das schon Gescheh'ne mit dem Künft'gen
Verbunden und im Stillen ausgelegt.
Vielleicht reift in der Götter Rath schon lange
Das große Werk. Diana sehnet sich
Von diesem rauhen Ufer der Barbaren
Und ihren blut'gen Menschenopfern weg.
Wir waren zu der schönen That bestimmt,
Uns wird sie auferlegt, und seltsam sind
Wir an der Pforte schon gezwungen hier.

Orest.

Mit selt'ner Kunst flichtst du der Götter Rath
Und deine Wünsche klug in Eins zusammen.

Pylades.

Was ist des Menschen Klugheit, wenn sie nicht
Auf Jener Willen droben achtend lauscht?
Zu einer schweren That beruft ein Gott
Den edeln Mann, der viel verbrach, und legt
Ihm auf, was uns unmöglich scheint zu enden.
Es siegt der Held, und büßend dienet er
Den Göttern und der Welt, die ihn verehrt.

Orest.

Bin ich bestimmt zu leben und zu handeln,
So nehm' ein Gott von meiner schweren Stirn
Den Schwindel weg, der auf dem schlüpfrigen,
Mit Mutterblut besprengten Pfade fort
Mich zu den Todten reißt! Er trockne gnädig
Die Quelle, die, mir aus der Mutter Wunden
Entgegen sprudelnd, ewig mich befleckt.

Pylades.

Erwart' es ruhiger! Du mehrst das Uebel
Und nimmst das Amt der Furien auf dich.
Laß mich nur sinnen, bleibe still! Zuletzt,
Bedarf's zur That vereinter Kräfte, dann
Ruf' ich dich auf, und Beide schreiten wir
Mit überlegter Kühnheit zur Vollendung.

Orest.

Ich hör' Ulyssen reden.

Pylades.

Spotte nicht!
Ein Jeglicher muß seinen Helden wählen,
Dem er die Wege zum Olymp hinauf
Sich nacharbeitet. Laß es mich gestehn:
Mir scheinen List und Klugheit nicht den Mann
Zu schänden, der sich kühnen Thaten weiht.

Orest.

Ich schätze den, der tapfer ist und g'rad.

Pylades.

Drum hab' ich keinen Rath von dir verlangt.

Schon ist ein Schritt gethan. Von unsern Wächtern
Hab' ich bisher gar Vieles ausgelockt.
Ich weiß, ein fremdes, göttergleiches Weib
Hält jenes blutige Gesetz gefesselt;
Ein reines Herz und Weihrauch und Gebet
Bringt sie den Göttern dar. Man rühmet hoch
Die Gütige; man glaubet, sie entspringe
Vom Stamm der Amazonen, sey geflohn,
Um einem großen Unheil zu entgehn. ·

Orest.

Es scheint, ihr lichtes Reich verlor' die Kraft
Durch des Verbrechers Nähe, den der Fluch
Wie eine breite Nacht verfolgt und deckt.
Die fromme Blutgier löf't den alten Brauch
Von seinen Fesseln los, uns zu verderben.
Der wilde Sinn des Königs tödtet uns;
Ein Weib wird uns nicht retten, wenn er zürnt.

Pylades.

Wohl uns, daß es ein Weib ist! denn ein Mann,
Der beste selbst, gewöhnet seinen Geist
An Grausamkeit, und macht sich auch zuletzt
Aus dem, was er verabscheut, ein Gesetz,
Wird aus Gewohnheit hart und fast unkenntlich;
Allein ein Weib bleibt stät auf Einem Sinn,
Den sie gefaßt. Du rechnest sicherer
Auf sie im Guten wie im Bösen. — Still!
Sie kommt; laß uns allein. Ich darf nicht gleich
Ihr unsre Namen nennen, unser Schicksal
Nicht ohne Rückhalt ihr vertrau'n. Du gehst,
Und eh' sie mit dir spricht, treff' ich dich noch.

Zweiter Auftritt.

Iphigenie. Pylades.

Iphigenie.

Woher du seyst und kommst, o Fremdling, sprich!
Mir scheint es, daß ich eher einem Griechen

Als einem Scythen dich vergleichen soll.

(Sie nimmt ihm die Ketten ab.)

Gefährlich ist die Freiheit, die ich gebe;
Die Götter wenden ab, was euch bedroht!

Pylades.

O süße Stimme! Vielwillkommner Ton
Der Muttersprach' in einem fremden Lande!
Des väterlichen Hafens blaue Berge
Seh' ich Gefangner neu willkommen wieder
Vor meinen Augen. Laß dir diese Freude
Versichern, daß auch ich ein Grieche bin!
Vergessen hab' ich einen Augenblick,
Wie sehr ich dein bedarf, und meinen Geist
Der herrlichen Erscheinung zugewendet.
O sage, wenn dir ein Verhängniß nicht
Die Lippe schließt, aus welchem unsrer Stämme
Du deine göttergleiche Herkunft zählst.

Iphigenie.

Die Priesterin, von ihrer Göttin selbst
Gewählet und geheiligt, spricht mit dir.
Das laß dir g'nügen; sage, wer du seyst
Und welch unselig=waltendes Geschick
Mit dem Gefährten dich hierher gebracht.

Pylades.

Leicht kann ich dir erzählen, welch ein Uebel
Mit lastender Gesellschaft uns verfolgt.
O könntest du der Hoffnung frohen Blick
Uns auch so leicht, du Göttliche, gewähren!
Aus Kreta sind wir, Söhne des Adrasts:
Ich bin der jüngste, Cephalus genannt,
Und er Laodamas, der älteste
Des Hauses. Zwischen uns stand rauh und wild
Ein mittlerer, und trennte schon im Spiel
Der ersten Jugend Einigkeit und Lust.
Gelassen folgten wir der Mutter Worten,
So lang' des Vaters Kraft vor Troja stritt;
Doch als er beutereich zurücke kam

Und kurz darauf verschied, da trennte bald
Der Streit um Reich und Erbe die Geschwister.
Ich neigte mich zum Aeltesten. Er erschlug
Den Bruder. Um der Blutschuld willen treibt
Die Furie gewaltig ihn umher.
Doch diesem wilden Ufer sendet uns
Apoll, der Delphische, mit Hoffnung zu.
Im Tempel seiner Schwester hieß er uns
Der Hülfe segensvolle Hand erwarten.
Gefangen sind wir und hierher gebracht,
Und dir als Opfer dargestellt. Du weißt's.

Iphigenie.

Fiel Troja? Theurer Mann, versich'r es mir.

Pylades.

Es liegt. O sich're du uns Rettung zu!
Beschleunige die Hülfe, die ein Gott
Versprach. Erbarme meines Bruders dich.
O sag' ihm bald ein gutes holdes Wort;
Doch schone seiner, wenn du mit ihm sprichst,
Das bitt' ich eifrig: denn es wird gar leicht
Durch Freud' und Schmerz und durch Erinnerung
Sein Innerstes ergriffen und zerrüttet.
Ein fieberhafter Wahnsinn fällt ihn an,
Und seine schöne freie Seele wird
Den Furien zum Raube hingegeben.

Iphigenie.

So groß dein Unglück ist, beschwör' ich dich,
Vergiß es, bis du mir genug gethan.

Pylades.

Die hohe Stadt, die zehen lange Jahre
Dem ganzen Heer der Griechen widerstand,
Liegt nun im Schutte, steigt nicht wieder auf.
Doch manche Gräber unsrer Besten heißen
Uns an das Ufer der Barbaren denken.
Achill liegt dort mit seinem schönen Freunde.

Iphigenie.

So seyd ihr Götterbilder auch zu Staub!

Pylades.

Auch Palamedes, Ajax Telamons;
Sie sahn des Vaterlandes Tag nicht wieder.

Iphigenie.

Er schweigt von meinem Vater, nennt ihn nicht
Mit den Erschlag'nen. Ja! er lebt mir noch!
Ich werd' ihn sehn! O hoffe, liebes Herz!

Pylades.

Doch selig sind die Tausende, die starben
Den bittersüßen Tod von Feindes Hand!
Denn wüste Schrecken und ein traurig Ende
Hat den Rückkehrenden statt des Triumphs
Ein feindlich aufgebrachter Gott bereitet.
Kommt denn der Menschen Stimme nicht zu euch?
So weit sie reicht, trägt sie den Ruf umher
Von unerhörten Thaten, die geschah'n.
So ist der Jammer, der Mycenens Hallen
Mit immer wiederholten Seufzern füllt,
Dir ein Geheimniß? — Klytemnestra hat
Mit Hülf' Aegisthens den Gemahl berückt,
Am Tage seiner Rückkehr ihn ermordet! —
Ja, du verehrest dieses Königshaus!
Ich seh' es, deine Brust bekämpft vergebens
Das unerwartet ungeheure Wort.
Bist du die Tochter eines Freundes? bist
Du nachbarlich in dieser Stadt geboren?
Verbirg' es nicht und rechne mir's nicht zu,
Daß ich der erste diese Gräuel melde.

Iphigenie.

Sag' an, wie ward die schwere That vollbracht?

Pylades.

Am Tage seiner Ankunft, da der König
Vom Bad' erquickt und ruhig, sein Gewand
Aus der Gemahlin Hand verlangend, stieg,
Warf die Verderbliche ein faltenreich
Und künstlich sich verwirrendes Gewebe
Ihm auf die Schultern, um das edle Haupt;

Und da er wie von einem Netze sich
Vergebens zu entwickeln strebte, schlug
Aegisth ihn, der Verräther, und verhüllt
Ging zu den Todten dieser große Fürst.

Iphigenie.

Und welchen Lohn erhielt der Mitverschworne?

Pylades.

Ein Reich und Bette, das er schon besaß.

Iphigenie.

So trieb zur Schandthat eine böse Lust?

Pylades.

Und einer alten Rache tief Gefühl.

Iphigenie.

Und wie beleidigte der König sie?

Pylades.

Mit schwerer That, die, wenn Entschuldigung
Des Mordes wäre, sie entschuldigte.
Nach Aulis lockt' er sie und brachte dort,
Als eine Gottheit sich der Griechen Fahrt
Mit ungestümen Winden widersetzte,
Die älteste Tochter, Iphigenien,
Vor den Altar Dianens, und sie fiel
Ein blutig Opfer für der Griechen Heil.
Dies, sagt man, hat ihr einen Widerwillen
So tief in's Herz geprägt, daß sie dem Werben
Aegisthens sich ergab und den Gemahl
Mit Netzen des Verderbens selbst umschlang.

Iphigenie (sich verhüllend.)

Es ist genug. Du wirst mich wiedersehn.

Pylades (allein.)

Von dem Geschick des Königshauses scheint
Sie tief gerührt. Wer sie auch immer sey,
So hat sie selbst den König wohl gekannt
Und ist, zu unserm Glück, aus hohem Hause
Hierher verkauft. Nur stille, liebes Herz,
Und laß dem Stern der Hoffnung, der uns blinkt,
Mit frohem Muth uns klug entgegen steuern.

12*

Dritter Aufzug.

Erster Auftritt.
Iphigenie. Oreſt.

Iphigenie.
Unglücklicher, ich löſe deine Bande
Zum Zeichen eines ſchmerzlichen Geſchicks.
Die Freiheit, die das Heiligthum gewährt,
Iſt wie der letzte, lichte Lebensblick
Des ſchwer Erkrankten, Todesbote.   Noch
Kann ich es mir und darf es mir nicht ſagen,
Daß ihr verloren ſeyd!   Wie könnt' ich euch
Mit mörderiſcher Hand dem Tode weihen?
Und Niemand, wer es ſey, darf euer Haupt,
So lang' ich Prieſterin Dianen's bin,
Berühren.   Doch verweigr' ich jene Pflicht,
Wie ſie der aufgebrachte König fordert;
So wählt er eine meiner Jungfrau'n mir
Zur Folgerin, und ich vermag alsdann,
Mit heißem Wunſch allein euch beizuſtehn.
O werther Landsmann!   Selbſt der letzte Knecht,
Der an den Herd der Vatergötter ſtreifte,
Iſt uns in fremdem Lande hoch willkommen:
Wie ſoll ich euch genug mit Freud' und Segen
Empfangen, die ihr mir das Bild der Helden,
Die ich von Eltern her verehren lernte,
Entgegen bringet und das innre Herz
Mit neuer ſchöner Hoffnung ſchmeichelnd labet!

Oreſt.
Verbirgſt du deinen Namen, deine Herkunft
Mit klugem Vorſatz? oder darf ich wiſſen,
Wer mir, gleich einer Himmliſchen, begegnet?

Iphigenie.

Du sollst mich kennen. Jetzo sag' mir an,
Was ich nur halb von deinem Bruder hörte,
Das Ende derer, die von Troja kehrend
Ein hartes unerwartetes Geschick
Auf ihrer Wohnung Schwelle stumm empfing.
Zwar ward ich jung an diesen Strand geführt;
Doch wohl erinnr' ich mich des scheuen Blicks,
Den ich mit Staunen und mit Bangigkeit
Auf jene Helden warf. Sie zogen aus,
Als hätte der Olymp sich aufgethan
Und die Gestalten der erlauchten Vorwelt
Zum Schrecken Ilion's herabgesendet,
Und Agamemnon war vor allen herrlich!
O sage mir: Er fiel, sein Haus betretend,
Durch seiner Frauen und Aegisthens Tücke?

Orest.

Du sagst's!

Iphigenie.

Weh dir, unseliges Mycen!
So haben Tantal's Enkel Fluch auf Fluch
Mit vollen wilden Händen ausgesät!
Und gleich dem Unkraut, wüste Häupter schüttelnd
Und tausendfält'gen Samen um sich streuend,
Den Kindeskindern nahverwandte Mörder
Zur ew'gen Wechselwuth erzeugt! Enthülle,
Was von der Rede deines Bruders schnell
Die Finsterniß des Schreckens mir verdeckte.
Wie ist des großen Stammes letzter Sohn,
Das holde Kind, bestimmt des Vaters Rächer
Dereinst zu seyn, wie ist Orest dem Tage
Des Bluts entgangen? Hat ein gleich Geschick
Mit des Avernus Netzen ihn umschlungen?
Ist er gerettet? Lebt er? Lebt Elektra?

Orest.

Sie leben.

Iphigenie.

Goldne Sonne, leihe mir
Die schönsten Strahlen, lege sie zum Dank
Vor Jovis Thron! denn ich bin arm und stumm.

Orest.

Bist du gastfreundlich diesem Königshause,
Bist du mit nähern Banden ihm verbunden,
Wie deine schöne Freude mir verräth:
So bändige dein Herz und halt es fest!
Denn unerträglich muß dem Fröhlichen
Ein jäher Rückfall in die Schmerzen seyn.
Du weißt nur, merk' ich, Agamemnon's Tod.

Iphigenie.

Hab' ich an dieser Nachricht nicht genug?

Orest.

Du hast des Gräuels Hälfte nur erfahren.

Iphigenie.

Was fürcht' ich noch? Orest, Elektra leben.

Orest.

Und fürchtest du für Klytemnestren nichts?

Iphigenie.

Sie rettet weder Hoffnung, weder Furcht.

Orest.

Auch schied sie aus dem Land der Hoffnung ab.

Iphigenie.

Vergoß sie reuig wüthend selbst ihr Blut?

Orest.

Nein, doch ihr eigen Blut gab ihr den Tod.

Iphigenie.

Sprich deutlicher, daß ich nicht länger sinne.
Die Ungewißheit schlägt mir tausendfältig
Die dunkeln Schwingen um das bange Haupt.

Orest.

So haben mich die Götter ausersehn
Zum Boten einer That, die ich so gern

In's klanglos=dunkle Höllenreich der Nacht
Verbergen möchte? Wider meinen Willen
Zwingt mich dein holder Mund; allein er darf
Auch etwas Schmerzlich's fordern und erhält's.
Am Tage, da der Vater fiel, verbarg
Elektra rettend ihren Bruder: Strophius,
Des Vaters Schwäher, nahm ihn willig auf,
Erzog ihn neben seinem eignen Sohne,
Der, Pylades genannt, die schönsten Bande
Der Freundschaft um den Angekommnen knüpfte.
Und wie sie wuchsen, wuchs in ihrer Seele
Die brennende Begier des Königs Tod
Zu rächen. Unversehen, fremd gekleidet,
Erreichten sie Mycen, als brächten sie
Die Trauernachricht von Orestens Tode
Mit seiner Asche. Wohl empfänget sie
Die Königin; sie treten in das Haus.
Elektren gibt Orest sich zu erkennen;
Sie bläs't der Rache Feuer in ihm auf,
Das vor der Mutter heil'ger Gegenwart
In sich zurückgebrannt war. Stille führt
Sie ihn zum Orte, wo sein Vater fiel,
Wo eine alte leichte Spur des frech
Vergoßnen Blutes oftgewaschnen Boden
Mit blassen ahnungsvollen Streifen färbte.
Mit ihrer Feuerzunge schilderte
Sie jeden Umstand der verruchten That,
Ihr knechtisch elend durchgebrachtes Leben,
Den Uebermuth der glücklichen Verräther,
Und die Gefahren, die nun der Geschwister
Von einer stiefgewordnen Mutter warteten. —
Hier drang sie jenen alten Dolch ihm auf,
Der schon in Tantal's Hause grimmig wüthete,
Und Klytemnestra fiel durch Sohnes Hand.

Iphigenie.

Unsterbliche, die ihr den reinen Tag
Auf immer neuen Wolken selig lebet,

Habt ihr nur darum mich so manches Jahr
Von Menschen abgesondert, mich so nah
Bei euch gehalten, mir die kindliche
Beschäftigung, des heil'gen Feuers Gluth
Zu nähren, aufgetragen, meine Seele,
Der Flamme gleich, in ew'ger frommer Klarheit
Zu euern Wohnungen hinaufgezogen,
Daß ich nur meines Hauses Gräuel später
Und tiefer fühlen sollte? — Sage mir
Vom Unglückſel'gen! Sprich mir von Orest! —

Oreſt.

O könnte man von seinem Tode sprechen!
Wie gährend stieg aus der Erschlagnen Blut
Der Mutter Geist
Und ruft der Nacht uralten Töchtern zu:
„Laßt nicht den Muttermörder entfliehn!
Verfolgt den Verbrecher! Euch ist er geweiht!"
Sie horchen auf, es schaut ihr hohler Blick
Mit der Begier des Adlers um sich her.
Sie rühren sich in ihren schwarzen Höhlen,
Und aus den Winkeln schleichen ihre Gefährten,
Der Zweifel und die Reue, leis' herbei.
Vor ihnen steigt ein Dampf vom Acheron;
In seinen Wolkenkreisen wälzet sich
Die ewige Betrachtung des Gescheh'nen
Verwirrend um des Schuld'gen Haupt umher,
Und sie, berechtigt zum Verderben, treten
Der gottbesäten Erde schönen Boden,
Von dem ein alter Fluch sie längst verbannte.
Den Flüchtigen verfolgt ihr schneller Fuß;
Sie geben nur, um neu zu schrecken, Rast.

Iphigenie.

Unseliger, du bist in gleichem Fall,
Und fühlst, was er, der arme Flüchtling leidet!

Oreſt.

Was sagst du mir? Was wähnst du gleichen Fall?

Iphigenie.

Dich drückt ein Brudermord wie jenen; mir
Vertraute dies dein jüngster Bruder schon.

Orest.

Ich kann nicht leiden, daß du große Seele
Mit einem falschen Wort betrogen werdest.
Ein lügenhaft Gewebe knüpf' ein Fremder
Dem Fremden, sinnreich und der List gewohnt,
Zur Falle vor die Füße; zwischen uns
Sey Wahrheit!
Ich bin Orest! und dieses schuld'ge Haupt
Senkt nach der Grube sich und sucht den Tod;
In jeglicher Gestalt sey er willkommen!
Wer du auch seyst, so wünsch' ich Rettung dir
Und meinem Freunde; mir wünsch' ich sie nicht.
Du scheinst hier wider Willen zu verweilen;
Erfindet Rath zur Flucht und laßt mich hier.
Es stürze mein entseelter Leib vom Fels,
Es rauche bis zum Meer hinab mein Blut,
Und bringe Fluch dem Ufer der Barbaren!
Geht ihr, daheim im schönen Griechenland,
Ein neues Leben freundlich anzufangen.

(Er entfernt sich.)

Iphigenie.

So steigst du denn, Erfüllung, schönste Tochter
Des größten Vaters, endlich zu mir nieder!
Wie ungeheuer steht dein Bild vor mir!
Kaum reicht mein Blick dir an die Hände, die
Mit Frucht und Segenskränzen angefüllt
Die Schätze des Olympus niederbringen.
Wie man den König an dem Uebermaß
Der Gaben kennt: denn ihm muß wenig scheinen,
Was Tausenden schon Reichthum ist; so kennt
Man euch, ihr Götter, an gesparten, lang'
Und weise zubereiteten Geschenken.
Denn ihr allein wißt, was uns frommen kann,
Und schaut der Zukunft ausgedehntes Reich,

Wenn jedes Abends Stern und Nebelhülle
Die Aussicht uns verdeckt. Gelassen hört
Ihr unser Flehn, das um Beschleunigung
Euch kindisch bittet; aber eure Hand
Bricht unreif nie die goldnen Himmelsfrüchte;
Und wehe dem, der ungeduldig sie
Ertrotzend saure Speise sich zum Tod'
Genießt. O laßt das lang erwartete,
Noch kaum gedachte Glück nicht, wie den Schatten
Des abgeschiednen Freundes, eitel mir
Und dreifach schmerzlicher vorübergehn!

O r e ſt (tritt wieder zu ihr.)

Rufst du die Götter an für dich und Pylades,
So nenne meinen Namen nicht mit eurem.
Du retteſt den Verbrecher nicht, zu dem
Du dich gesell'ſt, und theileſt Fluch und Noth.

Iphigenie.

Mein Schickſal iſt an deines feſt gebunden.

Oreſt.

Mit nichten! Laß allein und unbegleitet
Mich zu den Todten gehn. Verhülltest du
In deinen Schleier selbst den Schuldigen;
Du birgst ihn nicht vorm Blick der Immerwachen
Und deine Gegenwart, du Himmliſche,
Drängt sie nur seitwärts und verscheucht sie nicht.
Sie dürfen mit den ehrnen frechen Füßen
Des heil'gen Waldes Boden nicht betreten;
Doch hör' ich aus der Ferne hie und da
Ihr gräßliches Gelächter. Wölfe harren
So um den Baum, auf den ein Reisender
Sich rettete. Da draußen ruhen sie
Gelagert; und verlaſſ' ich dieſen Hain,
Dann steigen sie, die Schlangenhäupter schüttelnd,
Von allen Seiten Staub erregend auf,
Und treiben ihre Beute vor sich her.

Iphigenie.

Kannst du, Oreſt, ein freundlich Wort vernehmen?

Oreſt.

Spar' es für einen Freund der Götter auf.

Iphigenie.

Sie geben dir zu neuer Hoffnung Licht.

Oreſt.

Durch Rauch und Qualm ſeh' ich den matten Schein
Des Todtenfluſſes mir zur Hölle leuchten!

Iphigenie.

Haſt du Elektren, Eine Schweſter nur?

Oreſt.

Die Eine kannt' ich; doch die ältſte nahm
Ihr gut Geſchick, das uns ſo ſchrecklich ſchien,
Bei Zeiten aus dem Elend unſers Hauſes.
O laß dein Fragen, und geſelle dich
Nicht auch zu den Erinnyen; ſie blaſen
Mir ſchadenfroh die Aſche von der Seele,
Und leiden nicht, daß ſich die letzten Kohlen
Von unſers Hauſes Schreckensbrande ſtill
In mir verglimmen. Soll die Gluth denn ewig,
Vorſetzlich angefacht, mit Höllenſchwefel
Genährt, mir auf der Seele marternd brennen?

Iphigenie.

Ich bringe ſüßes Rauchwerk in die Flamme.
O laß den reinen Hauch der Liebe dir
Die Gluth des Buſens leiſe wehend kühlen!
Oreſt, mein Theurer, kannſt du nicht vernehmen?
Hat das Geleit der Schreckensgötter ſo
Das Blut in deinen Adern aufgetrocknet?
Schleicht, wie vom Haupt der gräßlichen Gorgone,
Verſteinernd dir ein Zauber durch die Glieder?
O wenn vergoſſ'nen Mutterblutes Stimme
Zur Höll' hinab mit dumpfen Tönen ruft:
Soll nicht der reinen Schweſter Segenswort
Hülfreiche Götter vom Olympus rufen?

Oreſt.

Es ruft! es ruft! So willſt du mein Verderben?
Verbirgt in dir ſich eine Rachegöttin?

Wer bist du, deren Stimme mir entsetzlich
Das Innerste in seinen Tiefen wendet?

Iphigenie.

Es zeigt sich dir im tiefsten Herzen an:
Orest, ich bin's! Sieh Iphigenien!
Ich lebe!

Orest.

Du!

Iphigenie.

Mein Bruder!

Orest.

Laß! Hinweg!
Ich rathe dir, berühre nicht die Locken!
Wie von Kreusa's Brautkleid zündet sich
Ein unauslöschlich Feuer von mir fort.
Laß mich! Wie Herkules will ich Unwürd'ger
Den Tod voll Schmach, in mich verschlossen, sterben.

Iphigenie.

Du wirst nicht untergehn! O daß ich nur
Ein ruhig Wort von dir vernehmen könnte!
O löse meine Zweifel, laß des Glückes,
Des lang' erflehten, mich auch sicher werden.
Es wälzet sich ein Rad von Freud' und Schmerz
Durch meine Seele. Von dem fremden Manne
Entfernet mich ein Schauer; doch es reißt
Mein Innerstes gewaltig mich zum Bruder.

Orest.

Ist hier Lyäens Tempel? und ergreift
Unbändig=heil'ge Wuth die Priesterin?

Iphigenie.

O höre mich! O sieh mich an, wie mir
Nach einer langen Zeit das Herz sich öffnet
Der Seligkeit, dem Liebsten, was die Welt
Noch für mich tragen kann, das Haupt zu küssen,
Mit meinen Armen, die den leeren Winden
Nur ausgebreitet waren, dich zu fassen!

O laß mich! Laß mich! Denn es quillet heller
Nicht vom Parnaß die ew'ge Quelle sprudelnd
Von Fels zu Fels in's goldne Thal hinab,
Wie Freude mir vom Herzen wallend fließt,
Und wie ein selig Meer mich rings umfängt.
Orest! Orest! Mein Bruder!

> ### Orest.
>
> Schöne Nymphe,
Ich traue dir und deinem Schmeicheln nicht.
Diana fordert strenge Dienerinnen
Und rächet das entweihte Heiligthum.
Entferne deinen Arm von meiner Brust!
Und wenn du einen Jüngling rettend lieben,
Das schöne Glück ihm zärtlich bieten willst;
So wende meinem Freunde dein Gemüth,
Dem würd'gern Manne zu. Er irr't umher
Auf jenem Felsenpfade; such' ihn auf,
Weis' ihn zurecht und schone meiner.

> ### Iphigenie.
>
> Fasse
Dich, Bruder, und erkenne die Gefund'ne!
Schilt einer Schwester reine Himmelsfreude
Nicht unbesonnene, strafbare Lust.
O nehmt den Wahn ihm von dem starren Auge,
Daß uns der Augenblick der höchsten Freude
Nicht dreifach elend mache! Sie ist hier,
Die längst verlorne Schwester. Vom Altar
Riß mich die Göttin weg und rettete
Hierher mich in ihr eigen Heiligthum.
Gefangen bist du, dargestellt zum Opfer,
Und findest in der Priesterin die Schwester.

> ### Orest.
>
Unselige! So mag die Sonne denn
Die letzten Gräuel unsers Hauses sehn!
Ist nicht Elektra hier? damit auch sie
Mit uns zu Grunde gehe, nicht ihr Leben
Zu schwererem Geschick' und Leiden friste.

Gut, Priesterin! ich folge zum Altar:
Der Brudermord ist hergebrachte Sitte
Des alten Stammes; und ich danke, Götter,
Daß ihr mich ohne Kinder auszurotten
Beschlossen habt.   Und laß dir rathen, habe
Die Sonne nicht zu lieb und nicht die Sterne:
Komm, folge mir in's dunkle Reich hinab!
Wie sich vom Schwefelpfuhl' erzeugte Drachen
Bekämpfend die verwandte Brut verschlingen,
Zerstört sich selbst das wüthende Geschlecht;
Komm kinderlos und schuldlos mit hinab!
Du siehst mich mit Erbarmen an? Laß ab!
Mit solchen Blicken suchte Klytemnestra
Sich einen Weg nach ihres Sohnes Herzen;
Doch sein geschwung'ner Arm traf ihre Brust.
Die Mutter fiel! — Tritt auf, unwill'ger Geist!
Im Kreis geschlossen tretet an, ihr Furien,
Und wohnet dem willkommnen Schauspiel bei,
Dem letzten, gräßlichsten, das ihr bereitet!
Nicht Haß und Rache schärfen ihren Dolch!
Die liebevolle Schwester wird zur That
Gezwungen.   Weine nicht! Du hast nicht Schuld.
Seit meinen ersten Jahren hab' ich nichts
Geliebt, wie ich dich lieben könnte, Schwester.
Ja, schwinge deinen Stahl, verschone nicht,
Zerreiße diesen Busen, und eröffne
Den Strömen, die hier sieden, einen Weg!

(Er sinkt in Ermattung.)

Iphigenie.

Allein zu tragen dieses Glück und Elend
Vermag ich nicht. — Wo bist du, Pylades?
Wo find' ich deine Hülfe, theurer Mann?

(Sie entfernt sich suchend.)

Zweiter Auftritt.

Oreſt
(aus seiner Betäubung erwachend und sich aufrichtend).

Noch Einen! reiche mir aus Lethe's Fluthen
Den letzten kühlen Becher der Erquickung!
Bald ist der Krampf des Lebens aus dem Busen
Hinweggespült; bald fließet still mein Geist,
Der Quelle des Vergessens hingegeben,
Zu euch, ihr Schatten, in die ew'gen Nebel.
Gefällig laßt in eurer Ruhe sich
Den umgetriebnen Sohn der Erde laben!
Welch ein Gelispel hör' ich in den Zweigen,
Welch ein Geräusch aus jener Dämmrung säuseln? —
Sie kommen schon, den neuen Gast zu sehn!
Wer ist die Schaar, die herrlich mit einander
Wie ein versammelt Fürstenhaus sich freut?
Sie gehen friedlich, Alt' und Junge, Männer
Mit Weibern; göttergleich und ähnlich scheinen
Die wandelnden Gestalten.   Ja, sie sind's,
Die Ahnherrn meines Hauses — Mit Thyesten
Geht Atreus in vertraulichen Gesprächen;
Die Knaben schlüpfen scherzend um sie her.
Ist keine Feindschaft hier mehr unter euch?
Verlosch die Rache wie das Licht der Sonne?
So bin auch ich willkommen, und ich darf
In euern feierlichen Zug mich mischen.
Willkommen, Väter! euch grüßt Orest,
Von eurem Stamme der letzte Mann;
Was ihr gesä't, hat er geerntet.
Mit Fluch beladen stieg er herab,
Doch leichter träget sich hier jede Bürde:
Nehmt ihn, o nehmt ihn in euren Kreis!
Dich, Atreus, ehr' ich, auch dich Thyesten:
Wir sind hier Alle der Feindschaft los. —
Zeigt mir den Vater, den ich nur Einmal
Im Leben sah! — Bist du's, mein Vater?
Und führst die Mutter vertraut mit dir?

Darf Klytemnestra die Hand dir reichen;
So darf Orest auch zu ihr treten
Und darf ihr sagen: sieh deinen Sohn! —
Seht euren Sohn! Heißt ihn willkommen.
Auf Erden war in unserm Hause
Der Gruß des Mordes gewisse Losung,
Und das Geschlecht des alten Tantalus
Hat seine Freuden jenseits der Nacht.
Ihr ruft: Willkommen! und nehmt mich auf!
O führt zum Alten, zum Ahnherrn mich!
Wo ist der Alte? daß ich ihn sehe,
Das theure Haupt, das vielverehrte,
Das mit den Göttern zu Rathe saß.
Ihr scheint zu zaudern, euch wegzuwenden?
Was ist es? Leidet der Göttergleiche?
Weh mir! es haben die Uebermächt'gen
Der Heldenbrust grausame Qualen
Mit ehrnen Ketten fest aufgeschmiedet.

Dritter Auftritt.

Orest. Iphigenie. Pylades.

Orest.

Seyd ihr auch schon herabgekommen?
Wohl, Schwester, dir! Noch fehlt Elektra:
Ein güt'ger Gott send' uns die Eine
Mit sanften Pfeilen auch schnell herab.
Dich, armer Freund, muß ich bedauern!
Komm mit! komm mit! zu Pluto's Thron,
Als neue Gäste den Wirth zu grüßen.

Iphigenie.

Geschwister, die ihr an dem weiten Himmel
Das schöne Licht bei Tag und Nacht herauf
Den Menschen bringet, und den Abgeschiednen
Nicht leuchten dürfet, rettet uns Geschwister!
Du liebst, Diane, deinen holden Bruder
Vor Allem, was dir Erd' und Himmel bietet,

Und wendest dein jungfräulich Angesicht
Nach seinem ew'gen Lichte sehnend still,
O laß den einz'gen Spätgefundnen mir
Nicht in der Finsterniß des Wahnsinns rasen!
Und ist dein Wille, da du hier mich bargst,
Nunmehr vollendet, willst du mir durch ihn
Und ihm durch mich die sel'ge Hülfe geben:
So lös' ihn von den Banden jenes Fluchs,
Daß nicht die theure Zeit der Rettung schwinde.

Pylades.

Erkennst du uns und diesen heil'gen Hain
Und dieses Licht, das nicht den Todten leuchtet?
Fühlst du den Arm des Freundes und der Schwester,
Die dich noch fest und lebend halten? Faß'
Uns kräftig an; wir sind nicht leere Schatten.
Merk auf mein Wort! Vernimm es! Raffe dich
Zusammen! Jeder Augenblick ist theuer,
Und unsre Rückkehr hängt an zarten Fäden,
Die, scheint es, eine günst'ge Parze spinnt.

Orest (zu Iphigenien).

Laß mich zum Erstenmal mit freiem Herzen
In deinen Armen reine Freude haben!
Ihr Götter, die mit flammender Gewalt
Ihr schwere Wolken aufzuzehren wandelt,
Und gnädig=ernst den lang' erflehten Regen
Mit Donnerstimmen und mit Windes Brausen
In wilden Strömen auf die Erde schüttet;
Doch bald der Menschen grausendes Erwarten
In Segen auflöst und das bange Staunen
In Freudeblick und lauten Dank verwandelt,
Wenn in den Tropfen frischerquickter Blätter
Die neue Sonne tausendfach sich spiegelt,
Und Iris freundlich bunt mit leichter Hand
Den grauen Flor der letzten Wolken trennt,
O laßt mich auch an meiner Schwester Armen,
An meines Freundes Brust, was ihr mir gönnt,
Mit vollem Dank genießen und behalten!

Es löset sich der Fluch, mir sagt's das Herz.
Die Eumeniden ziehn, ich höre sie,
Zum Tartarus und schlagen hinter sich
Die ehrnen Thore fernabdonnernd zu.
Die Erde dampft erquickenden Geruch
Und ladet mich auf ihren Flächen ein,
Nach Lebensfreud' und großer That zu jagen.

Pylades.

Versäumt die Zeit nicht, die gemessen ist!
Der Wind, der unsre Segel schwellt, er bringe
Erst unsre volle Freude zum Olymp.
Kommt! Es bedarf hier schnellen Rath und Schluß.

Vierter Aufzug.

Erster Auftritt.

Iphigenie.

Denken die Himmlischen
Einem der Erdgebornen
Viele Verwirrungen zu,
Und bereiten sie ihm
Von der Freude zu Schmerzen
Und von Schmerzen zur Freude
Tief=erschütternden Uebergang;
Dann erziehen sie ihm
In der Nähe der Stadt,
Oder am fernen Gestade,
Daß in Stunden der Noth
Auch die Hülfe bereit sey,
Einen ruhigen Freund.
O segnet, Götter, unsern Pylades,
Und was er immer unternehmen mag!
Er ist der Arm des Jünglings in der Schlacht,
Des Greises leuchtend Aug' in der Versammlung:
Denn seine Seel' ist stille; bewahrt
Der Ruhe heil'ges unerschöpftes Gut,
Und den Umhergetriebenen reichet er
Aus ihren Tiefen Rath und Hülfe. Mich
Riß er vom Bruder los; den staunt' ich an
Und immer wieder an, und konnte mir
Das Glück nicht eigen machen, ließ ihn nicht
Aus meinen Armen los, und fühlte nicht
Die Nähe der Gefahr, die uns umgibt.

Jetzt gehn sie, ihren Anschlag auszuführen,
Der See zu, wo das Schiff, mit den Gefährten
In einer Bucht versteckt, aufs Zeichen lauert,
Und haben kluges Wort mir in den Mund
Gegeben, mich gelehrt, was ich dem König
Antworte, wenn er sendet und das Opfer
Mir dringender gebietet. Ach! ich sehe wohl,
Ich muß mich leiten lassen wie ein Kind.
Ich habe nicht gelernt zu hinterhalten,
Noch Jemand etwas abzulisten. Weh!
O weh der Lüge! Sie befreit nicht,
Wie jedes andre wahrgesprochne Wort,
Die Brust; sie macht uns nicht getrost, sie ängstet
Den, der sie heimlich schmiedet, und sie kehrt,
Ein losgedrückter Pfeil von einem Gotte
Gewendet und versagend, sich zurück
Und trifft den Schützen. Sorg' auf Sorge schwankt
Mir durch die Brust. Es greift die Furie
Vielleicht den Bruder auf dem Boden wieder
Des ungeweihten Ufers grimmig an.
Entdeckt man sie vielleicht? Mich dünkt, ich höre
Gewaffnete sich nahen! — Hier! — Der Bote
Kommt von dem Könige mit schnellem Schritt.
Es schlägt mein Herz, es treibt sich meine Seele,
Da ich des Mannes Angesicht erblicke,
Dem ich mit falschem Wort begegnen soll.

Zweiter Auftritt.

Iphigenie. Arkas.

Arkas.

Beschleunige das Opfer, Priesterin!
Der König wartet und es harrt das Volk.

Iphigenie.

Ich folgte meiner Pflicht und deinem Wink,
Wenn unvermuthet nicht ein Hinderniß
Sich zwischen mich und die Erfüllung stellte.

Arkas.

Was ist's, das den Befehl des Königs hindert?

Iphigenie.

Der Zufall, dessen wir nicht Meister sind.

Arkas.

So sage mir's, daß ich's ihm schnell vermelde:
Denn er beschloß bei sich der Beiden Tod.

Iphigenie.

Die Götter haben ihn noch nicht beschlossen.
Der älteste dieser Männer trägt die Schuld
Des nahverwandten Bluts, das er vergoß.
Die Furien verfolgen seinen Pfad,
Ja in dem innern Tempel faßte selbst
Das Uebel ihn, und seine Gegenwart
Entheiligte die reine Stätte.   Nun
Eil' ich mit meinen Jungfraun, an dem Meere
Der Göttin Bild mit frischer Welle netzend,
Geheimnißvolle Weihe zu begehn.
Es störe Niemand unsern stillen Zug!

Arkas.

Ich melde dieses neue Hinderniß
Dem Könige geschwind: beginne du
Das heil'ge Werk nicht eh', bis er's erlaubt.

Iphigenie.

Dies ist allein der Priest'rin überlassen.

Arkas.

Solch seltnen Fall soll auch der König wissen.

Iphigenie.

Sein Rath wie sein Befehl verändert nichts.

Arkas.

Oft wird der Mächtige zum Schein gefragt.

Iphigenie.

Erdringe nicht, was ich versagen sollte.

Arkas.

Versage nicht, was gut und nützlich ist.

Iphigenie.

Ich gebe nach, wenn du nicht säumen willst.

Arkas.

Schnell bin ich mit der Nachricht in dem Lager,
Und schnell mit seinen Worten hier zurück.
O könnt' ich ihm noch eine Botschaft bringen,
Die Alles lös'te, was uns jetzt verwirrt:
Denn du hast nicht des Treuen Rath geachtet.

Iphigenie.

Was ich vermochte, hab' ich gern gethan.

Arkas.

Noch änderst du den Sinn zur rechten Zeit.

Iphigenie.

Das steht nun einmal nicht in unsrer Macht.

Arkas.

Du hältst unmöglich, was dir Mühe kostet.

Iphigenie.

Dir scheint es möglich, weil der Wunsch dich trügt.

Arkas.

Willst du denn Alles so gelassen wagen?

Iphigenie.

Ich hab' es in der Götter Hand gelegt.

Arkas.

Sie pflegen Menschen menschlich zu erretten.

Iphigenie.

Auf ihren Fingerzeig kommt Alles an.

Arkas.

Ich sage dir, es liegt in deiner Hand.
Des Königs aufgebrachter Sinn allein
Bereitet diesen Fremden bittern Tod.
Das Heer entwöhnte längst vom harten Opfer
Und von dem blut'gen Dienste sein Gemüth.
Ja, Mancher, den ein widriges Geschick
An fremdes Ufer trug, empfand es selbst,
Wie göttergleich dem armen Irrenden,
Umhergetrieben an der fremden Gränze,

Ein freundlich Menschenangesicht begegnet.
O wende nicht von uns, was du vermagst!
Du endest leicht was du begonnen hast:
Denn nirgends baut die Milde, die herab
In menschlicher Gestalt vom Himmel kommt,
Ein Reich sich schneller, als wo trüb' und wild
Ein neues Volk, voll Leben, Muth und Kraft,
Sich selbst und banger Ahnung überlassen,
Des Menschenlebens schwere Bürden trägt.

Iphigenie.

Erschütt're meine Seele nicht, die du
Nach deinem Willen nicht bewegen kannst.

Arkas.

So lang' es Zeit ist, schont man weder Mühe
Noch eines guten Wortes Wiederholung.

Iphigenie.

Du machst dir Müh' und mir erregst du Schmerzen;
Vergebens Beides; darum laß mich nun.

Arkas.

Die Schmerzen sind's, die ich zu Hülfe rufe:
Denn es sind Freunde, Gutes rathen sie.

Iphigenie.

Sie fassen meine Seele mit Gewalt,
Doch tilgen sie den Widerwillen nicht.

Arkas.

Fühlt eine schöne Seele Widerwillen
Für eine Wohlthat, die der Edle reicht?

Iphigenie.

Ja, wenn der Edle, was sich nicht geziemt,
Statt meines Dankes mich erwerben will.

Arkas.

Wer keine Neigung fühlt, dem mangelt es
An einem Worte der Entschuld'gung nie.
Dem Fürsten sag' ich an, was hier gescheh'n.
O wiederholtest du in deiner Seele,
Wie edel er sich gegen dich betrug
Von deiner Ankunft an bis diesen Tag.

Dritter Auftritt.

Iphigenie allein.

Von dieses Mannes Rede fühl' ich mir
Zur ungelegnen Zeit das Herz im Busen
Auf einmal umgewendet. Ich erschrecke! —
Denn wie die Fluth mit schnellen Strömen wachsend
Die Felsen überspült, die in dem Sand'
Am Ufer liegen: so bedeckte ganz
Ein Freudenstrom mein Innerstes. Ich hielt
In meinen Armen das Unmögliche.
Es schien sich eine Wolke wieder sanft
Um mich zu legen, von der Erde mich
Empor zu heben und in jenen Schlummer
Mich einzuwiegen, den die gute Göttin
Um meine Schläfe legte, da ihr Arm
Mich rettend faßte. — Meinen Bruder
Ergriff das Herz mit einziger Gewalt:
Ich horchte nur auf seines Freundes Rath;
Nur sie zu retten drang die Seele vorwärts,
Und wie den Klippen einer wüsten Insel
Der Schiffer gern den Rücken wendet: so
Lag Tauris hinter mir. Nun hat die Stimme
Des treuen Manns mich wieder aufgeweckt,
Daß ich auch Menschen hier verlasse, mich
Erinnert. Doppelt wird mir der Betrug
Verhaßt. O bleibe ruhig, meine Seele!
Beginnst du nun zu schwanken und zu zweifeln?
Den festen Boden deiner Einsamkeit
Mußt du verlassen! Wieder eingeschifft
Ergreifen dich die Wellen schaukelnd, trüb'
Und bang' verkennest du die Welt und dich.

Vierter Auftritt.
Iphigenie. Pylades.

Pylades.

Wo ist sie? daß ich ihr mit schnellen Worten
Die frohe Botschaft unsrer Rettung bringe!

Iphigenie.

Du siehst mich hier voll Sorgen und Erwartung
Des sichern Trostes, den du mir versprichst.

Pylades.

Dein Bruder ist geheilt! Den Felsenboden
Des ungeweihten Ufers und den Sand
Betraten wir mit fröhlichen Gesprächen;
Der Hain blieb hinter uns, wir merkten's nicht.
Und herrlicher und immer herrlicher
Umloderte der Jugend schöne Flamme
Sein lockig Haupt; sein volles Auge glühte
Von Muth und Hoffnung, und sein freies Herz
Ergab sich ganz der Freude, ganz der Lust,
Dich, seine Retterin, und mich zu retten.

Iphigenie.

Gesegnet seyst du, und es möge nie
Von deiner Lippe, die so Gutes sprach,
Der Ton des Leidens und der Klage tönen!

Pylades.

Ich bringe mehr als das: denn schön begleitet,
Gleich einem Fürsten, pflegt das Glück zu nah'n.
Auch die Gefährten haben wir gefunden.
In einer Felsenbucht verbargen sie
Das Schiff und saßen traurig und erwartend.
Sie sahen deinen Bruder und es regten
Sich Alle jauchzend, und sie baten dringend
Der Abfahrt Stunde zu beschleunigen.
Es sehnet jede Faust sich nach dem Ruder,
Und selbst ein Wind erhob vom Lande lispelnd,
Von allen gleich bemerkt, die holden Schwingen.
Drum laß uns eilen, führe mich zum Tempel,

Laß mich das Heiligthum betreten, laß
Mich unsrer Wünsche Ziel verehrend fassen!
Ich bin allein genug, der Göttin Bild
Auf wohlgeübten Schultern wegzutragen:
Wie sehn' ich mich nach der erwünschten Last!

(Er geht gegen den Tempel unter den letzten Worten, ohne zu bemerken, daß
Iphigenie nicht folgt; endlich kehrt er sich um.)

Du stehst und zauderst — Sage mir — du schweigst!
Du scheinst verworren!   Widersetzet sich
Ein neues Unheil unserm Glück!   Sag' an!
Hast du dem Könige das kluge Wort
Vermelden lassen, das wir abgeredet?

Iphigenie.

Ich habe, theurer Mann; doch wirst du schelten.
Ein schweigender Verweis war mir dein Anblick.
Des Königs Bote kam, und wie du es
Mir in den Mund gelegt, so sagt's ich ihm.
Er schien zu staunen, und verlangte dringend
Die seltne Feier erst dem Könige
Zu melden, seinen Willen zu vernehmen;
Und nun erwart' ich seine Wiederkehr.

Pylades.

Weh' uns!   Erneuert schwebt nun die Gefahr
Um unsre Schläfe!   Warum hast du nicht
In's Priesterrecht dich weislich eingehüllt?

Iphigenie.

Als eine Hülle hab' ich's nie gebraucht.

Pylades.

So wirst du, reine Seele, dich und uns
Zu Grunde richten.   Warum dacht' ich nicht
Auf diesen Fall voraus und lehrte dich
Auch dieser Ford'rung auszuweichen!

Iphigenie.

                      Schilt
Nur mich, die Schuld ist mein, ich fühl' es wohl;
Doch konnt' ich anders nicht dem Mann begegnen,

Der mit Vernunft und Ernst von mir verlangte,
Was ihm mein Herz als Recht gestehen mußte.

Pylades.

Gefährlicher zieht sich's zusammen; doch auch so
Laß uns nicht zagen, oder unbesonnen
Und übereilt uns selbst verrathen.   Ruhig
Erwarte du die Wiederkunft des Boten
Und dann steh' fest, er bringe was er will:
Denn solcher Weihung Feier anzuordnen
Gehört der Priesterin und nicht dem König.
Und fordert er den fremden Mann zu sehn,
Der von dem Wahnsinn schwer belastet ist:
So lehn' es ab, als hieltest du uns Beide
Im Tempel wohl verwahrt.   So schaff' uns Luft,
Daß wir auf's Eiligste, den heil'gen Schatz
Dem rauh unwürd'gen Volk entwendend, flieh'n.
Die besten Zeichen sendet uns Apoll,
Und, eh' wir die Bedingung fromm erfüllen,
Erfüllt er göttlich sein Versprechen schon.
Orest ist frei, geheilt! — Mit dem Befreiten
O führet uns hinüber, günst'ge Winde,
Zur Felsen=Insel, die der Gott bewohnt;
Dann nach Mycen, daß es lebendig werde,
Daß von der Asche des verloschnen Herdes
Die Vatergötter fröhlich sich erheben,
Und schönes Feuer ihre Wohnungen
Umleuchte!   Deine Hand soll ihnen Weihrauch
Zuerst aus goldnen Schalen streuen.   Du
Bringst über jene Schwelle Heil und Leben wieder,
Entsühnst den Fluch und schmückest neu die Deinen
Mit frischen Lebensblüthen herrlich aus.

Iphigenie.

Vernehm' ich dich, so wendet sich, o Theurer,
Wie sich die Blume nach der Sonne wendet,
Die Seele, von dem Strahle deiner Worte
Getroffen, sich dem süßen Troste nach.
Wie köstlich ist des gegenwärt'gen Freundes

13*

Gewisse Rede, deren Himmelskraft
Ein Einsamer entbehrt und still versinkt!
Denn langsam reift, verschlossen in dem Busen,
Gedank' ihm und Entschluß; die Gegenwart
Des Liebenden entwickelte sie leicht.

Pylades.

Leb' wohl!   Die Freunde will ich nun geschwind
Beruhigen, die sehnlich wartend harren.
Dann komm' ich schnell zurück und lausche hier,
Im Felsenbusch versteckt, auf deinen Wink —
Was sinnest du?   Auf einmal überschwebt
Ein stiller Trauerzug die freie Stirne.

Iphigenie.

Verzeih'!   Wie leichte Wolken vor der Sonne,
So zieht mir vor der Seele leichte Sorge
Und Bangigkeit vorüber.

Pylades.

Fürchte nicht!
Betrüglich schloß die Furcht mit der Gefahr
Ein enges Bündniß; beide sind Gesellen.

Iphigenie.

Die Sorge nenn' ich edel, die mich warnt,
Den König, der mein zweiter Vater ward,
Nicht tückisch zu betrügen, zu berauben.

Pylades.

Der deinen Bruder schlachtet, dem entfliehst du.

Iphigenie.

Es ist derselbe, der mir Gutes that.

Pylades.

Das ist nicht Undank, was die Noth gebeut.

Iphigenie.

Es bleibt wohl Undank; nur die Noth entschuldigt's.

Pylades.

Vor Göttern und vor Menschen dich gewiß.

Iphigenie.

Allein mein eigen Herz ist nicht befriedigt.

Pylades.

Zu strenge Ford'rung ist verborgner Stolz.

Iphigenie.

Ich untersuche nicht, ich fühle nur.

Pylades.

Fühlst du dich recht, so mußt du dich verehren.

Iphigenie.

Ganz unbefleckt genießt sich nur das Herz.

Pylades.

So hast du dich im Tempel wohl bewahrt;
Das Leben lehrt uns, weniger mit uns
Und andern strenge seyn; du lernst es auch.
So wunderbar ist dies Geschlecht gebildet,
So vielfach ist's verschlungen und verknüpft,
Daß Keiner in sich selbst, noch mit den Andern
Sich rein und unverworren halten kann.
Auch sind wir nicht bestellt, uns selbst zu richten;
Zu wandeln und auf seinen Weg zu sehen
Ist eines Menschen erste, nächste Pflicht:
Denn selten schätzt er recht, was er gethan,
Und was er thut, weiß er fast nicht zu schätzen.

Iphigenie.

Fast überred'st du mich zu deiner Meinung.

Pylades.

Braucht's Ueberredung, wo die Wahl versagt ist?
Den Bruder, dich, und einen Freund zu retten
Ist nur Ein Weg; fragt sich's, ob wir ihn gehn?

Iphigenie.

O laß mich zaudern! denn du thätest selbst
Ein solches Unrecht keinem Mann gelassen,
Dem du für Wohlthat dich verpflichtet hieltest.

Pylades.

Wenn wir zu Grunde gehen, wartet dein
Ein härt'rer Vorwurf, der Verzweiflung trägt.
Man sieht, du bist nicht an Verlust gewohnt,
Da du dem großen Uebel zu entgehen,
Ein falsches Wort nicht einmal opfern willst.

Iphigenie.

O trüg' ich doch ein männlich Herz in mir!
Das, wenn es einen kühnen Vorsatz hegt,
Vor jeder andern Stimme sich verschließt.

Pylades.

Du weigerst dich umsonst; die ehrne Hand
Der Noth gebietet, und ihr erster Wink
Ist oberstes Gesetz, dem Götter selbst
Sich unterwerfen müssen.* Schweigend herrscht
Des ew'gen Schicksals unberathne Schwester.
Was sie dir auferlegt, das trage; thu',
Was sie gebeut! Das Andre weißt du. Bald
Komm' ich zurück, aus deiner heil'gen Hand
Der Rettung schönes Siegel zu empfangen.

Fünfter Auftritt.

Iphigenie allein.

Ich muß ihm folgen: denn die Meinigen
Seh' ich in dringender Gefahr. Doch ach!
Mein eigen Schicksal macht mir bang' und bänger.
O soll ich nicht die stille Hoffnung retten,
Die in der Einsamkeit ich schön genährt?
Soll dieser Fluch denn ewig walten? Soll
Nie dies Geschlecht mit einem neuen Segen
Sich wieder heben? — Nimmt doch Alles ab!
Das beste Glück, des Lebens schönste Kraft
Ermattet endlich, warum nicht der Fluch?
So hofft' ich denn vergebens, hier verwahrt,

---

* This is a purely Grecian idea, in whose theology Necessity was in fact the supreme power. This idea constitutes one of the principal features of the ancient drama. So Euripides Iphig. Taur. v. 1487. τὸ γὰρ χρεὼν σοῦ τε, καὶ θεῶν κρατεῖ, (where Barnes correctly makes τὸ χρεὼν = εἱμαρμένη et πεπρωμένον, rendering the passage: *Fatum enim, vel fatalis necessitas, etiam in teipsum et reliquos deos habet imperium; multo magis in me mortalem*). Æschylos Prom. 103. τὴν πεπρωμένην δὲ χρὴ αἶσαν φέρειν ὡς ῥᾷστα, γιγνώσκονθ', ὅτε τὸ τῆς ἀνάγκης ἔστ' ἀδήριτον σθένος. Euripides Helen. 513. δεινῆς ἀνάγκης οὐδὲν ἰσχύειν πλέον, et m. l. a.

Von meines Hauses Schicksal abgeschieden,
Dereinst mit reiner Hand und reinem Herzen
Die schwer befleckte Wohnung zu entsühnen!
Kaum wird in meinen Armen mir ein Bruder
Vom grimm'gen Uebel wundervoll und schnell
Geheilt; kaum naht ein lang' erflehtes Schiff,
Mich in den Port der Vaterwelt zu leiten;
So legt die taube Noth ein doppelt Laster
Mit ehrner Hand mir auf: das heilige
Mir anvertraute, viel verehrte Bild
Zu rauben und den Mann zu hintergehn,
Dem ich mein Leben und mein Schicksal danke.
O daß in meinem Busen nicht zuletzt
Ein Widerwille keime! der Titanen,
Der alten Götter tiefer Haß auf euch,
Olympier, nicht auch die zarte Brust
Mit Geierklauen fasse! Rettet mich,
Und rettet euer Bild in meiner Seele!

Vor meinen Ohren tönt das alte Lied —
Vergessen hatt' ich's und vergaß es gern —
Das Lied der Parcen, das sie grausam sangen,
Als Tantalus vom gold'nen Stuhle fiel:
Sie litten mit dem edeln Freunde; grimmig
War ihre Brust, und furchtbar ihr Gesang.
In unsrer Jugend sang's die Amme mir
Und den Geschwistern vor, ich merkt' es wohl.

Es fürchte die Götter
Das Menschengeschlecht!
Sie halten die Herrschaft
In ewigen Händen,
Und können sie brauchen
Wie's ihnen gefällt.

Der fürchte sie doppelt
Den je sie erheben!
Auf Klippen und Wolken
Sind Stühle bereitet
Um goldene Tische.

Erhebet ein Zwist sich:
So stürzen die Gäste
Geschmäht und geschändet
In nächtliche Tiefen,
Und harren vergebens,
Im Finstern gebunden,
Gerechten Gerichtes.

Sie aber, sie bleiben
In ewigen Festen
An goldenen Tischen.
Sie schreiten vom Berge
Zu Bergen hinüber:
Aus Schlünden der Tiefe
Dampft ihnen der Athem
Erstickter Titanen,
Gleich Opfergerüchen,
Ein leichtes Gewölke.

Es wenden die Herrscher
Ihr segnendes Auge
Von ganzen Geschlechtern,
Und meiden, im Enkel
Die eh'mals geliebten,
Still redenden Züge
Des Ahnherrn zu sehn.

So sangen die Parcen;
Es horcht der Verbannte,
In nächtlichen Höhlen
Der Alte die Lieder,
Denkt Kinder und Enkel
Und schüttelt das Haupt.

Fünfter Aufzug.

Erster Auftritt.

Thoas. Arkas.

Arkas.

Verwirrt muß ich gestehn, daß ich nicht weiß,
Wohin ich meinen Argwohn richten soll.
Sind's die Gefang'nen, die auf ihre Flucht
Verstohlen sinnen? Ist's die Priesterin,
Die ihnen hilft? Es mehrt sich das Gerücht:
Das Schiff, das diese Beiden hergebracht,
Sey irgend noch in einer Bucht versteckt.
Und jenes Mannes Wahnsinn, diese Weihe,
Der heil'ge Vorwand dieser Zög'rung, rufen
Den Argwohn lauter und die Vorsicht auf.

Thoas.

Es komme schnell die Priesterin herbei!
Dann geht, durchsucht das Ufer scharf und schnell
Vom Vorgebirge bis zum Hain der Göttin.
Verschonet seine heil'gen Tiefen, legt
Bedächt'gen Hinterhalt und greift sie an;
Wo ihr sie findet, faßt sie, wie ihr pflegt.

Zweiter Auftritt.

Thoas allein.

Entsetzlich wechselt mir der Grimm im Busen;
Erst gegen sie, die ich so heilig hielt;
Dann gegen mich, der ich sie zum Verrath
Durch Nachsicht und durch Güte bildete.

303

Zur Sklaverei gewöhnt der Mensch sich gut
Und lernet leicht gehorchen, wenn man ihn
Der Freiheit ganz beraubt. Ja, wäre sie
In meiner Ahnherrn rohe Hand gefallen,
Und hätte sie der heil'ge Grimm verschont:
Sie wäre froh gewesen, sich allein
Zu retten, hätte dankbar ihr Geschick
Erkannt und fremdes Blut vor dem Altar
Vergossen, hätte Pflicht genannt,
Was Noth war. Nun lockt meine Güte
In ihrer Brust verwegnen Wunsch herauf.
Vergebens hofft' ich, sie mir zu verbinden;
Sie sinnt sich nun ein eigen Schicksal aus.
Durch Schmeichelei gewann sie mir das Herz:
Nun widersteh' ich der; so sucht sie sich
Den Weg durch List und Trug, und meine Güte
Scheint ihr ein alt verjährtes Eigenthum.

Dritter Auftritt.

Iphigenie. Thoas.

Iphigenie.

Du forderst mich! was bringt dich zu uns her?

Thoas.

Du schiebst das Opfer auf; sag' an, warum?

Iphigenie.

Ich hab' an Arkas Alles klar erzählt.

Thoas.

Von dir möcht' ich es weiter noch vernehmen.

Iphigenie.

Die Göttin gibt dir Frist zur Ueberlegung.

Thoas.

Sie scheint dir selbst gelegen, diese Frist.

Iphigenie.

Wenn dir das Herz zum grausamen Entschluß
Verhärtet ist: so solltest du nicht kommen!

Ein König, der Unmenschliches verlangt,
Find't Diener g'nug, die gegen Gnad' und Lohn
Den halben Fluch der That begierig fassen;
Doch seine Gegenwart bleibt unbefleckt.
Er sinnt den Tod in einer schweren Wolke,
Und seine Boten bringen flammendes
Verderben auf des Armen Haupt hinab;
Er aber schwebt durch seine Höhen ruhig,
Ein unerreichter Gott, im Sturme fort.

Thoas.

Die heil'ge Lippe tönt ein wildes Lied.

Iphigenie.

Nicht Priesterin! nur Agamemnon's Tochter.
Der Unbekannten Wort verehrtest du;
Der Fürstin willst du rasch gebieten? Nein!
Von Jugend auf hab' ich gelernt gehorchen,
Erst meinen Eltern und dann einer Gottheit,
Und folgsam fühlt' ich immer meine Seele
Am schönsten frei; allein dem harten Worte,
Dem rauhen Ausspruch eines Mannes mich
Zu fügen, lernt' ich weder dort noch hier.

Thoas.

Ein alt Gesetz, nicht ich, gebietet dir.

Iphigenie.

Wir fassen ein Gesetz begierig an,
Das unsrer Leidenschaft zur Waffe dient.
Ein andres spricht zu mir, ein älteres,
Mich dir zu widersetzen, das Gebot,
Dem jeder Fremde heilig ist.

Thoas.

Es scheinen die Gefangnen dir sehr nah
Am Herzen: denn vor Antheil und Bewegung
Vergissest du der Klugheit erstes Wort,
Daß man den Mächtigen nicht reizen soll.

Iphigenie.

Red' oder schweig' ich, immer kannst du wissen,
Was mir im Herzen ist und immer bleibt.

Löf't die Erinnerung des gleichen Schicksals
Nicht ein verschlossnes Herz zum Mitleid auf?
Wie mehr dann meins! In ihnen seh' ich mich.
Ich habe vorm Altare selbst gezittert,
Und feierlich umgab der frühe Tod
Die Knieende; das Messer zuckte schon
Den lebenvollen Busen zu durchbohren;
Mein Innerstes entsetzte wirbelnd sich,
Mein Auge brach, und — ich fand mich gerettet.
Sind wir, was Götter gnädig uns gewährt,
Unglücklichen nicht zu erstatten schuldig?
Du weißt es, kennst mich, und du willst mich zwingen!

Thoas.
Gehorche deinem Dienste, nicht dem Herrn.

Iphigenie.
Laß ab! Beschönige nicht die Gewalt,
Die sich der Schwachheit eines Weibes freut.
Ich bin so frei geboren als ein Mann.
Stünd' Agamemnon's Sohn dir gegenüber,
Und du verlangtest, was sich nicht gebührt:
So hat auch Er ein Schwert und einen Arm,
Die Rechte seines Busens zu vertheid'gen.
Ich habe nichts als Worte, und es ziemt
Dem edeln Mann, der Frauen Wort zu achten.

Thoas.
Ich acht' es mehr als eines Bruders Schwert.

Iphigenie.
Das Loos der Waffen wechselt hin und her;
Kein kluger Streiter hält den Feind gering.
Auch ohne Hülfe gegen Trutz und Härte
Hat die Natur den Schwachen nicht gelassen:
Sie gab zur List ihm Freude, lehrt ihn Künste;
Bald weicht er aus, verspätet und umgeht.
Ja, der Gewaltige verdient, daß man sie übt.

Thoas.
Die Vorsicht stellt der List sich klug entgegen.

Iphigenie.

Und eine reine Seele braucht sie nicht.

Thoas.

Sprich unbehutsam nicht dein eigen Urtheil.

Iphigenie.

O sähest du, wie meine Seele kämpft,
Ein bös' Geschick, das sie ergreifen will,
Im ersten Anfall muthig abzutreiben!
So steh' ich denn hier wehrlos gegen dich?
Die schöne Bitte, den anmuth'gen Zweig,
In einer Frauen Hand gewaltiger
Als Schwert und Waffe, stößest du zurück:
Was bleibt mir nun, mein Inn'res zu vertheid'gen?
Ruf' ich die Göttin um ein Wunder an?
Ist keine Kraft in meiner Seele Tiefen?

Thoas.

Es scheint, der beiden Fremden Schicksal macht
Unmäßig dich besorgt. Wer sind sie? sprich,
Für die dein Geist gewaltig sich erhebt.

Iphigenie.

Sie sind — sie scheinen — für Griechen halt' ich sie.

Thoas.

Landsleute sind es? und sie haben wohl
Der Rückkehr schönes Bild in dir erneut?

Iphigenie (nach einigem Stillschweigen.)

Hat denn zur unerhörten That der Mann
Allein das Recht? Drückt denn Unmögliches
Nur Er an die gewalt'ge Heldenbrust?
Was nennt man groß? Was hebt die Seele schaudernd
Dem immer wiederholenden Erzähler,
Als was mit unwahrscheinlichem Erfolg
Der Muthigste begann? Der in der Nacht
Allein das Heer des Feindes überschleicht,
Wie unversehen eine Flamme wüthend
Die Schlafenden, Erwachenden ergreift,
Zuletzt gedrängt von den Ermunterten

Auf Feindes Pferden, doch mit Beute kehrt,
Wird der allein gepriesen? Der allein,
Der, einen sichern Weg verachtend, kühn
Gebirg' und Wälder durchzustreifen geht,
Daß er von Räubern eine Gegend säub're?
Ist uns nichts übrig? Muß ein zartes Weib
Sich ihres angebornen Rechts entäußern,
Wild gegen Wilde seyn, wie Amazonen
Das Recht des Schwerts euch rauben und mit Blute
Die Unterdrückung rächen? Auf und ab
Steigt in der Brust ein kühnes Unternehmen:
Ich werde großem Vorwurf nicht entgehn,
Noch schwerem Uebel, wenn es mir mißlingt;
Allein Euch leg' ich's auf die Knie! Wenn
Ihr wahrhaft seyd, wie ihr gepriesen werdet:
So zeigt's durch euern Beistand und verherrlicht
Durch mich die Wahrheit! — Ja, vernimm, o König,
Es wird ein heimlicher Betrug geschmiedet;
Vergebens fragst du den Gefangnen nach;
Sie sind hinweg und suchen ihre Freunde,
Die mit dem Schiff' am Ufer warten, auf.
Der Aeltste, den das Uebel hier ergriffen
Und nun verlassen hat — es ist Orest,
Mein Bruder, und der Andre sein Vertrauter,
Sein Jugendfreund, mit Namen Pylades.
Apoll schickt sie von Delphi diesem Ufer
Mit göttlichen Befehlen zu, das Bild
Dianens wegzurauben und zu ihm
Die Schwester hinzubringen, und dafür
Verspricht er dem von Furien Verfolgten,
Des Mutterblutes Schuldigen, Befreiung.
Uns Beide hab' ich nun, die Ueberbliebnen
Von Tantal's Hauf', in deine Hand gelegt:
Verdirb uns — wenn du darfst.

Thoas.

Du glaubst, es höre
Der rohe Scythe, der Barbar, die Stimme

Der Wahrheit und der Menschlichkeit, die Atreus,
Der Grieche, nicht vernahm?

Iphigenie.

Es hört sie Jeder,
Geboren unter jedem Himmel, dem
Des Lebens Quelle durch den Busen rein
Und ungehindert fließt. — Was sinnst du mir,
O König, schweigend in der tiefen Seele?
Ist es Verderben? so tödte mich zuerst!
Denn nun empfind' ich, da uns keine Rettung
Mehr übrig bleibt, die gräßliche Gefahr,
Worein ich die Geliebten übereilt
Vorsätzlich stürzte. Weh! ich werde sie
Gebunden vor mir sehn! Mit welchen Blicken
Kann ich von meinem Bruder Abschied nehmen,
Den ich ermorde? Nimmer kann ich ihm
Mehr in die vielgeliebten Augen schaun!

Thoas.

So haben die Betrüger, künstlich=dichtend,
Der lang Verschloßnen, ihre Wünsche leicht
Und willig Glaubenden, ein solch Gespinnst
Um's Haupt geworfen!

Iphigenie.

Nein! o König, nein!
Ich könnte hintergangen werden; diese
Sind treu und wahr. Wirst du sie anders finden,
So laß sie fallen und verstoße mich,
Verbanne mich zur Strafe meiner Thorheit
An einer Klippen=Insel traurig Ufer.
Ist aber dieser Mann der lang' erflehte,
Geliebte Bruder: so entlaß uns, sey
Auch den Geschwistern wie der Schwester freundlich!
Mein Vater fiel durch seiner Frauen Schuld,
Und sie durch ihren Sohn. Die letzte Hoffnung
Von Atreus Stamme ruht auf ihm allein.
Laß mich mit reinem Herzen, reiner Hand,
Hinübergehn und unser Haus entsühnen.

Du hältst mir Wort! — Wenn zu den Meinen je
Mir Rückkehr zubereitet wäre, schwurst
Du, mich zu lassen; und sie ist es nun.
Ein König sagt nicht, wie gemeine Menschen,
Verlegen zu, daß er den Bittenden
Auf einen Augenblick entferne; noch
Verspricht er auf den Fall, den er nicht hofft:
Dann fühlt er erst die Höhe seiner Würde,
Wenn er den Harrenden beglücken kann.

Thoas.

Unwillig, wie sich Feuer gegen Wasser
Im Kampfe wehrt und gischend seinen Feind
Zu tilgen sucht, so wehret sich der Zorn
In meinem Busen gegen deine Worte.

Iphigenie.

O laß die Gnade, wie das heil'ge Licht
Der stillen Opferflamme, mir, umkränzt
Von Lobgesang und Dank und Freude, lodern.

Thoas.

Wie oft besänftigte mich diese Stimme!

Iphigenie.

O reiche mir die Hand zum Friedenszeichen.

Thoas.

Du forderst viel in einer kurzen Zeit.

Iphigenie.

Um Gut's zu thun braucht's keiner Ueberlegung.

Thoas.

Sehr viel! denn auch dem Guten folgt das Uebel.

Iphigenie.

Der Zweifel ist's, der Gutes böse macht.
Bedenke nicht; gewähre wie du's fühlst.

Vierter Auftritt.

Orest gewaffnet. Die Vorigen.

Orest (nach der Scene gekehrt.)

Verdoppelt eure Kräfte! Haltet sie
Zurück! Nur wenig Augenblicke! Weicht

Der Menge, und deckt den Weg zum Schiffe
Mir und der Schwester.

(Zu Iphigenien, ohne den König zu sehen.)

    Komm, wir sind verrathen.
Geringer Raum bleibt uns zur Flucht. Geschwind!

(Er erblickt den König.)

Thoas (nach dem Schwerte greifend.)

In meiner Gegenwart führt ungestraft
Kein Mann das nackte Schwert.

Iphigenie.

    Entheiliget
Der Göttin Wohnung nicht durch Wuth und Mord.
Gebietet eurem Volke Stillstand, höret
Die Priesterin, die Schwester!

Orest.

    Sage mir!
Wer ist es, der uns droht?

Iphigenie.

    Verehr' in ihm
Den König, der mein zweiter Vater ward!
Verzeih' mir, Bruder! doch mein kindlich Herz
Hat unser ganz Geschick in seine Hand
Gelegt. Gestanden hab' ich euren Anschlag
Und meine Seele vom Verrath gerettet.

Orest.

Will er die Rückkehr friedlich uns gewähren?

Iphigenie.

Dein blinkend Schwert verbietet mir die Antwort.

Orest (der das Schwert einsteckt.)

So sprich! Du siehst, ich horche deinen Worten.

Fünfter Auftritt.

Pylades.

Verweilet nicht! Die letzten Kräfte raffen
Die Unsrigen zusammen; weichend werden
Sie nach der See langsam zurückgedrängt.
Welch ein Gespräch der Fürsten find' ich hier!
Dieß ist des Königes verehrtes Haupt!

Arkas.

Gelassen, wie es dir, o König, ziemt,
Stehst du den Feinden gegenüber.   Gleich
Ist die Verwegenheit bestraft; es weicht
Und fällt ihr Anhang, und ihr Schiff ist unser.
Ein Wort von dir, so steht's in Flammen.

Thoas.

                                        Geh!
Gebiete Stillstand meinem Volke! Keiner
Beschädige den Feind, so lang' wir reden.

                    (Arkas ab.)

Orest.

Ich nehm' es an.   Geh', sammle, treuer Freund,
Den Rest des Volkes; harret still, welch' Ende
Die Götter unsern Thaten zubereiten.

                    (Pylades ab.)

Sechster Auftritt.

Iphigenie. Thoas. Orest.

Iphigenie.

Befreit von Sorgen mich, eh' ihr zu sprechen
Beginnet.   Ich befürchte bösen Zwist,
Wenn du, o König, nicht der Billigkeit
Gelinde Stimme hörest; du, mein Bruder,
Der raschen Jugend nicht gebieten willst.

Thoas.

Ich halte meinen Zorn, wie es dem Aeltern

Geziemt, zurück. Antworte mir! Womit
Bezeugst du, daß du Agamemnon's Sohn
Und dieser Bruder bist?

Orest.
Hier ist das Schwert,
Mit dem er Troja's tapfre Männer schlug.
Dies nahm ich seinem Mörder ab, und bat
Die Himmlischen, den Muth und Arm, das Glück
Des großen Königes mir zu verleihn,
Und einen schönern Tod mir zu gewähren.
Wähl' Einen aus den Edeln deines Heers
Und stelle mir den Besten gegenüber.
So weit die Erde Heldensöhne nährt,
Ist keinem Fremdling dies Gesuch verweigert.

Thoas.
Dies Vorrecht hat die alte Sitte nie
Dem Fremden hier gestattet.

Orest.
So beginne
Die neue Sitte denn von dir und mir!
Nachahmend heiliget ein ganzes Volk
Die edle That der Herrscher zum Gesetz.
Und laß mich nicht allein für unsre Freiheit,
Laß mich, den Fremden für die Fremden, kämpfen.
Fall' ich, so ist ihr Unheil mit dem meinen
Gesprochen: aber gönnet mir das Glück
Zu überwinden; so betrete nie
Ein Mann dies Ufer, dem der schnelle Blick
Hülfreicher Liebe nicht begegnet, und
Getröstet scheide Jeglicher hinweg!

Thoas.
Nicht unwerth scheinest du, o Jüngling, mir,
Der Ahnherrn, deren du dich rühmst, zu seyn.
Groß ist die Zahl der edeln tapfern Männer,
Die mich begleiten; doch ich stehe selbst
In meinen Jahren noch dem Feinde, bin
Bereit mit dir der Waffen Loos zu wagen.

14

Iphigenie.

Mit nichten! Dieses blutigen Beweises
Bedarf es nicht, o König! Laßt die Hand
Vom Schwerte! Denkt an mich und mein Geschick.
Der rasche Kampf verewigt einen Mann:
Er falle gleich, so preiset ihn das Lied.
Allein die Thränen, die unendlichen
Der überbliebnen, der verlaßnen Frau,
Zählt keine Nachwelt, und der Dichter schweigt
Von tausend durchgeweinten Tag' und Nächten,
Wo eine stille Seele den verlornen,
Rasch abgeschied'nen Freund vergebens sich
Zurückzurufen bangt und sich verzehrt.
Mich selbst hat eine Sorge gleich gewarnt,
Daß der Betrug nicht eines Räubers mich
Vom sichern Schutzort reiße, mich der Knechtschaft
Verrathe. Fleißig hab' ich sie gefragt,
Nach jedem Umstand mich erkundigt, Zeichen
Gefordert, und gewiß ist nun mein Herz.
Sieh hier an seiner rechten Hand das Mahl
Wie von drei Sternen, das am Tage schon,
Da er geboren ward, sich zeigte, das
Auf schwere That mit dieser Faust zu üben
Der Priester deutete. Dann überzeugt
Mich doppelt diese Schramme, die ihm hier
Die Augenbraune spaltet. Als ein Kind
Ließ ihn Elektra, rasch und unvorsichtig
Nach ihrer Art, aus ihren Armen stürzen.
Er schlug auf einen Dreifuß auf — Er ist's —
Soll ich dir noch die Aehnlichkeit des Vaters,
Soll ich das inn're Jauchzen meines Herzens
Dir auch als Zeugen der Vesich'rung nennen?

Thoas.

Und hübe deine Rede jeden Zweifel
Und bändigt' ich den Zorn in meiner Brust:
So würden doch die Waffen zwischen uns
Entscheiden müssen; Frieden seh' ich nicht.

Sie sind gekommen, du bekennest selbst,
Das heil'ge Bild der Göttin mir zu rauben.
Glaubt ihr, ich sehe dies gelassen an?
Der Grieche wendet oft sein lüstern Auge
Den fernen Schätzen der Barbaren zu,
Dem goldnen Felle, Pferden, schönen Töchtern;
Doch führte sie Gewalt und List nicht immer
Mit den erlangten Gütern glücklich heim.

Orest.

Das Bild, o König, soll uns nicht entzweien!
Jetzt kennen wir den Irrthum, den ein Gott
Wie einen Schleier um das Haupt uns legte,
Da er den Weg hierher uns wandern hieß.
Um Rath und um Befreiung bat ich ihn
Von dem Geleit der Furien; er sprach:
„Bringst du die Schwester, die an Tauris Ufer
Im Heiligthume wider Willen bleibt,
Nach Griechenland, so löset sich der Fluch."
Wir legten's von Apollons Schwester aus,
Und er gedachte d i c h! Die strengen Bande
Sind nun gelöf't; du bist den Deinen wieder,
Du Heilige, geschenkt.   Von dir berührt
War ich geheilt; in deinen Armen faßte
Das Uebel mich mit allen seinen Klauen
Zum Letztenmal, und schüttelte das Mark
Entsetzlich mir zusammen; dann entfloh's
Wie eine Schlange zu der Höhle.   Neu
Genieß' ich nun durch dich das weite Licht
Des Tages.   Schön und herrlich zeigt sich mir
Der Göttin Rath.   Gleich einem heil'gen Bilde,
Daran der Stadt unwandelbar Geschick
Durch ein geheimes Götterwort gebannt ist,
Nahm sie dich weg, die Schützerin des Hauses;
Bewahrte dich in einer heil'gen Stille
Zum Segen deines Bruders und der Deinen.
Da alle Rettung auf der weiten Erde
Verloren schien, gibst du uns Alles wieder.

Laß deine Seele sich zum Frieden wenden,
O König! Hindre nicht, daß sie die Weihe
Des väterlichen Hauses nun vollbringe,
Mich der entsühnten Halle wiedergebe,
Mir auf das Haupt die alte Krone drücke!
Vergilt den Segen, den sie dir gebracht,
Und laß des nähern Rechtes mich genießen!
Gewalt und List, der Männer höchster Ruhm,
Wird durch die Wahrheit dieser hohen Seele
Beschämt, und reines kindliches Vertrauen
Zu einem edeln Manne wird belohnt.

Iphigenie.

Denk' an dein Wort, und laß durch diese Rede
Aus einem g'raden treuen Munde dich
Bewegen! Sieh' uns an! Du hast nicht oft
Zu solcher edeln That Gelegenheit.
Versagen kannst du's nicht; gewähr' es bald!

Thoas.

So geht!

Iphigenie.

        Nicht so, mein König! Ohne Segen,
In Widerwillen, scheid' ich nicht von dir.
Verbann' uns nicht! Ein freundlich Gastrecht walte
Von dir zu uns: so sind wir nicht auf ewig
Getrennt und abgeschieden. Werth und theuer,
Wie mir mein Vater war, so bist du's mir,
Und dieser Eindruck bleibt in meiner Seele.
Bringt der Geringste deines Volkes je
Den Ton der Stimme mir in's Ohr zurück,
Den ich an euch gewohnt zu hören bin,
Und seh' ich an dem Aermsten eure Tracht;
Empfangen will ich ihn wie einen Gott,
Ich will ihm selbst ein Lager zubereiten,
Auf einen Stuhl ihn an das Feuer laden,
Und nur nach dir und deinem Schicksal fragen.
O geben dir die Götter deiner Thaten

Und deiner Milde wohlverdienten Lohn!
Leb' wohl! O wende dich zu uns und gib
Ein holdes Wort des Abschieds mir zurück!
Dann schwellt der Wind die Segel sanfter an,
Und Thränen fließen lindernder vom Auge
Des Scheidenden.   Leb' wohl! und reiche mir
Zum Pfand der alten Freundschaft deine Rechte.

Thoas.

Lebt wohl!

PUSS IN BOOTS:

A NURSERY-TALE

IN THREE ACTS,

WITH INTERLUDES, A PROLOGUE AND AN EPILOGUE

BY

L. TIECK.

INTRODUCTION

TO

TIECK'S BOOTED PUSS.

·THIS comedy made its first appearance in the year ·1797, and was subsequently with some changes and additions incorporated into the author's *Phantasus*, a sort of æsthetical novel, in which a number of personages are made to recite a series of tales and dramas for their mutual instruction and amusement, the merits of each of which the party then discusses, each individual conveying in his turn the impression produced by the rehearsal, or the critical comments or exceptions suggested at the moment. It is thus, that the poet takes occasion (as did Goethe in his Meister) to advance and defend his own peculiar principles of taste and criticism, and at the same time to keep up both in serious and sportive strains a sharp polemic fire on the enemy. The piece before us is moreover the first and by far the freshest part of a comic trilogy. The complementary parts are : „Die verfehrte Welt,“ or *The World Turned Topsy-turvy*, which was composed in 1798; and „Zerbino,“ or *A Journey in Search of Taste*, written about the same time. In these compositions, which remind us of Shakespeare and of Sterne as often as they do of Aristophanes, the poet makes an attempt to exhibit in a poetically capricious, parodizing manner the follies and extravagancies of certain tendencies existing in his day both in society and in the world of letters. Born and educated in Berlin, and acquainted from his earliest youth with nearly all the learned and social circles of that northern metropolis of culture,-the poet enjoyed peculiar advantages for observation and reflection. A certain tone of arrogant omniscience, which according to the author's account, was at that time particularly·prevalent in that city, was as offensive to him as it was odious to foreigners. A certain

—14*

shallow enlightenment, which pronounced sentence of condemnation on everything, that would not submit to the metewand of its
artificial standard, had become the fashion of the day.

Unable and unwilling itself to comprehend the profounder
verities of art, of philosophy and of religion it yet arraigned them
all before the forum of its superficial common sense. This jejune
illuminatism, while it successfully exposed to merited ridicule
and contempt many a remaining vestige of superstition or of
obscurantistic abuses, assumed itself the intolerant attitude of
the parties supplanted and condescended even to inquisitorial
heretifications and to a malignant persecution of all, who ventured to dissent from its infallible decisions. Religion, especially
the mystical element of the Christian, was the object of special
and constant assaults. One of its positive and earnestly advo-
cated elements was educational reform. Many of its results
were commendable, but all this was blended with so much charla-
tanry, that on the whole there was more noise than wool in the re-
formatorial movement, of which the Berlin Monthly Magazine was
the oracle and organ. On all sides a boastful exaltation of the
astounding progress of the age and now and then a supercilious
hope, that soon no prejudices of any sort would trammel and tor-
ment this poor humanity of ours any longer! At this time
Goethe's advancing fame excited anew the attention of this Athens
of the North. The mediocre malevolence of some of the former
leaders of taste would not submit to the idea, that a poet should
even during his lifetime enjoy not only the reputation of a national
genius, but of one already in the secure possession of an enduring
name, of a permanent fame, which posterity itself could no longer
call in question. Tieck was by his own confession not only one
of those who warmly admired, studied, expounded, lauded and
circulated Goethe's writings, but one of the few, who were inspired by them to an honorable emulation.

An association of those of homogeneous views on these important matters of poetry and art soon sprung into existence, by
which the rising generation, which more particularly had espoused the liberal and genial cause, was enabled by mutual
encouragement and succor to show front to the more influential
and powerful party of the conservatives, who spared no effort to
discourage and even to persecute the fast and widely-spreading
heresy. Nearly all the learned celebrities of Berlin, many of
them veterans of scholarship, traditional oracles of taste, decried

and derided the ingenuous enthusiasm of the younger, nobler minds, denouncing them as the hare-brained chimeras of immature and inexperienced novices, and the new poetical church was under the constant odious *surveillance* of a jealous censorship conducted by this literary oligarchy. While Goethe's Stella and more particularly his Werter called forth the ire of the moralists, the followers and expositors of Lessing, and the coadjutors of the „Deutsche Bibliothek," among whom the publisher Nicolai was prominent, opposed the rusty weapons of their baldest rationalism to all the innovating inspirations of the Weimar school, and while the ultra-religionists pitied Goethe as a free-thinker, the ultra-democrats denounced him as an enemy to popular freedom! This remarkable controversy was kindled into a still fiercer blaze by the joint efforts of Goethe and Schiller, who in their *"Xenien"* discharged their epigrammatic shafts of the wittiest and sharpest irony at their septentrional enemies, while in their positive creations (particularly Goethe in his Meister, and in Hermann and Dorothea), they offered now weapons of immortal temper to their oppressed disciples and admirers. This memorable contest furnished the subject of this brief notice, who had a personal interest of no small importance in the movement, with many an opportunity of observing and applying the comic aspect of the story in his own dramatic compositions; and in the literary history of this titanic period he stands preëminent as the Aristophanic *persifleur* of the ridiculous aspect of things around him.

I give his own exposition of his experience and intentions. "The manifold relations of life, its varied entanglements, incongruities and contradictions, the necessary ineptitude, with which subaltern powers so frequently disfigure and impede the realization of the sublimest conceptions, offer to the poet ever new materials for his characterizations. The perversity of men finds its way and the means of its success in every sphere of life, and when the poet's eye, whose ken is sharpened by its impartiality and by an inherent sense of rectitude, looks into these various circles, it will ever meet with new subjects for satiric mirth and heart-relieving laughter, provided he properly understands the art of distinguishing the significant and the truthful from the trivial and the accidental, and provided in the bitterness of his sarcastic raillery the poet does not condescend to individual personalities for the purpose of annihilating with his persecutions that which he may deem an error in others." In such times and under such auspicious circumstances, the calm observer and the friend of humor could glean many a useful incident for his purposes, and the author assures us, that many of the drollest absurdities, many of the most extravagant and exaggerated follies of his comic trilogy are little more than verbal repetitions of what he accidentally saw and heard within the various circles of learned and social intercourse, in which he freely moved at the time of its composition. With such keen weapons the warfare against the exasperated enemy was carried on by our champion, whose comico-satiric talent threw more confusion into the hostile ranks, than the merely occasional levels of Goethe and Schiller put together.

But it is not merely the absurdities of a particular literary sect, that appear mirrored in the phantastic play before us. The shower of its volcanic ashes quietly descends on life in general, on all the comic phases, which the poet in the sportive caprices of his humor could fix and interweave into the motley contexture of his fable, without always either proximately or remotely referring to any body in particular. Tieck possessed the genuine talent of humor, joyous, light, phantastic, riant, in its widest, most genial and consequently inoffensive sense; so that the bitterest antagonist could hardly refrain from laughter at the sight of such a novel, such a glorious confusion, which in its ever-eddying and chaotic undulations still reflects the pure ether of celestial beauty and of an eternal serenity over-head.

The occasional allusions to living personalities, however, and the poet's somewhat unique and isolated position did not fail to draw on him the vengeance of some of the aggrieved parties, whose malice seized on what they termed a libellous caricature of certain peculiarities of the army, and who pretended to have discovered other dangerous tendencies of a political description. Kotzebue revenged the poet's indifference to his egotistic vanity by basely abusing his access to those in power, among whom he denounced the poet's droll creations as suspicious game for censorship and punishment. A certain painter Darbes, likewise, obstinately persisted in discovering in the most innocent sallies of the poet profoundly covered but no less deadly aims of satire on certain illustrious personages of the day, and the obtuseness of the quasi-artist, who was incapable of comprehending objective satire, or of an all-in-laughter-involving humor, subjected the author for years after to troublesome importunities and useless protestations. "Darbes like many other men could only comprehend sport, caprice and humor in their prosaic and personal application. Such a malignant bitterness, however, was always foreign to my nature, nor did it ever lie in my intention. In this department of culture, which can take a jest as a jest, and merely as such, the Germans are yet far behindhand." While it must therefore be conceded that many of the comic situations in this as well as in the remaining parts of the comic trilogy were suggested by the actual sayings, doings and writings of author's contemporaries, it must as emphatically be denied, that the malevolence of personal bitterness, the virulence of subjective satire was ever within the intention of the poet, or ever found an odious place within the limits of this incomparable phantasmagoria of caprice. In regard to those suggestions from actual life or rather those distant allusions, one or two have been indicated by the author himself.   Leander is the personification of pedantry and formalistic cant.   The absurd astronomer, who, destitute of the spirit of his science, seeks the sentiment of the Sublime, not in the moral profundity of his own inner nature, not in the soul-expanding *Idea of the Infinite*, of which the universe is but the outward garb, but in the *ad infinitum progression of cyphers*, in the piles of magnitudes and distances, and who consequently leaves the skull of the king as empty as his own, is handled with pitiless severity, and the poet's sallies at this slang of science are peculiarly happy.   No wonder, that the jester (whose folly shames the wisdom of the wise throughout the piece) deems the bowl of rice in his immediate proximity an object of sublimer interest! ———— The ludicrously sentimental love-scene of the comedy (Act II., Scene second), and its equally ludicrous conversion into a scene of bitter hatred (Act III., Scene second), was intended as a persiflage either on Werner or on Kotzebue, both of whom were corrupting the national taste by the dulcified and false morality, by the effeminate and worthless characters of their pieces, with which at that time the theatres were inundated.   The success of Kotzebue was partly owing to the shamelessness, with which he pampered and fed the weaknesses and vices of the multitude.   A number of poets of indifferent talent had by their productions given undue preponderance to an inferior comedy and to a certain species of belittled genre-pictures of domestic life, and their attempts to *instruct* and *to mend* their spectators, instead of elevating them by grand delineations of character and action, had gradually given rise to all sorts of unnatural and extravagant abortions. A persiflage on this sort of mannerism is furnished us by the introductory scene, and by the whole career of Gottlieb and his feline coadjutor. One of the most remarkable features (by no means uncommon in the world) of this dramaturgic corruption, which the poet makes the target of his missiles, was the naïve conceipt, that the Germans had at last attained to a veritable standard of a national stage—an opinion of which the selecter few, who witnessed the disorder, could not divest the multitude, who either spurned or drowned the voices of the protesting minority. The baldness and misery of the prevailing critical cant is portrayed in the most deliciously comic scenes, wherein the interlocutors of the pit *en passant* comment upon the probable nature of the piece, of which they themselves constitute an integral part. The value of their authority in matters of taste is for the most part already sufficiently indicated by the names of these petty celebrities. The misplaced and exaggerated encomiums bestowed on the histrionic performance of the actor, who is supposed to personate the feline hero of the piece, by two of these pit-critics, Bötticher and Schlosser, appear to have been provoked by a *brochure* on Iffland (one of the most prominent actors and stage-poets of that time), in which the most unimportant trivialities, the merest conventionalities of detail were set up as the most essential points of dramaturgic excellence. Strange enough, many of those who made pretensions to independent judgment in these matters, and whose knowledge of the drama should have taught them better, regarded a certain tremulous, whining utterance of the actor, which had its origin in a constitutional defect and weakness of his voice, as the manifestation of the highest artistic culture, the expression of unwonted power, and these idiosyncrasies which the artist himself would gladly have exchanged for a better vocal organ, were even imitated by the servile mass and for some time constituted the distinctive shiboleth of an histrionic school! The critical comments on the inimitable personification of this matchless *Felis Calceatus* which entail so severe a punishment on the unfortunate critic, are to be accounted for in this way (Act III., Scene first and seventh). On the peculiar standpoint of the æsthetic criticism of his day, at which the poet so often and so severely levels, he himself more especially remarks:—"From the models of the Ancients, from the poems of different ages and of unequal value, and from isolated, short, often unintelligible or ambiguous oracular responses of certain canonized masters a sort of theory of Art has been projected for the behoof of our modern times and with the intent of universal application—a theory, the laws of which are still quoted as authority in many countries and at ever recurring intervals. The critical writers of this school take it for granted, that Art has long ago reached the period of its consummation, and that all that is left for us, is the more or less servile imitation of those works, which pass for models—an error which betrays a gross misapprehension of art and history both. It is solely from experience, from living intuition and poetic inspiration, that sound criticism can proceed, and in doing so, it surely will not neglect to find and to establish the principles of its procedure, and while it understandingly appreciates the *dicta* of an Aristoteles, it will not forget to compare and harmonize them with the results of modern experience. Poetical criticism, the quizzing stage, which makes itself the object of its laughter, had already been elevated into an independent poetical form by the most powerful and bitterly sarcastic delineations of Aristophanes. In his works, however, the spirit of party-prejudice appears to take the lead of critical conviction and of the purely polemical attempts to produce the latter. At any rate the politician and the poet are so intimately blended in this personage, that it becomes next to impossible to separate his poetical creed from his political. Among the moderns the case is entirely different. They pedantically fight for an imaginary standard. With this false criticism, borrowed from the Ancients, whom he did not even fully comprehend, and yet sufficiently misunderstood, to blunt the vision of his mind in regard to the new phenomena of literature, Ben Johnson at an early period, disturbed the free development of the English stage, which in his day was bearing the most precious blossoms and the choicest fruits. His prejudices are at the same time mingled with bitter animosity, and he persecutes with a malignant hate the person of his antagonist. Fletcher is less severe and Holberg in his merry parodies is full of cheer. Gozzi understands the art of uniting to his pedantic admiration for what he calls the good old better times, the grace and boldness of the comic and the farcical. Like this latter poet, I myself was under the impression of having lived to witness the decline and the degenerate imbecilities of my country's stage."

With reference to the positive value of the Author's æsthetical creed, the limits of this introductory notice will not permit me to do justice to the claims of this important question. It may not be out of place here, however, to remark, that the so-called Romantic school, of which Tieck was the most productive and most genial representative, went so far as to elevate this purely negative principle of irony to the rank of the ultimate canon of art. The supreme egotism of this position and the utter insufficiency of this principle (which Solger and Frederick Schlegel have elaborately developed), to account for any of the graver and sublimer productions of literature, it would not be difficult to prove; far more difficult would it be for its advocates to show, wherein, for example, the irony of the Author's own "Genovieve" or of his "Kaiser Octavianus" resides—pieces, which he himself desires us to consider as the most perfect expression of his own peculiar views and aims in the poetic art. When elevated to such a rank, this principle of irony becomes a vicious error, a suicidal heresy, which art can never seriously entertain, in which it never can find its final resting-place. Nor will a rational criticism ever be willing to concede, that the same poetic law is to control or even account for the lofty inspirations of an Æschylos and the unlicenced ribaldry of the sarcastic Aristophanes. The Artist of the graver Muse does not evoke the airy images of his imagination for the sole purpose of exhibiting his skill, and that accomplished to consign them to their former nothingness, but with the serious intent of giving them a permanent local habitation and an enduring name; and this he can only accomplish by embodying in his works the positive and substantial elements of our universal humanity and by subjecting them to an ideal law of beauty. A total disregard for form involves the ruin of the contents; and the abnegation of principle, when it degenerates into lawlessness, becomes the very grave of Art. But whatever may be the value of this negative and polemic side of the play, its exquisite genial humor, its happy combinations of comic incidents and situations will ever elicit fresh delight from the reader, and it will maintain its place as a choice classic of the language long after the particular circumstances, to which it owes its origin, are consigned to oblivion.

Der gestiefelte Kater

Ein Kindermährchen in drei Akten

mit Zwischenspielen, einem Prologe und Epiloge,

von

L. Tieck.

Perſonen.

Der König.

Die Prinzeſſin, ſeine Tochter.

Prinz Nathanael von Malſinki.

Leander, Hofgelehrter.

Hanswurſt, Hofnau.

Ein Kammerdiener.

Der Koch.

Lorenz,
Barthel, } Brüder und Bauern.
Gottlieb,

Hinze, ein Kater.

Ein Wirth.

Kunz,
Michel, } Bauern.

Geſetz, ein Popanz.

Ein Beſänftiger.

Der Dichter.

Ein Soldat.

Zwei Huſaren.

Zwei Liebende.

Bediente.

Muſiker.

Ein Bauer.

Der Souffleur.

Ein Schuhmacher.

Ein Hiſtoriograph.

Fiſcher,
Müller,
Schloſſer,
Bötticher,
Leutner,
Wieſener,
Deſſen Nachbar, } Zuſchauer.

Elephanten.

Löwen.

Bären.

Ein Amtmann.

Adler und andere Vögel.

Ein Kaninchen.

Rebhühner.

Jupiter.

Tarkaleon.

Der Maſchiniſt.

Geſpenſter.

Affen.

Das Publikum.

Prolog.

Die Scene ist im Parterre, die Lichter sind schon angezündet, die Musiker sind im Orchester versammelt. — Das Schauspiel ist voll, man schwatzt durcheinander, mehr Zuschauer kommen, einige drängen, andere beklagen sich. Die Musiker stimmen.

Fischer, Müller, Schlosser, Bötticher im Parterre, eben so auf der andern Seite **Wiesener** und dessen **Nachbar.**

Fischer. Aber ich bin doch in der That neugierig. — Lieber Herr Müller, was sagen Sie zu dem heutigen Stücke?

Müller. Ich hätte mir eher des Himmels Einfall vermuthet, als ein solches Stück auf unserm großen Theater zu sehn — auf unserm National-Theater! Ei! ei! nach allen den Wochenschriften, den kostbaren Kleidungen, und den vielen, vielen Ausgaben!

Fischer. Kennen Sie das Stück schon?

Müller. Nicht im Mindesten. — Einen wunderlichen Titel führt es: Der gestiefelte Kater. — Ich hoffe doch nimmermehr, daß man die Kinderpossen wird auf's Theater bringen.

Schlosser. Ist es denn vielleicht eine Oper?

Fischer. Nichts weniger, auf dem Komödienzettel steht: ein Kindermährchen.

Schlosser. Ein Kindermährchen? Aber um's Himmels Willen, sind wir denn Kinder, daß man uns solche Stücke aufführen will? Es wird doch wohl nun und nimmermehr ein ordentlicher Kater auf's Theater kommen?

Fischer. Wie ich es mir zusammen reime, so ist es eine Nachahmung der neuen Arkadier,* und es kommt ein verruchter Bösewicht, ein katerartiges Ungeheuer vor, mit dem es fast solche Bewandniß, wie mit dem Tarkaleon hat, nur daß er etwa statt roth um's Maul, schwärzlich gefärbt ist.

Müller. Das wäre nun nicht übel, denn ich habe schon längst gewünscht, eine solche recht wunderbare Oper einmal ohne Musik zu sehn.

* The title of some play.

331

Fischer. Wie? Ohne Musik? Ohne Musik, Freund, ist dergleichen abgeschmackt, denn ich versichre Sie, Liebster, Bester, nur durch diese himmlische Kunst bringen wir alle die Dummheiten hinunter. Ei was, genau genommen sind wir über Fratzen und Aberglauben weg; die Aufklärung hat ihre Früchte getragen, wie sich's gehört.

Müller. So ist es wohl ein ordentliches Familiengemälde, und nur ein Spaß, gleichsam ein einladender Scherz mit dem Kater, nur eine Veranlassung, wenn ich so sagen darf, oder ein bizarrer Titel, Zuschauer anzulocken.

Schlosser. Wenn ich meine rechte Meinung sagen soll, so halte ich das Ganze für einen Pfiff, Gesinnungen, Winke unter die Leute zu bringen. Ihr werdet sehen, ob ich nicht Recht habe. Ein Revolutionsstück, so viel ich begreife, mit abscheulichen Fürsten und Ministern, und dann ein höchst mystischer Mann, der sich mit einer geheimen Gesellschaft tief, tief unten in einem Keller versammelt, wo er als Präsident etwa verlarvt geht, damit ihn der gemeine Haufe für einen Kater hält. Nun da kriegen wir auf jeden Fall tiefsinnige und religiöse Philosophie und Freimaurerei. Endlich fällt er als das Opfer der guten Sache. O du Edler! Freilich mußt du gestiefelt seyn, um allen den Schurken die vielen Tritte in den gefühllosen Hintern geben zu können!

Fischer. Sie haben gewiß die richtige Einsicht, denn sonst würde ja der Geschmack abscheulich vor den Kopf gestoßen. Ich muß wenigstens gestehn, daß ich nie an Hexen oder Gespenster habe glauben können, viel weniger an den gestiefelten Kater.

Müller. Es ist das Zeitalter für diese Phantome nicht mehr.

Schlosser. Doch, nach Umständen. Könnte nicht in recht bedrängter Lage ein großer Abgeschiedener unerkannt als Hauskater im Palast wandeln, und sich zur rechten Zeit wunderthätig zu erkennen geben? Das begreift sich ja mit der Vernunft, wenn es höheren und mystischen Endzwecken dient. — Da kömmt ja Leutner, der wird uns vielleicht mehr sagen können.

Leutner drängt sich durch. Guten Abend, guten Abend! Nun, wie geht's?

Müller. Sagen Sie uns nur, wie es mit dem heutigen Stücke beschaffen ist. Die Musik fängt an.

Leutner. Schon so spät? Da komm' ich ja gerade zur rech=
ten Zeit. — Mit dem Stücke? Ich habe so eben den Dichter ge=
sprochen, er ist auf dem Theater und hilft den Kater anziehn.

Viele Stimmen. Hilft? — der Dichter? — den Kater?
— Also kommt doch ein Kater vor?

Leutner. Ja freilich, und er steht ja auch auf dem Zettel.

Fischer. Wer spielt ihn denn?

Leutner. Je, der fremde Acteur, der große Mann.

Bötticher. Da werden wir einen Göttergenuß haben. Ei,
wie doch dieser Genius, der alle Charactere so innig fühlt und fein
nüancirt, dieses Individuum eines Katers heraus arbeiten wird!
Ohne Zweifel Ideal im Sinn der Alten, nicht unähnlich dem
Pygmalion, nur Soccus hier, wie dort Cothurn. Doch sind Stie=
feln freilich Cothurne, und keine Socken. Ich schwebe noch im
Dilemma des Zweifels. — O, meine Herren, nur ein wenig Raum
für meine Schreibtafel und Bemerkungen.

Müller. Aber wie kann man denn solches Zeug spielen?

Leutner. Der Dichter meint, zur Abwechselung. —

Fischer. Eine schöne Abwechselung! Warum nicht auch den
Blaubart, und Rothkäppchen oder Däumchen?* Ei! der vor=
trefflichen Sujets für's Drama!

Müller. Wie werden sie aber den Kater anziehn? — Und
ob er denn wirkliche Stiefeln trägt?

Leutner. Ich bin eben so begierig wie Sie alle.

Fischer. Aber wollen wir uns denn wirklich solch Zeug vor=
spielen lassen? Wir sind zwar aus Neugier hergekommen, aber
wir haben doch Geschmack.

Müller. Ich habe große Lust zu pochen.

Leutner. Es ist überdies etwas kalt. Ich mache den Anfang.
Er trommelt, die übrigen accompagniren.

Wiesener auf der andern Seite. Weßwegen wird denn gepocht?

Leutner. Den guten Geschmack zu retten.

---

* Blue-Beard, Red Ridinghood, Tom Thumb, and a number of other nur-
sery-tales have likewise been made the basis of dramatic compositions by the
Author, who has blended the original stories with modern elements and motives. Indeed most of his earlier (dramatic) works are reared on the ground-
work of mediæval legends and popular tales.

Wiesener. Nun, da will ich auch nicht der Letzte seyn.

Er trommelt.

Stimmen. Still! man kann ja die Musik nicht hören.

Alles trommelt.

Schlosser. Aber man sollte doch das Stück auf jeden Fall erst zu Ende spielen lassen, denn man hat sein Geld ausgegeben, und in der Komödie wollen wir doch einmal seyn; aber hernach wollen wir pochen, daß man es vor der Thür hört.

Alle. Nein, jetzt, jetzt, — der Geschmack, — die Regeln, — die Kunst, — Alles geht sonst zu Grunde.

Ein Lampenputzer erscheint auf dem Theater. Meine Herren, soll man die Wache herein schicken?

Leutner. Wir haben bezahlt, wir machen das Publikum aus, und darum wollen wir auch unsern eignen guten Geschmack haben und keine Possen.

Lampenputzer. Aber das Pochen ist ungezogen und beweis't, daß Sie keinen Geschmack haben. Hier bei uns wird nur geklatscht und bewundert; denn solch honettes Theater, wie das unsre hier, wächst nicht auf den Bäumen, müssen Sie wissen.

Der Dichter hinter dem Theater. Das Stück wird sogleich seinen Anfang nehmen.

Müller. Kein Stück, — wir wollen kein Stück, wir wollen guten Geschmack, —

Alle. Geschmack! Geschmack!

Dichter. Ich bin in Verlegenheit; — was meinen Sie, wenn ich fragen darf!

Schlosser. Geschmack! Sind Sie ein Dichter, und wissen nicht einmal, was Geschmack ist?

Dichter. Bedenken Sie, einen jungen Anfänger —

Schlosser. Wir wollen nichts von Anfänger wissen, — wir wollen ein ordentliches Stück sehn, — ein geschmackvolles Stück!

Dichter. Von welcher Sorte? Von welcher Farbe?

Müller. Familiengeschichten.

Leutner. Lebensrettungen.

Fischer. Sittlichkeit und deutsche Gesinnung.

Schlosser. Religiös erhebende, wohlthuende geheime Gesell= schaften!

Wieſener. Huſſiten und Kinder!

Nachbar. Recht ſo, und Kirſchen dazu, und Viertelsmeiſter!

Der Dichter kömmt hinter dem Vorhange hervor. Meine Herren —

Alle. Iſt der der Dichter?

Fiſcher. Er ſieht wenig wie ein Dichter aus.

Schloſſer. Naſeweis.

Dichter. Meine Herren, — verzeihen Sie meiner Keckheit —

Fiſcher. Wie können Sie ſolche Stücke ſchreiben? Warum haben Sie ſich nicht gebildet?

Dichter. Vergönnen Sie mir nur eine Minute Gehör, ehe Sie mich verdammen. Ich weiß, daß ein verehrungswürdiges Publikum den Dichter richten muß, daß vor Ihnen keine Appella=tion ſtatt findet; aber ich kenne auch die Gerechtigkeitsliebe eines verehrungswürdigen Publikums, daß es mich nicht von einer Bahn zurück ſchrecken wird, auf welcher ich ſeiner gütigen Leitung und ſeiner Einſichten ſo ſehr bedarf.

Fiſcher. Er ſpricht nicht übel.

Müller. Er iſt höflicher, als ich dachte.

Schloſſer. Er hat doch Reſpekt vor dem Publikum.

Dichter. Ich ſchäme mich, die Eingebung meiner Muſe ſo erleuchteten Richtern vorzuführen, und nur die Kunſt unſrer Schau=ſpieler tröſtet mich noch einigermaßen, ſonſt würde ich ohne weitere Umſtände in Verzweiflung verſinken.

Fiſcher. Er dauert mich.

Müller. Ein guter Kerl!

Dichter. Als ich Dero gütiges Pochen vernahm, — noch nie hat mich etwas dermaßen erſchreckt, ich bin noch bleich und zittre, und begreife ſelbſt nicht, wie ich zu der Kühnheit komme, ſo vor Ihnen zu erſcheinen.

Leutner. So klatſcht doch! Alle klatſchen.

Dichter. Ich wollte einen Verſuch machen, durch Laune, wenn ſie mir gelungen iſt, durch Heiterkeit, ja, wenn ich es ſagen darf, durch Poſſen zu beluſtigen, da uns unſre neueſten Stücke ſo ſelten zum Lachen Gelegenheit geben.

Müller. Das iſt auch wahr.

Leutner. Er hat Recht, — der Mann.

Schloſſer. Bravo! bravo! Sie klatſchen.

Dichter. Mögen Sie, Verehrungswürdige, jetzt entscheiden, ob mein Versuch nicht ganz zu verwerfen sey. Mit Zittern zieh' ich mich zurück, und das Stück wird seinen Anfang nehmen.

Er verbeugt sich sehr ehrerbietig und geht hinter den Vorhang.

Alle. Bravo! bravo!

Stimme von der Gallerie. Da Capo!

Alles lacht. Die Musik fängt wieder an, indem geht der Vorhang auf.

Erster Akt.

Erste Scene.

Kleine Bauernstube.

Lorenz, Barthel, Gottlieb. Der Kater Hinz liegt auf einem Schemel am Ofen.

Lorenz. Ich glaube, daß nach dem Ableben unsers Vaters unser kleines Vermögen sich bald wird eintheilen lassen. Ihr wißt, daß der selige Mann nur drei Stück von Belang zurück gelassen hat: ein Pferd, einen Ochsen und jenen Kater dort. Ich, als der älteste, nehme das Pferd, Barthel, der nächste nach mir, bekömmt den Ochsen, und so bleibt denn natürlicherweise für unsern jüngsten der Kater übrig.

Leutner, im Parterre. Um Gottes Willen! hat man schon eine solche Exposition gesehn! Man sehe doch, wie tief die dramatische Kunst gesunken ist!

Müller. Aber ich habe doch alles recht gut verstanden.

Leutner. Das ist ja eben der Fehler, man muß es dem Zuschauer so verstohlener Weise unter den Fuß geben, ihm aber nicht so geradezu in den Bart werfen.*

Müller. Aber man weiß doch nun, woran man ist.

Leutner. Das muß man ja durchaus nicht so geschwind wissen; daß man so nach und nach hineinkommt, ist ja eben der beste Spaß.

Schlosser. Die Illusion leidet darunter, das ist ausgemacht.

Barthel. Ich glaube, Bruder Gottlieb, Du wirst auch mit

---

* There lies precisely the error; the spectator must gradually, and as it were by stealth, become initiated into the subject; it should not be thrown at his teeth so all of a sudden.—Müller. We know now at least, what to make of it.

der Eintheilung zufrieden seyn; Du bist leider der jüngste, und da mußt Du uns einige Vorrechte lassen.*

Gottlieb. Freilich wohl.

Schlosser. Aber warum mischt sich denn das Pupillen=Collegium nicht in die Erbschaft? das sind ja Unwahrscheinlich=keiten, die unbegreiflich bleiben!

Lorenz. So wollen wir denn nur gehn, lieber Gottlieb, lebe wohl, laß Dir die Zeit nicht lang werden.

Gottlieb. Adieu! Die Brüder gehn ab. Gottlieb allein. Monolog. Sie gehn fort — und ich bin allein. — Wir haben alle drei unsre Hütten; Lorenz kann mit seinem Pferde doch den Acker bebauen, Barthel kann seinen Ochsen schlachten und einsalzen, und eine Zeitlang davon leben, — aber was soll ich armer Unglückseliger mit meinem Kater anfangen? — Höchstens kann ich mir aus sei=nem Felle für den Winter einen Muff machen lassen; aber ich glaube, er ist jetzt noch dazu in der Mauße. — Da liegt er und schläft ganz ruhig. — Armer Hinze! Wir werden uns bald trennen müssen. Es thut mir leid, ich habe ihn auferzogen, ich kenne ihn, wie mich selber, — aber er wird daran glauben müssen, ich kann mir nicht helfen, ich muß ihn wahrhaftig verkaufen. — Er sieht mich an, als wenn er mich verstände; es fehlt wenig, so fang' ich an zu weinen.

Er geht in Gedanken auf und ab.

Müller. Nun, seht Ihr wohl, daß es ein rührendes Fami=liengemälde wird? Der Bauer ist arm und ohne Geld, er wird nun in der äußersten Noth sein treues Hausthier verkaufen, an irgend ein empfindsames Fräulein, und dadurch wird am Ende sein

---

* The formally ceremonious use of the German Pronouns being of perpetual recurrence in the dialogues of this drama, i. e. the English *You*, being some-times Sie, sometimes Du or Ihr, and sometimes Er (according to Gram. § 91, Obs. 5), the Editor has deviated from the previous orthography of the volume and left *all* the pronouns relating to the person addressed with a capi-tal initial, which the Learner will find important to remember. The Sie, Ihnen of the critics, &c. denote polite equality; the Du, Dir of Barthel, &c. fa-miliarity and friendship; the Ihr, Euch, Euer, &c. of Hinze, deference, intended politeness; the Er in Was will Er, guter Freund? of Act II., Scene 2d, and in the King's An diesen Kaninchen läßt Er es mangeln! of Act II., Scene 3d, and in the King's talk with Leander of Act II., Scene 4th, (e. g. Meint Er.... Er denkt wohl.... Er und seines Gleichen.... &c.) expresses a contemptuous superiority on the part of the speaker.

Glück gegründet werden. Sie verliebt sich in ihn und heirathet
ihn. Es ist eine Nachahmung vom Papagei von Kotzebue;
aus dem Vogel ist hier eine Katze gemacht, und das Stück findet
sich von selbst.

Fischer. Nun es so kömmt, bin ich auch zufrieden.

Hinze der Kater richtet sich auf, dehnt sich, macht einen hohen
Buckel, gähnt und spricht dann: Mein lieber Gottlieb, ich habe ein
ordentliches Mitleiden mit Euch.

Gottlieb erstaunt. Wie, Kater, Du sprichst?

Die Kunstrichter im Parterre. Der Kater spricht? — Was
ist denn das?

Fischer. Unmöglich kann ich da in eine vernünftige Illu=
sion hinein kommen.

Müller. Eh' ich mich so täuschen lasse, will ich lieber zeit=
lebens kein Stück wieder sehn.

Hinze. Warum soll ich nicht sprechen können, Gottlieb?

Gottlieb. Ich hätt' es nicht vermuthet, ich habe zeitlebens
noch keine Katze sprechen hören.

Hinze. Ihr meint, weil wir nicht immer in Alles mitreden,
wären wir gar Hunde.

Gottlieb. Ich denke, Ihr seyd bloß dazu da, Mäuse zu
fangen.

Hinze. Wenn wir nicht im Umgange mit den Menschen eine
gewisse Verachtung gegen die Sprache bekämen, so könnten wir
alle sprechen.

Gottlieb. Nun, das gesteh' ich! — Aber warum laßt Ihr
Euch denn so gar nichts merken?

Hinze. Um uns keine Verantwortung zuzuziehen; denn
wenn uns sogenannten Thieren noch erst die Sprache angeprügelt
würde, so wäre gar keine Freude mehr auf der Welt. Was muß
der Hund nicht Alles thun und lernen! Wie wird das Pferd
gemartert! Es sind dumme Thiere, daß sie sich ihren Ver=
stand merken lassen, sie müssen ihrer Eitelkeit durchaus nachgeben;
aber wir Katzen sind noch immer das freieste Geschlecht, weil wir
uns bei aller unsrer Geschicklichkeit so ungeschickt anzustellen wissen,
daß es der Mensch ganz aufgibt, uns zu erziehen.

Gottlieb. Aber warum entdeckst Du mir das alles?

Hinze. Weil Ihr ein guter, ein edler Mann seyd, einer von den wenigen, die keinen Gefallen an Dienstbarkeit und Sklaverei finden; seht, darum entdecke ich mich Euch ganz und gar.

Gottlieb *reicht ihm die Hand.* Braver Freund!

Hinze. Die Menschen stehn in dem Irrthume, daß an uns jenes seltsame Murren, das aus einem gewissen Wohlbehagen entsteht, das einzige Merkwürdige sey; sie streicheln uns daher oft auf eine ungeschickte Weise, und wir spinnen dann gewöhnlich nur, um uns vor Schlägen zu sichern. Wüßten sie aber mit uns auf die wahre Art umzugehn, glaube mir, sie würden unsre gute Natur zu Allem gewöhnen, und Michel, der Kater bei Eurem Nachbar, läßt es sich ja auch zuweilen gefallen, für den König durch ein Tonnenband zu springen.

Gottlieb. Da hast Du Recht.

Hinze. Ich liebe Euch, Gottlieb, ganz vorzüglich. Ihr habt mich nie gegen den Strich gestreichelt, Ihr habt mich schlafen lassen, wenn es mir recht war, Ihr habt Euch widersetzt, wenn Eure Brüder mich manchmal aufnehmen wollten, um mit mir ins Dunkle zu gehn, und die sogenannten elektrischen Funken zu beobachten, — für alles dieses will ich nun dankbar seyn.

Gottlieb. Edelmüthiger Hinze! Ha, mit welchem Unrecht wird von Euch schlecht und verächtlich gesprochen, Eure Treue und Anhänglichkeit bezweifelt! Die Augen gehn mir auf: welchen Zuwachs von Menschenkenntniß bekomme ich so unerwartet!

Fischer. Freunde, wo ist unsre Hoffnung auf ein Familiengemälde geblieben?

Leutner. Es ist doch fast zu toll.

Schlosser. Ich bin wie im Traume.

Hinze. Ihr seyd ein braver Mann, Gottlieb, — nehmt's mir nicht übel, — Ihr seyd etwas eingeschränkt, bornirt, keiner der besten Köpfe, wenn ich frei heraus sprechen soll.

Gottlieb. Ach Gott nein.

Hinze. Ihr wißt zum Beispiel jetzt nicht, was Ihr anfangen wollt.

Gottlieb. Du hast ganz meine Gedanken.

Hinze. Wenn Ihr Euch auch einen Muff aus meinem Pelze machen ließet —

Gottlieb. Nimm's nicht übel, Kamerad, daß mir das vorher durch den Kopf fuhr.

Hinze. Ach nein, es war ein ganz menschlicher Gedanke. — Wißt Ihr kein Mittel, Euch durchzubringen?

Gottlieb. Kein einziges.

Hinze. Ihr könntet mit mir herumziehn und mich für Geld sehen lassen, — aber das ist immer keine sichre Lebensart.

Gottlieb. Nein.

Hinze. Ihr könntet vielleicht ein Naturdichter werden, aber dazu seyd Ihr zu gebildet; Ihr könntet an ästhetischen Journalen mitarbeiten, aber, wie gesagt, Ihr seyd keiner der besten Köpfe, die dazu immer verlangt werden; da müßtet Ihr noch Jahr und Tag abwarten, weil es nachher nicht mehr so genau genommen wird; denn nur die neuen Besen kehren scharf, — aber das Ding ist überhaupt zu umständlich.

Gottlieb. Ja wohl.

Hinze. Nun, ich will schon noch besser für euch sorgen; verlaßt Euch drauf, daß Ihr durch mich noch ganz glücklich werden sollt.

Gottlieb. O bester, edelmüthigster Mann! Er umarmt ihn zärtlich.

Hinze. Aber Ihr müßt mir auch trauen.

Gottlieb. Vollkommen, ich kenne ja jetzt Dein redliches Gemüth.

Hinze. Nun so thut mir den Gefallen und holt mir sogleich den Schuhmacher, daß er mir ein Paar Stiefeln anmesse.

Gottlieb. Den Schuhmacher? — Stiefeln?

Hinze. Ihr wundert Euch; aber bei dem, was ich für Euch zu thun gesonnen bin, habe ich so viel zu gehn und zu laufen, daß ich nothwendig Stiefeln tragen muß.

Gottlieb. Aber warum nicht Schuh'?

Hinze. Gottlieb, Ihr versteht das Ding nicht, ich muß dadurch ein Ansehn bekommen, ein imponirendes Wesen, kurz, eine gewisse Männlichkeit, die man in Schuhen zeitlebens nicht hat.

Gottlieb. Nun, wie Du meinst, — aber der Schuster wird sich wundern.

Hinze. Gar nicht, man muß nur nicht thun, als wenn es

etwas Besonders wäre, daß ich Stiefeln tragen will; man gewöhnt sich an Alles.

Gottlieb. Ja wohl, ist mir doch der Discurs mit Dir ordentlich ganz geläufig geworden. — Aber noch eins, da wir jetzt so gute Freunde geworden sind, so nenne mich doch Du; warum wollen wir noch Complimente mit einander machen; macht die Liebe nicht alle Stände gleich?

Hinze. Wie Du willst.

Gottlieb. Da geht gerade der Schuhmacher vorbei. — He! pst! Herr Gevatter Leichdorn! Will er wohl einen Augenblick bei mir einsprechen?

Der Schuhmacher kömmt herein. Prosit!* Was gibt's Neues?

Gottlieb. Ich habe lange keine Arbeit bei Ihm bestellt —

Schuhmacher. Nein, Herr Gevatter, ich habe jetzt überhaupt gar wenig zu thun.

Gottlieb. Ich möchte mir wohl wieder ein Paar Stiefeln machen lassen —

Schuhmacher. Setz' Er sich nur nieder, das Maaß hab' ich bei mir.

Gottlieb. Nicht für mich, sondern für meinen jungen Freund da.

Schuhmacher. Für den da? — Gut.

Hinze setzt sich auf einen Stuhl nieder, und hält das rechte Bein hin.

Schuhmacher. Wie beliebt Er denn, Musje?†

Hinze. Erstlich, gute Sohlen, dann braune Klappen, und vor allen Dingen steif.

Schuhmacher. Gut. — Er nimmt Maaß. — Will Er nicht so gut seyn, — die Krallen, — oder Nägel etwas einzuziehen? Ich habe mich schon gerissen.

Hinze. Und schnell müssen sie fertig werden. Da ihm das Bein gestreichelt wird, fängt er wider Willen an zu spinnen.

Schuhmacher. Der Musje ist recht vergnügt.

* Prosit is used by the author as a more general form of salutation than usual.

† Musje, a corruption of *monsieur*: And how do you like them, sir?

Gottlieb. Ja, er ist ein aufgeräumter Kopf, er ist erst von der Schule gekommen, was man so einen Vocativus nennt.

Schuhmacher. Na, Adjes.*   Ab.

Gottlieb. Willst du Dir nicht etwa auch den Bart scheeren lassen?

Hinze. Bei Leibe nicht, ich sehe so weit ehrwürdiger aus, und Du weißt ja wohl, daß wir Katzen dadurch unmännlich und verächtlich werden. Ein Kater ohne Bart ist nur ein jämmerliches Geschöpf.

Gottlieb. Wenn ich nur wüßte, was Du vorhast?

Hinze. Du wirst es schon gewahr werden. — Jetzt will ich noch ein wenig auf den Dächern spazieren gehn, es ist da oben eine hübsche freie Aussicht, und man erwischt auch wohl eine Taube.

Gottlieb. Als guter Freund will ich Dich warnen, daß sie Dich nicht dabei ertappen: die Menschen denken meist in diesem Punkt sehr unbillig.

Hinze. Sey unbesorgt, ich bin kein Neuling. — Adieu unterdessen.   Geht ab.

Gottlieb allein. In der Naturgeschichte steht, daß man den Katzen nicht trauen könne, und daß sie zum Löwengeschlechte gehören, und ich habe vor einem Löwen eine gar erbärmliche Furcht; auch sagt man im Sprichwort: falsch wie eine Katze; wenn also der Kater kein Gewissen hätte, so könnte er mit den Stiefeln nachher davon laufen, für die ich mein letztes Geld hingeben muß, und sie irgendwo vertröbeln, oder er könnte sich beim Schuhmacher dadurch beliebt machen wollen, und nachher bei ihm in Dienste treten. — Aber der hat schon einen Kater. — Nein, Hinz, meine Brüder haben mich betrogen, und deßwegen will ich es mit deinem Herzen versuchen. — Er sprach so edel, er war so gerührt, — da sitzt er drüben auf dem Dache und putzt sich den Bart, — vergib mir, erhabener Freund, daß ich an deinem Großsinn nur einen Augenblick zweifeln konnte. Er geht ab.

Fischer. Welcher Unsinn!

Müller. Warum der Kater nur die Stiefeln braucht, um besser gehn zu können! — dummes Zeug!

_____
* Adjes, a corruption of Adieu or Adjeu.

Schloſſer. Es iſt aber, als wenn ich einen Kater vor mir
ſähe!

Leutner. Stille! Es wird verwandelt!*

Zweite Scene.

Saal im königlichen Palaſt.

Der König mit Krone und Scepter. Die Prinzeſſin, ſeine Tochter.

König. Schon tauſend ſchöne Prinzen, werthgeſchätzte Toch=
ter, haben ſich um Dich beworben und Dir ihre Königreiche zu
Füßen gelegt, aber Du haſt ihrer immer nicht geachtet; ſage uns
die Urſach' davon, mein Kleinod.

Prinzeſſin. Mein allergnädigſter Herr Vater, ich habe im=
mer geglaubt, daß mein Herz erſt einige Empfindungen zeigen
müſſe, ehe ich meinen Nacken in das Joch des Eheſtandes beugte.
Denn eine Ehe ohne Liebe, ſagt man, iſt die wahre Hölle auf
Erden.

König. Recht ſo, meine liebe Tochter. Ach, wohl, wohl haſt
Du ein wahres Wort geſagt: eine Hölle auf Erden! Ach, wenn
ich doch nicht darüber mitſprechen könnte! Wär' ich doch lieber
unwiſſend geblieben! Aber ſo, theures Kleinod, kann ich ein
Liedchen davon ſingen, wie man zu ſagen pflegt. Deine Mutter,
meine höchſt ſelige Gemahlin, — ach, Prinzeſſin, ſieh, die Thrä=
nen ſtehn mir noch auf meinen alten Tagen in den Augen, — ſie
war eine gute Fürſtin, ſie trug die Krone mit einer unglaublichen
Majeſtät, — aber mir hat ſie gar wenige Ruhe gelaſſen. — Nun,
ſanft ruhe ihre Aſche neben ihren fürſtlichen Anverwandten!

Prinzeſſin. Ihre Majeſtät erhitzen ſich zu ſehr.

König. Wenn mir die Erinnerung davon zurückkömmt, — o
mein Kind, auf meinen Knieen möcht' ich Dich beſchwören, —
nimm Dich beim Verheirathen ja in Acht. — Es iſt eine große
Wahrheit, daß man Leinewand und einen Bräutigam nicht bei
Lichte kaufen müſſe; eine erhabene Wahrheit, die jedes Mädchen
mit goldenen Buchſtaben in ihr Schlafzimmer ſollte ſchreiben laſ=
ſen. — Was hab' ich gelitten! Kein Tag verging ohne Zank,
ich konnte nicht in Ruhe ſchlafen, ich konnte die Reichsgeſchäfte

---

* Es wird verwandelt, they are changing the scene.

nicht mit Bequemlichkeit verwalten, ich konnte über nichts denken,
ich konnte mit Verstand keine Zeitung lesen, — bei Tische, beim
besten Braten, beim gesundesten Appetit, immer mußte ich Alles
nur mit Verdruß hinunter würgen, so wurde gezankt, gescholten,
gegrämelt, gebrummt, gemault, gegrollt, geschmollt, gekeift, gebissen, genurrt, geknurrt und geschnurrt, daß ich mir oft an der Tafel mitten unter den Gerichten den Tod gewünscht habe. — Und
doch sehnt sich mein Geist, verewigte Klotilde, jezuweilen nach Dir
zurück. — Es beißt mir in den Augen, — ich bin ein rechter alter
Narr.

Prinzessin zärtlich. Mein Vater!

König. Ich zittere, wenn ich überhaupt an alle die Gefahren
denke, die Dir bevorstehen; denn wenn Du dich auch wirklich verlieben solltest, meine Tochter, wenn Dir auch die zärtlichste Gegenliebe zu Theil würde, — ach, Kind, sieh, so dicke Bücher haben
weise Männer voll geschrieben, oft eng gedruckt, um die Gefahren
der Liebe darzustellen; eben Liebe und Gegenliebe können sich doch
elend machen: das glücklichste, das seligste Gefühl kann uns zu
Grunde richten; die Liebe ist gleichsam ein künstlicher Vexier-
becher, statt Nektar trinken wir oft Gift, dann ist unser Lager von
Thränen naß, alle Hoffnung, aller Trost ist dahin. — Man hört blasen.
Es ist doch noch nicht Tischzeit? — Gewiß wieder ein neuer Prinz,
der sich in Dich verlieben will. — Hüte Dich, meine Tochter, Du
bist mein einziges Kind, und Du glaubst nicht, wie sehr mir Dein
Glück am Herzen liegt. Er küßt sie und geht ab, im Parterre wird geklatscht.

Fischer. Das ist doch einmal eine Scene, in der gesunder
Menschenverstand anzutreffen ist.

Schlosser. Ich bin auch gerührt.

Müller. Es ist ein trefflicher Fürst.

Fischer. Mit der Krone brauchte er nun gerade nicht aufzu-
treten.

Schlosser. Es stört die Theilnahme ganz, die man für ihn
als zärtlichen Vater hat.

Die Prinzessin allein. Ich begreife gar nicht, warum noch
keiner von den Prinzen mein Herz mit Liebe gerührt hat. Die
Warnungen meines Vaters liegen mir immer im Gedächtniß; er
ist ein großer Fürst, und dabei doch ein guter Vater; mein Glück

steht ihm beständig vor Augen; er ist vom Volke geliebt, er hat Talente und Reichthümer, er ist sanft, wie ein Lamm, aber plötz= lich kann ihn der wildeste Zorn übereilen, daß er sich und seine Bestimmung vergißt. Ja, so ist Glück immer mit Unglück ge= paart. Meine Freude sind die Wissenschaften und die Künste, Bücher machen all mein Glück aus.

Die Prinzeſſin, Leander, der Hofgelehrte.

Prinzeſſin. Sie kommen gerade recht, Herr Hofgelehrter.

Leander. Ich bin zu den Befehlen Euer Königlichen Hoheit.

Setzen sich.

Prinzeſſin. Hier ist mein Versuch, ich hab' ihn Nacht= gedanken überschrieben.

Leander liest. Trefflich! Geistreich! — Ach, mir ist, als hör' ich die mitternächtliche Stunde Zwölfe schlagen. Wann haben Sie das geschrieben?

Prinzeſſin. Gestern Mittag, nach dem Essen.

Leander. Schön gedacht! Wahrlich schön gedacht! — Aber, mit gnädigster Erlaubniß: — „Der Mond scheint betrübt in der Welt herein," — wenn Sie es nicht ungnädig vermerken wollen, so muß es heißen: in die Welt.

Prinzeſſin. Schon gut, ich will es mir für die Zukunft merken. Es ist einfältig, daß einem das Dichten so schwer ge= macht wird; man kann keine Zeile schreiben, ohne einen Sprach= fehler zu machen.

Leander. Das ist der Eigensinn unsrer Sprache.

Prinzeſſin. Sind die Gefühle nicht zart und fein gehalten?

Leander. Unbeschreiblich, o so, wie soll ich sagen? — so zart und lieblich ausgezaselt, so fein gezwirnt; alle die Pappeln und Thränenweiden, und der goldne Mondenschein hineinweinend, und dann das murmelnde Gemurmel des murmelnden Gießbachs, — man begreift kaum, wie ein sanfter weiblicher Geist den großen Gedanken nicht hat unterliegen müssen, ohne sich vor dem Kirchhofe und den blaß verwaschenen Geistern der Mitternacht bis zur Ver= nichtung zu entsetzen.

Prinzeſſin. Jetzt will ich mich nun in die griechischen und antiken Versmaße werfen; ich möchte einmal die romantische Un=

15*

bestimmtheit verlassen, und mich an der plastischen Natur versuchen.

Leander. Sie kommen nothwendig immer weiter, Sie steigen
immer höher.

Prinzessin. Ich habe auch ein Stück angefangen: Der
unglückliche Menschenhasser; oder: verlorne Ruhe
und wiedererworbne Unschuld.*

Leander. Schon der bloße Titel ist bezaubernd.

Prinzessin. Und dann fühle ich einen unbegreiflichen
Drang in mir, irgend eine gräßliche Geistergeschichte zu schreiben.
— Wie gesagt, wenn nur die Sprachfehler nicht wären!

Leander. Kehren Sie sich daran nicht, Unvergleichliche, die
lassen sich leicht ausstreichen.

Kammerdiener tritt auf. Der Prinz von Malsinki, der eben
angekommen ist, will Ew. Königlichen Hoheit seine Aufwartung
machen.   Ab.

Leander. So empfehle ich mich unterthänigst.   Geht ab.
        Prinz Nathanael von Malsinki und der König kommen.

König. Hier, Prinz, ist meine Tochter, ein junges einfältiges
Ding, wie Sie sie da vor sich sehn. — Beiseit. Artig, meine Tochter, höflich! er ist ein angesehener Prinz, weit her, sein Land steht
gar nicht einmal auf meiner Landkarte, ich habe schon nachgesehn;
ich habe einen erstaunlichen Respekt vor ihm.

Prinzessin. Ich freue mich, daß ich das Vergnügen habe,
Sie kennen zu lernen.

Nathanael. Schöne Prinzessin, der Ruf Ihrer Schönheit
hat so sehr die ganze Welt durchdrungen, daß ich aus einem weit
entlegenen Winkel hieher komme, Sie von Angesicht zu Angesicht
zu sehn.

König. Es ist doch erstaunlich, wie viele Länder und Königreiche es gibt! Sie glauben nicht, wie viel tausend Kronprinzen
schon hier gewesen sind, sich um meine Tochter zu bewerben; zu
Dutzenden kommen sie oft an, besonders wenn das Wetter schön
ist, — und Sie kommen nun gar, — verzeihen Sie, die Topographie
ist eine weitläufige Wissenschaft, — in welcher Gegend liegt ihr
Land?

---

* The caricatured titles of some contemporaneous plays; probably of Kotzebue's Menschenhaß und Reue.

Nathanael. Mächtiger König, wenn Sie von hieraus reisen, erst die große Chaussee hinunter, dann schlagen Sie sich rechts und immer fort so; wenn Sie aber an einen Berg kommen, dann wieder links, dann geht man zur See und fährt immer nördlich (wenn es der Wind nämlich zugibt), und so kömmt man, wenn die Reise glücklich geht, in anderthalb Jahren in meinem Reiche an.

König. Der Tausend!* das muß ich mir von meinem Hofgelehrten deutlich machen lassen. — Sie sind wohl vielleicht ein Nachbar vom Nordpol, oder Zodiakus, oder dergleichen?

Nathanael. Daß ich nicht wüßte. †

König. Vielleicht so nach den Wilden zu?

Nathanael. Ich bitte um Verzeihung, alle meine Unterthanen sind sehr zahm.

König. Aber Sie müssen doch verhenkert weit wohnen. Ich kann mich immer noch nicht daraus finden.

Nathanael. Man hat noch keine genaue Geographie von meinem Lande; ich hoffe täglich mehr zu entdecken, und so kann es leicht kommen, daß wir am Ende noch Nachbarn werden.

König. Das wäre vortrefflich! Und wenn uns am Ende ein paar Länder noch im Wege stehen, so helfe ich Ihnen mit entdecken. Mein Nachbar ist so nicht mein guter Freund und er hat ein vortreffliches Land; alle Rosinen kommen von dort her, das möcht' ich gar zu gerne haben. — Aber noch eins, sagen Sie mir nur, da Sie so weit weg wohnen, wie Sie unsre Sprache so geläufig sprechen können?

Nathanael. Still!.

König. Wie?

Nathanael. Still! Still!

König. Ich versteh' nicht.

Nathanael *leise zu ihm.* Seyn Sie doch ja damit ruhig, denn sonst merkt es ja am Ende das Publikum da unten, daß das eben sehr unnatürlich ist.

König. Schadet nicht, es hat vorher geklatscht und da kann ich ihm schon etwas bieten.

---

* Instead of Ei, der Tausend! an exclamation of surprise or wonder; something like the English: The deuce!

† Daß ich nicht wüßte, not that I know of.

Nathanael. Sehn Sie, es geschieht ja bloß dem Drama zu Gefallen, daß ich Ihre Sprache rede, denn sonst ist es allerdings unbegreiflich.

König. Ach so! Ja freilich, den Damen und den Dramen thut man Manches zu gefallen, und muß oft Fünfe gerade seyn lassen.—Nun kommen Sie, Prinz, der Tisch ist gedeckt! Der Prinz führt die Prinzessin ab, der König geht voran.

Fischer. Verfluchte Unnatürlichkeiten sind da in dem Stück!

Schlosser. Und der König bleibt seinem Charakter gar nicht getreu.

Leutner. Am meisten erboßen mich immer Widersprüche und Unnatürlichkeiten. Warum kann denn nun der Prinz nicht ein Bißchen eine fremde Sprache reden, die sein Dolmetscher verdeutschte? warum macht denn die Prinzessin nicht zuweilen einen Sprachfehler, da sie selber gesteht, daß sie unrichtig schreibt?

Müller. Freilich! freilich! — das Ganze ist ausgemacht dummes Zeug; der Dichter vergißt immer selber, was er den Augenblick vorher gesagt hat.

Dritte Scene.
Vor einem Wirthshause.

Lorenz, Kunz, Michel, sitzen auf einer Bank, der **Wirth.**

Lorenz. Ich werde wohl gehn müssen, denn ich habe noch einen weiten Weg bis nach Hause.

Wirth. Ihr seyd ein Untherthan des Königs?

Lorenz. Ja wohl. — Wie nennt Ihr Euren Fürsten?

Wirth. Man nennt ihn nur Popanz.

Lorenz. Das ist ein närrischer Titel. Hat er denn sonst keinen Namen?

Wirth. Wenn er die Edicte ausgehn läßt, so heißt es immer: zum Besten des Publikums verlangt das Gesetz. — Ich glaube daher, das ist sein eigentlicher Name: alle Bittschriften werden auch immer beim Gesetz eingereicht. Es ist ein fürchtbarer Mann.

Lorenz. Ich stehe doch lieber unter einem Könige, ein König ist doch vornehmer. Man sagt, der Popanz sey ein sehr ungnädiger Herr.

Wirth. Gnädig ist er nicht besonders, das ist nun wohl wahr, dafür ist er aber auch die Gerechtigkeit selbst; von auswärts sogar werden ihm oft die Prozesse zugeschickt, und er muß sie schlichten.

Lorenz. Man erzählt wunderliche Sachen von ihm; er soll sich in alle Thiere verwandeln können.

Wirth. Das ist wahr, und so geht er oft incognito umher, und erforscht die Gesinnungen seiner Unterthanen; wir trauen daher auch keiner fremden Katze, keinem unbekannten Hunde, weil wir immer denken, unser Herr könnte wohl dahinter stecken!

Lorenz. Da sind wir doch auch besser dran; unser König geht nie aus, ohne Krone, Mantel und Zepter anzuziehn, man kennt ihn daher auch auf tausend Schritt. — Nun, gehabt Euch wohl.

Geht ab.

Wirth. Nun ist er schon in seinem Lande.

Kunz. Ist die Gränze so nah?

Wirth. Freilich, jener Baum gehört schon dem König; man kann von hier Alles sehn, was im Lande dort vorfällt. Die Gränze hier macht noch mein Glück, ich wäre schon längst bankerott geworden, wenn mich nicht noch die Deserteurs von drüben erhalten hätten; fast täglich kommen etliche.

Michel. Ist der Dienst so schwer?

Wirth. Das nicht, aber das Weglaufen ist so leicht, und bloß weil es so scharf verboten ist, kriegen die Kerle die erstaunliche Lust zum Desertiren. — Seht, ich wette, daß da wieder einer kömmt!

Ein Soldat kömmt gelaufen. Eine Kanne Bier, Herr Wirth! geschwind!

Wirth. Wer seyd Ihr?

Soldat. Ein Deserteur.

Michel. Vielleicht gar aus Kindesliebe; der arme Mensch; nehmt Euch doch seiner an, Herr Wirth.

Wirth. Je, wenn er Geld hat, soll's am Bier nicht fehlen.

Geht in's Haus.

Zwei Husaren kommen geritten und steigen ab.

Erster Husar. Nu, Gottlob, daß wir so weit sind. — Prosit Nachbar.

Soldat. Hier ist die Gränze.

Zweiter Husar. Ja, dem Himmel sey Dank, — Haben wir des Kerls wegen nicht reiten müssen — Bier, Herr Wirth!

Wirth, mit mehrern Gläsern. Hier, meine Herren, ein schöner frischer Trunk; Sie sind alle drei recht warm.

Erster Husar. Hier, Halunke! auf deine Gesundheit!

Soldat. Danke schönstens; ich will Euch die Pferde unterweilen halten.

Zweiter Husar. Der Kerl kann laufen! Es ist gut, daß die Grenze nicht gar so weit ist, denn sonst wäre das ein Hundedienst.

Erster Husar. Nun, wir müssen wohl wieder zurück. Adieu, Deserteur! viel Glück auf den Weg! —
Sie steigen wieder auf und reiten davon.

Wirth. Werdet Ihr hier bleiben?

Soldat. Nein, ich will fort, ich muß mich ja beim benachbarten Herzog wieder anwerben lassen.

Wirth. Sprecht doch wieder zu, wenn Ihr wieder desertirt.

Soldat. Gewiß. — Lebt wohl. —
Sie geben sich die Hände, der Soldat und die Gäste gehn ab, der Wirth in's Haus.
Der Vorhang fällt.

Zwischenakt.

Fischer. Es wird doch immer toller und toller. — Wozu war denn nun wohl die letzte Scene?

Leutner. Zu gar nichts, sie ist völlig überflüssig; bloß um einen neuen Unsinn hinein zu bringen. Den Kater verliert man ganz aus den Augen und behält nirgend einen festen Standpunkt.

Schlosser. Mir ist völlig so, als wenn ich betrunken wäre.

Müller. In welchem Zeitalter mag denn das Stück spielen sollen? Die Husaren sind doch offenbar eine neuere Erfindung?

Schlosser. Wir sollten's nur nicht leiden und derbe trommeln. Man weiß durchaus jetzt gar nicht, woran man mit dem Stücke ist.

Fischer. Und auch keine Liebe! Nichts für's Herz darin, für die Phantasie!

Leutner. Sobald wieder so etwas Tolles vorkömmt, fang' ich für meine Person wenigstens an zu pochen und zu zischen.

Wiesener zu seinem Nachbar. Mir gefällt jetzt das Stück.

Nachbar. Sehr hübsch, in der That hübsch, ein großer Mann, der Dichter, — hat die Zauberflöte gut nachgeahmt.

Wiesener. Die Husaren gefielen mir besonders; es sind die Leute selten so dreist, Pferde auf's Theater zu bringen, — und warum nicht? Sie haben oft mehr Verstand als die Menschen. Ich mag lieber ein gutes Pferd sehn, als so manchen Menschen in den neueren Stücken.

Nachbar. Im Kotzebue die Mohren, — ein Pferd ist am Ende nichts, als eine andere Art von Mohren.

Wiesener. Wissen Sie nicht, von welchem Regiment die Husaren waren?

Nachbar. Ich habe sie nicht einmal genau betrachtet, — Schade, daß sie so bald wieder weggingen; ich möchte wohl ein ganzes Stück von Husaren sehn, — ich mag die Caballerie so gern.

Leutner zu Bötticher. Was sagen Sie zu dem Allen?

Bötticher. Ich habe nur immer noch das vortreffliche Spiel des Mannes im Kopfe, welcher den Kater darstellt. Welches Studium! Welche Feinheit! Welche Beobachtung! Welcher Anzug!

Schlosser. Das ist wahr, er sieht natürlich aus wie ein großer Kater.

Bötticher. Und bemerken Sie nur seine ganze Maske, wie ich seinen Anzug lieber nennen möchte; denn da er so ganz sein natürliches Aussehn verstellt hat, so ist dieser Ausdruck weit passender. Gott segne mir doch auch bei der Gelegenheit die Alten! Sie wissen wahrscheinlich nicht, daß diese Alten alle Rollen ohne Ausnahme in Masken spielen, wie Sie im Athenäus, Pollux und Andern finden werden.* Es ist schwer, sehn Sie, das alles so genau zu wissen, weil man mitunter diese Bücher deswegen selber nachschlagen muß; doch hat man freilich nachher auch den Vortheil, daß man sie anführen kann. Es ist eine schwierige Stelle im Pausanias.

* Athenæus and Pollux, voluminous writers on Grecian Antiquities. The *Deipnosophistæ* (the sophists or scholars at supper) of the former, and the *Onomastikon* (a sort of Encyclopedia) of the latter are among the most important sources of our knowledge of ancient life and manners. Pausanias is an ancient traveller, who has left a description of Greece and of the remains of Art, as they were to be seen in his day.

Fischer. Sie wollten so gut seyn, von dem Kater zu sprechen.

Bötticher. Ja so, — Ich will auch alles Vorhergehende nur so nebenher gesagt haben; ich bitte Sie daher alle inständigst, es als eine Note anzusehn, und — um wieder auf den Kater zu kommen, — haben Sie wohl bemerkt, daß er nicht einer von den schwarzen Katern ist? Nein, im Gegentheil, er ist fast ganz weiß und hat nur einige schwarze Flecke; das drückt seine Gutmüthig= keit ganz vortrefflich aus; man sieht gleichsam den Gang des gan= zen Stückes, alle Empfindungen, die es erregen soll, schon im Vor= aus in diesem Pelze.

Fischer. Der Vorhang geht wieder auf.

Zweiter Akt.

Erste Scene.

Bauernstube.

Gottlieb, Hinze, Beide sitzen an einem kleinen Tisch und essen.

Gottlieb. Hat's Dir geschmeckt?

Hinze. Recht gut, recht schön.

Gottlieb. Nun muß sich aber mein Schicksal bald entschei= den, weil ich sonst nicht weiß, was ich anfangen soll.

Hinze. Habe nur noch ein paar Tage Geduld, das Glück muß doch auch einige Zeit haben, um zu wachsen; wer wird denn so aus dem Stegreif glücklich seyn wollen! Mein guter Mann, das kommt nur in Büchern vor, in der wirklichen Welt geht das nicht so geschwinde.

Fischer. Nun hört nur, der Kater untersteht sich, von der wirklichen Welt zu sprechen! — Ich möchte fast nach Hause gehn, denn ich fürchte toll zu werden.

Leutner. Es ist beinahe, als wenn es der Verfasser darauf angelegt hätte.

Müller. Ein excellenter Kunstgenuß, toll zu seyn, das muß ich gestehn!

Schlosser. Es ist zu arg. Statt daß er froh seyn sollte, daß er nur, wenn auch in imaginärer Welt, wenigstens existiren darf, will er den andern von phantastischen Hoffnungen abbringen, und behandelt ihn als Schwärmer, der doch wenigstens als Bauer nicht den Gesetzen unserer gewöhnlichen Welt widerspricht!

Gottlieb. Wenn ich nur wüßte, lieber Hinze, wo du die viele Erfahrung, den Verstand herbekommen hast.

Hinze. Glaubst Du denn, daß man Tagelang umsonst unterm Ofen liegt und die Augen fest zumacht? Ich habe dort immer im Stillen fortstudirt. Heimlich und unbemerkt wächst die Kraft des Verstandes; daher hat man dann am wenigsten Fortschritte gemacht, wenn man manchmal Lust kriegt, sich mit einem recht langen Halse nach der zurückgelegten Bahn umzusehn. — Uebrigens sey doch so gut und binde mir die Serviette ab.

Gottlieb thut's. Gesegnete Mahlzeit! — Sie küssen sich. Nimm so vorlieb.

Hinze. Ich danke von ganzem Herzen.

Gottlieb. Die Stiefeln sitzen recht hübsch, und Du hast einen scharmanten* kleinen Fuß.

Hinze. Das macht bloß, weil unser eins immer auf den Zehn geht, wie Du auch wirst in der Naturgeschichte gelesen haben.

Gottlieb. Ich habe einen großen Respekt vor Dir, — von wegen der Stiefeln.

Hinze hängt sich einen Tornister um. Ich will nun gehn. — Sieh, ich habe mir auch einen Sack mit einer Schnurre gemacht.

Gottlieb. Wozu das alles?

Hinze. Laß mich nur, ich will einen Jäger vorstellen. — Wo ist denn mein Stock?

Gottlieb. Hier.

Hinze. Nun so lebe wohl. Geht ab.

Gottlieb. Einen Jäger? — Ich kann aus dem Manne nicht klug werden. Ab.

Zweite Scene.

Freies Feld.

Hinze mit Stock, Tornister und Sack.

Hinze. Herrliches Wetter! — Es ist ein schöner warmer Tag, ich will mich auch hernach ein wenig in die Sonne legen. —

* scharmanten for charmanten, charming, elegant.

Er spreitet seinen Sack aus. Nun, Glück, stehe mir bei! — Wenn ich freilich bedenke, daß diese eigensinnige Göttin so selten die klug an= gelegten Plane begünstigt, daß sie immer darauf ausgeht, den Ver= stand der Sterblichen zu Schanden zu machen, so möcht' ich allen Muth verlieren. Doch, sey ruhig, mein Herz, ein Königreich ist schon der Mühe werth, etwas dafür zu arbeiten und zu schwitzen! — Wenn nur keine Hunde hier in der Nähe sind. Ich kann diese Geschöpfe gar nicht vor Augen leiden; sie sind ein Geschlecht, das ich verachte, weil sie sich so gutwillig unter der niedrigsten Knecht= schaft der Menschen bequemen; sie können nichts als schmeicheln und beißen, sie haben gar nichts von dem Ton, welcher im Um= gange so nothwendig ist. — Es will sich nichts fangen.* — *Er fängt an ein Jägerlied zu singen:* Im Felde schleich' ich still und wild u. s. w., *eine Nachtigall im benachbarten Busch fängt an zu schmettern.* Sie singt trefflich, die Sängerin der Haine, — wie delicat muß sie erst schmecken! — Die Großen der Erde sind doch darin recht glücklich, daß sie Nachtigallen und Lerchen essen können, so viel sie nur wollen, — wir armen gemeinen Leute müssen uns mit dem Gesange zufrieden stellen, mit der schönen Natur, mit der unbe= greiflich süßen Harmonie. — Es ist fatal, daß ich nichts kann sin= gen hören, ohne Lust zu kriegen, es zu fressen. — Natur! Natur! Warum störst du mich dadurch immer in meinen allerzartesten Empfindungen, daß du meinen Geschmack für Musik so pöbelhaft eingerichtet hast? — Fast krieg' ich Lust, mir die Stiefeln auszuziehn und sacht den Baum dort hinauf zu klettern! sie muß dort sitzen. — *Im Parterre wird getrommelt.* Die Nachtigall hat eine gute Na= tur; ich habe immer nicht glauben wollen, daß sie am liebsten bei Sturm und Ungewitter singe, aber jetzt erleb' ich die Wahrheit dieser Behauptung. — Ei! so singe und schmettre, daß dir der Athem vergeht! —Delicat muß sie schmecken. Ich vergesse meine Jagd über diesen süßen Träumen. — Es fängt sich wahrhaftig nichts. — Wer kömmt denn da?

Zwei Liebende treten auf.

Er. Hörst du wohl die Nachtigall, mein süßes Leben?
Sie. Ich bin nicht taub, mein Guter.

---

* Es will sich nichts fangen, *lit.* nothing will be caught, i. e. there is no pros= pect of getting any game. In the same way below Es läßt sich nichts fangen, and Es fängt sich wahrhaftig nichts, there is really nothing to be caught.

Er. Wie wallt mein Herz vor Entzücken über, wenn ich die ganze harmonische Natur so um mich her versammelt sehe, wenn jeder Ton nur das Geständniß meiner Liebe wiederholt, wenn sich der ganze Himmel nieder beugt, um Aether auf mich auszuschütten.

Sie. Du schwärmst, mein Lieber.

Er. Nenne die natürlichsten Gefühle meines Herzens nicht Schwärmerei. *Kniet nieder.* Sieh, ich schwöre Dir hier vor dem Angesicht des heitern Himmels.

Hinze *höflich hinzu tretend.* Verzeihen Sie gütigst, — wollen Sie sich nicht gefälligst anders wohin bemühn? Sie stören hier mit Ihrer holdseligen Eintracht eine Jagd.

Er. Die Sonne soll mein Zeuge, die Erde, — und was sonst noch; Du selbst, mir theurer als Erde, Sonne und alle Planeten. — Was will Er,* guter Freund?

Hinze. Die Jagd, — ich bitte demüthigst.

Sie. Barbar, wer bist Du, daß Du es wagst, die Schwüre der Liebe zu unterbrechen? Dich hat kein Weib geboren, Du gehörst jenseits der Menschheit zu Hause.

Hinze. Wenn Sie nur bedenken wollten —

Sie. So wart' Er doch nur einen Augenblick, Er sieht ja wohl, daß der Geliebte, in Trunkenheit verloren, auf seinen Knieen liegt.

Er. Glaubst Du mir nun?

Sie. Ach! hab' ich Dir nicht schon geglaubt, noch ehe Du ein Wort gesprochen hattest? *Sie beugt sich liebevoll zu ihm hinab.* Theurer! — ich — liebe Dich! — o unaussprechlich!

Er. Bin ich unsinnig? — O und wenn ich es nicht bin, warum werd' ich Elender, Verächtlicher, es nicht urplötzlich vor übergroßer Freude? — Ich bin nicht mehr auf der Erde; sieh mich doch recht genau an, o Theuerste, und sage mir, ob ich nicht vielleicht im Mittelpunkte jener unsterblichen Sonne dort oben wandle.

Sie. In meinen Armen bist Du, und die sollen Dich auch nicht wieder lassen.

Er. O komm, dieses freie Feld ist meinen Empfindungen zu

---

* See page 337, note.

enge, wir müssen den höchsten Berg erklettern, um der ganzen
Natur zu sagen, wie glücklich wir sind! —

*Sie gehen schnell und voll Entzücken ab. Lautes Klatschen und Bravorufen im
Parterre.*

Wiesener klatschend. Der Liebhaber griff sich tüchtig an. —
O weh! da hab' ich mir selber einen Schlag in die Hand gegeben,
daß sie ganz aufgelaufen ist.

Nachbar. Sie wissen sich in der Freude nicht zu mäßigen.

Wiesener. Ja, so bin ich immer.

Fischer. Ah! — das war doch etwas für's Herz! — Das
thut einem wieder einmal wohl!

Leutner. Eine wirklich schöne Diction in der Scene.

Müller. Ob sie aber zum Ganzen wird nothwendig seyn?

Schlosser. Ich kümmere mich nie um's Ganze; wenn ich
weine, so wein' ich, und damit gut; es war eine göttliche Stelle.

Hinze. O Liebe, wie groß ist deine Macht, daß deine
Stimme die Ungewitter besänftigt, ein pochendes Publikum be-
schwichtigt, und das Herz kritischer Zuschauer so umwendet, daß sie
ihren Zorn und alle ihre Bildung vergessen — Es läßt sich nichts
fangen. *Ein Kaninchen kriecht in den Sack, er springt schnell hinzu und schnürt
ihn zusammen.* Sieh da, guter Freund! ein Wildpret, das eine Art
von Geschwisterkind mit mir ist; ja, das ist der Lauf der heutigen
Welt, Verwandte gegen Verwandte, Bruder gegen Bruder; wenn
man selbst durch die Welt will, muß man andre aus dem Wege
stoßen. — *Er nimmt das Kaninchen aus dem Sacke und steckt es in den Tornister.*
Halt! Halt! — Ich muß mich wahrhaftig in Acht nehmen, daß
ich das Wildpret nicht selber auffresse. Ich muß nur geschwinde
den Tornister zubinden, damit ich meine Affecten bezähme. —
Pfui! schäme dich, Hinz! — Ist es nicht die Pflicht des Edlen,
sich und seine Neigungen dem Glück seiner Mitgeschöpfe aufzu-
opfern? Dies ist der Endzweck, zu welchem wir geschaffen worden, und wer das nicht kann, — o ihm wäre besser, daß seine
Mutter ihn nie geboren hätte. —

*Er will abgehn, man klatscht heftig und ruft allgemein da Capo, er muß die letzte
schöne Stelle noch einmal hersagen, dann verneigt er sich ehrerbietig und
geht mit dem Kaninchen ab.*

Fischer. O welcher edle Mann!

Müller. Welche schöne menschliche Gesinnung!

Schlosser. Durch so etwas kann man sich doch noch bessern, — aber wenn ich Narrenpossen sehe, möcht' ich gleich drein schlagen.

Leutner. Mir ist auch ganz wehmüthig geworden, — die Nachtigall, die Liebenden, — die letzte Tirade, — das Stück hat denn doch wahrhaftig schöne Stellen!

Dritte Scene.

Saal im Palast.

Große Audienz. Der König, die Prinzessin, der Prinz Nathanael, der Koch in Galla.

König sitzt auf dem Thron. Hieher, Koch, jetzt ist es Zeit, Rede und Antwort zu geben; ich will die Sache selbst untersuchen.

Koch läßt sich auf ein Knie nieder. Ihre Majestät geruhen, Ihre Befehle über Dero getreuesten Diener auszusprechen.

König. Mann kann nicht genug dahin arbeiten, meine Freunde, daß ein König, dem das Wohl eines ganzen Landes und unzähliger Unterthanen auf dem Halse liegt, immer bei guter Laune bleibe; denn wenn er in eine üble Laune geräth, so wird er gar leicht ein Tyrann, ein Unmensch; denn gute Laune befördert die Fröhlichkeit, und Fröhlichkeit macht nach den Beobachtungen aller Philosophen den Menschen gut, dahingegen die Melancholie deßwegen für ein Laster zu achten ist, weil sie alle Laster befördert. Weiß, frag' ich nun, liegt es so nahe, in wessen Gewalt steht es wohl so sehr, die Laune eines Monarchen zu befördern, als eben in den Händen eines Kochs? — Sind Kaninchen nicht sehr unschuldige Thiere? Wer anders denken oder sprechen könnte, von dem müßte ich fürchten, daß er selbst den reinsten Schmuck seiner Seele, seine Unschuld, verloren hätte. — Durch diese sanften Thierchen könnte ich dahin kommen, es gar nicht überdrüßig zu werden, mein Land glücklich zu machen, — und an diesen Kaninchen läßt Er* es mangeln! — Spanferkeln und alle Tage Spanferkeln, — Bösewicht, das bin ich endlich überdrüßig.

Koch. Verdamme mich, mein König, nicht ungehört. Der Himmel ist mein Zeuge, daß ich mir alle Mühe nach jenen niedlichen weißen Thierchen gegeben habe; ich habe sie zu allen Preisen

einkaufen wollen, aber durchaus sind keine zu haben. — Sollten
Sie an der Liebe Ihrer Unterthanen zweifeln können, wenn man
nur irgend dieser Kaninchen habhaft werden könnte?

König. Laß die schelmischen Worte, schier Dich fort in die
Küche und beweise durch die That, daß Du deinen König liebst!
— Der Koch geht ab. — Jetzt wend' ich mich zu Ihnen, mein Prinz,
und zu Dir, meine Tochter. — Ich habe erfahren, werther Prinz,
daß meine Tochter Sie nicht liebt, daß sie Sie nicht lieben kann;
sie ist ein unbesonnenes, unvernünftiges Mädchen; aber ich traue
ihr doch so viel Verstand zu, daß sie einige Ursachen haben wird.
Sie macht mir Sorgen und Gram, Kummer und Nachdenken, und
meine alten Augen fließen von häufigen Thränen über, wenn ich
daran denke, wie es nach meinem Tode mit ihr werden soll. — Du
wirst sitzen bleiben, hab' ich ihr tausendmal gesagt; greif' zu, so
lange es Dir geboten wird! Aber sie will nicht hören; nun so
wird sie sich gefallen lassen müssen, zu fühlen.

Prinzessin. Mein Vater, —

König weinend und schluchzend. Geh, Undankbare, Ungehorsame,
— Du bereitest meinem grauen Kopfe durch Dein Weigern ein,
ach! nur allzufrühzeitiges Grab! — Er stützt sich auf den Thron, verdeckt
mit dem Mantel das Gesicht und weint heftig.

Fischer. Der König bleibt seinem Charakter doch nicht einen
Augenblick getreu.

Ein Kammerdiener kömmt herein. Ihro Majestät, ein
fremder Mann ist draußen und bittet vor Ihro Majestät gelassen
zu werden.

König schluchzend. Wer ist's?

Kammerdiener. Verzeihung, mein König, daß ich diese
Frage nicht beantworten kann. Seinem langen weißen Barte
nach sollte er ein Greis seyn, und sein ganz mit Haaren bedecktes
Gesicht sollte einen fast in dieser Vermuthung bestärken, aber dann
hat er wieder so muntre jugendliche Augen, einen so dienstfertigen
geschmeidigen Rücken, daß man an ihm irre wird. Er scheint ein
wohlhabender Mann, denn er trägt ein Paar vortreffliche Stiefeln,
und so viel ich irgend aus seinem Aeußern abnehmen kann, möcht'
ich ihn für einen Jäger halten.

König. Führt ihn herein, ich bin neugierig ihn zu sehn.
Kammerdiener geht ab und kommt sogleich mit Hinze zurück.

Hinze. Mit Ihrer Majestät gnädigster Erlaubniß ist der Graf von Carabas so frei, Ihnen ein Kaninchen zu übersenden.

König entzückt. Ein Kaninchen? — Hört Ihr's wohl, Leute? — O das Schicksal hat sich wieder mit mir ausgesöhnt! — Ein Kaninchen?

Hinze nimmt es aus dem Tornister. Hier, großer Monarch.

König. Da, — halten Sie mal* das Scepter einen Augenblick, Prinz, — Er befühlt das Kaninchen — fett! hübsch fett! — Vom Grafen von —

Hinze. Carabas.

König. Ei, das muß ein vortrefflicher Mann seyn, den Mann muß ich näher kennen lernen. — Wer ist der Mann? Wer kennt ihn von Euch? — Warum hält er sich verborgen? Wenn solche Köpfe feiern, wie viel Verlust für meinen Staat! Ich möchte vor Freuden weinen; schickt mir ein Kaninchen! Kammerdiener, gebt es gleich dem Koch.

Kammerdiener empfängt's und geht ab.

Nathanael. Mein König, ich nehme meinen demüthigsten Abschied.

König. Ja so, das hätt' ich über die Freude bald vergessen. — Leben Sie wohl, Prinz. Ja, Sie müssen andern Freiwerbern Platz machen, das ist nicht anders. — Adieu! Ich wollte, Sie hätten Chaussee bis nach Hause.

Nathanael küßt ihm die Hand und geht ab.

König schreiend. Leute! — Mein Historiograph soll kommen!

Der Historiograph erscheint.

König. Hier, Freund, kommt, hier giebt's Materie für unsre Weltgeschichte. — Ihr habt doch Euer Buch bei Euch?

Historiograph. Ja, mein König.

König. Schreibt gleich hinein, daß wir an dem und dem Tage (welch Datum wir nun heut schreiben) der Graf von Carabas ein sehr delicates Kaninchen zum Präsent überschickt hat.

Historiograph setzt sich nieder und schreibt.

König. Vergeßt nicht anno currentis. — Ich muß an Alles denken, sonst wird's doch immer schief ausgerichtet. Man hört blasen.

* Halten Sie mal das Scepter, ꝛc. Pray, hold me the sceptre for a moment. Mal is here for the unaccented einmal, as elsewhere in the play.

— Ah, das Eſſen iſt fertig. — Komm, meine Tochter, weine nicht,
iſt's nicht der Prinz, ſo iſt's ein anderer. — Jäger, wir danken
für Deine Mühe; willſt du uns nach dem Speiſeſaal begleiten?

Sie gehen ab; Hinze folgt.

Leutner. Bald halt' ich's nicht mehr aus. Wo iſt denn
der Vater geblieben, der erſt gegen ſeine Tochter ſo zärtlich war,
und uns alle ſo rührte?

Fiſcher. Was mich nur ärgert, iſt, daß ſich kein Menſch im
Stück über den Kater wundert; der König und Alle thun, als
müßte es ſo ſeyn.

Schloſſer. Mir geht der ganze Kopf von dem wunderlichen
Zeuge herum.

Vierte Scene.
Königlicher Speiſeſaal.

Große ausgerüſtete Tafel. Unter Pauken und Trompeten treten ein: der König,
die Prinzeſſin, Leander, Hinze, mehrere vornehme Gäſte und
Hanswurſt, Bediente, welche aufwarten.

König. Setzen wir uns, die Suppe wird ſonſt kalt. — Iſt
für den Jäger geſorgt?

Ein Bedienter. Ja, Ihro Majeſtät; er wird mit dem Hof‐
narren hier am kleinen Tiſchchen eſſen.

Hanswurſt zu Hinze. Setzen wir uns, die Suppe wird ſonſt
kalt.

Hinze ſetzt ſich. Mit wem habe ich die Ehre zu ſpeiſen?

Hanswurſt.* Der Menſch iſt, was er iſt, Herr Jäger, wir

* The *Hanswurst* was formerly a standing character of the German
mountebank (and subsequently of the regular) stage, and is closely allied to
the *Clown* of the English, the *Gracioso* of the Spaniards, the *Arlequin* of
the French, and the *Arlechino* and the *Scapin* of the Italians. The ances‐
tral progenitor of all these comic figures seems to have been the Italian Arle‐
chino, unless the lineage of their pedigree be pursued still further to the Ro‐
man pantomimic characters, whose *Planipes* and *Sannio* appear to have ful‐
filled a similar function on their stage. The Planipes (= *bare-foot*, accord‐
ing to some) seems to have been a sort of mime, who derived his name from
the circumstance, that he wore neither the *cothurnus* nor the *soccus* of the
regular actors. Sannio was originally the name of a servant (Cicero ad He‐
renn. IV. 50. ed. Ernesti), which subsequently acquired the generic significa‐
tion of grotesque stupidity and drollery in general. This appears from Cicero

könnten nicht Alle daſſelbe treiben. Ich bin ein armer verbannter Flüchtling, ein Mann, der vor langer Zeit einmal ſpaßhaft war,

De Oratore II. 61 :—*Quid enim potest esse tam ridiculum, quam* Sannio *est? Sed ore, vultu, immitandis moribus, voce, denique ipso corpore ridetur.* That this Roman Sannio was the veritable archetype of all those later European imitations, is evident not only from the foregoing description of Cicero, which characterizes all of them, but also from the etymological fact, that the best Italian writers apply the term *Zanni* (the English *Zany*) to both their Scapin and their Arlechino.

The first mention of the German Hanswurst is made in one of Luther's pamphlets, entitled : " Wider den Hanswurst," which was written against the duke of Brunswick-Wolfenbüttel. From this it appears that this comic personage of the Germans (who at that time were particularly all fond of good living) was represented usually by a man of a well-fed and somewhat more than comfortably obese bodily condition :—"It is true, that some are of opinion, that you regard my gracious liege and master as a Hanswurst for no other reason, than that from the liberal participation of the divine bounties he is possessed of a stout, fat, well-filled corporation." This gluttonizing propensity of the character is already indicated by his name, which among the different nations is directly taken from that of some favorite popular dish :—English *Jack Pudding*, Dutch *Pickleherring*, French *Jean Potage*, Italian *Macaroni*, and the German Hanswurst, which by interpretation = *John Sausage* (from which it would appear that sausages, like watches, gun-powder, printing and other inventions were of German origin). The result of this voracity, however, was different among the different nations. With the Germans, its consequence was a jovial outward Falstaff obesity, while among the Italians and the French it had no material effect whatever, and their harlequin remains lean and flexible. The primitive Arlechino was strutfully extravagant in gesture, action and buffoonery, and his language was low and saucy. At a later period he appears as the standing representative of the ignorant simpleton, cowardly and sycophantic, though faithful and cringingly servile, ever busy to conceal the baseness of his nature by the drollery of his coarsely witty improvisations, ever ready to resent an injury. The great fort of the character lay in his extemporaneous sallies, and yet it would seem, that certain stereotype pantomimes and witticisms were handed down from century to century for his behoof. The harlequin appears moreover, modified to some extent by the peculiar national taste of the people, to whose amusement he contributed, and the Frenchman was not only droll, but gallant, pliable and versatile. The witticisms and the grotesque gesticulations of the German Hanswurst, most of which were originally done extempore, had always made him a favorite of the masses, who were ever fond of seeing sights, and he was long the Merry Andrew of the ambulatory mountebank stages. In the carnival-farces and mysteries he occupied a comic middle-ground between the devils and the saints. At the beginning of the eighteenth century, the regular stage made its first attempt to give a sort of histrionic finish to the rôle of the German clown, which still consisted chiefly in mimic improvisations, and he was

den man nachher für dumm, abgeschmackt und unanständig hielt, und der nun in einem fremden Lande wieder in Dienst getreten ist, wo man ihn von neuem auf einige Zeit für unterhaltend ansieht.

Hinze. So? — Was seid Ihr für ein Landsmann?

Hanswurst. Leider nur ein Deutscher. Meine Landsleute wurden um eine gewisse Zeit so klug, daß sie allen Spaß bei Strafe verboten; wo man mich nur gewahr ward, gab man mir unaus= stehliche Ekelnamen, als: gemein, pöbelhaft, niederträchtig, ja mein guter ehrlicher Name Hanswurst ward zu einem Schimpf= worte herab gewürdigt. O edle Seele, die Thränen stehn Dir in den Augen, und Du knurrst vor Schmerz, oder macht es der Ge= ruch des Bratens, der Dir in die Nase zieht? Ja, lieber Em= pfindsamer, wer sich damals nur unterstand, über mich zu lachen, der wurde eben so verfolgt, wie ich, und so mußt' ich denn wohl in die Verbannung wandern.

Hinze. Armer Mann.

Hanswurst. Es giebt wunderliche Handthierungen in der Welt, Herr Jäger; Köche leben vom Appetit, Schneider von der Eitelkeit, ich vom Lachen der Menschen; wenn sie nicht mehr la= chen, so ist meine Nahrung verloren.

Hinze. Das Gemüse ess' ich nicht.

Hanswurst. Warum? Seyd nicht blöde, greift zu.

Hinze. Ich sage Euch, ich kann den weißen Kohl nicht ver= tragen.

---

to appear more of a nationalized harlequin of the more recent and more po- lished Italian and French type. About the middle of that century, however, when the regular drama began to supplant the former extemporaneous comedy, a deadly warfare was commenced against this popular idol, until at last he was entirely banished from the boards. This victory was chiefly due to the efforts of Gottsched and his school (1700—1766). It is against the puristic zealotry of this new school and its contemporary followers, that Tieck here de- fends and restores the pristine honor of the droll figure of the ancient gour- mand-type. Among the vindicators of Hanswurst, Lessing and Moser were prominent, and the latter went even so far, as to maintain, that no popular comedy could ever exist, without some similar representative of the grotesque- comic element. And indeed the character seems to be possessed of a sort of metamorphosic immortality. Even after the name had vanished, the person still continued in variously modified transmutations, as in the Viennese *Lari- fari, Casperle,* &c.; and in the most recent times, the droll standing figures of certain fairy extravaganzas are of a similar description.

Hanswurst. Mir wird er desto besser schmecken. — Gebt mir Eure Hand, ich muß Euch näher kennen lernen, Jäger.

Hinze. Hier.

Gemurmel im Parterre: ein Hanswurst! ein Hanswurst!

Hanswurst. Empfangt hier die Hand eines deutschen Biedermanns; ich schäme mich nicht, wie so viele meiner Landsleute, ein Deutscher zu seyn.

Er drückt dem Kater die Hand sehr heftig.

Hinze. Au! au! —

Er sträubt sich, knurrt und klaut den Hanswurst.

Hanswurst. O weh! Jäger! plagt Euch der Teufel? — *Er steht auf und geht weinend zum König.* Ihro Majestät, der Jäger ist ein treuloser Mann, seht nur, wie er mir ein Andenken von seinen fünf Fingern hinterlassen hat.

König, essend. Wunderlich, — nun, setz Dich nur wieder hin, trage künftig Handschuh', wenn Du mit ihm gut Freund seyn willst. Es giebt vielerlei Arten von Freunden, man muß jedes Gericht zu essen und jeden Freund zu behandeln verstehn. Halt! Ich habe gleich gedacht, daß hinter dem Jäger was Besonderes steckt! sieh! sieh! er ist ein Freimaurer, und hat Dir nur das Zeichen in die Hand schreiben wollen, um zu sehn, ob Du auch von der Brüderschaft bist.

Hanswurst. Man muß sich vor Euch hüten.

Hinze. Warum kneift Ihr mich so? Hole der Henker Euer biederes Wesen.

Hanswurst. Ihr kratzt ja wie eine Katze.

Hinze lacht boshaft.

König. Aber was ist denn das heute? Warum wird denn kein vernünftiges Tischgespräch geführt? Mir schmeckt kein Bissen, wenn nicht auch der Geist einige Nahrung hat. — Hofgelehrter, seyd Ihr denn heute auf den Kopf gefallen?

Leander, essend. Ihro Majestät geruhn —

König. Wie weit ist die Sonne von der Erde?

Leander. Zweimal hundert tausend, fünf und siebenzig und eine Viertel Meile, fünfzehn auf einen Grad gerechnet.

König. Und der Umkreis, den die Planeten so insgesammt durchlaufen?

Leander. Wenn man rechnet, was jeder einzelne laufen muß,

so kommen in der Total=Summa etwas mehr als tausend Millionen Meilen heraus.

König. Tausend Millionen! — Man sagt schon, um sich zu verwundern: Ei, der Tausend! und nun gar tausend Millionen! Ich mag auf der Welt nichts lieber hören, als so große Nummern, — Millionen, Trillionen, — da hat man noch dran zu denken. — Es ist doch meiner Seel' ein Bißchen viel, so tausend Millionen.

Leander. Der menschliche Geist wächst mit den Zahlen.

König. Sagt mal, wie groß ist wohl so die ganze Welt im Umfange, Firsterne, Milchstraßen, Nebelkappen und allen Plun= der mitgerechnet?

Leander. Das läßt sich gar nicht aussprechen.

König. Du sollst es aber aussprechen, oder —

Mit dem Zepter drohend.

Leander. Wenn wir eine Million wieder als Eins ansehn, dann ohngefähr zehnmal hundert tausend Trillionen solcher Ein= heiten, die jede an sich schon eine Million Meilen ausmachen . . .

König. Denkt nur, Kinder, denkt! — Sollte man meinen, daß das Ding von Welt so groß seyn könnte? Aber wie das den Geist beschäftigt!

Hanswurst. Ihro Majestät, das ist eine curiose Erhabenheit, davon krieg' ich noch weniger in den Kopf als in den Magen; mir kommt die Schüssel mit Reiß hier viel erhabener vor.

König. Wie so, Narr?

Hanswurst. Bei solchen ungeheuren Zahlen kann man gar nichts denken, denn die höchste Zahl wird ja am Ende wieder die kleinste. Man darf sich ja nur alle Zahlen denken, die es geben kann. Wir können nicht leicht, ohne uns zu verirren, bis Fünfe zählen.

König. Aber da ist was Wahres drin. Der Narr hat seine Einfälle. — Gelehrter, wie viel Zahlen giebt es denn?

Leander. Unendlich viel.

König. Sagt mal geschwind die höchste Zahl.

Leander. Es giebt gar keine höchste, weil man zur höchsten noch immer wieder eine neue hinzufügen kann; der menschliche Geist kennt hier gar keine Einschränkung.

König. Es ist doch wahrhaftig ein wunderliches Ding um diesen menschlichen Geist.

Hinze. Es muß Dir hier sauer werden, ein Narr zu seyn.

Hanswurst. Man kann gar nichts Neues aufbringen, es arbeiten zu viele in dem Fache.

König. Und Du sagst also auch, daß die Erde immer rund=um, immer rundum geht, bald so, bald so, wie ein besoffener Mensch?

Leander. Nicht eigentlich auf diese Weise, sondern mehr einem Walzenden ähnlich.

König. Und sie ist, wie Ihr meint, eine Kugel?

Leander. Allerdings, so daß unter uns Menschen wohnen, die ihre Füße gegen die unsrigen richten oder unsre Antipoden sind, so wie wir wiederum die Antipoden von ihnen sind.

König. Wie? Ich auch?

Leander. Allerdings.

König. Ich verbitte mir aber dergleichen: meint Er, daß ich mich so wegwerfen werde?" Er und seines Gleichen mögen An=tipoden seyn, so viel sie wollen; aber ich halte mich zu gut, Jeman=des Antipode zu seyn, und wenn es selbst der große Mogul wäre. Er denkt wohl, weil ich mich manchmal herablasse, mit Ihm zu disputiren, so werde ich mir auch Alles bieten lassen. Ja, ja, ich sehe, wer sich zum Schaf macht, den fressen die Wölfe; man darf solche Gelehrte nur ein Weniges um sich greifen lassen, so mengen sie nach ihren Systemen Kraut und Rüben durcheinander, und entblöden sich nicht, den regierenden Herrn selbst unter die Anti=poden zu werfen. Daß dergleichen niemals wieder geschieht!

Leander. Wie Ihro Majestät befehlen.

König. Doch um nicht einseitig bei einem Gegenstande zu verweilen, so bringt mir nun einmal mein Mikroskop herein! Leander ab. Ich muß Ihnen sagen, meine Herren, daß ich es als eine Andacht treibe, in das kleine Ding hinein zu gucken, und daß es mich in der That erbaut, und mein Herz erhebt, wenn ich sehe, wie ein Wurm so ungeheuer vergrößert wird, wie eine Made und Fliege so seltsamlich construirt sind, und wie sie in ihrer Pracht mit einem Könige wetteifern können. — Leander kommt zurück. Gebt her! Ist nicht eine Mücke bei der Hand, ein Gewürm, sey es, was es sey, um es zu beobachten?

* See p. 337, note.

Hanswurst. Sonst findet sich dergleichen oft, ohne daß man's wünscht, und nun es zur Geistesbildung dienen soll, läßt sich nichts betreffen: aber ich schlage Ihro Majestät unmaßgeblich vor, eins von den seltsamen Barthaaren des fremden Jägers zu observiren, was sich gewiß der Mühe verlohnt.

König. Seht, der Narr hat heut einen luminösen Tag. Ein trefflicher Gedanke! Damit der Jäger sich aber nicht über Gewalt zu beschweren habe, soll ihm das ansehnlichste Haar durch Niemand anders als durch zwei Kammerherren ausgerauft werden. Macht Euch dran, Leute.

Hinze zu den Kammerherren. Das scheint mir ein Eingriff in das Völkerrecht. — Sie ziehn ihm das Haar aus. Au! Mau! Miau! Prrrst!

König. Hört, er maut fast wie eine Katze.

Hanswurst. O ja, auch hat er eben so geprustet; er scheint überhaupt eine merkwürdige Organisation zu besitzen.

König durch das Glas sehend. Ei! Ei! wie höchst wunderbar! Da ist doch auch kein Riß, keine unebene Stelle, keine Rauhigkeit wahrzunehmen. Ja, das sollen mir einmal die Englischen Fabriken nachahmen! · Ei! ei! wo der Jäger nur die kostbaren Barthaare hergenommen hat!

Hanswurst. Sie sind ein Werk der Natur, mein König. Dieser fremde Mann hat noch eine andre große Naturmerkwürdigkeit an sich, die gewiß eben so unterhaltend als nachdenklich ist. Ich nahm vorhin wahr, als die Braten hereingebracht wurden und der angenehme Duft den ganzen Saal erfüllte, daß sich in seinem Körper ein gewisses Orgelwerk in Bewegung zu setzen anfing, das mit lustigen Passagen auf und nieder schnurrte, wobei er die Augen aus Wohlgefallen eindrückte und ihm die Nase lebhaft zitterte. Ich fühlte ihn zu der Zeit an, und der Tremulant war in seinem ganzen Körper unter Nacken und Rücken fühlbar.

König. Ist es möglich? Komm mal her, trete zu mir, Jäger.

Hinze. An diesen Mittag werd' ich gedenken.

Hanswurst. Kommt, edler Freund. · Indem er ihn führt. Nicht wahr? Ihr werdet wieder kratzen?

König. Hier tretet her. — Nun? — Legt sein Ohr an ihn. Ich höre nichts, es ist ja mäuschenstill in seinem Leibe.

Hanswurst. Er hat es verloren, seit ihm das Haar ausge-rissen wurde; es scheint nur zu orgeln, wenn ihm wohl ist. Jä-ger, denkt einmal recht was Wohlgefälliges, stellt Euch doch was Anmuthiges vor, sonst glaubt man, es ist nur Tücke, daß es jetzt nicht in Euch spielt.

König. Haltet ihm den Braten vor die Nase. — So. — Seht Jäger, davon sollt Ihr sogleich bekommen. Nun? — Ich will ihm indeß etwas den Kopf und die Ohren streicheln; hoffent-lich wirkt diese Gnade auf sein Zufriedenheits-Organ. — Richtig! Hört, hört, Leute, wie es schnurrt, auf und ab, ab und auf, in recht hübschen Läufen! Und in seinem ganzen Körper fühl' ich die Erschütterung. — Hm! hm! äußerst sonderbar! — Wie ein solcher Mensch inwendig muß beschaffen seyn! Ob es eine Walze seyn mag, die sich umdreht, oder ob es nach Art der Claviere ein-gerichtet ist? Wie nur die Dämpfung angebracht wird, daß au-genblicks das ganze Werk still steht? — Sagt mal, Jäger: (Euch acht' ich und bin wohlwollend gegen Euch gesinnt) aber habt Ihr nicht vielleicht in der Familie einen Vetter oder weitläuftigen An-verwandten, an dem nichts ist, an dem die Welt nichts verlöre, und den man so ein weniges aufschneiden könnte, um ein Einsehn in die Maschinerie zu bekommen?

Hinze. Nein, Ihro Majestät, ich bin der einzige meines Ge-schlechts.

König. Schade! — Hofgelehrter, denkt einmal nach, wie der Mensch innerlich gebaut seyn mag, und les't es uns alsdann in der Akademie vor.

Hanswurst. Kommt, Jäger, setzen wir uns wieder und speisen.

Hinze. Ich sehe, mit Dir muß ich Freundschaft halten.

Leander. Es wird mir eine Ehre seyn, mein König; ich habe auch schon eine Hypothese im Kopf, die mir von der höchsten Wahrscheinlichkeit ist; ich vermuthe nämlich, daß der Jäger ein unwillkührlicher Bauchredner ist, der wahrscheinlich bei strenger Erziehung sich früh angewöhnt hat, sein Wohlgefallen und seine Freude, die er nicht äußern durfte, in seinem Innern zu verschlie-ßen; dorten aber, weil sein starkes Naturell zu mächtig war, hat es in den Eingeweiden für sich selbst den Ausdruck der Freude getrieben, und sich so diese innerliche Sprache gebildet, die wir jetzt als eine seltsame Erscheinung an ihm bewundern.

König. Läßt sich hören.

Leander. Nun klingt es deshalb in ihm mehr wie ein verhaltner Grimm, als wie ein Ausdruck der Lust. Ihrer Natur nach steigt die Freude nach oben, öffnet den Mund weit und spricht in den offensten Vokalen, am liebsten in A, I oder Ei, wie wir in der ganzen Schöpfung, an Kindern, Schafen, Eseln, Stieren und Betrunkenen wahrnehmen können; er aber, bei seinen tyrannischen Eltern und Vormündern, wo er nichts durfte laut werden lassen, mußte innerlich nur ein O und U brummen, und so angesehn muß diese Erscheinung alles Wunderbare verlieren, und ich glaube aus diesen Gründen nicht, daß er eigene Walzen oder ein Orgelwerk in seinem Leibe besitze.*

Hanswurst. Wenn es nun einmal dem Herrn Leander verboten würde, laut zu philosophieren, und seine tiefsinnigen Gedanken müßten sich auch, statt oben, in der Tiefe aussprechen, welche Sorte von Knarrwerk sich wohl in seinem Bauche etabliren würde?

Leander. Der Narr, mein König, kann vernünftige Gedanken nie begreifen; mich wundert überhaupt, daß sich Ihro Majestät noch von seinen geschmacklosen Einfällen belustigen lassen. Man sollte ihn geradezu fortjagen, denn er bringt Ihren Geschmack nur in einen üblen Ruf.

König, wirft ihm das Zepter an den Kopf. Herr Naseweis von Gelehrter! was untersteht Er sich denn?† In Ihn ist ja heut ein satanischer Rebellionsgeist gefahren! Der Narr gefällt mir, mir, seinem Könige, und wenn ich Geschmack an ihm finde, wie kann Er sich unterstehn zu sagen, daß der Mann abgeschmackt sei? Er ist Hofgelehrter und der andere Hofnarr; Ihr steht beide in einem Gehalte; der einzige Unterschied ist, daß er an dem kleinen Tischchen mit dem fremden Jäger speist. Der Narr macht dummes Zeug bei Tische und Er führt einen vernünftigen Discurs bei Tische, Beides soll mir nur die Zeit vertreiben und machen, daß mir

---

* An evident persiflage on certain philosophers, who attempt to explain the origin of language by the theory of a gradual development from interjectional sounds.

† See page 337, note.

das Essen gut schmeckt; wo ist denn also der große Unterschied? —
Und dann thut's einem Herrn, wie mir, auch wohl, einen Narren
zu sehn, der dummer ist, der die Gabe und die Bildung nicht hat,
man fühlt sich mehr und ist dankbar gegen den Himmel. Schon
deswegen ist ein Dummkopf ein angenehmer Umgang. — Wenn
Er aber meint, daß der Narr in Religion und Philosophie zurück
ist, daß er zu sehr in der Irre wandelt, kann Er sich denn nicht
(da der Dumme doch gewiß Sein Nächster ist) menschenfreundlich zu
ihm setzen und liebreich sagen: Sieh, Schatz, das ist so, und jenes
so, Du bist hierin zurück, ich will Dich mit Liebe auf den Weg des
Lichtes bringen, und dann etwas gründliche Logik, Metaphysik und
Hydrostatik ihm vorsprechen, daß der Dumme in sich schlägt und
sich bekehrt? So müßte einer handeln, der ein Weltweiser
heißen will.

Der Koch trägt das Kaninchen auf und entfernt sich.

König. Das Kaninchen! — Ich weiß nicht, — die andern
Herren essen es wohl nicht gerne? — *Alle verneigen sich.* Nun, so
will ich es denn mit Ihrer Erlaubniß für mich allein behalten. —
Er ißt.

Prinzessin. Mich dünkt, der König zieht Gesichter, als
wenn er seine Zufälle wieder bekäme.

König, *aufstehend in Wuth.*

Das Kaninchen ist verbrannt! —
O Herr des Himmels! Erde? — Was noch sonst!
Nenn' ich die Hölle mit? —

Prinzessin. Mein Vater —

König. Wer ist das?
Durch welchen Mißverstand hat dieser Frembling
Zu Menschen sich verirrt? — Sein Aug' ist trocken!

*Alle erheben sich in Besorgniß, Hanswurst läuft geschäftig hin und wieder. Hinze
bleibt sitzen und ißt heimlich.*

Gieb diesen Todten mir heraus. Ich muß
Ihn wieder haben!

Prinzessin. Hole doch Einer schnell den Besänftiger.

König. Der Koch Philipp sei Jubelgeschrei der Hölle, wenn
ein Undankbarer verbrannt wird!

Prinzessin. Wo nur der Musikus bleibt.

16*

König.

Die Todten stehen nicht mehr auf. Wer darf
Mir sagen, daß ich glücklich bin? O wär' er mir gestorben!
Ich hab' ihn lieb gehabt, sehr lieb.

Der **Besänftiger** tritt mit einem Glockenspiele auf, das er sogleich spielt.

König. Wie ist mir? Weinend. Ach, ich habe schon wieder
meinen Zufall gehabt. — Schafft mir den Anblick des Kaninchens
aus den Augen. —

Er legt sich voll Gram mit dem Kopf auf den Tisch und schluchzt.

Ein Hofmann. Seine Majestät leiden viel.

Es entsteht ein gewaltiges Pochen und Pfeifen im Parterre; man hustet, man zischt,
die Gallerie lacht; der König richtet sich auf, nimmt den Mantel in Ordnung
und setzt sich mit dem Scepter in größter Majestät hin. Alles ist umsonst, der
Lärm wird immer größer, alle Schauspieler vergessen ihre Rollen; auf dem Theater eine fürchterliche Pause — Hinze ist eine Säule hinan geklettert. Der **Dichter** kömmt bestürzt auf's Theater:

Meine Herren, — verehrungswürdigstes Publikum, — nur einige
Worte.

Im Parterre. Still! still! der Narr will sprechen.

Dichter. Ums Himmelswillen machen Sie mir die Schande
nicht, der Akt ist ja gleich zu Ende. — Sehn Sie doch nur, der
König ist ja auch wieder zur Ruhe, nehmen Sie an dieser großen
Seele ein Beispiel, die gewiß mehr Ursache hatte, außer sich zu
seyn, als Sie.

Fischer. Mehr als wir?

Wiesener, zum Nachbar. Aber warum trommeln Sie denn?
Uns beiden gefällt ja das Stück.

Nachbar. Ist auch wahr, — in Gedanken, weil es Alle thun.
Klatscht aus Leibeskräften.

Dichter. Einige Stimmen sind mir doch noch günstig; lassen Sie sich aus Mitleid mein armes Stück gefallen, ein Schelm
giebt's besser, als er's hat; es ist auch bald zu Ende. — Ich bin
so verwirrt und erschrocken, daß ich Ihnen nichts Anders zu sagen
weiß.

Alle. Wir wollen nichts hören, nichts wissen.

Dichter, reißt wüthend den Besänftiger hervor. Der König ist besänftigt, besänftige nun auch diese tobende Fluth, wenn Du es
kannst!

Stürzt außer sich ab.

Der Besänftiger spielt auf den Glocken, das Pochen schlägt dazu den Takt. Er winkt: Affen und Bären erscheinen, und tanzen freundlich um ihn her, Adler und andere Vögel; ein Adler sitzt Hinzen auf dem Kopf, der in der größten Angst ist, zwei Elephanten und zwei Löwen tanzen auch.

Ballet und Gesang.

Die Vierfüßigen.

Das klinget so herrlich, —

Die Vögel.

Das klinget so schön, —

Vereinigtes Chor.

Nie hab' ich so etwas gehört noch gesehn.

Hierauf wird von allen Anwesenden eine künstliche Quadrille getanzt, der König und sein Hofstaat wird in die Mitte genommen, Hinze und den Hanswurst nicht ausgeschlossen; allgemeines Applaudiren. Gelächter. Man steht im Parterre auf, um recht genau zu sehn; einige Hüte fallen von der Gallerie herunter.

Der Besänftiger

singt während dem Ballet und der allgemeinen Freude der Zuschauer:

Könnte jeder brave Mann
Solche Glöckchen finden,
Seine Feinde würden dann
Ohne Mühe schwinden,
Und er lebte ohne sie
In der schönsten Harmonie.

Der Vorhang fällt, Alles jauchzt und klatscht, man hört noch das Ballet eine Zeitlang.

Zwischenakt.

Wiesener. Herrlich! herrlich!

Nachbar. Das heiß ich mir noch ein heroisch Ballet.

Wiesener. Und so schön in die Haupthandlung einge= flochten!

Leutner. Schöne Musik!

Fischer. Göttlich!

Schlosser. Das Ballet hat das Stück noch gerettet.

Bötticher. Ich bewundere nur immer das Spiel des Ka= ters. — An solchen Kleinigkeiten erkennt man den großen und geübten Schauspieler; so oft er zum Beispiel das Kaninchen aus der Tasche nahm, hob er es jederzeit bei den Ohren, — es stand ihm nicht vorgeschrieben; haben sie wohl bemerkt, wie es der Kö= nig sogleich an dem Leib packte? Aber man hält diese Thiere bei ben Ohren, — weil sie es dort am besten vertragen können. Das nenn' ich den Meister!

Müller. Das ist sehr schön auseinandergesetzt.

Fischer, heimlich. Man sollte ihn selbst dafür bei den Ohren nehmen.

Bötticher. Und die Angst, als ihm der Adler auf dem Kopfe saß! Wie er sich aus Furcht so gar nicht bewegte, sich weder rührte noch regte, — nein, eine solche vollendete Kunst kann keine Beschreibung ausdrücken.

Müller. Sie gehen sehr gründlich.

Bötticher. Ich schmeichle mir, nur ein klein wenig Kenner zu seyn; das ist freilich mit Ihnen allen nicht der Fall, und darum muß man es Ihnen ein wenig entwickeln.

Fischer. Sie geben sich viele Mühe.

Bötticher. Wenn man die Kunst so liebt, wie ich, ist das eine angenehme Mühe. — Mir ist auch jetzt über die Stiefeln des Katers ein sehr scharfsinniger Gedanke eingefallen, und ich bewundre darin das Genie des Schauspielers. — Sehn Sie, er ist anfangs Kater, deshalb muß er seine natürliche Kleidung ablegen, um die passende Maske einer Katze zu nehmen; jetzt soll er nun wieder ganz als Jäger erscheinen (dies schließe ich daraus, daß ihn Jeder so nennt, sich auch kein Mensch über ihn verwundert), ein ungeschickter Schauspieler würde sich auch gewiß in einen Jagd=habit geworfen haben: — aber — wie würde es um unsre Illusion aussehn? Wir hätten vielleicht darüber vergessen, daß er doch im Grunde ein Kater ist, und wie unbequem müßte dem Schauspieler eine neue Kleidung über dem schon vorhandenen Pelze seyn? Durch die Stiefeln aber deutet er sehr geschickt die Jägeruniform* nur an, und daß solche Andeutungen vollkommen kunstgemäß sind, beweisen uns ganz vorzüglich die Alten, die oft —

Fischer. Schon wieder die Alten!

---

* See Introduction, page 326. Iffland had written a play, called die Jäger, and excelled in that character on the stage. These remarks of Bötticher have evidently reference both to his acting and to the *brochure* mentioned above. The following Xenion of Goethe or Schiller is here in place:

IMITATION OF NATURE.

What one only can do, that one should delineate only,
  Voss but the parson should paint, Iffland the hunter alone.

Bötticher. Verzeihen Sie, es ist eine angenehme, sonst löbliche Gewohnheit, die ich mir zugelegt habe, verträgt sich auch mit aller möglichen modernen Eleganz. Ich bin übrigens gesonnen, meine Herren, ein eignes Buch über die dargestellte Rolle des Katers herauszugeben (wozu ich mir auch nachher von Ihnen allerseits einige scharfsinnige Bemerkungen ausbitten werde), und darum wünschte ich wohl, daß das Stück nicht so oft unterbrochen würde. Die Scene, in welcher er dem Könige das Kaninchen mit so großer Kunst überliefert, schien mir fast sein Triumph, wenn ich die letzte ausnehme, in welcher sich sein Genie noch glänzender zeigte; denn jene spielte er ganz und gar mit dem linken Zeigefinger und einer geringen Bewegung des rechten Fußes. Was würde da mancher Schauspieler sich heftig bewegt und laut geschrieen haben? Aber er, er steht ruhig auf sich selber da, sich kennend, seiner Größe vertrauend, wohl wissend, daß das Kaninchen im Tornister steckt, den er nur aufknöpfen darf, um sein Glück zu machen.

Schlosser. Uns dünkt der Mensch aber sehr langweilig.

Bötticher. Sie sind vielleicht nur verwöhnt, meine Herren. Waren Sie denn nicht tief erschüttert in jener einzigen, unnachahmlichen Scene, als dem Würdigsten seines Geschlechtes auf Befehl des Tyrannen sein ehrwürdiger Bart ausgerauft ward? Nicht wahr, hier hätten Sie Geschrei, Fußstampfen, Zähneknirschen erwartet? Wie mancher Schreier unsrer Bühnen, der in Heldenrollen gerühmt wird, hätte hier die ganze Kraft seines Organs aufgeboten, um sich den Beifall des Haufens zu ertoben? Nicht so unser großer origineller Künstler. Da stand er, still in sich gezogen, seinen Schmerz zurück zwängend; während die rechte Hand in der aufgeknöpften Weste unter dem Jabot ruhig steckt, ist die linke mit der ausgestreckten Fläche nach oben gewandt, sie drückte seinen Unwillen aus, und forderte gleichsam des Himmels Unterstützung; sein Gesicht war ruhig, fast lächelnd, in Verachtung gegen die Diener des Tyrannen, nur eine zwinkelnde Bebung zuckte im aufwärtsrollenden Auge, in der man sein ganzes Gefühl erkannte, und nun ertönt aus gehobener Brust das herzdurchschneidende Au Mau, Miau, so gedehnt, so gezogen, so wimmernd klagend, daß uns Allen der Athem verging; doch das Gefühl des

Unwillens läßt sich nicht ganz zurückhalten, und nun der plötzlich
kühne Uebergang in jenen Ausruf des Zornes, den der Narr ein
Prusten nannte, und vor dem selbst die schamlosen Despotenknechte
zurückfuhren. Wahrlich, dies war der Gipfel aller Kunst. Ja,
in diesem marrenden, quarrenden, prustigen Tone möcht' ich von
diesem einzigen Manne einmal den König Lear, oder den Wallen=
stein spielen sehn; ich bin überzeugt, diese Darstellungen wären
etwas Unerhörtes, und würden gegen jene Schreier grell abstechen,
die die tragischen Rollen immer nur mit sogenannter Kraft und
mit Nachdruck zu spielen suchen.

Fischer. Das fehlt uns noch! Es ist aber unausstehlich,
wenn es da oben einmal still ist, so martert uns der Kenner hier
fast eben so sehr. — Der Vorhang geht auf!

Dritter Akt.

Bauernstube.

Der Dichter, der Maschinist.

Maschinist. Meinen Sie denn wirklich, daß das etwas hel=
fen wird?

Dichter. O mein verehrtester Herr Maschinist, ich bitte Sie,
ich beschwöre Sie, schlagen Sie mir meine Bitte nicht ab; meine
letzte Hoffnung, meine Rettung beruht nur darauf.

Leutner. Was ist denn das wieder? — Wie kommen denn
diese Menschen in Gottliebs Stube?

Schlosser. Ich zerbreche mir über nichts mehr den Kopf.

Maschinist. Aber, lieber Freund, Sie verlangen auch wahr=
haftig zu viel, daß das alles so in der Eil', ganz aus dem Stege=
reife zu Stande kommen soll.

Dichter. Sie verfolgen mich auch; einverstanden mit meinen
Freunden drunten, erfreuen Sie sich meines Unglücks.

Maschinist. Nicht im mindesten.

Dichter fällt vor ihm nieder. Nun so beweisen Sie es mir da=
durch, daß Sie meinen Bitten nachgeben; wenn das Mißfallen
des Publikums bei irgend einer Stelle wieder so laut ausbricht, so
lassen Sie auf einen Wink von mir alle Maschinen spielen! Der

zweite Akt ist so schon ganz anders geschlossen, als er in meinem Manuscripte steht.

Maschinist. Was ist denn das? — Wer hat denn die Gardine aufgezogen?

Dichter. Alles Unglück strömt auf mich ein, ich bin verloren!
Er flieht beschämt hinter die Coulissen.

Maschinist. Solche Verwirrung ist noch an keinem Abende gewesen. *Geht ab. — Eine Pause.*

Wiesener. Gehört denn das zum Stück?

Nachbar. Natürlich, das motivirt ja die nachherigen Verwandlungen.

Fischer. Den heutigen Abend sollte man doch wirklich im Theater-Calender beschreiben.

König hinter der Scene. Nein, ich geh' nicht vor, durchaus nicht; ich kann es nicht vertragen, wenn ich ausgelacht werde.

Dichter. Aber Sie, — theuerster Freund, — es ist doch einmal nicht zu ändern.

Hanswurst. Nun, ich will mein Glück versuchen.
Er tritt hervor, und verbeugt sich possierlich gegen das Publikum.

Müller. Wie kommt denn der Hanswurst nun in die Bauernstube?

Schlosser. Er wird gewiß einen abgeschmackten Monolog halten wollen.

Hanswurst. Verzeihen Sie, wenn ich mich erkühne, ein paar Worte vorzutragen, die eigentlich nicht zum Stücke gehören.

Fischer. O Sie sollten nur ganz stille schweigen, Sie sind uns schon im Stücke zuwider, vielmehr nun gar so —

Schlosser. Ein Hanswurst untersteht sich mit uns zu reden?

Hanswurst. Warum denn nicht? denn, wenn ich ausgelacht werde, so thut mir das nichts, sondern es ist im Gegentheil mein heißester Wunsch, daß Sie geruhen möchten, über mich zu lachen. Nein, nein, ich bitte, geniren Sie sich nur gar nicht, wir sind hier unter uns.

Leutner. Das ist ziemlich possierlich.

Hanswurst. Was dem Könige freilich wenig ansteht, schickt sich desto besser für mich; er wollte daher auch gar nicht vorkommen, sondern überließ mir diese wichtige Ankündigung.

Müller. Wir wollen aber nichts hören.

Hanswurst. Meine lieben deutschen Landsleute —

Schlosser. Ich denke, das Stück spielt draußen in Asien?

Hanswurst. Kann seyn, ich weiß nicht; jetzt aber, verstehn Sie mich, jetzt rede ich ja zu Ihnen als bloßer Schauspieler zu den Zuschauern, nicht als Hanswurst, sondern als Mensch zu einem Publikum, das nicht in der Illusion begriffen ist, sondern sich außerhalb derselben befindet; kühl, vernünftig, bei sich, vom Wahnsinn der Kunst unberührt. Capiren Sie mich? Können Sie mir folgen? Distinguiren Sie?*

Schlosser. Adieu! Nun geht's fort mit mir, ich schnappe über. Richtig, wie ich immer vorher gesagt habe.

Müller. Wir verstehn Sie gar nicht.

Schlosser. Sagen Sie doch nicht zu einem Hanswurste Sie.†

Müller. Er sagt ja aber, daß er jetzt nur einen Menschen vorstellt.

Hanswurst. Geruhen Sie doch zu vernehmen (und das ist die Ursach, weßhalb ich komme), daß die vorige Scene, die Sie eben sahen, gar nicht zum Stücke gehört.

Fischer. Nicht zum Stücke? Wie kömmt sie denn aber hinein?

Hanswurst. Der Vorhang war zu früh aufgezogen. Es war eine Privatunterredung, die gar nicht auf dem Theater vorgefallen wäre, wenn man zwischen den Coulissen etwas mehr Raum hätte. Sind Sie also illudirt gewesen ‡, so ist es wahrlich um so schlimmer, und es hilft nichts, Sie müssen dann so gütig seyn und die Mühe daran setzen, diese Täuschung aus sich wieder auszurotten; denn von jetzt an, verstehen Sie mich, von dem Augenblicke, daß ich werde abgegangen seyn, nimmt der dritte Akt erst seinen Anfang. Unter uns: alles Vorhergehende gehört nicht zur Sache; es ist eine Zugabe, die wir uns jetzt wieder von Ihnen

---

* Capiren Sie mich?... Distinguiren Sie? pedantically for Verstehen Sie mich?... Begreifen Sie?

† On the use of the pronouns of the person addressed, see p. 337. Note.

‡ Sie sind also illudirt gewesen, then you have been in a state of illusion; a side-cut at the doctrine of actual illusion in art.

zurück erbitten. Aber Sie sollen entschädigt werden; es wird im Gegentheil bald Manches kommen, das ziemlich zur Sache gehört, denn ich habe den Dichter selbst gesprochen und er hat's mir zugeschworen.

Fischer. Ja, Euer Dichter ist der rechte Kerl.

Hanswurst. Nicht wahr, er ist nichts werth?

Müller. Gar nichts, Hanswurst; es ist mir lieb, daß Sie die Einsicht haben.

Hanswurst. Nun, das freut mich von Herzen, daß noch Jemand anders meinen Geschmack hat.

Das Parterre. O, wir Alle, wir Alle, keiner denkt anders.

Hanswurst. Gehorsamer Diener, gar zu viel Ehre. — Ja, es ist, weiß Gott, ein elender Dichter, — nur, um ein schlechtes Beispiel zu geben: welche armselige Rolle hat er mir zugetheilt? Wo bin ich denn witzig und spaßhaft? Ich komme in so wenigen Scenen vor, und ich glaube, wenn ich nicht noch jetzt durch einen glücklichen Zufall herausgetreten wäre, ich erschiene gar nicht wieder.

Dichter hervorstürzend. Unverschämter Mensch —

Hanswurst. Sehn Sie! Sogar auf die kleine Rolle, die ich jetzt spiele, ist er neidisch.

Dichter, auf der andern Seite des Theaters, mit einer Verbeugung. Verehrungswürdige! ich hätte es nie wagen dürfen, diesem Manne eine größere Rolle zu geben, da ich Ihren Geschmack kenne —

Hanswurst auf der andern Seite. Ihren Geschmack! — Nun sehn Sie den Neid. — Und so eben haben Sie erklärt, daß mein Geschmack und der Ihrige in Einer Form gegossen seien.

Dichter. Ich wollte Sie durch gegenwärtiges Stück nur vorerst zu noch ausschweifenderen Geburten der Phantasie vorbereiten.

Alle im Parterre. Wie? — Was?

Dichter. Denn stufenweise nur kann die Ausbildung geschehn, die den Geist das Phantastische und Humoristische lieben lehrt.

Hanswurst. Humoristische! Was er die Backen voll nimmt, und es ist doch lauter Wind. Aber Geduld, er hat gut Rollen-Schreiben, wir machen im Spielen doch ganz andre daraus.

Dichter. Ich empfehle mich indeß, um den Gang des Stückes

nicht länger zu unterbrechen, und bitte der vorigen Störung wegen nochmals um Verzeihung. *Geht ab.*

Hanswurst. Adieu, meine Theuren, bis auf Wiedersehn. — *Er geht ab, und kömmt schnell wieder.* Apropos! noch eins! — Auch was jetzt unter uns vorgefallen ist, gehört, genau genommen, nicht zum Stück. *Ab.*

Das Parterre lacht.

Hanswurst kömmt schnell zurück. Lassen Sie uns heut das miserable Stück zu Ende spielen; thun Sie, als merken Sie gar nicht, wie schlecht es ist, und so wie ich nach Hause komme, setze ich mich hin und schreibe eins für Sie nieder, das Ihnen gewiß gefallen soll. *Ab. Viele klatschen.*

Erste Scene.
Gottlieb und Hinze treten auf.

Gottlieb. Lieber Hinze, es ist wahr, Du thust sehr viel für mich, aber ich kann immer noch nicht einsehn, was es mir helfen soll.

Hinze. Auf mein Wort, ich will dich glücklich machen, und ich scheue keine Mühe und Arbeit, keine Schmerzen, keine Aufopferungen, um diesen Endzweck durchzusetzen.

Gottlieb. Bald, sehr bald muß es geschehn, sonst ist es zu spät, — es ist schon halb acht, und um acht ist die Komödie aus.

Hinze. Was Teufel ist denn das?

Gottlieb. Ach, ich war in Gedanken! sonst, wollte ich sagen, verschmachten wir beide. Aber sieh, wie schön die Sonne aufgegangen ist, — der verdammte Souffleur spricht so undeutlich, und wenn man denn manchmal extemporiren will, geht's immer schief.

Hinze leise. Nehmen Sie sich doch zusammen, das ganze Stück bricht sonst in tausend Stücke.

Schlosser. Was sprach der von Komödie und halb Acht?

Fischer. Ich weiß nicht: mir däucht, wir sollten Acht geben, es würde bald aus seyn.

Schlosser. Ja wohl, Acht! gottlob, um Acht werden wir erlöst; wenn wir Acht geben, so wird es um Acht für uns ein Losgeben; bis Neun, Neun, könnt' es Keiner aushalten; um Zehn würd' ich mit Zähnen um mich beißen.

Müller. Bester, Sie phantasieren schon in der Manier des Stücks.

Schlosser. Ja, ich bin auf lange ruinirt.

Gottlieb. Also heut noch soll sich mein Glück entscheiden?

Hinze. Ja, lieber Gottlieb, noch ehe die Sonne untergeht. — Sieh, ich liebe Dich so sehr, daß ich für Dich durch's Feuer laufen möchte, — und Du zweifelst an meiner Freundschaft?

Wiesener. Haben Sie's wohl gehört? — Er wird durch's Feuer laufen. — Schön! da bekommen wir noch die Decoration aus der Zauberflöte, mit dem Wasser und Feuer.

Nachbar. Katzen gehn aber nicht ins Wasser.

Wiesener. Desto größer ist ja des Katers Liebe für seinen Herrn: merken Sie, das will uns ja der Dichter eben dadurch zu verstehn geben.

Hinze. Was hast Du denn wohl Lust zu werden in der Welt?

Gottlieb. Das ist schwer zu sagen.

Hinze. Möchtest Du wohl Prinz oder König werden?

Gottlieb. Das noch am ersten.

Hinze. Fühlst Du auch die Kraft in Dir, ein Volk glücklich zu machen?

Gottlieb. Warum nicht? Wenn ich nur erst glücklich bin.

Hinze. Nun so sey zufrieden; ich schwöre Dir, Du sollst den Thron besteigen.   *Geht ab.*

Gottlieb. Wunderlich müßt' es zugehn. — Doch kömmt ja in der Welt so Manches unerwartet.   *Geht ab.*

Bötticher. Bemerken Sie doch die unendliche Feinheit, mit der der Kater seinen Stock hält, so zart, so leutselig.

Fischer. Sie sind uns mit ihren Feinheiten schon längst zur Last, Sie sind noch langweiliger als das Stück.

Müller. Ja es ist recht verdrießlich, immer diese Entwicklungen und Lobpreisungen anhören zu müssen.

Bötticher. Aber der Kunst-Enthusiasmus sucht sich doch auszusprechen.

Schlosser. O, es soll nun gleich zu Ende seyn! Fassen Sie an, bester Herr Leutner; Herr Müller, halten Sie ihm den

Kopf, ich habe hier eine Maschine, die ihm den Mund schließen
und das Sprechen untersagen wird.

Bötticher. Sie werden doch nimmermehr —

Schlosser. So, nun steckt ihm der Knebel schon im Munde:
Herr Fischer, lassen Sie die Feder zuschnappen, so ist die Sache
gemacht. *Sie knebeln ihn.*

Bötticher. Das ist doch himmelschreiend, daß ein Kunst=
ke — —

Schlosser. Kunstkenner will er sagen. So, jetzt wird doch
von der Seite Ruhe seyn. Nun sehn Sie hübsch still und be=
dächtlich zu.

Zweite Scene.
Freies Feld.

Hinze *mit Tornister und Sack.* Ich bin der Jagd ganz gewohnt
worden, alle Tage fang' ich Rebhühner, Kaninchen und derglei=
chen, und die lieben Thierchen kommen auch immer mehr in die
Uebung, sich fangen zu lassen. —*Er spreitet seinen Sack aus.* — Die
Zeit mit den Nachtigallen ist nun vorbei. Ich höre keine einzige.
Die beiden Liebenden treten auf.

Er. Geh', Du bist mir zur Last.

Sie. Du bist mir zuwider.

Er. Eine schöne Liebe!

Sie. Jämmerlicher Heuchler, wie hast Du mich betrogen!

Er. Wo ist Deine unendliche Zärtlichkeit geblieben?

Sie. Und Deine Treue?

Er. Deine Wonnetrunkenheit?

Sie. Deine Entzückungen?

Er. Der Teufel hat's geholt! Das kommt vom Heirathen

Hinze. So ist die Jagd noch nie gestört worden. — Wenn
Sie doch geruhen wollten, zu bemerken, daß dieses freie Feld für
Ihre Schmerzen offenbar zu enge ist, und irgend einen Berg
bestiegen....

Er. Schlingel! *Gibt Hinzen eine Ohrfeige.*

Sie. Flegel! *Gibt ihm von der andern Seite eine.*

Hinze *knurrt.*

Sie. Ich dächte, wir ließen uns scheiden.

Er. Ich stehe zu Befehl. Die Liebenden gehen ab.

Hinze. Niedliches Volk, die sogenannten Menschen. — Sieh da, zwei Rebhühner, ich will sie schnell hintragen. — Nun, Glück, tummle dich, denn fast wird mir die Zeit auch zu lang. — Jetzt hab' ich gar keine Lust mehr, die Rebhühner zu fressen. So gewiß ist es, daß wir durch bloße Gewohnheit unserer Natur alle möglichen Tugenden einimpfen können. Geht ab.

Bötticher unterm Knebel. Himm — himm — li — sch!

Schlosser. Strengen Sie sich nicht so an; es ist doch vergeblich.

Dritte Scene.

Saal im Palast.

Der König auf seinem Thron mit der Prinzessin, Leander auf einem Katheder, ihm gegenüber Hanswurst auf einem andern Katheder; in der Mitte des Saales steckt auf einer hohen Stange ein Hut, der mit Gold besetzt und mit bunten Federn geschmückt ist; der ganze Hof ist versammelt.

König. Noch nie hat sich ein Mensch um das Vaterland so verdient gemacht, als dieser liebenswürdige Graf von Carabas. Einen dicken Folianten hat unser Historiograph schon voll geschrieben, so oft hat er mir durch seinen Jäger niedliche und wohlschmeckende Präsente übermacht, manchmal sogar an Einem Tage zweimal. Meine Erkenntlichkeit gegen ihn ist ohne Grenzen, und ich wünsche nichts so sehnlich, als irgend einmal eine Gelegenheit zu finden, etwas von meiner großen Schuld gegen ihn abzutragen.

Prinzessin. Liebster Herr Vater, wollten Dieselben nicht gnädigst erlauben, daß jetzt die gelehrte Disputation ihren Anfang nehmen könnte? Mein Herz schmachtet nach dieser Geistesbeschäftigung.

König. Ja, es mag jetzt seinen Anfang nehmen. — Hofgelehrter, — Hofnarr, — Ihr wißt beide, daß demjenigen von Euch, der in dieser Disputation den Sieg davon trägt, jener kostbare Hut beschieden ist; ich habe ihn auch deßwegen hier aufrichten lassen, damit Ihr ihn immer vor Augen habt und es Euch nie an Witz gebricht.

Leander und Hanswurst verneigen sich.

Leander. Das Thema meiner Behauptung ist, daß ein neuerlich erschienenes Stück: Der gestiefelte Kater, ein gutes Stück sey.

Hanswurst. Das ist gerade das, was ich leugne.

Leander. Beweise, daß es schlecht sey.

Hanswurst. Beweise, daß es gut sey.

Leutner. Was ist denn das wieder? — die Rede ist ja wohl von demselben Stücke, das hier gespielt wird, wenn ich nicht irre.

Müller. Freilich von demselben.

Leander. Das Stück ist, wenn nicht ganz vortrefflich, doch in einigen Rücksichten zu loben.

Hanswurst. In gar keiner Rücksicht.

Leander. Ich behaupte, es ist Witz darin.

Hanswurst. Ich behaupte, es ist keiner drin.

Leander. Du bist ein Narr; wie willst Du über Witz urtheilen?

Hanswurst. Und Du bist ein Gelehrter, was willst Du von Witz verstehn?

Leander. Manche Charaktere sind gut durchgeführt.

Hanswurst. Kein einziger.

Leander. So ist, wenn ich auch alles Uebrige fallen lasse, das Publikum gut darin gezeichnet.

Hanswurst. Ein Publikum hat nie einen Charakter.

Leander. Ueber diese Frechheit möcht' ich fast erstaunen.

Hanswurst gegen das Parterre. Ist es nicht ein närrischer Mensch? Ich und das verehrungswürdige Publikum stehn nun beide gleichsam auf Du und Du,* und sympathisiren in Ansehung des Geschmacks, und doch will er gegen meine Meinung behaupten, das Publikum im gestiefelten Kater sey gut gezeichnet.

Fischer. Das Publikum? Es kommt ja kein Publikum in dem Stücke vor?

Hanswurst. Noch besser! Also kömmt gar kein Publikum darin vor?

* I and the worshipful public are now, as it were, on terms of the most familiar intimacy, we are *thee-and-thouing* each other.

Müller. Je bewahre!* Wir müßten ja doch auch darum wissen.

Hanswurst. Natürlich. Nun siehst Du, Gelehrter? Was die Herren da unten sagen, muß doch wohl wahr seyn.

Leander. Ich werde confus, — aber ich lasse Dir noch nicht den Sieg.

Hinze tritt auf.

Hanswurst. Herr Jäger, ein Wort! —

Hinze nähert sich, Hanswurst spricht heimlich mit ihm.

Hinze. Wenn es weiter nichts ist. — Er zieht die Stiefeln aus und klettert die Stange hinauf, nimmt den Hut, springt herunter, und zieht die Stiefeln wieder an.

Hanswurst den Hut schwenkend. Sieg! Sieg!

König. Der Tausend! Wie ist der Jäger geschickt!

Leander. Es betrübt mich nur, daß ich von einem Narren überwunden bin, daß Gelehrsamkeit vor Thorheit die Segel streichen muß.

König. Sey ruhig; Du wolltest den Hut haben, er wollte den Hut haben, da seh' ich nun wieder keinen Unterschied. — Aber was bringst Du, Jäger?

Hinze. Der Graf von Carabas läßt sich Eurer Majestät demüthigst empfehlen, und nimmt sich die Freiheit, Ihnen diese beiden Rebhühner zu überschicken.

König. Zu viel! zu viel! Ich erliege unter der Last der Dankbarkeit. Schon lange hätte ich meine Pflicht beobachten sollen, ihn zu besuchen, heute will ich es nun nicht länger aufschieben. — Laßt geschwind meine Staatscarosse in Ordnung bringen, acht Pferde vor, ich will mit meiner Tochter ausfahren! — Du, Jäger, sollst uns den Weg nach dem Schlosse des Grafen zeigen. Geht mit seinem Gefolge ab.

Hinze, Hanswurst.

Hinze. Worüber war denn Eure Disputation?

Hanswurst. Ich behauptete, ein gewisses Stück, das ich übrigens gar nicht kenne: Der gestiefelte Kater, sey ein erbärmliches Stück.

Hinze. So?

---

* For Je Gott bewahre! lit. God forfend! here only a strong negation: *Not in the least, by no means!*

Hanswurst. Adieu, Herr Jäger, viel Dank.

Setzt den Hut auf und geht.

Hinze *allein.* Ich bin ganz melancholisch. — Ich habe selbst dem Narren zu einem Siege verholfen, ein Stück herabzusetzen, in welchem ich die Hauptrolle spiele! — Schicksal! Schicksal! In welche Verwirrungen führst Du so oft den Sterblichen! Doch mag es hingehn, wenn ich es nur dahin bringe, meinen geliebten Gottlieb auf den Thron zu setzen, so will ich herzlich gern alles Ungemach vergessen; will vergessen, daß ich mir und meiner Existenz zu nahe trete, indem ich die bessere Kritik entwaffnete und der Narrheit Waffen gegen mich selbst in die Hände gegeben; will vergessen, daß man mir den Bart ausgerauft und fast den Leib aufgeschnitten hätte; ja ich will nur im Freunde leben und der Nachwelt das höchste Muster uneigennütziger Freundschaft zur Bewunderung zurück lassen. — Der König will den Grafen besuchen? das ist noch ein schlimmer Umstand, den ich in's Reine bringen muß. — In seinem Schlosse, das bis jetzt noch nirgend in der Welt liegt? — Nun ist der große wichtige Tag erschienen, an dem ich Euch, ihr Stiefeln, ganz vorzüglich brauche! Verlaßt mich heut' nicht, zerreißt nur heut' nicht, zeigt nun, von welchem Leder ihr seyd, von welchen Sohlen! Auf denn, Füß' und Stiefeln, an das große Werk, denn noch heut' muß sich Alles entscheiden!

Geht ab.

Schlosser. Was würgen Sie denn so?

Bötticher. G — Gr — Großß!!

Fischer. Sagt mir nur, wie das ist, — das Stück selbst, — das kommt wieder als Stück im Stücke vor?

Schlosser. Ich habe jetzt keinen mehr, an dem ich meinen Zorn, in welchen mich das Stück versetzt hat, auslassen könnte; da steht er, ein stummes Denkmal meiner eignen Verzweiflung.

Vierte Scene.

Vor dem Wirthshause.

Der Wirth, *der mit einer Sense Korn mäht.* Das ist eine schwere Arbeit! — Je nun, die Leute können auch nicht alle Tage desertiren; an den guten Kindern liegt's gewiß nicht, sie haben den besten Willen, es geht aber halt nicht immer an. Das Leben besteht doch aus lauter Arbeit: bald Bier zapfen, bald Gläser rein machen, bald einschenken, nun gar mähen. Leben heißt arbeiten. Es kam mal ein Gelehrter hier durch, der sagte, um recht zu leben, müsse sich der Mensch den Schlaf abgewöhnen, weil er im Schlaf seine Bestimmung verfehle und nicht arbeite; der Kerl muß gewiß noch niemals müde gewesen seyn, und noch keinen guten Schlaf gethan haben, denn ich kenne doch nichts Herrlicher's und Ausbündiger's als den Schlaf. Ich wollte, es wäre erst so weit, daß ich mich niederlegen könnte.

Hinze tritt auf. Wer etwas Wunderbares hören will, der höre mir jetzt zu. Wie ich gelaufen bin! Erstlich von dem königlichen Palast zu Gottlieb; zweitens mit Gottlieb nach dem Palast des Popanzes, wo ich ihn draußen im Walde gelassen habe; drittens von da wieder zum Könige; viertens lauf' ich nun vor dem Wagen des Königes wie ein Läufer her und zeige ihm den Weg. O Beine, o Füße, o Stiefeln, wie viel müßt ihr heut' verrichten! — He! guter Freund!

Wirth. Wer ist da? — Landsmann, Ihr müßt wohl fremde seyn, denn die hiesigen Leute wissen's schon, daß ich um die Zeit kein Bier verkaufe, ich brauch's für mich selber; wer solche Arbeit thut, wie ich, der muß sich auch stärken; es thut mir leid, aber ich kann Euch nicht helfen.

Hinze. Ich will kein Bier, ich trinke gar kein Bier, ich will Euch nur ein paar Worte sagen.

Wirth. Ihr müßt wohl ein rechter Tagedieb seyn, daß Ihr die fleißigen Leute in ihrem Beruf zu stören sucht.

Hinze. Ich will Euch nicht stören. Hört nur: der benachbarte König wird hier vorbeifahren, er steigt vielleicht aus und erkundigt sich, wem diese Dörfer hier gehören; wenn Euch Euer Leben lieb ist, wenn Ihr nicht gehängt oder verbrannt seyn wollt, so antwortet ja: dem Grafen von Carabas.

Wirth. Aber, Herr, wir sind ja dem Gesetz unterthan.

Hinze. Das weiß ich wohl, aber, wie gesagt, wenn Ihr nicht umkommen wollt, so gehört diese Gegend hier dem Grafen von Carabas. Geht ab.

Wirth. Schön Dank! — das wäre nun die schönste Gele-

17

genheit, von aller Arbeit loszukommen, ich dürfte nur dem Könige
sagen, das Land gehöre dem Popanz. Aber nein. Müßiggang
ist aller Laster Anfang. Ora et labora ist mein Wahlspruch.

Eine schöne Kutsche mit acht Pferden, viele Bedienten hinten; der Wagen hält, der König und die Prinzessin steigen aus.

Prinzessin. Ich fühle eine gewisse Neugier, den Grafen
zu sehn.

König. Ich auch, meine Tochter. — Guten Tag, mein
Freund! wem gehören diese Dörfer hier?

Wirth. *für sich.* Er frägt, als wenn er mich gleich wollte
hängen lassen. — Dem Grafen von Carabas, Ihro Majestät.

König. Ein schönes Land. — Ich habe immer gedacht, daß
das Land ganz anders aussehn müßte, wenn ich über die Gränze
käme, so wie es auf der Landkarte ist. — Helft mir doch einmal.
Er klettert schnell auf einen Baum hinauf.

Prinzessin. Was machen Sie, mein königlicher Vater?

König. Ich liebe in der schönen Natur die freien Aussichten.

Prinzessin. Sieht man weit?

König. O ja, und wenn mir die fatalen Berge hier nicht
vor der Nase ständen, so würde ich noch weiter sehn. — O weh!
der Baum ist voller Raupen. *Er steigt wieder hinunter.*

Prinzessin. Das macht, es ist eine Natur, die noch nicht
idealisirt ist; die Phantasie muß sie erst veredeln.

König. Ich wollte, Du könntest mir mit der Phantasie die
Raupen abnehmen. — Aber steig' ein, wir wollen weiter fahren.

Prinzessin. Lebe wohl, guter unschuldiger Landmann.
Sie steigen ein, der Wagen fährt weiter.

Wirth. Wie die Welt sich umgekehrt hat! — Wenn man
so in alten Büchern lies't, oder alte Leute erzählen hört, so kriegte
man immer Goldstücke, oder herrliche Kostbarkeiten, wenn man
mit einem Könige oder Prinzen sprach. Aber jetzt! — Wie soll
man noch sein Glück unverhoffter Weise machen, wenn es sogar
mit den Königen nichts mehr ist? Wenn ich ein König wäre, ich
unterstände mich nicht, den Mund aufzuthun, wenn ich den Leuten
nicht erst Geld in die Hand gesteckt hätte. — Unschuldiger Land=
mann! Wollte Gott, ich wäre nichts schuldig. — Aber das ma=
chen die neuen empfindsamen Schilderungen vom Landleben. So
ein König ist capabel und beneidet unser einen noch. Ich muß

nur Gott danken, daß er mich nicht gehängt hat. Der fremde Jäger war am Ende unser Popanz selber. — Wenigstens kömmt es nun doch in die Zeitung, daß der König gnädig mit mir ge= sprochen hat.   Geht ab.

Fünfte Scene.
Eine andere Gegend.

Kunz, der Korn mäht. Saure Arbeit! Und wenn ich's noch für mich thäte, aber der Hofedienst! Da muß man für den Popanz schwitzen, und er dankt es einem nicht einmal. — Es heißt wohl immer in der Welt, die Gesetze sind nothwendig, um die Leute in Ordnung zu halten, aber warum da u n s e r G e s e t z nothwendig ist, der uns alle auffrißt, kann ich nicht einsehen.

Hinze kömmt gelaufen. Nun hab' ich schon Blasen unter den Füßen! — Nun, es thut nichts; Gottlieb, Gottlieb muß dafür auf den Thron! — He! guter Freund!

Kunz. Was ist denn das für ein Kerl?

Hinze. Hier wird sogleich der König vorbeifahren; wenn er Euch fragt, wem dies alles gehört, so müßt Ihr antworten, dem Grafen von Carabas, sonst werdet Ihr in tausend Millionen Stück= chen gehackt. Zum Besten des Publikums will es so das Gesetz.

Fischer. Wie? zum Besten des Publikums?

Schlosser. Natürlich. weil sonst das Stück gar kein Ende hätte.

Hinze. Euer Leben wird Euch lieb seyn!   Geht ab.

Kunz. Das ist so, wie die Edicte immer klingen. Nun, mir kann's recht seyn, wenn nur keine neuen Auflagen daraus ent= stehen, daß ich das sagen soll. Man darf keiner Neuerung trauen.

Die Kutsche fährt vor und hält, **König** und **Prinzessin** steigen aus.

König. Auch eine hübsche Gegend. Wir haben doch schon eine Menge hübscher Gegenden gesehn. — Wem gehört das Land hier?

Kunz. Dem Grafen von Carabas.

König. Er hat herrliche Länder, das muß wahr seyn, und so nahe an den meinigen. Tochter, das wäre so eine Parthie für Dich. Was meinst Du?

Prinzessin. Sie beschämen mich, Herr Vater. — Aber was man doch auf Reisen Neues sieht. Sagt mir doch einmal, guter Bauer, warum haut Ihr denn das Stroh so um?

Kunz lachend. Das ist ja die Ernte, Mamsell Königin, das Getraide.

König. Das Getraide? — Wozu braucht Ihr denn das?

Kunz lachend. Daraus wird ja das Brod gebacken.

König. Bitt' ich Dich um Gotteswillen, Tochter! — daraus wird Brod gebacken! — Wer sollte wohl auf solche Streiche kommen? — Die Natur ist doch etwas Wunderbares. — Hier, guter Freund, habt Ihr ein klein Trinkgeld, es ist heute warm. —

Er steigt mit der Prinzessin wieder ein, der Wagen fährt fort.

Kunz. Kennt kein Getraide! Alle Tage erfährt man doch mehr Neues. — Wenn er mir nicht ein blankes Goldstück gegeben hätte, und wenn er kein König wäre, so sollte man denken, er wäre ein ganz einfältiger Mensch. — Ich will mir nur gleich eine Kanne gutes Bier holen. Kennt kein Getraide! Geht ab.

Sechste Scene.
Eine andere Gegend an einem Flusse.

Gottlieb. Da steh' ich nun hier schon seit zwei Stunden und warte auf meinen Freund Hinze. — Er kömmt immer noch nicht. — Da ist er! Aber wie er läuft! Er scheint ganz außer Athem.

Hinze kömmt gelaufen. Nun, Freund Gottlieb, zieh' Dir geschwind die Kleider aus.

Gottlieb. Die Kleider?

Hinze. Und dann springe hier in's Wasser. —

Gottlieb. In's Wasser?

Hinze. Und dann werf' ich die Kleider in den Busch. —

Gottlieb. In den Busch?

Hinze. Und dann bist Du versorgt!

Gottlieb. Das glaub' ich selber; wenn ich ersoffen bin, und die Kleider weg sind, bin ich versorgt genug.

Hinze. Es ist nicht Zeit zum Spaßen. —

Gottlieb. Ich spaße gar nicht. Hab' ich darum hier warten müssen?

Hinze. Zieh' Dich aus!

Gottlieb. Nun, ich will Dir Alles zu Gefallen thun.

Hinze. Komm, du sollst Dich nur ein wenig baden. Er geht mit ihm ab, und kömmt mit den Kleidern zurück, die er in den Busch hineinwirft. — Hülfe! Hülfe! Hülfe!

Die Kutsche fährt vor, der König sieht aus dem Schlage.

König. Was gibt's denn, Jäger? Warum schreist Du so?

Hinze. Hülfe, Ihro Majestät, der Graf von Carabas ist ertrunken.

König. Ertrunken!

Prinzessin im Wagen. Carabas!

König. Meine Tochter in Ohnmacht! — Der Graf ertrunken!

Hinze. Er ist vielleicht noch zu retten, er liegt dort im Wasser.

König. Bediente! wendet Alles, Alles an, den edlen Mann zu erhalten.

Ein Bedienter. Wir haben ihn gerettet, Ihro Majestät.

Hinze. Unglück über Unglück, mein König. — Der Graf hatte sich hier in dem klaren Wasser gebadet, und ein Spitzbube hat ihm die Kleider gestohlen.

König. Schnall' gleich meinen Koffer ab! Gebt ihm von meinen Kleidern! — Ermuntre Dich, Tochter, der Graf ist gerettet.

Hinze. Ich muß eilen. Geht ab.

Gottlieb in den Kleidern des Königs. Ihro Majestät —

König. Das ist der Graf! Ich kenne ihn an meinen Kleidern! — Steigen Sie ein, mein Bester, — was machen Sie? — Wo kriegen Sie all' die Kaninchen her? — Ich weiß mich vor Freude nicht zu lassen! — Zugefahren, Kutscher! —

Der Wagen fährt schnell ab.

Ein Bedienter. Da mag der Henker so schnell hinauf kommen, — nun hab' ich das Vergnügen zu Fuße nachzulaufen, und naß bin ich überdies noch wie eine Katze. Geht ab.

Leutner. Wie oft wird denn der Wagen noch vorkommen! — Diese Situation wiederholt sich auch gar zu oft.

Wiesener. Herr Nachbar! — Sie schlafen ja.

Nachbar. Nicht doch, — ein schönes Stück!

Siebente Scene.

Palast des Popanzes.

Der Popanz steht als ein Rhinozeros da, ein armer Bauer vor ihm.

Bauer. Geruhn Ihr Gnaden Popanz —

Popanz. Gerechtigkeit muß seyn, mein Freund.

Bauer. Ich kann jetzt noch nicht zahlen —

Popanz. Aber Er hat doch den Prozeß verloren, das Gesetz fordert Geld und Seine Strafe; Sein Gut muß also verkauft werden, es ist nicht anders, und das von Rechtswegen! Bauer geht ab.

Popanz, der sich wieder in einen ordentlichen Popanz verwandelt. Die Leute würden allen Respekt verlieren, wenn man sie nicht so zur Furcht zwänge.

Ein Amtmann tritt mit vielen Bücklingen herein. Geruhen Sie, — gnädiger Herr — ich —

Popanz. Was ist Ihm, mein Freund?

Amtmann. Mit Ihrer gütigsten Erlaubniß, ich zittre und bebe vor Dero furchtbarem Anblick.

Popanz. O, das ist noch lange nicht meine entsetzlichste Gestalt.

Amtmann. Ich kam eigentlich, — in Sachen, — um Sie zu bitten, sich meiner gegen meinen Nachbar anzunehmen, — ich hatte auch diesen Beutel mitgebracht, aber der Anblick des Herrn Gesetzes ist mir zu schrecklich.

Popanz verwandelt sich plötzlich in eine Maus, und sitzt in einer Ecke.

Amtmann. Wo ist denn der Popanz geblieben?

Popanz mit einer feinen Stimme. Legen Sie nur das Geld auf den Tisch dort hin; ich sitze hier, um Sie nicht zu erschrecken.

Amtmann. Hier. — Legt das Geld hin. O das ist eine herrliche Sache mit der Gerechtigkeit. — Wie kann man sich vor einer solchen Maus fürchten? Geht ab.

Popanz nimmt seine natürliche Gestalt an. Ein ziemlicher Beutel, — man muß auch mit den menschlichen Schwachheiten Mitleid haben.

Hinze tritt herein. Mit ihrer Erlaubniß, — Für sich: Hinze,
Du mußt dir ein Herz fassen, — Ihro Excellenz —

Popanz. Was wollt Ihr?

Hinze. Ich bin ein durchreisender Gelehrter, und wollte mir
nur die Freiheit nehmen, Ihro Excellenz kennen zu lernen.

Popanz. Gut, so lern' Er mich kennen.

Hinze. Sie sind ein mächtiger Fürst, Ihre Gerechtigkeitsliebe
ist in der ganzen Welt bekannt.

Popanz. Ja, das glaub' ich wohl. — Setz' Er sich doch.

Hinze. Man erzählt viel Wunderbares von Ihro Hoheit —

Popanz. Die Leute wollen immer was zu reden haben, und
da müssen denn die regierenden Häupter zuerst dran.

Hinze. Aber eins kann ich doch nicht glauben, daß dieselben
sich nämlich in Elephanten und Tiger verwandeln können.

Popanz. Ich will Ihm gleich ein Exempel davon geben.
　　　　　　　　　　　　Er verwandelt sich in einen Löwen.

Hinze zieht zitternd eine Brieftasche heraus. Erlauben Sie mir, daß
ich mir diese Merkwürdigkeit notire. — Aber nun geruhen Sie
auch, Ihre natürliche anmuthige Gestalt wieder anzunehmen, weil
ich sonst vor Angst vergehe.

Popanz in seiner Gestalt. Gelt, Freund, das sind Kunststücke?

Hinze. Erstaunliche. Aber, noch eins! man sagt auch, Sie
könnten sich in ganz kleine Thiere verwandeln; das ist mir mit
Ihrer Erlaubniß noch weit unbegreiflicher; denn, sagen Sie mir
nur, wo bleibt dann Dero ansehnlicher Körper?

Popanz. Auch das will ich machen. Er verwandelt sich in eine
Maus; Hinze springt hinter ihm her auf allen Vieren: Popanz erschreckt, entflieht
in ein anderes Zimmer, Hinze ihm nach.

Hinze zurückkommend. Freiheit und Gleichheit! — Das Gesetz
ist aufgefressen! Nun wird ja wohl der Tiers état Gottlieb zur
Regierung kommen.
　　　　　Allgemeines Pochen und Zischen im Parterre.

Schlosser. Halt! Ein Revolutionsstück! Ich wittere Alle=
gorie und Mystik in jedem Wort! Halt! halt! Zurück möcht'
ich nun Alles denken und empfinden, um all die großen Winke, die
tiefen Andeutungen zu fassen, die religiöse Tiefe zu ergründen!
Halt! Nur nicht gepocht! Es sollte lieber von vorn gespielt wer=
den! Nur nicht weltlich getrommelt!

Das Pochen dauert fort; Wiesener und manche Andre klatschen, Hinze ist sehr verlegen.

Bötticher. Ich — muß —

Fischer. Halten Sie sich nur ruhig.

Bötticher. Muß — muß —

Müller. Was er drückt! Wie er sich aufbläst!

Fischer. Ich fürchte, er platzt in der Anstrengung.

Bötticher. Muß — muß —

Fischer. Ums Himmels Willen, Sie gehn zu Grunde.

Bötticher. Lo — lo — *sehr laut,* loben!! —

Der Knebel fliegt ihm aus dem Munde, über das Orchester weg auf das Theater, und dem Hinze an den Kopf.

Hinze. O weh! o weh! sie werfen mit Steinen nach mir! Ich bin tödtlich am Kopfe blessirt! *Er entflieht.*

Bötticher. Muß loben, preisen, vergöttern und auseinandersetzen das himmlische, das einzige Talent dieses unvergleichlichen Mannes, dem ähnlich nichts in unserm Vaterlande noch den übrigen Reichen anzutreffen ist. Und, o Jammer! er muß nun glauben, daß meine Anstrengung, ihn zu erheben, ihn hat beschädigen wollen, weil dieser verruchte Knebel ihm an sein ehrwürdiges, lorbeerumkränztes Haupt geflogen ist.

Fischer. Es war wie ein Kanonenschuß.

Müller. Lassen Sie ihn nur schwatzen und loben, und halten Sie den Herrn Schlosser, welcher auch wüthig geworden ist.

Schlosser. O Tiefe, Tiefe der mystischen Anschauungen! O gewiß, gewiß wird der sogenannte Kater nun in der letzten Scene auf dem Berge im Aufgang der Sonne knieen, daß ihm das Morgenroth durch seinen transparenten Körper scheint! O weh! o weh! und darum kommen wir nun. Horcht! das Pochen währt immer fort. Nein, Kerle, laßt mich los, — weg da!

Leutner. Hier, Herr Fischer, habe ich zum Glück einen starken Bindfaden im Orchester gefunden; da, binden Sie ihm die Hände.

Müller. Die Füße auch, er stößt wie ein Rasender um sich.

Bötticher. Wie wohl, wie leicht ist mir, nun du Knebel fort, fort flogest, weit in die Welt hinein, und die Lobpreisungen, einem Strome ähnlich, der seinen Damm zerreißt, wieder ergiebig, wortüberflüssig, mit Anspielungen und Citaten spielend, Stellen

aus alten Autoren wälzend, dahin fluthen kann! O welchen An=
stand hat dieser Mann! Wie drückte er die Ermüdung so sinn=
reich aus, daß er ein Weniges mit den Knieen knickte und knackte,
wenn er zum Stillstehn kam; nichts da vom Schweißabtrocknen,
wie ein ordinärer Künstler gethan haben würde; nein, dazu hatte
er keine Zeit, der Erste, Einzige, Uebermenschliche, Riesenhafte,
Titanenmäßige!

Fischer. Er fällt ordentlich in den Hymnus, nun das Sperr=
werk fort ist.

Müller. Lassen Sie ihn, mit dem Herrn Schlosser steht es
viel schlimmer.

Schlosser. Ach! nun würde die geheime Gesellschaft kom=
men, die für das Wohl der Menschheit thätig ist; die Freiheit
wird nun proclamirt, und ich bin hier gebunden. *Das Getümmel
vermehrt sich, so wie das Geschrei im Parterre und auf der Gallerie.*

Leutner. Das ist ja ein höllischer Spectakel, als wenn das
ganze Haus einbrechen wollte.

Dichter *hinter der Scene.* Ei was! laßt mich zufrieden, — wo=
hin soll ich mich retten? — *Er stürzt außer sich auf das Theater.* Was
fang' ich an, ich Elendester? — das Stück ist sogleich zu Ende —
Alles wäre vielleicht gut gegangen — ich hatte nun gerade von
dieser moralischen Scene so vielen Beifall erwartet. — Wenn es
nur nicht so weit von hier — nach dem Palast des Königs wäre,
so holt' ich den Besänftiger, — er hat mir schon am Schluß des
zweiten Aktes — alle Fabeln vom Orpheus glaublich gemacht. —
Doch, bin ich nicht Thor? — Ich bin ja völlig confuse; — auf
dem Theater steh' ich, — und der Besänftiger muß irgendwo —
zwischen den Coulissen stecken. — Ich will ihn suchen, — ich muß
ihn finden, — er soll mich retten! — *Er geht ab, kömmt schnell zurück.*
Dort ist er nicht. — Herr Besänftiger! — Ein hohles Echo spot=
tet meiner. — Kommen Euer Wohlgeboren! — Nur ein wenig
vermittelnde Kritik — und das ganze Reich, — das jetzt empört
ist, — kömmt zur Ruhe wieder. — Wir meinen es ja Alle gut,
— wir haben ja nur den Mittelpunkt verfehlt, — Publikum, wie
ich! — Herr Vermittler! Herr Besänftiger! — Etwas bessere
Kritik, die Anarchie zu enden! — — O weh, er hat mich verlas=
sen. — Ha!! — dort seh' ich ihn, er muß hervor!

Die Pauſen werden vom Parterre aus mit Pochen ausgefüllt, und der Dichter
ſpricht dieſen Monolog recitativiſch, ſo daß dadurch eine Art von Melodram entſteht.

Beſänftiger hinter der Scene.   Nein, ich gehe nicht vor.

Dichter.   Kommen Sie, ſeyn Sie nur dreiſt, Sie werden ge=
wiß Glück machen.

Beſänftiger.   Der Lärm iſt zu ungeheuer.

Dichter, ſtößt ihn mit Gewalt hervor.   Die Welt wartet auf Sie!
Hinaus! Vermitteln Sie! Beſänftigen Sie!

Beſänftiger tritt vor mit dem Glockenſpiel.   Ich will mein Heil
verſuchen. — Er ſpielt auf den Glocken und ſingt:

> In dieſen heil'gen Hallen
>   Kennt man die Rache nicht,
> Und iſt ein Menſch gefallen,
>   Führt Liebe ihn zur Pflicht;
> Dann wandelt er an Freundes Hand
> Vergnügt und froh ins beſſ're Land.
>
> Wozu dies wilde Brüllen,
>   Die Excentricität?
> Das alles muß ſich ſtillen,
>   Wenn die Kritik entſteht;
> Dann wiſſen wir woran wir ſind,
> Das Ideal fühlt jedes Kind.

Das Parterre fängt an zu klatſchen, indem verwandelt ſich das Theater; das Feuer
und das Waſſer aus der Zauberflöte fängt an zu ſpielen, oben ſieht man den
offnen Sonnentempel, der Himmel iſt offen, und Jupiter ſitzt darin,
unten die Hölle mit Tarkaleon; Kobolde und Heren auf dem Theater,
viel Licht.   Das Publikum klatſcht unmäßig, Alles iſt in Aufruhr.

Wieſener.   Nun muß der Kater noch durch Feuer und Waſ=
ſer gehn, und das Stück iſt fertig.

Der **König,** die **Prinzeſſin, Gottlieb, Hinze,** mit verbundenem Kopfe, Be=
diente treten herein.

Hinze.   Dies iſt der Palaſt des Grafen von Carabas. — Die
Henker, hat ſich's denn hier verändert?

König.   Ein ſchön Palais.

Hinze.   Weil's denn doch einmal ſo weit iſt, Gottlieb bei der
Hand nehmend, ſo müſſen Sie erſt hier durch das Feuer, und dann
durch das Waſſer gehn.   Gottlieb geht nach einer Flöte und Pauke durch

Feuer und Wasser. Sie haben die Prüfung überstanden; nun, mein
Prinz, sind Sie ganz der Regierung würdig.

Gottlieb. Das Regieren, Hinze, ist eine curiose Sache.
Mir ist heiß und kalt dabei geworden.

König. Empfangen Sie nun die Hand meiner Tochter.

Prinzessin. Wie glücklich bin ich!

Gottlieb. Ich ebenfalls. — Mein König, ich wünschte nun
auch meinen Diener zu belohnen.

König. Allerdings; ich erhebe ihn hiermit in den Adelstand.
Er hängt dem Kater einen Orden um. Wie heißt er eigentlich?

Gottlieb. Hinze; seiner Geburt nach ist er nur aus einer
geringen Familie, aber seine Verdienste erheben ihn.

Leander tritt schnell herein. Platz! Platz! Er drängt sich durch.
Ich bin mit Extrapost nachgereis't, um meiner anbetungswürdigen
Prinzessin und ihrem Herrn Gemahl Glück zu wünschen. Er tritt
vor, verbeugt sich gegen das Publikum.

Vollendet ist die That, trotz thät'gen Tatzen
Der Bosheit glänzt sie in der Weltgeschichten
Jahrhunderten, die nach Verdiensten richten;
Wenn dann vergessen sind hochprahl'nde Fratzen,

Die oft im stolzen Dünkel gleichsam platzen:
Dann tönt im Lied, in lieblichen Gedichten
Von schönen Lippen noch das Lob der schlichten
Schmeich'lhaften, stillen, duldungsreichen Katzen.

Der große Hinz hat sein Geschlecht geadelt,
Er achtet nicht an Bein und Kopf der Wunden,
Nicht Popanz, Ungethüm, die ihn angrinzen.

Wenn Unbill nun das Katzgeschlecht blöd tadelt,
Irrwähnend Vorzug geben möchte Hunden, —
Man widerlegt nicht, — nein! — nennt Ihr nur — Hinzen!
Lautes allgemeines Pochen, der Vorhang fällt.

Epilog.

Der König tritt hinter dem Vorhang hervor. Morgen werden wir
die Ehre haben, die heutige Vorstellung zu wiederholen.

Fischer. Welche Unverschämtheit! Alles pocht.

König geräth in Confusion, geht zurück und kömmt dann wieder. Morgen! — Allzuscharf macht schartig.

Alle. Ja wohl! ja wohl! — Applaudiren, der König geht ab.

Man schreit: Die letzte Decoration!. Die
letzte Decoration!

Hinter dem Vorhange. Wahrhaftig! Da wird die
Decoration hervorgerufen! Der Vorhang geht auf, das Theater ist leer,
man sieht nur die Decoration.

Hanswurst tritt mit Verbeugungen hervor. Verzeihen Sie, daß
ich so frei bin, mich im Namen der Decoration zu bedanken; es
ist nicht mehr als Schuldigkeit, wenn die Decoration nur halbweg
höflich ist. Sie wird sich bemühen, auch künftig den Beifall eines
erleuchteten Publikums zu verdienen; daher wird sie es gewiß we=
der an Lampen, noch an den nöthigen Verzierungen fehlen lassen,
denn der Beifall einer solchen Versammlung wird sie so — so —
so anfeuern, — o Sie sehn ja, sie ist vor Thränen so gerührt, daß
sie nicht weiter sprechen kann. — Er geht schnell ab und trocknet sich die
Augen, einige im Parterre weinen, die Decoration wird weggenommen, man sieht
die kahlen Wände des Theaters, die Leute fangen an fortzugehn; der Souffleur
steigt aus seinem Kasten; — der Dichter erscheint demüthig auf der Bühne.

Dichter. Ich bin noch einmal so frei —

Fischer. Sind Sie auch noch da?

Müller. Sie sollten doch ja nach Hause gegangen seyn.

Dichter. Nur noch ein paar Worte mit Ihrer gütigen Er=
laubniß! Mein Stück ist durchgefallen —

Fischer. Wem sagen Sie denn das?

Müller. Wir haben's bemerkt.

Dichter. Die Schuld liegt vielleicht nicht ganz an mir —

Müller. An wem denn sonst, daß wir hier einen würdigen
jungen Mann gebunden halten müssen, der sonst wie ein Rasender
um sich schlägt? Wer hat denn sonst wohl Schuld, als Sie, daß
wir alle confuse im Kopfe sind?

Schlosser. Erleuchteter Mann! nicht wahr, Ihr hohes

Schauspiel ist eine mystische Theorie und Offenbarung über die Natur der Liebe?

Dichter. Daß ich nicht wüßte; ich wollte nur den Versuch machen, Sie alle in die entfernten Empfindungen Ihrer Kinderjahre zurück zu versetzen, daß sie dadurch das dargestellte Märchen empfunden hätten, ohne es doch für etwas Wichtigeres zu halten, als es seyn sollte.

Leutner. Das geht nicht so leicht, mein guter Mann.

Dichter. Sie hätten dann freilich Ihre ganze Ausbildung auf zwei Stunden beiseit legen müssen. —

Fischer. Wie ist denn das möglich?

Dichter. Ihre Kenntnisse vergessen —

Müller. Warum nicht gar!

Dichter. Eben so, was sie in Journalen gethan haben.

Müller. Seht nur die Forderungen!

Dichter. Kurz, Sie hätten wieder zu Kindern werden müssen.

Fischer. Aber wir danken Gott, daß wir es nicht mehr sind.

Leutner. Unsere Ausbildung hat uns Mühe und Angstschweiß genug gekostet.

Man trommelt von Neuem.

Soufleur. Versuchen Sie ein paar Verse zu machen, Herr Dichter; vielleicht bekommen sie dann mehr Respect vor Ihnen.

Dichter. Vielleicht fällt mir eine Xenie ein.

Soufleur. Was ist das'?

Dichter. Eine neuerfundene Dichtungsart, die sich besser fühlen als beschreiben läßt.

Gegen das Parterre.

Publikum, soll mich dein Urtheil nur einigermaßen belehren,
Zeig' erst, daß du mich nur einigermaßen verstehst.

Es wird aus dem Parterre mit verdorbenen Birnen und Aepfeln und zusammengerolltem Papier nach ihm geworfen.

Die Herren da unten sind mir in dieser Dichtungsart zu stark.

Müller. Kommen Sie, Herr Fischer und Herr Leutner, daß wir den Herrn Schlosser als ein Opfer der Kunst nach seinem Hause schleppen.

Schlosser, indem sie ihn fortschleppen. Zieht nur, wie Ihr wollt, Ihr gemeinen Seelen, das Licht der Liebe und der Wahrheit wird dennoch die Welt durchdringen.   Alle gehn ab.

Dichter. Ich gehe auch nach Hause.

Bötticher. St! St! Herr Poet!

Dichter. Was ist Ihnen gefällig?

Bötticher. Ich bin nicht unter Ihren Gegnern gewesen, aber das hinreißende Spiel des einzigen Mannes, welcher den tugendhaften Hinze dargestellt, hat mich ganz gehindert, die Kunst der dramatischen Composition ganz zu fassen, der ich aber auch ohne das gern ihr Recht widerfahren lasse; jetzt wollte ich nur fragen, ob dieser große Mensch noch auf dem Theater verweilt?

Dichter. Nein. Was wollten Sie aber mit ihm?

Bötticher. Nichts als ihn ein Weniges anbeten und seine Größe erläutern. — Reichen Sie mir doch gefälligst den Knebel dort her, den ich als ein Denkmal von der Barbarei meines Zeit= alters und unsrer Landsleute aufbewahren will.

Dichter. Hier.

Bötticher. Ich werde mich Ihrer Gefälligkeit immer mit Dankbarkeit erinnern. Geht ab.

Dichter. O du undankbares Jahrhundert!

Geht ab. Die wenigen, die noch im Theater waren, gehn nach Hause.

SELECTIONS

FROM THE

XENIA OF GOETHE AND SCHILLER.

INTRODUCTION.

THE composition of the Xenia being nearly synchronous with that of Tieck's polemic comedies, of which we have just exhibited a specimen, and their object being precisely the same (the schism between the Romantic and the Classical schools not having as yet become complete), it may not be deemed out of place to add here a selection from these epigrams, which at the time of their publication created so great a sensation in all the learned circles of Germany, and which were productive of such decisive effects on the taste and culture of the nation, that independently of their intrinsic merit, they have become inseparably interwoven with the literary history of that period.—In the language itself, from which these epigrams derive their name, the term is never applied to any sort of literary production whatsoever, its only signification being a present or pledge of friendship given by a guest to his host in return for his kindly hospitalities, or a memento presented by the latter to the former at the moment of departure from the friendly roof—a custom generally prevalent among the Greeks of the heroic age. Not unfrequently there was a mutual interchange of these gifts. The reader may at once surmise the motive, which induced the German poets to select this term to designate their new species of poetic composition.* Their Xenia were short epigrammatic monodistichs, of which the first line was a hexameter and the second a pentameter verse. In regard to their contents, they were partly of a serious, partly (and mostly) of a satyrico-polemic character. Their whole number amounts to about seven hundred, all of which made their first appearance in the 𝔐 u f e n a l m a n a ɕ edited by Schiller. They were composed after the manner of Martial, and at first intended as a defense of the 𝔥 o r e n, a literary monthly, likewise

---

*   MARTIAL.—(No. 155.)
Xenia are ye ycleped and come from the kitchen as presents:
Pray, is it custom with you hot Spanish pepper to eat?
                 XENIA—(No. 156).
No, not at all! But the many slip-slop dishes had weakened
So long the stomach, that now pepper and wormwood must help.

399

under the direction of Schiller. The poets, however, who in the midst of their own arduous labours could neither afford the time nor condescend to refute the many clamorous attacks of insignificant but no less venomous men, soon found these spicy presents an effectual method of repelling the assaults of their antagonists and of fortifying themselves in their own peculiar position. In regard to their authorship, there has recently been much dispute, they having been for the most part the joint product of both poets, and published in such a manner, that subsequently it became next to impossible for the authors themselves to recognize their own property. Nay some of them were even the work of both at once, one having written one verse, and the other the other; sometimes one invented the wit and the other gave it the form, and *vice versa*. From the correspondence between Goethe and Schiller and from an album-copy of the poems, formerly owned by Schiller's wife, it appears that only about one-half of these monodistichs can with any degree of certainty be assigned to their respective authors. They seem to have themselves desired to leave the matter forever problematical. Their honor is mutual and as inseparable as were the interests of their common cause. Goethe, however, makes somewhere the perhaps too modest confession, that Schiller's contributions were always cutting and *piquant*, while his own were generally harmless and more insignificant.

Both the poets were at the very outset of the opinion, that these poignant satires, which they were forced to write in defence of their own honor, should remain as free as possible from any thing like virulent malice or criminal inculpations : "the domain of good-natured humor," says Goethe, " should in this quarrel of ours be departed from as little as possible. We must remember that the Muses are no executioners. And yet we must not let these gentlemen escape without settling their scores with us."

The play-ground on which the Xenia perform their evolutions is of illimitable extent. Ascending up to the heavens, they sweep through the whole literary zodiac, halting and discharging a volley at every one of the signs of its constellations ; again alighting, their march advances through the whole extent of the German provinces, and their rivers are all remembered by the hospitable liberality of the visitors ; nay they at last descend to visit the lower regions even, and Dante-like pursue the shades of living and departed enemies beyond the Styx ! It is thus that no notable phenomenon, no characteristic trait of the age remains untouched, no folly and no literary vice unpunished. The leading periodicals of the day particularly, were, with few exceptions, subjected to a fiery ordeal (cf. Xenion No. 97), and the inept and invidious perversion of critical justice, which had so often annoyed the poets, was visited with a merited retribution. The Bibliothek der schönen Wissenschaften, edited by Weisse and Dyk (cf. No. 27, 28), the Reichsanzeiger, conducted by the Aulic counsellor Becker (No. 115, 134–138), the Urania of Ewald (No. 118), the Kalender der Musen und Grazien, edited by pastor Schmidt (No. 112), and more especially the Deutsche Bibliothek, conducted by the unfortunate Nicolai (No. 116), were all rewarded for their services to the cause of letters by suitable presents according to their several merits.

Among the living personalities, who were subjected to the united scourge of the Dioscuri of Weimar, the Berlin publisher Nicolai was prominent. He had some years before audaciously travestied Goethe's Werther, and was now making his journal the theatre of perpetual assaults on both the poets. He had also allowed himself a violent invective against the Horen in a book of travels, written about that time. These hints may serve to elucidate Xenia No. 43, 64, 65, 83–94, 102, 116.

The poignantly severe distichs on Manso's translation of Tasso and on his Kunst zu lieben, or "Art of loving" (No. 19–22) were likewise intended as a punishment for libellous assaults.

The musical composer and „Kapellmeister" Reichardt had formerly been on terms of friendly intercourse, with Goethe particularly. He was the first, who had set the poet's lyric compositions to music. His subsequent aggressive conduct, however, his political radicalism, and more especially his maliciously arrogant animadversion on one o Goethe's novels had rendered him obnoxious to the poets, who gave him No. 66–68, 104.

No. 53, 54 are directed against Stollberg, the younger, who had severely handled Schiller's Gods of Greece, and who in a preface to his translation of one of Plato's dialogues had inserted a Eulogy on Christ. No. 39 is against both the brothers Stollberg; it is a persiflage on their apostasy from protestantism.

Lavater's former friendly relations with Goethe could not save him from the castigation, which his theurgic reveries and his fanatic extravagancies so highly merited (No. 13, 14.).

The hyper-puristic ineptitudes of certain Grammarians and Lexicographers, the critical scepsis of certain philologists (e. g. of Heyne and Wolf with particular reference to the Homeric question) are likewise remembered by the hospitable hosts, and their presents to such are highly flavored dishes. Nor are the *niaiseries* of certain learned associations forgotten (No. 33, 63, 69, 80, 119, 124, 125.). The bookseller's advertisement (No. 128) is a persiflage on Spalding's book: " On the destiny of man."

Schlichtegroll the editor of the Nekrolog merkwürdiger verstorbener Deutschen is castigated for his many funeral puffs on insignificant men (No. 42, 79.)

The political Xenia were for the most part furnished by Goethe, but owing to their aristocratic tone, which was characteristic of the poet, and to a general lack of fire, they are not among the happiest. The same may be said of those directed against Newton's theory of light. Neither of these proceeded from that free and open humor which marks the rest (No. 72, 100, 101, 107, 108, 126.).

The person of the illustrious sage of Königsberg, whose writings were at that time producing a complete revolution in the philosophy of Europe is treated with deferential reverence by Schiller at least, who himself was at one time profoundly interested in the grand problems propounded by that school (especially as regards the moral and æsthetical part of the critical philosophy); but the numerous disciples and inept expounders of the new system are handled without gloves, as are also those who, in the opinion of the poet, attempted to bring about a premature union between a priori speculation and the results of the particular physical sciences founded on observation and experiment. In several of his epigrams on academic men and methods, Schiller brings out the light and humorous side of the profession, of which he himself was then a member and an ornament (No. 17, 30–38, 73–76, 81, 82, 108, 109, 128, 130, 160–164.).

The friendly and laudatory Xenia are but scantily interspersed among those of a satiric and hostile character. Lessing appears as Achilles in the lower world, and again as Tiresias in connection with the shade of Shakespeare, the Hercules of the poetic art (No. 146–150, 178.). Voss is called the noble Eutinean Lion in the Zodiac (No. 40.); his Louise and his spirited imitations of the Ancients are highly lauded (No. 58.), but his Almanach is censured (No. 113.). Wieland is gently reprimanded for the elegantly polished, but too elaborate and drawling structure of the periods of his prose (No. 41, 122.).

The arrangement of the Xenia is on the whole incoherent, as might be expected from the nature of the epigram. Nevertheless there are several groups of them, relating to one and the same subject and bearing a common superscription. Thus the group entitled "The Philosophers" (composed of nineteen Xenia) was originally a dialogue in the lower world in the style of Lucian, wherein the shades of Aristoteles, of Des Cartes, Spinoza, Berkley, Leibnitz, Hume, Puffendorf, Kant and Fichte once more successively appear in defense of their several systems (No. 160–174.).

The Jeremiaden of ten distichs were a persiflage on the tone of a certain journal, the Reichsanzeiger conducted by Becker (No. 134–138,). The literary Zodiac consisted of twenty three, the Rivers of sixteen monodistichs.

Like the Philosophers there is yet another group of thirty-nine Xenia, which constitutes another scene in the lower world. The shade of Lessing appears under the name of Achilles (No. 146–156.) for the purpose of enquiring into the progress of literature since his exit from life. Ajax, Tantalos, Agamemnon, Sisyphos (who likewise represent certain literary celebrities in disguise), Lucian, Martial, Sulzer, Haller, Mendelsohn, and even young Werther are prominent among the interlocutors of the motley crowd. Five epigrams entitled the "Rhapsodists" (No. 157—159.) are a parody on the homeric question, as treated by Heyne and Wolf. The poet in a third scene encounters at last the shade of Shakespeare, the "powerful Hercules" of the dramatic muse. He informs the hero, that he had once more been obliged to descend into Hades for the purpose of consulting the prophet Tiresias (i. e. Lessing) on the subject of Taste, which had recently vanished from the earth, and then proceeds to give the venerable bard an account of the present state of dramatic literature in Germany, and complains of the lamentable degeneracy of his noble art (No. 175–188.). This dialogue concludes the collection. The Muse interposing her authority commands the Xenia to pause ; at the same time assuring the suitors (as she homerically terms the combattants), that all this warfare was but sport, that they were still alive and that the bow and a place for honorable manly contest was awaiting their command! (No. 189. 190.)

From this succinct account of the origin and intent of this novel species of satiric epigrams, and from the specimens which I have selected for this volume, the Reader may readily infer the nature and extent of their effect on those for whose special benefit they were composed. The devastation produced by these "incendiary foxes," which the poets had sent into the land of the Philistines, was immense. The conflagration was universal. Says a distinguished contemporary : "I well remember that time and may say without exaggeration that from November, 1796, till about Easter of 1797 the mania for the Xenia was so great, that they absorbed completely the interest of the reading public to the exclusion of all other literary productions."* Of the wondering and guessing in all the doubtful allusions, of the bitter mortifications, the angry and clamorous retorts in journals and pamphlets, anonymous and avowed, there was no end, and the full elucidation of these poems would now be a matter of no little difficulty.

The contest, however, ended greatly to the advantage of the poets. Indeed, most of their antogonists were incapable of coping with them even in the field of parody and satire, and many of them spoiled their cause by the grossest violations of moral decency. Goethe and Schiller had, moreover, now clearly defined the *negative* side of their position. They had indicated, what they did *not* want. The positive ground, which they occupied, the goal for which they strove, while they avoided the rocks, on which their enemies were making perpetual shipwreck, is

* Franz Horn.

set forth in a smaller collection of more general epigrams, entitled *Tabulæ Votivæ*. These, as will be remembered, were tables of inscriptions containing accounts of deliverance from sickness, shipwreck and other perils, which the ancient Romans were wont to offer to the gods as tokens of a pious gratitude. That the poets were animated by similar motives may be inferred from the introductory distich :

> That which the god hath taught me, which helped me in life through,
> Grateful, in sacred place I suspend here, with pious intent.

These are the *Aurea Carmina*, the golden maxims of the poets, wherein with terse conciseness they lay down their own method of looking at nature and at life, in opposition to the perverse methods and the scholastic formalism of certain men of science on the one hand, and to the turgid and lazy mysticism of certain religionists on the other; revealing now with some sudden flash of light the principles of their own poetic art, and then again unfolding with philosophic calmness the secret workings of our inner moral nature, or propounding general lessons of wisdom for the proper regulation of the heart and life. Of these impersonal and more general epigrams, there are in fact three different collections, arranged by the poets themselves and published among their minor poems.

The first and most extensive bore the superscription already named : Die Botivtafeln. Of the two smaller groups the first bears the title Die Bielen and the second Einer. Goethe has collected a wreath of these Xenia in his Jahreszeiten. Most of these had also originally been composed for the Musenalmanach, and it is equally impossible to determine their authorship with any degree of certainty. A selection from them may be found in their various new combinations among the lyric poems of Goethe and Schiller, to which the Reader is referred. The few specimens at the close of this collection will suffice to give some idea of their character. The general metrical formula of the epigram runs thus :

Xenien

von

J. W. v. Goethe und Fr. Schiller.

1. Der ästhetische Thorschreiber.

Halt, Passagiere! Wer seyd ihr? Weß Stands und Characters?
Niemand passiret hier durch, bis er den Paß mir gezeigt.

2. Xenien.

Distichen sind wir. Wir geben uns nicht für mehr noch für minder,
Sperre du immer, wir ziehn über den Schlagbaum hinweg.

3. Der Mann mit dem Klingelbeutel.

Messieurs! Es ist der Gebrauch, wer diese Straße bereiset,
Legt für die Dummen was, für die Gebrechlichen, ein.

4. Helf Gott.

Das verwünschte Gebettel! Es haben die vorderen Kutschen
Reichlich für uns mit bezahlt. Geben nichts. Kutscher, fahr' zu!

5. Der Glückstopf.

Hier ist Messe, geschwind, packt aus und schmücket die Bude,
Kommt, Autoren, und zieht, jeder versuche sein Glück.

6. Die Kunden.

Wenige Treffer sind gewöhnlich in solchen Boutiquen,
Doch die Hoffnung treibt frisch und die Neugier herbei.

7. Das Desideratum.

Hättest du Phantasie, und Witz und Empfindung und Urtheil,
Wahrlich, dir fehlte nicht viel, Wieland und Lessing zu seyn!

8. An einen gewissen moralischen Dichter.

Ja der Mensch ist ein ärmlicher Wicht, ich weiß — doch das wollt ich
Eben vergessen, und kam, ach wie gereut mich's, zu dir.

9. Das Verbindungsmittel.

Wie verfährt die Natur um Hohes und Niedres im Menschen
Zu verbinden? Sie stellt Eitelkeit zwischen hinein.

10. Der Kunstgriff.

Wollt ihr zugleich den Kindern der Welt und den Frommen gefallen?
  Malet die Wollust — nur malet den Teufel dazu.

11. Der Teleolog.

Welche Verehrung verdient der Weltenschöpfer, der gnädig,
  Als er den Korkbaum schuf, gleich auch die Stöpsel erfand!

12. Erreurs et Verité.

Irrthum wolltest du bringen und Wahrheit, o Bote, von Wandsbeck;
  Wahrheit, sie war dir zu schwer; Irrthum, den brachtest du fort!

13. Der Prophet.

Schade, daß die Natur nur einen Menschen aus dir schuf,
  Denn zum würdigen Mann war und zum Schelmen der Stoff.

14. Der erhabene Stoff.

Deine Muse besingt, wie Gott sich der Menschen erbarmte,
  Aber ist das Poesie, daß er erbärmlich sie fand?

15. Neueste Schule.

Ehemals hatte man Einen Geschmack. Nun giebt es Geschmäcke.
  Aber sagt mir, wo sitzt dieser Geschmäcke Geschmack?

16. Zur Abwechslung.

Einige steigen als leuchtende Kugeln und Andere zünden,
  Manche auch werfen wir nur spielend, das Aug' zu erfreun.

17. Der Zeitpunkt.

Eine große Epoche hat das Jahrhundert geboren,
  Aber der große Moment findet ein kleines Geschlecht.

18. Goldnes Zeitalter.

Ob die Menschen im Ganzen sich bessern? ich glaub' es, denn einzeln
  Suche man, wie man auch will, sieht man doch gar nichts davon.

19. Manso von den Grazien.

Heren lassen sich wohl durch schlechte Sprüche citiren,
  Aber die Grazie kommt nur auf der Grazie Ruf.

20. Tasso's Jerusalem von demselben.

Ein asphaltischer Sumpf bezeichnet hier noch die Stätte,
  Wo Jerusalem stand, das uns Torquato besang.

21. Die Kunst zu lieben.

Auch zum Lieben bedarfst du der Kunst? Unglücklicher Manso,
  Daß die Natur auch nichts, gar nichts für dich noch gethan!

22. Der zweite Ovid.

Armer Naso, hätteſt du doch wie Manſo geſchrieben,
Nimmer, du guter Geſell, hätteſt du Tomi geſehn.

23. Jean Paul Richter.

Hielteſt du deinen Reichthum nur halb ſo zu Rathe, wie jener
Seine Armuth, du wärſt unſrer Bewundrung werth.

24. An ſeinen Lobredner.

Meinſt du, er werde größer, wenn du die Schulter ihm leiheſt?
Er bleibt klein wie zuvor, du haſt den Höcker davon.

25. Feindlicher Einfall.

Fort ins Land der Philiſter, ihr Füchſe mit brennenden Schwänzen!
Und verderbet der Herrn reife papierene Saat.

26. Nekrolog.

Unter Allen, die von uns berichten, biſt du mir der liebſte:
Wer ſich lieſet in dir, lieſ't dich zum Glücke nicht mehr.

27. Bibliothek der ſchönen Wiſſenſchaften.

Jahre lang ſchöpfen wir ſchon in das Sieb und brüten den Stein aus,
Aber der Stein wird nicht warm, aber das Sieb wird nicht voll.

28. Dieſelbe.

Invaliden Poeten iſt dieſer Spittel geſtiftet,
Gicht und Waſſerſucht wird hier von der Schwindſucht gepflegt.

29. Die neueſten Geſchmacksrichter.

Dichter, ihr armen, was müßt ihr nicht Alles hören, damit nur
Sein Exercitium ſchnell leſe gedruckt der Student!

30. Kant und ſeine Ausleger.

Wie doch ein einziger Reicher ſo viele Bettler in Nahrung
Setzt! Wenn die Könige baun, haben die Kärrner zu thun.

31. Die Stockblinden.

Blinde, weiß ich wohl, fühlen und Taube ſehen viel ſchärfer,
Aber mit welchem Organ philoſophirt denn das Volk?

32. Analytiker.

Iſt denn die Wahrheit ein' Zwiebel, von dem man die Häute nur abſchält?
Was ihr hinein nicht gelegt, ziehet ihr nimmer heraus.

33. Der Geiſt und der Buchſtabe.

Lange kann man mit Marken, mit Rechenpfennigen zahlen,
Endlich, es hilft nichts, ihr Herrn, muß man den Beutel doch ziehn.

34. Wissenschaftliches Genie.

Wird der Poet nur geboren? Der Philosoph wird's nicht minder,
　Alle Wahrheit zuletzt wird nur gebildet, geschaut.

35. Wissenschaft.

Einem ist sie die hohe, die himmlische Göttin, dem Andern
　Eine tüchtige Kuh, die ihn mit Butter versorgt.

36. Der kurzweilige Philosoph.

Eine spaßhafte Weisheit docirt hier ein lustiger Doctor,
　Bloß dem Namen nach Ernst, und in dem lustigsten Saal.

37. Verfehlter Beruf.

Schade, daß ein Talent hier auf dem Katheder verhallet,
　Das auf höherm Gerüst hätte zu glänzen verdient.

38. Das philosophische Gespräch.

Einer, das höret man wohl, spricht nach dem Andern, doch Keiner
　Mit dem Andern: wer nennt zwei Monologe Gespräch?

39. Zeichen der Zwillinge.

Kommt ihr den Zwillingen nah, so sprecht nur: Gelobet sey J —
　C — !* „In Ewigkeit," giebt man zum Gruß euch zurück.

40. Zeichen des Löwen.

Jetzo nehmt euch in Acht vor dem wackern Eutinischen Leuen,
　Daß er mit griechischem Zahn euch nicht verwunde den Fuß.

41. Zeichen der Jungfrau.

Bückt euch, wie sich's geziemt, vor der zierlichen Jungfrau zu Weimar,
　Schmollt sie auch oft — wer verzeiht Launen der Grazie nicht?

42. Zeichen des Raben.

Vor dem Raben nur sehet euch vor, der hinter ihr krächzet,
　Das nekrologische Thier setzt auf Kadaver sich nur.

43. Zeichen des Steinbocks.

Im Vorbeigehn stutzt mir den alten Berlinischen Steinbock,
　Das verdrießt ihn, so giebt's etwas zu lachen für's Volk.

44. Wohlfeile Achtung.

Selten erhaben und groß und selten würdig der Liebe
　Lebt er doch immer, der Mensch, und wird geehrt und geliebt.

---

* „Gelobet sey Jesus Christus," is a general form of salutation among the Romanists; „in Ewigkeit" is the usual reply of the person saluted.

45. Revolutionen.

Was das Lutherthum war, ist jetzt das Franzthum in diesen
Letzten Tagen, es drängt ruhige Bildung zurück.

46. Partheigeist.

Wo Partheien entstehn, hält Jeder sich hüben und drüben,
Viele Jahre vergehn, eh' sie die Mitte vereint.

47. Das deutsche Reich.

Deutschland? aber wo liegt es? Ich weiß das Land nicht zu finden,
Wo das gelehrte beginnt, hört das politische auf.

48. Rhein.

Treu, wie dem Schweizer gebührt, bewach' ich Germaniens Grenze,
Aber der Gallier hüpft über den duldenden Strom.

49. Gesundbrunnen zu ***

Seltsames Land! Hier haben die Flüsse Geschmack und die Quellen,
Bei den Bewohnern allein hab' ich noch keinen verspürt.

50. Die **chen Flüsse.

Unser Einer hat's halter gut in **cher Herren
Ländern, ihr Joch ist sanft und ihre Lasten sind leicht.

51. Der anonyme Fluß.

Fastenspeisen dem Tisch des frommen Bischofs zu liefern,
Goß der Schöpfer mich aus durch das verhungerte Land.

52. Les fleuves indiscrets.

Jetzt kein Wort mehr, ihr Flüsse. Man sieht's, ihr wißt euch so wenig
Zu bescheiden, als einst Diderot's Schätzchen gethan.

53. Dialogen aus dem Griechischen.

Zur Erbauung andächtiger Seelen hat F*** S***
Graf und Poet und Christ diese Gespräche verdeutscht.

54. Der Ersatz.

Als du die griechischen Götter geschmäht, da warf dich Apollo
Von dem Parnasse: dafür gehst du ins Himmelreich ein.

55. Nachbildung der Natur.

Was nur Einer vermag, das sollte nur Einer uns schildern,
Voß nur den Pfarrer und nur Iffland den Förster allein.

56. Nachäffer.

Aber da meinen die Pfuscher, ein jeder Schwarzrock und Grünrock
Sei auch, an und für sich, unsrer Beschauung schon werth.

18

57. An die Moralisten.

Richtet den herrschenden Stab auf Leben und Handeln, und lasset
Amorn, dem lieblichen Gott, doch mit der Muse das Spiel!

58. Louise von Voß.

Wahrlich, es füllt mit Wonne das Herz, dem Gesange zu horchen,
Ahmt ein Sänger, wie der, Töne des Alterthums nach.

59. Jupiters Kette.

Hängen auch alle Schmierer und Reimer sich an dich, sie ziehen
Dich nicht hinunter, doch du ziehst sie auch schwerlich hinauf.

60. Aus einer der neuesten Episteln.

Klopstock, der ist mein Mann, der in neue Phrasen gestoßen,
Was er im höllischen Pfuhl Hohes und Großes vernahm.

61. Ein deutsches Meisterstück.

Alles an diesem Gedicht ist vollkommen, Sprache, Gedanke,
Rhythmus, das Einzige nur fehlt noch, es ist kein Gedicht.

62. Beispielsammlung.

Nicht bloß Beipielsammlung, nein, selber ein warnendes Beispiel,
Wie man nimmermehr soll sammeln für guten Geschmack.

63. Der Sprachforscher.

Anatomiren machst du die Sprache, doch nur ihr Cadaver,
Geist und Leben entschlüpft flüchtig dem groben Scalpell.

64. Geschichte eines dicken Mannes.

(Man sehe die Recension davon in der N. deutschen Bibliothek).

Dieses Werk ist durchaus nicht in Gesellschaft zu lesen,
Da es, wie Recensent rühmet, die Blähungen treibt.

65. Literaturbriefe.

Auch Nicolai schrieb an dem trefflichen Werk? Ich will's glauben,
Mancher Gemeinplatz steht in dem trefflichen Werk.

66. Gewisse Melodien.

Dies ist Musik für's Denken! So lang' man sie hört, bleibt man eiskalt,
Vier, fünf Stunden darauf macht sie erst rechten Effect.

67. Ueberschriften dazu.

Frostig und herzlos ist der Gesang, doch Sänger und Spieler
Werden oben am Rand höflich zu fühlen ersucht.

68. Der böse Geselle.

Dichter, bitte die Musen, vor ihm dein Lied zu bewahren,
Auch dein leichtestes zieht nieder der schwere Gesang.

69. Der Purist.

Sinnreich bist du, die Sprache von fremden Wörtern zu säubern,
  Nun, so sage doch, Freund, wie man Pedant uns verdeutscht.

70. An **.

Gerne plagt' ich auch dich, doch es will mir mit dir nicht gelingen,
  Du bist zum Ernst mir zu leicht, bist für den Scherz mir zu plump.

71. An ***.

Nein! Du erbittest mich nicht. Du hörtest dich gerne verspottet,
  Hörtest du dich nur genannt, darum verschon' ich dich, Freund.

72. Stoßgebet.

Vor dem Aristokraten in Lumpen bewahrt mich, ihr Götter,
  Und vor dem Sansculott auch mit Epauletten und Stern.

73. Triumph der Schule.

Welch erhabner Gedanke! Uns lehrt der unsterbliche Meister,
  Künstlich zu theilen den Strahl, den wir nur einfach gekannt.

74. Die Möglichkeit.

Liegt der Irrthum nur erst, wie ein Grundstein, unten im Boden,
  Immer baut man darauf, nimmermehr kömmt er an Tag.

75. Wiederholung.

Hundertmal werd' ich's euch sagen und tausendmal: Irrthum ist Irrthum!
  Ob ihn der größte Mann, ob ihn der kleinste beging.

76. Wer glaubt's?

Newton hat sich geirrt? ja, doppelt und dreifach! und wie denn?
  Lange steht es gedruckt, aber es liest es kein Mensch.

77. Der Widerstand.

Aristokratisch gesinnt ist mancher Gelehrte, denn gleich ist's,
  Ob man auf Helm und Schild oder auf Meinungen ruht.

78. Moralische Zwecke der Poesie.

„Bessern, bessern soll uns der Dichter!" So darf denn auf eurem
  Rücken des Büttels Stock nicht einen Augenblick ruhn?

79. Sections-Wuth.

Lebend noch exenteriren sie euch, und seid ihr gestorben,
  Passet im Nekrolog noch ein Prosector euch auf.

80. Kritische Studien.

Schneidet, schneidet, ihr Herrn, durch Schneiden lernet der Schüler,
  Aber wehe dem Frosch, der euch den Schenkel muß leihn!

81. Der astronomische Himmel.
So erhaben, so groß ist, so weit entlegen der Himmel!
　　Aber der Kleinigkeitsgeist fand auch bis dahin den Weg.

82. Naturforscher und Transscendental=Philo=
sophen.
Feindschaft sey zwischen euch, noch kommt das Bündniß zu frühe,
　　Wenn ihr im Suchen euch trennt, wird erst die Wahrheit erkannt.

83. Nicolai.
Nicolai reiset noch immer, noch lang wird er reisen,
　　Aber in's Land der Vernunft findet er nimmer den Weg.

84. Der Wichtige.
Seine Meinung sagt er von seinem Jahrhundert, er sagt sie,
　　Nochmals sagt er sie laut, hat sie gesagt und geht ab.

85. Der Plan des Werks.
Meine Reis' ist ein Faden, an dem ich drei Lustra die Deutschen
　　Nützlich führe, so wie formlos die Form mir's gebeut.

86. Der Todfeind.
Willst du Alles vertilgen, was deiner Natur nicht gemäß ist,
　　Nicolai, zuerst schwöre dem Schönen den Tod!

87. Philosophische Querköpfe.
Querkopf! schreiet ergrimmt in unsere Wälder Herr Nickel,
　　Leerkopf! schallt es darauf lustig zum Walde heraus.

88. Empirischer Querkopf.
Armer empirischer Teufel! du kennst nicht einmal das Dumme
　　In dir selber, es ist, ach! a priori so dumm.

89. Der Quellenforscher.
Nicolai entdeckt die Quellen der Donau! Welch Wunder!
　　Sieht er gewöhnlich doch sich nach der Quelle nicht um

90. Derselbe.
Nichts kann er leiden, was groß ist und mächtig. drum, herrliche Donau,
　　Spürt dir der Häscher so lang' nach, bis er seicht dich ertappt.

91. N. Reisen, XI. Band, S. 177.
A propos Tübingen! Dort sind Mädchen, die tragen die Zöpfe
　　Lang geflochten, auch dort giebt man die Horen heraus.

92. Der Glückliche.
Sehen möcht' ich dich, Nickel, wenn du ein Späßchen erhaschest,
　　Und, von dem Fund entzückt, drauf dich im Spiegel bestehst

93. Pfahl im Fleisch.

Nenne Leſſing nur nicht, der Gute hat Vieles gelitten,
Und in des Märtyrers Kranz warſt du ein ſchrecklicher Dorn.

94. Fichte und Er. (Sc. Nicolai).

Freilich tauchet der Mann kühn in die Tiefe des Meeres,
Wenn du, auf leichtem Kahn ſchwankeſt und Heringe fängſt.

95. Das grobe Organ.

Was du mit Händen nicht greifſt, das ſcheint dir Blinden ein Unding,
Und betaſteſt du was, gleich iſt das Ding auch beſchmutzt.

96. Vorſatz.

Den Philiſter verdrieße, den Schwärmer necke, den Heuchler
Quäle der fröhliche Vers, der nur das Gute verehrt.

97. Nur Zeitſchriften.

Frankreich faßt er mit einer, das arme Deutſchland gewaltig
Mit der andern, doch ſind beide papieren und leicht!

98. Das Motto.

Wahrheit ſag' ich euch, Wahrheit und immer Wahrheit, verſteht ſich:
Meine Wahrheit; denn ſonſt iſt mir auch keine bekannt.

99. Der Wächter Zions.

Meine Wahrheit beſteht im Bellen, beſonders wenn irgend
Wohlgekleidet ein Mann ſich auf der Straße mir zeigt.

100. Verſchiedene Dreſſuren.

Ariſtokratiſche Hunde, ſie knurren auf Bettler, ein ächter
Demokratiſcher Spitz klafft nach dem ſeidenen Strumpf.

101. Böſe Geſellſchaft.

Ariſtokraten mögen noch gehn, ihr Stolz iſt doch höflich
Aber du, löbliches Volk, biſt ſo voll Hochmuth und grob.

102. Verdienſt.

Haſt du auch wenig genug verdient um die Bildung der Deutſchen
Fritz Nicolai, ſehr viel haſt du dabei doch verdient.

103. Der Halbvogel.

Fliegen möchte der Strauß, allein er rudert vergeblich,
Ungeſchickt rühret der Fuß immer den leidigen Sand.

104. Kunſtgriff.

Schreib die Journale nur anonym, ſo kannſt du mit vollen
Backen deine Muſik loben, es merkt es kein Menſch.

105. Das züchtige Herz.
Gern erlaffen wir dir die moralifche Delicateffe,
  Wenn du die zehen Gebot' nur fo nothdürftig befolgft.

106. Abfcheu.
Heuchler, ferne von mir! Befonders du widriger Heuchler,
  Der du mit Grobheit glaubft Falfchheit zu decken und Lift.

107. Der Patriot.
Daß Verfaffung fich überall bilde! Wie fehr ift's zu wünfchen,
  Aber ihr Schwätzer verhelft uns zu Verfaffungen nicht!

108. Die drei Stände.
Sagt, wo fteht in Deutfchland der Sansculott? In der Mitte,
  Unten und oben befitzt Jeglicher, was ihm behagt.

109. Einladung.
„Glaubft du denn nicht, man könnte die fchwache Seite dir zeigen?"
  Thu' es mit Laune, mit Geift, Freund, und wir lachen zuerft.

110. An die Philifter.
Freut euch des Schmetterlings nicht, der Böfewicht zeugt euch die Raupe,
  Die euch den herrlichen Kohl, faft aus der Schüffel, verzehrt.

111. Hausrecht.
Keinem Gärtner verdenk' ich's, daß er die Sperlinge fcheuchet,
  Doch nur Gärtner ift er, jene gebar die Natur.

112. Kalender der Mufen und Grazien.
Mufen und Grazien! oft habt ihr euch fchrecklich verirret,
  Doch dem Pfarrer noch nie felbft die Perücke gebracht.

113. Voffens Almanach.
Immer zu, du redlicher Voß! Beim neuen Kalender
  Nenne der Deutfche dich doch, der dich im Jahre vergißt.

114. Das Journal Deutfchland.
Alles beginnt der Deutfche mit Feierlichkeit und fo zieht auch
  Diefem deutfchen Journal blafend ein Spielmann voran.

115. Reichsanzeiger.
Edles Organ, durch welches das deutfche Reich mit fich felbft fpricht,
  Geiftreich, fo wie es hinein fchallet, fo fchallt es heraus.

116. A. D. B.*
Zehnmal gelefne Gedanken auf zehnmal bedrucktem Papiere,
  Auf zerriebenem Blei ftumpfer und bleierner Witz.

* A. D. B. stands for Allgemeine Deutfche Bibliothek, the periodical edited
by Nicolai. Cf. p. 401.

117. Deutsche Monatschrift.

Deutsch in Künsten gewöhnlich heißt mittelmäßig! und bist du,
Deutscher Monat, vielleicht auch so ein deutsches Product?

118. Urania.

Deinen heiligen Namen kann nichts entehren, und wenn ihn
Auf sein Sudelgefäß Ewald, der frömmelnde, schreibt.

119. Der Wolfische Homer.

Sieben Städte zanken sich drum, ihn geboren zu haben,
Nun, da der Wolf ihn zerriß, nehme sich jede ihr Stück.

120. M***.

Weil du doch Alles beschreibst, so beschreib' uns zu gutem Beschluffe
Auch die Maschine noch, die dich so fertig bedient.

121. Menschenhaß und Reue.

Menschenhaß? Nein, davon verspürt' ich beim heutigen Stücke
Keine Regung, jedoch Reue, die hab' ich gefühlt.

122. Zum Geburtstag.

Möge dein Lebensfaden sich spinnen, wie in der Prosa
Dein' Periode, bei dem leider die Lachesis schläft.

123. Verleger von P** Schriften.

Eine Maschine besitz' ich, die selber denkt, was sie drucket,
Obengenanntes Werk zeig' ich zur Probe hier vor.

124. Preisfrage der Akademie nützlicher Wissenschaften.

Wie auf dem Ü fortan der theure Schnörkel zu sparen?
Auf die Antwort sind dreißig Ducaten gesetzt.

125. G. G.*

Jeder, siehst du ihn einzeln, ist leiblich klug und verständig,
Sind sie in Corpore, gleich wird dir ein Dummkopf daraus.

126. Hörsäle auf gewissen Universitäten.

Prinzen und Grafen sind hier von den übrigen Hörern gesondert,
Wohl! Denn trennte der Stand nirgends, er trennte doch hier.

127. Sachen, so gesucht werden.

Einen Bedienten wünscht man zu haben, der leserlich schreibet
Und orthographisch, jedoch nichts in Bell-Letters gethan.

* G. G. = Gelehrte Gesellschaften.

128. Buchhändler-Anzeige.

Nichts ist der Menschheit so wichtig, als ihre Bestimmung zu kennen;
  Um zwölf Groschen Courant wird sie bei mir jetzt verkauft.

129. Auction.

Da die Metaphysik vor Kurzem unbeerbt abging,
  Werden die Dinge an sich* morgen sub hasta verkauft.

130. Sachen, so gestohlen worden.

(Immanuel Kant spricht:)

Zwanzig Begriffe wurden mir neulich diebisch entwendet,
  Leicht sind sie kenntlich, es steht sauber mein I. K. darauf.

131. Professor Historiarum.

Breiter wird immer die Welt und immer mehr Neues geschiehet,
  Ach! die Geschichte wird stets länger und kürzer das Brod!

132. Recension.

Sehet, wie artig der Frosch nicht hüpft! Doch sind' ich die hintern
  Füße um Vieles zu lang, so wie die vordern zu kurz.

133. Literarischer Adreßcalender.

Jeder treibe sein Handwerk, doch immer steh' es geschrieben:
  Dies ist das Handwerk, und der treibet das Handwerk geschickt.

134. Chorus.

Alles in Deutschland hat sich in Prosa und Versen verschlimmert,
  Ach! und hinter uns liegt weit schon die goldene Zeit.

135. Böse Zeiten.

Philosophen verderben die Sprache, Poeten die Logik,
  Und mit dem Menschenverstand kommt man durch's Leben nicht mehr.

136. Scandal.

Aus der Aesthetik, wohin sie gehört, verjagt man die Tugend,
  Jagt sie, den lästigen Gast, in die Politik hinein.

137. Das goldene Alter.

Schöne Naivetät der Stubenmädchen zu Leipzig,
  Komm doch wieder, o komm! witzige Einfalt, zurück!

138. Deutliche Prosa.

Alte Prosa komm wieder, die Alles so ehrlich heraussagt,
  Was sie denkt und gedacht, auch was der Leser sich denkt.

* The term Ding an sich, *thing or object per se*, i. e. substance, the substratum of the phenomena of experience, is a term frequently employed by Kant.

139. Die zwei Fieber.

Kaum hat das kalte Fieber der Gallomanie uns verlassen,
  Bricht in der Gräcomanie gar noch ein hitziges aus.

140. Griechheit.

Griechheit, was war sie? Verstand und Maaß und Klarheit! drum
dächt' ich,
  Etwas Geduld noch, ihr Herrn, eh' ihr von Griechheit uns sprecht.

141. Entgegengesetzte Wirkung.

Wir Modernen, wir gehn erschüttert, gerührt aus dem Schauspiel,
  Mit erleichterter Brust hüpfte der Grieche heraus.

142. Die höchste Harmonie.

Oedipus reißt die Augen sich aus, Jokasta erhenkt sich,
  Beide schuldlos; das Stück hat sich harmonisch gelöst.

143. Geschwindschreiber.

Was sie gestern gelernt, das wollen sie heute schon lehren
  Ach! was haben die Herrn doch für ein kurzes Gedärm!

144. Die Sonntagskinder.

Jahre lang bildet der Meister und kann sich nimmer genug thun,
  Dem genialen Geschlecht wird es im Traume bescheert!

145. Acheronta movebo.

Hölle, jetzt nimm dich in Acht, es kommt ein Reisebeschreiber,
  Und die Publicität deckt auch den Acheron auf.

146. Achilles.*

Vormals im Leben ehrten wir dich, wie einen der Götter,
  Nun du todt bist, so herrscht über die Geister dein Geist.

147. Trost.

Laß dich den Tod nicht reuen, Achill. Es lebet dein Name
  In der Bibliothek schöner Scientien-hoch.

148. Seine Antwort.

Lieber möcht' ich fürwahr dem Aermsten als Ackerknecht dienen,
  Als des Gänsegeschlechts Führer seyn, wie du erzählst.

149. Frage.

Du verkündige mir von meinen jungen Nepoten,
  Ob in der Literatur beide noch walten und wie?

* Achilles, i. e. Lessing. See p. 402.

18*

150. Antwort.

Freilich walten sie noch und bedrängen hart die Trojaner,
  Schießen manchmal wohl blind in das Blaue hinein.

151. Sisyphus.

Auch noch hier nicht zur Ruh', du Unglücksel'ger! Noch immer
  Rollst du Bergauf wie einst, da du regiertest, den Stein!

152. Dioscuren.

Einen wenigstens hofft' ich von euch hier unten zu finden,
  Aber beide sebt ihr sterblich, drum lebt ihr zugleich.

153. Unvermuthete Zusammenkunft.

Sage, Freund, wie find' ich denn dich in des Todes Behausung,
  Ließ ich doch frisch und gesund dich in Berlin noch zurück?

154. Der Leichnam.

Ach, das ist nur mein Leib, der in Almanachen noch umgeht,
  Aber es schiffte schon längst über den Lethe der Geist.

155. Martial.

Xenien nennet ihr euch? Ihr gebt euch für Küchenpräsente?
  Ißt man denn, mit Vergunst, spanischen Pfeffer bei euch?

156. Xenien.

Nicht doch! Aber es schwächten die vielen wäsfrigten Speisen
  So den Magen, daß jetzt Pfeffer und Wermuth nur hilft.

157. Rhapsoden.

Wer von euch ist der Sänger der Ilias? Weil's ihm so gut schmeckt,
  Ist hier von Heynen ein Pack Göttinger Würste für ihn.

158. Viele Stimmen.

Mir her, ich sang der Könige Zwist! Ich die Schlacht bei den Schiffen,
  Mir die Würste! ich sang, was auf dem Ida geschah!

159. Rechnungsfehler.

Friede! Zerreißt mich nur nicht! die Würste werden nicht reichen,
  Der sie schickte, er hat sich nur auf Einen versehn.

160. Philosophen.

Gut, daß ich euch, ihr Herren, in pleno beisammen hier finde,
  Denn das Eine, was noth, treibt mich herunter zu euch.

161. Aristoteles.

Gleich zur Sache, mein Freund. Wir halten die Jenaer Zeitung
  Hier in der Hölle und sind längst schon von Allem belehrt.

162. Dringend.

Desto besser! So gebt mir, ich geh' euch nicht eher vom Leibe,
  Einen allgültigen Satz, und der auch allgemein gilt.

163. Einer aus dem Haufen.

Cogito ergo sum: Ich denke, und mithin, so bin ich,
  Ist das Eine nur wahr, ist das Andre gewiß.

164. Ich.

Denk' ich, so bin ich! Wohl! Doch, wer wird immer auch denken?
  Oft schon war ich, und hab' wirklich an gar Nichts gedacht!

165. Ein Zweiter.

Weil es Dinge doch giebt, so giebt es ein Ding aller Dinge,
  In dem Ding aller Ding schwimmen wir, wie wir so sind.

166. Ein Dritter.

Just das Gegentheil sprech' ich. Es giebt kein Ding als mich selber!
  Alles Andre, in mir steigt es als Blase nur auf.

167. Ein Vierter.

Zweierlei Dinge laß ich passiren, die Welt und die Seele,
  Keins weiß vom Andern und doch deuten sie beide auf Eins.

168. Ein Fünfter.

Von dem Ding weiß ich nichts, und weiß auch nichts von der Seele,
  Beide erscheinen mir nur, aber sie sind doch kein Schein.

169. Ein Sechster.

Ich bin ich, und setze mich selbst, und setz' ich mich selber,
  Als nicht gesetzt, nun gut! setz' ich ein Nicht Ich dazu.

170. Ein Siebenter.

Vorstellung wenigstens ist; ein Vorgestelltes ist also,
  Ein Vorstellendes auch, macht, mit der Vorstellung, drei!

171. Ich.

Damit lock' ich, ihr Herrn, noch keinen Hund aus dem Ofen,
  Einen erklecklichen Satz will ich, und der auch was setzt.

172. David Hume.

Rede nicht mit dem Volk, der Kant hat sie alle verwirret,
  Mich frag', ich bin mir selbst auch in der Hölle noch gleich.

173. Rechtsfrage.

Jahre lang schon bedien' ich mich meiner Nase zum Riechen,
  Hab ich denn wirklich an sie auch ein erweisliches Recht?

174. Puffendorf.

Ein bedenklicher Fall! doch die erste Possession scheint
 Für dich zu sprechen, und so brauche sie immerhin fort.

175. Hercules.*

Endlich erblick' ich auch den gewaltigen Hercules! Seine
 Uebersetzung! Er selbst leider war nicht mehr zu sehn.

176. Heracliden.

Rings um schrie, wie Vögelgeschrei, das Geschrei der Tragöden
 Und das Hundegebell der Dramaturgen um ihn.

177. Er.

Welche noch kühnere That, Unglücklicher, wagest du jetzo,
 Zu den Verstorbenen selbst niederzusteigen in's Grab!

178. Ich.

Wegen Tiresias mußt' ich herab, den Seher zu fragen,
 Wo ich den guten Geschmack fände, der nicht mehr zu sehn.

179. Er.

Glauben sie nicht der Natur und den alten Griechen, so holst du
 Eine Dramaturgie ihnen vergeblich herauf.

180. Ich.

O die Natur, die zeigt auf unsern Bühnen sich wieder,
 Splitternackend, daß man jegliche Rippe ihr zählt.

181. Er.

Also sieht man bei euch den leichten Tanz der Thalia
 Neben dem ernsten Gang, welchen Melpomene geht?

182. Ich.

Keines von Beiden! Uns kann nur das Christlich=Moralische rühren,
 Und was recht populär, häuslich und bürgerlich ist.

183. Er.

Was? Es dürfte kein Cesar auf euren Bühnen sich zeigen,
 Kein Anton, kein Orest, kein Andromacha mehr?

184. Ich.

Nichts! Man siehet bei uns nur Pfarrer, Kommerzienräthe,
 Fähndriche, Sekretär's oder Husarenmajor's.

185. Er.

Woher nehmt ihr denn aber das große gigantische Schicksal,
 Welches den Menschen erhebt, wenn es den Menschen zermalmt?

* Hercules, i. e. Shakspeare, see p. 403.

186. Ich.

Das sind Grillen! Uns selbst und unsre guten Bekannten,
    Unsern Jammer und Noth suchen und finden wir hier.

187. Er.

Also eure Natur, die erbärmliche, trifft man auf euren
    Bühnen, die große nur nicht, nicht die unendliche, an?

188. Er.

Der Poet ist der Wirth, und der letzte Actus die Zeche,
    Wenn sich das Laster erbricht, setzt sich die Tugend zu Tisch.

189. Muse zu den Xenien.

Aber jetzt rath' ich euch, geht, sonst kommt noch gar der Gorgona
    Fratze oder ein Band Oden von Haschka hervor.

190. An die Freier.

Alles war nur ein Spiel! Ihr Freier lebt ja noch alle,
    Hier ist der Bogen und hier ist zu dem Ringen der Platz.

Goethe.

Frühling.

191.

Auf, ihr Distichen, frisch! ihr muntern lebendigen Knaben!
    Reich ist der Garten und Feld: Blumen zum Kranze herbei!

192.

Reich ist an Blumen die Flur; doch einige sind nur dem Auge,
    Andre dem Herzen nur schön: Wähle dir, Leser, nun selbst!

193.

Sagt! was füllet das Zimmer mit Wohlgerüchen? Reseda,
    Farblos, ohne Gestalt, stilles bescheidenes Kraut.

194.

Deine liebliche Kleinheit, dein holdes Auge, sie sagen
    Immer: Vergiß mein nicht! immer: Vergiß nur nicht mein.

Sommer.

195.

Das ist die wahre Liebe, die immer und immer sich gleich bleibt,
    Wenn man ihr Alles gewährt, wenn man ihr Alles versagt.

196.

Warum bin ich vergänglich, o Zeus? so fragte die Schönheit.
Macht' ich doch, sagte der Gott, nur das Vergängliche schön.

Herbst.

197.

Freunde, treibet nur Alles mit Ernst und Liebe; die beiden
Stehen dem Deutschen so schön, den ach! so Vieles entstellt.

198.

Immer strebe zum Ganzen, und kannst du selber kein Ganzes
Werden, als dienendes Glied schließ an ein Ganzes dich an.

199.

Alle Blüthen müssen vergehn, daß Früchte beglücken:
Blüthen und Frucht zugleich gebet ihr Musen allein.

200.

Irrthum verläßt uns nie; doch ziehet ein höher Bedürfniß
Immer den strebenden Geist leise zur Wahrheit hinan.

201.

Wo Parteien entstehn, hält Jeder sich hüben und drüben:
Viele Jahre vergehn, eh' sie die Mitte vereint.

202.

Wer ist der edlere Mann in jedem Stande?   Der stets sich
Neiget zum Gleichgewicht, was er auch habe voraus.

203.

Was ist heilig?   Das ist's, was viele Seelen zusammen
Bindet, bänd' es auch nur leicht wie die Binse den Kranz.

204.

Was ist das Heiligste?   Das, was heut und ewig die Geister,
Tiefer und tiefer gefühlt, immer nur einiger macht.

Winter.

205.

Wasser ist Körper und Boden der Fluß.   Das neuste Theater
Thut in der Sonne Glanz zwischen den Ufern sich auf.

206.

Eingefroren sahen wir so Jahrhunderte starren,
Menschengefühl und Vernunft schlich nur verborgen am Grund.

207.

Durch einander gleiten sie her, die Schüler und Meister..
Und das gewöhnliche Volk, das in der Mitte sich hält.

208.

Gleite fröhlich dahin, gib Rath dem werdenden Schüler,
Freue des Meisters.dich, und so genieße des Tags.

209.

Siehe, schon nahet der Frühling: das strömende Wasser verzehret
Unten, der sanftere Blick oben der Sonne, das Eis.

210.

Mache der Schwärmer sich Schüler wie Sand am Meere — der Sand ist
Sand, die Perle sey mein, du, o vernünftiger Freund!

211.

Schüler macht sich der Schwärmer genug und rühret die Menge,
Wenn der vernünftige Mann einzelne Liebende zählt.
Wunderthätige Bilder sind meist nur schlechte Gemälde:
Werke des Geists und der Kunst sind für den Pöbel nicht da.

212.

Diese Gondel vergleich' ich der sanft einschaukelnden Wiege,
Und das Kästchen darauf scheint ein geräumiger Sarg.
Recht so! Zwischen der Wieg' und dem Sarg' wir schwanken und schweben
Auf dem großen Canal sorglos durch's Leben dahin.

213.

Was mit mir das Schicksal gewollt? Es wäre verwegen
Das zu fragen; denn meist will es mit Vielen nicht viel.
Einen Dichter zu bilden, die Absicht wär' ihm gelungen,
Hätte die Sprache sich nicht unüberwindlich gezeigt.

Schiller.

214. Das Distichon.

Im Hexameter steigt des Springquells silberne Säule,
Im Pentameter drauf fällt sie melodisch herab.

215. Der epische Hexameter.

Schwindelnd trägt er dich fort auf rastlos strömenden Wogen:
Hinter dir siehst du, du siehst vor dir nur Himmel und Meer.

216. Deutscher Genius.

Ringe, Deutscher, nach römischer Kraft, nach griechischer Schönheit!
　Beides gelang dir: doch nie glückte der gallische Sprung.

217. Das Kind in der Wiege.

Glücklicher Säugling! Dir ist ein unendlicher Raum noch die Wiege:
　Werde Mann, und dir wird eng die unendliche Welt.

218. Menschliches Wirken.

An dem Eingang der Bahn liegt die Unendlichkeit offen,
　Doch mit dem engsten Kreis höret der Weiseste auf.

219. Falscher Studirtrieb.

O wie viel Feinde der Wahrheit! Mir blutet die Seele,
　Seh' ich das Eulengeschlecht, das zu dem Lichte sich drängt.

220. Die Philosophieen.

Welche noch bleibt von allen den Philosophieen? Ich weiß nicht:
　Aber die Philosophie, hoff' ich, soll ewig bestehn.

221. Das Unwandelbare.

„Unaufhaltsam enteilet die Zeit!" — Sie sucht das Beständ'ge.
　Sey getreu, und du legst ewige Fesseln ihr an!

222. Unsterblichkeit.

Vor dem Tod erschrickst du! Du wünschest unsterblich zu leben?
　Leb' im Ganzen! Wenn du lange dahin bist, es bleibt.

223. Die zwei Tugendwege.

Zwei sind der Wege, auf welchen der Mensch zur Tugend emporstrebt;
　Schließt sich der eine dir zu, thut sich der andre dir auf:
　Handelnd erringt der Glückliche sie, der Leidende duldend.
　Wohl ihm, den sein Glück liebend auf beiden geführt!

APPENDIX:

SPECIMENS OF GERMAN PROSE,

FROM THE MIDDLE OF THE SIXTEENTH TO THE MIDDLE OF THE

NINETEENTH CENTURIES.

SPECIMENS OF GERMAN PROSE,

FROM THE MIDDLE OF THE SIXTEENTH TO THE MIDDLE OF THE
NINETEENTH CENTURIES.

Jacob Boehme.

1. Aus der Morgenröthe im Aufgang.[1]

Ich vergleiche die ganze Philosophiam,[d] Astrologiam und Theologiam
samt ihrer Mutter einem köstlichen Baum der in einem schönen Lustgarten

[1] This piece and the following can not properly be said to come under the
category of modern high German prose of the classical period, as the Reader
will at once perceive from the difference of style and of orthography even, in
comparing these extracts with those of a later date. Both these writers belong
to the transition-state, when the language, although its *usus* had been already
become somewhat established by the illustrious precedent of Luther, was yet
far from the grammatical precision and the versatile elegance of the more
recent prose, of which Lessing was the father and (in his day) the most
classic representative. Boehme and Sancta Clara, however, are not
only remarkable, the former for his mystic profundity, the latter for satiric
humor, and both for unequalled originality, but also for their style,
which already exhibits the exhaustless resources of the language, its plastic
flexibility, and its perfect adaptedness to all the purposes of poetry and speculation. This will justify the admission of the two introductory specimens.
Among the orthographical peculiarities will be noticed :—a.) the reduplication
of certain consonants, especially of f in Safft, auff, Apffel, Gifft, Teuffel, hilfft,
boshafftigen, Kupffer, Kopff, schlaffen, unterwerffen, Straff, seufftzet, gantz, &c.,
instead of Saft, auf, Apfel, &c., schlafen, Strafe, ganz, &c.   b.) the use of a
single consonant for a double one, especially of n for nn, in wan, fan, dan,
komt, tönt, herschet, &c., instead of wann (or wenn), kann, dann (or denn), kommt,
könnet, herrschet, &c.   c.) the use of w for u in abgehawen, Mülthaw (in
Boehme only) for abgehauen, Mehlthau.   d.) the original form in words of Latin
origin in Philosophiam, Theologiam, Elementa, Thesibus, &c. for Philosophie,
Elemente, Thesen, &c.   e.) other obsolete forms, especially of verbs, as seind
for sind, bedeut for bedeutet, umb for um, verbrandt for verbrannt, darzu for dazu,
denen (dat. pl. article) for den, dahero for daher, and the relative so for der or
welcher (frequently) &c.   f.) a difference of gender, as in höllischen Loh for höllische Lohe, mit seiner Gifft for mit seinem Gift, &c., &c.   Those who are not
sufficiently familiar with the language to distinguish the archaisms from the
modern grammatical forms, may begin with No. 3.—*The references a, b, c, d,
e, f, relate to the explanations of this note.*

wächſt. Nun gibt die Erde, da der Baum inne ſtehet,[2] dem Baum immer
Safft,[a] davon der Baum ſeine lebendige Qualität hat: der Baum aber in
ſich ſelbſt wächſt von dem Safft der Erden[3] und wird groß und breitet ſich
aus mit ſeinen Äſten.   Nun gleich wie die Erde mit ihrer Krafft[a] an dem
Baum arbeitet, daß derſelbe wachſe und zunehme, alſo arbeitet der Baum
ſtäts mit ſeinen Äeſten aus gantzem Vermögen, daß er möchte immer
viel guter Früchte bringen.   Wenn aber der Baum wenig Früchte bringet,
darzu[4] gantz klein, madig und wurmſtichicht, ſo iſt die Schuld nicht an des
Baumes Willen, daß derſelbe vorſätzlich begehre böſe Früchte zu tragen,
dieweil er ein köſtlicher Baum guter Qualität iſt, ſondern die Schuld iſt
daß offt[a] große Kälte, Hitze, Mülthaw,[c] Raupen und Ungeziefer auff ihn
fället, denn die Qualität in der Tieffe,[a] von den Sternen ausgeworffen,
verderbet ihn, daß er wenig guter Früchte bringet   Nun hat aber der
Baum dieſe Art an ſich, daß je größer und älter der Baum wird, je ſüßere
Frucht träget er: in ſeiner Jugend träget er wenig Früchte, denn das
macht die raue[5] und wilde Art des Erdbodems und die überlei[6] Feuchte in
dem Baum, und ob er gleich ſchön blühet, ſo fallen doch im Gewächſe ſeine
Äpffel[a] meiſtentheil abe,[7] es ſey dan Sache[8] daß er gar in einem guten
Acker ſtehet.   Nun hat der Baum auch eine gute ſüße Qualität an ſich, dar=
gegen[9] auch drei andere deme[10] zuwider, als bitter, ſauer und herbe. Nun
wie der Baum iſt, alſo werden auch ſeine Früchte, bis ſie die Sonne
würcket[11] und ſüße machet, daß ſie einen lieblichen Geſchmack bekommen,
und müſſen ſeine Früchte beſtehen im Regen, Wind und Ungewitter.
Wan[b] aber der Baum alt wird, daß ſeine Äſte verdorren, daß der Safft
nicht mehr in die Höhe kan,[b] ſo wachſen unten umb den Stamm viel
grüne Zweiglein aus, letzlich[12] auch auff[a] der Wurtzel, und verklären den
alten Baum, wie er auch ein ſchönes grünes Zweiglein und Bäumlein ge=
weſen iſt und nun gar alt worden.   Dan die Natur oder der Safft wehret
ſich, bis der Stamm gar dürre wird, dan wird er abgehawen[c] und im
Feuer verbrandt.[13]

Nun merke was ich mit dieſem Gleichnis angedeutet habe: Der Garten
dieſes Baumes bedeut[14] die Welt, der Acker die Natur, der Stamm des
Baumes die Sternen, die Äſte die Elementa,[c] die Früchte ſo auff dieſem
Baume wachſen bedeuten die Menſchen, der Safft in dem Baume be=
deut[14] die klare Gottheit.   Nun ſeind[c] die Menſchen aus der Natur, Ster=
nen und Elementen gemacht worden, Gott der Schöpffer[a] aber herſchet[b] in

---

2. Instead of darinnen der Baum ſtehet. — 3. der Erden is the old inflected genitive,
for der Erde. — 4. dazu. — 5. rauhe. — 6. übermäßige Feuchtigkeit. — 7. ab. — 8. es ſei
dan Sache, unless it be the case, unless it happens, &c. — 9. dagegen, but on the
other hand; the r in compounds of da and wo is frequent in the prose of this
period. — 10. dem. — 11. until the sun mellows them, &c. — 12. for zuletzt, at last.
finally. — 13. verbrannt. — 14. bedeutet, *signifies*.

allem, gleich wie der Safft in dem gantzen Baume. Die Natur aber hat
zwei Qualitäten in sich bis in das Gerichte Gottes, eine liebliche, himm=
lische und heilige, und eine grimmige, höllische und durstige. Nun quali=
ficieret und arbeitet die gute immer mit gantzem Fleiß, daß sie gute Früchte
bringe, darinnen herschet der heilige Geist, und gibt darzu Safft und Leben:
die böse quillet und treibet auch mit gantzem Fleiße daß sie immer böse
Früchte bringt, darzu[9] gibt ihr der Teuffel[a] Safft und höllischen Loh.[f]
Nun dieses beides ist in dem Baum der Natur, und die Menschen seind[e] aus
dem Baum gemacht und leben in dieser Welt in diesem Garten zwischen
beiden in großer Gefahr und fället auff sie bald Sonnenschein, bald Regen,
Wind und Schnee. Das ist, so[15] der Mensch seinen Geist erhebet in die
Gottheit, so quillet und qualificieret in ihme der heilige Geist: so[15] er aber
seinen Geist sinken lässet in diese Welt, in Lust des Bösen, so quillet und
herschet in ihme der Teuffel und der höllische Safft. Gleich wie der Apffel
auf dem Baum madig und wurmstichicht wird, wan Frost, Hitze und Mül=
thaw auff ihn fället, und leicht abfället und verdirbet, also auch der Mensch,
wan[b] er lässet den Teuffel mit seiner Gifft[f] in ihm herschen. Nun gleich
wie in der Natur Gutes und Böses quillet, herschet und ist, also auch im
Menschen: der Mensch aber ist Gottes Kind, den er aus dem besten Kern
der Natur gemacht hat, zu herschen in dem Guten und zu überwinden das
Böse. Ob ihm gleich das Böse anhanget, gleich wie in der Natur das
Böse am Guten hanget, so kan[b] er doch das Böse überwinden; so er
seinen Geist in Gott erhebet, so quillet in ihm der heilige Geist und
hilfft[a] ihm siegen. Gleich wie die gute Qualität in der Natur mächtig ist
zu siegen über die böse, dan[16] sie ist und komt[b] auß Gott, und der heilige
Geist ist Herscher darinnen, also auch ist die grimme Qualität mächtig zu
siegen in der boßhafftigen[a] Seelen, dan[16] der Teuffel ist ein mächtiger
Herscher in der Grimmigkeit und ist ein ewiger Fürst derselben.

Abraham a Sancta Clara.

2. Der Kupferstecher.

Wie alt diese Kunst, kan[b] man es eigentlich nicht wissen. Mir gefällt
zwar daß etliche wollen, Martin Schoen, ein Deutscher, habe diese erfun=
den. Es seye nun Martin Schoen, oder Caspar Hübsch, oder Christoph
Sauber ein Urheber dieser Kunst gewesen, liegt endlich so viel nicht daran,
dann[16] es für sich selbst ein saubere Kunst, ein hübsche Kunst, ein schöne
Kunst, und gibt den Mahlern[17] nicht viel nach, ja sie essen das Brot mit

15. The so here = wenn. — 16. Dan is here for the causal denn (*for*); as the cor-
relative wan for wenn (*if*). — 17. Mahlern, as throughout the piece.

einander, wie die zwei Jünger Lucas und Cleophas in dem Flecken Emaus,
und pflegen ſie meiſtens neben einander zu ziehen, wie die zwei Kühe, welche
den Bundeskaſten von den Philiſtäern hinweg geführet, dann[16] ohne Mah=
ler gar offt[a] der Kupfferſtecher[a] nicht beſtehen kan, zuweilen aber auch ein
Mahler von Kupfferſtecher etwas abſticht[18] und in die Farben legt.

Laurentius Beyrlinck gibt das Lob der vornehmen Reichsſtadt Nürnberg,
daß ſie wegen Menge und Unterſchied der Künſten die ganze Chriſtenheit
übertreffe, worvon[9] etwann[19] herrühret das gemeine Sprichwort wegen des
Trachters von Nürnberg, als ſeye ſelbes ein ſolches Ort wo alle Künſten
können ergriffen werden. Weit mehrer[20] Künſtler ſeind von dieſer Stadt
herkommen[21] als gewaffnete Soldaten geſtiegen aus dem großen Trojani=
ſchen Pferd, daß man alſo ſchier ſolle dieſe Stadt nicht mehr Nürnberg
ſondern Hirnberg[22] nennen, zumalen ſo viel vernünftige und zu allen Kün=
ſten capable Köpff anzutreffen.[23] Vor allen aber muß man doch meines
Erachtens den Vorzug vergönnen dem weltbefandten[24] Albrecht Dürer als
einem gebornen Nürnberger, der nicht allein ein Mahler, Bildhauer, ſondern
forderiſt[25] ein ſo künſtlicher Kupfferſtecher geweſt,[26] daß, wofern er dieſe
Kunſt, wie doch einige wollen, nicht erfunden, wenigiſt[27] in die größte Voll=
kommenheit gebracht, daß man alſo ſeine noch übrige Kupfferplatten faſt
über Silber und Gold ſchätzet.

Jene gute Mutter hat einen Korb bekommen von unſerm Herrn, wie ſie
ihn bittlich erſucht, er möchte doch ihre zwei Söhn beſter Maßen promo=
vieren, und zwar damit einer ſitze zur rechten der andere zur linken Hand:
dann[16] es glaubte die fromme Haut, daß er ein Reich auf Erden werde be=
ſitzen. Es hat aber hieruber[28] das gute Weib ein[29] abſchlägige Antwort
erhalten, dann[16] der heilige Ambroſius ſpricht, daß dieſer Mutter Anbrin=
gen ſeye gar närriſch und ungereimt geweſt,[26] indem ſie begehret, die Söhn
ſollen ſitzen ꝛc. Dann[16] unſerm Hern faſt kein Ding alſo mißfällig als
das Sitzen und Faullentzen; bei ihm iſt otiosus ſoviel als odiosus, da=
hero[30] der Menſch ein rechter Limmel wann er nicht iſt wie ein Himmel; ein
Himmel iſt in einer ſtetten[31] Bewegung, alſo ſoll der Menſch auch nicht
anders geſitt[32] ſein.

Wie Petrus durch einen Engel aus dem Herodianiſchen Kercker erledigt
worden da hat er vermeint,[33] es ſeye nur ein Traum, und glaubte An=
fang[34] gar nicht daß er wahrhaftig ſeye auf freien Fuß geſtellt; die Urſach
war dieſe, er gedachte, weil er die gantze[a] Nacht hindurch habe geſchlaf=

---

18. etwas abſticht, *copies something.* — 19. etwann for etwa, *perhaps.* — 20. mehr.
21. hergekommen. — 22. a play on the word Nürnberg, Hirnberg = *brain-hill.* —
23. Supply ſind, *are to be met with, found* — 24 weltbekannten. — 25. zuvörderſt, haupt=
ſächlich, *especially.* — 26. geweſt for geweſen, sc. iſt. — 27. for wenigſtens, *at least.* —
28. hierüber. — 29. eine; see f., Note 1. — 30. daher. — 31. ſteten, *continual,* see Note 1, a.
— 32. geſittet — 33. gemeint, *supposed, imagined.* — 34. Anfangs, *at first.*

fen,ᵃ daß solches von Gott nicht herkommen, dann Gott pflege keine Gut=
thaten erweisen denjenigen die da schlaffenᵃ und faullentzen; daheroᵉ³⁵ die
gute Mutter einen Fehler begangen indem sie begehrt, ihre zwei Soehn
möchten sitzen. Das Sitzen und Faullentzen ist Gott nicht lieb, aber sitzen
und zugleich arbeiten gilt viel bei unserem Herren, absonderlich wann die
Arbeit ist zu größerer Ehr Gottes, wie da meistens bei den Kupfferstechern
zu sehen. Diese sitzen die gantzeᵃ Zeit, aber ihr Sitzen ist nicht ohne Mühe
und Arbeit. Jener Partiten=Macher und ungerechte Verwalter im Evan=
gelio,ᵈ nachdem er von seinem Dienst verstoßen worden, hat selbst bekennt:
graben kann ich nicht. Ei du fauler Dieb, du hätteft sagen sollen: gra=
ben will ich nicht, dann¹⁶ die Bärenhaut ist dein Unterbett; schaue nur die
embsige³⁶ Kupfferstecher an, ob sie nicht den gantzenᵃ Tag, die gantze Wo=
chen, das gantze Jahr, sogar die meiste Zeit ihres Lebens mit Graben zu=
bringen, und zwar graben sie in das harte Kupffer hinein, fürwahr aber,
ihr Graben ist ein rechtes Schatzgraben; dann was seindᵉ die heilige Bil=
der so von ihren Händen verfertigt werden anderst³⁷ als ein Schatz der
Kirchen; die Bilder welche die Mahler entwerffen,ᵃ seind zwar auch ein
Schatz, aber ehe und bevor ein Mahler ein einiges Bild vollendet, da ist
die Kupfferstecherkunst so glückseelig, daß sie unterdessen durch stellen³¹ Ab=
druck etlich tausend unter die Leut ausgesprengt. Moses hat mit seinem
Ertz oder Glockenspeis dem Volck Israel sehr großen Nutzen gebracht,
dann¹⁶ wie selbiges durch billige Straffᵃ von feuerigen Schlangen gebissen
worden, da hat er aus Befehl des Allerhöchsten ein eherne Schlangen
gießen lassen, und solche muß einer absonderlichen Größe gewest²⁶ sein,
weil sie auf etliche Meil herum ist gesehen worden; diese hat Moses
erhöcht,³⁸ und wer solche nur hat angeschaut, der ist augenblicklich von sei=
nem Biß geheilet worden. Viel hat Moses genützt mit seinem Ertz, aber
fast noch mehrer²⁰ die Kupfferstecher mit ihrem Kupffer, dann vielmal durch
ein einigen Anblick eines Kupfferstichs, worauf etwann der gekreutzigte
Jesus, oder das jüngste Gericht, oder die erschröckliche³⁹ Pein der Höl=
len entworffen,ᵃ ist mancher in sich selbsten gangen,⁴⁰ seine Sünd und
Missethat beweinet, und folgsam⁴¹ an der Seelen Wunden curiert worden.

  Es ist einer der sicht⁴² einen Kupfferstich worauf die Stadt Sodoma
und Gomorrha entworffen,ᵃ wie selbige mit Feuer und Flammen ver=
zehrt worden; des Loths Weib aber, um weil sie aus unartigem Vor=
witz nur umgeschaut, in ein Saltzsaul⁴³ verkehrt worden. Dieser Kupf=
ferstich ist ihme schon ein Stich ins Hertz.ᵃ O mein Gott! seufftzet er

35. daher. — 36. emsigen, busy, diligent, assiduous. — 37. anders. — 38. erhöht. —
39. erschreckliche. — 40. gegangen; the auxiliary iſt belongs properly only to this verb
and to curiert worden; with beweinet, hat has to be supplied. — 41. folglich, consequently. An der Seelen for an der Seele. — 42. sieht, sees. — 43. in eine Salzsäule, cf.
Note 1, f.

hierüber, hat Gott wegen einer einigen so geringen Übertrettung also gestrafft, was hab ich dann zu erwarten, der ich so viel schwere Misse=thaten begangen?

Ein anderer sicht einen Kupfferstich, auf deme da abgebildet die Dalila, wie sie dem Samson seine Haar, und folgsam [41] die Stärcke abgeschnitten; dieser Kupfferstich ist ihm schon ein Stich ins Herz, dann [16] er betracht [44] in was Unheil schon manchen ein Weib habe gestürzt. Der Adam hat nur ein Weib gehabt, die hat ihn und uns alle ins Elend gestürzt; wann er mehrer Weiber hätt gehabt, wie bei den Türcken im Brauch, wie wär es nachmals erst hergangen! Wie viel Weiberzöpff in der Welt, so viel seind schier Fallstrick, darum weit darvon [9] ist gut vor dem Schuß, welcher von dem blinden Buben zu fürchten.

Auf solche Weis' verursacht der Kupffersstecher ihre [45] schöne Arbeit sehr viel Guts in der Welt, ja sie geben mehrmal stille Prediger ab, welche da mit ihren stummen Bildern denen [46] Leuten gleichwol in das Herz reden und folgsam [41] zu guten und heiligen Gedancken leiten. Daß des Loths Weib in ein Salzsaulen, [47] und die Ägyptischen Wässer zu Zeiten Mosis in Blut, und die Ruten [48] Aarons in ein Schlang [49] seye verkehrt worden, das glaub ich gar gern, aber daß die Alchimisten oder alte Kühemister zuweilen Eisen, Blei, Kupffer und dergleichen Metall in feines und reines Gold ver=wandlen sollen, bin ich nicht schuldig zu glauben, weil man es meistens handgreifflich ertappt, daß sie leere Kohlenblaser, lappische Tägelhüter, lächerliche Rauchschlücker und vergebliche Feuerhund abgeben; soll es aber seyn, daß etwann ein Deutscher Theophrastus, so aus Cärnden von Villach gebürtig, soll es seyn, daß er mit anderen und andere mit ihm haben ge=wußt, die Metallen zu verwandlen, so halt ich diesfalls mit ihm, daß man kein Metall könne leichter zu Gold machen als das Kupffer, aber ich versteh das Kupffer unter den Händen der Kupfferstecher, dann fürwahr solche Kupffer offt und vielfältig zu Gold werden, ja mehr als Gold zu schätzen seind, indeme sie der gantzen Welt den größten Nutzen bringen.

Jene wunderliche Statua oder Bildnus [50] (Daniel II, 32) welche der übermüthige König Nabuchodonosor gesehen, hatte ein Haupt von Gold, ein Brust [51] von Silber, Bauch und Lenden von Erz, Schenckel von Eisen und woraus dann klar abzunehmen, daß Gold und Silber unter denen [46] Metallen in allweg [52] den Vorzug haben, welches dann leider bei denen [46] geldgierigen Adams=Kindern und bei denen [46] unersättlichen Geizhälsen allenthalben zu sehen. Bei jetziger Welt aber ist das Kupffer in solchen

---

44. betrachtet. — 45. The pronoun ihre is redundant: die schöne Arbeit der Kupfer-stecher is the present proper mode of expression. So also above: dem Samson seine Haar, &c. — 46. denen for den, dat. pl. — 47. in eine Salzsäule, cf. f. Note 1. — 48. Ru-then. — 49. in eine Schlange, Note 1, f. — 50. Bildniß. — 51. eine Brust, cf. f. Note first. — 52. for in jeder Beziehung, durchaus, immer.

Preis gestiegen, daß es ein Kunstliebender über Gold und Silber pflegt zu schätzen, ich verstehe aber ein solches Kupffer, worein die erfahrene Künstler mit sonderer Wissenschaft allerlei Form und Bildnussen[53] einstechen, forderist[54] ist die schwartze Arbeit absonderlich zu loben, so[55] zwar vor wenig Jahren erfunden worden, selbige aber hat bei jetziger Zeit der berühmte Mann Elias Christophorus Heiß in Augspurg zu einer solchen Vollkommenheit gebracht, daß auch ein Protogenes, wann[16] er sollt auf Erden erscheinen, seine von damaliger Welt fast angebettete Kunststuck[56] möchte mit einer Kotzen oder Roßdecken verhüllen. Die schwartze Kunst, welche der gewissenlose Doctor Faustus getrieben verdient nichts anderst[37] als ein Teuffelskunst genennt zu werden; die schwartze Kunst aber welche obberührter Künstler dem gantzen Deutschland vor Augen stellt, ist werth und würdig, daß sie den Namen einer Englischen Kunst trage, zumal mit seiner Arbeit die berühmteste Universitäten und hohe Schulen prangen, weil nemlich in dero öffentlichen thesibus sein schwartze Kunst oder Arbeit so manche Candidatos vorstellet.

Moses der große Führer des Israelitischen Volcks hatte ein Weib, dessen Namen Sephora; diese aber ware[57] ein Mohrin, und weil ihr Mann von Gott in ein so große Amtsverwaltung gesetzt worden, also hat sie vermög schwacher Weiber Art sich in etwas übernommen und ihren Mann, den Mosen, allen andern vorgezogen, auch dem Aaron selbst und der Mariä als dessen Schwester, welches dann dieser nicht ein wenig in die Nasen gerauchtt, maßen[58] der Weiber Natur mit dem Pantoffelholtz gleichet, so in allweg[59] nur will oben schwimmen, ja die meiste[60] arten den Storchen nach, welche nicht allein öffters knaftern und schnadern, sondern auch ihr Residenz allzeit in die Höhe setzen; dahero[35] diese Maria in einen Weiberzanck ausgebrochen, die Sephoram etwann eine Dintenfresserin, oder ein Kohlenkramerin genennt, dann an dergleichen Prädicaten die Weiberzungen einen großen Vorrath haben; ja sie hat in allweg den Bruder Aaron nicht um ein Haar geringer gehalten als den Mosen, so gar hat diese disgustierte Maria ihren Bruder Aaron dahin veranlaßt und aufgewicklet,[61] daß solcher ebenfalls wider den großen Mann Gottes schmählich geredt. Auf solche Weis' vertretten[a] die Weiberzungen und Zindtruthen ein Amt und seind beede ein Ursach[62] eines öffteren Feuers: in Summa, Maria hat geschmähet wider die schwartze Sephora. Num. XII.

Aber bei dieser unserer Zeit wird wohl Niemand wider die so bekandte[63] schwartze Arbeit schimpfflich reden, sondern vielmehr dieselbe mit tausend

53. Bildnisse, Abbildungen. — 54. forderist instead of zuvörderst, hauptsächlich. — 55. so = die or welche, cf. Note 1. e. — 56. seine . . . . . fast angebeteten Kunststücke &c. — 57. war. — 58. for immaßen, da, weil. — 59. so in allweg &c. = die (sc. der Weiber Natur) immer nur will oben schwimmen, &c. — 60. die meisten (sc. Weiber), &c. — 61. veranlaßt und aufgewiegelt. — 62. beide eine Ursache, &c. — 63. bekannte.

Lobſprüchen hervorſtreichen[64] dann ſogar der großen Frauen ihre Geſichter, welche ſonſt aus natürlichem Antrieb nach der Weiße ſtreben, wollen durch dieſe ſchwarze Arbeit entworffen* werden, wie dann dergleichen mehrere Contrafeit von obbenenntem Künſtler verfertiget worden.

Weil nun mehrer,[65] wie an unterſchiedlichen Orten zu ſehen, dieſer ſchönen Kunſt ſich befleißen und ſolche Stuck durch die ſchwarze Arbeit ans Licht geben, deren eins und anders mit der Salomoniſchen Braut wol könt[b] ſagen: "nigra sum sed formosa," alſo ſeind ſie doch anbei[66] erinnert, daß ſie in allweg[52] ein ſolchen frommen Wandel führen, damit ſie bei Gott nicht in das ſchwarze Buch kommen.

Dann wie im Himmel nicht lauter stellæ fixæ ſondern auch errantes, im Garten nicht lauter Roſen ſondern auch Knöpff,[67] auf dem Acker nicht lauter Waitz ſondern auch Unkraut: alſo ſeind unter den Kufferſtechern nicht gar alle lobwürdig. Dann wer kan diejenige loben, welche in ihrer Kunſt ſo unerfahren, daß ſie ſich beſſer ſollen Keſſelſlicker als Kupferſtecher nennen; wer kan diejenige loben, welche wider alles Gewiſſen nackende[68] und ärgerliche Bildnuſſen auf das Kupffer tragen, wordurch die ohnedies ſchlüpffrige Jugend zu allerlei Schandthaten veranleitet wird; wer kan diejenige loben, welche ſich beſſer verſtehen auf das Octoberwaſſer als auf das Scheidwaſſer, und darum nicht allein Kupffer unter den Händen haben, ſondern auch Kupffer auf der Naſen führen. Weilen[69] aber nicht viel dergleichen gefunden werden, ſondern die meiſte ein lobwürdigſte Wiſſenſchafft und ehrlichen Wandel führen, alſo will ſich nicht gebühren, daß man dieſer wertheſten Profeſſion den geringſten Flecken anhencke,[70] zumalen gegenwärtiges Buch ſeinen Ruhm und Werth allein gewinnt von der Hand eines Kupfferſtechers, den ich für diesmal mit keinem Fuchsſcepter zu beleidigen ſuche.

Was anbelangt die Kupfferdrucker, iſt es ebenfalls ein lobwürdiges Weſen, worzu[9] großer Fleiß und Arbeit erfordert wird, und ſeind ſie diejenige, ſo ein ziemliches Trumm von dem Filtz ererbt, welchen Gott dem Adam hat geben: im Schweiß deines Angeſichts ſollſt du das Brot eſſen. Es können auch dieſe Kupfferdrucker ſo bald keine Nudeldrucker abgeben, dann[71] ſie durch ihr Arbeit gar zu großen Gewinn nicht erhäſchen, und folgſam über die tägliche Unterhaltung und ehrliches Auskommen wenig erſparen, außer daß ſie zuweilen für ſich ein hundert Exemplaria zuſchießen und mit ſolchen die Zech bezahlen am Sonn- und Feiertag, damit ſie die ſchwarze Farb, mit der ſie ein gantze Woche beſudelt ſeind, mögen abwaſchen.

---

64. herausſtreichen; dann = denn, *for*, as often before. — 65. mehrere, viele, verſchiedene. — 66. dabei. — 67. Knöpff = Knoſpen, buds; Waitz = Weizen. — 68. nackte und ärgerliche Bildniſſe, &c. — 69. weil, da. — 70. anhänge. — 71. dann seems here = da, since.

Gottlieb Wilhelm Rabener.

3. Wem Gott ein Amt giebt, dem giebt er auch Verstand.

Wenn irgend ein Sprichwort ist, dessen Wahrheit durch die tägliche Erfahrung bestätigt wird, so ist es dieses, wenn man sagt: Wem Gott
ein Amt giebt, dem giebt er auch Verstand. Da ich Gelegenheit gehabt habe, die Verfassung meines Vaterlandes sehr genau kennen
zu lernen, so getraue ich mir sehr wohl zu behaupten, daß wenigstens zwei
Drittheile meiner Mitbürger ihren Verstand nicht eher erlangt haben, als
bis sie das Amt bekommen; und kaum ein Drittheil ist, ich weiß nicht durch
was für einen Zufall, vor Erlangung des Amtes mit Verstande begabt gewesen. Ich sage mit gutem Vorbedachte: kaum ein Drittheil. Denn ich
muß noch für diejenigen ein wenig Platz lassen, welche die Ausnahme von
dem Sprichwort machen und das Amt zwar seit langer Zeit, noch bis diese
Stunde aber nicht den geringsten Verstand haben.

Ich finde von unserem Sprichworte verschiedene Lesarten. Ein altes
Manuscript, welches, wie ich aus einigen Umständen vermuthe, zu Hein-
richs des Voglers Zeiten geschrieben worden, lies't ausdrücklich: Wem
Gott ein Amt giebt, dem giebt er Verstand, und dieser
Lesart habe ich mich bedient. Die meisten der neueren Schriftsteller sagen
hingegen nur: Wem er ein Amt giebt ıc. Beide Lesarten haben
ihren guten Grund und beide sind in ihrer Art merkwürdig. In den damaligen rohen und unaufgeklärten Zeiten war es noch hier und da Mode,
daß Gott die Aemter gab, und daher läßt sich die Art zu reden: wem Gott
ein Amt giebt, noch wohl entschuldigen. Jetzt braucht man diese Weitläuftigkeit nicht mehr, und man hat Mittel gefunden die Aemter zu erlangen,
ohne daß man nöthig hat, Gott mit der Austheilung derselben beschwerlich
zu fallen. Dieses mag auch Gelegenheit gegeben haben, das alte Sprichwort einigermaßen zu ändern. Inzwischen muß ich doch zum Ruhme unsrer
Zeiten erinnern, daß man wieder anfängt die alte Lesart hervor zu suchen,
und aus einer andächtigen Höflichkeit so zu thun, als habe man das Amt
von Gott, ob man sich gleich in Acht nimmt, der, über rechtsverwährte Zeit
wohl erlangten Gerechtsamen sich zu begeben und das Amt von Gott zu erwarten, da man es näher haben kann. Ich freue mich, so oft ich Jemanden
also reden höre, von dem ich sonst sehr wohl weiß, daß ihn die göttliche
Fügung am wenigsten beunruhiget. Es ist dieses ein Zeugniß, daß die
Religion bei uns noch nicht ganz abgekommen ist. Man darf mir nicht
einwenden, daß diese Art, von Gott zu reden, nur ein Ehrenwort sey; ich
glaube es selbst, aber das thut nichts. Dieses hat mich bewogen, das
Sprichwort nach seiner alten Lesart beizubehalten und ich habe mich deut-

lich genug darüber erklärt, ohne zu besorgen, daß mich diejenigen, welche
stärker denken als der fromme Pöbel, mich für einen Quäker halten werden.

Ich nehme es also für bekannt an, daß Gott das Amt giebt. Es hebt dieser
Satz dasjenige gar nicht auf, was man aus der Erfahrung dawider ein=
wenden möchte. Recht wahrscheinlich ist es freilich nicht, aber ein guter
Ausleger weiß alles zusammen zu reimen. Ich halte mich in einem sehr
kleinen Städtchen auf, und doch ist es noch immer groß genug meinen Satz
zu behaupten. Außer dem Nachtwächter weiß ich Niemanden, welcher auf
eine erlaubte Weise zu seinem Amte gekommen wäre. Er würde als ein
alter, wohl verdienter und abgedankter Soldat haben verhungern müssen
(denn dieses ist immer die gewisse Belohnung derer, welche sich für das Va=
terland verstümmeln lassen), wenn er nicht zu diesem wichtigen Posten zu
eben der Zeit erhoben worden wäre, als die Bürgerschaft so weit gebracht
war, daß sie ihn als einen Hausarmen ernähren sollte. Man machte ihn
ohne sein Ansuchen zum Nachtwächter, und sein Beruf muß wohl recht=
mäßig sein, weil er den Amtmann nicht bestochen hat und von keinem Raths=
herrn ein Vetter ist. Dieses ist der einzige Mann in der Stadt, der sein
Amt auf eine billige Art erlangt hat, und im Vorbeigehen muß ich auch
erinnern, daß er zugleich der einzige in unserm Orte ist, welcher den Ver=
stand eher hatte als das Amt.

Mit den Übrigen ist es ganz anders beschaffen. Der Stadtschreiber
hatte als Advocat das Unglück, daß er wegen seiner Geschicklichkeit, die
verschiedene Obere aus Unverstand Betrügerei nannten, in die Inquisition
kommen sollte. Seine Sache war so beschaffen, daß er nach dem Eigen=
sinne altväterischer Rechte gewiß den Staupbesen würde bekommen haben;
aber ein edler wohlweiser Rath sah die unvermeidliche Folge davon ein.
Der größte Theil von ihnen stand in einer so genauen Verbindung mit ihm,
daß sie gewiß an seinem Staupbesen hätten Antheil nehmen und des regie=
renden Herrn Bürgermeisters Hochedlen am Galgen ersticken müssen,
wenn man diesen wackern Mann nicht den Händen der blinden Gerechtig=
keit entrissen hätte. Man überlegte mit der Frau Amtmännin die Sache
genau, und eine Kleinigkeit von etlichen Ellen brabanter Spitzen legte seine
Unschuld dergestalt an den Tag, daß er sich mit Ehren von seinem Handel
befreit sah. Der Frau Bürgermeisterin war der Hals ihres theuren Ge=
mahls so lieb, daß sie vor Freuden nicht eher ruhete, bis diesem angefochte=
nen Mann die Gerechtigkeit der Stadt und das Wohl der ganzen Bürger=
schaft anvertraut und er ungesäumt zum Stadtschreiber erwählt wurde.
Ein jeder seiner Vorgesetzten glaubte, er sei diesen Dienst sich selbst schuldig,
weil ein jeder wünschte, daß man sich bei dergleichen besorglichen Fällen auf
gleiche Weise seiner annehmen möchte.

Wie der Amtmann zu seinem Dienste gelangte, weiß die ganze Stadt.

Er hatte durch seine patriotischen Bemühungen es so weit gebracht, daß ganze Dörfer wüste und eine ansehnliche Menge nichtswürdiger Bauern mit Weib und Kind Bettler geworden waren. Die Beute, die er dabei gemacht, setzte ihn in den Stand unverschämter zu seyn als sein Vorfahr, welcher einfältig genug war sich einzubilden, daß man es mit dem Landesherrn nicht redlich meinen könne, wenn man es nicht zugleich mit den Unterthanen redlich meine. Er stürzte diesen gewissenhaften Tropf und bemächtigte sich seines Amtes auf eine Art, welche zu gewöhnlich ist, als daß man sie tadeln sollte.

Es sind nicht mehr als zween Priester in unsrer Stadt; der oberste wäre vielleicht noch jetzt Candidat, wenn er nicht die Geschicklichkeit besessen hätte, alle diejenigen zu verkleinern und ihre Lebensart verdächtig zu machen, welche mit ihm um ein geistliches Amt ansuchten. Er meinte es aber mit seiner christlichen Gemeinde so gut, daß er sich den Capellan zu seinem Collegen selbst ausersah und ihm dazu beförderlich war, weil die natürliche Dummheit dieses lieben Mannes ihm vortheilhaft zu seyn schien, und weil er das Herz hatte, des Herrn Pastors Jungfer Muhme zu heirathen, welcher sehr viel daran lag, einen dummen Ehemann zu haben.

Sogar bis auf den Küster erstreckt sich in meinem Städtchen diese Art des Berufs. Denn weil er in der ganzen Gegend den besten Branntwein brennt, so hat es der Kirchenvorsteher für billig gehalten, ihm das Küsteramt und die Unterweisung der Jugend anzuvertrauen. — Diese wenigen Exempel beweisen schon genug, wie wunderbar oftmals die Wege sind zu einem Amte zu gelangen. Die Ausschweifung würde überflüssig seyn, wofern ich nicht versichern könnte, daß der Stadtschreiber, der Amtmann und die Geistlichen in Gesellschaften niemals von ihrem Amte reden, ohne Gott mit darin zu mengen, der es ihnen gegeben haben soll.

Diejenigen, welche sich dieses Sprichwortes: Wem Gott das Amt giebt, dem giebt er auch den Verstand, auf eine bequeme Art zu bedienen wissen, sind als ein überzeugender Beweis wider diejenigen Lästerer anzuführen, welche uns vorwerfen, daß in unsern Zeiten das Vertrauen auf die göttliche Vorsorge nur gar zu matt geworden und fast gänzlich abgekommen sey. Ich freue mich, daß ich hier eine Gelegenheit finde, das Christenthum meiner Landsleute zu vertheidigen, und ich erwarte dafür alle Erkenntlichkeit. Denn ich nehme eine Sache über mich, bei der auch der beste Advocat verzweifeln würde.

Ich finde besonders dreierlei Gattungen von Leuten, welche dieses sagen. Es sind entweder diejenigen, durch welche, nach ihrer Sprache zu reden, Gott die Aemter austheilt, oder es sind die selbst, welche die Aemter bekommen, oder es sind endlich die, welche als Zuschauer über die wunderbare Führung und Besetzung der Aemter erstaunen. Die letzten fühlen dabei in ihrem

Herzen den Troſt, daß Gott, welcher nach ihrer Meinung ſo vielen Narren
Aemter giebt, auch ſie nicht unverſorgt laſſen und wenn ſie verſorgt ſind, auch
ſie alsdann mit dem nöthigſten Verſtande ausrüſten wird, den ſie nicht ha=
ben und den ſie ohne ein Wunderwerk auch nicht zu erlangen hoffen. Dieſe
Betrachtungen zeugen von ihrer Demuth, und ſie beſchämen dadurch eine
unzählige Menge Leute, welche doppelt unglücklich ſind, da ſie keinen Ver=
ſtand haben und ihn doch nicht vermiſſen.

Noch weit ſtärker aber iſt das Vertrauen zur göttlichen Vorſorge bei den=
jenigen, welche die Pflicht auf ſich haben die Aemter zu beſetzen. Bei ver=
ſchiedenen von ihnen würde ihr Betragen unſinnig ſeyn ; man würde ſie
für Betrüger, für heimliche Verräther ihres eigenen Vaterlandes, für die
gefährlichſten Böſewichter halten, wenn man ſieht, wie unbedachtſam ſie bei
der Beſetzung der Aemter verfahren. Aber man darf nur denken, daß ſie
überzeugt ſind : Wem Gott das Amt giebt, dem giebt er auch Verſtand, ſo
iſt dieſer Widerſpruch gehoben. Sie können dieſes mit einer deſto gewiſſern
Zuverſicht hoffen, als ſie an ihren eignen Perſonen ein ſo erſtaunendes
Wunder erfahren, und nach dem glaubwürdigen Zeugniſſe aller ihrer de=
müthigen Clienten gegenwärtig die verſtändigſten Männer, die weiſeſten
Väter der Stadt ſind, ungeachtet ſie vor der Erlangung ihres Amtes die
unverſtändigſten Narren waren. Dieſe wichtige Erfahrung wirket in ihnen
eine wahre Freudigkeit, ſo oft ſie ein Amt beſetzen müſſen.

Ich weiß nicht, ob irgend ein Amt wichtiger iſt als das Amt eines Seel=
ſorgers. Die üble Beſetzung eines ſolchen Amtes kann eine ganze Ge=
meinde unglücklich machen und das Verderben von mehr als einer Nach=
kommenſchaft nach ſich ziehen. Wenigſtens würde ich ſehr unruhig ſeyn,
wenn ich für die Beſetzung eines ſolchen Amtes ſorgen ſollte. Aber wie
glücklich ſind nicht diejenigen, welche ſich darauf verlaſſen, daß der Verſtand
ſich ſchon mit dem Amte finden werde. Ich habe vor wenigen Tagen das
Schickſal gehabt, einer Prieſterwahl auf dem Lande beizuwohnen. Der
Kirchenpatron hatte in kurzer Zeit das Unglück erfahren, daß ihm ſein
Pfarrer und bald darauf, welches noch weit wichtiger war, ſein Schäfer ge=
ſtorben war. Einen guten Schäfer zu finden, welcher das Vieh ſorgfältig
wartete, die Kunſt verſtände Krankheiten zu heilen, und welcher bei ſeinem
Amte ehrlich wäre, dieſen ausfindig zu machen, war freilich eine ſchwere
Sache, die alle mögliche Behutſamkeit erforderte. Denn wenn eine Schä=
ferei durch Verwahrloſung ausſtirbt, ſo iſt dieſes manchem Gerichtsherrn
weit empfindlicher, als wenn durch ein unexemplariſches Leben oder durch
Unachtſamkeit des Pfarrherrns die Hälfte der Bauern zum Teufel fährt.
Und ökonomiſch davon zu urtheilen, hat der Gerichtsherr Recht. Ich kam
eben zu der Zeit an, als mein Landedelmann einen geſchickten Schäfer aus=
findig gemacht und in ſeine Dienſte genommen hatte. Er erzählte mir die=

ses mit Freuden und that dabei viele gute Wünsche für seine Schäferei. Morgen, fuhr er fort, morgen müssen Sie noch bei mir bleiben, mein neuer Pfarrer thut seine Anzugspredigt, und wir wollen tausend Spaß mit ihm haben. Da ich ein Bürger bin, der die Art zu leben noch nicht recht weiß, und da mir die Einfalt meines Urältervaters noch immer anhängt, so kann ich nicht leugnen, ich erschrak ungemein über die edle Gleichgültigkeit meines Wirths. Ich erwartete den folgenden Tag mit Ungeduld; ich kam in die Kirche und erstaunte als ich einen großen, schwarzgekleideten Körper auf die Kanzel steigen sah. Sein Gang, seine Miene, seine Bewegung mit den Händen, seine Sprache selbst war so pöbelmäßig, daß ich den Kirchenpatron im Verdacht hielt, er habe aus einem leichtsinnigen Scherze seinen Reit=knecht verkleidet und der Gemeine vorgestellt. Ich sagte ihm meinen Zwei=fel. Allein er lachte mit solcher Heftigkeit über mich, daß ihm der Bauch schütterte. Mein Reitknecht? sagte er endlich. Zerreiß mich der Teufel, wenn es nicht mein Informator ist! Er ist ein Magister und nicht unge=schickt. Er will noch heuer ein Gesangbuch für mein Dorf zusammen drucken lassen und es meiner Gemahlin zueignen. Er ist ein guter Narr, ich wollte Holz auf ihm hacken. Ein vortrefflicher Character! dachte ich bei mir selbst und schwieg ganz beschämt still. Ich hörte ihm zu, weil ich sonst nichts zu hören hatte, und hielt bei seinem albernen Gewäsche eine Stunde lang geduldig aus. Ich getraue mir indessen ohne Eigenruhm zu behaupten, daß dasjenige, was mein lieber Urältervater Sancho Pansa mit seinem Esel geredet hat, weit vernünftiger gewesen ist als dieses neuen Seelsorgers heilige Rede an seine Gemeine war. Wir eilten aus der Kirche auf's Schloß. Sogleich stellte sich unser Seelenhirt auch ein, und das erste Compliment, das ihm der gnädige Herr zum Glückwunsche bei dem Eintritte in die Stube machte, war, daß er sagte: Komm Er, komm Er, Herr Magister, trink er das Glas Branntwein, es ist Ihm sauer geworden; aber er hat auch, der Teufel hol' mich! gepredigt wie ein Superintendent. Nur das verfluchte Schmälen gewöhne Er sich ab, das leide ich mein Seele nicht; und wenn Er einmal auf mich schmält, so soll mich der Donner zer=schlagen, wenn ich Ihn nicht über die Kanzel herunter werfen lasse, daß Er die Beine in die Höhe kehrt. Da! trink Er! Und darauf trank der theure Kirchenvater lächelnd auf einen Zug ein großes Glas aus. Wir setzten uns zu Tische; ich war demungeachtet ganz kleinmüthig und sah die armen Bauern als eine verrathene Heerde an. Ich aß wenig. Weiß Er denn, Herr Magister, sagte der Edelmann, wofür Ihn Herr Pansa angesehen hat? Für meinen Reitknecht! Das wundert mich nicht, rief der schon halb trunkene Pfarrer aus: Die Diener des Herrn sind den rohen Weltkindern immer ein Anstoß, und Herr Pansa hat noch ketzerisches Blut in seinen Adern. Wäre er wie seine Eltern verbrannt worden, so hätte unsere Re=

ligion auch einen Verächter weniger.   Ich entfärbte mich über diesen Un=
sinn und war eben im Begriffe ihm nach seiner Narrheit zu antworten, als
unser Wirth merkte, daß sich dieser Auftritt mit Verdruß endigen würde.
Er unterbrach mich mit einem Deckelglase und brachte es seinem Pfarrer
auf die Gesundheit aller hübschen Mädchen zu, welcher redlich Bescheid
that; und auf diese Weise ward bis gegen Abend fortgefahren.   Ihre
Wohlehrwürden hatten das Vergnügen zu sehen, daß Ihro Gnaden nebst
dem Gerichtsverwalter trunken unter den Tisch sanken, ohne daß er
selbst auf eine merkliche Art unvernünftiger geworden wäre als er schon
vor Tische war.   Ich schlich mich fort, weil ich merkte, daß er einen Reli=
gionsstreit mit mir anfangen wollte.   Am folgenden Morgen fragte mich
der Gerichtsherr, was ich nun eigentlich von seinem Pfarrer hielte?   Ich
halte ihn, sagte ich, für einen Mann ohne Verstand, ohne... Ach, sagte er,
was Verstand! Wem Gott ein Amt giebt, dem giebt er auch Verstand. Er
ist mein Informator gewesen; ich habe ihm die Pfarre schon lange ver=
sprochen, und um deswillen hat er meine Kinder für ein Spottgeld unter=
richtet. Was ich verspreche, das halte ich als ein Cavalier. Der Kerl
wird schon werden. Saufen kann er wie ein Teufel. Hier verstummte ich
auf einmal. Ich sah, daß der Herr das Wohl und die Unterweisung seiner
Kinder nicht für so wichtig gehalten als die Ersparung einiger Thaler
Geld; ich schloß, daß er es mit seinen Bauern nicht so boshaft, als ich an=
fangs geglaubt, meinen müsse, weil er ihnen einen Mann zum Lehrer gab,
dem er seine eignen Kinder anvertraut hatte; daß er doch immer glaubte,
Gott habe dieses Amt seinem Pfarrer gegeben, und daß er gewiß hoffte, er
werde den Verstand, der ihm fehlte, schon zu rechter Zeit aus der Hand des
Herrn empfangen.

Ich habe mich bei der Erzählung dieses Abentheuers länger aufgehalten
als ich Willens gewesen und als es vielleicht einigen meiner Leser lieb sein
wird, welche von der Ehrwürdigkeit des geistlichen Standes eben so ortho=
doxe Begriffe haben als der neue Pfarrer. Aber es schien mir um desto
nöthiger hievon etwas umständlicher zu reden, je leichter es nunmehr zu
begreifen sein wird, wie es komme, daß man bei Besetzung anderer Aemter,
welche nicht die Seele, sondern den Leib oder den Beutel der Unterthanen
betreffen, so sorglos seyn und nach allem eher als nach dem Verstande und
der Geschicklichkeit der Candidaten fragen kann. Alle Stände sind voll
von Beweisen meines Satzes. Ich habe nicht den Vorsatz, für mein jetzt
lebendes Vaterland zu schreiben, sonst würde ich mit leichter Mühe noch
hundert Exempel anführen können.

Es ist noch übrig, daß ich von der zweiten Gattung der Menschen ein
paar Worte sage, denen unser Sprichwort bei allen möglichen Fällen zum
kräftigsten Trost gereichet. Es sind dieses diejenigen, welche Aemter suchen.

Sie sind so vorsichtig, daß sie keine mühsame Untersuchung anstellen, ob sie auch den nöthigen Verstand haben, der zu den Aemtern erfordert wird. Eine solche Untersuchung verriethe ein Mißtrauen, welches ihrer männlichen und gesetzten Religion zuwider, dem geliebten Vaterlande aber sehr schädlich wäre. Denn dem Vaterlande liegt sehr viel daran, daß diese Herren Aemter kriegen; und wenn sie sich nicht eher darum bewerben sollten als bis sie von ihrem Verstande und ihrer Fähigkeit innerlich überzeugt wären, so würde ungeachtet unsers sehr bevölkerten Landes eine große Menge Aemter unbesetzt bleiben müssen. Und was wäre dem Vaterlande wohl nachtheiliger als dieses? Sie ängstigen sich daher gar nicht mit dergleichen kindischen und unpatriotischen Fragen: Wo werden wir den Verstand her= nehmen? Der dem Vieh sein Futter giebt, der wird auch für ihren Verstand sorgen; und sie genießen bei dieser nahrhaften Gemüthsruhe eben diejenige wahre Glückseligkeit, die ein Mastschwein hat, welches um Weihnachten feist ist, ohne daß es den Sommer über für seine Mastung gesorgt hat. Wenn ich drei Candidaten beisammen stehen sehe, so kann ich ohne die Liebe des Nächsten zu beleidigen gewiß glauben, daß zwei davon keinen Verstand haben, und bei dem dritten ist es noch vielmals ungewiß. Unsre Eltern sind gemeiniglich gegen die Vorsorge des Himmels so erkenntlich, daß sie bei der Erziehung ihrer Kinder nicht den geringsten Vorwitz bezeigen, wenn es auf die Frage ankömmt: ob ihre Kinder auch Gelegenheit haben, ihren Verstand so zu bilden, daß er dereinst zur Uebernehmung eines Amtes und zu dessen würdiger Bekleidung fähig ist. Es wäre dieses unverantwortlich. Ihre Väter dachten eben so, und dennoch haben die Kinder dieser Väter Aemter bekommen, ohne daß Jemand die unbescheidene Frage aufzuwerfen das Herz gehabt, ob sie auch Verstand genug besäßen. Solche Kleinigkeiten geben sich von sich selbst. Sie haben nunmehr Verstand genug, und sie haben zu viel Verstand, als daß sie in diesem Falle wegen ihrer eignen Kinder bekümmert sein sollten. Ja sie machten sich ein Gewissen daraus, und sie sind deswegen zu loben. Es ist unverantwortlich die Natur in ihrem Laufe zu stören, oder in ihrem Werke zu meistern. Sie haben wohl= gestaltete Kinder gezeugt, und die Natur hat sie ohne ihre Vorsorge so wohlgestaltet hervorgebracht. Und da der Körper das vornehmste an dem Menschen wenigstens heut zu Tage ist, so überlassen sie auch der gütigen Natur lediglich die Bildung des Verstandes als eines sehr zufälligen und nicht unentbehrlichen Theils des Menschen. Ich kenne den Sohn eines vornehmen Officiers. Er ist noch in seiner zarten Kindheit von achtzehn Jahren; deswegen hat der gnädige Papa noch nicht so grausam sein und ihn der Aufsicht der Französin entreißen wollen, welche ihn noch alle Morgen anziehen und waschen muß. Er ist ein vortrefflicher Kenner von der Näherei und versteht die Schattirung der bunten Naht besser als irgend

14*

ein Sohn eines Officiers. Der Koch ist ein Sudler gegen ihn. Er weiß
alle Gerichte zu beurtheilen; er kocht selbst die schmackhaftesten Speisen,
und unter der ganzen Armee ist Niemand, der die Pasteten so leckerhaft
backen kann, als dieser junge Herr. Wäre er der Sohn eines Unterofficiers
oder elenden Gemeinen, so würde man ihn nach der Gewohnheit des bürgerlichen Pöbels zu einer Kenntniß des Christenthums, der nöthigsten
Wissenschaften und der Welt angeführt und durch beständige Arbeit zu
seinen künftigen Diensten abgehärtet haben. Aber so niederträchtig erzieht
man den Sohn eines großen Officiers nicht. Aus Liebe zum Vaterlande
schont man diesen theuren Körper; zu seiner Gemüthsergötzung läßt man
ihn kochen, nähen und sticken. Er ist ein junger feuriger Herr, welchen
man nicht zu früh anstrengen muß, wenn es ihm nicht gehen soll wie den
jungen hitzigen Ochsen, welche sich leicht verrücken, wenn man sie zu früh
anspannt. Seine gnädige Mama hat mit mütterlichem Vergnügen zu-
gesehen, mit was für einer edlen Unverschämtheit er nur ohnlängst gegen
das Kammermädchen sich benahm. Der lose Schelm! sagte die zärtliche
Mutter, und nunmehr glaubte sie, daß es Zeit wäre ihn in die Welt zu
lassen. Sie überlegte die Sache mit ihrem Gemahle. Man kaufte ihm
eine Compagnie, und bei der ersten Gelegenheit wird dieser allerliebste Sohn
eine Anzahl bärtiger und tapferer Männer, die unter ihm stehen, wider den
Feind anführen. Er hatte kaum eine Stunde lang den Ringkragen an-
gehabt, als er recht eigentlich spürte, wie ihm der Verstand, der zu einem
solchen Commando gehört, aus dem Magen in alle Glieder des Leibes
drang. Er kann fluchen wie der älteste Musketier, er säuft wie ein Cor-
poral, hat sich schon zweimal mit dem Lieutenant geschlagen, seinem Obersten
sich einigemal widersetzt und Alles gethan, was man von ihm hat hoffen
können. Ist nicht dieses Alles ein Beweis, daß der Verstand mit dem Amt
kömmt? Und hätte wohl Jemand geglaubt, daß bei einer solchen Erziehung derjenige mit so vieler anscheinender Hoffnung für sein Vaterland
fechten sollte, welcher menschlichem Ansehen nach nur geboren war, für sein
Vaterland zu kochen?

Wie glücklich muß das Land seyn, in welchem ein Ueberfluß von solchen
Personen vorhanden ist, bei denen man ungewiß bleibt, ob sie sich besser
vor die Spitze ihrer Truppen oder hinter den Nährahm schicken! Indessen
muß ich gestehen, daß nicht der Militärstand allein sich dieses Vorzugs
rühmen kann, sondern daß wir durch die weise Sorglosigkeit unsrer Eltern
und Vorgesetzten und durch die natürliche sich selbst gelassene Dummheit
des größten Theils unsrer hoffnungsvollen Jugend denjenigen glücklichen
Zeiten sehr nahe gekommen sind, wo man einen Candidaten, welcher die
nöthige Geschicklichkeit und den Verstand eher hat als ein Amt, bald als
ein Wunderthier für Geld in Messen sehen lassen wird. Ich bin verschie-

denen werthen Freunden, welche in meiner Gegend wohnen, für das Ver=
gnügen, das ich in ihrem erbaulichen Umgange täglich genieße, so vielen Dank
schuldig, daß ich mir ein Gewissen daraus mache, diese Abhandlung zu schlie=
ßen, ohne sie im Vorbeigehen ein wenig zu verewigen, und der Nachwelt ihre
Verdienste um das Vaterland nach meinem Vermögen kenntbar zu machen.

Cajus ist werth, daß ich ihn zuerst nenne. Seinen wahren Namen muß
ich verschweigen, um seine Bescheidenheit nicht zu beleidigen. Vielleicht
aber findet man ihn nächstens im Anhang der Zeitungen, nebst einer ge=
nauen Beschreibung seiner Person und Kleidung. Denn wenn er in seinem
Vorhaben glücklich ist, wie seine Anstalten nicht anders vermuthen lassen,
so wird man das Vergnügen haben, ihn entweder unter dem Galgen, oder
doch aus einem Steckbriefe kennen zu lernen. Es sind ihm landesherr=
schaftliche Cassen anvertraut. Ob er nun gleich weder schreiben noch rechnen
kann, so kennt er doch das Geld sehr gut, und ist in seinem Amte so uner=
müdet, daß er nirgends keine Reste außer in seiner Casse leiden kann.
Unter andern Wohlthaten des Himmels, welche dieser wackere Mann ver=
dient, ist diese nicht die geringste, daß er einen Sohn erzogen hat, welcher
recht zum Galgen geboren zu seyn scheint. Als ein unschuldsvoller Knabe
von zwölf Jahren empfand er seinen innerlichen Beruf und bediente sich
mit vieler Geschicklichkeit einer Gelegenheit, seiner Mutter einen Theil ihres
Geschmeides zu entwenden. Zweimal hat er bei zunehmenden Jahren
seinem werthgeschätzten Herrn Vater die Casse erbrochen. Im ganzen
Städtchen ist Keiner, der mit einer so witzigen Art die Schnupftücher aus
der Tasche ziehen kann, als er thut. Diese Beschäftigungen haben ihm von
Jugend auf nicht so viel Zeit gelassen etwas zu lernen, und ich kann es ihm
ohne Ruhm nachsagen, daß er jetzo, da er zwanzig Jahre alt ist, seinen
Namen nicht zu schreiben weiß, noch das Geringste von Rechnungssachen
versteht. Dieses hat seinen Papa ganz natürlicher Weise auf die Gedanken
gebracht, daß es sehr wohl gethan seyn würde, sich den lieben Sohn ad=
jungieren zu lassen. Und ich sehe nicht die geringste Schwierigkeit, welche
diese väterliche Absicht hindern sollte. Wem Gott ein Amt gibt, dem gibt
er auch den Verstand; und da der Herr Vater so lange Zeit sein Amt hat
verwalten können, ohne ehrlich zu seyn, so hoffe ich gewiß, der Herr Ad=
junctus wird es mit der Zeit noch höher bringen.

Der Pachter von einem benachbarten Landgute hat einen Sohn, welcher
so dumm ist, als man es nur verlangen kann. Sein Vater hat viel Ein=
sicht, und ist daher im Stande gewesen, sich mit einer Menge gelehrter
Männer bekannt zu machen, welche, so viel er hat wahrnehmen können, in
ihrer Jugend wenigstens so dumm gewesen sind als sein Sohn, und noch
jetzo dem Verstand eines Pächters nicht gleichkommen. Da sich sein Sohn
zu gar nichts schickt, so hat er dem gnädigen Herrn sein Anliegen erzählt,

und beide sind einmüthig darauf gefallen, der Junge soll ein Doctor werden.
Und er fängt auch nunmehr an, ein Doctor zu werden. Der Vater schmei=
chelt sich, daß ihm Gott gewiß mit der Zeit eine Professur und sodann
wenigstens so viel Verstand geben werde, als seiner Meinung nach zu
einem Canonicat erfordert wird. In der That sehe ich nicht, was ihn in
seinem frommen Vertrauen stören sollte.

Der Organist in einem Marktflecken, der ungefähr eine halbe Meile von
mir liegt, hat einen Sohn, der wohl gewachsen ist, reiche Westen trägt, über
alle Sachen ein entscheidendes Urtheil fällt und nichts gelernt hat. Der
Vater, der den Sohn väterlich bewundert, wünscht sehr, ihn als Hofmeister
bei einem Jungen von Adel zu sehen. Er glaubt, daß er alle Fähigkeiten
besitze, die dazu erfordert werden, und ich glaube, daß er in Kurzem eine
einträgliche Hofmeisterstelle bekommen wird. Es ist wahr, daß er von
Allem dem nichts versteht, was ein junger Cavalier lernen soll. Er ist
auch niemals, so wenig als jetzo, im Stande gewesen, sich selbst zu regieren.
Er ist, wie ihm einige mürrische Leute nachsagen, in seinen Ausschweifungen
niederträchtig, in seiner Wirthschaft unordentlich, in seinen Urtheilen pöbel=
haft. Was schadet das? Wie viele junge Herren würden allein auf
Reisen gehen müssen, wenn diese Eigenschaften hinderten, ein Hofmeister zu
seyn! Genug, er spielt gut l'Hombre; er kann die Kunst, mit vieler
Unterthänigkeit einen gnädigen Rock zu küssen; er ist unverschämt, und hat
er gleich keinen Verstand, so wird sich das schon geben.

Weil vielleicht einige nicht begreifen möchten, warum ich mich bei einer
so ausgemachten Sache, als das Sprichwort ist: Wem Gott ein Amt gibt,
dem gibt er auch Verstand, so lange aufgehalten habe, so will ich hier den
Schlüssel dazu geben. Es betrifft meine eigene Leibes= und Seelenruhe,
und es liegt mir viel daran, daß alle Leute von der Wahrheit dieses Sprich=
worts überzeugt sind. Man hat mir unter der Hand angetragen, Ballet=
meister an einem gewissen Hofe zu werden. Es sind viele Vortheile bei
dieser Station, und mancher große Gelehrte verdient in seinem Leben so
viel nicht bei aller sauern Mühe mit seinem Kopfe, als ich sodann unter
Tanzen und Springen in einem Jahre mit meinen Füßen verdienen könnte.
Ich bin um deswillen nicht ganz abgeneigt, die Stelle anzunehmen. Es ist
wahr! es scheint nicht, als wenn mich die Natur zu einem Tanzmeister er=
koren hätte. Mein linker Fuß ist ungeheuer dick; auf dem rechten hinke
ich ein wenig: die rechte Schulter ist etwas höher als die linke; auf dem
einen Auge habe ich einen Stern, auf dem andern schiele ich; die Arme sind
durch die englische Krankheit sehr verwachsen, und weil ich einen Ansatz zur
Wassersucht habe, so zweifle ich fast, daß ich solche hohen Capriolen werde
machen können, als mein seliger Urältervater machte, da er geprellt ward.
Inzwischen verzweifle ich nicht ganz. Wenn es ausgemacht ist, daß Gott

demjenigen Verstand gibt, dem er ein Amt gibt, so ist es eben so leicht zu hoffen, daß er einem Krüppel gesunde Gliedmaßen geben wird, den er zum Tanzmeister machen will. Es gehört, dünkt mich, noch weniger dazu, als wenn aus einem gebornen Narren ein verständiger Mann werden soll. Und wenn ich auch wider Vermuthen ein Krüppel bliebe: so würde doch das gemeine Wesen von einem gebrechlichen Tanzmeister bei weitem nicht so viel Schaden zu besorgen haben, als es von einem Manne befürchten muß, der zu einem öffentlichen Amte ungeschickt und bei dessen Verwaltung ohne Verstand ist. Mit einem Worte, ich halte den Antrag für einen rechtmäßigen Beruf. Ich werde ihn also wohl annehmen; und gar der geneigte Leser wird künftige Messe das Vergnügen haben, eine systematische Abhandlung von den Regeln der Tanzkunst von mir zu erhalten. Verstehe ich gleichwohl nicht das Geringste davon; so habe ich doch das Recht, mir eine gütige Aufnahme meines Werkes mit eben der Zuversicht zu verspre- chen, mit welcher sich so viele Schriftsteller schmeicheln, die sich zum Bücher- schreiben so wenig schicken, als ich mich zum Tanzmeister. Was mich noch abhält, meine endliche Erklärung von mir zu geben, ist die Furcht vor dem Hofe. Es geschieht zuweilen, daß die vornehmsten Damen einen wunder- lichen Appetit haben, und mein scarronischer Körper stellt mich vor ihren verführerischen Liebkosungen nicht in völlige Sicherheit. Ich weiß mehr Exempel, daß ein plumper Stallknecht die Stelle eines liebenswürdigen Gemahls hat vertreten müssen. Ich wäre des Todes, wenn ich mich in solche gefährliche Umstände verwickelt sehen sollte. Denn keusch bin ich wie meine Väter, und diese unzeitige Keuschheit hat mich mehr als einmal um mein Glück gebracht. Ich will es überlegen. Ein Balletmeister zu seyn, wäre gleichwohl eine hübsche Sache.

Johann Winckelmann.
4. Beschreibung des Torso im Belvedere zu Rom.

Ich theile hier eine Beschreibung des berühmten Torso im Belvedere mit, welcher insgemein der Torso vom Michael Angelo genennet wird, weil die- ser Künstler dieses Stück besonders hochgeschätzet und viel nach demselben studiret hat. Es ist eine verstümmelte Statue eines sitzenden Hercules, wie bekannt ist, und der Meister desselben ist Apollonius, des Nestors Sohn, von Athen. Diese Beschreibung gehet nur auf das Ideal der Statue, son- derlich da sie idealisch ist, und ist ein Stück von einer ähnlichen Abbildung mehrerer Statuen.
   Die erste Arbeit, an welche ich mich in Rom machete, war, die Statuen im

Belvedere, nämlich den Apollo, den Laokoon, den sogenannten Antinous und diesen Torso als das vollkommenste der alten Bildhauerei zu beschreiben. Die Vorstellung einer jeden Statue sollte zween Theile haben: der erste in Absicht des Ideals, der andere nach der Kunst; und meine Meinung war, die Werke selbst von dem besten Künstler zeichnen zu lassen. Diese Unternehmung aber ging über mein Vermögen. —

Ich führe dich jetzo zu dem so viel gerühmten und niemals genug gepriesenen Trunk eines Hercules, zu einem Werke, welches das schönste in seiner Art und unter die höchsten Hervorbringungen der Kunst zu zählen ist, von denen, welche bis auf unsere Zeit gekommen sind. Wie werde ich dir den beschreiben, da er der schönsten und der bedeutendsten Theile der Natur beraubet ist! So wie von einer prächtigen Eiche, welche umgehauen und von Zweigen und Aesten entblößet worden, nur der Stamm allein übrig geblieben ist, so gemißhandelt und verstümmelt sitzet das Bild des Helden; Kopf, Arme und Beine und das Oberste der Brust fehlen.

Der erste Anblick wird dir vielleicht nichts als einen verunstalteten Stein entdecken: vermagst du aber in die Geheimnisse der Kunst einzudringen, so wirst du ein Wunder derselben erblicken, wenn du dieses Werk mit einem ruhigen Auge betrachtest. Alsdann wird dir Hercules wie mitten in allen seinen Unternehmungen erscheinen, und der Held und der Gott werden in diesem Stücke zugleich sichtbar werden.

Da, wo die Dichter aufgehört haben, hat der Künstler angefangen: jene schwiegen, sobald der Held unter die Götter aufgenommen und mit der Göttin der ewigen Jugend ist vermählet worden; dieser aber zeiget uns denselben in einer vergötterten Gestalt und mit einem gleichsam unsterblichen Leibe, welcher dennoch Stärke und Leichtigkeit zu den großen Unternehmungen, die er vollbracht, behalten hat.

Ich sehe in den mächtigen Umrissen dieses Leibes die unüberwundene Kraft des Besiegers der gewaltigen Riesen, die sich wider die Götter empöreten und in den Phlagräischen Feldern von ihm erlegt wurden; und zu gleicher Zeit stellen mir die sanften Züge dieser Umrisse, die das Gebäude des Leibes leicht und gelenksam machen, die geschwinden Wendungen desselben in dem Kampfe mit dem Achelous vor, der mit allen vielförmigen Verwandlungen seinen Händen nicht entgehen konnte.

In jedem Theile dieses Körpers offenbart sich wie in einem Gemälde der ganze Held in einer besondern That, und man sieht so wie die richtigen Absichten in dem vernünftigen Baue eines Palastes hier den Gebrauch, zu welcher That ein jedes Theil gedient hat.

Ich kann das Wenige, was von der Schulter noch zu sehen ist, nicht betrachten, ohne mich zu erinnern, daß auf ihrer ausgebreiteten Stärke wie auf zwei Gebirgen die ganze Last der himmlischen Kreise geruht hat. Mit

was für einer Großheit wächst die Brust an, und wie prächtig ist die an=
hebende Rundung ihres Gewölbes! Eine solche Brust muß diejenige ge=
wesen seyn, auf welcher der Riese Antäus und der dreileibige Geryon
erdrückt worden. Keine Brust eines drei= und viermal gekrönten olym=
pischen Siegers, keine Brust eines spartanischen Kriegers, von Helden gebo=
ren, muß sich so prächtig und erhöhet gezeiget haben.

Fraget diejenigen, die das Schönste in der Natur der Sterblichen ken=
nen, ob sie eine Seite gesehen haben, die mit der linken Seite zu vergleichen
ist. Die Wirkung und Gegenwirkung ihrer Muskeln ist mit einem weis=
lichen Maße von abwechselnder Regung und schneller Kraft wunderwürdig
abgewogen, und der Leib mußte durch dieselbe zu Allem, was er vollbringen
wollen, tüchtig gemacht werden. So wie in einer anhebenden Bewegung
des Meeres, die zuvor stille Fläche in einer neblichen Unruhe mit spielen=
den Wellen anwächset, wo eine von der andern verschlungen und aus dersel=
ben wiederum hervorgewälzet wird, eben so sanft aufgeschwellet und schwe=
bend gezogen, fließet hier eine Muskel in die andere, und eine dritte, die sich
zwischen ihnen erhebet und ihre Bewegung zu verstärken scheinet, verliert sich
in jene, und unser Blick wird gleichsam mit verschlungen.

Hier möchte ich stille stehen, um unseren Betrachtungen Raum zu geben,
der Vorstellung ein immerwährendes Bild von dieser Seite einzudrücken;
allein die hohen Schönheiten sind hier in einer unzertrennlichen Mitthei=
lung. Was für ein Begriff erwächset zugleich hieher aus den Hüften, deren
Feistigkeit andeuten kann, daß der Held niemals gewanket und nie sich beu=
gen müssen?

In diesem Augenblicke durchfährt mein Geist die entlegensten Gegenden
der Welt, durch welche Hercules gezogen ist, und ich werde bis an die Gren=
zen seiner Mühseligkeiten und bis an die Denkmale und Säulen, wo sein
Fuß ruhete, geführet durch den Anblick der Schenkel von unerschöpflicher
Kraft und von einer den Gottheiten eigenen Länge, die den Held durch hun=
dert Länder und Völker bis zur Unsterblichkeit getragen haben. Ich fing
an, diese entfernten Züge zu überdenken, da mein Geist zurückgerufen wird
durch einen Blick auf seinen Rücken. Ich wurde entzücket, da ich diesen
Körper von hinten ansahe, so wie ein Mensch, der nach Bewunderung des
prächtigen Portals an einem Tempel auf die Höhe desselben geführet würde,
wo ihn das Gewölbe desselben, welches er nicht übersehen kann, von Neuem
in Erstaunen setzet.

Ich sehe hier den vornehmsten Bau der Gebeine dieses Leibes, den Ur=
sprung der Muskeln und den Grund ihrer Lage und Bewegung, und dieses
Alles zeigt sich wie eine von der Höhe der Berge entdeckte Landschaft, über
welche die Natur mannigfaltigen Reichthum ihrer Schönheiten ausgegos=
sen. So wie die lustigen Höhen derselben sich mit einem sanften Abhange

in geſenkte Thäler verlieren, die hier ſich ſchmälern und dort erweitern, ſo
mannigfaltig, prächtig und ſchön erheben ſich hier ſchwellende Hügel von
Muskeln, um welche ſich oft unmerkliche Tiefen gleich dem Strome des
Mäanders krümmen, die weniger dem Geſichte als dem Gefühle offenbar
werden.

Scheinet es unbegreiflich, außer dem Haupte in einem andern Theile des
Körpers eine denkende Kraft zu zeigen, ſo lernet hier, wie die Hand eines
ſchöpferiſchen Meiſters die Materie geiſtig zu machen vermögend iſt. Mich
deucht, es bilde mir der Rücken, welcher durch hohe Betrachtungen gekrümmt
ſcheinet, ein Haupt, das mit einer frohen Erinnerung ſeiner erſtaunenden
Thaten beſchäftigt iſt, und indem ſich ſo ein Haupt voll von Majeſtät und
Weisheit vor meinen Augen erhebet, ſo fangen ſich an in meinen Gedanken
die übrigen mangelhaften Glieder zu bilden: es ſammelt ſich ein Ausfluß
aus dem gegenwärtigen und wirket gleichſam eine plötzliche Ergänzung.

Die Macht der Schulter deutet mir an, wie ſtark die Arme geweſen, die
den Löwen auf dem Gebirge Cithäron erwürget, und mein Auge ſucht ſich
diejenigen zu bilden, die den Cerberus gebunden und weggeführet haben.
Seine Schenkel und das erhaltene Knie geben mir einen Begriff von den
Beinen, die niemals ermüdet ſind und den Hirſch mit Füßen von Erze ver-
folget und erreichet haben.

Durch eine geheime Kunſt aber wird der Geiſt durch alle Thaten ſeiner
Stärke bis zur Vollkommenheit ſeiner Seele geführt, und in dieſem Sturze
iſt ein Denkmal derſelben, welches ihm keine Dichter, die nur die Stärke
ſeiner Arme beſingen, errichtet: der Künſtler hat ſie übertroffen. Sein
Bild des Helden gibt keinen Gedanken von Gewaltthätigkeit und ausgelaſ-
ſener Liebe Platz. In der Ruhe und Stille des Körpers offenbaret ſich der
geſetzte große Geiſt, der Mann, welcher ſich aus Liebe zur Gerechtigkeit den
größten Gefährlichkeiten ausgeſetzt, der den Ländern Sicherheit und den
Einwohnern Ruhe geſchafft.

In dieſe vorzügliche und edle Form einer ſo vollkommenen Natur iſt
gleichſam die Unſterblichkeit eingehüllet, und die Geſtalt iſt bloß wie ein Gefäß derſelben; ein höherer Geiſt ſcheinet den Raum der ſterblichen Theile
eingenommen und ſich an die Stelle derſelben ausgebreitet zu haben. Es
iſt nicht mehr der Körper, welcher annoch wider Ungeheuer und Friedens-
ſtörer zu ſtreiten hat: es iſt derjenige, der auf dem Berge Oeta von den
Schlacken der Menſchheit gereinigt worden, die ſich von dem Urſprunge der
Aehnlichkeit des Vaters der Götter abgeſondert.

O möchte ich dieſes Bild in der Größe und Schönheit ſehen, in welcher
es ſich dem Verſtande des Künſtlers geoffenbaret hat, um nur allein von
dem Ueberreſte ſagen zu können, was er gedacht hat und wie ich denken
ſollte! Mein großes Glück nach dem ſeinigen würde ſeyn, dieſes Werk wür-

dig zu beschreiben. Voller Betrübniß aber bleibe ich stehen, und so wie
Psyche anfing die Liebe zu beweinen, nachdem sie dieselbe kennen gelernt, so
bejammere ich den unersetzlichen Schaden dieses Hercules, nachdem ich zur
Einsicht der Schönheit desselben gelangt bin.

Die Kunst weint zugleich mit mir: denn das Werk, welches sie den größ=
ten Erfindungen des Witzes und Nachdenkens entgegensetzen, und durch wel=
ches sie noch jetzt ihr Haupt wie in ihren goldenen Zeiten zu der größten
Höhe menschlicher Achtung erheben könnte, dieses Werk, welches vielleicht
das letzte ist, in welches sie ihre äußersten Kräfte gewandt hat, muß sie halb
vernichtet und grausam gemißhandelt sehen. Wem wird nicht der Verlust
so vieler hundert anderer Meisterstücke derselben zu Gemüthe geführet! Aber
die Kunst, welche uns weiter unterrichten will, rufet uns von diesen trau=
rigen Ueberlegungen zurück, und zeigt uns, wieviel noch aus dem Uebrig=
gebliebenen zu lernen ist und mit was für einem Auge es der Künstler an=
sehen müsse.

Gottfried Ephraim Lessing.

5. Laokoon.

Es giebt Kenner des Alterthums, welche die Gruppe Laokoon zwar für
ein Werk Griechischer Meister, aber aus der Zeit der Kaiser halten, weil sie
glauben, daß der Virgilische Laokoon dabei zum Vorbilde gedient habe. Ich
will von den älteren Gelehrten, die dieser Meinung gewesen sind, nur den
Bartholomäus Marliani, und von den neuen den Montfaucon nennen.
Sie fanden ohne Zweifel zwischen dem Kunstwerke und der Beschreibung
des Dichters eine so besondere Uebereinstimmung, daß es ihnen unmöglich
dünkte, daß beide von ungefähr auf einerlei Umstände sollten gefallen seyn,
die sich nichts weniger als von selbst darbieten. Dabei setzten sie voraus,
daß, wenn es auf die Ehre der Erfindung und des ersten Gedankens an=
komme, die Wahrscheinlichkeit für den Dichter ungleich größer sey als für
den Künstler. Nur scheinen sie vergessen zu haben, daß ein dritter Fall
möglich sei. Denn vielleicht hat der Dichter eben so wenig den Künstler
als der Künstler den Dichter nachgeahmt, sondern beide haben aus einerlei
älteren Quellen geschöpft. Bewiesen oder nicht bewiesen, daß die Bild=
hauer dem Virgil nachgeahmt haben; ich will es bloß annehmen, um zu se=
hen, wie sie ihm sodann nachgearbeitet hätten. Ueber das Geschrei habe
ich mich schon erklärt. Vielleicht daß mich weitere Vergleichung auf nicht
weniger unterrichtende Bemerkungen leitet. Der Einfall, den Vater mit
seinen beiden Söhnen durch die mörderischen Schlangen in einen Knoten
zu schürzen, ist ohnstreitig ein sehr glücklicher Einfall, der von einer unge=

mein maleriſchen Phantaſie zeuget.   Wem gehört er? dem Dichter oder
den Künſtlern? Montfaucon will ihn bei dem Dichter nicht finden.   Aber
ich meine, Montfaucon hat den Dichter nicht aufmerkſam genug geleſen.
Der Dichter hat die Schlangen von einer wunderbaren Länge geſchildert.
Sie haben die Knaben umſtrickt, und da der Vater ihnen zu Hülfe kommt,
ergreifen ſie auch ihn.   Nach ihrer Größe konnten ſie ſich nicht auf einmal
von den Knaben loswinden; es mußte alſo einen Augenblick geben, da ſie
den Vater mit ihren Köpfen und Vordertheilen ſchon angefallen hatten
und mit ihren Hintertheilen die Knaben noch verſchlungen hielten.   Dieſer
Augenblick iſt in der Fortſchreitung des poetiſchen Gemäldes nothwendig;
der Dichter läßt ihn ſattſam empfinden; nur ihn anzumalen, dazu war jetzt
die Zeit nicht.   Daß ihn die alten Ausleger auch wirklich empfunden haben, ſcheint eine Stelle des Donatus zu bezeugen.   Wie viel weniger wird
er den Künſtlern entwiſcht ſeyn, in deren verſtändiges Auge Alles, was ihnen
vortheilhaft werden kann, ſo ſchnell und deutlich einleuchtet?   In den
Windungen ſelbſt, mit welchen der Dichter die Schlangen um den Laocoon
führet, vermeidet er ſehr ſorgfältig die Arme, um den Händen alle ihre
Wirkſamkeit zu laſſen.
    Hierin mußten ihm die Künſtler nothwendig folgen.   Nichts giebt mehr
Ausdruck und Leben als die Bewegung der Hände; im Affecte beſonders
iſt das ſprechende Geſicht ohne ſie unbedeutend.   Arme durch die Ringe
der Schlangen feſt an den Körper geſchloſſen, würden Froſt und Tod über
die ganze Gruppe verbreitet haben.   Alſo ſehen wir ſie an der Hauptfigur
ſowohl als an den Nebenfiguren in völliger Thätigkeit und da am meiſten
beſchäftigt, wo gegenwärtig der heftigſte Schmerz iſt.   Weiter aber auch
nichts als dieſe Freiheit der Arme, fanden die Künſtler zuträglich in Anſe=
hung der Verſtrickung der Schlangen von dem Dichter zu entlehnen.   Virgil
läßt die Schlangen doppelt um den Leib und doppelt um den Hals des
Laocoon ſich winden und hoch mit ihren Köpfen über ihn herausragen.
Dieſes Bild füllet unſre Einbildungskraft vortrefflich.   Die edelſten Theile
ſind bis zum Erſticken gepreßt, und das Gift gehet gerade nach dem Ge=
ſichte.   Demohngeachtet war es kein Bild für Künſtler, welche die Wirkun=
gen des Giftes und des Schmerzes in dem Körper zeigen wollten.   Denn
um dieſe bemerken zu können, mußten die Haupttheile ſo frei ſeyn als mög=
lich, und durchaus mußte kein äußerer Druck auf ſie wirken, welcher das
Spiel der leidenden Nerven und der arbeitenden Muskeln verändern und
ſchwächen könnte.   Die doppelten Windungen der Schlangen würden den
ganzen Leib verdeckt haben, und jene ſchmerzliche Einziehung des Unterlei=
bes, welche ſo ſehr ausdrückend iſt, würde unſichtbar geblieben ſeyn.   Was
man über oder unter oder zwiſchen den Windungen von dem Leibe noch er=
blickt hätte, würde unter Preſſungen und Aufſchwellungen erſchienen ſeyn,

die nicht von dem innern Schmerze, sondern von der äußern Last gewirkt
worden. Der eben so oft umschlungene Hals würde die pyramidalische Zu-
spitzung der Gruppe, welche dem Auge so angenehm ist, gänzlich verdorben
haben; und die aus dieser Wulst ins Freie hinaus ragenden spitzen Schlan-
genköpfe hätten einen so plötzlichen Abfall von Mensur gemacht, daß die
Form des Ganzen äußerst anstößig geworden wäre. Es giebt Zeichner,
welche unverständig genug gewesen sind, sich demohngeachtet an den Dichter
zu binden. Was denn aber auch daraus geworden, läßt sich unter andern
aus dem Blatte des Franz Cleyn mit Abscheu erkennen. Die alten Bildhauer übersahen es mit einem Blicke, daß ihre Kunst hier eine gänzliche
Abänderung erforderte. Sie verlegten alle Windungen von dem Leibe und
Halse um die Schenkel und Füße. Hier konnten diese Windungen dem
Ausdrucke unbeachtet, so viel decken und pressen als nöthig war. Hier er-
regten sie zugleich die Idee der gehemmten Flucht und einer Art von Unbe-
weglichkeit, die der künstlichen Fortdauer des nämlichen Zustandes sehr vortheilhaft ist. Ich weiß nicht, wie es gekommen, daß die Kunstrichter diese
Verschiedenheit, welche sich in den Windungen der Schlangen zwischen dem
Kunstwerke und der Beschreibung des Dichters so deutlich zeiget, gänzlich
mit Stillschweigen übergangen haben. Sie erhebet die Weisheit der Künstler eben so sehr als die andre, auf die sie alle fallen, die sie aber nicht sowohl anzupreisen wagen, als vielmehr nur zu entschuldigen suchen. Ich
meine die Verschiedenheit in der Bekleidung. Virgil's Laokoon ist in seinem priesterlichen Ornate, und in der Gruppe erscheinet er mit seinen beiden Söhnen völlig nackend. Man sagt, es gäbe Leute, welche eine große
Ungereimtheit darin fänden, daß ein Königssohn, ein Priester, bei einem
Opfer nackend vorgestellet werde. Und diesen Leuten antworten Kenner
der Kunst in allem Ernst, daß es allerdings ein Fehler wider das Uebliche
sey, daß aber die Künstler dazu gezwungen worden, weil sie ihren Figuren
keine anständige Kleidung geben können. Die Bildhauerei, sagen sie,
könne keine Stoffe nachahmen; dicke Falten machten eine üble Wirkung;
aus zwei Unbequemlichkeiten habe man also die geringste wählen und lieber
gegen die Wahrheit selbst verstoßen, als in den Gewändern tadelhaft werden müssen. Wenn die alten Artisten bei dem Einwurfe lachen würden,
so weiß ich nicht, was sie zu der Beantwortung sagen dürften. Man kann
die Kunst nicht tiefer herabsetzen, als es dadurch geschiehet. Denn gesetzt,
die Sculptur könnte die verschiedenen Stoffe eben so gut nachahmen als die
Malerei: würde sodann Laokoon nothwendig bekleidet seyn müssen?
Würden wir unter dieser Bekleidung nichts verlieren? Hat ein Gewand,
das Werk sclavischer Hände, eben so viel Schönheit als das Werk der ewigen Weisheit im organisirten Körper? Erfordert es einerlei Fähigkeiten,
ist es einerlei Verdienst, bringt es einerlei Ehre, jenes oder diesen nachzu-

ahmen? Wollen unsre Augen nur getäuscht seyn, und ist es ihnen gleich-
viel, womit sie getäuscht werden? Bei dem Dichter ist ein Gewand kein
Gewand; es verdeckt nichts; unsere Einbildungskraft sieht überall hindurch. Laokoon habe es bei dem Virgil oder habe es nicht: sein Leiden ist
ihr an jedem Theile seines Körpers einmal so sichtbar als das andre. Die
Stirne ist mit der priesterlichen Binde für sie umbunden, aber nicht um-
hüllet. Ja sie hindert nicht allein nicht diese Binde, sie verstärkt auch den
Begriff, den wir uns von dem Unglücke des Leidenden machen. Nichts
hilft ihm seine priesterliche Würde, selbst das Zeichen derselben, das ihm
überall Ansehn und Verehrung verschafft, wird von dem giftigen Geifer
durchnetzt und entheiligt. Aber diesen Nebenbegriff mußte der Artist aufgeben, wenn das Hauptwerk nicht leiden sollte. Hätte er dem Laokoon auch
nur diese Binde gelassen, so würde er den Ausdruck um ein Großes ge-
schwächt haben. Die Stirne wäre zum Theil verdeckt worden, und die
Stirne ist der Sitz des Ausdrucks. Wie er also dort bei dem Schreien
den Ausdruck der Schönheit aufopferte, so opferte er hier das Uebliche dem
Ausdrucke auf. Ueberhaupt war das Uebliche bei den Alten eine sehr ge-
ringschätzige Sache. Sie fühlten, daß die höchste Bestimmung ihrer Kunst
sie auf die völlige Entbehrung desselben führte. Schönheit ist diese höchste
Bestimmung; Noth erfand die Kleider, und was hat die Kunst mit der
Noth zu thun? Ich gebe es zu, daß es auch eine Schönheit der Bekleidung
giebt, aber was ist sie gegen die Schönheit der menschlichen Form? Und
wird der, der das größere erreichen kann, sich mit dem kleineren begnügen?
Ich fürchte sehr, der vollkommenste Meister in Gewändern zeigt durch diese
Geschicklichkeit selbst, woran es ihm fehlt.

Johann Georg Hamann.

6. Aus den biblischen Betrachtungen.

Ich will einige allgemeine Anmerkungen über die göttliche Offenbarung
machen, die mir einfallen werden. Gott hat sich geoffenbart dem Menschen
in der Natur und in seinem Wort. Man hat die Aehnlichkeiten und Beziehungen dieser beiden Offenbarungen noch nicht so weit auseinander gesetzt und so deutlich erklärt, noch auf diese Harmonie gedrungen, worin
eine gesunde Philosophie sich ein weites Feld öffnen könnte. Beide Offenbarungen müssen auf eine gleiche Art in unzähligen Fällen gegen die größten Einwürfe gerettet werden; beide Offenbarungen erklären, unterstützen
sich einander und können sich nicht widersprechen, so sehr es auch die Aus-
legungen thun mögen, die unsere Vernunft darüber macht. Es ist vielmehr
der größte Widerspruch und Mißbrauch derselben, wenn sie sich selbst offen-

baren will. Ein Philosoph, welcher, der Vernunft zu Gefallen, das gött=
liche Wort aus den Augen setzt, ist in dem Falle der Juden, die desto hart=
näckiger das neue Testament verwerfen, je fester sie an dem alten zu han=
gen scheinen.   An diesen wird die Prophezeihung erfüllt, daß dasjenige ein
Aergerniß und eine Thorheit in ihren Augen ist, was zur Bestätigung und
zur Erfüllung ihrer übrigen Einsichten dienen sollte.   Die Naturkunde und
Geschichte sind die zwei Pfeiler, auf welchen die wahre Religion beruht.
Der Unglaube und der Aberglaube gründen sich auf eine seichte Physik und
seichte Historie.   Die Natur ist so wenig einem blinden Ungefähr oder
ewigen Gesetzen unterworfen, als sich alle Begebenheiten durch Charaktere
und Staatsgründe aufschließen lassen.   Ein Newton wird als Naturkun=
diger von der weisen Allmacht Gottes, ein Geschichtsschreiber von der wei=
sen Regierung Gottes gleich stark gerührt werden.

Gott offenbart sich — der Schöpfer der Welt ist ein Schriftsteller. —
Was für ein Schicksal werden seine Bücher erfahren müssen; was für
strengen Urtheilen, was für scharfsinnigen Kunstrichtern werden seine Bücher
unterworfen seyn?   Wie viele armselige Religionsspötter haben ihr täg=
lich Brob von seiner Hand genossen; wie viele starke Geister, wie Herostra=
tus, in der Verwegenheit ihrer Schande eine Unsterblichkeit gesucht, deren
Todesangst um eine bessere gefleht hat! — Gott ist gewohnt seine Weisheit
von den Kindern der Welt getadelt zu sehen.   Moses Stab war in keiner
Gefahr, ohngeachtet ihn die Zauberstäbe der weisen Aegyptier umzingelt
anzischten.   Diese Tausendkünstler waren endlich genöthigt, den Finger Got=
tes in dem verächtlichsten Ungeziefer zu erkennen und dem Propheten des
wahren Gottes auszuweichen.   Der Begriff, daß das höchste Wesen selbst
die Menschen einer besonderen Offenbarung gewürdigt hat, scheint dem
Witzling so fremde und außerordentlich zu seyn, daß er mit Pharao fragt,
was dieser Gott haben will und worin sein Gesuch besteht.   Mit diesem
Begriff sollte man aber nothwendiger Weise eine Betrachtung derjenigen
verbinden, denen diese Offenbarung zu Gut geschehen.   Gott hat sich
Menschen offenbaren wollen; er hat sich durch Menschen offenbart.
Er hat die Mittel, diese Offenbarung den Menschen nützlich zu machen, sie
für solche einzunehmen, sie unter den Menschen auszubreiten, fortzupflanzen
und zu erhalten, auf die Natur der Menschen, seiner Weisheit am gemäße=
sten, gründen müssen.   Ein Philosoph, der Gott in der Wahl aller dieser
Umstände und Wege, in welchen Gott seine Offenbarung hat mittheilen
wollen, tadeln und verbessern wollte, würde immer vernünftiger handeln,
wenn er seinem Urtheil hierin zu wenig zutrauete, damit er nicht Gefahr
liefe, wie jener gekrönte Sternkundige das Ptolomäische System oder seine
Erklärung des Sternenlaufs für den wahren Himmelsbau anzusehen.   Hat
Gott sich den Menschen und dem ganzen menschlichen Geschlechte zu offen=

baren die Absicht gehabt, so fällt die Thorheit derjenigen desto mehr in die
Augen, die einen eingeschränkten Geschmack und ihr eigenes Urtheil zum
Probestein des göttlichen Wortes machen wollen. Die Rede ist nicht von
einer Offenbarung, die ein Voltaire, ein Bolingbroke, ein Shaftesbury an-
nehmungswerth finden würden; die ihren Vorurtheilen, ihrem Witz, ihren
moralischen, politischen und epischen Grillen am meisten ein Genüge thun
würde: sondern von einer Entdeckung solcher Wahrheiten, an deren Gewiß-
heit, Glaubenswürdigkeit und Wichtigkeit dem ganzen menschlichen Geschlechte gelegen wäre. Leute, die sich Einsicht genug zutrauen, um eines
göttlichen Unterrichts entbehren zu können, würden in jeder anderen Offenbarung Fehler gefunden haben, und haben keine nöthig. Sie sind die Gesunden, die des Arztes nicht bedürfen. Gott hat es unstreitig seiner Weisheit am gemäßesten gefunden, diese nähere Offenbarung seiner selbst erst
an einen einzigen Menschen, hierauf an sein Geschlecht und endlich an ein
besonderes Volk zu binden, ehe er erlauben wollte selbige allgemeiner zu
machen. Die Gründe dieser Wahl lassen sich eben so wenig von uns erfor-
schen, als warum es ihm gefallen in sechs Tagen zu schaffen, was sein Wille
eben so füglich in einem einzigen Zeitpunkte hätte wirklich machen können.
Ferner, Gott hat sich, so viel möglich, bequemt und zu der Menschen Neigungen und Begriffen, ja selbst Vorurtheilen und Schwachheiten herunter-
gelassen. Dieses vorzügliche Merkmal seiner Menschenliebe, davon die heilige Schrift voll ist, dient den schwachen Köpfen zum Spott, die eine
menschliche Weisheit oder eine Genugthuung ihrer Neugierde, ihres Vor-
witzes, eine Uebereinstimmung mit dem Geschmack der Zeit, in der sie leben,
oder der Seite, zu der sie sich bekennen, im göttlichen Worte zum Voraus
setzen. Kein Wunder, wenn sie in ihrer Vorstellung sich hintergangen
sehen, und wenn der Geist der Schrift mit eben der Gleichgültigkeit zurück-
gewiesen wird, ja, wenn dieser Geist eben so stumm und unnütz scheint, als
der Heiland dem Herodes, der ihn, ungeachtet seiner Neugierde und Erwartung zu sehen, mit mehr als Kaltsinn zu Pilatus bald zurückschickte. Wer
sollte sich einbilden, daß man in den Büchern Mosis eine Geschichte der
Welt hat suchen wollen? Viele scheinen ihn bloß deßwegen zu lästern, daß
er ihnen nicht Mittel gibt, die Fabeln eines Herodotus zu erklären, zu
ergänzen oder zu widerlegen. Wie lächerlich, wie unglaublich würde ihnen
vielleicht die Geschichte der alten Welt vorkommen, wenn wir sie so vollkommen hätten, als sie selbige wünschen?

Matthias Claudius.

7. Ueber's Genie.

Mein Vetter hat eine sehr gelehrte Abhandlung über's Genie angefangen. Er fängt oft an, und kömmt ihm dann eine Grille, da läßt er's gut seyn und denkt nicht weiter dran. Ich pfleg' ihm denn wohl zuweilen unter vier Augen seine Narrheit je zu verweisen, aber er schämt und grämt sich nicht, und oft giebt er mir noch allerhand spitzfindige Redensarten zum Lohn. Neulich gab ich ihm zu verstehen, daß er, was er angefangen hätte, auch — „Wohl wahr, Vetter, fiel er mir in die Rede, doch setzt ihr's fort!" Ich gab natürlicherweise zur Antwort, daß ich nichts von der Materie verstehe. „Desto besser werdet ihr davon schreiben, Vetter, es ist Vieles in der Natur verborgen." Was soll ich thun? will ich's fortgesetzt haben, muß ich dran, es mag denn auch gehen wie's geht. — Will nun zuvor den den letzten Perioden nachlesen: „und nun herunter zum modernen Genius oder zum Genie," — herunter denn, und gleich im Fallen angefangen. Empfange mich, du liebreicher Hain am Helikonberg! Ich komme gefallen, zu hören deinen Silbersturm und dein sanfteres Geräusche, und ihr im leichten Rosengewand mit dem blassen Munde, der so holdselig sprechen kann, Gesellen des Hains! seyd mir gegrüßt — Ha! der Schwindel ist über, und ich habe wieder festen Grund unter'n Füßen. Wenn einer 'n * Buch geschrieben hat, und man lies't in dem Buch, und's wirkt so sonderbar als ob man in Doctor Faust's Mantel davon sollte, daß man aufsteht und sich reisefertig macht, und wenn man wieder zu sich selbst kömmt, dankbar zum Buche zurückkehrt, dann, sollt' ich glauben, habe der Author mit Genie geschrieben. Aber mein Vetter wird sagen, daß das nichts gesagt sey; daß man nicht wissen will, wer Genie habe, sondern was das Genie sey, das einer hat. Das Genie also ist — ist — weiß nicht — ist 'n * Wallfisch! So recht, das Genie ist 'n Wallfisch, der eine Idee drei Tage und drei Nächte in seinem Bauch halten kann, und sie dann lebendig an's Land speit; ist 'n Wallfisch, der bald durch die Tiefe in stiller Größe daher fährt, daß den Völkern der Wasserwelt 'n kaltes Fieber ankömmt, bald herauf fährt in die Höhe und mit Dreimastern spielt, auch wohl mit Ungestüm aus dem Meer plötzlich hervorbricht und große Erscheinungen macht. Das Nichtgenie aber ist 'n Wallfischgeripp ohne Fett und Bein, das auf'm Wasser vom Winde hin und her getrieben wird, eine Witterung für die schwarzen und weißen Bären (Journalisten und Zeitungsschreiber), die über die Eisschollen herkommen und dran nagen. Ich will's nur bei Zeiten sagen, daß ich über meines Vetters Papiere gewesen bin; der geneigte Leser

* 'n stands for ein.

würd's doch bald merken; hab's gemacht * wie die Andern: Fremd Kraut und meine Brühe drüber.

Der menschliche Körper voll Nerven und Adern, in deren Centro die menschliche Seele sitzt wie eine Spinne im Centro ihres Gewebes, ist einer Harfe zu vergleichen und die Dinge in der Welt um ihn den Fingern, die auf der Harfe spielen. Alle Harfensaiten beben und geben einen Ton, wenn sie berührt werden. Einige Harfen aber sind von einem so glücklichen Bau, daß sie gleich unter dem Finger des Künstlers sprechen, und ihre Saiten sind so innig zum Beben aufgelegt, daß sich der Ton von der Saite losreißt und ein leichtes ätherisches Wesen für sich ausmacht, das in der Luft umher wallt, und die Herzen mit süßer Schwermuth anfüllt. Und dies leichte ätherische Wesen, das so frei für sich in der Luft umher wallt, wenn die Saite schon aufgehört hat zu beben, und das die Herzen mit süßer Schwermuth anfüllt, kann nicht anders als mit dem Namen Genie getauft werden, und der Mann, dem es sich auf'n † Kopf setzt wie die Eule auf'n Kopf der Minerva, ist ein Mann, der Genie hat; und der geneigte Leser wird nun hoffentlich besser, als ich, wissen, was Genie ist. Dies Genie, fahren die oberwähnten Papiere fort, das bis so weit eine bloße Gabe der Natur ist, erhält nun eine verschiedene Richtung, nachdem der ganze individuelle Zustand, in dem der Mensch sich befindet und befunden hat, verschieden ist. Da thun Wiege und Amme und Fiebel und Wohnung und Sprache und Schlafmütze und Religion und Gelehrsamkeit u.s.w. das Ihrige, es zu erdrücken, oder in Gang zu helfen. Ein ganz besonderes Verdienst im Erdrücken hat die Philosophie, wie sie auf den Schulen gang und gebe ist: Vita Caroli, mors Conradini! Die Herren Philosophen, die von Allgemeinheiten gehört haben, die tief in der Natur verborgen liegen sollen und durch Hebammenkünste zur Welt gebracht werden müssen, abstrahieren der Natur das Fell über die Ohren, und geben ihre nackten Gespenster für jene Allgemeinheiten aus; und ihre Zuhörer, die an diese Gespenster gewöhnt werden, verlieren nach und nach die Gabe, Eindrücke von einer Welt zu empfangen, in der sie sind. Alle Haken ihrer Seele, die an die Eindrücke der wirklichen Natur anpacken sollen, werden abgeschliffen, und alle Bilder fallen ihnen nun perspectivisch und dioptrisch in Aug und Herz u.s.w.

Aber das kostet Kopfbrechen, von einer Sache zu schreiben, von der man nichts versteht; und da pflegen wir Gelehrte denn wohl zur Abwechselung und Erholung eine Spielstunde zu machen. Der selige Isaak Newton schrieb in seinen Spielstunden eine Chronologie, und ich pflege wohl an meinen alten Freund und Schulcameraden Andres zu schreiben.

---

* Ich habe es gemacht. — † auf'n = auf den.

Johann Jakob Engel. 457

Mein lieber Andres!

Ich habe das Leichdornpflaster erhalten, die Würzpillen aber nicht, arbeite auch jetzo an einem Buch, das ich dem Druck übergeben will. Er glaubt nicht, Andres, wie einem so wohl ist, wenn man was schreibt, das gedruckt werden soll, und ich wollt' Ihm die Freude auch 'nmal* gönnen. Er könnte etwa das Recept zu dem Pflaster herausgeben, etwas vom Ursprung der Leichdörner herraisoniren und am Ende einige Errata hinzuthun. Sieht Er, es kömmt bei einer Schrift auf den Inhalt eben nicht groß an, wenn nur Schwarz auf Weiß ist; Einige loben's doch, und am Ende läßt sich von Leichdörnern und Pflaster schon was schreiben. Ich besinne mich, daß es Ihm in der Schule immer so schwer ward, die Commata und Puncta recht zu setzen. Sieht er, Andres, wo der Verstand halb aus ist, setzt Er ein Comma; wo er ganz aus ist, ein Punctum, und wo gar keiner ist, kann Er setzen, was Er will, wie Er auch in vielen Schriften findet, die herauskommen. Was Er Seinem Buch für einen Titel geben will, das muß Er wissen; meines heißt: Secum portans, und ich kann Ihm nichts weiter davon sagen, als daß es Anfang und Ende hat.

Sein Diener.

Johann Jakob Engel.

8. Der Traum des Galilei.

Galilei, der sich um die Wissenschaften so unsterblich verdient gemacht hatte, lebte jetzt in einem ruhigen und ruhmvollen Alter zu Arcetri im Florentinischen. Er war bereits seines edelsten Sinnes beraubt, aber er freute sich dennoch des Frühlings: theils um der wiederkehrenden Nachtigall und der duftenden Blüthen willen, theils um der lebhaftern Erinnerung willen, die er an ehemaligen Freuden hatte.

Einst in seinem letzten Frühling ließ er sich von Viviani, seinem jüngsten und dankbarsten Schüler, in das Feld um Arcetri führen. Er merkte, daß er sich für seine Kräfte zu weit entfernte und bat daher im Scherz seinen Führer, ihn nicht über das Gebiet von Florenz zu bringen. „Du weißt," sagte er, „was ich dem heiligen Gericht habe geloben müssen." Viviani setzte ihn zum Ausruhen auf eine kleine Erhebung des Erdreichs nieder; und da er hier den Blumen und Kräutern näher gleichsam in einer Wolke von Wohlgeruch saß, erinnerte er sich der heißen Sehnsucht nach Freiheit, die ihn einst zu Rom bei Annäherung des Frühlings befallen hatte. Er wollte jetzt eben den letzten Tropfen Bitterkeit, der ihm noch übrig war, gegen seine grausamen Verfolger ausschütten, als er schnell wieder einhielt

* einmal.

20

und sich selbst mit den Worten bestrafte: „Der Geist des Copernicus möchte zürnen."

- Viviani, der noch von dem Traum nicht wußte, auf den sich Galilei be=
zog, bat ihn um Erläuterung dieser Worte. Aber der Greis, dem der
Abend zu kühl und für seine kranken Nerven zu feucht ward, wollte erst zu=
rückgeführt seyn, eh' er sie gäbe. „Du weißt," fing er dann nach einer kur=
zen Erholung an, „wie hart mein Schicksal in Rom war, und wie lange sich
meine Befreiung verzögerte. Als ich fand, daß auch die kräftigste Für=
sprache meiner Beschützer, der Medici, und selbst der Widerruf, zu dem ich
mich herabließ, noch ohne Wirkung blieben, warf ich mich einst voll feind=
seliger Betrachtungen über mein Schicksal und voll innerer Empörung
gegen die Vorsehung auf mein Lager nieder. „So weit du nur denken
kannst," rief ich aus, „wie untadelhaft ist dein Leben gewesen! Wie mühsam
bist du im Eifer für deinen Beruf die Irrgänge einer falschen Weisheit
durchwandert, um das Licht zu suchen, das du nicht finden konntest! Wie
hast du alle Kraft deiner Seele dran gesetzt, um hindurch zur Wahrheit zu
brechen, und sie alle vor dir zu Boden zu kämpfen, die verjährten mächtigen
Vorurtheile, die dir den Weg vertraten! Wie karg gegen dich selbst hast
du oft die Tafel gefloh'n, nach der dich gelüstete, und den Becher, den du
ausleeren wolltest, von deinen Lippen gezogen, um nicht träge zu den Ar=
beiten des Geistes zu werden! Wie hast du mit den Stunden des Schlafs
gedarbt, um sie der Weisheit zu schenken! Wie oft, wenn Alles um dich
her in sorgloser Ruhe lag und den ermüdeten Leib zu neuen Wollüsten
stärkte, wie oft hast du vor Frost gezittert, um die Wunder des Firmaments
zu betrachten! oder in trüben, umwölkten Nächten beim Schimmer der
Lampe gewacht, um die Ehre der Gottheit zu verkündigen und die Welt zu
erleuchten! Elender! Und was ist nun die Frucht deiner Arbeit? Was
für Gewinn hast du nun für alle Verherrlichung deines Schöpfers und alle
Aufklärung der Menschheit? Daß der Gram über dein Schicksal die
Säfte aus deinen Augen trocknet; daß sie dir täglich mehr absterben, diese
treusten Gehülfen der Seele; daß nun bald diese Thränen, die du nicht
halten kannst, ihr dürftiges Licht auf ewig vertilgen werden! So sprach
ich zu mir selbst, Viviani, und dann warf ich einen Blick voll Neids auf
meine Verfolger. Diese Unwürdigen, rief ich, die in geheimnißreiche For=
meln ihren Aberwitz und in ehrwürdiges Gewand ihre Laster hüllen, die
zur schnöden Ruhe für ihre Trägheit sich menschliche Lügen zu Aussprüchen
Gottes heiligten, und den Weisen, der die Fackel der Wahrheit empor hält,
wüthend zu Boden schlagen, daß nicht sein Licht sie in ihrem wollüstigen
Schlummer störe; diese Niederträchtigen, die nur thätig für ihre Lüste und
das Verderben der Welt sind: wie lächeln sie in ihren Palästen des Kum=
mers! wie genießen sie in unaufhörlichem Taumel des Lebens! wie haben

sie dem Verdienste Alles geraubt: auch das heiligste seiner Güter, die Ehre!
wie stürzt vor ihnen andächtig das Volk hin, das sie um die Frucht seiner
Aecker betrügen, und sich Freudenmahle von dem Fett seiner Heerden und
dem Most seiner Trauben bereiten. Und du, Unglücklicher! der du nur
Gott und deinem Berufe lebtest, der du nie in deiner Seele eine Leidenschaft
aufkommen ließest, als die reinste und heiligste für die Wahrheit; der du
ein besserer Priester Gottes, seine Wunder im Weltsystem, seine Wunder
im Wurm offenbartest: mußt du jetzt auch das Einzige missen, wornach du
schmachtest? Das Einzige, was selbst den Thieren des Waldes und den
Vögeln des Himmels gegeben ist — Freiheit? Welches Auge wacht über
die Schicksale der Menschen? Welche gerechte, unpartheiische Hand theilt
die Güter des Lebens aus? Den Unwürdigen läßt sie Alles an sich reißen; dem Würdigen Alles entziehen!" Ich klagte fort, bis ich einschlief;
und alsbald kam es mir vor, als ob ein ehrwürdiger Greis an mein Lager
träte. Er stand und betrachtete mich mit stillschweigendem Wohlgefallen,
indeß mein Auge voll Verwunderung auf seiner denkenden Stirne und den
silbernen Locken seines Haupthaars ruhte. „Galilei!" sagte er endlich:
„was du jetzt leidest, das leidest du um Wahrheiten, die ich dich lehrte; und
eben der Aberglaube, der dich verfolgt, würde auch mich verfolgen, hätte
nicht der Tod mich in jene ewige Freiheit gerettet." — „Du bist Copernicus!" rief ich, und schloß ihn, noch eh' er mir antworten konnte, in meine
Arme. O, sie sind süß, Viviani, die Verwandschaften des Bluts, die schon
selbst die Natur stiftet; aber wie viel süßer sind die Verwandtschaften der
Seele! Wie viel theurer und inniger als selbst die Bande der Bruder-
liebe sind die Bande der Wahrheit! Mit wie seligen Vorgefühlen des
erweiterten Wirkungskreises, der erhöheten Seelenkraft, der freien Mittheilung aller Schätze der Erkenntniß eilt man dem Freund entgegen, der
an der Hand der Weisheit hereintritt! „Siehe!" sprach nach erwiederter
Umarmung der Greis: „ich habe diese Hülle zurückgenommen, die mich ehemals einschloß, und will dir schon jetzt seyn, was ich dir künftig seyn werde,
dein Führer. Denn dort, wo der entfesselte Geist in rastloser Thätigkeit
unermüdet fortwirkt; dort ist die Ruhe nur Tausch der Arbeit: eigenes
Forschen in den Tiefen der Gottheit wechselt nur mit dem Unterricht, den
wir den spätern Ankömmlingen der Erde geben; und der erste, der einst
deine Seele in die Erkenntniß des Unendlichen leitet, bin ich." Er führte
mich bei der Hand zu einer niedergesunkenen Wolke, und wir nahmen unsern Flug in die unermeßliche Weite des Himmels. Ich sah hier den
Mond, Viviani, mit seinen Anhöhen und Thälern; ich sah die Gestirne
der Milchstraße, der Plejaden und des Orion; ich sah die Flecken der
Sonne und die Monden des Jupiter: Alles, was ich hienieden zuerst sah,
das sah ich dort besser mit unbewaffnetem Auge, und wandelte am Himmel

voll Entzückens über mich selbst unter meinen Entdeckungen, wie auf Erden
ein Menschenfreund unter seinen Wohlthaten wandelt. Jede hier durch=
arbeitete mühvolle Stunde ward dort fruchtbar an Glückseligkeit, an einer
Glückseligkeit, die der nie fühlen kann, der leer an Erkenntniß in jene Welt
tritt. Und darum will ich nie, Viviani, auch nicht in diesem zitternden
Alter, aufhören nach Wahrheit zu forschen: denn wer sie hier suchte, dem
blüht dort Freude hervor, wo er nur hinblickt; aus jeder bestätigten Ein=
sicht, aus jedem vernichteten Zweifel; aus jedem enthüllten Geheimniß,
aus jedem verschwindenden Irrthum. — Siehe! ich fühlte dies Alles in
jenen Augenblicken der Wonne; aber auch nur dies Einzige, daß ich es
fühlte, ist mir geblieben: denn meine zu überhäufte Seele verlor jede ein=
zelne Glückseligkeit in dem Meere ihrer aller. Indem ich so sah und
staunte und mich in Dessen Größe verlor, der dies Alles voll allmächtiger
Weisheit schuf und durch seine ewig wirksame Liebe trägt und erhält, erhob
mich das Gespräch meines Führers zu noch höhern Begriffen. „Nicht die
Grenzen deiner Sinne," sagte er, „sind auch die Grenzen des Weltalls, ob=
gleich aus undenklichen Fernen ein Heer von Sonnen zu dir herüberschim=
mert: noch viele tausende leuchten deinem Blick unbemerkbar im endlosen
Aether; und jede Sonne, wie jede sie umkreisende Sphäre ist mit empfin=
denden Wesen, ist mit denkenden Seelen bevölkert. Wo nur Bahnen mög=
lich waren, da rollen Weltkörper, und wo nur Wesen sich glücklich fühlen
konnten, da wallen Wesen! Nicht eine Spanne blieb in der ganzen Uner=
meßlichkeit des Unendlichen, wo der sparsame Schöpfer nicht Leben hinschuf,
oder dienstbaren Stoff für das Leben; und durch diese ganze zahllose Man=
nigfaltigkeit von Wesen hindurch herrscht bis zum kleinsten Atom herab
unverbrüchliche Ordnung: ewige Gesetze stimmen Alles von Himmel zu
Himmel, und von Sonne zu Sonne, und von Erde zu Erde in entzückende
Harmonie. Unergründlich ist für den unsterblichen Weisen in die Ewigkeit
aller Ewigkeiten der Stoff zur Betrachtung, und unerschöpflich der Quell
seiner Seligkeiten. Zwar, was sag' ich dir das schon jetzt, Galilei? Denn
diese Seligkeiten faßt doch ein Geist nicht, der noch gefesselt an einen trä=
gen Gefährten in seiner Arbeit nicht weiter kann, als der Gefährte mit
ausdauert, und sich schon zum Staube zurückgerissen fühlt, wenn er kaum
anfing sich zu erheben!" — „Er mag sie nicht fassen," rief ich, „diese Selig=
keiten, nach ihrer ganzen göttlichen Fülle; aber gewiß, er kennt sie, Coper=
nicus, nach ihrer Natur, ihrem Wesen. Denn welche Freuden schafft nicht
schon in diesem irdischen Leben die Weisheit! Welche Wonne fühlt nicht
schon in diesen sterblichen Gliedern ein Geist, wenn es nun anfängt in der
ungewissen Dämmerung seiner Begriffe zu tagen, und sich immer weiter
und weiter der holde Schimmer verbreitet, bis endlich das volle Licht der
Erkenntniß aufgeht, das dem entzückten Auge Gegenden zeigt voll unend=

licher Schönheit! Erinnere dich, der du selbst so tief in die Geheimnisse
Gottes schautest und den Plan seiner Schöpfung enthüllest; erinnere dich
jenes Augenblicks, als der erste kühne Gedanke in dir heraufstieg und sich
freudig alle Kräfte deiner Seele hinzudrängten, ihn zu fassen, zu bilden, zu
ordnen; erinnere dich, als nun Alles in herrlicher Uebereinstimmung vollendet stand, mit wie trunkener Liebe du noch einmal das schöne Werk deiner Seele überschautest, und deine Aehnlichkeit mit dem Unendlichen fühl-
test, dem du nachdenken könntest! O ja, mein Führer! Auch schon hienieden ist die Weisheit an himmlischen Freuden reich; und wäre sie's
nicht, warum säh'n wir aus ihrem Schooße so ruhig allen Eitelkeiten der
Welt zu?"

„Die Wolke, die uns trug, war zurück zur Erde gesunken, und ließ sich
jetzt, wie es mir däuchte, auf einen der Hügel vor Rom nieder. Die Hauptstadt der Welt lag vor uns; aber voll tiefer Verachtung streckt' ich aus
meiner Höhe die Hand hin und sprach: „Sie mögen sich groß dünken, die
stolzen Bewohner dieser Paläste! weil Purpur ihre Glieder umhüllt, und
Gold und Silber auf ihren Tafeln das Kostbarste beut, was Europa und
Indien tragen! Aber wie der Adler auf die Raupe im Seidengespinnst,
so sieht auf diese Blöden der Weise herab; denn sie sind Gefangene an
ihrer Seele, die über das Blatt nicht hinaus können, an dem sie kleben:
indeß der freie Weise auf seine Höhen tritt und die Welt überschaut, oder
sich auf Flügeln der Betrachtung hinauf zu Gott schwingt und unter Sternen einhergeht."

„Da ich so sprach, Viviani, da umwölfte sich mit feierlichem Ernst die
Stirn meines Führers; sein brüderlicher Arm sank von meinen Schultern
herab und sein Auge schoß einen drohenden Blick bis ins Innerste meiner
Seele. „Unwürdiger! rief er: so hast du sie schon auf Erden gefühlt,
jene Freuden des Himmels? hast deinen Namen herrlich gemacht vor den
Weisen der Nationen? hast sie alle erhöht, deine Seelenkräfte, daß sie bald
freier und mächtiger fortwirken in Erkenntniß der Wahrheit, eine Ewigkeit
durch? Und nun dich Gott würdigt, Verfolgung zu leiden, nun dir deine
Weisheit Verdienst werden soll, und dein Herz sich mit Tugenden schmücken,
wie dein Geist mit Erkenntniß: nun ist es ohne Spur vertilgt, das Gedächtniß des Guten, und deine Seele empört sich wider Gott?" Hier
erwacht' ich von meinem Traum, sah mich aus aller Herrlichkeit des Himmels in mein ödes Gefängniß zurückgeworfen, und überschwemmte mit
einer Fluth von Thränen mein Lager. Dann erhob ich mitten durch die
Schatten der Nacht mein Auge und sprach: „O Gott voll Liebe! Hat das
Nichts, das durch dich Etwas ward, deine Wege getadelt? Hat der Staub,
dem du Seele gabst, hat er auf die Rechnung seiner Verdienste geschrieben,
was Geschenke deiner Erbarmung waren? Hat der Unwürdige, den du

in deinem Busen, an deinem Herzen nährtest, dem du so manchen Tropfen
Seligkeit reichtest aus deinem eigenen Becher; hat er deiner Gnaden und
seiner Vorzüge vergessen?   Schlage sein Auge mit Blindheit! laß ihn nie
wieder die Stimme der Freundschaft hören! laß ihn grau werden im Kerker! Mit willigem Geist soll er's tragen, dankbar gegen die Erinnerung
seiner-genoss'nen Freuden, und selig in Erwartung der Zukunft!"
        Es war meine ganze Seele, Viviani, die ich in diesem Gebete hingoß;
aber nicht das Murren des Unzufriednen, nur die willige Ergebung des
Dankbaren, hatte der Gott vernommen, der mich zu so viel Seligkeit schuf!
Denn siehe! ich lebe hier frei zu Arcetri, und nur heute noch hat mich mein
Freund unter die Blumen des Frühlings geführt."   Er tappte nach der
Hand seines Schülers, um sie dankbar zu drücken; aber Viviani ergriff die
seinige und führte sie ehrerbietig an seine Lippen.

Johann Gottfried Herder.

9. Unsre Humanität ist nur Vorübung, die Knospe zu einer zukünftigen Blume.

Wir sahen, daß der Zweck unsers jetzigen Daseyns auf Bildung der Humanität gerichtet sei, der alle niedrigen Bedürfnisse der Erde nur dienen und selbst zu ihr führen sollen.   Unsere Vernunftfähigkeit soll zur
Vernunft, unsre feinern Sinne zur Kunst, unsre Triebe zur echten Freiheit
und Schöne, unsre Bewegungskräfte zur Menschenliebe gebildet werden.
Entweder wissen wir nichts von unsrer Bestimmung, und die Gottheit
täuschte uns mit allen ihren Anlagen von Innen und Außen, (welche
Lästerung auch nicht einmal einen Sinn hat), oder wir können dieses Zwecks
so sicher seyn als Gottes und unsers Daseyns.
        Und wie selten wird dieser ewige, dieser unendliche Zweck hier erreicht!
Bei ganzen Völkern liegt die Vernunft unter der Thierheit gefangen, das
Wahre wird auf den irresten Wegen gesucht, und die Schönheit und Auf-
richtigkeit, zu der uns Gott erschuf, durch Vernachläßigung und Ruchlosig-
keit verderbet.   Bei wenigen Menschen ist die gottähnliche Humanität im
reinen und weiten Umfange des Worts eigentliches Studium des Lebens;
die meisten fangen nur spät an daran zu denken, und auch bei den besten
ziehen niedrige Triebe den erhabenen Menschen zum Thier hinunter.   Wer
unter den Sterblichen kann sagen, daß er das reine Bild der Menschheit,
das in ihm liegt, erreiche oder erreicht habe?
        Entweder irrte sich also der Schöpfer mit dem Ziel, das er uns vorsteckte,
und mit der Organisation, die er zu Erreichung desselben so künstlich zu-
sammengeleitet hat, oder dieser Zweck geht über unser Daseyn hinaus, und

die Erde ist nur ein Uebungsplatz, eine Vorbereitungsstätte. Auf ihr mußte freilich noch viel Niedriges dem Erhabensten zugesellet werden, und der Mensch im Ganzen ist nur eine kleine Stufe über das Thier erhoben. Ja, auch unter dem Menschen selbst mußte die größeste Verschiedenheit stattfinden, da Alles auf der Erde so vielartig ist und in manchen Gegenden und Zuständen unser Geschlecht so tief unter dem Joch des Klimas und der Nothdurft lieget. Der Entwurf der bildenden Vorsehung mußte also alle diese Stufen, diese Zonen, diese Abartungen mit einem Blick umfaßt haben, und den Menschen in ihnen allen weiter zu führen wissen, wie er die niedrigen Kräfte allmählig und ihnen unbewußt höher führet. Es ist befremdend und doch unleugbar, daß unter allen Erdbewohnern das menschliche Geschlecht dem Ziel seiner Bestimmung am meisten fern bleibt. Jedes Thier erreicht, was es in seiner Organisation erreichen soll: der einzige Mensch erreicht's nicht, eben weil sein Ziel so hoch, so weit, so unendlich ist, und er auf unsrer Erde so tief, so spät, mit so viel Hindernissen von Außen und Innen anfängt. Dem Thier ist die Muttergabe der Natur, sein Instinct, der sichre Führer; es ist noch als Knecht im Hause des obersten Vaters und muß gehorchen. Der Mensch ist schon als Kind in demselben und soll außer einigen nothdürftigen Trieben Alles, was zur Vernunft und Humanität gehört, erst lernen. Er lernet's also unvollkommen, weil er mit dem Samen des Verstandes und der Tugend auch Vorurtheile und üble Sitten erbet und in seinem Gange zur Wahrheit und Seelenfreiheit mit Ketten beschwert ist, die vom Anfange seines Geschlechts herreichen. Die Fußstapfen, die göttliche Menschen vor und um ihn gezeichnet, sind mit so viel andern verwirrt und zusammengetreten, in denen Thiere und Räuber wandelten und leider oft wirksamer waren als jene wenigen erwählten, großen und guten Menschen. Man würde also (wie es auch Viele gethan haben) die Vorsehung anklagen müssen, daß sie den Menschen so nah' an's Thier grenzen lassen und ihm, da er dennoch nicht Thier sein sollte, den Grad von Licht, Festigkeit und Sicherheit versagt habe, der seiner Vernunft statt des Instincts hätte dienen können, oder dieser dürftige Anfang ist eben seines unendlichen Fortganges Zeuge. Der Mensch soll sich nämlich diesen Grad des Lichts und der Sicherheit durch Uebung selbst erwerben, damit er unter der Leitung seines Vaters ein edler Freier durch eigne Bemühung werde — und er wird's werden. Auch der Menschenähnliche wird Mensch sein, auch die durch Kälte und Sonnenbrand erstarrte und verdorrte Knospe der Humanität wird aufblühen zu ihrer wahren Gestalt, zu ihrer eigentlichen und ganzen Schönheit.

Und so können wir auch leicht ahnen, was aus unserer Menschheit allein in jene Welt übergehen kann: es ist eben diese gottähnliche Humanität, die verschlossene Knospe der wahren Gestalt der Menschheit.

Alles Nothdürftige dieser Erde ist nur für sie: wir lassen den Kalk unsrer
Gebeine den Steinen und geben den Elementen das Ihrige wieder.   Alle
sinnlichen Triebe, in denen wir wie die Thiere der irdischen Haushaltung
dienten, haben ihr Werk vollbracht; sie sollten bei dem Menschen die
Veranlassung edlerer Gesinnungen und Bemühungen werden, und damit ist
ihr Werk vollendet.   Das Bedürfniß der Nahrung sollte ihn zur Arbeit,
zur Gesellschaft, zum Gehorsam gegen Gesetze und Einrichtungen erwecken,
und ihn unter ein heilsames, der Erde unentbehrliches Joch fesseln.   Der
Trieb der Geschlechter sollte Geselligkeit, väterliche, eheliche, kindliche Liebe
auch in die harte Brust des Unmenschlichen pflanzen, und schwere, langwie-
rige Bemühungen für sein Geschlecht ihm angenehm machen, weil er sie ja
für die Seinen, für sein Fleisch und Blut übernehme.   Solche Absicht
hatte die Natur bei allen Bedürfnissen der Erde: jedes derselben sollte
eine Mutterhülle seyn, in der ein Keim der Humanität sproßte.   Glücklich,
wenn er gesproßt ist!   Er wird unter dem Strahl einer schönern Sonne
Blüthe werden.   Wahrheit, Schönheit und Liebe waren das Ziel, nach dem
der Mensch in jeder seiner Bemühungen, auch ihm selbst unbewußt und oft
auf so unrechten Wegen, strebte.   Das Labyrinth wird sich entwirren, die
verführenden Zaubergestalten werden schwinden, und ein Jeder wird, fern
oder nahe, nicht nur den Mittelpunkt sehen, zu dem sein Weg geht, sondern
du wirst ihn auch, mütterliche Vorsehung, unter der Gestalt des Genius
und Freundes, deß er bedarf, mit verzeihender, sanfter Hand selbst zu ihm
leiten.

Also auch die Gestalt jener Welt hat uns der gute Schöpfer verborgen,
um weder unser schwaches Gehirn zu betäuben, noch zu ihr eine falsche Vorliebe zu reizen.   Wenn wir indeß den Gang der Natur bei den Geschlechtern unter uns betrachten und bemerken, wie die Bildnerin Schritt vor
Schritt das Uneblere wegwirft und die Nothdurft mildert, wie sie dagegen
das Geistige anbaut, das Feine feiner ausführt und das Schönere schöner
belebt, so können wir ihrer unsichtbaren Künstlerhand gewiß zutrauen, daß
auch die Efflorescenz unsrer Knospe der Humanität in jenem Daseyn gewiß
in einer Gestalt erscheinen werde, die eigentlich die wahre göttliche Men-
schengestalt ist, und die kein Erdensinn in ihrer Herrlichkeit und Schöne zu
dichten vermöchte.   Vergeblich ist also auch, daß wir dichten; und ob ich
wohl überzeugt bin, daß, da alle Zustände der Schöpfung auf's Genaueste
zusammenhangen, auch die organische Kraft unsrer Seele in ihren reinsten
und geistigen Uebungen selbst den Grund zu ihrer künftigen Erscheinung
lege, oder daß sie wenigstens ihr selbst unwissend das Gewebe anspinne, das
ihr so lange zur Bekleidung dienen wird, bis der Strahl einer schönern
Sonne ihre tiefsten, ihr selbst hier verborgnen Kräfte weckt, so wäre es doch
Kühnheit, dem Schöpfer Bildungsgesetze zu einer Welt vorzuzeichnen, deren

Verrichtungen uns noch so wenig bekannt sind. Genug, daß alle Verwand=
lungen, die wir in den niedrigen Reichen der Natur bemerken, Vervoll=
kommnungen sind, und daß wir also wenigstens Winke dahin haben, wohin
wir, höherer Ursachen wegen, zu schauen unfähig waren. Die Blume
erscheint unserm Auge als ein Samensprößchen, sodann als Keim, der
Keim wird Knospe, und nun erst gehet das Blumengewächs hervor, das
sein Lebensalter in dieser Oekonomie der Erde anfängt. Aehnliche Aus=
wirkungen und Verwandlungen giebt es bei mehrern Geschöpfen, unter de=
nen der Schmetterling ein bekanntes Sinnbild geworden. Siehe, da kriecht
die häßliche, einem groben Nahrungstriebe dienende Raupe; ihre Stunde
kommt, und Mattigkeit des Todes befällt sie: sie stemmet sich an, sie win=
det sich ein, sie hat das Gespinnst zu ihrem Todtengewande, sowie zum
Theil die Organe ihres neuen Daseyns schon in sich. Nun arbeiten die
Ringe, nun streben die inwendigen organischen Kräfte. Langsam geht die
Verwandlung zuerst und scheint Zerstörung: zehn Füße bleiben an der ab=
gestreiften Haut, und das neue Geschöpf ist noch unförmlich an seinen Glie=
dern. Allmählig bilden sich diese und treten in Ordnung, das Geschöpf
aber erwacht nicht eher, bis es ganz da ist: nun dränget es sich an's Licht,
und schnell geschiehet die letzte Ausbildung. Wenige Minuten, und die
zarten Flügel werden fünfmal größer, als sie noch eben unter der Todes=
hülle waren: sie sind mit elastischer Kraft und mit allem Glanz der Strah=
len begabt, der unter dieser Sonne nur stattfand, zahlreich und groß, um
das Geschöpf wie auf Schwingen des Zephyrs zu tragen. Sein ganzer
Bau ist verändert: statt der groben Blätter, zu denen es vorhin gebildet
war, genießt es jetzt Nektarthau vom goldnen Kelch der Blumen. Seine
Bestimmung ist verändert: statt des groben Nahrungstriebes dient es
einem feinern, der Liebe. Wer würde in der Raupengestalt den künftigen
Schmetterling ahnen? Wer würde in beiden ein und dasselbe Geschöpf
erkennen, wenn es uns die Erfahrung nicht zeigte? Und beide Existenzen
sind nur Lebensalter eines und desselben Wesens auf einer und derselben
Erde, wo der organische Kreis gleichartig wieder anfängt. Wie schöne Ab=
bildungen müssen im Schooß der Natur ruhn, wo ihr organischer Cirkel
weiter ist, und die Lebensalter, die sie ausbildet, mehr als Eine Welt um=
fassen? Hoffe also, o Mensch, und weissage nicht! Der Preis ist dir vor=
gesteckt, um den kämpfe! Wirf ab, was unmenschlich ist, strebe nach Wahr=
heit, Güte und Gott=ähnlicher Schönheit: so kannst du deines Ziels nicht
verfehlen.

Und so zeigt uns die Natur auch in diesen Analogieen werdender, d. i.
übergehender Geschöpfe, warum sie den Todesschlummer in ihr Reich der
Gestalten einwebte. Er ist die wohlthätige Betäubung, die ein Wesen um=
hüllet, in dem jetzt die organischen Kräfte zur neuen Ausbildung streben.

20*

Das Geschöpf selbst, mit seinem wenigern oder mehrern Bewußtseyn, ist nicht stark genug, ihren Kampf zu übersehn oder zu regieren; es entschlummert also und erwacht nur, wenn es ausgebildet da ist. Auch der Todesschlaf ist also eine väterliche milde Schonung, er ist ein heilsames Opium, unter dessen Wirkung die Natur ihre Kräfte sammelt und der entschlummerte Kranke geneset.

Johann Wolfgang Goethe.

10. Bekenntnisse einer schönen Seele.

Philo war schon in gewissen Jahren, und meinem Vater, dessen Kräfte abzunehmen anfingen, in gewissen Geschäften von der größten Beihülfe. Er war bald der innige Freund unseres Hauses, und da er, wie er sagte, an mir eine Person fand, die nicht das Ausschweifende und Leere der großen Welt und nicht das Trockene und Aengstliche der Stillen im Lande habe, so waren wir bald vertraute Freunde. Er war mir sehr angenehm und sehr brauchbar. Ob ich gleich nicht die mindeste Anlage noch Neigung hatte, mich in weltliche Geschäfte zu mischen und irgend einen Einfluß zu suchen, so hörte ich doch gern davon, und wußte gern, was in der Nähe und Ferne vorging. Von weltlichen Dingen liebte ich mir eine gefühllose Deutlichkeit zu verschaffen; Empfindung, Innigkeit, Neigung bewahrte ich für meinen Gott, für die Meinigen und meine Freunde. Diese letzten waren, wenn ich so sagen darf, auf meine neue Verbindung mit Philo eifersüchtig, und hatten dabei von mehr als einer Seite Recht, wenn sie mich hierüber warnten. Ich litt viel in der Stille, denn ich konnte selbst ihre Einwendungen nicht ganz für leer oder eigennützig halten. Ich war von jeher gewohnt meine Einsichten unterzuordnen, und doch wollte diesmal meine Ueberzeugung nicht nach. Ich flehte zu meinem Gott, auch hier mich zu warnen, zu hindern, zu leiten, und da mich hierauf mein Herz nicht abmahnte, so ging ich meinen Pfad getrost fort.

Philo hatte im Ganzen eine entfernte Aehnlichkeit mit Narcissen; nur hatte eine fromme Erziehung sein Gefühl mehr zusammengehalten und belebt. Er hatte weniger Eitelkeit, mehr Charakter, und wenn jener in weltlichen Geschäften fein, genau, anhaltend und unermüdlich war, so war dieser klar, scharf, schnell, und arbeitete mit einer unglaublichen Leichtigkeit. Durch ihn erfuhr ich die innersten Verhältnisse fast aller der vornehmen Personen, deren Aeußeres ich in der Gesellschaft hatte kennen lernen, und ich war froh, von meiner Warte dem Getümmel von Weitem zuzusehen. Philo konnte mir nichts mehr verhehlen: er vertraute mir nach und nach seine äußern und innern Verbindungen. Ich fürchtete für ihn, denn ich

faß gewiſſe Umſtände und Verwickelungen voraus, und das Uebel kam
ſchneller als ich vermuthet hatte; denn er hatte mit gewiſſen Bekenntniſſen
immer zurückgehalten, und auch zuletzt entdeckte er mir nur ſo viel, daß ich
das Schlimmſte vermuthen konnte. Welche Wirkung hatte das auf mein
Herz! Ich gelangte zu Erfahrungen, die mir ganz neu waren. Ich ſah
mit unbeſchreiblicher Wehmuth einen Agathon, der, in den Hainen von
Delphi erzogen, das Lehrgeld noch ſchuldig war und es nun mit ſchweren
rückſtändigen Zinſen abzahlte, und dieſer Agathon war mein genau verbun-
dener Freund. Meine Theilnahme war lebhaft und vollkommen; ich litt
mit ihm und wir befanden uns beide in dem ſonderbarſten Zuſtande.

Nachdem ich mich lange mit ſeiner Gemüthsverfaſſung beſchäftigt hatte,
wendete ſich meine Betrachtung auf mich ſelbſt. Der Gedanke: du biſt
nicht beſſer als er, ſtieg wie eine kleine Wolke vor mir auf, breitete ſich nach
und nach aus und verfinſterte meine ganze Seele. Nun dachte ich nicht
mehr bloß: du biſt nicht beſſer als er; ich fühlte es, und fühlte es ſo, daß
ich es nicht noch einmal fühlen möchte: und es war kein ſchneller Uebergang. Mehr als ein Jahr mußte ich empfinden, daß, wenn mich eine un-
ſichtbare Hand nicht umſchränkt hätte, ich ein Girard, ein Cartouche, ein
Damiens, und welches Ungeheuer man nennen will, hätte werden können:
die Anlage dazu fühlte ich deutlich in meinem Herzen. Gott, welche Entdeckung! Hatte ich nun bisher die Wirklichkeit der Sünde in mir durch die
Erfahrung, nicht einmal durch das leiſeſte Gefühl gewahr werden können,
ſo war mir jetzt die Möglichkeit derſelben in der Ahnung auf's Schrecklichſte
deutlich geworden, und doch kannte ich das Uebel nicht, ich fürchtete es nur;
ich fühlte, daß ich ſchuldig ſeyn könnte, und hatte mich nicht anzuklagen.
So tief ich überzeugt war, daß eine ſolche Geiſtesbeſchaffenheit, wofür ich
die meinige anerkennen mußte, ſich nicht zu einer Vereinigung mit dem höchſten Weſen, die ich nach dem Tode hoffte, ſchicken könne; ſo wenig fürchtete
ich in eine ſolche Trennung zu gerathen. Bei allem Böſen, was ich in mir
entdeckte, hatte ich ihn lieb und haßte, was ich fühlte, ja ich wünſchte es
noch ernſtlicher zu haſſen, und mein ganzer Wunſch war, von dieſer Krankheit und dieſer Anlage zur Krankheit erlöſt zu werden, und ich war gewiß,
daß mir der große Arzt ſeine Hilfe nicht verſagen würde. Die einzige
Frage war: was heilt dieſen Schaden? Tugendübungen? an die konnte
ich nicht einmal denken; denn zehn Jahre hatte ich ſchon mehr als nur
bloße Tugend geübt, und die nun erkannten Gräuel hatten dabei tief in
meiner Seele verborgen gelegen. Hätten ſie nicht auch wie bei David los-
brechen können, als er Bathſeba erblickte? und war er nicht auch ein Freund
Gottes, und war ich nicht im Innerſten überzeugt, daß Gott mein Freund
ſey? Sollte es alſo wohl eine unvermeidliche Schwäche der Menſchheit
ſeyn? Müſſen wir uns nun gefallen laſſen, daß wir irgend einmal die

Herrschaft unserer Neigung empfinden, und bleibt uns bei dem besten Wil=
len nichts Andres übrig, als den Fall, den wir gethan, zu verabscheuen, und
bei einer ähnlichen Gelegenheit wieder zu fallen? Aus der Sittenlehre
konnte ich keinen Trost schöpfen. Weder ihre Strenge, wodurch sie unsere
Neigung meistern will, noch ihre Gefälligkeit, mit der sie unsere Neigungen
zu Tugenden machen möchte, konnte mir genügen. Die Grundbegriffe, die
mir der Umgang mit dem unsichtbaren Freunde eingeflößt hatte, hatten für
mich schon einen viel entschiedenern Werth.

Indem ich einst die Lieder studirte, welche David nach jener häßlichen
Katastrophe gedichtet hatte, war mir sehr auffallend, daß er das in ihm
wohnende Böse schon in dem Stoff, woraus er geworden war, erblickte;
daß er aber entsündigt seyn wollte, und daß er auf das Dringendste um ein
reines Herz flehte. Wie nun aber dazu zu gelangen? Die Antwort aus
den ·symbolischen Büchern wußte ich wohl; es war mir auch eine Bibel=
wahrheit, daß das Blut Jesu Christi uns von allen Sünden reinige. Nun
aber bemerkte ich erst, daß ich diesen so oft wiederholten Spruch noch nie
verstanden hatte. Die Fragen: was heißt das? wie soll das zugehen?
arbeiteten Tag und Nacht in mir sich durch. Endlich glaubte ich bei einem
Schimmer zu sehen, daß das, was ich suchte in der Menschenwerdung des
ewigen Worts, durch das Alles und auch wir erschaffen sind, zu suchen sey.
Daß der Uranfängliche sich in die Tiefen, in denen wir stecken, die er durchschaut
und umfaßt, einstmal als Bewohner begeben habe, durch unser Verhältniß
von Stufe zu Stufe, von der Empfängniß und Geburt bis zu dem Grabe
durchgegangen sey, daß er durch diesen sonderbaren Umweg wieder zu den
lichten Höhen aufgestiegen, wo wir auch wohnen sollten, um glücklich zu
seyn: das ward mir wie in einer dämmernden Ferne offenbart. O warum
müssen wir, um von solchen Dingen zu reden, Bilder gebrauchen, die nur
äußere Zustände anzeigen! Wo ist vor ihm etwas Hohes oder Tiefes,
etwas Dunkles oder Helles? wir nur haben ein Oben und Unten, einen
Tag und eine Nacht. Und eben darum ist er uns ähnlich geworden, weil
wir sonst keinen Theil an ihm haben könnten. Wie können wir aber an
dieser unschätzbaren Wohlthat Theil nehmen? Durch den Glauben, ant=
wortet uns die Schrift. Was ist denn Glauben? Die Erzählung einer
Begebenheit für wahr halten, was kann mir das helfen? Ich muß mir
ihre Wirkungen, ihre Folgen zueignen können. Dieser zueignende Glaube
muß ein eigener, dem natürlichen Menschen ungewöhnlicher Zustand des
Gemüths sein. Nun, Allmächtiger! so schenke mir Glauben! flehte ich
einst in dem größten Druck des Herzens. Ich lehnte mich auf einen kleinen
Tisch, an dem ich saß und verbarg mein bethräntes Gesicht in meinen Hän=
den. Hier war ich in der Lage, in der man seyn muß, wenn Gott auf unser
Gebet achten soll, und in der man selten ist. Ja, wer nur schildern könnte,

was ich da fühlte. Ein Zug brachte meine Seele nach dem Kreuze hin, an
dem Jesus einst erblaßte; ein Zug war es, ich kann es nicht anders nennen,
demjenigen völlig gleich, wodurch unsere Seele zu einem abwesenden Ge=
liebten geführt wird, ein Zunahen, das vermuthlich viel wesentlicher und
wahrhafter ist, als wir vermuthen. So nahte meine Seele dem Menschge=
wordenen und am Kreuz Gestorbenen, und in dem Augenblick wußte ich,
was Glaube war.

Friedrich Schiller.

11. Ueber das Erhabene und das Schöne.

Zwei Genien sind es, die uns die Natur zu Begleitern durch's Leben gab.
Der Eine, gesellig und hold, verkürzt uns durch sein munteres Spiel die
mühevolle Reise, macht uns die Fesseln der Nothwendigkeit leicht und führt
uns unter Freude und Scherz bis an die gefährlichen Stellen, wo wir als
reine Geister handeln und alles Körperliche ablegen müssen, bis zur Erkennt=
niß der Wahrheit und zur Ausübnng der Pflicht. Hier verläßt er uns,
denn nur die Sinnenwelt ist sein Gebiet; über diese hinaus kann ihn sein
irdischer Flügel nicht tragen. Aber jetzt tritt der andere hinzu, ernst und
schweigend, und mit starkem Arm trägt er uns über die schwindliche Tiefe.

In dem ersten dieser Genien erkennt man das Gefühl des Schönen, in
dem Zweiten das Gefühl des Erhabenen. Zwar ist schon das Schöne ein
Ausdruck der Freiheit, aber nicht derjenigen, welche uns über die Macht der
Natur erhebt und von allem körperlichen Einfluß entbindet, sondern derje=
nigen, welche wir innerhalb der Natur als Menschen genießen. Wir fühlen
uns frei bei der Schönheit, weil die sinnlichen Triebe mit dem Gesetz der
Vernunft harmonieren; wir fühlen uns frei beim Erhabenen, weil die
sinnlichen Triebe auf die Gesetzgebung der Vernunft keinen Einfluß haben,
weil der Geist hier handelt, als ob er unter keinen andern als seinen eige=
nen Gesetzen stünde.

Das Gefühl des Erhabenen ist ein gemischtes Gefühl. Es ist eine Zu=
sammensetzung von Wehseyn, das sich in seinem höchsten Grad als ein
Schauer äußert, und von Frohseyn, das bis zum Entzücken steigen kann,
und ob es gleich nicht eigentlich Lust ist, von feinen Seelen aller Lust doch
weit vorgezogen wird. Diese Verbindung zweier widersprechender Empfin=
dungen in einem einzigen Gefühl beweis't unsere moralische Selbstständigkeit
auf eine unwiderlegliche Weise. Denn da es absolut unmöglich ist, daß
der nämliche Gegenstand in zwei entgegengesetzten Verhältnissen zu uns
stehe. so folgt daraus, daß wir selbst in zwei verschiedenen Verhältnissen zu
dem Gegenstand stehen, daß folglich zwei entgegengesetzte Naturen in uns

vereinigt seyn müssen, welche bei Vorstellung desselben auf ganz entgegenge=
setzte Art interessirt sind. Wir erfahren also durch das Gefühl des Erha=
benen, daß sich der Zustand unsers Geistes nicht nothwendig nach dem Zu=
stand des Sinnes richtet, daß die Gesetze der Natur nicht nothwendig auch
die unsrigen sind, und daß wir ein selbstständiges Principium in uns haben,
welches von allen sinnlichen Rührungen unabhängig ist.

Der erhabene Gegenstand ist von doppelter Art. Wir beziehen ihn ent=
weder auf unsre Fassungskraft, und erliegen bei dem Versuch, uns ein Bild
oder einen Begriff von ihm zu bilden; oder wir beziehen ihn auf unsre Le=
benskraft, und betrachten ihn als eine Macht, gegen welche die unsrige in
Nichts verschwindet. Aber ob wir gleich in dem einen wie in dem andern
Fall durch seine Veranlassung das peinliche Gefühl unsrer Grenzen enthal=
ten, so fliehen wir ihn doch nicht, sondern werden vielmehr mit unwider=
stehlicher Gewalt von ihm angezogen. Würde dieses wohl möglich seyn,
wenn die Grenzen unserer Phantasie zugleich die Grenzen unsrer Fassungs=
kraft wären? Würden wir wohl an die Allgewalt der Naturkräfte gern
erinnert seyn wollen, wenn wir nicht noch etwas Andres im Rückhalt hätten,
als was ihnen zum Raube werden kann? Wir ergötzen uns an dem Sinn=
lich=Unendlichen, weil wir denken können, was die Sinne nicht mehr fassen
und der Verstand nicht mehr begreift. Wir werden begeistert von dem
Furchtbaren, weil wir wollen können, was die Triebe verabscheuen, und ver=
werfen, was sie begehren. Gern lassen wir die Imagination im Reich der
Erscheinungen ihren Meister finden, denn endlich ist es doch nur eine sinn=
liche Kraft, die über eine andere sinnliche triumphirt, aber an das absolut
Große in uns selbst kann die Natur in ihrer ganzen Grenzenlosigkeit nicht
reichen. Gern unterwerfen wir der physischen Nothwendigkeit unser Wohl=
seyn und unser Daseyn, denn das erinnert uns eben, daß sie über unsere
Grundsätze nicht zu gebieten hat. Der Mensch ist in ihrer Hand, aber des
Menschen Willen ist in der seinigen.

Und so hat die Natur sogar ein sinnliches Mittel angewendet, uns zu
lehren, daß wir mehr als bloß sinnlich sind, so mußte sie selbst Empfin=
dungen dazu zu benutzen, uns der Entdeckung auf die Spur zu führen, daß
wir der Gewalt der Empfindungen nichts weniger als sklavisch unterwor=
fen sind, und dies ist eine ganz andere Wirkung, als durch das Schöne ge=
leistet werden kann; durch das Schöne der Wirklichkeit nämlich: denn im
Idealschönen muß sich auch das Erhabene verlieren. Bei dem Schönen
stimmen Vernunft und Sinnlichkeit zusammen, und nur um dieser Zusam=
menstimmung willen hat es Reiz für uns. Durch die Schönheit allein
würden wir also ewig nie erfahren, daß wir bestimmt und fähig sind, uns
als reine Intelligenzen zu beweisen. Beim Erhabenen hingegen stimmen
Vernunft und Sinnlichkeit nicht zusammen, und eben in diesem Widerspruch

zwischen beiden liegt der Zauber, womit es unser Gemüth ergreift. Der physische und der moralische Mensch werden hier auf's Schärfste von einander geschieden, denn gerade bei solchen Gegenständen, wo der erste nur seine Schranken empfindet, macht der andere die Erfahrung seiner Kraft, und wird durch eben das unendlich erhoben, was den andern zu Boden drückt.

Ein Mensch, will ich annehmen, soll alle die Tugenden besitzen, deren Vereinigung den schönen Charakter ausmacht. Er soll in der Ausübung der Gerechtigkeit, Wohlthätigkeit, Mäßigkeit, Standhaftigkeit und Treue seine Wohllust finden; alle Pflichten, deren Befolgung ihm die Umstände nahe legen, sollen ihm zum leichten Spiel werden, und das Glück soll ihm keine Handlung schwer machen, wozu nur immer sein menschenfreundliches Herz ihn auffordern mag. Wem wird dieser schöne Einklang der natürlichen Triebe mit den Vorschriften der Vernunft nicht entzückend seyn, und wer sich enthalten können, einen solchen Menschen zu lieben? Aber können wir uns wohl bei aller Zuneigung zu demselben versichert halten, daß er wirklich ein tugendhafter ist, und daß es überhaupt eine Tugend giebt? Wenn es dieser Mensch auch bloß auf angenehme Empfindungen angelegt hätte, so könnte er, ohne ein Thor zu seyn, schlechterdings nicht anders handeln, und er müßte seinen eigenen Vortheil hassen, wenn er lasterhaft seyn wollte. Es kann seyn, daß die Quelle seiner Handlungen rein ist, aber das muß er mit seinem eignen Herzen ausmachen; wir sehen nichts davon. Wir sehen ihn nicht mehr thun, als auch der bloß kluge Mann thun müßte, der das Vergnügen zu seinem Gott macht. Die Sinnenwelt also erklärt das ganze Phänomen seiner Tugend, und wir haben gar nicht nöthig, uns jenseits derselben nach einem Grunde davon umzusehen.

Dieser nämliche Mensch soll aber plötzlich in ein großes Unglück gerathen. Man soll ihn seiner Güter berauben man soll seinen guten Namen zu Grunde richten; Krankheiten sollen ihn auf ein schmerzhaftes Lager werfen; Alle, die er liebt, soll der Tod ihm entreißen; Alle, denen er vertraut, ihn in der Noth verlassen. In diesem Zustande suche man ihn wieder auf und fordere von dem Unglücklichen die Ausübung der nämlichen Tugenden, zu denen der Glückliche einst so bereit gewesen war. Findet man ihn in diesem Stück noch ganz als den Nämlichen, hat die Armuth seine Wohlthätigkeit, der Undank seine Dienstfertigkeit, der Schmerz seine Gleichmüthigkeit, eigenes Unglück seine Theilnehmung an fremdem Glücke nicht vermindert, bemerkt man die Verwandlung seiner Umstände in seiner Gestalt, aber nicht in seinem Betragen, in der Materie, aber nicht in der Form seines Handelns — dann freilich reicht man mit keiner Erklärung aus dem Naturbegriff mehr aus, (nach welchem es schlechterdings nothwendig ist, daß das Gegenwärtige als Wirkung sich auf etwas Vergangenes als seine Ursache gründet), weil nichts widersprechender seyn kann, als daß die Wir-

kung dieſelbe bleibe, wenn die Urſache ſich in ihr Gegentheil verwandelt
hat.   Man muß alſo jeder natürlichen Erklärung entſagen, muß es ganz
und gar aufgeben, das Betragen aus dem Zuſtande abzuleiten, und den
Grund des erſtern aus der phyſiſchen Weltordnung heraus in eine ganz
andere verlegen, welche die Vernunft zwar mit ihren Ideen erfliegen, der
Verſtand aber mit ſeinen Begriffen nicht erfaſſen kann.   Dieſe Entdeckung
des abſoluten moraliſchen Vermögens, welches an keine Naturbedingung
gebunden iſt, giebt dem wehmüthigen Gefühl, wovon wir beim Anblick eines
ſolchen Menſchen ergriffen werden, den ganz eignen unausſprechlichen Reiz,
den keine Luſt der Sinne, ſo veredelt ſie auch ſeyen, dem Erhabenen ſtreitig
machen kann.

Das Erhabene verſchafft uns alſo einen Ausgang aus der ſinnlichen
Welt, worin uns das Schöne gern immer gefangen halten möchte.   Nicht
allmählig (denn es giebt von der Abhängigkeit keinen Uebergang zur Freiheit),
ſondern plötzlich und durch eine Erſchütterung reißt es den ſelbſtſtändigen
Geiſt aus dem Netze los, womit die verfeinerte Sinnlichkeit ihn umſtrickte,
und das um ſo feſter bindet, je durchſichtiger es geſponnen iſt.   Wenn ſie
durch den unmerklichen Einfluß eines weichlichen Geſchmacks auch noch ſo
viel über die Menſchen gewonnen hat, wenn es ihr gelungen iſt, ſich in
der verführeriſchen Hülle des geiſtigen Schönen in den innerſten Sitz der
moraliſchen Geſetzgebung einzudrängen und dort die Heiligkeit der Maxi=
men an ihrer Quelle zu vergiften, ſo iſt oft eine einzige erhabene Rührung
genug, dieſes Gewebe des Betrugs zu zerreißen, dem gefeſſelten Geiſt ſeine
ganze Schnellkraft auf einmal zurückzugeben, ihm eine Revelation über ſeine
wahre Beſtimmung zu ertheilen, und ein Gefühl ſeiner Würde wenigſtens
für den Moment aufzunöthigen.   Die Schönheit unter der Geſtalt der
Göttin Calypſo hat den tapfern Sohn des Ulyſſes bezaubert, und durch die
Macht ihrer Reizungen hält ſie ihn lange Zeit auf ihrer Inſel gefangen.
Lange glaubt er einer unſterblichen Gottheit zu huldigen, da er doch nur
in den Armen der Wolluſt liegt, — aber ein erhabener Eindruck ergreift
ihn plötzlich unter Mentors Geſtalt: er erinnert ſich ſeiner beſſern Be=
ſtimmung, wirft ſich in die Wellen, und iſt frei.

Das Erhabene wie das Schöne iſt durch die ganze Natur verſchwende=
riſch ausgegoſſen, und die Empfindungsfähigkeit für beides in alle Men=
ſchen gelegt; aber der Keim dazu entwickelt ſich ungleich, und durch die
Kunſt muß ihm nachgeholfen werden.   Schon der Zweck der Natur bringt
es mit ſich, daß wir der Schönheit zuerſt entgegeneilen, wenn wir noch vor
dem Erhabenen fliehen; denn die Schönheit iſt unſere Wärterin im kindi=
ſchen Alter und ſoll uns ja aus dem rohen Naturſtande zur Verfeinerung
führen.   Aber ob ſie gleich unſere erſte Liebe iſt und unſere Empfindungs=
fähigkeit für dieſelbe zuerſt ſich entfaltet, ſo hat die Natur doch dafür ge=

sorgt, daß sie langsamer reif wird und zu ihrer völligen Entwickelung erst die Ausbildung des Verstandes und Herzens abwartet. Erreichte der Ge= schmack seine völlige Reife, ehe Wahrheit und Sinnlichkeit auf einem bessern Weg, als durch ihn geschehen kann, in unser Herz gepflanzet wären, so würde die Sinnenwelt ewig die Grenzen unsrer Bestrebungen bleiben. Wir wür= den weder in unsern Begriffen noch in unsern Gesinnungen über sie hin= ausgehen, und was die Einbildungskraft nicht darstellen kann, würde auch keine Realität für uns haben. Aber glücklicherweise liegt es schon in der Einrichtung der Natur, daß der Geschmack, obgleich er zuerst blüht, doch zuletzt unter allen Fähigkeiten des Gemüths seine Zeitigung erhält. In dieser Zwischenzeit wird Frist genug gewonnen, einen Reichthum von Be= griffen in dem Kopf und einen Schatz von Grundsätzen in der Brust anzu= pflanzen, und dann besonders auch die Empfindungsfähigkeit für das Große und Erhabene aus der Vernunft zu entwickeln.

---

12. Selbstkritik über die Räuber.

Man nehme dieses Schauspiel für nichts Anderes als eine dramatische Geschichte, welche die Vortheile der dramatischen Methode, die Seele gleich= sam bei ihren geheimsten Operationen zu ertappen, benutzt, ohne sich übri= gens in die Schranken eines Theaterstücks einzuzäunen oder nach dem so zweifelhaften Gewinne bei theatralischer Verkörperung zu geizen. Man wird mir einräumen, daß es eine widersinnige Zumuthung ist, binnen drei Stun= den drei außerordentliche Menschen zu erschöpfen, deren Thätigkeit von viel= leicht tausend Räderchen abhängt, sowie es in der Natur der Dinge unmöglich kann gegründet seyn, daß sich drei außerordentliche Menschen auch dem durchdringendsten Geisterkenner innerhalb vierundzwanzig Stunden entblö= ßen. Hier war Fülle ineinander gedrungener Realitäten vorhanden, die ich unmöglich in die allzu engen Pallisaden des Aristoteles und Batteur einkeilen konnte. Nun ist es aber nicht sowohl die Masse meines Schau= spiels, als vielmehr sein Inhalt, der es von der Bühne verbannt. Die Oekonomie desselben machte es nothwendig, daß mancher Charakter auf= treten mußte, der das feinere Gefühl der Tugend beleidigt und die Zärt= lichkeit unserer Sitten empört. Jeder Menschenmaler ist in diese Nothwen= digkeit gesetzt, wenn er anders eine Copie der wirklichen Welt und keine idealischen Affectationen, keine Compendien=Menschen will geliefert haben. Es ist einmal so die Mode in der Welt, daß die guten durch die bösen schattirt werden, und die Tugend im Contraste mit dem Laster das leben= digste Colorit erhält. Wer sich den Zweck vorgezeichnet hat, das Laster zu stürzen und Religion, Moral und bürgerliche Gesetze an ihren Feinden zu

rächen, ein Solcher muß das Laster in seiner nackten Abscheulichkeit ent=
hüllen und in seiner kolossalischen Größe vor das Auge der Menschheit
stellen, — er selbst muß augenblicklich seine nächtlichen Labyrinthe durch=
wandern, — er muß sich in Empfindungen hineinzuzwingen wissen, unter
deren Widernatürlichkeit sich seine Seele sträubt. Das Laster wird hier
mit sammt seinem ganzen innern Räderwerk entfaltet. Es löst in Fran=
zen all' die verworrenen Schauer des Gewissens in unmächtige Abstractio=
nen auf, skeletisirt die richtende Empfindung, und scherzt die ernsthafte
Stimme der Religion hinweg. Wer es einmal so weit gebracht hat (ein
Ruhm, den wir ihm nicht beneiden), seinen Verstand auf Unkosten seines
Herzens zu verfeinern, dem ist das Heiligste nicht heilig mehr, — dem ist
die Menschheit, die Gottheit nichts, — beide Welten sind nichts in seinen
Augen. Ich habe versucht, von einem Mißmenschen dieser Art ein treffen=
des, lebendiges Conterfei hinzuwerfen, die vollständige Mechanik seines
Lastersystems auseinander zu gliedern — und ihre Kraft an der Wahrheit
zu prüfen. Man unterrichte sich demnach im Verfolg dieser Geschichte, wie
weit ihr's gelungen hat. — Ich denke, ich habe die Natur getroffen.

Nächst an diesem stehet ein anderer, der vielleicht nicht wenige meiner
Leser in Verlegenheit setzen möchte. Ein Geist, den das äußerste Laster
nur reizet, um der Größe willen, die ihm anhängt; um der Kraft willen,
die es erheischet; um der Gefahren willen, die es begleiten. Ein merk=
würdiger, wichtiger Mensch, ausgestattet mit aller Kraft, nach der Rich=
tung, die diese bekommt, nothwendig entweder ein Brutus oder ein Cata=
lina zu werden. Unglückliche Conjuncturen entscheiden für das zweite, und
erst am Ende einer ungeheuren Verirrung gelangt er zu dem ersten. Falsche
Begriffe von Thätigkeit und Einfluß, Fülle von Kraft, die alle Gesetze über=
sprudelt, mußten sich natürlicher Weise an bürgerlichen Verhältnissen zer=
schlagen, und zu diesen enthusiastischen Träumen von Größe und Wirksam=
keit durfte sich nur eine Bitterkeit gegen die unidealische Welt gesellen. So
war der seltsame Don Quixote fertig, den wir im Räuber Moor verab=
scheuen und lieben, bewundern und bedauern. Ich werde es hoffentlich
nicht erst anmerken dürfen, daß ich dieses Gemälde so wenig nur allein
Räubern vorhalte, als die Satyre des Spaniers nur allein Ritter geißelt.

Auch ist jetzt der große Geschmack, seinen Witz auf Kosten der Religion
spielen zu lassen, daß man beinahe für kein Genie mehr passirt, wenn man
nicht seinen gottlosen Satyr auf ihren heiligsten Wahrheiten sich herum=
tummeln läßt. Die edle Einfalt der Schrift muß sich in alltäglichen Af=
sembleen von den sogenannten witzigen Köpfen mißhandeln und in's Lächer=
liche verzerren lassen; denn was ist so heilig und ernsthaft, daß, wenn man
es falsch verdreht nicht belacht werden kann? — Ich kann hoffen, daß ich
der Religion und der wahren Moral keine gemeine Rache verschafft habe,

wenn ich diese muthwilligen Schriftverächter in der Person meiner schänd=
lichsten Räuber dem Abscheu der Welt überliefere. Aber noch mehr. Diese
unmoralischen Charaktere, von denen vorhin gesprochen wurde, mußten von
gewissen Seiten glänzen, ja oft von Seiten des Geistes gewinnen, was sie
von Seiten des Herzens verlieren. Hierin habe ich nur die Natur gleich=
sam wörtlich abgeschrieben. Jedem, auch dem Lasterhaftesten, ist gewisser=
maßen der Stempel des göttlichen Ebenbildes aufgedrückt, und vielleicht
hat der große Bösewicht keinen so weiten Weg zum Großen, Rechtschaffenen,
als der kleine; denn die Moralität hält gleichen Gang mit den Kräften,
und je weiter die Fähigkeit, desto weiter und ungeheurer ihre Verirrung,
desto imputabler ihre Verfälschung.

Jean Paul Friedrich Richter.

13. Ueber die Unsterblichkeit der Seele.

Die Sonne sank immer tiefer auf die Gebirge nieder und Riesenschatten
stiegen wie Nachtraubvögel aus ihrem ewigen Schnee kalt zu uns herein.
Ich nahm mit heißer Hand Karlson's seine und sah ihm mit nassen Augen
in sein männlich=schönes Angesicht und sagte: „O Karlson, auf welche
blühende große Welt werfen Sie einen unermeßlichen Leichenstein, den keine
Zeit abwälzt! Sind zwei Schwierigkeiten, die sich noch dazu auf eine
nothwendige Unwissenheit des Menschen gründen, hinreichend einen Glau=
ben zu überwältigen, der tausend größere Schwierigkeiten allein auflöset,
ohne den unsere Existenz ohne Ziel, unsere Schmerzen ohne Erklärung und
die göttliche Dreieinigkeit in unserer Brust drei Plagegöttinnen und drei
fürchterliche Widersprüche bleiben? — Vom gestaltlosen Erdwurm bis zum
strahlenden Menschenangesicht, vom chaotischen Volke des ersten Tages bis
zum jetzigen Weltalter, von der ersten Krümmung des unsichtbaren Her=
zens bis zu seinem alten kühnen Schlag im Jüngling geht eine pflegende
Gotteshand, die den innern Menschen (den Säugling des äußern) führt
und nährt, ihn gehen und sprechen lehrt und ihn erzieht und verschönert —
und warum? damit, wenn er als ein schöner Halbgott sogar mitten in den
Ruinen seines veralteten Körper=Tempels aufrecht und erhaben steht, die
Keule des Todes den Halbgott auf ewig zerschlage? Und auf dem unend=
lichen Meere, worin der kleinste Tropfenfall unermeßliche Kreise wirft, auf
diesem hat ein lebenslanges Steigen des Geistes und ein lebenslanges Fal=
len desselben einerlei Folge, nämlich das Ende der Folgen, die Vernichtung?
Und da mit unserm Geiste nach demselben Grunde auch die Geister aller
andern Welten fallen und sterben müssen, und nichts auf der von dem Lei=

chenſchleier und der Trauerſchleppe überhüllten Unermeßlichkeit übrig bleibt
als der ewig ſäende und niemals erntende einſame Weltgeiſt, der eine
Ewigkeit die andere betrauern ſieht: ſo iſt im ganzen geiſtigen All kein
Ziel und Zweck, weil der in ein Univerſum aus ſuccedirenden und ſucceſſi-
ven Ephemeren, in eine unſterbliche Legion aus ſterbenden zertheilte und
zertragene Zweck der Entwicklung ja keiner für die verſchwundenen Ephemeren, höchſtens für die letzte wäre, die nie kommen kann. — Und alle, alle
dieſe Widerſprüche und Räthſel, wodurch nicht blos alle Wohllaute, ſondern alle Saiten der Schöpfung zerriſſen werden, müſſen Sie annehmen,
bloß weil ſich zwei Schwierigkeiten, die unſere Vergänglichkeit eben ſo wenig auflöſet, vor Sie ſtellen .... Geliebter Karlſon, in dieſe Harmonie
der Sphären, nicht über ſondern neben uns wollen Sie Ihren ewig ſchrei-
enden Mißton bringen! Sehen Sie, wie ſanft und gerührt der Tag geht,
wie erhaben die Nacht kommt — o dachten Sie nicht daran, daß unſer
Geiſt glänzend einmal eben ſo aus der Grube voll Aſche ſteigen werde, da
Sie einmal den milden und lichten Mond groß aus dem Krater des Ve-
ſuv's aufgehen ſahen?'' ...

Die Sonne ſtand ſchon roth auf den Gebirgen, um ſich in's Meer zu
ſtürzen und in die neue Welt zu ſchwimmen. Nadine umfing unendlich gerührt die Schweſter und ſagte: „O wir lieben uns ewig und unſterblich,
gute Schweſter.'' Karlſon rührte zufällig die Saiten der Laute an, die er
trug: Gione nahm ſie mit der einen Hand und gab ihm die andere und
ſagte: „Unter uns allen werden Sie allein von dieſem triſten Glauben ge-
quält — und Sie verdienen einen ſo ſchönen!'' Dieſes Wort der ver-
hüllten Liebe ſtürzte ſein lang gefülltes Herz um, und zwei heiße Tropfen
wanden ſich aus den geblendeten Augen, und die Sonne vergoldete die reinen Thränen, und er ſagte, indem er nach dem Gebirge hinüberſchaute:
„Ich kann keine Vernichtung ertragen als nur meine — mein ganzes Herz
iſt Ihrer Meinung und mein Kopf wird ihm langſam folgen.'' Laſſe mich
nun nicht mehr eines andern Mannes erwähnen, den ich ſo oft getadelt
habe. Wir ſtanden gerade vor einem Schloſſe, worin des Abendſcheins
ungeachtet alle Fenſter ſich von Girandolen verſilbern und (wenn es dunkler geworden) vergolden ließen. Oben über der italieniſchen Platteforme
deſſelben hingen zwei Montgolfieren, die eine am weſtlichen, die andere am
öſtlichen Ende, gefeſſelt am Aether. Ohne dieſe ſchönen Globen, in denen
ſich gleichſam die zwei herrlichen im Himmel, der Mond und die Sonne
wiederholten, hätt' ich im Glanz höherer Scenen dieſe nähern kaum bemerkt. O Theuerſter, wie ſchön war die Stelle und die Zeit! Die Pyrenäen ruhten groß, halb in Nächte, halb in Tage gekleidet, um uns und bückten
ſich nicht wie der veraltende Menſch vor der Zeit, ſondern erhoben ſich
ewig; und ich fühlte, warum die großen Alten die Gebirge für Giganten

hielten. Die Häupter der Berge trugen Kränze und Ketten von Rosen aus
Wolken gemacht; aber so oft sich Sterne aus dem leeren tiefen Aethermeer
herausdrängten und aus den blauen Wellen glänzten, so erblichen Rosen
an den Bergen und fielen ab. Nur das Mittaghorn schauete wie ein hö=
herer Geist lange der tiefen einsamen Sonne nach und glühte entzückt.
Ein tieferes Amphitheater aus blühenden Citronenbäumen zog uns mit
Wohlgerüchen auf die eingehüllte Erde zurück und machte aus ihr ein
dunkles Paradies. Und Gione drang voll stillem Entzücken in ihre Lau=
tensaiten und Nadine sang den gleitenden Tönen leise nach. Und die
Nachtigallen wachten in den Rosenhecken am Wasser auf und zogen mit den
Tönen ihres kleinen Herzens tief in das große menschliche, und glimmende
Johanniswürmchen schweiften um sie von Rose zu Rose, und im spiegeln=
den Wasser schwebten nur fliegende Goldkörner über gelben Blumen. —
Aber da wir gen Himmel sahen, schimmerten schon alle seine Sterne und
die Gebirge trugen statt der Rosenketten ausgelöschte Regenbogen, und der
Riese unter den Pyrenäen war statt der Rosen mit Sternen gekrönt. —
O mein Geliebter, mußte dann nicht jeder entzückten Seele seyn, als falle
von der gedrückten Brust die irdische Last, als gebe uns die Erde aus ih=
rem Mutterarm reif in die Vaterarme des unendlichen Genius — als sey
das leichte Leben verweht? — Wir kamen uns wie Unsterbliche und erha=
bener vor; wir wähnten, das Sprechen über die Unsterblichkeit habe bei uns,
wie bei jenen zwei edeln Menschen,* den Anfang der unsrigen bedeutet.

------

14. Das Verhältniß der Griechen und der Neuern.

Keine Zeit ist mit der Zeit zufrieden; das heißet, die Jünglinge halten
die künftige für idealer als die gegenwärtige, die Alten die vergangene. In
Rücksicht der Literatur denken wir wie Jünglinge und Greise zugleich. Da
der Mensch für seine Liebe dieselbe Einheit sucht, die er für seine Vernunft
begehrt: so ist er so lange für oder wider Völker parteiisch, als er ihre
Unterschiede unter einer höhern Einheit auszugleichen weiß. Daher mußte
in Frankreich und noch mehr in England die Vergleichung der Alten und
Neuern allzeit entweder im Wider oder im Für parteiisch werden. Der
Deutsche, zumal im 19ten Jahrhundert, ist im Stande, gegen alle Nationen
— seine eigene verkannte ausgenommen — unparteiisch zu seyn. Wir
wollen daher das Bild der Griechen noch mit folgenden Zusätzen ergänzen.
Erstlich ihr Musenberg stand gerade auf der Morgenseite in Blüthe, die
schönsten, einfachsten Menschenverhältnisse und Verwickelungen der Tapfer=

------

* Raphael starb, da er die Verklärung vollendet hatte; und der genialische Hamann starb
mitten im Drucke einer Abhandlung „über Verklärung und Entkörperung.‟

feit, der Liebe, der Aufopferung, des Glücks und Unglücks nahmen die
Glücklichen weg und ließen den spätern Dichtern bloß deren Wiederholung
übrig und die mißliche Darstellung der künſtlichern . Ferner erscheinen sie
als höhere Todte uns heilig und verklärt. Sie müſſen auf uns ſtärker als
auf ſich ſelber wirken, weil uns neben dem Gedicht noch der Dichter ent=
zückt; weil die ſchöne reiche Einfalt des Kindes nicht das zweite Kind,
ſondern den bezaubert, der ſie verloren, und weil eben die welke Ausein=
anderblätterung durch die Hitze der Cultur uns fähig macht, in den grie=
chiſchen Knoſpen mehr die zuſammengedrungene Fülle zu ſehen, als ſie
ſelber konnten.   Ja auf ſo beſtimmte Kleinigkeiten erſtreckt ſich der Zauber,
daß uns der Olymp und der Helikon und das Tempe=Thal und jeder
Tempel ſchon außerhalb des Gedichtes poetiſch glänzen, weil wir ſie nicht
zugleich in nackter Gegenwart vor unſern Fenſtern haben; ſo wie ähnlicher
Weiſe Honig, Milch und andere arkadiſche Wörter uns als Bilder mehr
anziehen denn als Urbilder.   Schon der Stoff der griechiſchen Gedichte,
von der Götter= und Menſchengeſchichte an bis zur kleinſten Münze und
Kleidung, liegt vor uns als poetiſcher Demant da, ohne daß noch die poe=
tiſche Form ihm Sonne und Faſſung gegeben.   Drittens vermengt man,
wie es ſcheint, das griechiſche Maximum der Plaſtik mit dem Maximum
der Poeſie.   Die körperliche Geſtalt, die körperliche Schönheit hat Grenzen
der Vollendung, die keine Zeit weiter rücken kann; und ſo hat das Auge
und die außen geſtaltende Phantaſie die ihrigen.   Hingegen ſowohl den
äußern als den innern Stoff der Poeſie häufen die Jahrhunderte reicher
auf; und die geiſtige Kraft, die ihn in ihre Formen nöthigt, kann an der
Zeit ſich immer ſtärker üben.   Daher kann man richtiger ſagen: dieſer
Apollo iſt die ſchönſte Geſtalt, als: dieſes Gedicht iſt das ſchönſte Gedicht.
Malerei wie Gedicht iſt ſchon weit mehr der romantiſchen Endloſigkeit ver=
wandt, und verſchwimmt ſich oft ſogar bei Landſchaften ganz in dieſelbe.
Endlich iſt's ein alter Fehler der Menſchen, daß ſie bei dem ewigen Schau=
ſpiele der Zeit Wiederholungen des Schönen (ancora) befehlen, als könne
in der überreichen Natur etwas, auch nur das Schlimmſte, wiederkommen.
Eine Volks=Doublette wäre ein größeres Wunder, als ein Wolkenhimmel,
der mit ſeinen abentheuerlichen Bildungen ganz irgend einem dageweſenen
gliche; nicht einmal in Griechenland könnte das Alte auferſtehen.   Ja es
iſt ſogar leer, wenn ein Volk über Geiſterreichthum das andere zur Rede
ſetzt und z. B. das franzöſiſche uns fragt, wo ſind euere Voltaire's, Rouſ=
ſeau's, Diderot's, Büffon's?   Wir haben ſie nicht (ſagen wir), aber wo
ſind bei euch unſere Leſſinge, Winkelmanne, Herder, Goethe ꝛc.?   Wahr=
lich nicht einmal elende Autoren finden ihre Nebenaffen im Auslande.   In
ganz England und Frankreich hat unter allen Schriftſtellern, welche Ro=

mane schreiben, doch der bekannte * * * (in * *) keinen Zwillingsbruder; und
es ist freilich für die Länder ein Glück.

Wir priesen oben die Kraft der griechischen Götter= und Heroen=Lehre!
Nur aber mache man doch nie im vielgliederigen Leben eines Volks irgend
ein Glied zur Seele und nicht nährende Früchte und Eier sogleich zu auf=
gehenden und ausgebrüteten! Ging nicht der Zug der Götterschaar aus
Aegyptens traurigen Labyrinthen über Griechenlands helle Berge auf
Roms sieben Hügel? Aber wo schlug sie ihren poetischen Himmel auf, als
nur auf dem Helikon, auf dem Parnaß und an den Quellen beider Berge?
— Dasselbe gilt von der Heroenzeit, welche auf Aegypter, Peruaner und
fast alle Völker herüberglänzte, ohne doch in irgend einem so wie im grie=
chischen einen poetischen Widerschein nachzulassen. Wenn nicht einmal die
zeit= und religionverwandten Römer durch Nachahmen griechisch dichten
lernten, — welche überhaupt als handelnde Theaterdichter und Acteurs
der Erde mehr als Volk denn als Individuen, mehr mit Thaten als Wor=
ten, mehr daher in ihren Geschichtschreibern als in ihren Dichtern poetisch
waren — : so ist unser Abstand und unser Mißglück der Nachahmung noch
natürlicher. Die griechischen Götter sind uns nur flache Bilder und leere
Kleider unserer Empfindungen, nicht lebendige Wesen. Ja, anstatt daß es
damals kaum falsche Götter auf der Erde gab — und jedes Volk in dem
Tempel des andern ein Gast seyn konnte — so kennen wir jetzt fast nur
falsche; die kalte Zeit wirft gleichsam den ganzen Weltenhimmel zwischen
den Menschen und seinen Gott. — Sonderlich heiter ist das nordische
Leben so wenig als der Himmel darüber; mitten in unsern hellesten
Wintermittagen werden lange Abendschatten geworfen, moralisch und phy=
sisch; und daß die Sonne als Phöbus ein Land nicht licht=, holz=, dach=, kost=
und pelzfrei hält, das spüren die Phöbussöhne am ersten. In den schönen
Ländern fliegen die Schiffe singend am Ufer hin, wo ein Hafen am andern
ist. — Was unsere Heroenzeit anlangt, so steht sie — ungleich der griechischen,
mit Götterzeichen geschmückten — theils in der Bärenhaut vor uns da;
theils durch Religion in die Eichenhaine zurückgejagt, so daß wir uns mit
dem Adam und Noah viel verwandter glauben als mit Hermann, und den
Jupiter mehr anbeten als den Gott Thor. Doch seit Klopstock setzen wir
uns einander mehr darüber herab, daß wir uns nicht stärker hinauf setzen,
und dringen mit mehr Selbstbewußtseyn auf mehr Selbstbewußtseyn. Und
endlich (um den bösen Genius der Kunst zu nennen), sonst war die Poesie
Gegenstand des Volks, so wie das Volk Gegenstand der Poesie; jetzt singt
man aus einer Studierstube in eine andere hinüber, das Interessanteste in
beiden betreffend. Um parteiisch zu werden, müßte man jetzt nichts weiter
dazu setzen. Aber wie viel gehet hier der Wahrheit noch zur Rundung ab!
— Eigentlich ist's schon unnütz, alle Völker — und noch dazu ihre Zeiten

— und vollends die ewig wechselnden Farbenspiele ihrer Genieen — d. h. ein großes, vielgegliedertes, ewig anders blühendes Leben an ein paar weite Allgemeinheiten (wie plastische und romantische Poesie, oder objective und subjective) gleichsam am Kreuze zweier Hölzer festzuheften; denn allerdings ist die Abtheilung wahr und so wahr als die ähnliche der ganzen Natur in gerade und krumme Linien (die krumme als die unendliche ist die romantische Poesie); oder als die in Quantität und Qualität, so richtig als die, welche alle Musik in solche zerfällte, worin Harmonie, und in solche, worin Melodie vorklingt, oder kürzer in's simultane und in's successive Uebergewicht; so richtig als die polarisirenden leeren Classificationen der Schelling'schen Aesthetiker; aber was ist aus dieser atomistischen Dürre für das dynamische Leben zu gewinnen? So kann z.B. durch die Schiller'sche Abtheilung in naive Poesie (wofür objective klarer wäre) und in die sentimentale (womit nur ein Verhältniß „moderner" Subjectivität ausgesprochen wird), die verschiedene Romantik eines Shakspeare's, Petrarch's, Ariost's, Cervantes 2c., eben so wenig bezeichnet, noch geschieden werden, als durch „naiv" die verschiedene Objectivität eines Homer's, Sophokles, Hiob's, Cäsar's. Jedes einzelne Volk und seine Zeit ist ein klimatisches Organ der Poesie, und es ist sehr schwer, den verschlungenen Reichthum der Organisation so für ein System auseinander zu wickeln, daß man für dasselbe nicht eben so viel Lebenstheile fallen lasse als aufnehme. Indeß kann dies die große Absonderung der griechischen und romantischen Poesie so wenig aufheben, als die Wesenleiter der Thiere deren Ordnen in Fächer.

August Wilhelm Schlegel.

15. Unterschied des Classischen und Romantischen.

Die menschliche Natur ist in ihrer Grundlage einfach; aber alle Nachforschungen zeigen uns, keine Grundkraft in der gesammten Natur sey auf solche Weise einfach, daß sie sich nicht in sich selbst spalten und in entgegengesetzte Richtungen auseinandergehen könnte. Das ganze Spiel lebendiger Bewegung beruht auf Einstimmung und Gegensatz. Warum sollte sich diese Erscheinung nicht auch in der Geschichte der Menschheit im Großen wiederholen? Vielleicht wäre mit diesem Gedanken der wahre Schlüssel zur alten und neuen Geschichte der Poesie und der schönen Künste gefunden. Die, welche dies annahmen, haben für den eigenthümlichen Geist der modernen Kunst, im Gegensatz mit der antiken oder classischen, den Namen romantisch erfunden; allerdings nicht unpassend: das Wort kommt her von romance, der Benennung der Volkssprachen, welches sich durch die Vermischung des Lateinischen mit den Mundarten des Altdeut-

ſchen gebildet hatten, gerade wie die neuere Bildung aus den fremdartigen
Beſtandtheilen der nordiſchen Stammesart und der Bruchſtücke des Alter=
thums zuſammengeſchmolzen iſt, da hingegen die Bildung der Alten weit
mehr aus einem Stücke war.

Dieſe vorläuſig nur ſo hingeſtellte Anſicht würde in hohem Grade ein=
leuchtend werden, wenn ſich zeigen ließe, daß derſelbe Gegenſatz zwiſchen
dem Streben der Alten und Neueren ſymmetriſch, ja ich möchte ſagen ſy=
ſtematiſch, durch alle Außerungen des künſtleriſchen Vermögens (ſo weit
wir ſie bei jenen kennen) hindurch geht; ſich in der Muſik und den bilden=
den Künſten wie in der Poeſie offenbart: welche Aufgabe in ihrem ganzen
Umfange noch zu löſen ſteht, wiewohl manches Einzelne vortrefflich be=
merkt und angedeutet worden iſt.

Um Schriftſteller zu nennen, welche im Auslande geſchrieben haben und
früher, als in Deutſchland dieſe ſogenannte Schule aufgekommen: in der
Muſik hat Rouſſeau den Gegenſtand anerkannt und gezeigt, wie Rhythmus
und Melodie das herrſchende Princip der antiken, Harmonie der modernen
Muſik ſey. Er verwirft aber einſeitig die letztere, worin wir ganz und gar
nicht mit ihm einig ſeyn können. Ueber die bildenden Künſte thut Hem=
ſterhuys den ſinnreichen Ausſpruch: die alten Maler ſeyen vermuthlich
zu ſehr Bildhauer geweſen, die neueren Bildhauer ſeyen zu ſehr Maler.
Dies trifft den eigentlichen Punkt: denn, wie ich es in der Folge deutlicher
entwickeln werde, der Geiſt der geſammten antiken Kunſt und Poeſie iſt
p l a ſt i ſ ch, ſo wie der modernen p i t t o r e s k.

Für unſern Zweck, nämlich um die Haupteintheilung zu rechtfertigen,
welche wir in der Kunſtgeſchichte machen und wonach wir folglich auch die
Geſchichte der dramatiſchen Literatur abzuhandeln gedenken, möchte es hin=
reichen, dieſe ſo in die Augen fallende Entgegenſetzung des Antiken oder
Claſſiſchen und des Romantiſchen nur aufgeſtellt zu haben. Da indeſ=
ſen einſeitige Bewunderer der Alten immer fortfahren zu behaupten, alle
Abweichung von ihnen ſey nichts als eine Grille der neueſten Kritiker, wel=
che geheimnißvoll davon ſprächen, ihm aber keinen gültigen Begriff unter=
zulegen wüßten; ſo will ich eine Erklärung über den Urſprung und Geiſt
des Romantiſchen zu geben verſuchen, und man urtheile alsdann, ob der
Gebrauch des Wortes und die Anerkennung der Sache dadurch gerechtfer=
tigt wird.

Die Bildung der Griechen war vollendete Naturerziehung. Von ſchö=
nem und edlem Stamme, mit empfänglichen Sinnen und einem heitern
Geiſte begabt, unter einem milden Himmel, lebten und blühten ſie in voll=
kommener Geſundheit des Daſeyns und leiſteten durch die ſeltenſte Begün=
ſtigung der Umſtände Alles, was der in den Schranken der Endlichkeit be=
fangene Menſch leiſten kann. Ihre geſammte Kunſt und Poeſie iſt der

21

Ausdruck vom Bewußtseyn dieser Harmonie aller Kräfte. Sie haben die Poetik der Freude ersonnen.

Ihre Religion war Vergötterung der Naturkräfte und des irdischen Lebens; aber dieser Dienst, der bei andern Völkern die Phantasie mit scheußlichen Bildern verdüsterte und das Herz zur Grausamkeit abhärtete, gestaltete sich hier groß, würdig und milde. Der Aberglaube, sonst der Tyrann der menschlichen Anlagen, schien zu deren freiester Entwickelung die Hand bieten zu wollen: er hegte die Kunst, die ihn schmückte, und aus Götzen wurden Ideale.

Allein wie weit die Griechen auch im Schönen und selbst im Sittlichen gediehen, so können wir ihrer Bildung doch keinen höheren Charakter zugestehen, als den einer geläuterten, veredelten Sinnlichkeit. Es versteht sich, daß dies im Ganzen und Großen genommen werden muß. Einzelne Ahnungen der Philosophen, Blitze der dichterischen Begeisterung, machen eine Ausnahme. Der Mensch kann sich nie ganz vom Unendlichen abwenden, einzelne verlorne Erinnerungen werden von der eingebüßten Heimath zeugen; aber es kommt auf die herrschende Richtung seiner Bestrebungen an.

Die Religion ist die Wurzel des menschlichen Daseyns. Wäre es dem Menschen möglich, alle Religion, auch die unbewußte und unwillkürliche zu verläugnen; so würde er ganz Oberfläche werden, und kein Inneres mehr haben. Wenn dieses Centrum verrückt wird, so muß sich folglich darnach die gesammte Wirksamkeit der Gemüths- und Geisteskräfte anders bestimmen.

Und dies ist denn auch im neuern Europa durch die Einführung des Christenthums geschehen. Diese eben so erhabene als wohlthätige Religion hat die erschöpfte und versunkene alte Welt wiedergeboren, sie ist das lenkende Princip in der Geschichte der neueren Völker geworden; und noch jetzt, da Viele ihrer Erziehung entwachsen zu seyn wähnen, werden sie in der Ansicht aller menschlichen Dinge weit mehr durch deren Einfluß bestimmt, als sie selbst wissen.

Nächst dem Christenthum ist die Bildung Europa's seit dem Anfang des Mittelalters durch die germanische Stammesart der nordischen Eroberer, welche in ein ausgeartetes Menschengeschlecht neue Lebensregung brachten, entschieden worden. Die strenge Natur des Nordens drängt den Menschen mehr in sich selbst zurück, und was der spielenden freien Entfaltung der Sinne entzogen wird, muß bei edlen Anlagen dem Ernst des Gemüths zu Gute kommen. Daher die biedre Herzlichkeit, womit die altdeutschen Völkerschaften das Christenthum aufnahmen, so daß es nirgends so tief in's Innere gedrungen ist, sich so kräftig wirksam bewährt und mit allen menschlichen Gefühlen verwebt hat.

Aus dem rauhen aber treuen Heldenmuth der nordischen Eroberer ent-

stand durch Beimischung christlicher Gesinnungen das Ritterthum, dessen
Zweck darin bestand, die Uebung der Waffen durch heilig geachtete Gelübde
vor jedem rohen und niedrigen Mißbrauch der Gewalt zu bewahren, worein
sie so leicht verfällt.

Zu der ritterlichen Tugend gesellte sich ein neuer und sittsamerer Geist
der Liebe, als einer begeisterten Huldigung für ächte Weiblichkeit, die nun
erst als der Gipfel der Menschheit verehrt wurde und unter dem Bilde
jungfräulicher Mütterlichkeit von der Religion selbst aufgestellt, alle Her=
zen das Geheimniß reiner Güte ahnen ließ.

Da das Christenthum sich nicht wie der heidnische Götterdienst mit ge=
wissen äußern Leistungen begnügte, sondern den ganzen innern Menschen
mit seinen leisesten Regungen in Anspruch nahm; so rettete sich das Ge=
fühl der sittlichen Selbstständigkeit in das Gebiet der Ehre hinüber; gleich=
sam einer weltlichen Sittenlehre neben der religiösen, die sich oft im Wi=
derspruche mit dieser behauptete, aber ihr dennoch insofern verwandt war,
daß sie niemals die Folgen berechnete, sondern unbedingt Grundsätze des
Handelns heiligte, als Glaubens=Wahrheiten über die Untersuchung grü=
belnder Vernunft erhaben.

Ritterthum, Liebe und Ehre sind nebst der Religion selbst die Gegen=
stände der Naturpoesie, welche sich im Mittelalter in unglaublicher Fülle
ergoß und einer mehr künstlerischen Bildung des romantischen Geistes vor=
anging. Diese Zeit hatte auch ihre Mythologie, aus Ritterfabeln und Le=
genden bestehend, allein ihr Wunderbares und ihr Heroismus war dem der
alten Mythologie ganz entgegengesetzt.

Einige Denker, die übrigens die Eigenthümlichkeit der Neueren ebenso
begreifen und ableiten wie wir, haben das Wesen der nordischen Poesie in
die Melancholie gesetzt, und, gehörig verstanden, haben wir nichts hiegegen
einzuwenden.

Bei den Griechen war die menschliche Natur selbstgenügsam: sie ahnete
keinen Mangel und strebte nach keiner andern Vollkommenheit, als die sie
wirklich durch ihre eigenen Kräfte erreichen konnte. Eine höhere Weisheit
lehrt uns. die Menschheit habe durch eine große Verirrung die ihr ur=
sprünglich bestimmte Stelle eingebüßt, und die ganze Bestimmung ihres
irdischen Daseyns sey, dahin zurückzustreben; welches sie jedoch, sich selbst
überlassen, nicht vermöge. Jene sinnliche Religion wollte nur äußere ver=
gängliche Segnungen erwerben; die Unsterblichkeit, insofern sie geglaubt
wurde, stand in dunkler Ferne wie ein Schatten, ein abgeschwächter Traum
dieses wachen hellen Lebenstages. In der christlichen Ansicht hat sich
Alles umgekehrt: die Anschauung des Unendlichen hat das Endliche ver=
nichtet; das Leben ist zur Schattenwelt und zur Nacht geworden, und erst
jenseits geht der ewige Tag des wesentlichen Daseyns auf. Eine solche

Religion muß die Ahnung, die in allen gefühlvollen Herzen schlummert, zum deutlichen Bewußtseyn wecken, daß wir nach einer hier unerreichbaren Glückseligkeit trachten, daß kein äußerer Gegenstand jemals unsre Seele ganz wird erfüllen können, daß aller Genuß eine flüchtige Täuschung ist. Und wenn nun die Seele, gleichsam unter den Trauerweiden der Verbannung ruhend, ihr Verlangen nach der fremdgewordenen Heimath ausathmet, was anders kann der Grundton ihrer Lieder seyn als Schwermuth? So ist es denn auch: die Poesie der Alten war die des Besitzes, die unsrige ist die der Sehnsucht; jene steht fest auf dem Boden der Gegenwart, diese wiegt sich zwischen Erinnerung und Ahnung. Man mißverstehe dies nicht, als ob Alles in einförmige Klage verfließen und die Melancholie sich immer vorlaut aussprechen müßte. Wie in der heitern Weltansicht der Griechen die herbe Tragödie dennoch möglich war: so kann auch die aus der oben geschilderten entsprungene romantische Poesie alle Stimmungen bis zur fröhlichsten durchgehen, aber sie wird immer in einem namenlosen Etwas Spuren ihrer Quelle an sich tragen. Das Gefühl ist im Ganzen bei den Neueren inniger, die Phantasie unkörperlicher, der Gedanke beschaulicher geworden. Freilich laufen in der Natur die Grenzen ineinander, und die Dinge scheiden sich nicht so strenge, als man es thun muß, um einen Begriff festzuhalten.

Das griechische Ideal der Menschheit war vollkommene Eintracht und Ebenmaß aller Kräfte, natürliche Harmonie. Die Neueren hingegen sind zum Bewußtseyn der innern Entzweiung gekommen, welche ein solches Ideal unmöglich macht; daher ist das Streben ihrer Poesie, diese beiden Welten, zwischen denen wir uns getheilt fühlen, die geistige und sinnliche, miteinander auszusöhnen und unauflöslich zu verschmelzen. Die sinnlichen Eindrücke sollen durch ihr geheimnißvolles Bündniß mit höheren Gefühlen gleichsam geheiligt werden, der Geist hingegen will seine Ahnungen oder unnennbaren Anschauungen vom Unendlichen in der sinnlichen Erscheinung sinnlich niederlegen.

In der griechischen Kunst und Poesie ist ursprüngliche bewußtlose Einheit der Form und des Stoffes; in der neueren, sofern sie ihrem eigenthümlichen Geiste treu geblieben, wird innigere Durchdringung beider als zweier Entgegengesetzten gesucht. Jene hat ihre Aufgabe bis zur Vollendung gelöset; diese kann ihrem Streben in's Unendliche hin nur durch Annäherung Genüge leisten, und ist wegen eines gewissen Scheins von Unvollendung um so eher in Gefahr verkannt zu werden.

Friedrich Schlegel.

16. Charakteristik des neuen Testaments.

Die Griechen sind und bleiben unser Vorbild in aller Kunst und Wissen=
schaft, die Römer dagegen bilden nur den Uebergang zwischen dem Alter=
thum und der neuen Welt, doch galten sie dem Mittelalter zugleich auch als
nächste Quelle, bis jenes höhere und entferntere Vorbild erst später wieder
gefunden ward. Das nordische Naturgefühl, sowie es sich einestheils in
der alten Sage, die selbst im Christenthum blieb und nur in neuer Form
wieder auferstand, und anderntheils in der Germanischen Lebenseinrichtung
zwiefach ergoß, wurde die Wurzel, aus welcher das Gebilde des neuen Gei=
stes der abendländischen Völker emporwuchs. Das Christenthum aber,
nicht bloß an sich, sondern auch in seiner schriftlichen Abfassung, oder das
Evangelium ist das Licht von Oben gewesen, durch welches jene andern
Elemente neu verklärt und auch für die Kunst und Wissenschaft in Eins
gestaltet worden sind. Wir müssen hier des neuen Testaments um so mehr
gedenken, da der literarische Einfluß desselben für das Mittelalter und selbst
für die neuere Zeit durch Inhalt und Form, nicht bloß in der Moral und
Philosophie, sondern auch in der Kunst und Poesie unberechenbar groß ge=
wesen ist. Durch dieses göttliche Licht von Oben, welches das Evangelium
in seiner Einfalt und Klarheit in die Welt gebracht hat, wird der künstle=
rische Verstand und philosophische Scharfsinn der Griechen, der praktische
Weltverstand der Römer und der prophetische Tiefsinn der Hebräer erst zu
einem vollständigen Ganzen wahrhafter Erleuchtung und Einsicht für das
Leben, wie für die Wissenschaft, vollendet und beschlossen. Die Bibel,
welche wir nach ihrer innern Structur und dem organischen Zusammen=
hang der einzelnen Glieder und Theile derselben, als Ein Gebilde und gött=
liches Ganzes schon oben, so weit der hebräische Antheil desselben reicht, zu
betrachten suchten, wird als solches und als Ein Buch wahrhaft und völlig
erst durch das neue Testament vollendet. Ein Buch, wie es in Wahrheit
genannt werden muß, obwohl wunderbarer Weise aus zweiundsiebenzig
einzelnen Büchern, fünfmal neun des alten, dreimal neun des neuen Bun=
des, als eben so vielen Lebensgliedern und Geistesorganen, oder auch Glau=
benssternen und Lichtpunkten des ganzen Gottesgebildes bestehend. Es ist
auch das neue Testament wie das alte in einigen der dazu gehörigen Bücher
zunächst auf das ewige Wort des Lebens, in andern auf die göttliche Glau=
bensgemeinde und Kirche gerichtet und sich beziehend. Jenes Geheimniß
der Liebe, wie das ewige Wort zur bestimmten Zeit in der Mitte der welt=
historischen Entwickelung persönlich geworden und auf Erden erschienen ist,
schildert das Evangelium in einem vierfachen Abdruck, nach der gleichen
Vierzahl, in welcher auch im alten Bunde die Cherubim an der Arche das

Geheimniß der Verheißung bewachten. oder wie die vier Lebensströme aus
einer Quelle im Paradiese sich ergossen, und wie für jede Offenbarung der
göttlichen Herrlichkeit diese Vierzahl nach allen Weltgegenden und Dimen=
sionen ihrer sichtbaren Ausbreitung die wesentliche Form bildet, so daß man
wahrlich über diejenigen erstaunen und sich wohl wundern muß, welche sich
in diese so höchst natürliche und kaum anders denkbare Vierfachheit des
Evangeliums nicht finden können, oder gar einen Anstoß daran nehmen,
den sie wie ein seltsames Problem in ihrer gewöhnlichen Weise durch irgend
eine scharfsinnige Hypothese lösen und natürlich erklären möchten. Was
im Moses und in den Psalmen noch getrennt ist, nämlich die Offenbarung,
die bildliche Geschichte und bildliche Lehre vom Worte und die Begeisterung
und das lebendige Gefühl desselben, das ist im Evangelio vereint beisam=
men, welches uns das menschgewordene Wort in seinem Leben schildert.
Die übrigen Bücher des neuen Testaments aber gehen zunächst auf die
christliche Gemeinde und göttliche Kirche, indem sie uns die erste Gründung
und Ordnung derselben in der apostolischen Geschichte berichten, dann ihr
gegenseitiges Wirken und vereintes Leben in liebevoller Lehre und gläubiger
Hoffnung in dem ganzen Cyklus der mannigfachsten Episteln schildern, und
endlich auch noch die künftigen Schicksale derselben durch alle Zeiten ihrer
fernern Entwicklung in der Apokalypse hinstellen. Was in den Propheten
des alten Bundes noch ungesondert beisammen ist, die heilbringende Lehre
aus dem Geiste und die warnenden Gesichte des Geistes, die klare Lebens=
vorschrift und die verhüllte Weissagung, das ist hier in den Episteln und in
der Apokalypse abgesondert entfaltet, wie sich überhaupt die Schriften des
alten und des neuen Bundes überall entsprechen und gegenseitig ergänzen.
Der Prophet des neuen Bundes macht den vollständigen Schluß für das
ganze Gotteswerk, und dieses geheimnißvolle Buch der Zukunft bildet nebst
der Genesis oder der Offenbarung des Anfangs die andre Handhabe für
die heilige Arche der Schrift, in deren Umkreis das vierfache Evangelium
den lichten Mittelpunkt des Ganzen bildet. zu welchem aber Anfang und
Ende den eigentlichen Schlüssel des tieferen Sinns enthalten, so daß, wem
diese beiden Handhaben des ersten und letzten Buches der Bibel noch ganz
fremd oder völlig dunkel wären, sein Urtheil lieber zurückhalten und in red=
licher Unwissenheit stillschweigen sollte, wo von einem wissenschaftlichen
Verständniß der Offenbarung in ihrem Ganzen die Rede ist. In Form
und Schreibart ist das neue Testament allerdings ungleich einfacher als das
alte, und schon durch diese eigenthümliche Sprache der Einfalt, in welcher
der göttliche Tiefsinn sich hier in reinster Kindesklarheit ausspricht, ist das
wundervolle Volksbuch, wie man es wohl in gewissem Sinne nennen darf,
von dem entschiedensten Einfluß gewesen für die ganze Folgenreihe der
nachherigen Geistesentwicklung und aller neuern christlichen Belehrungs=

und Darstellungsformen. Der Geist der Allegorie ist übrigens im neuen
Testament nicht minder vorwaltend als im alten; besonders ist die eine be=
sondere Art derselben, welche Parabel genannt wird, obwohl sie auch schon
im alten Testamente vorkommt, hier am mannigfachsten angewandt und
entwickelt, und begründet recht eigentlich die kindliche Lehrart des Evange=
liums. Wenn der Spruch die natürliche Form ist für jegliche göttliche
Offenbarung im einfachen Ausdruck des ewigen Wortes, als das niederge=
schriebene Fiat, so ist die Parabel dagegen die menschliche und bildliche
Einkleidung und Entfaltung des einfachen göttlichen Lehrspruchs. Es ist
aber keine willkürliche oder künstlich gesuchte Dichterallegorie, oder eine
tiefsinnig verborgene Natursymbolik, sondern eine aus dem Leben und des=
sen gewöhnlichen Erscheinungen hergenommene Volksallegorie, in welcher sich
hier der göttliche Geist und die ewige Wahrheit wie in ein kindlich einfaches
Gewand einschließt. Es hat auch die einfache Parabel, sowie sie in der
Bibel angewandt und gebraucht wird, einen ganz eigenthümlichen göttlichen
Stempel, der sich nicht nachbilden noch erkünsteln läßt. Vorzüglich in die=
sen kindlichen Gleichnissen und sinnbildlichen Volksgeschichten und Parabeln
ist das Evangelium Urbild für alle spätern Legenden geworden, sowie diese
wiederum die Quelle und Vorrathskammer aller christlichen Kunst gewesen
sind, zunächst der bildenden, dann aber auch der Poesie. Indessen dürfen
wir über dieser kindlichen Einfalt im Vortrage des neuen Testaments doch
nie die innere Erhabenheit des göttlichen Verstandes, der darin niedergelegt
ist, verkennen oder übersehen. Wie aus der zornigen Löwengeberde, mit
der uns die Flammenschrift des alten Bundes mehrentheils entgegentritt,
im tiefsten Kern des innern Sinns und Herzens doch die fromme Lammes=
gestalt der duldenden Liebe emporsteigt, so erhebt sich in den Schriften des
neuen Bundes aus dem demuthsvollen Lammsgewande der kindlich ein=
fachen Lehre auch wiederum der Adler empor als höheres Sinnbild der ewi=
gen Anschauung Gottes. Und hier auf diesem Standpunkte tritt nun
eigentlich jene schon oben erwähnte dritte und höchste Auslegung und Er=
kenntniß der heiligen Schrift ein, nach dem geheimnißvollen Verständniß
der mit Gott vereinigten Seele, wo es das ewige Wort selbst ist, welches
sich in seinem eignen Lichte erfaßt und vernimmt. Denn alle Lehre und
Erkenntniß vom lebendigen Worte kann ja nach der dreifachen Geburt des
Wortes, der geschichtlichen, ewigen und der innerlichen in der Seele, auch
in der gleichen, dreifachen Beziehung erfaßt, verstanden und ausgelegt wer=
den. In jener höchsten Erkenntnißweise aber wird das Wort nun nicht
mehr nach einem bloß menschlichen Verstande getheilt und zerstückt erfaßt,
sondern wieder ganz und lebendig geworden wirkt es in den Wissenden als
Wort des Lebens und bringt auch Früchte des Lebens hervor. Da ver=
schwindet sodann jener mehrfache Sinn der Schrift, wie er auf den ersten

Stufen der annähernden Erkenntniß gesondert erhalten werden muß, und
geht, nachdem das Ziel gefunden ist, für das Wesentliche wieder über in den
einfachen Sinn der mit Gott vereinigten Seele, nach dem eignen vollen
Lichte des lebendigen Worts, welches in der Schrift selbst als das unge=
schriebene ewige Evangelium bezeichnet wird, durch welches auch das, was
noch früher verschlossen blieb, wenn die Zeit gekommen ist, entsiegelt wer=
den soll.

17. Der Minnegesang.

Das allgemeine Erwachen eines neuen Lebens und jugendlichen Gefühls
in dem Zeitalter der Kreuzzüge zeigte sich besonders in der plötzlichen Ent=
faltung jener Poesie, welche man bei den Provenzalen die fröhliche Wissen=
schaft nannte, und welche bei den geistvollsten Nationen des damaligen
Europa einen so verschwenderischen Reichthum von Rittergedichten und
Minneliedern hervorgebracht hat. Da der Geist des Minnegesangs aus
allen diesen Ritterdichtungen athmet, und dieser Geist vorzüglich sie von an=
dern bloß heroischen Heldengedichten unterscheidet; so mache ich mit dem
ersten den Anfang. Der Minnegesang blühte zuerst auf bei den Proven=
zalen und pflanzte sich von ihnen auf die Italiener fort, die anfangs selbst
wohl in provenzalischer Sprache dichteten. Jetzt ist diese Sprache wie
ausgestorben, daher die noch vorhandenen Denkmale derselben unbenutzt in
den Handschriften=Sammlungen daliegen. Nebst Frankreich blühte die
fröhliche Wissenschaft am frühesten in Deutschland, am meisten im zwölften
und dreizehnten Jahrhundert. Erst im vierzehnten Jahrhundert erreichte
der Minnegesang der Italiener durch Petrarka seine kunstreiche Vollendung,
und das fünfzehnte Jahrhundert war die eigentliche Zeit der spanischen Lie=
der. Ja, der letzte berühmte Dichter, der in dieser alten Art von Liebes=
liedern in Spanien einen großen Ruhm erreichte, lebte noch tief in das
sechszehnte Jahrhundert hinein. Es war Castillejo, der Ferdinand dem
Ersten aus seinem Vaterland nach Oestreich folgte.

Der Minnegesang hat sich bei jeder der genannten Nationen durchaus
eigenthümlich entwickelt, dem verschiedenen Nationalgeiste gemäß; und ich
glaube, daß hierin, mit Ausnahme der Italiener, keine Nation von der an=
dern so gar viel entlehnt hat; während die Ritterdichtungen allerdings
immer von einer Nation zur andern verpflanzt wurden und eine Art von
Allgemeingut für Alle waren. Selbst die Liederform hat sich bei jeder
Nation ganz verschieden gestaltet: in allen herrscht der Reim, und zwar
ein sehr musikalischer Gebrauch desselben, der ohne die Beziehung auf die
Musik fast verschwenderisch und spielend scheinen könnte. Wahrscheinlich

hat diese gemeinschaftliche Eigenschaft ihren Grund in der Beschaffenheit der damaligen Musik, da sie ursprünglich alle zum Gesange bestimmt waren.

Daß die deutschen Dichter ihre Minnelieder von den Provenzalen entlehnt hätten, wie man oft ohne allen Beweis behauptet und ohne Grund vorausgesetzt hat, ist um so weniger wahrscheinlich, da die Deutschen in viel früherer Zeit Minnelieder gehabt haben; denn schon unter Kaiser Ludwig dem Frommen fand man es nöthig, den Klosterfrauen das häufige Singen der deutschen Liebesgesänge, oder Wynelieder, zu untersagen. In der Ritterzeit haben allerdings einige deutsche Fürsten, die in Italien mehr einheimisch waren, auch in provenzalischer Sprache gedichtet; aber dies beweis't für den deutschen Minnegesang selbst nichts. Wäre dieser entlehnt, so würden die Sänger doch bisweilen ihre Vorbilder erwähnen, wie Petrarka seine geliebten Provenzalen so oft mit Ruhm anführt, um so mehr, da die deutschen Verfasser der erzählenden Rittergedichte ihre provenzalischen oder französischen Quellen fast jederzeit anführen.

Wie dem auch sey, in der Liederform und auch im Charakter, in dem Gedankengange und der Gefühlsweise sind die deutschen Minnelieder von den provenzalischen und französischen ganz verschieden, und von allen noch vorhandenen und schon bekannten Sammlungen der Art ist die deutsche die reichste.

Was darin zuerst auffällt, ist der sanfte Geist, den sie athmen; besonders Wunder nimmt es uns, wenn man einige dieser Fürsten und Ritter, von denen sie herrühren, in der Geschichte als die kühnsten Helden auftreten sieht. Aber dieser Gegensatz findet sich oft in der Natur und muß wohl dem menschlichen Herzen, wenn es edel ist, gemäß seyn: daß nämlich mitten in einem ganz kriegerischen Leben sanfte Neigungen erwachen, und aus der höchsten heroischen Kraft das feinste Zartgefühl wie eine schöne Blume emporsteigt. So ist auch jene alte Melodie, welche dem König Richard allgemein zugeschrieben wird, nur wie ein rührender Klagehauch, sanfter als man von dem löwenherzigen Helden irgend erwarten sollte.

Doch die Zartheit der Gefühle und auch die Anmuth und musikalische Weichheit in der Sprache hat man den deutschen Minneliedern noch nie abgesprochen, dagegen macht man ihnen den Vorwurf der Einförmigkeit und Tändelei. Der Vorwurf der Einförmigkeit ist eigentlich sonderbar: es ist, als ob man sich beklagen wollte, daß im Frühling oder in einem Garten der Blumen zu viel seyen. Freilich sollten Gedichte der Art nur wie einzelne Blumen den Weg des Lebens schmücken und nicht mit einem Male ausgeschüttet werden, was Ueberdruß erregt. Der Laura selbst hätte es zu viel werden mögen, wenn sie alle Gedichte, welche Petrarka noch bei ihrer Lebenszeit an sie gesungen hat, mit einem Male hätte lesen sollen. Der Eindruck der Einförmigkeit liegt aber bloß darin, daß wir ganze

Hunderte von folchen Liedern, weil fie jetzt eine Sammlung bilden, hinter=
einander lefen oder durchlaufen, wozu fie urfprünglich gar nicht beftimmt
waren. Denn find fie auch nicht alle an eine wirkliche Geliebte gerichtet
gewefen, fondern manche bloß erfonnen worden; fo war es doch immer für
den Gefang, und um gefungen, wo immer man Luft daran fand, das ge=
fellige Leben zu erheitern und zu verfchönern. Außerdem ift es unvermeid=
lich, daß nicht bloß Liebesgefänge, fondern überhaupt alle lyrifchen Ge=
dichte, wenn fie ganz Natur find und nur aus der eigenen Empfindung her=
vorgehen, fich in einem beftimmten Kreife von Gefühlen und Gedanken=
gange bewegen.

Dies ließe fich felbft in der ernfthaften lyrifchen Gattung durch Beifpiele
von allen Nationen bewähren. Das Gefühl muß eine gewiffe Hauptrich=
tung haben, wenn es fich eigenthümlich und poetifch ausfprechen foll, und
wo das Gefühl vorherrfchen foll, da kann der Gedankenreichthum nur eine
untergeordnete Stelle einnehmen. Die geforderte Mannigfaltigkeit der
lyrifchen Gedichte findet fich nur in den Zeitaltern der Nachbildung, wo
man denn oft alle mögliche Gegenftände in allen möglichen Formen behan=
delt und nicht felten den Ton und den Gefchmack der verfchiedenften Na=
tionen und Zeitalter in einer Sammlung beifammen und um fo mehr Ab=
wechslung zum hintereinander Durchlefen findet, je mehr das Lied und der
Gefang zum Gelegenheitsgedicht herabgefunken ift, oder fich in finnreiche
Kleinigkeit und Epigramme zerfplittert und aufgelöf't hat.

Der zweite Vorwurf, welchen man den Minneliedern macht, daß fie tän=
delnd feyen, ift nicht ungegründet; aber ich weiß nicht, ob es durchaus ein
Tadel ift. Selbft die Alten, obwohl fie in ihren erotifchen Gedichten mehr
die Gluth der Leidenfchaft in ihrer ganzen Stärke darzuftellen ftreben, ha=
ben doch erkannt, daß auch diefes Spielende in der Natur und in dem Ge=
fühl der Liebe liege, indem fie in ihrer Mythologie den Amor als ein Kind
darftellen und an diefen Begriff fo manche finnreiche Dichtungen und Bil=
der geknüpft haben. Daß die Liebe als die heftigfte Leidenfchaft auch in
der Ritterzeit oft tragifche Ereigniffe und Handlungen hervorgebracht hat,
läßt fich fchon aus dem lebendigen Charakter diefes Zeitalters vermuthen.
Die Gefchichte bietet eine Menge Beifpiele der Art dar. Aber diefe ernft=
hafte und leidenfchaftliche Seite der Liebe wird in den Minneliedern felten
hervorgehoben. So ganz ohne Sinnlichkeit, wie die platonifchen Sinn=
gedichte und Gefänge des Petrarka, find die deutfchen Minnelieder nicht.
Doch in den meiften wird auch diefe Seite nur zart berührt. Vorzüglich
und faft ausfchließend ergriffen diefe Dichter diejenige Seite des Gefühls,
welche dem Spiele der Phantafie einen freien Raum eröffnet. Es war
alfo der Geift des Minnegefangs überhaupt, und des deutfchen insbefon=
dere, etwa folgender. Aus der den Deutfchen urfprünglich eignen Achtung

vor den Frauen entwickelte sich bei mildern und verfeinerten Sitten und
nachdem auch das Christenthum strengere und reinere Begriffe von Sittlich=
keit allgemeiner verbreitet hatte, ein Zartgefühl, das nur da, wo es nicht
mehr empfunden ward, und die bloße Form davon übrig geblieben war, in
leere Galanterie entartete; was aber, so lange es wirklich gefühlt wird,
doch etwas unläugbar Edles und Schönes auch für die Poesie ist.

Die provenzalischen Liebeshöfe und Gerichte, die daselbst mit einer fast
metaphysischen Spitzfindigkeit durchgeführten Streitigkeiten und beantwor=
teten Fragen über die Liebe sind dem deutschen Minnegesang eigentlich durch=
aus fremd.   Er ist kunstlos im Vergleich mit dem sinnreichen Gedanken=
spiel des Petrarka oder der spanischen Lieder; dagegen aber ist er gefühl=
voller und besingt neben der Liebe gern auch die Natur und die Schönheit
des Frühlings.

Wilhelm von Humboldt.

18. Ueber Schiller und den Gang seiner Geistesentwickelung.

Schiller's Dichtergenie kündigte sich gleich in seinen ersten Arbeiten an;
ungeachtet aller Mängel der Form, ungeachtet vieler Dinge, die dem gereif=
ten Künstler sogar roh erscheinen mußten, zeugten die Räuber und
Fiesko von einer entschiednen großen Naturkraft.   Es verrieth sich
nachher durch die bei ganz verschiedenartigen philosophischen und historischen
Beschäftigungen immer durchbrechende, auch in diesen Briefen so oft ange=
deutete Sehnsucht nach der Dichtung, wie nach der eigenthümlichen Heimath
seines Geistes.   Es offenbarte sich endlich in männlicher Kraft und geläu=
terter Reinheit in den Stücken, die gewiß noch lange der Stolz und Ruhm
der deutschen Bühne bleiben werden.   Aber dies Dichtergenie war auf das
Engste an das Denken in allen seinen Tiefen und Höhen geknüpft, es tritt
ganz eigentlich auf dem Grunde einer Intellectualität hervor, die Alles er=
gründend spalten, und Alles verknüpfend zu einem Ganzen vereinen möchte.
Darin liegt Schiller's besondere Eigenthümlichkeit.   Er forderte von der
Dichtung einen tieferen Antheil des Gedankens, und unterwarf sie strenger
einer geistigen Einheit; letzteres auf zweifache Weise, indem er sie an eine
festere Kunstform band, und indem er jede Dichtung so behandelte, daß ihr
Stoff unwillkührlich und von selbst seine Individualität zum Ganzen einer
Idee erweiterte.   Auf diesen Eigenthümlichkeiten beruhen die Vorzüge,
welche Schiller charakteristisch bezeichnen.   Aus ihnen entsprang es, daß
er, das Größte und Höchste hervorzubringen, dessen er fähig war, erst eines
Zeitraums bedurfte, in welchem sich seine ganze Intellectualität, an die sein

Dichtergenie unauflöslich geknüpft war, zu der von ihm geforderten Klar=
heit und Bestimmtheit durcharbeitete. Diese Eigenthümlichkeiten endlich
erklären die tadelnden Urtheile derer, die in Schiller's Werken ihm die Frei=
willigkeit der Gabe der Musen absprechend, weniger die leichte glückliche
Geburt des Genies, als die sich ihrer selbst bewußte Arbeit des Geistes zu
erkennen meinen; worin allerdings das Wahre liegt, daß nur die intel=
lectuelle Größe Schillers die Veranlassung zu einem solchen Tadel darbie=
ten konnte.

Ich würde es für überflüssig halten, zur Rechtfertigung dieser Behauptun=
gen in eine Zergliederung der Schiller'schen Werke einzugehen, die Jedem
zu gegenwärtig sind, um nicht, welches auch seine Meinung seyn möchte, die
Anwendung selbst zu machen. Dagegen ist es vielleicht dem Leser des
Briefwechsels angenehm, wenn ich mit Wenigem zu entwickeln versuche, wie
diese meine Ansicht von Schillers Eigenthümlichkeit zugleich und besonders
durch meinen Umgang mit ihm, durch Erinnerungen aus seinen Gesprächen,
durch die Vergleichung seiner Arbeiten in ihrer Zeitfolge und den Nachfor=
schungen über den Gang seines Geistes entstand. Was jedem Beobachter
an Schiller am meisten als charakteristisch bezeichnend auffallen mußte,
war, daß in einem höheren und prägnanteren Sinn, als vielleicht je bei
einem Andern, der Gedanke das Element seines Lebens war. Anhaltend
selbstthätige Beschäftigung des Geistes verließ ihn fast nie, und wich nur
den heftigeren Anfällen seines körperlichen Uebels. Sie schien ihm Erho=
lung, nicht Anstrengung. Dieß zeigte sich am meisten im Gespräch, für das
Schiller ganz eigentlich geboren schien. Er suchte nie nach einem bedeu=
tenden Stoff der Unterredung, er überließ es mehr dem Zufall, den Gegen=
stand herbeizuführen, aber von jedem aus leitete er das Gespräch zu einem
allgemeinen Gesichtspunkt, und man sah sich nach wenigen Zwischenreden in
den Mittelpunkt einer den Geist anregenden Discussion versetzt. Er be=
handelte den Gedanken immer als ein gemeinschaftlich zu gewinnendes Re=
sultat, schien immer des Mitredenden zu bedürfen, wenn dieser auch sich
bewußt blieb, die Idee allein von ihm zu empfangen, und ließ ihn nie müßig
werden. Hierin unterschied sich sein Gespräch am meisten von dem Herder=
schen. Nie vielleicht hat ein Mann schöner gesprochen, als Herder, wenn
man, was bei Berührung irgend einer leicht bei ihm anklingenden Saite
nicht schwer war, ihn in aufgelegter Stimmung antraf. Alle seltenen
Eigenschaften dieses mit Recht bewunderten Mannes schienen, so geeignet
waren sie für dasselbe, im Gespräch ihre Kraft zu verdoppeln. Der Ge=
danke verband sich mit dem Ausdruck, mit der Anmuth und Würde, die, da
sie in Wahrheit allein der Person angehören, nur vom Gegenstande herzu=
kommen scheinen. So floß die Rede ununterbrochen hin in der Klarheit,
die doch noch dem eignen Erahnen übrig läßt, und in dem Helldunkel, das

doch nicht hindert, den Gedanken bestimmt zu erkennen. Aber wenn die Materie erschöpft war, so ging man zu einer neuen über. Man förderte nichts durch Einwendungen, man hätte eher gehindert. Man hatte gehört, man konnte nun selbst reden, aber man vermißte die Wechselthätigkeit des Gesprächs. Schiller sprach nicht eigentlich schön. Aber sein Geist strebte immer in Schärfe und Bestimmtheit einem neuen geistigen Gewinne zu, er beherrschte dies Streben, und schwebte in vollkommener Freiheit über seinem Gegenstande. Daher benutzte er in leichter Heiterkeit jede sich darbietende Nebenbeziehung, und daher war sein Gespräch so reich an den Worten, die das Gepräge glücklicher Geburten des Augenblicks an sich tragen. Die Freiheit that aber dem Gange der Untersuchung keinen Abbruch. Schiller hielt immer den Faden fest, der zu ihrem Endpunkt führen mußte, und wenn die Unterredung nicht durch einen Zufall gestört wurde, so brach er nicht leicht vor Erreichung des Zieles ab.

So wie Schiller im Gespräche immer dem Gebiete des Denkens neuen Boden zu gewinnen suchte, so war überhaupt seine geistige Beschäftigung immer eine von angestrengter Selbstthätigkeit. Auch seine Briefe zeigen dies deutlich. Er kannte sogar keine andere. Bloßer Lectüre überließ er sich nur spät Abends und in seinen, leider so häufig, schlaflosen Nächten. Seinen Tag nahmen seine Arbeiten ein, oder bestimmte Studien für dieselben, wo also der Geist durch die Arbeit und die Forschung zugleich in Spannung gehalten wird. Das bloße von keinem andern unmittelbaren Zweck, als dem des Wissens geleitete Studiren, das für den damit Vertrauten einen so unendlichen Reiz hat, daß man sich verwahren muß, dadurch nicht zu sehr von bestimmterer Thätigkeit abgehalten zu werden, kannte er nicht, und achtete es nicht genug. Das Wissen erschien ihm zu stoffartig, und die Kräfte des Geistes zu edel, um in dem Stoffe mehr zu sehen als ein Material zur Bearbeitung.

Nur weil er die allerdings höhere Anstrengung des Geistes, welche selbstthätig aus ihren eigenen Tiefen schöpft, mehr schätzte, konnte er sich weniger mit der geringeren befreunden. Es ist aber auch merkwürdig, aus welchem kleinen Vorrath des Stoffes, wie entblößt von den Mitteln, welche Andern ihn zuführen, Schiller eine sehr vielseitige Weltansicht gewann, die, wo man sie gewahr wurde, durch genialische Wahrheit überraschte; denn man kann die nicht anders nennen, die durchaus auf keinem äußerlichen Wege entstanden war. Selbst von Deutschland hatte er nur einen Theil gesehen, nie die Schweiz, von der sein Tell doch so lebendige Schilderungen enthält. Wer einmal am Rheinfall steht, wird sich beim Anblick unwillkührlich an die schöne Strophe des Tauchers erinnern, welche dies verwirrende Wassergewühl malt, das den Blick gleichsam fesselnd verschlingt; doch lag auch dieser keine eigne Ansicht zum Grunde. Aber was Schiller durch

eigne Erfahrung gewann, das ergriff er mit einem Blick, der ihm hernach
auch das anschaulich machte, was ihm bloß fremde Schilderung zuführte.
Dabei versäumte er nie, zu jeder Arbeit Studien durch Lectüre zu machen;
auch was er in dieser Art Dienliches zufällig fand, prägte sich seinem Gedächtniß fest ein, und seine rastlos angestrengte Phantasie, die in beständi-
ger Lebendigkeit bald diesen bald jenen Theil des irgend je gesammelten
Stoffes bearbeitete, ergänzte das Mangelhafte einer so mittelbaren Auffassung.

Auf ganz ähnliche Weise eignete er sich den Geist der griechischen Dichtung an, ohne sie je anders als aus Uebersetzungen zu kennen. Er scheute
dabei keine Mühe; er zog die Uebersetzungen vor, die darauf Verzicht leisten,
für sich zu gelten; am liebsten waren ihm die wörtlichen lateinischen Para-
phrasen. So übersetzte er die Scenen und die Hochzeit der Thetis
aus dem Euripides. Ich gestehe, daß ich diesen Chor immer mit großem
Vergnügen wieder lese. Es ist nicht bloß eine Uebertragung in eine andere Sprache, sondern in eine andere Gattung von Dichtung. Der
Schwung, in den die Phantasie von den ersten Versen an versetzt wird, ist
ein verschiedener, also gerade das, was die rein poetische Wirkung ausmacht.
Denn diese kann man nur in die allgemeine Stimmung der Phantasie und
des Gefühles setzen, die der Dichter unabhängig von dem Ideengehalte bloß
durch den seinen Werken beigegebenen Hauch seiner Begeisterung im Leser
hervorruft. Der antike Geist blickt wie ein Schatten durch das ihm ge-
liehene Gewand. Aber in jeder Strophe sind einige Züge des Originals
so bedeutsam herausgehoben und so rein hingestellt, daß man dennoch vom
Anfang bis zum Ende beim Antiken festgehalten wird. Ich meinte indeß
nicht vorzugsweise diese Uebersetzung, wenn ich von Schillers Eingehen in
griechischen Dichtergeist sprach, sondern zwei seiner späteren Stücke. Auch
hierin hatte Schiller bedeutende Fortschritte gemacht. Die Kraniche
des Ibykus und das Siegesfest tragen die Farben des Alterthums
so rein und treu an sich, als man es nur von irgend einem modernen Dichter erwarten kann, und zwar auf die schönste und geistvollste Weise. Der
Dichter hat den Sinn des Alterthums in sich aufgenommen, er bewegt
sich darin mit Freiheit, und so entspringt eine neue, in allen ihren Theilen
nur Eine athmende Dichtung. Beide Stücke stehen aber wieder in einem
merkwürdigen Gegensatz gegen einander. Die Kraniche des Ibykus erlaubten eine ganz epische Ausführung; was den Stoff dem Dichter
innerlich werth machte, war die daraus entspringende Idee der Gewalt
künstlerischer Darstellung über die menschliche Brust. Diese Macht der
Poesie, einer unsichtbaren, bloß durch den Geist geschaffnen, in der Wirklichkeit verfliegenden Kraft, gehörte wesentlich in den Ideenkreis, der Schiller lebendig beschäftigte. Schon acht Jahre, ehe er sich zur Ballade in ihm

gestaltete, schwebte ihm dieser Stoff vor, wie deutlich aus den **Künstlern** aus den Versen hervorgeht:

> Vom Eumenidenchor geschrecket,
> Zieht sich der Mord, auch nie entdecket,
> Das Loos des Todes aus dem Lied.

Diese Idee erlaubte aber auch eine vollkommen antike Ausführung; das Alterthum besaß Alles, um sie in ihrer ganzen Reinheit nnd Stärke hervortreten zu lassen. Daher ist Alles in der ganzen Erzählung unmittelbar aus ihm entnommen, besonders das Erscheinen und der Gesang der Eumeniden. Der Aeschylische bekannte Chor ist so kunstvoll in die moderne Dichtungsform in Reim und Silbenmaß verwebt, daß nichts von seiner stillen Größe aufgegeben scheint. Das Siegesfest ist lyrischer und betrachtender Natur. Hier konnte und mußte der Dichter aus der Fülle seines Busens hinzufügen, was nicht im Ideen- und Gefühlskreise des Alterthums lag. Aber im Uebrigen ist Alles im Sinne der Homerischen Dichtung eben so rein als in dem andern Gedicht. Das Ganze ist nur, wie in einer höheren mehr abgesondert gehaltenen Geistigkeit ausgeprägt, als dem alten Sänger eigen ist, und erhält gerade dadurch seine größten Schönheiten. An einzelnen, aus den Alten entnommenen Zügen, in die aber oft eine höhere Bedeutung gelegt ist, sind auch frühere Gedichte Schiller's reich. Ich erwähne hier nur die Schilderung des Todes aus den **Künstlern** „den sanften Bogen der Nothwendigkeit", der so schön an die ἀγανὰ βέλεα (die sanften Geschosse) bei Homer erinnert, wo aber die Uebertragung des Beiworts vom Geschoß auf den Bogen selbst dem Gedanken einen zarteren und tieferen Sinn giebt.

Die Zuversicht in das Vermögen der menschlichen Geisteskraft, gesteigert zu einem dichterischen Bilde, ist in den „**Columbus**" überschriebenen Distichen ausgedrückt, die zu dem Eigenthümlichsten gehören, was Schiller gedichtet hat. Dieser Glaube, an die dem Menschen unsichtbar inwohnende Kraft, die erhabene und so tief wahre Ansicht, daß es eine innere geheime Uebereinstimmung geben muß zwischen ihr und der das ganze Weltall ordnenden und regierenden, da alle Wahrheit nur Abglanz der ewigen, ursprünglichen seyn kann, war ein charakteristischer Zug in Schiller's Ideensystem. Ihm entsprach auch die Beharrlichkeit, mit der er jeder intellectuellen Aufgabe so lange nachging, bis sie befriedigend gelös't war. Schon in den **Briefen Raphaels an Julius** in der **Talia** in dem kühnen aber schönen Ausdruck: „als Columbus die bedenkliche Wette mit einem unbefahrenen Meer einging," findet sich der gleiche Gedanke an dasselbe Bild geknüpft.

Dem Inhalte und der Form nach, waren Schiller's philosophische Ideen ein getreuer Abdruck seiner ganzen geistigen Wirksamkeit überhaupt. Beide bewegten sich immer im nämlichen Gleise und strebten dem gleichen Ziele zu, allein auf eine Weise, daß die lebendigere Aneignung immer reicheren Stoffs und die Kraft des ihn beherrschenden Gedankens sich unaufhörlich zu wechselseitiger Steigerung bestimmten. Der Endpunkt, an den er Alles knüpfte, war die T o t a l i t ä t in der menschlichen Natur durch das Zusammenstimmen ihrer geschiedenen Kräfte in ihrer absoluten Freiheit. Beide dem Ich, das nur eins und ein untheilbares seyn kann, angehörend, aber die eine Mannigfaltigkeit und Stoff, die andere Einheit und Form suchend, sollten sie durch ihre freiwillige Harmonie schon hier auf einen über alle Endlichkeit hinaus liegenden Ursprung hindeuten. Die Vernunft, unbedingt herrschend in der Erkenntniß und Willensbestimmung, sollte die Anschauung und Empfindung mit schonender Achtung behandeln, und nirgends in ihr Gebiet übergreifen; dagegen sollten diese sich aus ihrem eigenthümlichen Wesen, und auf ihrer selbst gewählten Bahn zu einer Gestalt emporbilden, in welcher jene bei aller Verschiedenheit des Prinzips sich der Form nach wiederfände. Diese nicht auf entdeckbaren Wegen entstehende, sondern wie durch plötzliches Wunder überraschende Uebereinstimmung zu vermitteln, den in sich unabweisbaren Widerspruch beider Naturen durch einen in ihrer Wechselbeziehung auf einander gegründeten Schein aufzuheben, und dem Menschen dadurch in der Erscheinung ein Bild desjenigen zu geben, was außer aller Erscheinung liegt, vermag allein die Richtung in ihm, welche wir die ä st h e t i s ch e nennen. Denn sie behandelt den Stoff mit einer auf dem Gebiete der Sinnlichkeit entsprungenen, nicht von der Idee erborgten und dennoch als Freiheit erscheinenden Selbstthätigkeit.

Johann Gottlieb Fichte.

19. Ueber die Bestimmung des Gelehrten.

Der Gelehrte ist ganz vorzüglich für die Gesellschaft bestimmt: er ist, insofern er Gelehrter ist, mehr als irgend ein Stand, ganz eigentlich nur durch die Gesellschaft und für die Gesellschaft da; er hat demnach ganz besonders die Pflicht, die gesellschaftlichen Talente, Empfänglichkeit und Mittheilungsfertigkeit, vorzüglich und in dem höchst möglichen Grade in sich auszubilden. Die Empfänglichkeit sollte in ihm, wenn er auf die gehörige Art sich die gehörigen empirischen Kenntnisse erworben hat, schon vorzüglich ausgebildet seyn. Er soll bekannt seyn mit demjenigen in seiner Wissenschaft, was schon vor ihm da war: das kann er nicht anders als durch Unterricht, sey es nun mündlicher oder Bücherunterricht, gelernt, nicht aber durch Nachdenken aus bloßen Vernunftgründen entwickelt haben. Aber er soll durch stätes Hinzulernen sich diese Empfänglichkeit erhalten und sich otgn.ht.

vor der oft und bisweilen bei vorzüglichen Selbstdenkern vorkommenden gänzlichen Verschlossenheit vor fremden Meinungen und Darstellungsarten zu verwahren suchen; denn Niemand ist so unterrichtet, daß er nicht immer noch hinzulernen könnte und bisweilen noch etwas sehr Nöthiges zu lernen hätte; und selten ist Jemand so unwissend, daß er nicht selbst dem Gelehrtesten etwas sollte sagen können, was derselbe nicht weiß. Der Mittheilungsfertigkeit bedarf der Gelehrte immer: denn er besitzt seine Kenntniß nicht für sich selbst, sondern für die Gesellschaft. Diese hat er von Jugend auf zu üben, sie hat er in stäter Thätigkeit zu erhalten: durch welche Mittel, werden wir zu seiner Zeit untersuchen.

Seine für die Gesellschaft erworbene Kenntniß soll er nun wirklich zum Nutzen der Gesellschaft anwenden; er soll die Menschen zum Gefühl ihrer wahren Bedürfnisse bringen und sie mit den Mitteln ihrer Befriedigung bekannt machen. Das heißt nun aber nicht, er soll sich mit ihnen in die tiefen Untersuchungen einlassen, die er selbst unternehmen mußte, um etwas Gewisses und Sicheres zu finden. Dann ginge er darauf aus, alle Menschen zu so großen Gelehrten zu machen, als er etwa selbst sein mag; und das ist unmöglich und zweckwidrig. Das Uebrige muß auch gethan werden, und dazu sind andere Stände; und wenn diese ihre Zeit gelehrten Untersuchungen widmen sollten, so würden auch die Gelehrten bald aufhören müssen Gelehrte zu seyn. Wie kann und soll er denn aber seine Kenntnisse verbreiten? Die Gesellschaft könnte ohne Zutrauen auf die Redlichkeit und Geschicklichkeit Anderer nicht bestehen, und dieses Zutrauen ist demnach tief in unser Herz geprägt, und wir haben es durch eine besondere Wohlthat der Natur nie in einem höheren Grade, als da, wo wir der Redlichkeit und Geschicklichkeit des Andern am dringendsten bedürfen. Er darf auf dieses Vertrauen zu seiner Redlichkeit und Geschicklichkeit rechnen, wenn er es sich erworben hat, wie er soll. — Ferner ist in allen Menschen ein Gefühl des Wahren, welches freilich allein nicht hinreicht, sondern entwickelt, geprüft, geläutert werden muß; und das eben ist die Aufgabe des Gelehrten. Es würde dem Ungelehrten nicht hinreichen, um ihn auf alle Wahrheiten zu führen, deren er bedürfte; aber wenn es nur sonst — und das geschieht oft gerade durch Leute, die sich zu den Gelehrten zählen — wenn es nur sonst nicht etwa künstlich verfälscht worden ist: wird es immer hinreichen, daß er die Wahrheit, wenn ein Anderer ihn darauf hinführt, auch ohne tiefe Gründe für Wahrheit anerkenne. — Auf dieses Wahrheitsgefühl darf der Gelehrte gleichfalls rechnen. — Also der Gelehrte ist, insoweit wir den Begriff desselben bis jetzt entwickelt haben, seiner Bestimmung nach der Lehrer des Menschengeschlechts.

Aber er hat die Menschen nicht nur im Allgemeinen mit ihren Bedürfnissen und den Mitteln, dieselben zu befriedigen, bekannt zu machen; er hat

sie insbesondere zu jeder Zeit und an jedem Orte auf die eben jetzt, unter
diesen bestimmten Umständen eintretenden Bedürfnisse und auf die bestimm=
ten Mittel, die jetzt aufgegebenen Zwecke zu erreichen, zu leiten. Er sieht
nicht bloß das Gegenwärtige, er sieht auch das Künftige; er sieht nicht
bloß den jetzigen Standpunkt, er sieht auch, wohin das Menschengeschlecht
nunmehr schreiten muß, wenn es auf dem Wege zu seinem letzten Ziele
bleiben, und nicht von demselben abirren oder auf ihm zurückkehren soll.
Er kann nicht verlangen, es auf einmal bis zu dem Punkte fortzureißen,
der etwa ihm in die Augen strahlt: es kann seinen Weg nicht überspringen;
er hat nur zu sorgen, daß es nicht stille stehe, und daß es nicht zurückgehe.
In dieser Rücksicht ist der Gelehrte der Erzieher der Menschheit. — Ich
merke hierbei ausdrücklich an, daß der Gelehrte bei diesem Geschäft, sowie
bei allen seinen Geschäften, unter den Gebiete des Sittengesetzes, der gebo=
tenen Uebereinstimmung mit sich selbst, stehe. Er wirkt auf die Gesellschaft:
diese gründet sich auf den Begriff der Freiheit; sie und jedes Mitglied der=
selben ist frei, und er darf sie nicht anders behandeln als durch moralische
Mittel. Der Gelehrte wird nicht in die Versuchung kommen, die Menschen
durch Zwangsmittel, durch Gebrauch physischer Gewalt, zur Annahme seiner
Ueberzeugungen zu bringen: gegen diese Thorheit sollte man doch in unserm
Zeitalter kein Wort mehr zu verlieren haben; aber er soll sie auch nicht
täuschen. Abgerechnet, daß er dadurch sich an sich selbst vergeht, und daß
die Pflichten des Menschen in jedem Falle höher seyn würden als die
Pflichten des Gelehrten; vergeht er dadurch sich zugleich gegen die Gesell=
schaft. Jedes Individuum in derselben soll aus freier Wahl und aus einer
von ihm selbst als hinlänglich beurtheilten Ueberzeugung handeln; es soll
sich selbst bei jeder seiner Handlungen als Mitzweck betrachten können, und
als solcher von jedem Mitglied behandelt werden. Wer getäuscht wird,
wird als bloßes Mittel behandelt.

Der letzte Zweck jedes einzelnen Menschen sowohl als der ganzen Gesell=
schaft, mithin auch aller Arbeiten des Gelehrten an der Gesellschaft, ist
sittliche Veredlung des ganzen Menschen. Es ist die Pflicht des Gelehr=
ten, diesen letzten Zweck immer aufzustellen und ihn bei Allem, was er in
der Gesellschaft thut, vor Augen zu haben. Niemand aber kann mit Glück
an sittlicher Veredlung arbeiten, der nicht selbst ein guter Mensch ist. Wir
lehren nicht bloß durch Worte; wir lehren auch weit eindringender durch
unser Beispiel; und Jeder, der in der Gesellschaft lebt, ist ihr ein gutes
Beispiel schuldig, weil die Kraft des Beispiels erst durch unser Leben in der
Gesellschaft entsteht. Wie vielmehr ist der Gelehrte dies schuldig, der in
allen Stücken der Cultur den übrigen Ständen zuvor seyn soll? Ist er in
dem Ersten und Höchsten, demjenigen, was auf alle Cultur abzweckt, zurück,
wie kann er Muster seyn, das er doch seyn soll; und wie kann er glauben,

daß die andern seinen Lehren folgen werden, denen er vor Aller Augen durch jede Handlung seines Lebens widerspricht? (Die Worte, die der Stifter der christlichen Religion an seine Schüler richtete, gelten ganz eigentlich für den Gelehrten: „Ihr seyd das Salz der Erde; wenn das Salz seine Kraft verliert, womit soll man salzen? wenn die Auswahl unter den Menschen verdorben ist, wo soll man noch sittliche Güte suchen?" —) Also der Gelehrte in der letzten Rücksicht betrachtet, soll der sittlichbeste Mensch seines Zeitalters seyn: er soll die höchste Stufe der bis auf ihn möglichen sittlichen Ausbildung in sich darstellen.

Dies ist unsre gemeinschaftliche Bestimmung, M. H.,* dies unser gemeinschaftliches Schicksal: ein glückliches Schicksal noch durch seinen besonderen Beruf bestimmt zu seyn, dasjenige zu thun, was man schon um seines allgemeinen Berufs willen, als Mensch, thun müßte; seine Zeit und seine Kräfte auf nichts wenden zu sollen als darauf, wozu man sich sonst Zeit und Kraft mit kluger Kargheit absparen müßte; zur Arbeit, zum Geschäfte, zum einzigen Tagwerk seines Lebens zu haben, was Andern süße Erholung von der Arbeit seyn würde. Es ist ein stärkender, seelenerhebender Gedanke, den jeder unter Ihnen haben kann, welcher seiner Bestimmung werth ist: auch mir an meinem Theile ist die Cultur meines Zeitalters und der folgenden Zeitalter anvertraut; auch aus meinen Arbeiten wird sich der Gang der künftigen Geschlechter, die Weltgeschichte der Nationen, die noch werden sollen, entwickeln. Ich bin dazu berufen, der Wahrheit Zeugniß zu geben; an meinem Leben und an meinen Schicksalen liegt nichts; an den Wirkungen meines Lebens liegt unendlich viel. Ich bin ein Priester der Wahrheit; ich bin in ihrem Solde; ich habe mich verbindlich gemacht, Alles für sie zu thun und zu wagen und zu leiden. Wenn ich um ihretwillen verfolgt und gehaßt werden, wenn ich in ihrem Dienste gar sterben sollte; was thät' ich dann Sonderliches, was thät' ich dann weiter als das, was ich schlechthin thun mußte?

Ich weiß es, M. H.! wieviel ich jetzt gesagt habe: ich weiß es eben so gut, daß ein entmanntes und nervenloses Zeitalter diese Empfindung und diesen Ausdruck derselben nicht erträgt; daß es alles dasjenige, wozu es sich nicht selbst zu erheben vermag, mit schüchterner Stimme, durch welche die innere Schaam sich verräth, Schwärmerei nennt; daß es mit Angst seine Augen von einem Gemälde zurückreißt, in welchem es nichts sieht als seine Entnervung und seine Schande; daß alles Starke und Erhebende einen solchen Eindruck auf dasselbe macht, wie jede Berührung auf den an allen Gliedern Gelähmten: ich weiß das alles; aber ich weiß auch, wo ich rede. Ich rede vor jungen Männern, die schon durch ihre Jahre vor dieser gänzlichen Nervenlosigkeit gesichert sind, und ich möchte neben und ver-

* Meine Herren, Gentlemen.

mittelſt einer männlichen Sittenlehre zugleich Empfindungen in ihre Seele
ſenken, die ſie auch in Zukunft vor derſelben verwahren könnten. Ich ge-
ſtehe es freimüthig, daß ich eben von dieſem Punkte aus, auf den die Vor-
ſehung mich ſtellte, etwas beitragen möchte, um eine männlichere Denkungsart, ein ſtärkeres Gefühl für Erhabenheit und Würde, einen feurigern Eifer
ſeine Beſtimmung auf jede Gefahr zu erfüllen, nach allen Richtungen hin,
ſo weit die deutſche Sprache reicht, und weiter, wenn ich könnte, zu verbreiten; damit ich einſt, wenn Sie dieſe Gegenden werden verlaſſen und ſich
nach allen Enden werden verſtreut haben, in Ihnen an allen Enden, wo
Sie leben werden, Männer wüßte, deren auserwählte Freundin die Wahrheit iſt; die an ihr hangen im Leben und im Tode; die ſie aufnehmen,
wenn ſie von aller Welt ausgeſtoßen iſt; die ſie öffentlich in Schutz nehmen,
wenn ſie verläumdet und verläſtert wird; die für ſie den ſchlauverſteckten
Haß des Großen, das fade Lächeln des Aberwitzes, und das bemitleidende
Achſelzucken des Kleinſinnes freudig ertragen. In dieſer Abſicht habe ich
geſagt, was ich geſagt habe, und in dieſer Endabſicht werde ich Alles ſagen,
was ich unter ihnen ſagen werde.

Georg Wilhelm Friedrich Hegel.

20. Ueber den Werth und die Nothwendigkeit des Studiums der griechiſchen und römiſchen Sprache und Literatur auf Gymnaſien.

Der Geiſt und Zweck unſerer Anſtalt iſt die Vorbereitung zum
gelehrten Studium, und zwar eine Vorbereitung, welche auf
den Grund der Griechen und Römer erbaut iſt. Seit
einigen Jahrtauſenden iſt dies der Boden, auf dem alle Cultur geſtanden
hat, aus dem ſie hervorgeſproßt und mit dem ſie in beſtändigem Zuſam-
menhange geweſen iſt. Wie die natürlichen Organiſationen, Pflanzen und
Thiere, ſich der Schwere entwinden, aber dieſes Element ihres Weſens nicht
verlaſſen können: ſo iſt alle Kunſt und Wiſſenſchaft jenem Boden ent-
wachſen; und obgleich auch in ſich ſelbſtſtändig geworden, hat ſie ſich von
der Erinnerung jener ältern Bildung nicht befreit. Wie Antäus ſeine
Kräfte durch die Berührung der mütterlichen Erde erneuerte: ſo hat jeder
neue Aufſchwung und Bekräftigung der Wiſſenſchaft und Bildung ſich aus
der Rückkehr zum Alterthum an's Licht gehoben.

So wichtig aber die Erhaltung dieſes Bodens iſt; ſo weſentlich iſt die
Abänderung des Verhältniſſes, in welchem er ehemals geſtanden hat.
Wenn die Einſicht in das Ungenügende, Nachtheilige alter Grundſätze und
Einrichtungen überhaupt, und damit der mit ihnen verbundenen vorigen

Bildungszwecke und Bildungsmittel eintritt; so ist der Gedanke, der sich zunächst auf der Oberfläche darbietet, die gänzliche Beseitigung und Abschaffung derselben. Aber die Weisheit der Regierung, erhaben über diese leichtscheinende Hülfe, erfüllt auf die wahrhafteste Art das Bündniß der Zeit dadurch, daß sie **das Alte in ein neues Verhältniß zu dem Ganzen setzt und dadurch das Wesentliche desselben eben so sehr erhält, als sie es verändert und erneuert.** —

Ich brauche nur mit wenigen Worten an die bekannte Stellung zu erinnern, welche das Erlernen der lateinischen Sprache ehemals hatte: daß dasselbe nicht sowohl für ein Moment des gelehrten Studiums galt, sondern den wesentlichsten Theil desselben ausmachte und das einzige höhere Bildungsmittel war, welches demjenigen dargeboten wurde, der nicht bei dem allgemeinen, ganz elementarischen Unterrichte stehen bleiben wollte; daß für die Erwerbung anderer Kenntnisse, welche für's bürgerliche Leben nützlich oder an und für sich von Werth sind, kaum ausdrückliche Anstalten gemacht waren, sondern es im Ganzen der Gelegenheit der Erlernung jener Sprache überlassen war, ob etwas und wieviel dabei von ihnen anflog; daß jene Kenntnisse zum Theil für eine besondere Kunst, nicht zugleich für ein Bildungsmittel galten und größtentheils in jene Schale gehüllt waren.

Die allgemeine Stimme erhob sich gegen jenes unselig gewordene Lateinlernen; es erhob sich das Gefühl vornehmlich, daß ein Volk nicht als gebildet angesehen werden kann, welches nicht alle Schätze der Wissenschaft in seiner eigenen Sprache ausdrücken und sich in ihr mit jedem Inhalt frei bewegen kann. Diese Innigkeit, mit welcher die eigene Sprache uns angehört, fehlt den Kenntnissen, die wir nur in einer fremden besitzen; sie sind durch eine Scheidewand von uns getrennt, welche sie dem Geiste nicht wahrhaft einheimisch seyn läßt.

Dieser Gesichtspunkt, die fehlerhaften, oft zum durchgängigen Mechanismus herabsinkenden Methoden, die verabsäumte Erwerbung vieler wichtiger Sachkenntnisse und geistiger Fertigkeiten, hat nach und nach die Kenntniß der lateinischen Sprache von ihrem Anspruche als Hauptwissenschaft zu gelten, und von ihrer lange behaupteten Würde, allgemeines und fast ausschließendes Bildungsmittel zu seyn, abgesetzt. Sie hat aufgehört als Zweck betrachtet zu werden, und diese geistige Beschäftigung hat dagegen sogenannte Sachen, und darunter alltägliche, sinnliche Dinge, die keinen Bildungsstoff abzugeben fähig sind, über sich mächtig werden sehen müssen. Ohne in diese Gegensätze und deren weitere Bestimmungen, ihre Uebertreibungen oder äußerliche Collisionen einzugehen, genüge es hier uns des weisen Verhältnisses zu freuen, das unsere allerhöchste Regierung hierin festgesetzt hat.

Erſtlich hat dieſelbe, durch die **Vervollkommnung der deutſchen Volksſchulen**, die allgemeine Bürgerbildung erweitert; es
werden dadurch Allen die Mittel verſchafft, das ihnen als Menſchen We-
ſentliche und für ihren Stand Nützliche zu erlernen; denen, die das Beſ-
ſere bisher entbehrten, wird daſſelbe hierdurch gewährt; denen aber, die
um etwas Beſſeres, als den ungenügenden allgemeinen Unterricht zu erhalten, nur zu den genannten Bildungsmittel greifen konnten, wird daſſelbe
entbehrlicher gemacht und durch zweckmäßigere Kenntniſſe und Fertigkeiten
erſetzt. —

Zweitens hat das Studium der Wiſſenſchaften und die Erwerbung höherer geiſtiger und nützlicher Fertigkeiten, **in ihrer Unabhängigkeit
von der alten Literatur**, in einer eigenen Schweſteranſtalt ihr
vollſtändiges Mittel bekommen.

Drittens endlich iſt das **alte Sprachen-Studium** erhalten.
Es ſteht theils nach wie vor, als höheres Bildungsmittel, Jedem offen;
theils aber iſt es zur gründlichen Baſis des gelehrten Studiums befeſtigt
worden. Indem daſſelbe nun **neben** jene Bildungsmittel und wiſſen-
ſchaftliche Weiſen getreten iſt, iſt es ſeiner Ausſchließlichkeit verluſtig geworden und kann den Haß gegen ſeine vorherigen Anmaßungen getilgt haben. So auf die Seite getreten, hat es um ſo mehr das Recht zu fordern,
daß es in ſeiner Abſcheidung frei gewähren dürfe und von fremdartigen,
ſtörenden Einmiſchungen ferner unberuhigt bleibe.

Durch dieſe Ausſcheidung und Einſchränkung hat es ſeine wahrhafte
Stellung und die Möglichkeit erhalten, ſich um ſo freier und vollſtändiger
ausbilden zu können. Das ächte Kennzeichen der Freiheit und Stärke einer
Organiſation beſteht darin, wenn die unterſchiedenen Momente, die ſie enthält, ſich in ſich vertiefen und zu vollſtändigen Syſtemen machen, ohne
Neid und Furcht nebeneinander ihr Werk treiben und es ſich treiben ſehen,
und daß alle nur wieder Theile eines großen Ganzen ſind. Nur was ſich
abgeſondert in ſeinem Princip vollkommen macht, wird ein conſequentes
Ganzes; d. h. es wird Etwas; es gewinnt Tiefe und die kräftige Möglichkeit der Vielſeitigkeit. Die Beſorgniß und Aengſtlichkeit über Einſei-
tigkeit pflegt zu häufig der Schwäche anzugehören, die nur der vielſeitigen
inconſequenten Oberflächlichkeit fähig iſt.

Wenn nun das Studium der alten Sprachen, wie vorher, die Grundlage
der gelehrten Bildung bleibt, ſo iſt es auch in dieſer Einſchränkung ſehr in
Anſpruch genommen worden. Es ſcheint eine gerechte Forderung zu ſein,
daß die Cultur, Kunſt und Wiſſenſchaft eines Volks auf ihre eigenen Beine
zu ſtehen komme. Dürfen wir von der Bildung der neuern Welt, unſerer
Aufklärung und den Fortſchritten aller Künſte und Wiſſenſchaften nicht
glauben, daß ſie die griechiſchen und römiſchen Kinderſchuhe vertreten ha-

ben, ihrem alten Gängelbande entwachsen, auf eigenem Grund und Boden
fußen können? Den Werken der Alten möchte immer ihr größer oder geringer angeschlagener Werth bleiben; aber sie hätten in die Reihe von
Erinnerungen, gelehrter mäßiger Merkwürdigkeiten, unter das bloße Geschichtliche zurückzutreten, das man aufnehmen könnte oder auch nicht, das
aber nicht schlechthin für unsere höhere Geistesbildung Grundlage und Anfang ausmachen müßte. —

Lassen wir es aber gelten, daß überhaupt vom Vortrefflichen auszugehen
ist; so hat für das höhere Studium die Literatur der Griechen vornehmlich,
und dann die der Römer, die Grundlage zu seyn und zu bleiben. Die
Vollendung und Herrlichkeit dieser Meisterwerke muß das geistige Bad, die
profane Taufe sein, welche der Seele den ersten und unverlierbaren Ton
und Tinctur für Geschmack und Wissenschaft gebe. Und zu dieser Ein-
weihung ist nicht eine allgemeine, äußere Bekanntschaft mit den Alten hinreichend; sondern wir müssen uns ihnen in Kost und Wohnung geben, um
ihre Luft, ihre Vorstellungen, ihre Sitten, selbst, wenn man will, ihre Irr-
thümer und Vorurtheile einzusaugen, und in dieser Welt einheimisch zu
werden: der schönsten, die gewesen ist. Wenn das erste Paradies das Paradies der Menschennatur war, so ist dies das zweite, das höhere,
das Paradies des Menschengeistes, der in seiner schönern Natür-
lichkeit, Freiheit, Tiefe und Heiterkeit, wie die Braut aus ihrer Kammer,
hervortritt. Die erste wilde Pracht seines Aufgangs im Morgenlande ist
durch die Herrlichkeit der Form umschrieben und zur Schönheit gemildert;
er hat seine Tiefe nicht mehr in der Verworrenheit, Trübseligkeit oder Auf-
geblasenheit, sondern sie liegt in unbefangener Klarheit offen; seine Heiterkeit ist nicht ein kindisches Spielen, sondern über die Wehmuth hergebreitet,
welche die Härte des Schicksals kennt, aber durch sie nicht aus der Freiheit
über sie und aus dem Maße getrieben wird. Ich glaube nicht zu viel zu
behaupten, wenn ich sage, daß, wer die Werke der Alten nicht gekannt hat,
gelebt hat, ohne die Schönheit zu kennen.

In einem solchen Elemente nun, in dem wir uns einhausen, geschieht es
nicht nur, daß alle Kräfte der Seele angeregt, entwickelt und geübt werden;
sondern dasselbe ist ein eigenthümlicher Stoff, durch welchen wir
uns bereichern und unsere bessere Substanz bereiten.

Es ist gesagt worden, daß die Geistesthätigkeit an jedem
Stoffe geübt werden könne, und als zweckmäßigster Stoff erschienen
theils äußerlich nützliche, theils die sinnlichen Gegenstände, die dem jugendlichen oder kindlichen Alter am angemessensten seyen, indem sie dem Kreise
und der Art des Vorstellens angehören, welche dies Alter schon an und für
sich selbst habe.

Wenn vielleicht, vielleicht auch nicht, das Formelle von der Materie, das

Ueben selbst von dem gegenständlichen Kreise, an dem es geschehen soll, so
trennbar und gleichgültig dagegen seyn könnte, so ist es jedoch nicht um das
Ueben allein zu thun. Wie die Pflanze die Kräfte ihrer Reproduction an Licht
und Luft nicht nur übt, sondern in diesem Prozesse zugleich ihre Nahrung ein=
saugt: so muß der Stoff, an dem sich der Verstand und das Vermögen
der Seele überhaupt entwickelt und übt, zugleich eine Nahrung seyn. Nicht
jener sogenannte nützliche Stoff, jene sinnliche Materiatur, wie sie unmittel=
bar in die Vorstellungsweise des Kindes fällt; nur der geistige Inhalt,
welcher Werth und Interesse in und für sich selbst hat, stärkt die Seele und
verschafft dieser unabhängigen Halt: diese substanzielle Innerlichkeit, welche
die Mutter von Fassung, von Besonnenheit, von Gegenwart und Wachen
des Geistes ist; er erzeugt die an ihm großgezogene Seele zu einem Kern
von selbstständigem Werthe, von absolutem Zwecke, der erst die Grundlage
von Brauchbarkeit zu Allem ausmacht, und den es wichtig ist in allen
Ständen zu pflanzen.   Haben wir nicht in neuern Zeiten sogar Staaten
selbst, welche solchen innern Hintergrund in der Seele ihrer Angehörigen
zu erhalten und auszubauen vernachläßigten und verachteten, sie auf die
bloße Nützlichkeit und auf das Geistige nur als auf ein Mittel richteten, in
Gefahren haltungslos dastehen und in der Mitte ihrer vielen nützlichen
Mittel zusammenstürzen sehen?   Den edelsten Nahrungsstoff nun und in der edelsten Form, die goldenen
Aepfel in silbernen Schalen, enthalten die Werke der Alten, und unver=
gleichbar mehr als jede anderen Werke irgend einer Zeit und Nation. Ich
brauche an die Großheit ihrer Gesinnungen, an ihre plastische, von mora=
lischer Zweideutigkeit freie Tugend und Vaterlandsliebe, an den großen
Styl ihrer Thaten und Charaktere, das Mannigfaltige ihrer Schicksale,
ihrer Sitten und Verfassungen nur zu erinnern, um die Behauptung zu
rechtfertigen, daß in dem Umfange keiner Bildung so viel Vortreffliches,
Bewundernswürdiges, Originelles, Vielseitiges und Lehrreiches verei=
nigt war.

Dieser Reichthum aber ist an die Sprache gebunden, und nur durch
und in dieser erreichen wir ihn in seiner ganzen Eigenthümlichkeit. Den
Inhalt geben uns etwa Uebersetzungen, aber nicht die Form, nicht die äthe=
rische Seele desselben. Sie gleichen den nachgemachten Rosen, die an Ge=
stalt, Farbe, etwa auch Wohlgeruch, den natürlichen ähnlich seyn können;
aber die Lieblichkeit, Zartheit und Weichheit des Lebens erreichen jene nicht.
Oder die sonstige Zierlichkeit und Feinheit der Copie gehört nur dieser an,
an welcher ein Contrast zwischen dem Inhalte und der nicht mit ihm erwach=
senen Form sich fühlbar macht. Die Sprache ist das musikalische Element,
das Element der Innigkeit, das in der Uebertragung verschwindet; der

feine Duft, durch den die Sympathie der Seele sich zu genießen giebt, aber ohne den ein Werk der Alten nur schmeckt wie Rheinwein, der verduftet ist.

Dieser Umstand legt uns die hart scheinende Nothwendigkeit auf, die Sprachen der Alten gründlich zu studiren und sie uns geläufig zu machen, um ihre Werke in dem möglichsten Umfang aller ihrer Seiten und Vorzüge genießen zu können. Wenn wir uns über die Mühe, die wir hierzu anwenden müssen, beschweren wollten, und es fürchten oder bedauern könnten, die Erwerbung anderer Kenntnisse und Fertigkeiten darüber zurückzusetzen zu müssen: so hätten wir das Schicksal anzuklagen, das uns in unserer eigenen Sprache nicht diesen Kreis classischer Werke hat zu Theil werden lassen, die uns die mühevolle Reise zu dem Alterthum entbehrlich machten und den Ersatz für dasselbe gewährten. Nachdem ich von dem Stoffe der Bildung gesprochen, führt dieser Wunsch darauf, noch einige Worte über das Formelle zu sagen, das in ihrer Natur liegt.

Das Fortschreiten der Bildung ist nämlich nicht als das ruhige Fortsetzen einer Kette anzusehen, an deren frühere Glieder die nachfolgenden zwar mit Rücksicht auf sie gefügt würden, aber aus eigener Materie, und ohne daß diese weitere Arbeit gegen die erstere gerichtet wäre; sondern die Bildung muß einen frühern Stoff und Gegenstand haben, über den sie arbeitet, den sie verändert und neu formirt. Es ist nöthig, daß wir uns die Welt des Alterthums erwerben, so sehr, um sie zu besitzen, als noch mehr, um etwas zu haben, das wir verarbeiten. — Um aber zum Gegenstande zu werden, muß die Substanz der Natur und des Geistes uns gegenüber getreten seyn, sie muß die Gestalt von etwas Fremdartigem erhalten haben. — Unglücklich der, dem seine unmittelbare Welt der Gefühle entfremdet wird: denn dies heißt nichts anders, als daß die individuellen Bande, die das Gemüth und den Gedanken heilig mit dem Leben befreunden, Glauben, Liebe und Vertrauen, ihm zerrissen wird! — Für die Entfremdung, welche Bedingung der theoretischen Bildung ist, fordert diese nicht diesen sittlichen Schmerz, nicht das Leiden des Herzens, sondern den leichtern Schmerz und Anstrengung der Vorstellung, sich mit einem Nicht-Unmittelbaren, einem Fremdartigen, mit etwas der Erinnerung, dem Gedächtnisse und dem Denken Angehörigen zu beschäftigen. — Diese Forderung der Trennung aber ist so nothwendig, daß sie sich als ein allgemeiner und bekannter Trieb in uns äußert. Das Fremdartige, das Ferne führt das anziehende Interesse mit sich, das uns zur Beschäftigung und Bemühung lockt, und das Begehrenswerthe steht im umgekehrten Verhältnisse mit der Nähe, in der es steht und gemein mit uns ist. Die Jugend stellt es sich als ein Glück vor, aus dem Einheimischen weg zu kommen und mit Robinson eine ferne Insel zu bewohnen. Es ist eine nothwendige Täuschung, das Tiefe zuerst in der Gestalt der Entfernung suchen zu müssen, aber die Tiefe und Kraft, die

22

wir erlangen, kann nur durch die Weite gemessen werden, in die wir von dem Mittelpunkte hinwegflohen, in welchen wir uns zuerst versenkt befanden und dem wir wieder zustreben.

Auf diesen Centrifugal=Trieb der Seele gründet sich nun überhaupt die Nothwendigkeit, die Scheidung, die sie von ihrem natürlichen Wesen und Zustand sucht, ihr selbst darreichen und eine ferne, fremde Welt in den jungen Geist hineinstellen zu müssen. Die Scheidewand aber, wodurch diese Trennung für die Bildung, wovon hier die Rede ist, bewerkstelligt wird, ist Welt und Sprache der Alten; aber sie, die uns von uns trennt, enthält zugleich alle Anfangspunkte und Fäden der Rückkehr zu uns selbst, der Befreundung mit ihr und des Wiederfindens unsrer selbst, aber unsrer nach dem wahrhaften allgemeinen Wesen des Geistes.

Wenn wir diese allgemeine Nothwendigkeit, welche die Welt der Vorstellung so sehr als die Sprache als solche umfaßt, auf die Erlernung der letztern anwenden, so erhellt von selbst, daß die mechanische Seite davon mehr als bloß ein nothwendiges Uebel ist. Denn das Mechanische ist das dem Geiste Fremde, für den es Interesse hat, das in ihn hineingelegte Unverdaute zu verdauen, das in ihm noch Leblose zu verständigen und zu seinem Eigenthume zu machen.

Mit diesem mechanischen Momente der Spracherlernung verbindet sich ohnehin sogleich das grammatische Studium, dessen Werth nicht hoch genug angeschlagen werden kann: denn es macht den Anfang der logischen Bildung aus; — eine Seite, die ich noch zuletzt berühre, weil sie beinahe in Vergessenheit gekommen zu seyn scheint. Die Grammatik hat nämlich die Kategorien, die eigenthümlichen Erzeugnisse und Bestimmungen des Verstandes zu ihrem Inhalte; in ihr fängt also der Verstand selbst an, gelernt zu werden. Diese geistigsten Wesenheiten, mit denen sie uns zuerst bekannt macht, sind etwas höchst Faßliches für die Jugend, und wohl nichts Geistiges faßlicher als sie: denn die noch nicht umfassende Kraft dieses Alters vermag das Reiche in seiner Mannigfaltigkeit nicht aufzunehmen; jene Abstractionen aber sind das ganz Einfache. Sie sind gleichsam die einzelnen Buchstaben, und zwar die Vocale des Geistigen, mit denen wir anfangen, um es buchstabiren und dann lesen zu lernen. — Alsdann trägt die Grammatik sie auch auf eine diesem Alter angemessene Art vor, indem sie dieselben durch äußerliche Hülfsmerkmale, welche die Sprache meist selbst enthält, unterscheiden lehrt; um etwas besser, als Jedermann roth und blau unterscheiden kann, ohne die Definitionen dieser Farben nach der Newtonischen Hypothese oder einer sonstigen Theorie angeben zu können, reicht jene Kenntniß vorerst hin, und es ist höchst wichtig, auf diese Unterschiede aufmerksam gemacht worden zu seyn. Denn wenn die Verstandes=bestimmungen, weil wir verständige Wesen sind, in uns sind, und wir dieselben unmittelbar verstehen; so besteht die erste Bildung darin, sie zu haben, d. h. sie zum Gegenstande des Bewußtseyn gemacht zu haben und sie durch Merkmale unterscheiden zu können.

Indem wir durch die grammatische Terminologie uns in Abstractionen bewegen lernen, und dies Studium als die elementarische Philosophie an= zusehen ist; so wird es wesentlich nicht bloß als Mittel, sondern als Zweck — sowohl bei dem lateinischen als bei dem deutschen Sprachunterricht — betrachtet. Der allgemeine oberflächliche Leichtsinn, den zu vertreiben der ganze Ernst und die Gewalt der Erschütterungen, die wir erlebt, erforder= lich war, hatte, wie im Uebrigen, so bekanntlich auch hier, das Verhältniß von Mittel und Zweck verkehrt und das materielle Wissen einer Sprache höher, als ihre verständige Seite, geachtet. — Das grammatische Erlernen einer alten Sprache hat zugleich den Vortheil, anhaltende und unaus= gesetzte Vernunftthätigkeit seyn zu müssen, indem hier nicht, wie bei der Muttersprache, die unreflectirte Gewohnheit die richtige Wortfügung her= beiführt, sondern es nothwendig ist, den durch den Verstand bestimmten Werth der Redetheile vor Augen zu nehmen und die Regel zu ihrer Verbin= dung zu Hülfe zu rufen. Somit aber findet ein beständiges Subsumiren des Besondern unter das Allgemeine und Besonderung des Allgemeinen statt, als worin ja die Form der Vernunftthätigkeit besteht. — Das strenge grammatische Studium ergiebt sich also als eines der allgemeinsten und edelsten Bildungsmittel.

Dies zusammen, das Studium der Alten in ihrer eigenthümlichen Sprache und das grammatische Studium, macht die Grundzüge des Princips aus, welches unsere Anstalt charakterisirt. Dieses wichtige Gut, so reich es schon an sich selbst ist, begreift da= rum nicht den ganzen Umfang der Kenntnisse, in welche unsere vorberei= tende Anstalt einführt. — — —

Friedrich Wilhelm Joseph Schelling.
21. Ueber das Studium der Historie.

Wie das Absolute selbst in der Doppelgestalt der Natur und Geschichte als ein und dasselbige erscheint, zerlegt die Theologie, als Indifferenzpunkt der realen Wissenschaften, sich von der einen Seite in die Historie, von der andern in die Naturwissenschaft, deren jede ihren Gegenstand getrennt von dem andern und eben damit auch von der obersten Einheit betrachtet. Dies verhindert nicht, daß nicht jede derselben in sich den Centralpunkt her= stellen, und so in das Urwissen zurückgehen könne. Die gemeine Vorstel= lung der Natur und Geschichte ist, daß in jener Alles durch empirische Noth=

wendigkeit, in dieser Alles durch Freiheit geschehe. Aber eben dies sind
selbst nur die Formen oder Arten, außer dem Absoluten zu seyn. Die Ge=
schichte ist in so fern die höhere Potenz der Natur, als sie im Idealen aus=
drückt, was diese im Realen: dem Wesen nach aber ist eben deßwegen das=
selbe in beiden nur verändert durch die Bestimmung oder Potenz, unter der
es gesetzt ist. Könnte in Beiden das reine An=sich erblickt werden, so wür=
den wir dasselbe, was in der Geschichte ideal, in der Natur real vorgebildet
erkennen. Die Freiheit als Erscheinung kann nichts erschaffen; es ist ein
Universum, welches die zweifache Form der abgebildeten Welt jede für sich
und in ihrer Art ausdrückt. Die vollendete Welt der Geschichte wäre dem=
nach selbst eine ideale Natur, der Staat, als der äußere Organismus einer
in der Freiheit selbst erreichten Harmonie der Nothwendigkeit und der Frei=
heit. Die Geschichte, so fern sie die Bildung dieses Vereins zum vorzüg=
lichsten Gegenstand hat, wäre Geschichte im engern Sinn des Wortes.

Die Frage, welche uns hier zunächst entgegenkommt, nämlich ob Historie
Wissenschaft sein könne? scheint wegen ihrer Beantwortung keinen Zweifel
zuzulassen. Wenn nämlich Historie als solche, und von dieser ist die Rede,
der letzten entgegengesetzt ist, wie im Vorhergehenden allgemein angenom=
men wurde, so ist klar, daß sie nicht selbst Wissenschaft seyn könne, und
wenn die realen Wissenschaften Synthesen des Philosophischen und Histo=
rischen sind, so kann eben deßwegen die Historie selbst nicht wieder eine
solche seyn, so wenig als es Philosophie seyn kann. Sie träte also in der
letzten Beziehung mit dieser auf gleichen Rang.

Um dieses Verhältniß noch bestimmter einzusehen, unterscheiden wir die
verschiedenen Standpunkte, auf welchen Historie gedacht werden könnte.
Der höchste, der von uns im Vorhergehenden erkannt wurde, ist der reli=
giöse oder derjenige, in welchem die ganze Geschichte als Werk der Vor=
sehung begriffen wird. Daß dieser nicht in der Historie als solcher geltend
gemacht werden könne, folgt daraus, daß er von dem philosophischen nicht
wesentlich verschieden ist. Es versteht sich, daß ich hiemit weder die reli=
giöse noch die philosophische Construction der Geschichte läugne; allein
jene gehört der Theologie, diese der Philosophie an, und ist von der Historie
als solcher nothwendig verschieden. Der entgegengesetzte Standpunkt des
absoluten ist der empirische, welcher wieder zwei Seiten hat. Die der rei=
nen Aufnahme und Ausmittlung des Geschehenen, welche Sache des Ge=
schichtsforschers ist, der von dem Historiker als solchem nur eine Seite re=
präsentirt. Die der Verbindung des empirischen Stoffs nach einer Ver=
standes=Idealität, oder, weil die letztere nicht in den Begebenheiten an und
für sich selbst liegen kann, indem diese empirisch viel mehr zufällig und nicht
harmonisch erscheinen, der Anordnung nach einem durch das Subject ent=
worfenen Zweck, der in so fern didaktisch oder politisch ist. Diese Behand=

lung der Geschichte in ganz bestimmter, nicht allgemeiner Absicht ist, was der von den Alten festgesetzten Bedeutung zufolge, die pragmatische heißt. So ist Polybius, der sich über diesen Begriff ausdrücklich erklärt, pragmatisch wegen der ganz bestimmten, auf die Technik des Kriegs gerichteten Absicht seiner Geschichtsbücher: so Tacitus, weil er Schritt vor Schritt an dem Verfall des römischen Staats die Wirkungen der Sittenlosigkeit und des Despotismus darstellt.

Die Modernen sind geneigt, den pragmatischen Geist für das Höchste in der Historie zu halten, und zieren sich selbst unter einander mit dem Prädicat desselben, als mit dem größten Lob. Aber eben wegen ihrer subjectiven Abhängigkeit wird Niemand, der Sinn hat, die Darstellungen der beiden angeführten Geschichtschreiber in den ersten Rang der Historie setzen. Bei den Deutschen hat es nun überdies mit dem pragmatischen Geist in der Regel die Bewandtniß, wie bei dem Famulus in Goethe's Faust: „Was sie den Geist der Zeiten nennen, ist ihr eigner Geist, worin die Zeiten sich bespiegeln." In Griechenland ergriffen die erhabensten, gereiftesten, erfahrungsreichsten Geister den Griffel der Geschichte, um sie wie mit ewigen Charakteren zu schreiben. Herodotus ist ein wahrhaft homerischer Kopf, im Thukydides concentrirt sich die ganze Bildung des Perikleischen Zeitalters zu einer göttlichen Anschauung. In Deutschland, wo die Wissenschaft immer mehr eine Sache der Industrie wird, wagen sich gerade die geistlosesten Köpfe an die Geschichte. Welch' ein widerlicher Anblick, das Bild großer Begebenheiten und Charaktere im Organe eines kurzsichtigen und einfältigen Menschen entworfen, besonders, wenn er sich noch Gewalt anthut Verstand zu haben, und diesen etwa darein setzt, die Größe der Zeiten und Völker nach beschränkten Ansichten, z. B. Wichtigkeit des Handels, diesen oder jenen nützlichen oder verderblichen Erfindungen, zu schätzen und überhaupt einen so viel möglich gemeinen Maßstab an alles Erhabene zu legen: oder wenn er auf der andern Seite den historischen Pragmatismus darin sucht, sich selbst durch Räsonniren über die Begebenheiten oder Ausschmücken des Stoffs mit leeren rhetorischen Floskeln geltend zu machen, z. B. von den beständigen Fortschritten der Menschheit, und wie wir's denn zuletzt so herrlich weit gebracht. Dennoch ist selbst unter dem Heiligsten nichts, das heiliger wäre als die Geschichte, dieser große Spiegel des Weltgeistes, dieses ewige Gedicht des göttlichen Verstandes: nichts, das weniger die Berührung unreiner Hände ertrüge.

Der pragmatische Zweck der Geschichte schließt von selbst die Universalität aus und fordert nothwendig auch einen beschränkten Gegenstand. Der Zweck der Belehrung verlangt eine richtige und empirisch begründete Verknüpfung der Begebenheiten, durch welche der Verstand zwar aufgeklärt wird, die Vernunft aber ohne andere Zuthat unbefriedigt bleibt. Auch Kant's Plan

einer Gefchichte im weltbürgerlichen Sinn beabfichtigt eine bloße Verftan=
desgefetzmäßigkeit im Ganzen derfelben, die nur höher, nämlich in der all=
gemeinen Nothwendigkeit der Natur gefucht wird, durch welche aus dem
Krieg der Friede, zuletzt fogar der ewige und aus vielen andern Verirrun=
gen endlich die echte Rechtsverfaffung entftehen foll. Allein diefer Plan
der Natur ift felbft nur der empirifche Widerfchein der wahren Nothwen=
digkeit, fo wie die Abficht einer darnach geordneten Gefchichte nicht fowohl
eine weltbürgerliche als eine bürgerliche heißen müßte, den Fortgang näm=
lich der Menfchheit zum ruhigen Verkehr, Gewerbe und Handelsbetrieb
unter fich, und diefes fonach überhaupt als die höchften Früchte des Men=
fchenlebens und feiner Anftrengungen darzuftellen. Es ift klar, daß, da
die bloße Verknüpfung der Begebenheiten nach empirifcher Nothwendigkeit
immer nur pragmatifch feyn kann, die Hiftorie aber in ihrer höchften Idee
von aller fubjectiven Beziehung unabhängig und befreit feyn muß, auch
überhaupt der empirifche Standpunkt nicht der höchfte ihrer Dichtungen
feyn könne. Auch die wahre Hiftorie beruht auf einer Synthefis des Ge=
gebenen und Wirklichen mit dem Idealen, aber nicht durch Philofophie, da
diefe die Wirklichkeit vielmehr aufhebt und ganz ideal ift: Hiftorie aber ganz
in jener und doch zugleich Ideal feyn foll. Diefes ift nirgends als in der
Kunft möglich, welche das Wirkliche ganz beftehen läßt, wie die Bühne reale
Begebenheiten oder Gefchichten, aber in einer Vollendung und Einheit dar=
ftellt, wodurch fie Ausdruck der höchften Ideen werden. Die Kunft alfo ift
es, wodurch die Hiftorie, indem fie Wiffenfchaft des Wirklichen als folchen
ift, zugleich über daffelbe auf das höhere Gebiet des Idealen erhoben wird,
auf dem die Wiffenfchaft fteht; und der dritte und abfolute Standpunkt der
Hiftorie ift demnach der der hiftorifchen Kunft.

Wir haben das Verhältniß deffelben zu den vorher angegebenen zu zei=
gen. Es verfteht fich, daß der Hiftoriker nicht einer vermeinten Kunft zu
lieb den Stoff der Gefchichte verändern kann, deren oberftes Gefetz Wahr=
heit feyn foll. Eben fo wenig kann die Meinung feyn, daß die höhere
Darftellung den wirklichen Zufammenhang der Begebenheiten vernach=
läßige, es hat vielmehr hiermit ganz diefelbe Bewandtniß wie mit der Be=
gründung der Handlungen im Drama, wo zwar die einzelne aus der vor=
hergehenden und zuletzt Alles aus der erften Synthefis mit Nothwendigkeit
entfpringen muß, die Aufeinanderfolge felbft aber nicht empirifch, fondern
nur aus einer höhern Ordnung der Dinge begreiflich feyn muß. Erft dann
erhält die Gefchichte ihre Vollendung für die Vernunft, wenn die empiri=
fchen Urfachen, indem fie den Verftand befriedigen, als Werkzeuge und
Mittel der Erfcheinung einer höhern Nothwendigkeit gebraucht werden. In
folcher Darftellung kann die Gefchichte die Wirkung des größten und erftau=

nenswürdigsten Drama nicht verfehlen, das nur in einem unendlichen Geiste gedichtet seyn kann.

Wir haben die Historie auf die gleiche Stufe mit der Kunst gesetzt. Aber was diese darstellt, ist immer eine Identität der Nothwendigkeit und Freiheit, und diese Erscheinung, vornehmlich in der Tragödie, ist der eigentliche Gegenstand unserer Bewunderung. Dieselbe Identität aber ist zugleich der Standpunkt der Philosophie und selbst der Religion für die Geschichte, da diese in der Vorsehung nichts Anders als die Weisheit erkennt, welche in dem Plane der Welt die Freiheit der Menschen mit der allgemeinen Nothwendigkeit, und umgekehrt diese mit jener vereinigt. Nun soll aber die Historie wahrhaft weder auf dem philosophischen noch auf dem religiösen Standpunkt stehen. Sie wird demnach auch jene Identität der Freiheit und Nothwendigkeit in dem Sinne darstellen müssen, wie sie vom Gesichtspunkt der Wirklichkeit aus erscheint, den sie auf keine Weise verlassen soll. Von diesem aus ist sie aber nur als unbegriffene und ganz objective Identität erkennbar, als Schicksal. Die Meinung ist nicht, daß der Geschichtschreiber das Schicksal im Munde führe, sondern daß es durch die Objectivität seiner Darstellung von selbst und ohne sein Zuthun erscheine. Durch die Geschichtbücher des Herodotus gehen Verhängniß und Vergeltung als unsichtbare, überall waltende Gottheiten; in dem höheren und völlig unabhängigen Styl des Thukydides, der sich schon durch die Einführung der Reden dramatisch zeigt, ist jene höhere Einheit in der Form ausgedrückt und ganz bis zur äußern Erscheinung gebracht.

Ueber die Art, wie Historie studirt werden soll, möge Folgendes hinreichen. Sie muß im Ganzen nach Art des Epos betrachtet werden, das keinen bestimmten Anfang und kein bestimmtes Ende hat: man nehme denjenigen Punkt heraus, den man für den bedeutendsten oder interessantesten hält, und von diesem aus bilde und erweitere sich das Ganze nach allen Richtungen. Man meide die sogenannten Universalhistorien, die nichts lehren; andere giebt es noch nicht. Die wahre Universalgeschichte müßte im epischen Styl, also in dem Geiste verfaßt seyn, dessen Anlage im Herodotus ist. Was man jetzt so nennt, sind Compendien, darin alles Besondere und Bedeutende verwischt ist: auch derjenige aber, der Historie nicht zu seinem besondern Fach wählt, gehe so viel möglich zu den Quellen und den Particulargeschichten, die ihn bei Weitem mehr unterrichten. Er lerne für die neuere Geschichte die naive Einfalt der Chroniken liebgewinnen, die keine prätensionellen Charakterschilderungen machen, oder psychologisch motiviren. Wer sich zum historischen Künstler bilden will, halte sich einzig an die großen Muster der Alten, welche nach dem Zerfall des allgemeinen und öffentlichen Lebens nie wieder erreicht werden konnten. Wenn wir von Gibbon absehen, dessen Werk die umfassende Conception und die ganze

Macht des großen Wendepunktes der neuern Zeit für ſich hat, obgleich er
nur Redner, nicht Geſchichtſchreiber iſt, exiſtiren bloß wahrhaft nationelle
Hiſtoriker, unter denen die ſpätere Zeit nur Macchiavelli und Johannes
Müller nennen wird.   Welche Stufen derjenige zu erklimmen hat, der
würdiger Weiſe die Geſchichte verzeichnen will, könnten die, ſo dieſem Be=
ruf ſich weihen, vorerſt nur aus den Briefen, welche dieſer als Jüngling
geſchrieben, ohngefähr ermeſſen.   Aber überhaupt Alles, was Wiſſenſchaft
und Kunſt, was ein erfahrungreiches und öffentliches Leben vermögen, muß
dazu beitragen den Hiſtoriker zu bilden.   Die erſten Urbilder des hiſtoriſchen
Styls ſind das Epos in ſeiner urſprünglichen Geſtalt und die Tragödie ;
denn wenn die univerſelle Geſchichte, deren Anfänge wie die Quellen des
Nils unerkennbar, die epiſche Form und Fülle liebt, will die beſondere da=
gegen mehr concentriſch um einen gemeinſchaftlichen Mittelpunkt gebildet
ſeyn ; davon zu ſchweigen, daß für den Hiſtoriker die Tragödie die wahre
Quelle großer Ideen und der erhabenen Denkungsart iſt, zu welcher er ge=
bildet ſeyn muß.   Als den Gegenſtand der Hiſtorie im engern Sinne be=
ſtimmten wir die Bildung eines objectiven Organismus der Freiheit oder
des Staats.   Es gibt eine Wiſſenſchaft deſſelben, ſo nothwendig es eine
Wiſſenſchaft der Natur giebt.   Seine Idee kann um ſo weniger aus der
Erfahrung genommen ſeyn, da dieſe hier vielmehr ſelbſt erſt nach Ideen
geſchaffen und der Staat als Kunſtwerk erſcheinen ſoll.

Barthold Georg Niebuhr.
22. Ueber römiſche Geſchichte.

Ich habe es unternommen, die Geſchichte Roms zu erzählen; ich werde
in der Nacht des tiefen Alterthums beginnen, wo angeſtrengte Forſchung
bei dem ſchwachen Licht ſpäter und zweifelhafter Sagen kaum einige der
Hauptmaſſen des uralten Italiens zu unterſcheiden vermag, und wünſche
bis zu den Zeiten hinabzugehen, in denen eine zweite Nacht Alles, was wir
in der langen Reihe von Jahrhunderten entſtehen und altern ſahen, in
Gräber und Trümmer verſunken, mit beinahe gleich tiefer Finſterniß ver=
deckt.   Allgemein iſt dieſe Geſchichte in ihren großen Umriſſen, und ſehr
Vielen wenigſtens zum Theil unmittelbar aus den claſſiſchen Werken rö=
miſcher Schriftſteller bekannt, ſo weit uns in ihnen die Schilderung vieler
der glänzendſten oder merkwürdigſten Epochen des republikaniſchen und kai=
ſerlichen Roms erhalten iſt.   Wären dieſe Werke in ihrem ganzen Umfange
vorhanden; beſäßen wir in Livius und Tacitus Geſchichten eine, Auguſt's
letzte Jahre ausgenommen, zuſammenhängende Geſchichte vom Anfang der
Stadt bis auf Nerva; ſo würde es thöricht und zweckwidrig ſeyn, die Er=

zählung derselben Begebenheiten, welche diese Historiker vorgetragen haben,
zu unternehmen. Thöricht, weil ihre Schönheit uns unerreichbar bleiben
muß; zweckwidrig, weil neben der historischen Belehrung nichts Vollkomm-
neres, in der Jugend zur Bildung des Sinnes, im späteren Alter zu seiner
Erhaltung unter den mannigfaltigen barbarischen Einwirkungen unsrer
Umgebungen und Verhältnisse, uns durch das Leben begleiten könnte als
eine solche, für die Nation selbst in Fülle geschriebene Geschichte von neunte-
halb Jahrhunderten. Es bedürfte nur für die Zeit der früheren einer Kritik des Verfälschten, einer Absonderung der eingemischten Dichtungen von
dem historisch Sichern und Begründeten: ohne die Kühnheit, mit alten
Meistern scheinbar zu wetteifern, könnten wir die Verfassung und die Entwicklung einzelner Zeiten in reinen Umrissen zeichnen, wo Livius uns ohne
Kunde verläßt oder irre führt. Weil aber jene Werke nur in Bruchstücken
erhalten sind; weil sie uns über Epochen verstummen, die durch die Wichtigkeit ihrer Begebenheiten vielleicht noch über diejenigen hervorragen,
welche wir durch sie lebendig sehen; weil die Geschichtserzählung dieser
Zeiträume, von Neueren unternommen, unbefriedigend und oft voll Irr-
thümer ist; so schien es angemessen, die Kenntnisse der römischen Geschichte
durch ihr gewidmete Vorlesungen zu erleichtern. Es konnte zweifelhaft
seyn, ob einer zusammenhängenden Erzählung der Vorzug gebühre, oder ob
es besser sey, nur diejenigen Zeiträume vorzutragen, in denen wir jene beiden Historiker entbehren. Ich habe mich, in dem Vertrauen, daß keiner
meiner Leser sich verführen lassen werde, ein Studium der classischen Geschichtschreiber Roms für entbehrlich zu halten, wenn er einen Begriff von
den Begebenheiten erhalten hat, welche sie schildern, und in der Hoffnung,
dieses Studium zu erleichtern und zu vervollkommnen, für jene Methode
entschieden.

Vieles von dem, was der Römer in den Jahrbüchern seines Volks nieder-
schrieb, muß der Neuere aus der Fülle der Begebenheiten ausschließen, woran
diese Geschichte die aller übrigen Völker weit übertrifft. Genöthigt, Vieles
zu übergehen und für die Beschränkungen ein Gesetz festzustellen, werde ich
Männer und Vorfälle, die ohne innere Größe und äußere Folgenwichtigkeit
in einem todten Andenken erhalten sind, nicht erwähnen; obgleich dem Gelehrten vollständige Kenntniß unentbehrlich ist, und manche dürre Oede
Quellen verschließt, die es ihm, früher oder später, hervorzurufen gelingt.
Ich werde hingegen suchen die Kritik der Geschichte, besonders während der
fünf ersten Jahrhunderte, nicht nach dunkeln Gefühlen, sondern forschend
auszuführen, nicht ihre Resultate, welche nur blinde Meinungen stiften, sondern die Untersuchungen selbst in ihrem ganzen Umfange vortragen; ich
werde streben, die überbauten und versteckten, von den uns erhaltenen alten
Schriftstellern oft ganz verkannten, Grundfesten des alten römischen Volks

22*

und ſeines Staats zu entdecken, Gerechtigkeit zu Lob und Tadel, zu Liebe
und Haß, wo Parteigeiſt falſche Darſtellung, dieſe nach Jahrtauſenden fal=
ſches Urtheil geboren hat, in Kraft zu ſetzen; die Ausbreitung des Reichs,
die Entwicklung der Verfaſſung, den Zuſtand der Verwaltung, der Sitten
und Bildung, wie er ſich von Zeit zu Zeit überſehen läßt, darſtellen. Ich
werde die Männer näher bekannt machen, welche zum Guten oder Böſen in
ihrem Zeitalter mächtig waren oder ſich doch vor Anderen auszeichneten:
ich werde die Geſchichte der Kriege, ſo weit ſie nicht eine wiederkehrende
Einförmigkeit darbietet, genau erzählen, und ſo weit es unſere Nachrichten
geſtatten, ein treues und beſtimmtes Bild der Völker entwerfen, welche die
ſich ausdehnende Sphäre der römiſchen Gewalt allmählig erreichte: auch
die Literatur, ſowohl der erhaltnen als verlornen Schriftſteller, bei ihren
Hauptepochen betrachten.

Als Salluſt mit beruhigtem Gemüth nach vielem und bitterm in den
Geſchäften des Staats erlittnen Kummer ſich ihnen zu entziehen beſchloſſen
hatte, und, zu ſeinen Lieblingsforſchungen zurückgekehrt, einzelne Ereigniſſe
der vaterländiſchen Geſchichte auswählend zu erzählen unternahm, fand er
es nöthig, ſeinen Mitbürgern — denn nur einzelne Griechen und wenige von
den Weſteuropäern laſen lateiniſch — darzuthun, daß die Thaten der Rö=
mer von denen der Griechen nicht verdunkelt würden. Ein Jahrhundert
früher hatte Polybius wohl vergeblich den Griechen anſchaulich zu machen
geſtrebt, wie weit die römiſche Größe nicht allein, noch vorzüglich durch den
Umfang ihres Reichs, Alles übertreffe, was die frühere Geſchichte gekannt
habe. Daß die Griechen, wenn auch nicht Erbitterung und Haß gegen die
fremden Beherrſcher ſie verblendet hätten, eine Geſchichte geringſchätzten,
der damals jene Anmuth und das Leben beredter Erzählung fehlte, welche
die ihnen verwandten Thaten ihrer Vorfahren verſchönerte, und ohne die
auch die größte im Andenken erhaltene Geſchichte ſo wenig ganz empfunden
werden kann, als ein lyriſches Gedicht ohne eine entſprechende Muſik: dies
war die Folge ihres leichtſinnig lebhaften, der Schönheit hingegebenen
Sinnes. Auffallend aber iſt es, daß bei dem literariſchen Publikum Roms,
deſſen Beifall Salluſt ſuchte, wie hochmüthig auch der römiſche National=
ſtolz war, ähnliche Stimmung und Verkennen der vorväterlichen Größe
herrſchte. Doch, wie ſonderbar es auch erſcheint, ſo iſt dies nicht ſchwer
zu erklären, und er ſelbſt hat wohl die Erklärung mit dem ſtillen Bewußtſeyn
niedergeſchrieben, daß von ſeinen Geſchichten eine andere Anſicht bei den
Römern ſelbſt anheben würde. Dieſe fanden damals in ihrer eigenen
Sprache, Cato's Urgeſchichten ausgenommen, welche den Reiz der Kräftig=
keit unſrer beſſern alten Chroniken gehabt haben müſſen, keinen ihrer Ge=
ſchichtſchreiber lesbar. Allerdings mögen auch die meiſten ſehr armſelig
und geiſtlos geweſen ſeyn; doch waren ſelbſt die treuherzigen und ehrwür=

digen Alten eben für jene Zeit ungenießbar, da die Lesenden zu Rom ganz
durch griechische Literatur erzogen, und in dieser nicht durch die Erhaben=
heit der classischen Werke gebildet waren, sondern durch den Glanz und
Firniß einer ausgearteten, witzigen Literatur, welche damals unter den
Griechen, mit denen sie als Lehrern und lebendigen Mustern umgingen, mo=
disch war, den Sinn für Einfalt ganz verloren hatten. Wie die Dichter
die Heroen, so hat der große einheimische Geschichtschreiber, dem Sallust
voranging, Roms Thaten und seine Helden der Nacht entrissen. Es ist
wohl keine gewagte Behauptung, daß die Römer erst durch Livius inne
wurden, welche Geschichte sie hatten. Verschönert durch den Wunsch in
den Zeiten der Vorfahren, ein noch nicht lange ganz erstorbenes ehernes
Alter zu schauen, umgab jetzt im Reiz der lieblichsten Rede die Größe ihrer
Thaten und Siege der herrlichste Schmuck republikanischer und bürgerlicher
Tugenden; ein Ernst und eine Erhabenheit, welche die großen Männer
Athens mit ihren unverhüllten menschlichen Fehlern und Schwächen eben
so demüthigend übertraf, als die Besiegung ganzer Welttheile und furcht=
barer Völker die leidenschaftlichen Kämpfe kleiner Republiken: denn der
Perserkrieg galt den Römern bald für ein dreistes Mährchen. Das Mit=
telalter und das verjüngte Italien, denen die Anmuth griechischer Historiker
verborgen war, bewunderten Roms Geschichte ausschließend: als ob das
Schicksal jenen alten Helden Ersatz für die Gleichgültigkeit ihrer Nachkom=
men des Zeitalters geben wollte, welches sich zu fremder Cultur gewandt
hatte. Es ist eine ungelehrte, aber eine desto einfältigere und ungeschmink=
tere Verehrung, mit der die alten Italiener des erwachenden Mittelalters
die großen Namen Roms nennen: vielleicht waren sie ihnen um so näher,
weil sie sich ohne Klügeln, ohne Rücksicht auf die Verschiedenheit der Sit=
ten und der Zeiten, ihre großen Seelen in den Verhältnissen und fast in
der Gestalt von Zeitgenossen und Landsleuten dachten, so wie sie in dem
Kaiserthum ihrer Zeit eine unveränderte Fortsetzung des alten Reichs der
Cäsaren sahen. Virgil war Danten ein Lombarde, wie noch spätere Ma=
ler den Römern ihrer Kunstwerke das Gewand ihrer Tage anlegten: das
Volk ehrte Virgil's Grab und Andenken als eines mächtigen und wohlthä=
tigen Zauberers. Selbst Petrarca hegt noch, und wohl mit Absicht, die
Täuschung einer nur durch die Zeit getrennten Einheit der Nationaliät: er
sieht in Stephan Colonna einen alten Patricier, wie in Rienzi einen Tri=
bun des Volks. Erst im folgenden Jahrhundert schied das Alterthum aus
der Vermischung mit der Gegenwart; und bei der ungeheuren Macht, wo=
mit damals sich Alles entwickelte, erreichten Einzelne schnell die schärfste
und lebendigste Anschauung der Eigenthümlichkeit altrömischer Zeiten,
welche wir im Ganzen zu gewinnen hoffen dürfen, wie Vieles auch seitdem
an das Licht gebracht ist, woran wir genauere Einsicht erwerben können.

Aber nach Sigonius verdankt die Geschichte des alten Roms den Philolo-
gen nur noch wenig: sie entwich ihren Händen, und ward das Eigenthum
in wenigen glücklichen Fällen großer Staatsmänner; meistens aber gewöhn-
licher Historiker.

Friedrich Wilken.
23. Richard's Löwenherz Gefangenschaft.

Die Nachricht von des verhaßten Königs von England Ankunft auf deut-
schem Boden kam bald zu den Ohren des Herzogs Leopold von Oestreich,
welcher erfreuet über diese unerwartete Gelegenheit, die im gelobten Lande
empfangene Beschimpfung zu rächen, sogleich auf allen Straßen nach seinem Feinde spähen ließ. Richard aber kam auf leichtere Weise in des Herzogs Gewalt als erwartet werden konnte. Nachdem er drei Tage und drei
Nächte ohne Nahrung umhergeirrt war, führte ihn sein Unglück in die
Nähe von Wien, wo er in dem Dorfe Erdburg an der Donau in einer elenden Herberge seine Wohnung nahm und mehrere Tage sich auszuruhen beschloß. Auch hier beschränkte Richard seinen Aufwand nicht auf hinrei-
chende Weise, benahm sich überhaupt nicht mit Vorsicht und legte einen kostbaren Ring nicht ab, welcher zu seiner geringen Kleidung nicht paßte. Der
Diener, welcher ihn begleitete, zeigte, als er nach Wien kam, um einzukau-
fen, morgenländische Goldstücke oder Byzantien, welche ihn verdächtig machten; erregte durch eitles und anmaßliches Betragen Aufsehen und wurde
angehalten, half sich aber aus der Verlegenheit durch die Ausrede, daß er
der Diener eines reichen Kaufmanns sey, welcher nach drei Tagen selbst in
die Stadt kommen würde, und machte den König aufmerksam auf die Gefahr eines längern Aufenthalts. Doch Richard konnte sich noch nicht entschließen, seine Reise fortzusetzen; und nachdem der Diener noch mehrere
Male nach Wien gekommen war und durch den Einkauf ausgesuchterer
Speisen als für einen geringen Mann sich ziemten, von Neuem Aufmerksamkeit erregt hatte, so verriethen ihn endlich wenige Tage vor Weihnachten die Handschuhe des Königs, welche er im Gürtel trug, und er bekannte
den Beamten des Herzogs Leopold auf der Folter die Wahrheit. Hierauf
wurde unverzüglich die Herberge des Königs Richard mit Bewaffneten umringt, und der Schultheiß von Wien trat ein mit den Worten: „Sey gegrüßt, König von England, du verkleidest dich vergeblich, dein Gesicht macht
dich kenntlich;" und als Richard nach seinem Schwerte griff, fuhr der
Schultheiß fort: „Sey nicht ängstlich und begehe keine Unbesonnenheit, du
bist hier sicherer als sonst irgendwo, und wenn du in die Hände der Freunde
des Markgrafen, welche überall dir nachstellen, fielest, so würdest du nicht
hundert Leben davon bringen können." Der König aber erklärte, daß er

nur dem Herzog Leopold sich ergeben würde, und als dieser erschien, ging er ihm entgegen und überreichte ihm sein Schwert. Leopold behandelte zwar anfangs seinen königlichen Gefangenen mit Ehrerbietung, überantwortete ihn aber hernach dem Ritter Hademar von Chunring zur Bewahrung in der Burg Tierenstein an der Donau, zwischen Wien und Linz, wo Richard in strengem Gewahrsam gehalten und Tag und Nacht von Bewaffneten mit gezogenen Schwertern bewacht wurde.

Der Herzog von Oestreich gab nicht nur sogleich dem Kaiser Heinrich VI. von der Gefangenschaft des Königs Richard Nachricht, sondern führte auch seinen Gefangenen nach Regensburg, wo der Kaiser am Weihnachtstage einen Hoftag versammelt hatte, doch wurde die Verhandlung der Sache des Königs Richard noch verschoben; da aber Heinrich es ungebührlich fand, daß ein König in der Gewalt eines Herzogs bleibe, so versprach Leopold, den gefangenen König zu Ostern nächsten Jahres in die Hände des Kaisers zu liefern. Heinrich beeilte sich dem Könige Philipp August von Frankreich die Verhaftung des Königs Richard zu melden.

Am Dienstage nach dem Palmsonntage, den 23. März des Jahres 1193, übergab zu Mainz der Herzog Leopold, welcher sich zu dem nach Speier berufenen Reichstage begab, den König Richard dem Kaiser Heinrich, und Richard wurde zuerst in die Burg Trifels, später nach Worms in anständigen, jedoch strengen Gewahrsam geführt. Er verlor aber, auf Befreiung hoffend, in seiner Gefangenschaft nicht den Muth, war, obgleich getrennt von seinen Begleitern, stets heiter, oft muthwillig, neckte seine Wächter durch mancherlei Kurzweil, setzte sie durch seine gewaltige Leibeskraft in Furcht, oder machte sie trunken.

In England war längere Zeit der Ort, wo Richard aufbewahrt wurde, unbekannt; die englischen Pilger, welche um Weihnachten aus Syrien in ihre Heimath zurückkamen, erstaunten, als sie ihren König noch nicht in England fanden, und meldeten, daß sie das Schiff, auf welchem Richard von Ptolemais abgefahren war, zu Brundusium angetroffen hätten; und die erste sichere Nachricht von des Königs Schicksale erhielt der Erzbischof Walter von Rouen durch die abschriftliche Mittheilung des von dem Kaiser Heinrich an den König von Frankreich erlassenen Schreibens, worauf der Erzbischof die Getreuen des Königs nach Orford auf den Sonntag vor Lätare (den 28. Februar) zur Berathung rief und zwei Geistliche nach Deutschland reisen ließ, um den König aufzusuchen und über seinen Zustand sich zu erkundigen. Diese trafen ihren König in Baiern, als er durch den Herzog Leopold nach Mainz geführt wurde, fanden ihn heiter, guten Muths und ein würdevolles Benehmen behauptend, und Richard führte gegen sie keine andere Klage als über die Untreue seines Bruders Johann. Auch Blondel de Nesle, der Sänger aus Arras, soll seinen königlichen

Freund aufgesucht, bei dem Vogt der Burg, wo Richard gefangen gehalten
wurde, Dienste genommen und demselben durch sein Saitenspiel sich ange=
nehm gemacht haben; nachdem aber der König, indem er mit lauter und
schöner Stimme den ersten Vers eines Liedes sang, welches sie mit einan=
der gemacht hatten, und welches nur ihnen beiden bekannt war, sich ihm
kund gegeben hatte, begab sich Blondel nach England und betrieb, so viel
er vermochte, die Befreiung des Königs. Richard selbst schrieb an alle
Prälaten, Fürsten, Grafen, Barone und Freie seiner Länder bewegliche
Briefe, in welchen er sie aufforderte, für seine Befreiung aus der Gefangen=
schaft Sorge zu tragen.

Der König Philipp August von Frankreich, als er die Gefangenschaft
des Königs Richard vernahm, zog sogleich alle früheren Beschwerden gegen
denselben wieder hervor, und nahm die Weigerung des Seneschalls der
Normandie, die Prinzessin Alix auszuliefern, zum Vorwande, von dem
Versprechen, welches er zu Ptolemais dem Könige Richard gegeben, sich für
entbunden zu erklären, den Frieden mit dem Könige von England aufzu=
kündigen und in die Normandie mit seinem Heere einzufallen, und bestärkte
zugleich den Prinzen Johann in der Feindseligkeit gegen seinen Bruder und
dessen Freunde. Bei dem Kaiser Heinrich VI., welcher dem Könige Ri=
chard gegen ein ansehnliches Lösegeld die Freiheit schon zugesagt, fanden
die Anträge des Königs von Frankreich wegen längerer Gefangenhaltung des
Königs Richard anfangs kein Gehör, sondern Heinrich gab den französischen
Botschaftern, welche ihm den Fehdebrief ihres Königs an Richard überbrach=
ten, zur Antwort, daß, wer den König von England verletze, den Kaiser zum
Feinde habe. Der Kaiser Heinrich beharrte aber in dieser Gesinnung nicht
lange; in der Hoffnung, das Lösegeld zu steigern, verlängerte er unter man=
cherlei Vorwänden die Gefangenschaft des Königs Richard, und gab daher
auch in seinem Briefe, in welchem er den Lehnmännern des Königs Richard
damals kund that, daß ihr Herr für Geld seine Freiheit wieder erhalten
werde, den Betrag des Lösegeldes noch nicht an.

Das Unglück des Königs Richard begann aber Theilnahme selbst bei
solchen, welche ehemals nicht seine Freunde gewesen waren, zu erwecken;
die Dichter beklagten seine Leiden in mancherlei Gesängen und regten das
Mitleid des Adels und des Volkes auf, und von vielen Seiten wurde Für=
sprache eingelegt. Der gelehrte Peter von Blois, Archidiakonus zu Bath,
forderte den Erzbischof von Mainz, seinen Schulfreund, auf, das geistliche
Schwert unverdrossen und ohne Menschenfurcht zu gebrauchen, damit der
ungerechten und unverdienten Gefangenschaft eines Königs, welcher als
Kreuzfahrer unter dem Schutze der Kirche stehe, ein Ende gemacht werde,
und der sehr geachtete Abt von Clügny ermahnte den Kaiser Heinrich drin=
gend zur Beobachtung der Gerechtigkeit und Billigkeit gegen den König von

England. Richard selbst suchte auf den Rath seiner Mutter Eleonora den
Kaiser dadurch zu gewinnen, daß er sich erbot, von ihm, als dem Herrn
aller Könige, seine Krone zu Lehen zu nehmen, und einen jährlichen Lehen-
zins von fünf Tausend Pfund Sterling zu bezahlen; und diese Verabre-
dung wurde dadurch vollzogen, daß Richard in Gegenwart mehrerer deutscher und englischer Herren von dem Kaiser vermittelst eines zwiefachen goldenen Kreuzes die sinnbildliche Belehnung mit dem Königreiche England
empfing.

Nach diesem Schritte des Königs Richard glaubte Heinrich sich vollkommen berechtigt, die Sache seines Gefangenen einer öffentlichen Verhandlung zu unterwerfen, und indem er den König feierlich vor seinen Richter-
stuhl forderte, seine lehensherrliche Richtergewalt und die alte kaiserliche
Weltherrschaft geltend zu machen. Richard wurde angeklagt dadurch gefrevelt zu haben, daß er Tankred, dem unrechtmäßigen König von Sicilien,
Hilfe gewährte, den Kaiser Isaak von Cypern, einen Verwandten des Kaisers, des Reiches und der Freiheit beraubte, den Markgrafen Konrad von
Montferrat und Tyrus, einen Vasallen des deutschen Reichs, durch Assas-
sinen ermorden ließ, die deutschen Kreuzfahrer mit Wort und That beleidigte, das Panier des Herzogs Leopold von Oestreich im gelobten Lande
beschimpfte, das heilige Land an Saladin verrieth und gegen den König
Philipp August von Frankreich mancherlei Untreue und Ungebühr übte.
Der König Richard aber, indem er zugab, daß seine natürliche Heftigkeit
ihn zu Zeiten auf Abwege gebracht haben könnte, vertheidigte sich gegen
diese Anklagen so bündig und mit solcher Beredtsamkeit, daß der Kaiser
Heinrich dadurch gerührt von seinem Throne herabstieg, den König umarmte und ihm seine Freundschaft zusagte; auch der Herzog Leopold, welcher anwesend war, und mit dem Gefangenen in der Mitte der Versammlung stand, soll durch die Rede des Königs bis zu Thränen erweicht worden seyn. Seit dieser Zeit hatte Richard nicht nur mehr Freiheit als
zuvor, sondern der Kaiser und die Kaiserin ehrten ihn auch zu Hagenau, wo
sie seinen Besuch empfingen, mit Geschenken, und der Kaiser wies ihm
einen angenehmern Aufenthalt zu Mainz an.

Die Unterhandlungen wegen des Lösegeldes wurden zuerst durch die beiden Geistlichen geführt, welche der Erzbischof von Rouen nach Deutschland
gesandt hatte, um den König aufzusuchen, dann durch den Bischof Hubert
von Salisbury fortgesetzt, welcher, als er in Sicilien das Unglück seines
Königs vernommen hatte, nach Deutschland geeilt war; und die Bischöfe
Savary von Bath und Wilhelm von Ely brachten endlich die Uebereinkunft
zu Stande, indem Richard, welcher von der bevorstehenden Zusammenkunft
des Kaisers mit dem Könige von Frankreich zu Vaucouleurs Schlimmes
für sich besorgte, den Abschluß des Vertrages auf jede Weise beschleunigte.

Der Kaiſer Heinrich dagegen, durch ſeine damalige Freundſchaft mit dem
Könige von Frankreich in ſeiner Anmaßung beſtärkt, erſchwerte wiederum
die Unterhandlungen, ſo viel er vermochte; und zu Worms, wo um Jo=
hannistag die engliſchen Unterhändler bei dem Kaiſer ſich wieder einfanden,
wurden von ihm noch ſo übertriebene Forderungen gemacht, daß alle anwe=
ſenden Freunde des Königs Richard an der Möglichkeit, deſſen Befreiung
zu erwirken, verzweifelten.　Da aber unterbeß die verabredete Zuſammen=
kunft des Kaiſers mit dem Könige von Frankreich vereitelt wurde, und
Richard durch die Verheißung ſeines Beiſtandes gegen den Herzog von
Sachſen den Kaiſer gewann, ſo kam am Tage Petri und Pauli, den 29.
Junius, die Uebereinkunft dahin zu Stande, daß der König von England
als Löſegeld hundert Tauſend Mark reinen Silbers nach Cölniſchem Ge=
wichte und außerdem noch fünfzig Tauſend Mark Silbers zum Behufe des in
Apulien bevorſtehenden Kriegs zahlen ſolle; in dieſe letztere Summe von
fünfzig Tauſend Mark ſollten aber zwanzig Tauſend Mark begriffen ſeyn,
welche dem Herzoge Leopold von Oeſtreich für die Ueberlieferung des Kö=
nigs von dem Kaiſer waren zugeſagt worden.　Auch wurde beſtimmt, daß
ſogleich in möglichſt kurzer Friſt hundert Tauſend Mark wohl gewogen und
wohl verſiegelt den Abgeordneten, welche der Kaiſer und der König von
England gemeinſchaftlich nach London ſenden würden, übergeben und inner=
halb der engliſchen Grenzen auf Gefahr des Königs Richard, in Deutſch=
land auf Gefahr des Kaiſers an den Ort ihrer Beſtimmung befördert wer=
den ſollten.　Sobald der König dieſe Summe entrichtet und für die übri=
gen fünfzig Tauſend Mark dem Kaiſer ſechzig und dem Herzoge Leopold
ſieben Geiſel geſtellt haben würde, ſollte er in Freiheit geſetzt werden.　Doch
ſollten dieſe fünfzig Tauſend Mark Silbers dem Könige erlaſſen ſeyn,
wenn er ſein Verſprechen in Hinſicht des Herzogs von Sachſen erfülle, und
für dieſen Fall übernahm der Kaiſer die Befriedigung des Herzogs Leopold
mit zwanzig Tauſend Mark.　Außerdem machte Richard ſich anheiſchig,
binnen ſieben Monaten nach ſeiner Freilaſſung ſeine Nichte Eleonora, die
Schweſter des Herzogs Arthur von Bretagne, Friedrich, dem Sohne des
Herzogs Leopold, zur Gemahlin zu geben, und den Kaiſer Iſaak und deſſen
Tochter ohne Löſegeld dem Herzoge von Oeſtreich, ihrem nahen Verwand=
ten, zu überliefern.　Als der König Philipp von dieſer Uebereinkunft hörte,
ſo ſchrieb er an den Grafen Johann von Mortaigne, des Königs Richard
Bruder, er möge wohl auf ſeiner Hut ſeyn, denn der Teufel ſey wieder
losgelaſſen.

Doch Richard blieb nach dem Abſchluſſe dieſes Vertrages noch länger als
ſieben Monate in der Gefangenſchaft.　Ein Theil des Löſegeldes wurde
zwar in England zuſammengebracht, indem von jedem ritterlichen Lehen
zwanzig Schillinge, von allen Einkünften der Laien der vierte Theil, und

von den geiſtlichen Pfründen an einigen Kirchen der vierte und an andern
der zehnte Theil erhoben, und die ſilbernen und goldnen Kelche der Altäre,
die Reliquienkaſten und andere Schätze der Kirchen und ſelbſt das edle
Metall an den Grabmälern der Heiligen in Anſpruch genommen wurden;
und nachdem der Kaiſer das auf dieſe Weiſe geſammelte Geld empfangen
hatte, ſo beſtimmte er den vierten Montag nach Weihnachten, oder den 17.
Januar 1194 zum Termin der Entlaſſung des Königs Richard, und ſchmei-
chelte der Eitelkeit der Engländer und ihres Königs durch das Verſprechen,
den König von England mit der Krone des Reichs Arles zu belehnen. Obwohl das Geſchenk dieſes Reiches, in welchem der Kaiſer ſelbſt nicht einmal
als Oberherr anerkannt wurde, von keinem Werthe war, und die Anſprüche,
welche dadurch erworben wurden, nur dazu dienen konnten, der Feindſchaft
des Königs von Frankreich neue Nahrung zu geben, ſo nahm Richard dieſes Verſprechen doch dankbar an, und meldete die frohe Hoffnung, eine neue
Krone zu erwerben, mit Entzücken dem Erzbiſchof von Canterbury. Doch
bald gab Heinrich wieder Gehör den Anträgen des Königs von Frankreich,
welcher gemeinſchaftlich mit dem Grafen Johann von Mortaigne durch
große Verſprechungen ihn zu bewegen ſuchte, den König Richard wenigſtens
noch bis zum nächſten Michaelisfeſt in ſeiner Haft zu halten. Obgleich
Eleonora, des Königs Richard Mutter, ſelbſt nach Deutſchland kam, um
die Befreiung ihres Sohns zu bewirken, und die Geiſeln, welche zufolge des
Vertrags für den Reſt des Löſegeldes geſtellt werden mußten, bereit zur
Ablieferung gehalten wurden, ſo erhob der Kaiſer Heinrich zu Mainz, wo
am Feſte Mariä Reinigung über die Entlaſſung des Königs von England
von Neuem verhandelt wurde, mancherlei Schwierigkeiten, und zeigte die
von dem Könige von Frankreich und dem Prinzen Johann empfangenen
Briefe, ſo daß Richard und Eleonora genöthigt waren, die Hülfe der deutſchen Fürſten, welche die Bürgſchaft des Wormſer Vertrags übernommen
hatten, nachzuſuchen. Durch die nachdrücklichen Vorſtellungen dieſer Fürſten wurde endlich Heinrich bewogen, ſein gegebenes Wort zu erfüllen, und
am Freitage nach Mariä Reinigung (4. Februar) führten die Erzbiſchöfe
von Mainz und Cöln den König Richard als freien Mann zu ſeiner Mutter.

Mit ſicherm Geleite des Kaiſers reiſ'te Richard und ſein Gefolge über
Cöln, wo der Erzbiſchof Adolf mit großen Ehren ihn empfing und ſeine
Anweſenheit durch ein Hochamt feierte, nach Antwerpen, fuhr von dort
nach Swine, einem flandriſchen Hafen, und gewarnt durch die Meldung
eines ihm treuen Mannes, daß der Kaiſer Heinrich, es bereuend ihn ent-
laſſen zu haben, darauf denke, ſich ſeiner wieder zu bemächtigen, vertraute
Richard dem ſtürmiſchen Meere ſich an, und betrat am Sonntage, den 15.
März, bei Sandwich wieder den engliſchen Boden. Am Sonntage nach
Oſtern ließ Richard, auf den Rath der engliſchen Barone, damit alle

Schmach der Gefangenſchaft getilgt würde, jedoch nicht ohne Widerſtreben,
durch den Erzbiſchof von Canterbury zu Wincheſter ſich wieder krönen,
ſuchte dann durch nachdrückliche Maßregeln den in ſeinem Reiche eingeriſ=
ſenen Unordnungen zu ſteuern, und ordnete die Erhebung fernerer Beiträge
an, zur völligen Entrichtung des dem Kaiſer Heinrich und dem Herzoge
von Oeſtreich zugeſagten Löſegeldes.

Friedrich von Raumer.

24. Des Kaiſers Friedrich II. Charakter.

Friedrich war nicht groß, aber feſt gebaut, blond, und in allen körperli=
chen Uebungen, in allen mechaniſchen Künſten geſchickt.   An die ſchöne
Stirn ſchloß ſich die faſt antik gebildete Naſe auf feine Weiſe an; der
Mund war wohl geſtaltet, das rundliche Kinn keineswegs ſchwach abfal=
lend, und das Auge drückte in der Regel die freundliche Heiterkeit, auf ernſte
Veranlaſſung aber auch Ernſt und Strenge aus.   Merkwürdig iſt über=
haupt, um ſogleich von dem Aeußern auf das Innere überzugehen, die faſt
beiſpielloſe Verbindung des höchſten Ernſtes, der größten Strenge und Folge=
rechtheit mit der natürlichſten Heiterkeit und einem zu Luſt und Scherz aller
Art fähigen, überall geiſtreichen Gemüthe.   Wenn auch die bittern Erfah=
rungen eines langen Lebens allmählig im Alter die erſte Seite vielleicht
mehr hervorgehoben haben, ſo verſchwand doch nie der Glanz, welcher von
der zweiten ausging; und wenn auch die zweite bis an Gefahren und Ab=
wege führte, ſo richtete doch die ernſte Kraft ihn bald wiederum in die
Höhe, und ſeine durch ein halbes Jahrhundert ununterbrochene raſtloſe Re=
gierungsthätigkeit widerlegt am beſten die Anſchuldigung, als ſey der Kai=
ſer oft in Lüſten untergegangen.   Selbſt ſeine größten Feinde können ihm
ihr Lob nicht verſagen, ſondern geſtehen : er war ein kühner, tapferer, edelge=
ſinnter Mann von den größten natürlichen Anlagen, freigebig, aber doch
nicht verſchwenderiſch, voller Kenntniſſe, er verſtand Griechiſch, Lateiniſch,
Italieniſch, Deutſch, Franzöſiſch und Arabiſch.   Er gab nicht bloß die Ge=
ſetze, ſondern ließ auch genau unterſuchen, ob ſie gehalten wurden, und ſtrafte
die untauglichen Beamten ſo ſtreng, daß ſie von Unbilden möglichſt abge=
ſchreckt wurden.   Die Geringſten durften gegen ihn klagen, und Jeder über=
nahm ohne Furcht deren Vertheidigung.

Von dem Vorwurfe der Irreligioſität, welcher dem Kaiſer gemacht
wurde, muß in der weiteren Geſchichtserzählung mit Mehrem die Rede ſeyn.
Hier genüge die Bemerkung, daß er allerdings kein Chriſt war in dem
Sinne, wie es der Papſt von ihm verlangte, daß aber ein Kaiſer, der durch
Widerſtand gereizt, durch Erfahrung belehrt, durch Unterſuchungen aufge=

klärt und dadurch, wir möchten sagen, Protestant geworden war, im höhe=
ron Sinne immer noch Christ blieb, und um des Verwerfens einzelner
kirchlichen Formen willen keineswegs dem Judenthum oder dem Mahome=
danismus näher stand, oder gar in einen geistlos gleichgültigen Unglauben
hineingerieth. Vielmehr würden ihm Manche nach späteren Ansichten Vor=
würfe wegen seines Aberglaubens machen können, weil er Todtenmessen für
seine Vorfahren halten ließ, den Klöstern und Kirchen Schenkungen machte
und überhaupt unter dem Vorbehalt, daß man dem Kaiser gebe, was des
Kaisers ist, die christliche Kirche für höchst wichtig und schlechthin unent=
behrlich hielt. Sogar der Glaube an Wunder wird ihm, sonderbar genug,
neben seinem Unglauben zugeschrieben. Als er nämlich das ungehorsame
Katania strafen wollte, stand des Morgens Agatha, die Schutzheilige der
Stadt, auf seinem Gebetbuche und sagte ihm: beleidige mein Vaterland
nicht, denn ich räche die Unbilden; worauf Friedrich von seinem Vorhaben
abstand. Diese Erzählung ist indeß erfunden, und es liegen andere Gründe
zur Hand, warum der Kaiser seine eigene Stadt nicht zerstörte; dagegen
hat es keinen Zweifel, daß er nach damaliger Sitte Sterndeuter hielt und auch
befragte. Ihren Ausspruch fürchtend, daß er unter Blumen sterben werde,
habe er Florenz nicht betreten, und wie es wohl zu gehen pflegt, scheint
Spott über solche Weissagungen und eine dunkle, Vorsicht erzeugende Be=
sorgniß zugleich obgewaltet zu haben. Im Jahre 1227 gab ihm sein
Sterndeuter, wahrscheinlich auf Veranlassung spöttischer Zweifel, in Vi=
cenza einen versiegelten Zettel, worin stand, zu welchem Thore er hinaus=
gehen werde. Friedrich ließ, damit dieser Ausspruch zu Schanden werde,
ein Loch in die Wand brechen und ging hindurch; aber siehe, in dem Zettel
hieß es: der Kaiser wird durch ein neues Thor hinausgehen. Obschon
ein anderes Thor das neue hieß, ob der Kaiser Kenntniß, Zufall oder Be=
trug darin sah, ist schwer zu entscheiden. Ueberhaupt erhielt an Friedrich's
Hofe der Sterndeuter nie die große Bedeutung und verleitete nie zu so fin=
steren Schritten, wie etwa bei Ezelin von Romano. Vielmehr trieb der
Kaiser seinen Sterndeuter, Michael Skotus, zu mehrseitigem echten Erfor=
schen der Natur, und zum Uebersetzen der Thiergeschichte des Aristoteles.
Doch nicht Skotus, sondern Friedrich selbst war der Meister in diesem
Fache. Wir besitzen von ihm ein Werk über die Kunst, mit Vögeln zu ja=
gen, welches nicht etwa bloß dadurch eine oberflächliche Merkwürdigkeit er=
hält, daß es ein Kaiser schrieb, und eben so wenig ein Jagdbuch ist, wie es
viele Ritter damals hätten schreiben können, wenn sie überhaupt der Feder
mächtig gewesen wären. Jenes Werk enthält vielmehr neben einer, in der
That sehr scharfsinnigen Anweisung zum Behandeln der Jagdvögel und
zur edelsten aller Jagdarten, zur Falkenjagd, in seinem wichtigern Theile
so erstaunlich genaue und gründliche Forschungen über die Natur der Vö=

gel, daß Sachverständige selbst in unseren Tagen behaupten, der Kaiser
verdiene deßhalb den größten Männern in diesem Fache beigesellt zu wer=
den.   Er handelt von der Vögel Lebensweise, Nahrung, Nesterbau, Zeu=
gung, Jungenpflege, von ihren Krankheiten und den Heilmitteln derselben,
von ihren Zügen, wann, weßhalb und woher sie kommen, wohin sie gehen,
von Angriff und Vertheidigung, von allen äußern und innern Theilen ih=
res Leibes, Augen, Ohren, Schnabel, Knochen, Magen, Leber u. s. f., von
der Zahl und Stellung der Federn, der Art und Weise ihres mannigfachen
Fluges u. s. f.   Es fehlt nichts, was irgend zu einer vollkommenen Thier=
beschreibung gehört, und die geistreiche Rücksicht, welche dabei auf die ver=
gleichende Zergliederungskunst genommen wird, ist eine in jener Zeit noch
weniger erwartete, des Kaisers echte Sachkunde beweisende Erscheinung.—
Gleiche Aufmerksamkeit dürfte ein anderes, aber bisher vernachläßigtes
Werk über die Natur und Behandlung der Pferde verdienen, welches der
Stallmeister des Kaisers, Jordanus Rufus, nach dessen umständlichen Wei=
sungen zusammensetzte, und in der weiteren Anwendung überall trefflich
und bewährt fand.

Leopold Ranke.
25. Papst Sixtus V.

Es sollte zuweilen scheinen, als gäbe es in den Verwirrungen selbst eine
geheime Kraft, die den Menschen bildet und emporbringt, der ihnen zu
steuern fähig ist.   Während in der ganzen Welt erbliche Fürstenthümer
oder Aristokratieen die Herrschaft von Geschlecht zu Geschlecht überlieferten,
behielt das geistliche Fürstenthum das Ausgezeichnete, daß es von der unter=
sten Stufe der menschlichen Gesellschaft zu dem höchsten Range in dersel=
ben führen konnte.   Eben aus dem niedrigsten Stande erhob sich jetzt ein
Papst, der die Kraft und ganz die Natur dazu hatte, alle dem Unwesen ein
Ende zu machen.

Bei den ersten glücklichen Fortschritten der Osmanen in den illyrischen
und dalmatischen Provinzen flohen viele Einwohner derselben nach Italien.
Man sah sie ankommen, in Gruppen geschaart an dem Ufer sitzen und die
Hände gegen den Himmel ausstrecken.   Unter solchen Flüchtlingen ist
wahrscheinlich auch der Ahnherr Sixtus V., Zanetto Peretti, herüber ge=
kommen: er war von slavischer Nation.   Wie es aber Flüchtlingen geht:
weder er, noch auch seine Nachkommen, die sich in Montalto niedergelassen,
hatten sich in ihrem neuen Vaterlande eines besondern Glückes zu rühmen:
Peretto Peretti, der Vater Sixtus V., mußte sogar Schuldenhalber diese
Stadt verlassen: erst durch seine Verheirathung wurde er in Stand gesetzt,

einen Garten in Grotte a Mare bei Fermo zu pachten. Es war das eine merkwürdige Localität: zwischen den Gartengewächsen entdeckte man die Ruinen eines Tempels der Etruscischen Juno, der Cupra: es fehlte nicht an den schönsten Südfrüchten, wie denn Fermo sich eines mildern Klima's erfreut, als die übrige Mark. Hier ward dem Peretti am 18ten Dezember 1521 ein Sohn geboren. Kurz vorher war ihm im Traume vorgekommen, als werde er, indem er seine mancherlei Widerwärtigkeiten beklage, durch eine heilige Stimme mit der Versicherung getröstet, er werde einen Sohn bekommen, der sein Haus glücklich machen solle. Mit aller Lebhaftigkeit eines träumerischen, durch das Bedürfniß erhöhten, schon ohnehin den Regionen des Geheimnißvollen zugewandten Selbstgefühls ergriff er diese Hoffnung; er nannte den Knaben Felix.

In welchem Zustande die Familie war, sieht man wohl, wenn z. B. das Kind in einen Teich fällt, und die Tante, die an dem Teiche wäscht, es herauszieht: der Knabe muß das Obst bewachen, ja die Schweine hüten: die Buchstaben lernt er aus den Fibeln kennen, welche andere Kinder, die über Feld nach der Schule gegangen und von da zurückkommen, bei ihm liegen lassen: der Vater hat nicht die fünf Bajochi übrig, die der nächste Schulmeister monatlich fordert. Glücklicherweise hat die Familie ein Mitglied in dem geistlichen Stande, einen Franciscaner, Fra Salvatore, der sich endlich erweichen läßt das Schulgeld zu zahlen. Dann ging auch der junge Felix mit den übrigen zum Unterricht: er bekam ein Stück Brod mit: zu Mittag pflegte er dies an dem Brunnen sitzend zu verzehren, der ihm das Wasser dazu gab. Trotz so kümmerlicher Umstände waren doch die Hoffnungen des Vaters auch bald auf den Sohn übergegangen: als dieser sehr früh, im zwölften Jahr, denn noch verbot kein Tridentinisches Concilium so frühe Gelübde, in den Franciscanerorden trat, behielt er den Namen Felix bei. Fra Salvatore hielt ihn streng: er brauchte die Autorität eines Oheims, der zugleich Vaterstelle vertritt: doch schickte er ihn auch auf Schulen. Oft studirte Felix, ohne zu Abend gegessen zu haben, bei dem Schein einer Laterne im Kreuzgang, oder wenn diese ausging, bei der Lampe, die vor der Hostie in der Kirche brannte: es findet sich nicht gerade etwas bemerkt, was eine ursprüngliche religiöse Anschauung oder eine tiefere wissenschaftliche Richtung in ihm andeutete; wir erfahren nur, daß er rasche Fortschritte gemacht habe, sowohl auf der Schule zu Fermo als auf den Schulen und Universitäten zu Ferrara und Bologna: mit vielem Lob erwarb er die akademischen Würden. Besonders entwickelte er ein dialektisches Talent. Die Mönchsfertigkeit, verworrene theologische Fragen zu behandeln, machte er sich in hohem Grade eigen. Bei dem Generalconvent der Franciscaner im Jahre 1549, der zugleich mit literarischen Wettkämpfen begangen wurde, bestritt er einen Telestaner, Antonio Persico aus

Calabrien, der sich damals zu Perugia viel Ruf erworben, mit Gewandt=
heit und Geistesgegenwart. Dies verschaffte ihm zuerst ein gewisses Anse=
hen: der Protector des Ordens, Cardinal Pio von Carpi, nahm sich seit=
dem seiner eifrig an.

Sein eigentliches Glück aber schreibt sich von einem andern Vorfall her.
Im Jahre 1552 hielt er die Fastenpredigten in der Kirche S. Apostoli zu Rom
mit dem größten Beifall. Man fand seinen Vortrag lebhaft, wortreich,
fließend: ohne Floskeln: sehr wohl geordnet: er sprach deutlich und an=
genehm. Als er nun einst dort bei vollem Auditorium in der Mitte der
Predigt inne hielt, wie es in Italien Sitte ist, und nachdem er ausgeruht,
die eingelaufenen Eingaben ablas, welche Bitten und Fürbitten zu enthal=
ten pflegen, stieß er auf eine, die versiegelt auf der Kanzel gefunden worden
und ganz etwas Anderes enthielt. Alle Hauptsätze der bisherigen Predig=
ten Peretti's, vornehmlich in Bezug auf die Lehre von der Prädestination,
waren darin verzeichnet: neben einem jeden stand mit großen Buchstaben ::
du lügst. Nicht ganz konnte Peretti sein Erstaunen verbergen: er eilte
zum Schluß: so wie er nach Hause gekommen, schickte er den Zettel an die
Inquisition. Gar bald sah er den Großinquisitor, Michel Ghislieri, in
seinem Gemach anlangen. Die strengste Prüfung begann. Oft hat Pe=
retti später erzählt, wie sehr ihn der Anblick dieses Mannes mit seinen
strengen Brauen, den tiefliegenden Augen, den scharf markirten Gesichtszü=
gen in Furcht gesetzt habe. Doch faßte er sich, antwortete gut und gab
keine Blöße. Als Ghislieri sah, daß der Frater nicht allein unschuldig,
sondern in der katholischen Lehre so bewandert und fest war, wurde er
gleichsam ein anderer Mensch: er umarmte ihn mit Thränen: er ward
sein zweiter Beschützer.

Auf das Entschiedenste hielt sich seitdem Fra Felice Peretti zu der
strengen Partei, die so eben in der Kirche emporkam. Mit Ignatio, Fe=
lino, Filippo Neri, welche alle drei den Namen von Heiligen erworben, war
er in vertrautem Verhältniß. Daß er in seinem Orden, den er zu refor=
miren suchte, Widerstand fand und von den Ordensbrüdern einmal aus
Venedig vertrieben wurde, vermehrte nur sein Ansehen bei den Vertretern
der zur Macht gelangenden Gesinnung. Er ward bei Paul IV. einge=
führt und oft in schwierigen Fällen zu Rathe gezogen: er arbeitete als
Theolog in der Congregation für das Tridentinische Concilium, als Con=
sultor bei der Inquisition: an der Verurtheilung des Erzbischofs Caranza
hatte er großen Antheil: er hat sich die Mühe nicht verdrießen lassen, in
den Schriften der Protestanten die Stellen aufzusuchen, welche Caranza in
die seinen aufgenommen. Das Vertrauen Pius V. erwarb er völlig.
Dieser Papst ernannte ihn zum Generalvicar der Franciscaner — ausdrück=
lich in der Absicht, um ihn zur Reformation des Ordens zu autorisiren, —

und in der That fuhr Peretti gewaltig durch: er setzte die Generalcom=
miſſäre ab, die bisher die höchſte Gewalt in demſelben beſeſſen: er ſtellte
die alte Verfaſſung her, nach welcher dieſe den Provincialen zuſtand, und
führte die ſtrengſte Viſitation aus. Pius ſah ſeine Erwartungen nicht al=
lein erfüllt, ſondern noch übertroffen: die Zuneigung, die er für Peretti
hatte, hielt er für eine Art göttlicher Eingebung: ohne auf die Afterreden
zu hören, die denſelben verfolgten, ernannte er ihn zum Biſchof von St.
Agatha, im Jahre 1570 zum Cardinal. Auch das Bisthum Fermo ward
ihm ertheilt. In dem Purpur der Kirche kam Felice Peretti in ſein Va=
terland zurück, wo er einſt Obſt und Vieh gehütet: doch waren die Vorher=
ſagungen ſeines Vaters und ſeine eigenen Hoffnungen noch nicht völlig
erfüllt.

Es iſt zwar unzählige Mal wiederholt worden, welche Ränke Cardinal
Montalto — ſo nannte man ihn jetzt — angewendet habe, um zur Tiara
zu gelangen: wie demüthig er ſich angeſtellt, wie er gebeugt, huſtend und
am Stocke einhergeſchlichen: der Kenner wird von vorn herein erachten,
daß daran nicht viel Wahres iſt: nicht auf dieſe Weiſe werden die höchſten
Würden erworben. Montalto lebte ſtill, ſparſam und fleißig für ſich hin.
Sein Vergnügen war, in ſeiner Vigna bei Santa Maria Maggiore, die
man noch beſucht, Bäume, Weinſtöcke zu pflanzen und ſeiner Vaterſtadt
einiges Gute zu erweiſen. In ernſteren Stunden beſchäftigten ihn die
Werke des Ambroſius, die er 1580 herausgab. So vielen Fleiß er auch
darauf wandte, ſo war ſeine Behandlung doch etwas willkürlich. Uebri=
gens erſchien ſein Charakter gar nicht ſo harmlos, wie man geſagt hat: be=
reits eine Relation von 1574 bezeichnet Montalto als gelehrt und klug,
aber auch als argliſtig und boshaft. Doch zeigte er eine ungemeine Selbſt=
beherrſchung. Als ſein Neffe, der Gemahl der Vittoria Accorambuona er=
mordet worden, war er der erſte, der den Papſt bat, die Unterſuchung fallen
zu laſſen. Dieſe Eigenſchaft, die Jedermann bewunderte, hat vielleicht am
meiſten dazu beigetragen, daß, als die Intriguen des Conclaves von 1585
dahin gediehen, ihn nennen zu können, die Wahl wirklich auf ihn fiel. Auch
beachtete man, wie es in der unverfälſchten Erzählung des Vorgangs aus=
drücklich heißt, daß er nach den Umſtänden noch in ziemlich friſchem Alter,
nämlich 64 Jahre, und von ſtarker und guter Complexion war. Jeder=
mann geſtand, daß man unter den damaligen Umſtänden vor Allem eines
kräftigen Mannes bedurfte.

Und es ſah ſich Fra Felice an ſeinem Ziele. Es mußte auch ein men=
ſchenwürdiges Gefühl ſeyn, einen ſo erhabenen und legalen Ehrgeiz er=
füllt zu ſehen. Ihm ſtellte ſich Alles vor die Seele, worin er jemals eine
höhere Beſtimmung zu erkennen gemeint hatte. Er wählte zu ſeinem
Sinnſpruch: „Von Mutterleib an biſt du, o Gott, mein Beſchützer.“

Ludwig Uhland.

26. Ueber nordiſche Mythologie.

Aus den Tiefen einer Vorzeit, in die keine äußere Geſchichte hinabreicht, haben die Völker altnordiſchen Sprachſtamms ſich ein großartiges Geiſtes= denkmal gerettet: eine volle Mythologie, eine umfaſſende religiöſe Weltan= ſchauung in Sinnbildern.

Die beiden Hauptquellen dieſer Mythologie, die unter dem Namen ältere oder Sämund's Edda bekannte Sammlung altnordiſcher Götter= und Hel= denlieder, muthmaßlich in der erſten Hälfte des zwölften Jahrhunderts ver= anſtaltet, ſodann die jüngere oder Snorri's Edda, ein mythologiſch=poeti= ſches Handbuch, deſſen Grundlage dem Isländer Snorri in der vorderen Hälfte des dreizehnten Jahrhunderts zugeſchrieben wird, erhalten mannig= fache Ergänzung durch die vielen mythiſchen Ueberlieferungen, die in islän= ländiſchen Saga'n, in den Geſchichtwerken Saxo's und Snorri's, in Volks= liedern und Volksſagen, zum Theil noch jetzt gangbaren, aufbewahrt ſind.

Bei aller Reichhaltigkeit der vorhandenen Quellen, iſt jedoch in dieſen ſelbſt auf manches nun Verlorene hingewieſen, wovon oft nur noch dürftige Andeutungen oder die bloßen Namen übrig geblieben ſind. Aber auch die for= melle Beſchaffenheit jener Quellen erſchwert auf verſchiedene Weiſe den Gebrauch derſelben. Die älteſten Urkunden, die mythiſchen Eddalieder von unbekannten Verfaſſern aus heidniſcher Zeit, bedienen ſich einer ſehr ge= drängten Darſtellung, wobei der Gegenſtand größtentheils als ſchon bekannt vorausgeſetzt iſt; einige Lieder dieſer Art aber, die ſich durch ihre Annähe= rung an den Kunſtſtyl des nordiſchen Skaldengeſangs als ſpätere verkün= den, ſind eben darum auch theilweiſe mit den Dunkelheiten des gedachten Styls behaftet. In viel ſtärkerem Maße trifft dies die zahlreichen größe= ren und kleineren Bruchſtücke von Liedern genannter Skalden des neunten und der folgenden Jahrhunderte, welche der jüngern Edda als Belege der hier angegebenen dichteriſchen Ausdrücke eingeflochten ſind: die Sprache dieſer Skaldenlieder, in welchen alte Mythen entweder als Hauptgegen= ſtand behandelt, oder zum dichteriſchen Redeſchmucke benutzt waren, iſt durch künſtliche Bildlichkeit und durch die äußerſte Freiheit der Umſtellun= gen nicht ſelten ſo ſchwierig, daß die ſprachkundigſten Erklärer, geborne Isländer, rathlos davor ſtehen. Die proſaiſchen Erzählungen der jüngern Edda, meiſt Auszüge und Paraphraſen noch vorhandener oder verlorener Mythenlieder, ſind zwar an ſich deutlich, müſſen jedoch behutſam gebraucht werden, weil den Verfaſſern derſelben ſchwerlich mehr ein tieferes Ver= ſtändniß der Mythen zu Gebote ſtand, und deßhalb die Auffaſſung hin und wieder ungenau oder verfehlt iſt, wie man ſich da, wo die reineren Quellen noch zugänglich ſind, aus der Vergleichung überzeugen kann. Die mythi=

schen Rahmen, worein diese Erzählungen, nach dem Beispiel der alten Lieder,
gefaßt sind, und einige offenbare Einflüsse christlicher Ansicht müssen ohne=
dies in Abzug gebracht werden. Bei Saro hat man nicht bloß die Fär=
bung durch ein rhetorisches Latein, in das er die heimischen Sagen übertra=
gen hat, von diesen abzustreifen, sondern man muß auch bei ihm, wie in
Snorri's Geschichtsbuche, den historischen Gesichtspunkt, unter welchem beide
die alte Götterwelt aufgefaßt und dadurch nothwendig verdunkelt haben,
erst wieder auf den mythischen zurückführen. In den isländischen Saga'n
ist der ächte Mythenbestand häufig in das willkürlich Gefabelte hinüberge=
spielt und aufgelöst, in den späteren Volkssagen und Volksliedern aber ist
derselbe meist zum ergötzlichen Märchen geworden.

Zu diesen äußerlichen Schwierigkeiten kommt nun diejenige, die im We=
sen der Mythen selbst liegt. Jede Mythologie ist ihrem Begriffe nach
sinnbildlich; mögen daher auch ihre Bilder noch so vollständig und unge=
trübt erhalten seyn: so fragt es sich dann erst um die Ergründung ihres
Sinnes oder vielmehr um eine solche Aneignung derselben, wobei Bild und
Bedeutung in unmittelbarer, ungetheilter Anschauung wirken. Die nordi=
schen Mythen sind, nach dem Zeugnisse der Mythenquellen selbst, Runen,
Geheimreden, Geheimnisse: sie wollen, nach Räthselart, gelöst seyn.

Es kann unter solchen Umständen nicht befremden, daß diese Mythologie
sehr verschiedenartige Deutungen erfahren hat, und wer es, bei aller Aner=
kennung des durch vielfaches Verdienst bereits Geleisteten, nicht für über=
flüssig hält, hierin Weiteres zu versuchen, hat sein Augenmerk vorerst dar=
auf zu richten, welcher Weg zur Lösung durch die besondere Natur des Ge=
genstandes angezeigt sey. Hier bietet sich nun zunächst die unverkennbare
Bedeutsamkeit der mythischen Namen dar und zwar in einem Stufengange,
der von den unmittelbarsten und klarsten Bezeichnungen in stätiger Folge
zu entfernteren und versteckteren fortleitet. Unter den Namen der mythi=
schen Wesen sind manche noch im jetzigen Isländischen das gebräuchliche
und eigentliche Wort für denselben Gegenstand, den der Mythus damit be=
zeichnet; andre sind zwar nicht minder eigentlich, müssen aber, da sie schon
in den altnordischen Schriftdenkmälern nicht mehr in solchem Gebrauche
vorkommen, in andern, näher oder ferner verwandten Sprachen aufgesucht
werden; noch andere halten zwar das mehr oder weniger unmittelbar be=
zeichnende Wurzelwort fest, fügen aber Endformen bei, durch welche Person
und Geschlecht schärfer hervortreten; weiter giebt es solche, in denen Eigen=
schaften oder Thätigkeiten des damit benannten Wesens bald leicht erkennt=
lich und wieder eigentlich ausgesprochen, bald bildlich und in tieferliegenden
Beziehungen angedeutet sind. Von allen diesen Benennungsweisen oder
auch von Spielarten und Uebergängen derselben werden sich im Folgenden
Beispiele ergeben. Daß gleichwohl manche Namen, sey es etymologisch in

23

der Wurzel oder in der bestimmteren Beziehung zu ihrem Gegenstand, auch
der beharrlichsten Forschung sich verschließen mögen, hebt den Nutzen nicht
auf, der aus einem aufmerksamen Verfolgen der in den Namenbildungen
gegebenen Fingerzeige und aus einer vertrauteren Beobachtung des dabei
stattgefundenen Verfahrens für die Erklärung des inneren Mythengehaltes
gezogen werden kann.

Selbst der sprachlich unzweifelhafteste Name gewährt jedoch nur dann
eine sichere Mythendeutung, wenn das Wesen, dem er angehörte, auch durch
seine Erscheinung in Lied oder Sage, demselben wirklich entspricht. Weit
mehr noch ist man bei zweifelhaften oder gänzlich unerklärbaren Namen auf
die Anschauung des Gegenstandes verwiesen, aus welcher umgekehrt oft der
Name selbst erst deutlich wird. Schon bei der ersten unbefangenen Be=
trachtung lassen die nordischen Mythenbilder in ihrer Gesammtheit einen
entschiedenen Eindruck zurück, sie machen sich auf einen gewissen Grad ver=
ständlich und lassen weiteres Verständniß ahnen. Dies ist die Folge da=
von, daß sie aus dichterisch schaffendem Geiste hervorgegangen sind. Sie
können darum auch nur mit poetischem Auge richtig erfaßt werden; diesem
aber werden sie sich bei näherem Anblick immer voller und lebendiger ent=
falten. Jede Deutung dagegen, die in der Einbildungskraft keinen Anhalt
findet, die den Bildern einen Sinn unterlegt, durch welchen ihr anschauli=
cher Zusammenhang aufgehoben würde, muß eine unrichtige seyn, weil für
sie in der Natur des dichterischen Hervorbringens überall keine Möglichkeit
gegeben ist. Erst im Vereine mit der poetischen Anschauung wird nun auch
die etymologische Forschung ihre rechte Wirksamkeit üben, beide werden sich
wechselweise prüfen, bestätigen und ergänzen. Aber nicht blos die allge=
meinen Bedingungen des poetischen Gestaltens hat sich der Erklärer zur
Richtschnur zu nehmen; die mystische Symbolik hat sich bei verschiedenen
Völkern so verschiedenartig angelassen, ihre Plastik ist so mannigfach, die
Rechte des Bildes einerseits und der inwohnenden Idee andrerseits sind so
abweichend ausgetheilt, daß es nöthig ist, auch hierin je die Eigenthümlich=
keit der besonderen Götterlehre zu beachten, wenn die Deutung im Einzel=
nen glaubhaft und im Ganzen übereinstimmend werden soll.

Der Gesammtumfang nordischer Mythen ist allerdings von durchgreifen=
den Gedanken über göttliches Wesen und Wirken, über Leben und Schicksal
der Welt beherrscht; allein diese Gedanken sind vornherein auf die mythi=
sche Darstellung gerichtet; sie werden daher nicht als nackte Lehrsätze vor=
getragen, sondern sind durchaus in Bild und bildliche Handlung gesetzt, ja sie
treten oft ganz in den Hintergrund und überlassen das Feld der absichtloseren
Lust des dichterischen Gestaltens. Die vielen Mythen vom Wechsel der Jahres=
zeiten, des Lichtes und des Dunkels, vom Streite wohlthätiger und verderblicher
Naturkräfte, hängen zwar alle mit jenen Grundgedanken zusammen; soll=

ten aber auch fie durchaus in der Richtung erforſcht werden, Philoſopheme
oder phyſikaliſche Weisheit des Alterthums in ihnen zu ergründen: ſo
würde entweder die Ausbeute ſehr karg ausfallen, man würde unter der
ſinnbildlichen Verhüllung doch oft nur die bekannteſten Naturerſcheinungen
wiederfinden, oder man müßte, wie es wohl auch geſchehen iſt, Anſichten und
Denkweiſe einer viel ſpäteren Zeit in die Erzeugniſſe der früheren hinein-
legen. Der Drang des menſchlichen Geiſtes, ſich mittelſt der ihm eingebo-
renen Vermögen der Außenwelt zu bemächtigen, iſt in philoſophiſchen Zeitaltern vorzugsweiſe durch die Reflexion, in poetiſchen durch die Einbildungskraft thätig. Wie die Natur ſelbſt ihre Spiegel hat, im Waſſer und in der
Luft: ſo will auch die Dichterſeele von den äußeren Dingen ein Gegenbild
innerlich hervorbringen, und dieſe Aneignung für ſich ſchon iſt ein geiſtiger
Genuß, der ſich auch andern Betrachtern des Bildes mittheilt. Gewinnt
ja doch das Bekannteſte in irgend einer Widerſpieglung den Reiz des Fa-
belhaften, und ſtammen wohl eben daher die Wunder des Zauberſpiegels.
Das Innere des Menſchen aber ſtrahlt nichts zurück, ohne es mit ſeinem
eignen Leben, ſeinem Sinnen und Empfinden getränkt und damit mehr oder
weniger umgeſchaffen zu haben. So tauchen aus dem Borne der Phantaſie die Kräfte und die Erſcheinungen der unperſönlichen Natur als Perſonen und Thaten in menſchlicher Weiſe wieder auf. Die nordiſche Mythologie zeigt dieſen Hergang in allen Graden der Belebung und Geſtaltung, und wer ſie in ihrem eignen Sinne würdigen will, muß dieſer Wiedergeburt im Bilde, als ſolcher ſchon, ihre ſelbſtſtändige Geltung einräumen. Gleich den Kräften und Erſcheinungen der Natur ſind aber auch die
des Geiſtes in den Mythen perſönlich geworden: ſelbſt die abgezogenſten
Begriffe, namentlich die Formen und Verhältniſſe der Zeit, haben ſich als
handelnde Weſen geſtaltet. Indem ſo einerſeits die Natur durch Perſoni-
fication beſeelt wird, andererſeits der Geiſt durch daſſelbe Mittel äußere
Geſtaltung erlangt: werden beide fähig, auf dem gleichen Schauplatze ſinn-
bildlicher Darſtellung zuſammenzutreten.

Es macht ſich übrigens wohl fühlbar, daß die nordiſche Mythendichtung
nicht auf die bildende Kunſt gerichtet oder von letzterer beſtimmt war.
Wenn es gleich nicht an Beiſpielen fehlt, daß an heiliger Stätte Götterbilder aufgeſtellt, daß zur Weihung oder zum Schmucke des Hauſes, des
Ehrenſitzes, des Schiffes, des Schildes, Bildwerke aus der Götterwelt angebracht waren, ſo ſpricht doch nichts dafür, daß dieſe Kunſtübung ein all-
gemeineres Bedürfniß des Volkslebens geweſen ſey, oder irgend eine höhere
Stufe der Ausbildung erreicht habe. So blieb die mythiſche Symbolik
von den Bedingungen der künſtleriſchen Darſtellbarkeit unabhängig und nur
denen der innern Anſchauung unterworfen; ihr Inhalt konnte daher auch
nicht in der äußeren Vollendung des Bildes aufgehen. Der Gedanke in

seiner Versinnlichung, der Naturgegenstand in seiner Personification blieb doch zugleich er selbst. Nimmt man hiezu die vorbemerkte Bedeutsamkeit der Namen, so kann es nicht befremden, daß in manchen Fällen die Allegorie ziemlich unverschleiert heraustritt. Der Gebrauch der Sinnbilder erscheint als ein bewußter und ist eben deßhalb ein freierer: derselbe Gegenstand kann in verschiedenen Beziehungen auch unter verschiedenen Namen und Bildern aufgeführt seyn; es können sich Mythengruppen bilden, die unter sich wenig oder äußerlich gar nicht zusammenhängen; es kann selbst Widerspruch zwischen einzelnen Mythen oder mehrfachen Darstellungen des nämlichen Mythus stattfinden. Ob man geneigt sey oder nicht, ein solches Bewußtseyn der Mythenbildung im nordischen Alterthum anzuerkennen, die Thatsache liegt in den Mythen selbst. Diese Mythik ist darum doch nicht in trockenen Abstractionen erstarrt: denn da für Gegenstände der religiösen Weltbetrachtung noch keine andere Weise des Ausdrucks, ja des Denkens selbst, gefunden war als eben die bildliche; so steht der Gedanke doch niemals ausgeschieden neben dem Bilde, wohl aber theilt er den aus der Natur und der menschlichen Erscheinung entnommenen Gebilden seine eigene schrankenlosere Bewegung mit, und so erhält das Natürliche, indem es theils seinen gewohnten, theils fremden und höheren Gesetzen folgt, den Zauber des Wunderbaren, die Mythendichtung im Ganzen aber den Charakter des Tiefsinns und der sicheren Kühnheit.

Jene Thatsache der selbstbewußten oder sich fühlenden Symbolik hebt auch nicht den Glauben an göttliche Persönlichkeit auf, der überall als religiöses Bedürfniß vorauszusetzen ist, nur wird oft schwer zu bestimmen seyn, wo das Sinnbild aufhöre und der wahrhaft persönliche Gott eintrete. Im Allgemeinen befindet diese Frage sich in der Schwebung zwischen der dem sinnlichern Volksglauben und dem herkömmlichen Götterdienste zugewandten Außenseite und dem innersten Sinne des durchgebildeten Mythus. Der Mythenforscher wird somit zwar auch die rohere Volkssage und die zerstreuten Nachrichten über den heidnischen Cultus als Hülfsmittel zu gebrauchen haben, obwohl mit Vorsicht gegen die Befangenheit der christlichen Aufzeichner; stets aber werden ihm die Mythen selbst, sowie der eigentliche Gegenstand der Betrachtung, so auch die Hauptquelle der Erklärung seyn. Hier nun weichen allerdings die Persönlichkeiten größtentheils entweder nach Außen in die Natur oder nach Innen in den Begriff zurück; allein auch die bewußtsinnbildliche Personification zeugt von dem Verlangen und Erfühlen eines lebendigen Gottes, für dessen mannigfaches Walten und Wirken in Natur und Geisteswelt kein anderer Ausdruck genügt, als Gestalt und Bewegung lebendiger, begeisterter Wesen. Diese persönlichen Gestaltungen, besonders die bedeutenderen, durch älteste Ueberlieferung geheiligten, wurden denn auch fortwährend nicht rein bildlich genommen;

sondern sie wirkten mit dem Hauche des göttlichen Lebens, das in ihnen zur Erscheinung kam, und so vermittelte sich der tiefere Geist des Mythus mit der sinnlichern Volksansicht.

Während auf dem angezeigten Wege sich der etymologischen Forschung und der poetischen Anschauung die einzelnen Durchblicke lichten, wird zugleich der vorausgefaßte Gesammteindruck sich bestimmter gestalten, der Geist des Ganzen, von innen herausarbeitend, stets näher und vernehmbarer entgegenkommen und so die Genauigkeit im Besonderen mit der umfassenden Uebersicht zum rechten Verständnisse zusammenwirken.

Diese Bemerkungen über Mittel und Wege der Mythendeutung können zwar nur an der näheren Beleuchtung ihres Gegenstandes selbst sich bewähren; doch schienen sie geeignet, über manches Nachfolgende einleitend zu verständigen und die Wiederkehr allgemeinerer Betrachtungen abzuschneiden.

Die Erforschung des Einzelnen darf sich, wie eben bemerkt, vom Hinblick auf das Ganze, dem Jenes angehört, niemals lossagen; da aber die umfassendere Erkenntniß doch nicht mit einem Schritte zu erlangen ist: so wird es auch zu ihr am sichersten führen, wenn vom Leichteren zum Schwierigeren, vom Helleren zum Dunkleren fortgeschritten wird. Mythen, die im Naturgebiete verkehren, liegen nun gewiß dem Verständniß offener, als solche, die sich auf die innere Welt beziehen: dort sind die stoffartigen und greifbaren Dinge, hier die körperlosen und übersinnlichen. In der nordischen Götterlehre fällt auf diese Seite der Mythus von Odin, auf jene der von Thor; im ersteren Mythenkreise ist vorzugsweise das Geistesleben, im letzteren das Naturleben vergegenwärtigt. Schon die Anerkennug dieser verschiedenen Gebiete und die Auseinanderhaltung dessen, was der einen oder der anderen Seite angehört, ist ein erheblicher Schritt zur richtigen Auffassung des Ganzen. Thor waltet überall in der Natur und befindet sich im unabläßigen und mannigfachsten Zusammenstoße mit den gewaltsamsten Naturkräften, deren mythische Erscheinung denn auch am meisten in die Sinne fällt.

Wolfgang Menzel.

27. Nationalität.

Die Literatur ist in der neuesten Zeit so sehr die glänzendste Erscheinung unserer Nationalität geworden, daß wir diese eher aus jener erklären können, als umgekehrt. Es ist uns beinahe nichts übrig geblieben, wodurch wir unser Daseyn bemerklich machen, als eben Bücher. Wie die Griechen zuletzt durch nichts mehr ausgezeichnet waren, als durch Wissenschaften und

Künste: so haben auch wir nichts mehr was uns würdig machte, den deut=
schen Namen fortzuführen. Leben wir nicht als einige Nation wirklich nur
in Büchern? Versammelt sich das heilige Reich noch irgend anders wo als
auf der Leipziger Messe? Indeß scheint eben darum die geheime Wahlver=
wandtschaft mit den Büchern der tiefste Zug unseres Nationalcharakters:
wir wollen sie die Sinnigkeit nennen.

Schon in den ältesten Zeiten waren die Deutschen eine phantastische Na=
tion, im Mittelalter wurden sie mystisch, jetzt leben sie ganz im Verstande.
Zu allen Zeiten offenbarten sie eine überschwengliche Kraft und Fülle des
Geistes, die aus dem Innern hervorbrach und auf die Aeußerlichkeiten wenig
achtete. Zu allen Zeiten waren die Deutschen im praktischen Leben unbe=
hülflicher als andere Nationen, aber einheimischer in der innern Welt, und
alle ihre nationellen Tugenden und Laster können auf diese Innerlichkeit,
Sinnigkeit, Beschaulichkeit zurückgeführt werden. Sie ist es, die uns jetzt
vorzugsweise zu einem literarischen Volk macht und zugleich unserer Litera=
tur ein eigenthümliches Gepräge aufdrückt. Die Schriften anderer Na=
tionen sind praktischer, weil ihr Leben praktischer ist; die unsrigen haben
einen Anstrich von Uebernatürlichkeit oder Unnatürlichkeit, etwas Geister=
mäßiges, Fremdes, das nicht recht in die Welt passen will, weil wir immer
nur die wunderliche Welt unsres Innern im Auge haben. Wir sind phan=
tastischer als andere Völker, nicht nur weil unsere Phantasie in's Ungeheure
von der Wirklichkeit ausschweift; sondern auch weil wir unsere Träume
für wahr halten. Wie die Einbildungskraft, schweift unser Gefühl aus,
von der albernen Familiensentimentalität bis zur Ueberschwenglichkeit pie=
tistischer Secten. Am weitesten aber schweift der Verstand hinaus in's
Blaue und wir sind als Speculanten und Systemmacher überall verschrieen.
Indem wir aber unsre Theorien nirgends einigermaßen zu realisiren wissen,
als in der Literatur; so geben wir der Welt der Worte ein unverhältniß=
mäßiges Uebergewicht über das Leben selbst, und man nennt uns mit Recht
Bücherwürmer, Pedanten.

Dies ist indeß nur die Schattenseite, über die wir uns allerdings nicht
täuschen wollen. Ihr gegenüber behauptet unser sinniges literarisches
Treiben auch eine lichte Seite, die von den Fremden weit weniger gewürdigt
wird. Wir streben nach allseitiger Bildung des Geistes und bringen der=
selben nicht umsonst unsre Thatkraft und unsern Nationalstolz zum Opfer.
Die Erkenntnisse, die wir gewinnen, dürften dem menschlichen Geschlecht
leicht heilsamer seyn, als noch einige sogenannte große Thaten, und die Lust
von den Fremden zu lernen, dürfte uns mehr Ehre machen als ein Sieg
über dieselben. In unserem Nationalcharakter liegt ein ganz eigner Zug
zur Humanität. Wir wollen alle menschlichen Dinge recht im Mittelpunkt
ergreifen und in der unendlichen Mannigfaltigkeit des Lebens das Räthsel

der verborgenen Einheit lösen. Darum fassen wir das große Werk der Erkenntniß von allen Seiten an: die Natur verleiht uns Sinn für Alles, und unser Geist sammelt aus der größten Weite die Gegenstände seiner Wißbegierde und bringt in die innerste Tiefe aller Mysterien der Natur, des Lebens, der Seele. Es gibt keine Nation von so universellem Geist als die deutsche, und was dem Individuum nicht gelingt, wird in der Mannichfaltigkeit derselben erreicht. An die Masse sind die zahlreichen Organe vertheilt, durch welche die Erkenntniß Allen vermittelt wird.

Die deutsche Sinnigkeit war immer mit einer großen Mannigfaltigkeit eigenthümlicher Geistesblüthen gepaart. Der innere Reichthum schien sich nur in dem Maß entfalten zu können, als er an keine Norm gebunden war. Mehr als in irgend einer andern Nation, hat die Natur in der unsern die unerschöpfliche Fülle eigenthümlicher Geister aufgeschlossen. In keiner Nation gibt es so verschiedene Systeme, Gesinnungen, Neigungen und Talente, so verschiedene Manieren und Style zu denken und zu dichten, zu reden und zu schreiben. Man sieht, es mangelt diesen Geistern an aller Norm und Dressur, sie sind wild aufgewachsen hier und dort, verschieden von Natur und Bildung, und ihr Zusammenfluß in der Literatur gibt eine barocke Mischung. Sie reden in einer Sprache, wie sie unter einem Himmel leben; aber Jeder bringt einen eigenthümlichen Accent mit. Die Natur waltet vor, wie streng auch die Disciplin einzelner Schulen die sogenannte Barbarei ausrotten möchte. Der Deutsche besitzt wenig gesellige Geschmeidigkeit; doch um so stärker ist seine Individualität, und sie will frei sich äußern bis zum Eigensinn und bis zur Caricatur. Das Genie bricht durch alle Dämme und auch bei dem Gemeinen schlägt der Mutterwitz vor. Wenn man die Literatur anderer Völker überschaut; so bemerkt man mehr oder weniger Normalität, oder französische Gartenkunst; nur die deutsche ist ein Wald, eine Wiese voll wilder Gewächse. Jeder Geist ist eine Blume, eigenthümlich an Gestalt, Farbe, Duft. Nur die niedrigsten kommen in ganzen Gattungen vor, und nur die höchsten vereinigen in sich die Bildungen vieler andern; in einigen wird ein großer Theil der Nation gleichsam personificirt, und in seltenen Genien scheint die Menschheit selbst ihr großes Auge aufzuschlagen, Genien, die auf der Höhe des Geschlechts stehen und das Gesetz offenbaren, das in den Massen schlummert.

Der Genius wird immer nur geboren, und die reichen Originalitäten in der deutschen Geisterwelt sind unmittelbare Wirkungen der Natur. Mittelbar mag die große Verschiedenheit der deutschen Stämme, Stände, Bildungsstufen, durch die Erziehung und das Leben auf die Schriftsteller wirken; aber diese Verschiedenheit ist selbst nur eine Folge der Volksnatur. Diese hat unter allen Verhältnissen die Normalität unmöglich gemacht. Unter allen Völkern bot das deutsche von jeher die reichste Mannigfaltig-

keit, Gliederung und Abſtufung dar, wie äußerlich, ſo geiſtig. Dieſe Man=
nigfaltigkeit iſt durch die ewig junge Naturkraft von unten her aus dem
Volk beſtändig genährt worden und hat ſich nie einer von oben her gebote=
nen Regelmäßigkeit gefügt.   Mit ihr iſt zugleich alles Herrliche, was den
deutſchen Geiſt ausgezeichnet, von unten frei und wild hervorgewachſen.

Nur eins iſt der Maſſe unſerer Schriftſteller gemeinſam: die wenige
Rückſicht auf das praktiſche Leben, das Ueberwiegen der innern Beſchaulich=
keit; doch ſind gerade dadurch die Anſichten um ſo mehr vervielfältigt wor=
den.   In den engen Schranken des praktiſchen Lebens hätten ſich die Gei=
ſter in wenige Parteien und für einfache Zwecke vereinigen müſſen. In der
unendlichen Welt der Phantaſie und Speculation aber fand jeder eigen=
thümliche Geiſt den freieſten Spielraum.   Der Deutſche ſucht inſtinctartig
dies freie Element.   Kaum gehen wir einmal aus dem Traum heraus und
erfaſſen das praktiſche Leben, ſo geſchieht es nur, um es wieder in das Ge=
biet der Phantaſie und der Theorien zu ziehen; während umgekehrt die
Franzoſen von der Speculation und Einbildungskraft nur die Hebel für
das öffentliche Leben borgen.   Der Franzoſe braucht eine naturphiloſophi=
ſche Idee, um ſie auf die Medicin oder Fabrikation anzuwenden; der Deut=
ſche braucht die phyſikaliſchen Erfahrungen am liebſten, um wundervolle
Hypotheſen darauf zu bauen.   Der Franzoſe erfindet Tragödien, um auf
den politiſchen Sinn der Nation zu wirken; dem Deutſchen blieben von ſei=
nen Thaten und Erfahrungen eben nur Tragödien.   Die Franzoſen haben
eine arme Sprache, doch treffliche Redner; wir könnten weit beſſer ſprechen,
doch wir ſchreiben nur.   Jene reden, weil ſie handeln; wir ſchreiben, weil
wir nur denken.

Das originelle, phyſiognomiſche, aller Normalität widerſtrebende Weſen
in der deutſchen Literatur iſt noch immer wie in der Zeit der Chroniken,
wahre Naivetät, mehr als mancher Autor, der Griechen, Römer, Engländ=
der oder Franzoſen im Auge gehabt, ſelbſt wiſſen mag.   Wenn ſich nun
aber auch dieſe Naivetät der deutſchen Schriften ſtreng nachweiſen läßt,
ſo darf man doch damit ja nicht die ſogenannte deutſche Ehrlichkeit ver=
wechſeln.   Allerdings herrſcht noch eine große Gutmüthigkeit und Redlich=
keit unter den Autoren, und ſie ließe ſich ſchon aus dem eiſernen, wenn auch
oft fruchtloſen Fleiße und aus der Weitläuftigkeit, aus dem ſichtbaren Be=
ſtreben nach deutlicher Belehrung erkennen, wenn man auch den vielen Ver=
ſicherungen von Ehrlichkeit, und Liebe mit Recht mißtrauen dürfte.   Aber
eben dieſe ſentimentalen Schwüre zeigen nur zu deutlich, daß wir den
Stand der Unſchuld bereits verlaſſen haben.   Die deutſche Sprache iſt der
vollkommene Ausdruck des deutſchen Charakters.   Sie iſt dem Geiſt in
allen Tiefen und in dem weiteſten Umfang gefolgt.   Sie entſpricht vollkom=
men der Mannigfaltigkeit der Geiſter und hat jedem den eigenthümlichen

Ton gewährt, der ihn schärfer auszeichnet, als irgend eine andere Sprache vermöchte. Die Sprache selbst gewinnt durch diese Mannigfaltigkeit des Gebrauchs. Das bunte Wesen und die Vielgestaltigkeit ist ihr eigen und steht ihr schön. Ein Blumenfeld ist edler als ein einfaches Grasfeld, und gerade die schönsten Länder haben den reichsten Wechsel von Gegenden und Temperaturen. Alle Versuche, den deutschen Schriftstellern einen Normalsprachgebrauch aufzudrängen, sind schmählich gescheitert, weil sie der Natur widerstrebten. Jeder Autor schreibt, wie er mag. Jeder kann von sich mit Goethe sagen: „ich singe wie der Vogel singt, der auf den Zweigen lebt."

Es ist gewiß ein nationeller Zug, daß unsere Gelehrten und Dichter sogar noch keine durchgreifende Rechtschreibung haben, und, daß uns dies so selten auffällt. Wie viele Wörter werden nicht bald so, bald anders geschrieben, wie viele Willkühr herrscht in den zusammengesetzten Wörtern! und wer tadelt es, als hin und wieder die Grammatiker, von denen sich die Autoren so wenig belehren lassen, als die Künstler von den Aesthetikern.

Die grammatische Mannigfaltigkeit erscheint aber nur unbedeutend gegen die rhetorische und poetische, gegen den unendlichen Reichthum in Styl und Manier, worin uns kein Volk auf Erden gleich kommt. Es mag dahin gestellt seyn, ob keine andere Sprache so viel Physiognomik zuläßt; gewiß aber ist, daß in keiner so viel Physiognomik wirklich ausgedrückt wird. Diese ungebundene Weise der Aeußerung ist uns mit so manchem andern Zug unserer Natur aus den Wäldern angestammt, und auf ihr beruht die ganze freie Herrlichkeit unserer Poesie. Je besser der Conversationston, desto elender die Dichter, wie in Frankreich. Je schlechter der Kanzleistyl, desto origineller die Dichter, wie in Deutschland. Jeder neue Adelung wird vor einem neuen Goethe, Schiller, Tieck zu Spott werden. Titanen brauchen keine Fechtschule, weil sie doch jede Parade durchschlagen. Den großen Dichter und Denker hält sein Genie, den gemeinen seine angeborne Natur, alle der gänzliche Mangel einer Regel, eines gesetzgebenden Geschmacks und eines richtenden Publikums von dem Zwang einer attischen oder parisischen Censur entfernt.

Im Ganzen hat die deutsche Sprache im Fortschritt der Zeit auf der einen Seite gewonnen, auf der andern verloren. Die Reinheit, eine Menge Stammwörter, einen bewundernswürdigen Reichthum von feinen und wohllautenden Biegungen hat sie seit einem halben Jahrtausend verloren. Dagegen hat sie von dem, was ihr übrig geblieben, einen desto bessern Gebrauch gemacht. In der jetzt ärmern und klanglosern Sprache ist unendlich viel gedacht und gedichtet worden, das uns die verlornen Laute vermissen läßt. Ausgezeichnete Meister haben aber auch diese neue hochdeutsche Sprache durch Virtuosität des Gebrauchs zu einer eigenthümlichen

Schönheit zu bilden gewußt, und man hat angefangen, sie sogar auf's
Neue aus dem Schatz der Vorzeit zu schmücken. Es gehört nicht zu den
geringsten Verdiensten der Romantiker, daß sie die deutsche Sprache wieder
auf den alten Ton gestimmt haben, so weit es ihre gegenwärtige Instru=
mentation vertragen kann.

Diese lebendige, organische Wiedergeburt der reinen alten Sprache, durch
welche die fremden Schmarotzergewächse verdrängt werden, ist das schönste
Zeugniß von der angebornen Kraft unserer Nationalität, im Gegensatz
gegen die affectirte Kraft, womit wir es den Fremden gleich zu thun gestrebt
haben. Diese organische Entwickelung der deutschen Ursprache stellt zu=
gleich die mechanischen Versuche der Puristen gänzlich in den Schatten.
Nichts ist kläglicher als jener Purismus eines Campe und Anderer, welche
die aus der Philosophie verschwundene Atomenlehre noch einmal in der
Grammatik aufzufrischen und die atomistischen deutschen Silben nach einer
Cohärenz, die nicht im Organismus deutscher Sprachbildung, sondern nur
in der Analogie des fremden Wortes lag, zusammen zu schmieden versuch=
ten, die uns Wörter aus Sylben machten, wie Voß aus Wörtern eine
Sprache machte, die weder deutsch noch griechisch war, und die man erst
wieder in's Griechische übersetzen mußte, um sie zu verstehen.

Der Purismus ist löblich, wenn er uns denselben Begriff, den ein frem=
des Wort ausdrückt, ebenso umfassend und verständlich durch ein deutsches
ausdrücken lehrt, jederzeit aber zu verwerfen, wenn das fremde Wort um=
fassender oder verständlicher ist, oder wenn es einen unsrer Sprache gänz=
lich fremden Begriff bezeichnet: denn Mittheilung der Begriffe ist der erste
Zweck der Sprache, Deutlichkeit der Wörter das Mittel dazu. Wenn wir
nur unsere Begriffe durch einen fremden vermehren, so laßt uns immer das
fremde Wort dazu nehmen. Das Denken soll nicht verarmen, damit die
Sprache mit Reinheit prahlen könne.

Wenn der falsche Purismus zu verwerfen ist, so ist doch der wahre, wie
ihn schon Luther kräftig gehandhabt, höchst verdienstlich. Allerdings giebt
es unter den fremden Wörtern, die wir als das Kleid fremder und neuer
Begriffe ehren müssen, noch eine Menge anderer, die sich statt eben so guten
und desfalls für uns besserer, deutscher Wörter eingeschlichen haben, die
ganz bekannte alte Begriffe ausdrücken, und nur aus einer lächerlichen Ei=
telkeit oder Neuerungssucht von uns gebraucht werden. Der Gelehrte will
zeigen, daß er in alten Sprachen bewandert ist; der Reisende, daß er
fremde Zungen gehört hat; das übrige Volk, daß es mit weisen und erfah=
renen Menschen oder Büchern bekannt ist; oder die Vornehmeren wollen
ihre höheren Begriffe auch in einer fremden Sprache von der Denkungsart
des Pöbels geschieden wissen; und der Pöbel thut vornehm, indem er ihnen
die fremden Laute nachäfft. So ungefähr ist die deutsche Sprachmengerei

entſtanden, ſofern ſie nicht nothwendig mit fremden Begriffen auch fremde
Wörter borgen mußte, und ſo iſt ſie durchaus verwerflich, ein Schandfleck
der Nation und ihrer Literatur. Möchten die Puriſten uns für immer davon befreien können! Jedes Jahrhundert befreit uns wenigſtens von der
Thorheit der vorhergehenden. Klopſtock bemerkt ſehr richtig: „Zu Karl's
V. Zeiten miſchte man ſpaniſche Worte ein, vermuthlich aus Dankbarkeit
für den ſchönen kaiſerlichen Gedanken, daß die deutſche Sprache eine Pferde-
ſprache ſey, und damit ihm die Deutſchen etwas ſanfter wiehern möchten.
Wie es dieſen Worten ergangen iſt, wiſſen wir und ſehen daraus zugleich,
wie es künftig allen heutigstägigen Einmiſchungen ergehen werde, ſo arg
nämlich, daß dann einer kommen und erzählen muß, aus der oder der
Sprache wäre damals, zu unſrer Zeit nämlich, auch wieder eingemiſcht
worden; aber die Sprache, die das nun einmal ſchlechterdings nicht vertragen konnte, hätte auch damals wieder Uebelkeiten bekommen.“

Iſt nun aber auch die deutſche Sprache ſiegreich aus den Kämpfen mit
andern Sprachen hervorgegangen, ſo hat ſie doch darüber Manches an ihrer
innern Ausbildung vernachläßigt. In dem Zeitalter zwiſchen Luther und
Leſſing, alſo gerade in der Periode jenes Kampfes, drückte die vorüber-
gehende Langeweile der Zeit der deutſchen Sprache einen bleibenden Ausdruck von Phlegma auf. Aus dieſer Zeit ſtammt nämlich die heilloſe
Phraſeologie, die auf's Umſtändlichſte mit mehreren Wörtern ſagt, was ſie
weit einfacher und kräftiger mit einem einzigen ſagen würde, z. B. in Anſpruch nehmen, anſtatt anſprechen; in Unterſuchung ziehen, anſtatt unterſuchen; in Verſuchung führen, ſtatt verſuchen; in Anſchlag bringen, ſtatt
anrechnen u.ſ.w.

Wenn man dieſe weitſchweiſigen Phraſen aufgiebt, den Gebrauch des
„haben, ſeyn und werden“ durch erlaubte Auslaſſung möglichſt einſchränkt
und ſtatt der mißtönigen Imperfecte und Participien, z. B. fragte, biegte,
wägte, gedingt, entſprießt ꝛc. die vollautenden „frug, bog, wog, gedungen,
entſproſſen ꝛc.“ gebraucht, ſo muß unſere heute einmal übliche Sprachweiſe
um Vieles verſchönert werden.

Ein anderer Uebelſtand, der aus derſelben Zeit herrührt, iſt die Ueber-
treibung der gelehrten Terminologie. Man leſe manches philoſophiſche
Werk und frage ſich, ob es je in der Welt eine Nation geben wird, die eine
ſolche Sprache als die ihrige anerkennen würde.

Zwar hat ſich die deutſche Sprache ſeit Leſſing und Wieland und insbe-
ſondere im gegenwärtigen Jahrhundert ſehr ausgebildet, hat je mehr und
mehr dem alten langweiligen Phlegma und der gelehrten Pedanterei ent-
ſagt, iſt elaſtiſch und fließend worden und erfreut ſich namentlich eines
ſchnelleren Rhythmus; allein es ſcheint mir doch nicht, als ob ſie auf der
gegenwärtigen Stufe der Entwicklung werde ſtehen bleiben, und ich ſehe

im Geist den Leser lächeln, dem vielleicht nach fünfhundert Jahren einmal dieses Buch in die Hände und diese Stelle in die Augen fällt.

Der deutsche Genius und das deutsche Verdienst ist übrigens nicht von der Sprache abhängig. Mit Ausnahme der Poesie ist fast Alles, was die deutsche Literatur vor der Reformation in wissenschaftlicher Hinsicht Großes geleistet hat, lateinisch geschrieben, ohne darum weniger deutsch zu seyn. Zwar empfingen unsere Ahnen im Mittelalter wie die lateinische Sprache, so auch mit ihr die erste wissenschaftliche Anregung; aber sie bildeten dieselbe allmählig sehr eigenthümlich aus in dem naiven Styl der Chroniken, in den tiefsinnigen Systemen der Mystik, in den wunderbaren Naturansichten, in der gothischen Kunst und in der Legislatur und Jurisprudenz. Hier liegt im lateinischen Wort überall der deutsche Geist, und ich möchte daher nicht wie Wachter und Andre die lateinisch geschriebenen Werke unsrer Vorfahren von der deutschen Nationalliteratur ausschließen, wenn ich hier überhaupt von unsrer älteren Literatur handeln wollte.

Georg Gottfried Gervinus.

28. Regeneration der Poesie unter den Einflüssen der religiösen und weltlichen Moral, und der Kritik.

Wir sind bei dem Zeitraume angelangt, zu dem unsere Erzählung von allem Anfang an als zu ihrem Haupt- und Zielpunkte hingedrängt. Es ist die Zeit, wo unsere Dichtung jene Grade der Ausbildung erhielt, die ihr bei dem Auslande Stimme und Geltung verschafften, die sie befähigten mit den Literaturen der übrigen europäischen Nationen zu wetteifern und Einflüsse auf die Gestaltung der nordischen, der englischen, französischen und italienischen Poesien zu üben, wie sie ehmals diese auf die deutsche ihrerseits geübt hatten. Was ihr diesen Werth zu geben half und diese Wirkungen wesentlich erleichterte, war allerdings, daß sie die Zeitumstände begünstigten, indem sie ihre Blüthe entfaltete, als die der übrigen europäischen Literaturen vorüber war. War dies ein Vortheil, so war es doch keiner, den wir vor Anderen vorausgehabt hätten. Denn auch die anderen Literaturepochen der gebildeten Völker Europa's hatten zu ihrer Zeit keine gleichzeitigen Widerstände zu bekämpfen; nur die Höhepunkte der englischen und spanischen Poesie berührten sich der Zeit nach, sie haben sich aber grade dem Wesen und den Einflüssen nach so gut wie gar nicht berührt. Diese successive Folge der italienischen, spanischen, englischen, französischen und deutschen Literatur schreibt sich daher, daß die Entwickelung des europäischen Völkerkörpers nur eine gemeinsame ist, in der jene Glanzperioden

der jeweiligen Nationen, welche ihre Geschichte und Bildung vertreten und
darstellen, in einer nothwendigen Reihe liegen. Dies stellt sich in Bezug
auf die obige Folge der europäischen Dichtungen sehr einfach dar, sobald
wir das Drama als die eigenthümliche Gattung der neueren Zeit vorzugsweise
in's Auge fassen. Wir verlangen von jedem Kunstwerke, das auf einige
Vollkommenheit Anspruch macht, daß es den zwei contrastirenden Anforderungen an Natur und Cultur gleichmäßig genüge, und wir fanden im
Mittelalter darum so Weniges nach unserm Geschmacke, weil gewöhnlich
beiden Anforderungen nicht entsprochen war. Als Ariosto in Italien dich-
tete, fiel dies in die günstige Zeit, wo ein verjüngendes Naturleben durch
Europa fuhr, zugleich als die antike Bildung erweckt wurde. Wirklich
läßt sich weder Natur noch Cultur dem Sänger des rasenden Roland ab-
sprechen, allein Italien wandte sich damit, rückwärts schauend, auf die mittelalterlichen Epopöen und bildete ein eigenthümliches selbstständiges Drama
gar nicht aus. Spanien warf sich dagegen mit Macht auf diese neue Gattung, allein es blieb innerhalb derselben, weil es den europäischen Einflüssen allzusehr entzogen war, auf den mittelalterigen Ideen hängen und
konnte weder eine Cultur, noch eine Natur darin entwickeln, die der fort-
gehenden Bildung Europa's genügt hätte. Ein frischer Naturhauch durchdringt die englischen Schauspiele und hat ihnen bei jener reinen germanischen Hälfte Europa's, die Natur vor Kunst schätzt, die begeisterte Liebe
erwirkt, jener anderen aber, die in der Kunst die Formen vielleicht zu sehr
vor dem Inhalt achtet, hat der Mangel einer feineren Cultur sie ebenso
entfremdet gehalten. Ihr Gegensatz sind die französischen. Wie groß
der Mangel an Natur in ihnen ist, so hat sie doch eine gewisse Cultur immer auf allen Bühnen erhalten, und vorzugsweise auf jenen, die sich mit
dem englischen Drama nicht befreunden konnten. Das deutsche Schauspiel erst hat eigentlich jene harmonische Verbindung von Cultur und Natur dargestellt, auf die auch unsere ersten Dichter, bei denen beides Lieb-
lingsausdrücke waren, mit Bewußtseyn hinarbeiteten. Nachdem Göthe sich
in den gegensätzlichen Formen der Engländer und Griechen mit eigener
Freiheit versucht hatte, schmolz sie Schiller mit noch größerer Eigenthümlichkeit zusammen, und stellte sich in seiner dramatischen Architektur haar-
scharf in die Mitte von Shakspeare und Sophokles. Wann und wo auch
das Trauerspiel in den nächsten Zeiten sich fortpflanzte oder fortpflanzen
wird, da wird es sich der Form, die ihm Schiller gegeben hat, nur mit der
größten Gefahr entziehen dürfen.

Wenn diese Verbindung der dagewesenen Formen die Versöhnung strei-
tender Requisite, die Accommodation an die Dichtungen aller Zeiten und
Völker, die Höhe der Zeit, in der sich unsere Literatur ausbildete, ihr einen
so entschiedenen Werth vor allen anderen giebt, so sollte man denken, eben

dieſe Vorzüge müßten ihr auch eine noch größere erobernde Kraft mitthei=
len, als die übrigen Literaturen ihrer Zeit entwickelt haben und ſie ſelbſt
bisher kund gegeben. Allein, einmal hat das Beiſpiel von Frankreich ge=
zeigt, daß die größten literariſchen Eroberungen nach Außen zu machen, die
kriegeriſchen ganz beſonders behülflich ſind, und auf dieſen Beiſtand hat
denn die unſere wohl am wenigſten zu rechnen. Dann aber liegt auch in
dem Charakter unſerer Dichtung ſelbſt, was ſie ſchwerlich jemals anderen
Nationen anders zugänglich machen wird, als wenn zugleich mit ihr unſere
ſämmtliche Bildungsweiſe übertragen werden könnte. Wenn jene vorhin
berührten Eigenſchaften, jenes Anlehnen, jener Aufbau auf allen älteren
Literaturen ihr einen Charakter der Univerſalität geben, ſo trägt ſie dage=
gen auf der andern Seite einen eben ſo nationalen und eigenthümlichen
Zug, den ſie mit keiner andern vielleicht als der griechiſchen Dichtung theilt,
und der neben und mit jener Univerſalität ihr merkwürdigſtes Unterſchei=
dungszeichen bildet. Unſere Poeſie nämlich ſtand von jeher weit weniger
iſolirt als in andern Ländern, und beſonders im vorigen Jahrhundert griff
ſie mit ungemeinen Folgen in alle Fächer des Lebens und der Wiſſenſchaf=
ten ein und verzweigte ſich nach allen Richtungen mit den Beſtrebungen der
Zeit. Klopſtock wirkte auf die Religion, Wieland auf praktiſche Philoſo=
phie, Leſſing auf die geſammte Wiſſenſchaftlichkeit, Voß auf Philologie
und Alterthumskunde, Herder auf Geſchichte und Theologie. Bei Goethe
und Schiller fragen wir mehr nach Lebensanſichten faſt als nach Poeſie,
und wir behandeln ſie als Philoſophen, als Vertreter ganzer Richtungen
nicht der Dichtung ſowohl als des Geſammtlebens. Weder Lope noch
Cervantes, nicht Shakſpeare und nicht Corneille haben ſo ſcharfe Lebens=
tendenzen in ſolchem Maße aufgeregt, und man ließ auch überall die Le=
bensgeſchichte dieſer Dichter fallen, während bei uns ein gleiches Intereſſe
um biographiſche Notizen und um Nachleſe von Poeſieen fortwährend
eifert. Dieſe auffallende Verſchiedenheit unſerer Literatur rührt daher,
daß dieſe bei uns das ganze Leben der Nation gleichſam ausfüllte. Shak=
ſpeare ſtand neben Eliſabeth und England's junger Nationalmacht, Cer=
vantes und Lope dichteten, als Carl V. und Philipp II. die ganze Welt
umſpannten, Racine und Moliere, als Ludwig XIV. mit ſeinem Glanze
Alles verdunkelte. Dies ſpornte die Dichtung, ſich den großen Nationalbe=
gebenheiten gleich zu ſtellen, aber ſie konnte ſie nicht überragen! Wie an=
ders in Deutſchland! Der große Friedrich, von dem herrſchenden literari=
ſchen Geiſte des Jahrhunderts mitgeriſſen, meinte auch als Schriftſteller
groß ſeyn zu müſſen, ließ ſich gleichſam in einen Kampf mit der deutſchen
Literatur ein und unterlag vollkommen. Kaiſer Joſeph ließ ſich von eben
dieſem Geiſte verführen, nach deſſen Forderungen Politik und Regierungs=
weiſe zu richten, und verlor ſich in mannichfaltige Irren. Wir hatten in

Deutschland, wie noch jetzt, keine Geschichte, keinen Staat, keine Politik, wir hatten nur Literatur, nur Wissenschaft und Kunst. Sie überflügelte Alles, sie herrschte und siegte allerwege, sie dominirte daher in allen Bestrebungen der Zeit.

Diese großen Wirkungen machte unsere Literatur nur aus dem Trieb der eigenen Lebenskraft, sie war von dem ganzen Theile der Nation gefördert, der sich thätig oder empfangend für sie interessirte; kein Hof und keine Academie konnte dabei ein vorragendes Gewicht und Ansehen gewinnen, keine Nebenabsichten auf ästhetischen Luxus haben ihr falschen Glanz geliehen. Daher kommt es, daß sie eben so merkwürdig von anderen Literaturen durch jenen Charakter der Schrankenlosigkeit und Ungebundenheit unterschieden ist, den ihr das junge Naturleben, zu dem sie ungehindert aufschoß, mittheilte; und bis auf den heutigen Tag blieb unseren Literaten und literarischen Blättern der Ton der Freiheit und Rücksichtslosigkeit, der im vorigen Jahrhundert von tausend Kämpfen genährt ward, als ein Rest, ja als Fortdauer jenes revolutionären Umschwungs, dem wir das neue Leben Deutschlands allein zu danken haben, ohne dessen Vorausgang die französischen Einflüsse während des Kaiserreichs bei uns so wirkungslos vorübergegangen seyn würden, wie in Italien und Spanien. Es giebt nichts Großartigeres als das Schauspiel der geistigen Umwälzung; es setzt unsere Geschichte im vorigen Jahrhundert in den großen Verband mit den Weltbegebenheiten in Amerika und Frankreich und zeigt, nur in einem anderen Gebiete, dieselben Ideen, die übrigens auch bei uns außer einem ganz neuen Gesichtskreise der Bildung neue Staatsordnungen und eine neue Lebensordnung hervorriefen. Keine Literargeschichte einer anderen neueren Nation hat eine ähnliche Gestaltung und Entwickelung erfahren. Zwar die italienische im 15. und 16. Jahrhundert stellt in gleich großartiger Fülle einen ähnlichen Reichthum neuer Bildung dar; allein es war diese nur die Vollendung einer alten Civilisation, nicht der Beginn einer neuen. Auch Frankreich's wissenschaftliche Literatur im 17. und 18. Jahrhundert hat einen analogen Revolutionscharakter gehabt und war die natürliche Vorläuferin der späteren politischen Umwälzung; allein es ist grade das Schöne in unserer deutschen literarischen Bewegung, daß nicht die Religion oder Philosophie, die leicht fanatisiren, sondern daß die Dichtkunst der vorherrschende Zweig war, die überall mildert und versöhnt. An die Geschichte der Poesie muß also die Geschichte dieser Umwälzung geknüpft werden, obgleich dies nicht anders geschehen kann, als wenn wir gelegentlich auch auf andere Gebiete, der Theologie und Pädagogik, der Geschichte und Philosophie wenigstens hinüberblicken. Denn die Bewegung der Geister war durchaus eine gemeinsame und allgemeine, wie wir vorher schon andeuteten, und selbst die reinsten Dichtergenien konnten sich Thätigkeiten, die der Dichtung fremd waren, nicht entziehen. Unter diesen hat Schiller, dessen Seele allen feinsten Einwirkungen der historischen Witterung offen stand, sogar die Bedeutung unserer Dichtung für eine künftige politische Wiedergeburt mit einer merkwürdigen Ahnungsgabe vorausgesehen.

Den Revolutionscharakter unserer Literatur im vorigen Jahrhundert hat man bisher kaum im Allgemeinen nur erkannt; geschildert ist jene Bewegung, ihrem inneren Zusammhange nach, noch gar nicht worden, weil wir noch keine Literargeschichte hatten, die eigentlich das wäre, was sie ihrem Namen nach seyn will: Geschichte. Und es war doch so leicht, nur mit Uebertragung der Symptome einer politischen Revolution die ähnlichen Erscheinungen in unserem Literaturstaate zu gliedern. Freilich gehörte dazu erst eine Art des Ueberblicks derselben, wie wir ihn nicht gewohnt sind und wie er uns eben daher so schwer wird; ein Ueberblick, der auf jedes Buch wie auf eine Begebenheit, auf jeden Autor wie auf einen handelnden Menschen, auf kritische Urtheile wie auf Wirkungen des Geschehenen hinsähe, der also eine historische, chronologische Lectüre bedingte, nicht eine ästhetische und einfach genießende. Sollte ich also diese geschichtliche Betrachtung unserer Literatur hier übersichtlich erleichtern, so würde ich mich am kürzesten entschließen, jene Analogie zu skizziren, obwohl ich reichlich weiß, wie leicht eine solche Vergleichung mißdeutet oder durch Mißdeutung lächerlich wird. Ich würde also erinnern, daß unsere Poesie seit dem 16. Jahrhundert in den Händen der privilegirten Stände war, unter Geistlichen und Adel. Zuletzt noch werden wir sehen, daß selbst jene weltlichen Gelehrten, die aus den Leipziger Schulen wirken, dieser Verbindung mit Adel und Höfen sehnsüchtig nachstreben. Gegen eben diese beginnt nun zuerst eine durchaus bürgerliche Reaction von zwei Republiken aus, Hamburg und Zürich. Auf der Höhe dieser ersten Bewegungen steht Klopstock, der zwar vornehm und aristokratisch war, aber auch herablassend und frei, zwar noch gleichsam innerhalb des privilegirten Standes der Geistlichen sich bewegte, aber ein durchaus neues und populäres Element mitbrachte: Empfindsamkeit. Das Wesen der vornehmen Adels- und Hofdichtung war Esprit und Verstandesweisheit, das Eigenthum der höheren Stände; die Empfindung aber ist durchaus in den unteren Regionen herrschender. Eine Weile riß diese neue Richtung andächtiger Empfindsamkeit Alles mit, bis sich Wieland losfagte und sich etwas dem Verständigen wieder zuneigte, und sogleich auch eine annähernde Bewegung nach dem Hofe, nach dem Adel, nach Akademieen machte. Mit diesem Charakter seiner Werke steht sein persönlicher, durchaus schlicht und bürgerlicher fast ganz im Widerspruch, und so mischen sich in ihm und Klopstock offenbar die streitendsten Elemente: Klopstock lehnte sich an Höfe und Republiken zugleich, war Volksmann und Fürstendiener, und im Anfang ein ebenso begeisterter Vertheidiger als später ein zelotischer Gegner der französischen Revolution; Wieland suchte sich ähnlich mit Allen zu halten und predigt bald zu Jacobi's Aerger Ma=chiavellische Grundsätze, bald stellt er das Bild von Idealstaaten auf, die auf Menschenrechte und Tugend gegründet sind. Nun kommt Lessing: der eigentliche Beschwörer des jungen Geistes, der Deutschland erneute. Zwar dem gelehrten Stande angehörig, warf er das Standeskleid verachtend von sich, verschmähte, ob zwar in Büchern lebend, die Buchweisheit, brachte die gelehrtesten Gegenstände in der ungelehrtesten Behandlung vor's Volk, und statt auf Akademieen hinzusteuern, schreckte er vielleicht Maria Theresia von ihren Planen, die dahin gingen, ab. Er zerstörte alle die abgelebten poeti=schen Gattungen, die (wie das Lehrgedicht) nur Bedeutung für die oberen Stände hatten und warf sich mit aller Macht seines kolossalen Geistes auf das Schauspiel, nicht auf ein geschriebenes, sondern auf ein zur Verwirk=lichung und Darstellung gekommenes, auf die Bühne. Das Theater ist das eigentliche constitutionelle Gebäude in dem Reiche der Poesie, wenn es — wie Lessing strebte — Nationaltheater wird. Als Nationaltheater tra=ten die in Hamburg und Mannheim auf, zu denen Lessing mitwirken sollte, und Joseph taufte sein Hoftheater mit diesem populären Namen um. Les=sing brauchte keine Höfe mehr für die deutsche Literatur, wenn er für diese Form Sinn in dem Volke fand, wenn ihm gelang die Bühne als Vereini=gungspunkt der Nation zu gründen, wo die ausübenden, gesetzgebenden und richterlichen Gewalten geschieden sind, wo alle Stände in richtiger Gleich=stellung sitzen, für Jeden gesorgt wird und Jeder freies Stimmrecht hat. Es war uns eine Nationaldichtung gesichert, wenn die Nation diesen großen Mann in seinen Reformen nicht verließ! Aber sie verließ ihn! Er schei=terte in Hamburg an der Gleichgültigkeit des Volkes, gab die Bühne auf und hielt es nun für nöthig, fundamentaler, Alles, was die Kunstblüthe un=ter uns hemmte, wegzuräumen. Er griff daher die Orthodoxie an, die der Dichtung und besonders dem Theater entgegen waren, und ebenso das ver=ständige Prinzip in der bisherigen Poesie. Er legte jenes denkwürdige Zeugniß gegen seine eigene kritische Dichtung ab und ließ hinfort dem Ja=cobinismus in unserer Literatur, an dem er nicht Theil haben konnte, schweigend und nicht ohne geheimes Wohlgefallen den Lauf. Eine ganz neue Welt zerstörte nun hereinbrechend die alte. Die Vertreter der frühe=ren Dichtung, Haller, Klopstock und Andere traten ab, Wieland, wie vor=sichtig er lavirte, entging nicht heftigen Angriffen, selbst Lessing's Stellung ward hier und da über seinen Werken vergessen, die nach dem alten Regime schmeckten. In allen Fächern quoll nun ein neuer Geist heraus, anregend mehr als vollendend, und Herder ist der eigentliche Repräsentant dieser Zeit, der die Leidenschaft zuerst losband und gegen Alles, was dem alten Kastenwe=sen ähnlich war, gegen die Schulgelehrten, gegen die Schulpoeten, gegen die amtsstolzen Geistlichen, gegen jeden Druck und Usurpation gleich in frühester Jugend gewaffnet stand. Er brachte Schwung zu allen Wissenschaften, Vorliebe zur urältesten und einfachsten Dichtung des Volks, Freiheit der Forschung in Religionsdingen in vollen Händen mit. Die Jugend bemächtigte sich der ganzen Literatur, ein republikanischer Geist riß selbst jene Stolberge und Aehnliche, die ihrem Stand und Wesen nach den Privilegirten angehörten in den demagogischen Schwindel mit; die unerhörteste Preßfreiheit herrschte in den Journalen, in denen jener ungeheure Kampf geführt ward, Aller gegen Alle, wo Sentimentalität mit Humor, Patriotismus mit Weltbürgerthum, Mysticismus mit Freigeisterei, Originalität mit Classicismus, die gesammte Poesie mit dem Einfluß und Gegenstoß der Wissenschaften und der Weltbegebenheiten stritt, wo kalte Vernunft und prophetischer Enthusiasmus, Menschenverstand und Empfindsamkeit, Einfalt und Unnatur, Rücksichtslosigkeit und Pietät, Geschmack und Rohheit oft auf's Härteste sich stießen, oft auf's Wunderlichste nebeneinander lagen. Der Despotismus des französischen Geschmacks allein war es, was gemeinsam von Freund und Feind in diesen Bewegungen niedergeworfen ward, in denen die Einwirkungen von England her die wichtigste Rolle spielten. Es war eine eigentliche Schreckenszeit, jene Periode der Originalgenies, die jedes Herkommen verachteten, jede Autorität mit Füßen traten, auf dem erschütterten Ansehen Gellert's und Klopstock's der kaum erst allgemein angegriffenen Freigeisterei Altäre errichteten, die in der Poesie alles Gesetz und jede Regel verwarfen. Verknöchert und festgestanden dauerte der Charakter dieser sentimental-humoristischen, elegisch-satirischen Zeit in Jean Paul fort, dessen ganzes Wesen durchaus nur hier begründet ist, und er schlingt sich von dort an, durch die Wetzel, Falk und ähnliche Satiriker und misantropische Menschenfreunde bis auf die heutigen politisch-literarischen Freiheitsmänner herüber, welche Verbindung denn mit der ganzen schriftstellerischen und menschlichen Art der jetzigen Jugend wohl zeigt, daß wir die revolutionäre Stimmung noch nicht erstickt haben. Mitten in den Umwälzungen dieser Zeiten war auch das Drama nicht eben verschwunden, wohl aber von wilderen Gattungen und noch populäreren, von dem Romane, von der Prosa überfluthet. Allmählig besann man sich jetzt. Herder kehrte zurück und suchte Bande zwischen Regel und Freiheit zu knüpfen: Wien fiel ganz ab und warf sich wieder auf den französischen Theatergeschmack; von jenen aristokratischen Freiheitsmännern in Göttingen ging die feine Reaction des Classicismus aus, und die größte Persönlichkeit unter den jungen Dichtern jener Generation, Goethe, der vorhin ganz in dem demagogischen Sinne mitgewirkt hatte, ging dahin über. Ein Prinzip der Mäßigung faßte mitten unter den dauernden Stürmen Fuß. Zu Goethe gesellte sich Schiller. Sie waren schon ihren Schicksalen nach zweideutige

Männer der Mitte. Der eine, von den jungen Bewegungsmännern und
einer republikanischen Stätte ausgegangen, ging an einen Hof über, dem er
sich vielfach hingab; der andere, einer Despotie entronnen, ging zum Volke
über und ward auch, nach seiner Verbindung mit Goethe, von dem nahen
Hofe nicht angezogen. Sie regten noch in den Xenien eine allgemeine Be=
wegung auf, aber dann richteten sie sich ganz auf anständige Wirksamkeit,
und strebten für Lessing's Werk, für die Bühne. Sie standen mit Voß
wie ein Triumvirat eine Zeitlang, sie entledigten sich des dritten, und dies
war eine schöne Zeit, als die zwei so verschiedenen Männer im friedlichen
Consulate für das Drama arbeiteten. Leider auch sie erfuhren Lessing's
Schicksal. Die gemeine Popularität des Kotzebue riß die Majorität der
Bühnenwelt an sich; Schiller starb, und Goethe, obgleich ihn die Roman=
tiker erst zum Imperator und Alleinherrscher erklärten, dankte doch gleich=
sam ab und isolirte sich immer mehr, des poetischen Treibens müde. Daß
alsdann die Romantiker gegen die vulgäre Menge eine Restauration durch=
zufechten suchten, liegt der Vergleichung literarischer und politischer Begeben=
heiten so nahe, daß Friedrich Schlegel in Wien sogar in politischer Bezie=
hung vielfach als ein Werkzeug der Restauration erscheint.

Wem dieser Faden durch den labyrinthischen Gang unserer Literaturge=
schichte nicht sicher genug scheint, dem lassen sich zahllose andere von einfa=
cherem Gespinnste bieten. Unter diesen empfiehlt sich besonders einer auch
dem tieferen historischen Betrachter, weil er das Hauptsymptom einer Re=
volutionszeit darlegt. Das nämlich, was einer solchen Umwälzungspe=
riode ihre intensive Fülle und dadurch ihren Reiz giebt, ist die erhöhte Le=
bensthätigkeit in dem Volkskörper, kraft welcher in derselben alle Kreise
menschlicher Entwickelung, die im gewöhnlichen Laufe der Dinge Jahrhun=
derte ausfüllen, in verhältnißmäßig kürzester Zeit durchlaufen werden.
Wie die französische Revolution alle Staatsformen und Phasen politischer
Entwickelung rasch durchging, so recapitulirte sich im vorigen Jahrhun=
dert bei uns die ganze Geschichte unserer bisherigen Literatur bis zu den
Männern hin, die sie erst eine Stufe weiter rückten. Wer also zwischen
unserer alten und neuen Literatur so unübersteigliche Klüfte sähe, der
würde verrathen, daß er über geschichtliche Dinge nicht urtheilen dürfte.
Hier eben ist die Geschichte der Literatur am lehrreichsten, wo sie uns nach=
weis't, in welchem Verhältniß die ältere zur neueren ohne unser Wissen und
absichtliches Zuthun steht durch die bloßen gleichmäßigen Bildungen, die
der gleiche Volksgeist in verschiedenen Zeiten bedingte; denn erst, wenn wir
dieses Verhältniß durchschaut haben, lernen wir richtig darüber denken,
was unsere alte Literatur für uns Lebende war und forthin seyn wird.
Man kann also sagen, daß die Jahre, in denen ein neu entdeckter Dichter
der Urzeit, in denen Ossian und neben ihm Homer bei uns eingeführt

ward, und Klopstock den Bardenton anstimmte, das rasche Wiederbeleben und Wiederdurchleben unserer ganzen bisherigen Literatur eröffneten. Wie zur Zeit des niederdeutschen Heliand und Otfried's der kirchlichen Dichtung eine Art Kunstwerth gegeben werden sollte, so geschieht es jetzt durch Klopstock und Lavater, die in den ähnlichen Gegenden ähnliche Werke liefern, die unter sich im ähnlichen Verhältnisse liegen. Wieland beschreibt in einem großen Umfange den ganzen Kreis der alexandrinisch=mittelalterlichen Prosa und Dichtung, scheiternd an Dramen und Allem, was außerhalb dieser Sphäre liegt, und im Gedächtniß der Nation erhalten eigentlich nur durch ein episches Werk, dessen Stoff aus jenen Zeiten entlehnt ist. Ganz wie unsere mittelalterlichen Epiker individualisirt er Alles, was er entlehnt und übersetzt, nach sich, und färbt Alles mit einem französirenden Tone. Lessing stellt in allen Theilen die Reformationszeit dar, die, wie er wieder that, zuerst auf das Drama führte, die den antiken Sinn weckte, die Wissenschaft neu belebte und die Religion läuterte, wie Lessing, Luthern hart auf dem Fuß folgend, gethan haben würde, wenn nicht der Mangel an religiösem Interesse und die politischen Ereignisse gehindert hätten. Herder führt dies Werk weiter und leitet uns in den Geist des 17. Jahrhunderts zur Polyhistorie und Philosophie über. Ganz so unerwartet, wie man aus dem freien Geist der Volkspoesie im 16. Jahrhundert plötzlich in die gelehrte Poesie des 17. Jahrhunderts trat, ist man überrascht, Herdern nach und neben seiner Fürsprache für das Volkslied das Lehrgedicht cultiviren und anempfehlen zu sehen. Eben in diesen Zeiten steht auch Jean Paul in jenem ganz gleichen Gegensatze zu Wieland, in welchem die komischen Romane zu den Ritter=Epen stehen. Erst wenn man bei Goethe und Schiller angelangt ist, sehen wir uns auf eigenen Füßen. Man hat es auch sehr gut gefühlt, wie wenig jene älteren Koryphäen selbstständig waren; man fand überall ihre Anlehnungen aus. Ihre Zeit selbst gab ihnen jene Ehrennamen, die vielleicht nicht so ehrenvoll sind: sie nannte Klopstock unsern Milton, Wieland unsern Voltaire, Jean Paul unsern Sterne und jeden anderen anders, aber Goethe und Schiller blieben ewig sie selbst. So ist auch nichts leichter, als nach den fremden Influenzen und nach dem herrschenden Geiste der Nachahmung, nach dem Vorragen der französischen, englischen, griechischen und deutschthümlichen Tendenzen eine Ordnung in die Dinge des vorigen Jahrhunderts zu bringen. Auch diese Betrachtung würde überall die Abhängigkeit der früheren, und eigentliche Selbstständigkeit und Eigenthümlichkeit nur bei den allergrößten und letzten unserer schaffenden Geister darthun.

Auf das Mannigfaltigste ließen sich, wenn man dies wollte, die Merkmale der Verjüngung, d. h. der Revolution in unserer neueren Literatur variiren. Wie wir eben in der Poesie im Allgemeinen die rohen und An-

fangsgattungen wiederholen sehen, so läßt sich dies von dem Drama im
Besonderen nachweisen.   Wir haben alttestamentliche Stücke bei Klopstock,
eine Moralität bei Lessing, eine Historie im Götz, Mordspectakel bei Klin-
ger, den griechischen Kothurn bei den Stolbergen.   Natur und Jugend war
der laute Ruf des Jahrhunderts, und wie Rousseau zu dem Urstande der
Menschheit zurückwies, so klärte man uns die deutsche Anfangsgeschichte
und die Urwelt auf: man fing an ein Naturrecht neu zu begründen und
commentirte die Urgesetze der Barbaren und Hebräer, man schrieb für
Einsetzung der Juden und der Weiber in die Menschheitsrechte; und mit
allem diesem liegt das Wegringen von der conventionellen zur natürlichen
Poesie, wie es Voß im Leben Hölty's nennt, auf einer Linie.   Ebenso charakteristisch ist es, daß sich die neu auffeimende Poesie einen jungen Boden
suchte, der durch längeres Brachliegen neue Kräfte gesammelt hatte.   Sie
wich aus dem erschöpften Schlesien und Sachsen, sie concentrirte sich in
Preußen nach Berlin, und im katholischen Deutschland nach Wien, ohne
jedoch zum Flore kommen zu können.   Sie drängte aus dem gesammten
Osten weg nach der Schweiz, die nun nach langer Pause fortwährend geschäftig bleibt, nach Niedersachsen und dem Norden, wo von Brockes und
Hagedorn an durch Gleim und Klopstock bis auf Voß und Niebuhr, Dahl-
mann und Schlosser eine ungemein energische Thätigkeit herrschend ward,
die mit der Weichheit der schweizerischen Leistungen in einem sonderbaren
Contraste steht; und ferner nach dem Rheine hin, der seit zwei Jahrhunderten gefeiert hatte.   Nachdem auf diese Weise die Peripherie des Kreises
beschrieben war, strömte eine Zeit lang das Mark der deutschen Literatur
nach dem Mittelpunkte hin und sammelte sich in Weimar und Jena, und es
war ein Zeichen des schnellen Verfalls, als dann plötzlich eine neue Zersplitterung eintrat und die Dichterschulen im Norden, in Berlin, Wien und
Stuttgart entstanden, eine Zersplitterung, die in neuester Zeit noch größer
geworden ist, wo die junge Dichterrepublik, wie verabredet, ihre Prätoren
in alle Städte mäßiger Größe vertheilt.   Wer sich in noch gefährlichere
Tiefen dieses geheimnißvollen Wachsthums einer neuen Zeit versenken
wollte, der könnte in ihren Repräsentanten das Großwerden des jungen
Geistes physiologisch verfolgen, wie er embryonisch in dem räthselhaften
Hamann liegt, mit aller physischen Kraft einer Kindernatur in Herder vor-
tritt, dann als ein Bild der träumerischen Frühjugend in Jean Paul, der
reifen Spätjugend in Goethe, der umsichtigen Männlichkeit in Schiller erscheint.

Aber hier sey es genug mit diesen mißlichen Winken aus der Binnen-
lehre historischer Weisheit, die nicht mittheilbar sind, als dem, der sie schon
hat, und die Vielen eher ein verdunkelndes Räthsel als ein Aufschluß geben-
der Ueberblick seyn werden.   Wem es in einem Werke an Uebersichtlichkeit

gebricht, der muß mit Verzichtleiſtung auf das, was die hiſtoriſche Einſicht darin fördern kann, ſich an die Lichtpunkte des dargeſtellten Stoffes halten, wo es ihm nie an Klarheit fehlen kann.   Ich konnte in dieſem ſo ange= legten Werke, das eine Art Vollſtändigkeit bezweckt, leider den Vortheil nicht ganz benuͤtzen, den die Literaturgeſchichte beſonders des vorigen Jahrhun= derts darbietet.   Ihre Entwickelungen, Richtungen und Ideen haben außerordentlich ſcharfe Vertreter; der Gang unſerer Poeſie läßt ſich an Klopſtock und Wieland, Leſſing und Herder, Voß und Jean Paul, Schiller und Goethe vollkommen darſtellen.   Hätte ich mich der Gegenwart und ihrem Bedürfniſſe entfernter geſtellt, ein Werk von reinerer Form ſtatt eines von reicherem Stoffe zu ſchreiben gewählt, ſo wäre eine ſo klare und ein= fache Erzählung zu liefern geweſen, wie ſie nur irgend eine Periode der po= litiſchen Geſchichte des Alterthums duldet.   Durch die ungeheuren Maſſen der mittleren Talente hindurch iſt dieſer planere Weg allerdings ſchwerer zu bahnen.   Doch habe ich auch dieſe möglichſt um die Hauptführer zu gruppiren geſucht, was nur dort ſchwieriger war, wo die führerloſe Unord= nung und die Wirren der literariſchen Anarchie Selbſtzweck der Darſtellung wurden.